A REPORT

OF THE

DEBATES AND PROCEEDINGS

IN THE

SECRET SESSIONS

OF THE

CONFERENCE CONVENTION,

FOR PROPOSING

AMENDMENTS TO THE CONSTITUTION OF THE UNITED STATES,

HELD AT

WASHINGTON, D. C., IN FEBRUARY, A. D. 1861.

BY

L. E. CHITTENDEN,

ONE OF THE DELEGATES.

NEW YORK:

D. APPLETON & COMPANY,

443 & 445 BROADWAY.

1864.

INTRODUCTION.

If I had been guided by my judgment alone it is not probable that these notes of the debates in the Conference, held upon the invitation of Virginia, at Washington, in the month of February, 1861, would have been made public. From the commencement of its sessions, a portion of the members were in favor of the daily publication of the proceedings. I was disposed to go farther and have the sessions open to the public; but this proposition was opposed by a large majority. Strong reasons were urged for excluding the multitude which in the excitement of the time would have thronged the hall wherein the Conference held its sessions. But these reasons did not apply to the publication of the debates, and a considerable minority were strongly of opinion that the people should be informed daily, of the votes and remarks of their representatives in that body.

I commenced taking notes on the first day of the session. For the first few days, and until the reports were presented from the general committee, there was but little discussion, and that related to questions incidental to the general subject. On the 15th of February, and before the committee reported, Mr. Orth offered a resolution authorizing the admission of reporters, which, after some discussion, by a close vote was laid upon the table. On the 18th, finding the labor of taking notes greater than I had anticipated, and desiring that a complete record should be preserved; I introduced a resolution providing for the appointment of an official stenographer, who should report the proceedings and hold them subject to the order of the Conference. I urged the adoption of this resolution as strenuously as was proper, but the feeling of the majority appeared to be still adverse to its passage, and it shared the fate of its predecessor. I then revised the notes already taken, and finding them more complete than I had anticipated, determined to make as accurate a report as I was able of the general discussion. I could not then anticipate whether such a report would be useful to the country or not; but I thought if the Conference should propose amendments to the Constitution, and these should be ultimately submitted to the States for adoption, a knowledge of the motives and reasons which influenced the action of the Conference as well as the construction which the members gave to the propositions themselves, might become of as great importance as the same subjects were in the convention which framed the present Constitution. I attended every session of the Conference, and, so far as my strength would permit, made as full and accurate notes as I could, both of the action of the Conference and the observations of its members.

These notes were carefully examined and revised immediately after the close of each daily session. After the passage of the resolution introduced by Mr. BARRINGER, removing the injunction of secrecy and authorizing their publication, I determined to write them out for the press. I was engaged in this work when the rebellion commenced, and was shortly after called to the performance of the duties of an official position, which for many months left me no leisure for other employments.

My notes were then laid aside. As it was known by every member of the Conference that I had taken them, I was often pressed to permit selections from them to be made. These requests I invariably declined, as I desired the publication, if made at all, to be entire, as well as accurate. As time passed, these appeals became more frequent and pressing, and claims were made in relation to the course of several of the members which could only be sustained or refuted by a publication of their remarks. At length I was earnestly requested to write out one of these speeches, and after some weeks of delay consented to do so.

After the publication of this speech, which took place about the time of the fall elections of 1863, previous to which the action of the Conference had been much discussed, the desire to see a full report of the proceedings of that body appeared to be excited anew. Letters and personal interviews upon this subject became very numerous. I finally determined to take the advice of a number of gentlemen who were prominent in the convention and the country, as to the propriety of yielding to this desire, and to be guided by it. I did so, and found among them a remarkable unanimity of expression in favor of making the history of the Conference public.

When this question was settled, I desired to avail myself of every opportunity to secure the highest degree of accuracy and fidelity. I addressed notes to such of the members as were accessible, asking them to transmit to me such memoranda of the proceedings of the Conference as they had preserved. The response to these letters was very gratifying; not because the materials furnished were very full, but because so general a purpose was shown by all the members thus addressed, to furnish me every facility and aid in their power.

I have found much difficulty in determining what control each member ought to be permitted to exercise over his own remarks. The most agreeable course to me would have been, to have written out each speech and submitted it to its author for correction or revision; but to this there was a decisive objection. It would have depreciated, if not destroyed, the accuracy of the report. Although I do not believe that any gentleman would have been tempted to change the tenor of his remarks by subsequent events, the view of the public might not have been so charitable.

I have therefore made my own notes the standard of authority, and have admitted nothing into the report which has not been justified by them aided by my own recollection. The manuscript has not been changed or added to, except by my own hands. The few instances in which I have availed myself of the materials furnished by others, are distinctly stated either in the notes or the appendix.

During the sessions of the Conference I was able to secure but little practical assistance from the members. Although many of them desired that my purpose should be accomplished, and some were taking brief and general notes, I soon discovered that an accurate report of a speech required an amount of labor and a degree of attention to the subject, which few gentlemen were inclined to give. The work, therefore, was thrown almost exclusively upon myself. Some idea of its amount and severity may be formed when it is stated, that the sessions usually commenced at about ten o'clock in the morning, and with a brief intermission were continued late in the evening, in one instance as late as the hour of two o'clock, A. M. The necessity of these long daily sessions, arose from the fact, that the Congress then in existence terminated on the fourth of March, and but few days remained in which to discuss and perfect the report, and to submit it to that body for its action.

I do not claim to have furnished a *verbatim* report of the speeches delivered in the Conference of 1861, but I insist that I have given an accurate account of all its official proceedings, and the substance of the remarks made in the course of those proceedings. I think, also, that I have preserved nearly all the propositions made in the course of the debate, and generally have presented the ideas in the very language used. The gentlemen who have critically examined the report, all concur upon the question of its general accuracy, and I am content in this respect to rely upon their testimony.

I have suggested these considerations simply by way of explanation, and not for the purpose of avoiding criticism. I have endeavored to follow, so far as was in my power, the example of the illustrious Reporter of the Constitutional Convention of 1787; and while my notes lack the beauty and felicity which characterize his, I trust they are not less full and accurate. I submit them to the country as the best contribution which I can make to its history, at a most important and interesting period of our national existence.

The three short years which have passed since the Conference of 1861, have witnessed singular vicissitudes among its members. Many of them have entered into the military or civil service of the country, or of the rebellion which it was the avowed purpose of some members of that Conference to nourish into vigorous life. Death, also, has been busy with the roll. BALDWIN, BRONSON, SMITH, WOLCOTT, TYLER, and CLAY, are no more. ZOLLICOFFER fell at the head of a rebel army. HACKLEMAN sealed with his blood his devotion to the prin ciples he advocated upon the field of Corinth, and now, while I am writing these pages in a morning of beautiful spring, when tree, and shrub, and grass, and flower, are bursting into life and beauty; from the roar of cannon, the rattle of musketry, and the deadly storm of lead and iron, which bearing destruction upon its wings is waking the echoes of the "Wilderness," comes the mournful tidings that WADSWORTH has fallen. In that Conference or in the world, there was never a purer or a more ardent patriot. Those of us who were associated with him politically, had learned to love and respect him. His opponents admired his unflinching devotion to his country, and his manly frankness and candor. He was the type of a true American, able, unselfish, prudent, unambitious, and good. Other pens will do justice to his memory, but I thought as I heard the last account of him alive, as he lay within the rebel lines, his face wearing that calm serenity which grew more beautiful the nearer death approached, after having given so abundantly of his goods, now yielding his life to his country in the hour of her trial, that hereafter the good and true men of the nation would emulate the illustrious example of his patriotism, and would prize the blessings of a free government the more highly, as they remembered that it could only be maintained and perpetuated by such expensive sacrifices.

L. E. C.

May, 1864.

PROCEEDINGS OF THE CONFERENCE,

Washington, D. C.

MONDAY, *February 4th*, 1861.

COMMISSIONERS representing a number of the States, assembled at Willard's Hall, in the City of Washington, D. C., on the fourth day of February, A. D. 1861, at 12 o'clock M., in pursuance of the following preamble and resolutions, adopted by the General Assembly of the State of Virginia, on the nineteenth day of January, A. D. 1861:

" *Whereas*, It is the deliberate opinion of the General Assembly of Virginia, that unless the unhappy controversy which now divides the States of this confederacy, shall be satisfactorily adjusted, a permanent dissolution of Union is inevitable; and the General Assembly, representing the wishes of the people of the commonweath, is desirous of employing every reasonable means to avert so dire a calamity, and determined to make a final effort to restore the Union and the Constitution, in the spirit in which they were established by the fathers of the Republic: Therefore,

Resolved, That on behalf of the commonweath of Virginia, an invitation is hereby extended to all such States, whether slaveholding or non-slaveholding, as are willing to unite with Virginia in an earnest effort to adjust the present unhappy controversies, in the spirit in which the Constitution was originally formed, and consistently with its principles, so as to afford to the people of the slaveholding States adequate guarantees for the security of their rights, to appoint commissioners to meet on the fourth day of February next, in the City of Washington, similar commissioners appointed by Virginia, to consider, and if practicable, agree upon some suitable adjustment.

Resolved, That ex-President JOHN TYLER, WILLAM C. RIVES, Judge JOHN W. BROCKENBROUGH, GEORGE W. SUMMERS, and JAMES A. SEDDON are hereby appointed commissioners, whose duty it shall be to repair to the City of Washington, on the day designated in the foregoing resolution, to meet such commissioners as may be appointed by any of said States, in accordance with the foregoing resolution.

Resolved, That if said commissioners, after full and free conference, shall agree upon any plan of adjustment requiring amendments to the Federal Constitution, for the further security of the rights of the people of the slaveholding States, they be requested to communicate the proposed amendments to Congress, for the purpose of having the same submitted by that body, according to the forms of the Constitution, to the several States for ratification.

Resolved, That if said commissioners cannot agree on such adjustment, or if agreeing, Congress shall refuse to submit for ratification, such amendments as may be proposed, then the commissioners of this State shall immediately communicate the result to the executive of this commonwealth, to be by him laid before the convention of the people of Virginia and the General Assembly: *Provided*, That the said commissioners be subject at all times to the control of the General Assembly, or if in session, to that of the State convention.

Resolved, That in the opinion of the General Assembly of Virginia, the propositions embraced in the resolutions presented to the Senate of the United States by the Hon. JOHN J. CRITTENDEN, so modified as that the first article proposed as an amendment to the Constitution of the United States, shall apply to all the territory of the United States now held or hereafter acquired south of latitude thirty-six degrees and thirty minutes, and provide that slavery of the African race shall be effectually protected as property therein during the continuance of the territorial government, and the fourth article shall secure to the owners cf slaves the right of transit with their slaves between and through the non-slaveholding States and territories, constitute the basis of such an adjustment of the unhappy controversy which now divides the States of this confederacy, as would be accepted by the people of this commonwealth.

Resolved, That ex-President JOHN TYLER is hereby appointed, by the concurrent vote of each branch of the General Assembly, a commissioner to the President of the United States, and Judge JOHN ROBERTSON is hereby appointed, by a like vote, a commissioner to the State of South Carolina, and the other States that have seceded or shall secede, with instructions respectfully to request the President of the United States and authorities of such States to agree to abstain, pending the proceedings contemplated by the action of this General Assembly, from any and all acts calculated to produce a collision of arms between the States and the Government of the United States.

Resolved, That copies of the foregoing resolutions be forthwith telegraphed to the executives of the several States, and also to the President of the United States, and the Governor be requested to inform, without delay, the commissioners of their appointment by the foregoing resolutions.

[A copy from the rolls.] WM. F. GORDON, JR.,
C. H. D. and K. R. of Va.

The Conference was called to order by Mr. MOREHEAD, of Kentucky, who proposed the name of the honorable JOHN C. WRIGHT, of Ohio, as temporary Chairman.

The motion of Mr. MOREHEAD was unanimously adopted.

Mr. WRIGHT was conducted to the Chair by Mr. MEREDITH, of Pennsylvania, and Mr. CHASE, of Ohio, and proceeded to address the Conference as follows:

My warmest thanks are due to you, Gentlemen, for the undeserved honor which you have conferred upon me, in selecting me for the purpose of temporarily presiding over your deliberations. We have come together to secure a common and at the same time a most important object—to agree if we can upon some plan for adjusting the unhappy differences which distract the country, which will be satisfactory to ourselves and those we represent. We have assembled as friends, as brothers, each, I doubt not, animated by the most friendly sentiments.

If we enter upon, and with these sentiments carry through, a patient examination of the difficulties which now surround the Government, the result will be, it must be, a success, earnestly hoped for by every lover of his country; a result which will establish the Union according to the spirit of the Constitution.

For myself, I may say that I have come here with the earnest purpose of doing justice to all sections of the Union. I will hear with a patient and impartial mind all that may be said in favor of, or against such amendments of the Constitution as may be proposed. Such of them as will give to the Government permanence, strength, and stability, as will tend to secure to any State, or any number of States, the quiet and unmolested enjoyment of their rights under it, shall receive my cordial support. My confidence in republican institutions, in the capacity of the people for self-government, has been increased with every year of a life which has been protracted beyond the term usually allotted to man. That life is now drawing to a close, and I hope, when it ends, I may leave the Government more firmly established in the affections of my countrymen than it ever was before. To this end I have always labored, and shall continue to labor while I live. I pray GOD that He will be with us during our deliberations, and that He may guide them to a happy and wise conclusion.

Mr. BENJAMIN C. HOWARD, a commissioner from the State of Maryland, was unanimously appointed temporary Secretary.

The Roll of the States was then called over, and commissioners representing the following were found to be present:

New Hampshire,	Delaware,	Kentucky,
Rhode Island,	Maryland,	Ohio,
New Jersey,	Virginia,	Indiana.
Pennsylvania,	North Carolina,	

Mr. PRICE, of New Jersey:—I am informed that a number of Reporters for the press are at the door of the hall, desiring admittance to this Conference, for the purpose of reporting our proceedings. Whatever may be the ultimate action of the Conference in this respect, I can see no objection to the admission of reporters to-day, for our business will relate wholly to organization. I hope we shall admit them, and I make that motion.

Mr. SEDDON, of Virginia:—I hope this motion will not prevail. I do not see that any good can possibly come of giving publicity now, to our proceedings. On the contrary, in the present excited condition of the country, I can see how much harm might result from that publicity. It is not unlikely that wide differences of opinion will be found to exist among us at the outset. These we shall attempt to harmonize, and if we succeed, it will only be by mutual concessions and compromises. Every one should be left free to make these concessions, and not subject himself to unfavorable public criticism by doing so. If our deliberations are to attain the successful conclusion we so much desire, it certainly is the course of wisdom that we should follow the illustrious example of the framers of the present Constitution, and sit with closed doors.

The motion was thereupon, by *viva voce* vote, decided in the negative.

Mr. MEREDITH:—I move the appointment of a committee to consist of one member from each delegation present, to be named by the delegation and appointed by the President, who shall recommend permanent officers of this body, and also report rules for its government.

Which motion was agreed to.

The following gentlemen were then appointed such Committee on Rules and Organization:

Kentucky, Charles A. Wickliffe, *Chairman;* New Hampshire, Amos Tuck; Rhode Island, William W. Hoppin; New Jersey, Joseph F. Randolph; Pennsylvania, Thomas E. Franklin; Delaware, George B. Rodney; Maryland, John W. Crisfield; Virginia, William C. Rives; North Carolina, Thomas Ruffin; Ohio, Reuben Hitchcock; Indiana, Godlove S. Orth.

The Conference then adjourned to meet at 12 o'clock M. to-morrow.

SECOND DAY.

WASHINGTON, TUESDAY, *February 5th*, 1861.

THE Conference was called to order by the Chairman *pro tem.*, pursuant to adjournment, and the journal of the proceedings of the first day was read and approved.

Mr. FRANKLIN, of Pennsylvania:—It is usual in bodies of this description to take measures to ascertain who are and who are not duly accredited members. We should have the names of all the Commissioners present brought on to our records. I therefore move that a Committee of five be appointed by the Chairman, to whom all credentials of members shall be referred for examination and report.

The motion of Mr. FRANKLIN was adopted unanimously, and the Chairman announced as such Committee Mr. Summers, of Virginia; Mr. Franklin, of Pennsylvania; Mr. Guthrie, of Kentucky; Mr. Morehead, of North Carolina, and Mr. Smith, of Indiana.

Mr. WICKLIFFE, of Kentucky:—I rise at this time for the purpose of making the report of the Committee on Organization. I am instructed to report that we recommend that the permanent officers of the Convention be a President and Secretary, and that the Secretary have leave to appoint assistants, not exceeding two in number, to assist him in the discharge of his duties; and that the President of this Convention be JOHN TYLER, of Virginia, and that CRAFTS J. WRIGHT, of Ohio, be its Secretary.

The committee also report a series of rules for the government of the Convention.

Mr. CLAY, of Kentucky:—I move that the question upon accepting the report be divided, and that it be first taken on that part of the report which relates to the officers of the Convention.

Which was agreed to without objection.

It was then moved, and unanimously voted, that the part of the report relating to officers, be accepted, and the officers designated be appointed.

The President *pro tem.* then appointed Mr. EWING, of Ohio, and Mr. MEREDITH, of Pennsylvania, to conduct the President elect to the chair.

President TYLER upon taking his seat proceeded to address the Convention as follows:

Gentlemen, I fear you have committed a great error in appointing me to the honorable position you have assigned me. A long separation from all deliberative bodies has rendered the rules of their proceedings unfamiliar to me, while I should find, in my own state of health, variable and fickle as it is, sufficient reason to decline the honor of being your presiding officer. But, in times like these, one has but little option left him. Personal considerations should weigh but lightly in the balance. The country is in danger; it is enough; one must take the place assigned him in the great work of reconciliation and adjustment. The voice of Virginia has invited her co-States to meet her in council. In the initiation of this Government, that same voice was heard and complied with, and the results of seventy-odd years have fully attested the wisdom of the decisions then adopted. Is the urgency of her call now less great than it was then? Our godlike fathers created, we have to preserve. They built up, through their wisdom and patriotism, monuments which have eternized their names. You have before you, gentlemen, a task equally grand, equally sublime, quite as full of glory and immortality. You have to snatch from ruin a great and glorious Confederation, to preserve the Government, and to renew and invigorate the Constitution. If you reach the height of this great occasion, your children's children will rise up and call you blessed. I confess myself to be ambitious of sharing in the glory of accomplishing this grand and magnificent result.

To have our names enrolled in the Capitol, to be repeated by future generations with grateful applause—this is an honor higher than the mountains, more enduring than the monumental alabaster. Yes, Virginia's voice, as in the olden time, has been heard. Her sister States meet her this day at the council board. Vermont is here, bringing with her the memories of the past, and reviving in the memories of all, her Ethan Allen and his demand for the surrender of Ticonderoga, in the name of the Great Jehovah and the American Congress. New Hampshire is here, her fame illustrated by memorable annals, and still more lately as the birthplace of him who won for himself the name of defender of the Constitution, and who wrote that letter to John Taylor which has been enshrined in the hearts of his countrymen. Massachusetts is not here. (Some member said "She is coming.") I hope so, said Mr. TYLER, and that she will bring with her her daughter Maine. I did not believe it could well be that the voice which in other times was so familiar to her ears had been addressed to her in vain. Connecticut is here, and she comes, I doubt not, in the spirit of ROGER SHERMAN, whose name with our very children has become a household word, and who was in life the embodiment of that sound practical sense which befits the great lawgiver and constructer of governments. Rhode Island, the land of ROGER WILLIAMS, is here, one of the two last States, in her jealousy of the public liberty, to give in her adhesion to the Constitution, and among the earliest to hasten to its rescue. The great Empire State of New York, represented thus far but by one delegate, is expected daily in fuller force to join in the great work of healing the discontents of the times and restoring the reign of fraternal feeling. New Jersey is also here, with the memories of the past covering her all over. Trenton and Princeton live immortal in story, the plains of the last incrimsoned with the hearts blood of Virginia's sons. Among her delegation I rejoice to recognize a gallant son of a signer of the immortal Declaration which announced to the world that thirteen Provinces had become thirteen independent and sovereign States. And here, too, is Delaware, the land of the BAYARDS and the RODNEYS, whose soil at Brandywine was moistened by the blood of Virginia's youthful MONROE. Here is Maryland, whose massive columns wheeled into line with those of Virginia in the contest for glory, and whose state house at Annapolis was the theatre of the spectacle of a successful Commander, who, after liberating his country, gladly ungirthed his sword, and laid it down upon the altar of that country. Then comes Pennsylvania, rich in revolutionary lore, bringing with her the deathless names of FRANKLIN and MORRIS, and, I trust, ready to renew from the belfry of Independence Hall the chimes of the old bell, which announced *Freedom* and *Independence* in former days. All hail to North Carolina! with her Mecklenberg Declaration in her hand, standing erect on the ground of her own probity and firmness in the cause of public liberty, and represented in her attributes by her MACON, and in this assembly by her distinguished son at no great distance from me. Four daughters of Virginia also cluster around the council board on the invitation of their ancient mother—the eldest, Kentucky, whose sons, under the intrepid warrior ANTHONY WAYNE, gave freedon of settlement to the territory of her sister, Ohio. She extends her hand daily and hourly across *la belle riviere*, to grasp the hand of some one of kindred blood of the noble states of Indiana, and Illinois, and Ohio, who have grown up into powerful States, already grand, potent, and almost imperial. Tennessee is not here, but is coming—prevented only from being here by the floods which have swollen her rivers. When she arrives, she will wear the badges on her warrior crest of victories won in company with the Great West on many an ensanguined plain, and standards torn from the hands of the conquerors at Waterloo. Missouri, and Iowa, and Michigan, Wisconsin, and Minnesota, still linger behind, but it may be hoped that their hearts are with us in the great work we have to do.

Gentlemen, the eyes of the whole country are turned to this assembly, in expectation and hope. I trust that you may prove yourselves worthy of the great occasion. Our ancestors, probably, committed a blunder in not having fixed upon every fifth decade for a call of a general convention to amend and reform the Constitution. On the contrary, they have made the difficulties next to insurmountable to accomplish amendments to an instrument which was perfect for five millions of people, but not wholly so as to thirty millions. Your patriotism will surmount the difficulties, however great, if you will but accomplish one triumph in advance, and that is, a triumph over *party*. And what is party, when compared to the work of rescuing one's country from danger? Do that, and one long, loud shout of joy and gladness will resound throughout the land.

Mr. EWING:—I move that the remaining portion of the report of the Committee on Organization be postponed until to-morrow.

The motion of Mr. EWING was agreed to.

Mr. WICKLIFFE. I offer the following resolution:

Resolved, That the Conference shall be opened with prayer, and that the clergymen of the city of Washington be requested to perform that service.

The resolution offered by Mr. WICKLIFFE was adopted, and prayer was then offered by the Rev. Dr. P. D. GURLEY, of Washington.

The PRESIDENT:—I have received a communication from the Messrs. Willard, placing the Hall in which the Conference is now sitting at the service of the Conference, while its sessions may continue; also, a communication from the Mayor and Common Council of the City of Washington, offering police officers to attend our sittings.

It was moved, and agreed to, that these offers be severally accepted.

Mr. JOHNSON, of Maryland:—I move that the President of the Conference be requested to furnish a copy of his address to the Conference upon taking the Chair, that it be entered upon the journal as a part of this day's proceedings, and that the same be published.

Which motion was unanimously agreed to.

Mr. GRIMES, of Iowa:—I have received from the Governor of the State of Iowa a communication, requesting myself and my colleague in the Senate of the United States, and also the members representing that State in the House of Representatives, to represent the State of Iowa here. I desire to present his communication, that it may be referred to the Committee on Credentials.

The communication was so referred, and on motion of Mr. WRIGHT, of Ohio, the Conference adjourned.

THIRD DAY.

WASHINGTON, WEDNESDAY, *February 6th*, 1861.

THE Conference met at twelve o'clock, at noon, and was called to order by the PRESIDENT.

The Journal of yesterday was read, and after amendment, was approved.

Mr. SUMMERS:—I am instructed by the Committee on Credentials to make a report. That committee has examined the credentials which have been submitted to it, and finds the following-named gentlemen duly accredited as members of this Conference:

New Hampshire.—Amos Tuck, Levi Chamberlain, Asa Fowler.

Vermont.—Hiland Hall, Lucius E. Chittenden, Levi Underwood, H. Henry Baxter, B. D. Harris.

Rhode Island and Providence Plantations.—Samuel Ames, Alexander Duncan, William W. Hoppin, George H. Browne, Samuel G. Arnold.

Connecticut.—Roger S. Baldwin, Chauncey F. Cleveland, Charles J. McCurdy, James T. Pratt, Robbins Battell, Amos S. Treat.

New Jersey.—Charles S. Olden, Peter D. Vroom, Robert F. Stockton, Benjamin Williamson, Joseph F. Randolph, Frederick T. Frelinghuysen, Rodman M. Price, William C. Alexander, Thomas J. Stryker.

Pennsylvania.—Thomas White, James Pollock, William M. Meredith, David Wilmot, A. W. Loomis, Thomas E. Franklin, William McKennan.

Delaware.—George B. Rodney, Daniel M. Bates, Henry Ridgeley, John W. Houston, William Cannon.

Maryland.—John F. Dent, Reverdy Johnson, John W. Crisfield, Augustus W. Bradford, William T. Goldsborough, J. Dixon Roman, Benjamin C. Howard.

Virginia.—John Tyler, William C. Rives, John W. Brockenbrough, George W. Summers, James A. Seddon.

North Carolina.—George Davis, Thomas Ruffin, David S. Reid, Daniel M. Barringer, J. M. Morehead.

Kentucky.—William O. Butler, James B. Clay, Joshua F. Bell, Charles S. Morehead, James Guthrie, Charles A. Wickliffe.

Ohio.—John C. Wright, Salmon P. Chase, William S. Groesbeck, Franklin C. Backus, Reuben Hitchcock, Thomas Ewing, Valentine B. Horton.

Indiana.—Caleb B. Smith, Pleasant A. Hackleman, Godlove S. Orth, E. W. H. Ellis, Thomas C. Slaughter.

Iowa.—James W. Grimes, Samuel H. Curtis, William Vandever.

Mr. WICKLIFFE :—I move that the Secretary be authorized to employ one or more assistants. I am advised that the Secretary cannot perform his duties without assistance, and I see no objection to giving him this authority.

The motion of Mr. WICKLIFFE was agreed to.

Mr. WICKLIFFE :—I now desire to call up the remaining portion of the report of the Committee on Rules and Organization, and to move its adoption at the present time. These Rules are substantially the same as those which were adopted by the convention which proposed our present Constitution. The rule which we have reported securing secrecy, so far as our proceedings are concerned, has been made the subject of much discussion in the committee; and it was at first thought best to recommend a modification of it. But upon reflection and consideration, and in view of the fact that, while the rule reported requires that secrecy should be preserved in regard to all that is said or done in this Conference, it does not prevent any member from expressing his own hopes or predictions upon the final result of our deliberations, we have thought best to let it remain as it is.

Mr. SEDDON :—I desire to offer an amendment to this portion of the report of the committee, which I will read for the information of the Conference. It is as follows :

"*Resolved*, That no part of the Journal be published without the order or leave of the Conference, and that no copies of the whole or any part be furnished or allowed, except to members, who shall be privileged to communicate the same to the authorities or deliberative assemblies of their respective States, when deemed judicious or appropriate, under their instructions, and that nothing spoken in the House be printed or otherwise published; but private communications respecting the proceedings and debates, while recommended to be with caution and reserve, are allowed at the discretion of each member."

It may be thought, that in offering this resolution, I am seeking a different end from the one I proposed yesterday, when I advocated the proposition of excluding reporters from our sessions, and insisted that our proceedings should be at all times under the seal of secrecy. Such, however, is not my purpose. But some discretion must be allowed us, in order that we may conform to and carry out the spirit of the resolutions under which we respectively act. This is especially true in relation to myself and my colleagues. The resolutions under which we are acting, require that we should from time to time communicate to the legislature of Virginia the proceedings of this body, and to express our own opinions of the prospect which may exist of the settlement of existing difficulties. The Commissioners from Virginia would be placed in a delicate, not to say an awkward position, by the adoption of a rule here which would absolutely prohibit such communications. I hope my amendment may be adopted.

Mr. TUCK:—Would not the purpose of the gentleman from Virginia be answered by giving any delegation leave to communicate any action actually taken by the Conference, with their own opinions as to the probable result of our deliberations?

Mr. SEDDON:—Those opinions would possess no value, unless the facts and circumstances are communicated upon which they are founded. It is very clear to me, that the best course will be to entrust to the discretion of each member the privilege of making these communications, trusting that he will not abuse the confidence thus given.

Mr. WICKLIFFE:—I hope we have all come here with an earnest desire to harmonize our conflicting opinions, and to unite upon some plan which will settle our troubles and save the union of the States. The South has spoken of the North in very severe terms, and the North has not been slow in returning the compliment. If we come finally, to any definite result satisfactory to either side, it must be by mutual concessions, by confessing our sins to each other, and endeavoring to live harmoniously together in future. In my judgment, secrecy is absolutely indispensable to successful action here. I do not wish to be precluded from abandoning a position to-morrow, if I see cause for it, which I have taken to-day. If the proceedings, and especially the debates of this Conference, are made public from day to day, they will go into the newspapers and be made the subject of comment, favorable or otherwise. The necessary result will be, that when a member is understood to have committed himself to a particular proposition, or any special course of policy, that pride of opinion, which we all possess, will render any change of policy on his part difficult, if not impossible. I should sincerely regret the adoption of the resolution of the gentleman from Virginia.

Mr. RANDOLPH:—I move that the portion of the committee's report under consideration, together with the resolution of Mr. Seddon, be recommitted to the Committee on Rules and Organization.

The motion of Mr. Randolph was agreed to.

Mr. GUTHRIE:—I have an idea relating to the plan which should be adopted to carry into effect the purpose of this Conference. I wish to propose it. We have come together upon the invitation of the glorious old commonwealth of Virginia, the mother of States and Statesmen. We have come from the North and the South, from the East and the West, to see whether our wisdom can devise some means to avert the dangers which threaten to destroy this noble Republic, founded by the wisdom and patriotism of our ancestors. I hope we are animated by a common purpose. The storm is threatening. The horizon is covered with dark and portentous clouds. Section is arrayed against section, and already *seven* of our sister States have separated from us and are proceeding to establish an independent Confederation. War! Civil War! is impending over us. It must be averted! Who does not know that such a war, among such a people, must be, if it comes, a war of extermination.

Mr. President, I move the adoption of the resolution which I now send to the chair.

The resolution of Mr. Guthrie was read as follows:

Resolved, That a committee of one from each State be appointed by the Commissioners thereof, to be nominated to the President, and to be appointed by him, to whom shall be referred the resolutions of the State of Virginia, and the other States represented, and all propositions for the adjustment of existing difficulties between States, with authority to report what they may deem right, necessary, and proper to restore harmony and preserve the Union, and that they report on or before Friday next.

Mr. SEDDON:—It appears to me that the mode pointed out by the resolution introduced by the gentleman from Kentucky, is neither the one most appropriate nor expeditious for accomplishing the result desired. We are convened under the invitation of the State of Virginia; and the same invitation that brings us here, proposes the basis for our deliberation and action. Virginia has stated what will be satisfactory to her; not as an *ultimatum*, but as a basis of adjustment. It appears to me that the proper course would be, to take up the propositions of Virginia—propose amendments to them—discuss them, and in the end determine how far they shall be adopted. The adoption of the resolution proposed, transfers the labors of this Conference, not in itself too large for convenient deliberation, to a committee. That committee is to discuss the various propositions offered and report the result. What, in the mean time, is this Conference to do? Nothing whatever! We are to meet here from day to day and adjourn, no one knows how long, until this committee reports, and then the discussion will commence which ought to commence now. Mr. PRESIDENT, if any thing is accomplished, it must be accomplished speedily. Events are on the wing. Already in my State the delegates are elected to a Convention, which is to meet next week, to consider the subject which now engrosses the minds of the American people. I hope my suggestion may meet with favor in the Conference.

Mr. EWING:—I cannot agree with the gentleman from Virginia, for reasons which must be obvious to all. I do not think Virginia intended to dictate the terms upon which we were to act. I am in favor of the resolution, but would make one suggestion in relation to it. By its terms the committee is to report on Friday, if it can properly do so. I suggest that the committee should have leave to sit during the sessions of the Conference. In this way our business may be greatly expedited.

Mr. GUTHRIE:—It gives me pleasure to accept the modification proposed by the gentleman from Ohio. I should have incorporated it into my resolution.

The resolution as modified was then adopted by the Conference without a division.

The PRESIDENT:—I will take this occasion to announce a committee to carry into effect the determination of the Conference relating to the obtaining of the services of clergymen to open the proceedings of the Conference daily with prayer. The Chair appoints as such committee, Mr. RANDOLPH, of New Jersey, Mr. WICKLIFFE, of Kentucky, and Mr. JOHNSON, of Maryland.

Mr. JOHNSON:—It appears to me very appropriate, in view of the occasion which has brought us together, that the members of this Conference should pay their respects in a body to the President of the United States. I therefore move that we call upon him in a body at such a time as will be most agreeable to him; such time to be ascertained by the President of this Conference.

Which motion was unanimously agreed to.

Mr. CLAY:—I move the reconsideration of the vote by which the portion of the report of the Committee on Rules and Organization not yet adopted was recommitted to that committee. I do this in order that the Conference may now proceed to the consideration of those rules which may be adopted without much difference of opinion.

The vote was thereupon reconsidered, and the following rules were severally read and adopted. The remaining rules recommended were recommitted to the committee:

RULES.

I. A Convention to do business, shall consist of the Commissioners of not less than seven States; and all questions shall be decided by the greater number of those which be fully represented. But a less number than seven may adjourn from day to day.

II. Immediately after the President shall have taken the chair, and the members their seats, the minutes of the preceding day shall be read by the Secretary.

III. Every member, rising to speak, shall address the President; and while he shall be speaking none shall pass between them, or hold discourse with another, or read a book, pamphlet, or paper, printed or manuscript; and of two members rising to speak at the same time, the President shall name him who shall first be heard.

IV. A member shall not speak oftener than twice, without

special leave upon the same question; and not a second time before every other who had been silent shall have been heard, if he choose to speak upon the subject.

V. A motion made and seconded, shall be repeated; and if written, as it shall be when any member shall so require, read aloud by the Secretary before it shall be debated; and may be withdrawn at any time before the vote upon it shall have been declared.

VI. Orders of the day shall be read next after the minutes, and either discussed or postponed, before any other business shall be introduced.

VII. When a debate shall arise upon a question, no motion, other than to amend the question, to commit it, or to postpone the debate, shall be received.

VIII. A question which is complicated, shall, at the request of any member, be divided and put separately upon the propositions of which it is compounded.

IX. A writing which contains any matter brought on to be considered, shall be read once, throughout, for information; then by paragraphs, to be debated, and again with the amendments, if any, made on the second reading, and afterwards the question shall be put upon the whole, as amended or approved in the original form, as the case may be.

X. Committees shall be appointed by the President, unless otherwise ordered by the Convention.

XI. A member may be called to order by another member, as well as by the President, and may be allowed to explain his conduct or expressions supposed to be reprehensible. And all questions of order shall be decided by the President, without appeal or debate.

XII. Upon a question to adjourn for the day, which may be made at any time, if it be seconded, the question shall be put without debate.

XIII. When the Convention shall adjourn, every member shall stand in his place until the President pass him.

XIV. That no member be absent from the Convention, so as to interrupt the representation of the State, without leave.

XV. That Committees do not sit while the Convention shall be, or ought to be sitting, without leave of the Convention.

XVI. That no copy be taken of any entry on the Journal, during the sitting of the Convention, without leave of the Convention.

XVII. That members only be permitted to inspect the Journal.

XVIII. *Mode of Voting.* All votes shall be taken by States, and each State to give one vote. The yeas and nays of the members shall not be given or published—only the decision by States.

After the adoption of the foregoing Rules, the Conference adjourned until 10 o'clock to-morrow morning.

FOURTH DAY.

WASHINGTON, THURSDAY, *February 7th*, 1861.

THE Conference convened, pursuant to the adjournment yesterday, at 10 o'clock A. M.

It was called to order by President TYLER, and prayer was offered by Rev. Dr. PYNE, of Washington.

The Journal of yesterday was read, and after sundry amendments, was approved.

Messrs. J. H. PULESTON, JOHN STRYKER, W. W. HOPPIN, Jr., and ——— Olcott, took their places as Assistant Secretaries.

President TYLER:—Gentlemen of the Conference, as directed by the resolution which you adopted yesterday, I addressed a note to the President of the United States, asking at what hour it would be agreeable to him that this Conference should call on him in a body. To this note I have received a reply which will be read by the Secretary.

The Secretary then read the following note from the President:

EXECUTIVE MANSION, *February 6th*, 1861.

MY DEAR SIR:—I shall feel greatly honored to receive the gentlemen composing the Convention of Commissioners from the several States, on any day and at any hour most convenient to themselves. I shall name to-morrow

(Thursday) at 11 or 3 o'clock, though any other time would be equally agreeable to me. I shall at all times be prepared to give them a cordial welcome.

Yours, very respectfully,

JAMES BUCHANAN.

His Excellency, JOHN TYLER.

The PRESIDENT:—What order will the Conference take upon the subject?

Mr. GUTHRIE:—I move that the members of this Conference call in a body upon the President of the United States this morning, at 11 o'clock.

Mr. GUTHRIE's motion was adopted unanimously.

Mr. SUMMERS:—I am instructed by the Committee on Credentials further to report, that the committee have examined the credentials of the following gentlemen, and find them duly accredited as members of this body:

New York.—William E. Dodge.

Tennessee.—Samuel Milligan, Josiah M. Anderson, Robert L. Carruthers, Thomas Martin, Isaac R. Hawkins, R. J. McKinney, Alvin Cullom, William P. Hickerson, George W. Jones, F. K. Zollicoffer, William H. Stephens, A. W. O. Totten.

Illinois.—John Wood, Stephen T. Logan, John M. Palmer, Burton C. Cook, Thomas J. Turner.

Which report was accepted, and the names of the Commissioners were entered upon the record.

Mr. WICKLIFFE:—Certain printing has been ordered, but no provision has been made for paying for it. The Committee on Rules have therefore requested me to report the following resolution:

Resolved, That the Secretary procure for the use of the Convention the necessary stationery, and also provide for such printing as may be ordered. That the Journal, up to and including this day's proceeding, as well as the Rules, be printed for the use of the members.

The resolution of Mr. WICKLIFFE was agreed to.

The PRESIDENT:—The respective delegations have recommended, and the Chair announces the names of the following gentlemen to compose the committee ordered to be raised under the resolution of Mr. GUTHRIE, which was adopted yesterday:—New Hampshire, Asa Fowler; Vermont, Hiland Hall; Rhode

Island and Providence Plantations, Samuel Ames; Connecticut, Roger S. Baldwin; New Jersey, Joseph F. Randolph; Pennsylvania, Thomas White; Delaware, Daniel M. Bates; North Carolina, Thomas Ruffin; Kentucky, James Guthrie; Ohio, Thomas Ewing; Indiana, Caleb B. Smith; Illinois, Stephen T. Logan; Iowa, James Harlan; Maryland, Reverdy Johnson; Virginia, James A. Seddon.

Mr. WICKLIFFE:—The Committee on Rules have further considered the rule relating to the secrecy of the debates and proceedings of this body, and their convictions as to the necessity and propriety of its adoption remain unchanged. The prospect of an ultimate agreement among the Commissioners composing this body, in the opinion of the committee, would be materially lessened if all or any of its debates should be made public, for reasons which have already been stated. If any gentleman should desire to communicate with the Executive or Legislative authorities of his State any facts, during the progress of our business, I apprehend little difficulty would be experienced in obtaining the leave of the Convention. We therefore recommend the following Rule:

XIX. That nothing spoken in the Convention be printed, or otherwise published or communicated, without leave.

Mr. SEDDON:—I do not desire to discuss the adoption of the rule under consideration any further than I have already. The Commissioners from the State of Virginia are appointed under resolutions which make it their duty to communicate from time to time with her deliberative assemblies. We do not wish to have our right to do so subject to the action of this or any other body. It is no answer to this to say, that there is no doubt that the leave to make the necessary communications will be accorded to us when we ask it. We do not wish to ask it. We insist upon our rights in this respect, as it is our duty to the State that sent us here to do.

The rule was adopted upon a count of the members voting.

On motion, the Convention adjourned.

After the adjournment, the Convention in a body called upon

the President of the United States, when the several delegations were introduced by President Tyler, and the several Commissioners were presented by the chairmen of the several delegations.

FIFTH DAY.

Washington, Friday, *February 8th*, 1861.

The Convention was called to order at 12 o'clock by President Tyler. Prayer was offered by Rev. Dr. Butler. After sundry amendments, the Journal was approved.

Mr. SUMMERS:—I am directed by the Committee on Credentials to report that they find the following gentlemen duly accredited as members of the Convention:

New York.—David Dudley Field, William Curtis Noyes, James S. Wadsworth, Erastus Corning, Amaziah B. James, James C. Smith, Addison Gardner, Greene C. Bronson, John A. King, John E. Wool.

Massachusetts.—John Z. Goodrich, John M. Forbes, Richard P. Waters, Theophilus P. Chandler, Francis B. Crowninshield, George S. Boutwell, Charles Allen.

Missouri.—John D. Coalter, Alexander W. Doniphan, Waldo P. Johnson, Aylett H. Buckner, Harrison Hough.

On motion of the respective delegations the following gentlemen were added to the committee raised on the resolution of Mr. Guthrie:

New York.—Mr. Field.
Missouri.—Mr. Doniphan.
Tennessee.—Mr. Zollicoffer.

Mr. GUTHRIE:—I am instructed by the committee raised upon the resolution introduced by myself, to inform the Convention that that body is not able to report to-day, agreeable to the suggestion made at the time they were appointed. Several States are yet unrepresented on the committee, and delegations from some of them have only arrived this morning. I am therefore directed to ask for further time to make a report, assuring the Convention, at the same time, that a report will be made at soon as a proper regard to the interests of all sections will permit it to be done.

Mr. CLAY:—I move that the time for the report of the committee be extended until Monday next. As in the mean time there will be little business for the Convention to do, and that of a formal character, it might be as well to adjourn from this time until Monday; and I move further, that if delegates arrive from States now unrepresented, they may present their credentials to the committee, and if no question arises on them, they may then select a member of the committee on Mr. GUTHRIE's resolution, and report his name to the Secretary of that committee.

Mr. SEDDON:—I object to an adjournment until Monday. We can meet here to-morrow and do any business which may come before us.

The several motions of Mr. CLAY, with the alteration suggested by Mr. SEDDON, were then agreed to without a division.

Mr. ELLIS:—I move that the President be requested to issue cards of admission to the members and officers of this Convention.

Which motion was adopted.

Mr. HITCHCOCK:—I would like to understand whether we all construe the rule referring to the secrecy of our transactions alike. I am told that different constructions are placed upon it by different members, and would suggest the propriety of the PRESIDENT's giving his views of the meaning of the rule.

The PRESIDENT:—I understand, by the correct interpretation of the rule, that nothing which is said or done in the Convention having reference to any subject of business in it, can be spoken of or disclosed to any but members.

The Convention then adjourned.

SIXTH DAY.

WASHINGTON, SATURDAY, *February 9th*, 1861.

THE Convention was called to order by the PRESIDENT. Prayer was offered by Rev. Dr. BULLOCK. The Journal was read, corrected, and approved.

Mr. SUMMERS:—I am directed by the Committee on Credentials to report as members of this Convention the names of the following gentlemen from the State of Maine:—William P. Fessenden, Lot M. Morrill, Daniel E. Somes, John J. Perry, Ezra B. French, Freeman H. Morse, Stephen Coburn, Stephen C. Foster.

Mr. MORRILL, of Maine, and Mr. CROWNINSHIELD, of Massachusetts, were announced as members of the committee under the resolution of Mr. GUTHRIE.

Mr. TUCK:—I offer certain resolutions, which I desire to have printed and referred to the Committee on Resolutions.

The resolutions of Mr. TUCK were read, ordered to be printed, and referred. (These resolutions will be found on a subsequent page.)

Mr. CLAY:—I hold in my hand the proceedings of a very large Democratic meeting recently held at New Haven, in the State of Connecticut. Among them are certain resolutions, breathing a spirit of fervent devotion to the Union, and expressing an anxious desire for the settlement of the difficult questions now before the country. They have been sent to me with a request that I should lay them before this Convention. Why I was selected by them for the performance of this duty, I do not know, unless it was because, from my name and associations, they thought an assurance might be found that I participated in the sentiments expressed in the resolutions. I present them with great pleasure, and ask that they may be referred to the Committee on Resolutions.

The motion of Mr. CLAY was agreed to.

Mr. RANDOLPH:—I move that the Secretary be requested to furnish for the use of the members a printed list of the delegates to and officers of this Convention.

Which motion was adopted, and the Convention adjourned.

SEVENTH DAY.

WASHINGTON, MONDAY, *February* 11*th*, 1861.

THE Convention was called to order by the PRESIDENT. Prayer was offered by Rev. Dr. GURLEY.

After the reading and amendment of the Journal, Mr. GUTHRIE, from the Committee on Resolutions, asked for further time to make a general report of the matters submitted to them, which was given; and thereupon Mr. GUTHRIE, from the same Committee, made the following report upon the resolutions of a meeting in the State of Connecticut, which were referred to that committee on motion of Mr. CLAY:

The committee to whom were referred certain resolutions of the Democratic party of the State of Connecticut, report that in the opinion of the committee it is inexpedient for this Convention to act upon any resolution purporting to emanate from any political party whatever; and that the member of the Convention by whom they were presented have leave to withdraw the same.

The PRESIDENT:—I take this opportunity to announce to the Convention that the Door-keeper of the House of Representatives has transmitted to the Chair cards admitting members of this body on to the floor of the House. These cards will be delivered by the Secretary to such members as call for them.

Mr. CHASE:—I move that any propositions or resolutions which members of this Convention desire to have considered by the Committee on Resolutions and Propositions, may be presented to the committee through the Secretary, without being presented in Convention.

The motion was agreed to, and on motion the Convention adjourned until Wednesday the 13th instant, at 12 o'clock M.

EIGHTH DAY.

WASHINGTON, WEDNESDAY, *February* 13*th*, 1861.

THE Convention was called to order by the PRESIDENT, and prayer was offered by Rev. Dr. EDWARDS. The Journal, after sundry amendments, was approved.

Mr. GUTHRIE:—The Committee on Resolutions, &c., have labored diligently, and held protracted sessions, in the hope of being able to make their report to-day. This they find themselves unable to do. They are fully impressed with the necessity of immediate action, in view of the short time that will remain for Congress to consider the action of this Convention, if it shall become necessary to submit any proposition of this body to be acted upon by that. I have no doubt we shall be able to report on Friday, and I ask that we may have until that time to make a report.

The request of Mr. GUTHRIE was acceded to.

Mr. SEDDON:—The time has now arrived when, as one of the Commissioners from the State of Virginia, I find it necessary to ask the leave of the Convention to communicate to the Legislative authorities of Virginia, and to her Convention now in session, the state of the proceedings before this body, and the committee. I ask for liberty to do so, and believe that a proper regard to the instructions of the Legislature of the State under which my appointment is made, requires that my request should be granted.

Mr. BARRINGER offered the following resolution:

Resolved, That the Commissioners of any State represented in this Convention, upon their joint application, have leave to communicate to the Legislature, Governor, or Convention of said State, the proceedings of this body, or so much thereof as they may deem expedient.

Mr. SEDDON:—The passage of this resolution is all I ask.

Mr. FRELINGHUYSEN:—I move to amend the resolution by adding thereto: "But not to communicate what has transpired in the committee, before said committee has reported to the Convention.

Mr. SEDDON:—I do not deem the passage of the resolution at this moment as very important. At the suggestion of several gentlemen, I will move to lay it on the table, subject to be called up after Friday.

The Convention then adjourned to Friday at 12 o'clock.

On the evening of February 13th, the members of the Conference were informed of the death of Hon. JOHN C. WRIGHT, of Ohio, who officiated as temporary chairman previous to the permanent organization. In view of the anxious desire of all the members to recognize their appreciation of this act of Divine Providence, in removing from the sphere of his earthly labors one of the most valued Commissioners in attendance, President TYLER was requested to summon a special meeting of the Conference. In pursuance of his invitation, all the members attended on the morning of February 14th, when the following proceedings were had:

THURSDAY, WASHINGTON CITY, *February 14th*, 1861.

The Convention met in special session, pursuant to the call of the President.

The proceedings were opened with prayer by the Rev. Dr. HALL.

The following letter from the Secretary, CRAFTS J. WRIGHT, was read, and ordered to be entered upon the minutes:

WILLARD'S HOTEL,
WASHINGTON CITY, *February 13th*, 1861.

Hon. JOHN TYLER, *President of Conference Convention.*

DEAR SIR:—I grieve to communicate to you the fact, that the delegate from Ohio to this Conference Convention, the Hon. JOHN C. WRIGHT, departed this life this day, the 13th February, at half-past one o'clock.

Judge WRIGHT came to this Convention with a heart filled with fear for the safety of the Union. Though at an advanced age and nearly blind, he was filled with an earnest desire to add his efforts to that of others of the Convention called by the State of Virginia, and seek to agree on some measures honorable to each and all, to effect the object. Since the arrival of my father in Washington, he has been constant in his efforts to effect the end in view, and he has had his heart cheered with the belief that the object would be accomplished. Almost the last words that he uttered were, that he believed the Union would be preserved. He desired me to say, if the Union were preserved, he would die content. He called me to read to him, at 12 o'clock, the sections in the Constitution in regard to counting the votes, and this request, and this reading, terminated his knowledge on earth. In this desire of my father to do what he could, he pressed me to accompany him on account of his blindness. Since the Convention honored me with the appointment of Secretary, he required of me a promise that I would not leave the position. When I read the section of the Constitution to him, he required me then to leave him for the Convention. Whatever my personal feelings may be, I deem the pledge made sacred. I therefore ask that I may have leave of absence, until I carry the remains home to Ohio, and return to my duty.

Respectfully,

CRAFTS J. WRIGHT.

P. S.—J. HENRY PULESTON will act for me in my absence.

The PRESIDENT informed the Convention that the request of the Secretary had been complied with. The PRESIDENT asked what action the Convention proposed to take on the subject for which they had been specially assembled.

The Hon. SALMON P. CHASE, of Ohio, then said:—Mr. PRESIDENT, since we assembled yesterday in this Hall, it has pleased God to remove one of our number from all participation in the concerns of earth. It is my painful duty to announce to the Convention that JOHN C. WRIGHT, one of the Commissioners from Ohio, is no more. Full of years, honored by the confidence of the people, rich in large experience and ripened wisdom, and devoted in all his affections and all his powers to his country, and his whole country, he has been called from our midst at the very moment when the prudence and patriotism of his counsels seemed most needed. Such are the mysterious ways of Divine Providence. Judge WRIGHT was born in Wethersfield, Connecticut, on the 10th of August, 1784. The death of his parents made him an orphan in infancy; and he had little to depend upon in youth and early manhood, save his own energies and God's blessing. He was married, while young, to a daughter of Thomas Collier, of Litchfield, and for several years after resided at Troy, New York. When about twenty-six years old he removed to Steubenville, in Ohio, where he commenced the practice of the law, and rapidly rose to distinction in the profession. In 1822 he was elected a representative in Congress, where he became the associate and friend of Clay and Webster, and proved himself, on many occasions, worthy of their association and friendship.

After serving several terms in Congress, he was elected a Judge of the Supreme Court of Ohio, and, in 1834, removed from Steubenville to the city of Cincinnati. Resigning his seat soon afterwards, he resumed the labors of the bar, and, ever zealous for the improvement and elevation of the profession, established, in association with others, the Cincinnati law school.

In 1840, upon the dying request of CHARLES HAMMOND, the veteran editor of the "Cincinnati Gazette," Judge WRIGHT assumed the editorial control of that Journal, and retained that position until impaired vision, in 1853, admonished him of the necessity of withdrawing from labors too severe.

Thenceforward engaged in moderate labors, surrounded by affectionate relatives, enjoying the respect and confidence of his fellow-citizens, and manifesting always the liveliest concern in whatever related to the welfare and honor of his State and his country, he lived in tranquil retirement, until called by the Governor of Ohio, with the approbation of the Senate, to take part in the deliberations of this Conference Convention.

It was but a just tribute, sir, to his honored age, illustrated by abilities, by virtues, and by services, that he was unanimously selected as its temporary President. His interest in the great purpose of our assembling was profound and earnest. His labors to promote an auspicious result of its deliberations were active and constant. And when fatal disease assailed his life, and his enfeebled powers yielded to its virulence, his last utterances were of the Constitution and the Union.

Mr. PRESIDENT, Judge WRIGHT was my friend. His approval cheered and encouraged my own humble labors in the service of the State. Pardon me if I mingle private with public grief. He has gone from his last great labor. He was not permitted to witness upon earth the result of the mission upon which he and his associates, who here mourn his loss, were sent. God grant that the clouds which now darken over us may speedily disperse, and that through generous counsels and patriotic labors, guided by that good Providence which directed our fathers in its original formation, the Union of our States may be more than ever firmly cemented and established.

Mr. PRESIDENT, I offer the following resolutions:

Resolved, That in the death of our late venerable colleague, the Hon. JOHN C. WRIGHT, we mourn the loss to the State of Ohio, and to the nation at large, of one of our most sagacious statesmen and distinguished patriots; and to the cause of Union and conciliation, one of its most illustrious supporters.

Resolved, That while we deplore with saddened hearts the affliction with which an All-wise Providence has visited us, we know that no transition from life to immortality could have been more grateful to him who has fallen than this, in which his life has been offered a willing sacrifice in an effort to restore harmony to his distracted country.

Resolved, That the members of this Convention tender their heartfelt sympathies to the family of the deceased in this their great affliction.

Resolved, That these resolutions be spread upon the records of this body, and a copy of the same be transmitted to the family of the deceased.

Mr. CHARLES A. WICKLIFFE, of Kentucky, moved the adoption of the resolutions, and said:

Mr. PRESIDENT, I rise to tender my most cordial sanction and second to the resolutions which have just been read.

Mr. WRIGHT and myself entered the councils of this nation thirty-seven years ago. We served together during a period when party excitement ran high upon questions more of a personal than a constitutional character. I can bear witness not only to his ability, but to his personal integrity, and his purity of political action through our term of service in the House of Representatives. I have seldom met him since we separated at the termination of his service and mine in that body, which occurred at pretty near the same period; but whenever I have met him, I have found him the same stern advocate of the Union and of constitutional liberty. I rejoiced, therefore, when I found him in this hall on the day we first assembled here. I knew his conservative disposition and principles, and I promised myself that with his aid I could be more useful to my country and to my State than without him. In conversing with him upon the difficulties which now divide and distract our common country, I found him ready and willing, conscientiously and patriotically, to do that which I thought that portion of the country which I represent has a right to demand and expect of those who represent a different portion of our Union. And if my friend from Ohio (Mr. CHASE) and his colleagues will permit me to mingle my sorrow at the public loss, I will say nothing of the private bereavement of the family of our deceased colleague. I leave him to his country, and to you, with this testimony which I leave to his memory, his honesty of purpose and his patriotic love of country.

The Hon. A. W. LOOMIS, of Pennsylvania, said:

Mr. PRESIDENT, I desire to mingle my sincere regrets with those of the members of this assemblage at the sad and unexpected occurrence which deprived us of an able, experienced, and patriotic associate. My relations with the deceased were, for many years, probably more intimate than those which existed between him and any other member of this Convention. Forty years have elapsed since I first made his acquaintance. He was then in full, active, and extensive practice; a learned lawyer, an accomplished, skilful, and successful advocate. During the succeeding year I came to the bar, and resided and practiced in the same judicial circuit with our departed friend. For many years the most kind and intimate relations existed between us—sometimes colleagues, but usually opponents. So kind and genial was his nature, so fair and liberal his practice, that during our entire intercourse not an unkind word was uttered, and, so far as I know or believe, not an unpleasant feeling existed in the bosom of either.

Though not gifted with the highest order of eloquence, he was clear, distinct, and persuasive. His style of speaking resembled not the babbling brook or the dashing cataract, but usually the limpid stream, gliding gracefully amid fields and fruits and flowers, though sometimes assuming the power and proportions of the majestic river, cutting its sure and certain way to the mighty ocean.

His professional position, his kindness of heart, and genial humor, made him an object of high respect and warm regard among his professional brethren. And now, sir, as memory passes in review the pleasant incidents which marked our social and professional intercourse, the smitten heart shrinks in sadness and sorrow from the contemplation of our bereavement. He adorned, sir, the bar, the bench, and the halls of Legislation. He discharged, in all the relations of life, his obligations with fidelity. Of him it might be truly said:

> His life hath flowed a sacred stream, in whose calm depths
> The beautiful and pure alone are mirrored;
> Which, though shapes of ill may hover o'er the surface,
> Glides in light, and takes no shadows from them.

But, sir, the great crowning virtue and glory of his life was his acceptance of the mission which brought him here. Though whitened by the frosts of nearly eighty winters, neither lofty mountains nor intervening space could restrain his patriotic heart from a prompt response to the call of his country to mingle his influence in a sincere and sacred effort to save the Constitution and perpetuate the Union. He accepted the great trust; he mingled in our deliberations, and has fallen in the discharge of his duty. He has justly earned a title to the gratitude and respect of his country. May we not, sir, fondly hope that he, who was called from the discharge of such duties to the presence of his God, has passed from the sorrows of earth to the happiness of Heaven, and to the full fruition of joys pure, perfect, and eternal?

The Hon. THOMAS EWING, of Ohio, said:—I rise to bear my tribute of respect to the memory of the deceased. I have known him long. On my first entrance into active life, at the bar, I found him an able and distinguished member. Since that time down to the present day, he has been largely associated, in mind and person, with all the acts and progress, professional and political, of my life. I feel his loss intensely; and I feel it with more regret, because I know that on this occasion his voice would have been potential in our counsels, and would have been united with all of us who labor most earnestly for the preservation of the Union.

I tender my sympathies to the family of the deceased. I unite with them in their regrets and in their hopes of the happy future to which he may have attained,

The Hon. WILLIAM C. RIVES, of Virginia, said:—Though wholly unprepared to say any thing worthy of the solemnity of this occasion, I feel that I should be wanting, sir, in that sentiment of respect which is due to the character of a distinguished citizen, if I were not to add to what has been so eloquently spoken by others, a few words of personal recollection in regard to our deceased friend Judge WRIGHT. It so happened that we entered the public councils of the country at the same moment, and continued in them for the same period of time. It is now just thirty-seven years since I had the pleasure of meeting Judge WRIGHT, for the first time, in the House of Representatives of the United States. I may be permitted to say, that there were giants in those days. My honorable friend from Kentucky (Governor WICKLIFFE), who has already so feelingly addressed the Convention, will recollect that on the roll of the House of Representatives at that time stood the names of WEBSTER and EVERETT, of OAKLEY and STORRS, of SARGEANT and of HEMPHILL, of LEWIS MCLANE, of the immortal CLAY, and BARBOUR and RANDALL, and other gentlemen known to fame from the State which I have the honor to represent in this body, and LIVINGSTON of Louisiana, MCDUFFIE and HAMILTON of South Carolina, and other gentlemen who, on the spur of the occasion, I am not now able to recall, but whose names will forever shine upon the rolls of their country's glory. And yet in that body Judge WRIGHT, then in the maturity of his powers, though not previously known to the nation, vindicated an equal rank in debate with those gentlemen whose names I have mentioned. Sir, I shall never forget with what earnestness, with what manliness, with what integrity, with what ability, he ever uttered his convictions of public duty, whatever they were, in that consecrated hall.

After remaining here, I think, for six years, he retired to his own State for the purpose of assuming the duties of a highly-important and dignified office, which was soon followed by his retirement into the bosom of private life, where he met a rich and ample solace for the storms of his public career. He was followed there by the respect of his fellow-citizens throughout the country, and the confidence of his own State, as we have recently seen, by his being called from that honorable retirement to take part in the grave and solemn duties of this assembly. Sir, he came among us in obedience to the solemn call of patriotic duty, at a most exigent and distressing period in our national annals. He came here on an errand of peace, in the spirit of peace and conciliation. Such was the feeling entertained toward him by the whole of this assembly, that without the slightest preconcert, so far as I know, he was invited by general consent to preside during the preliminary stages of the organization of this Convention. I had an opportunity, from time to time, of private conversation with the aged statesman. I found no member of the assembly I met here, and, indeed, I have found nowhere any citizen of this wide Republic of ours, whose heart was more deeply imbued with the spirit of conciliation and of peace—of that spirit which was so solemnly and impressively uttered in his last prayer, "May the Union be preserved." Sir, it is not given to mortal man to choose the manner of his death; but if such were the privilege accorded to any human being, what more glorious end could he, appreciating a true fame, covet, than that which has been the lot of our departed friend? Sir, I speak what I feel, and I dare say I express a sentiment which has impressed itself upon many other bosoms in this assembly, when I say that his sudden death in the midst of our deliberations, seems to me to exalt—in some degree to canonize—our labors. This manifestation of the visible hand of God among us, brings us in the immediate presence of those solemn responsibilities which attach themselves to the discharge of our duties here. I doubt not that every member of this assembly is already deeply impressed with the solemnity of those duties, and I feel convinced that there are few, if any, in this assembly, who would not lay down their fleeting and feverish existence, and follow our deceased brother to his final account, if by doing so they could restore peace and harmony to this glorious Republic of ours.

It does not become me to make any professions of devotion to my country—to my whole country—but this I will say, in the spirit of the last prayer of my friend, that I should regard my poor life, such as it is, a cheap purchase—the cheapest imaginable purchase—for that great boon to our country, the restoration of its peace, of its harmony, of its unity, of its ancient confederated strength and glory.

The question was taken, and the resolutions were unanimously adopted.

The body of Judge WRIGHT was then brought into the hall, preceded by Rev. Dr. HALL, who read the impressive service of the Episcopal Church. A number of the members of the family, and of the friends of the deceased, were present during the services.

The funeral cortege proceeded from the hall to the depot of the Baltimore and Ohio Railroad.

The following gentlemen were designated to act as pall-bearers on the occasion:

Mr. Ewing,	Mr. Chase,
Mr. Hitchcock,	Mr. Loomis,

Mr. Backus,
Mr. Wolcott,
Mr. Sherman,
Mr. Vinton,
Mr. Groesbeck,
Mr. Stanton,
Mr. Harlan,
Mr. Gurley.

The proceedings upon the death of Judge WRIGHT were, by the Conference, ordered to be published, and the special session closed.

NINTH DAY.

WASHINGTON, FRIDAY, *February* 15*th*, 1861.

THE Convention was called to order by President TYLER, and prayer was offered by Rev. Mr. RENNER. The Journals of the 13th and 14th were read and approved.

The PRESIDENT:—I have this morning received several communications from different persons, which will be laid before the Convention. One is an invitation from HORATIO STONE, inviting the members of the Convention to visit his studio; also, a resolution of the House of Representatives, authorizing the admission of members of this Convention to the floor of the House. Also, a letter from J. E. SANDS, offering to the Convention certain flags which possess historical interest, from the fact that they were used in the convention which adopted the present Constitution of the United States. Also, a communication from HORATIO G. WARNER.

The communications were severally read and laid upon the table.

Mr. SUMMERS:—I am instructed by the Committee on Credentials to inform the Convention that the committee has received satisfactory evidence of the appointment by the Executive of Ohio of C. P. WOLCOTT, as a delegate to this Convention, in the place of JOHN C. WRIGHT, deceased.

Mr. ORTH:—I desire to offer the following resolutions, which I ask to have read for the information of the Convention. I have no purpose to admit spectators to seats on this floor, but in my judgment it is the right of the country to know what we are doing here. My constituents will not be satisfied with my course, unless I take means to give the public knowledge of all our transactions. I am aware that this is an invasion of the rule already adopted, requiring secresy, but in my opinion no possible harm can come from the daily publication of our debates. It is far better that true reports of these debates should be made, than that the distorted and perverted accounts which we see daily in the New York papers should be continued.

The resolutions were read, and are as follows:

Resolved, That Rules Sixteen (16) and Eighteen (18) of this Convention be, and the same hereby are, rescinded.

Resolved, That the President is hereby authorized to grant cards of admission to reporters of the press, not exceeding —— in number, which shall entitle them to seats on the floor of the Convention, for the purpose of reporting its proceedings.

Resolved, That no person be admitted to the floor of the Convention, except the members, officers, or reporters.

Mr. WICKLIFFE:—I do not wish to prolong this discussion myself, nor to cause it to be prolonged by others. I am sure that if we permit our debates to be reported, we shall never reach a conclusion which will in the slightest degree benefit the country. Every member will in that event wish to make a set speech, some of them three or four. I wish to have our time used in consultation and in action, not consumed in political speech-making. I do not care what the newspapers say of us. I know their accounts are distorted; but they would be distorted if we admitted reporters. Some of them assail us as a convention of compromisers—as belonging to the sandstone stratum of politics.

Mr. CHASE:—That is the formation which supports all others.

Mr. WICKLIFFE:—I know it, and I hope this Convention will prove to be the stratum which supports and preserves the Union and the country. Let us go on as we have begun, preserving secrecy; keeping our own counsels; making no speeches for outside consumption or personal reputation. Let us all keep steadily in mind the accomplishment of the great and good purpose which brought us here, and nothing else.

Mr. RANDOLPH:—New Jersey does not wish to have time consumed in making speeches. I think we should proceed at once to hear the report of the committee. I move that the resolutions offered be laid upon the table.

Mr. ORTH:—I suppose this motion cuts off debate. I should much have preferred to discuss the resolutions. I hope the motion will not prevail.

The motion to lay on the table passed in the affirmative by a *viva voce* vote.

The PRESIDENT:—Is the General Committee upon Propositions prepared to report? If it is, their report is now in order.

Mr. GUTHRIE:—That committee has given earnest and careful consideration to the subjects and propositions which have from time to time been presented to it. It has held numerous and protracted sessions, and the differences of opinion naturally existing between the members have been discussed in a spirit of candor and conciliation. The committee have not been so fortunate as to arrive at an unanimous conclusion. A majority of its members, however, have agreed upon a report which we think ought to be satisfactory to all sections of the Union, one which if adopted will, we believe, accomplish the purpose so much desired by every patriotic citizen. We think it will give peace to the country. In their behalf I have now the honor to submit, for the consideration of the Conference, the following:

PROPOSALS OF AMENDMENT TO THE CONSTITUTION OF THE UNITED STATES.

ARTICLE 1. In all the territory of the United States not embraced within the limits of the Cherokee treaty grant, north of a line from east to west on the parallel of 36 degrees 30 minutes north latitude, involuntary servitude, except in punishment of crime, is prohibited whilst it shall be under a Territorial government; and in all the territory south of said line, the status of persons owing service or labor, as it now exists, shall not be changed by law while such territory shall be under a Territorial government; and neither Congress nor the Territorial government shall have power to hinder or prevent the taking to said territory of persons held to labor or involuntary service, within the United States, according to the laws or usages of the State from which such persons may be taken, nor to impair the rights arising out of said relations, which shall be subject to judicial cognizance in the federal courts, according to the common law; and when any territory north or south of said line, within such boundary as Congress may prescribe, shall contain a population required for a member of Congress, according to the then federal ratio of representation, it shall, if its form of government be republican, be admitted into the Union on an equal footing with the original States, with or without involuntary service or labor, as the Constitution of such new State may provide.

ARTICLE 2. Territory shall not be acquired by the United States, unless by treaty; nor, except for naval and commercial stations and depots, unless such treaty shall be ratified by four-fifths of all members of the Senate.

ARTICLE 3. Neither the Constitution, nor any amendment thereof, shall be construed to give Congress power to regulate, abolish, or control within any State or Territory of the United States, the relation established or recognized by the laws thereof touching persons bound to labor or involuntary service therein, nor to interfere with or abolish involuntary service in the District of Columbia without the consent of Maryland and without the consent of the owners, or making the owners who do not consent just compensation; nor the power to interfere with or prohibit representatives and others from bringing with them to the City of Washington, retaining, and taking away, persons so bound to labor; nor the power to interfere with or abolish involuntary service in places under the exclusive jurisdiction of the United States within those States and Territories where the same is established or recognized; nor the power to prohibit the removal or transportation, by land, sea, or river, of persons held to labor or involuntary service in any State or Territory of the United States to any other State or Territory thereof where it is established or recognized by law or usage; and the right during transportation of touching at ports, shores, and landings, and of landing in case of distress, shall exist. Nor shall Congress have power to authorize any higher rate of taxation on persons bound to labor than on land.

ARTICLE 4. The third paragraph of the second section of the fourth article of the Constitution shall not be construed to prevent any of the States, by appropriate legislation, and through the action of their judicial and ministerial officers, from enforcing the delivery of fugitives from labor to the person to whom such service or labor is due.

ARTICLE 5. The foreign slave-trade and the importation of slaves into the United States and their Territories, from places beyond the present limits thereof, are forever prohibited.

ARTICLE 6. The first, second, third, and fifth articles, together with this article of these amendments, and the third paragraph of the second section of the first article of the Constitution, and the third paragraph of the second section of the fourth article thereof, shall not be amended or abolished without the consent of all the States.

ARTICLE 7. Congress shall provide by law that the United States shall pay to the owner the full value of his fugitive from labor, in all cases where the marshal or other officer, whose duty it was to arrest such fugitive, was prevented from so doing by violence or intimidation, or when, after arrest, such fugitive was rescued by force, and the owner thereby prevented and obstructed in the pursuit of his remedy for the recovery of such fugitive.

Mr. BALDWIN:—I have not been able to concur in opinion with those members of the committee who have presented the propositions just submitted. I do not deem them fair or equitable to the Free States, nor do I think they are likely to secure approval in those States. As one member of the minority, I have drawn up a report embodying my own views and perhaps those of some of my colleagues, which I now present for the consideration of the Conference:

MR. BALDWIN'S MINORITY REPORT.

The undersigned, one of the minority of the committee of one from each State, to whom was referred the consideration of the resolutions of the State of Virginia, and the other States represented, and all propositions for the adjustment of existing differences between the States, with authority to report what they deem right, necessary, and proper to restore harmony and preserve the Union, and report thereon, entered upon the duties of the committee with an anxious desire that they might be able to unite in the recommendation of some plan which, on due deliberation, should seem best adapted to maintain the dignity and authority of the Government of the United States, and at the same time secure to the people of every section that perfect equality of right to which they are entitled.

Convened, as we are, on the invitation of the Governor of Virginia, in pursuance of the resolutions of the General Assembly of that State, with an accompanying expression of the deliberate opinion of that body that, unless the unhappy controversy which now divides the States shall be satisfactorily adjusted, a permanent dissolution of the Union is inevitable; and, being earnestly desirous of an adjustment thereof, in concurrence with Virginia, in the spirit in which the Constitution was originally formed, and consistently with its principles, so as to afford to the people of all the States adequate security for all their rights, the attention of the undersigned was necessarily led to the consideration of the extent and equality of our powers, and to the propriety and expediency, under existing circumstances, of a recommendation by this Conference Convention of any specific action by Congress, whether of ordinary legislation, or in reference to constitutional amendments to be proposed by Congress on its own responsibility to the States.

A portion of the members of this Convention are delegated by the Legislatures of their respective States, and are required to act under their supervision and control, while others are the representatives only of the Executives of their States, and, having no opportunity of consulting the immediate representatives of the people, can only act on their individual responsibility.

Among the resolutions and propositions suggesting modes of adjustment appropriate to this occasion which were brought to the notice of the committee, were the resolutions of the State of Kentucky recommending to her sister States to unite with her in an application to Congress for the calling of a Convention in the mode prescribed by the Constitution for proposing amendments thereto.

The undersigned, for the reasons set forth in the accompanying resolution, and others which have been herein indicated, is of opinion that the mode of adjustment by a General Convention, as proposed by Kentucky, is the one which affords the best assurance of an adjustment acceptable to the people of every section, as it will afford to all the States which may desire amendments, an opportunity of preparing them with care and deliberation, and in such form as they may deem it expedient to prescribe, to be submitted to the consideration and deliberate action of delegates duly chosen and invested with equal powers from all the States.

The undersigned did not, therefore, deem it expedient that any of the measures of adjustment proposed by the majority of the committee, should be reported to this body to be discussed or acted upon by them, and he respectfully submits as a substitute for the articles of amendment to the Constitution, reported by the majority of the committee, the following preamble and resolution, and respectfully recommends the adoption thereof.

ROGER S. BALDWIN.

Whereas, unhappy differences exist which have alienated from each other portions of the people of the United States to such an extent as seriously to disturb the peace of the nation, and impair the regular and efficient action of the Government within the sphere of its constitutional powers and duties;

And whereas, the Legislature of the State of Kentucky has made application to Congress to call a Convention for proposing amendments to the Constitution of the United States;

And whereas, it is believed to be the opinion of the people of other States that amendments to the Constitution are or may become necessary to secure to the people of the United States, of every section, the full and equal enjoyment of their rights and liberties, so far as the same may depend for their security and protection on the powers granted to or withheld from the General Government, in pursuance of the national purposes for which it was ordained and established;

And whereas, it may be expedient that such amendments as any of the States may desire to have proposed, should be presented to the Convention in such form as the respective States desiring the same may deem proper;

This Convention does, therefore, recommend to the several States to unite with Kentucky in her application to Congress to call a convention for proposing amendments to the Constitution of the United States, to be submitted to the Legislatures of the several States, or to conventions therein, for ratification, as the one or the other mode of ratification may be proposed by Congress, in accordance with the provision in the fifth article of the Constitution.

Mr. FIELD:—I do not concur in the conclusions to which the majority of the committee have arrived. I may say that I wholly dissent from them. I have not deemed it necessary to make a separate report. At a suitable time I shall endeavor to make known to the Conference my views upon the topics which have occupied the attention of the committee.

Mr. CROWNINSHIELD:—I occupy substantially the same position as Mr. FIELD, and shall make my views known at a proper time.

Mr. SEDDON:—The report presented by the majority, I think, is a wide departure from the course we should have adopted. Virginia has prepared and presented a plan, and has invited this Conference to consider it. I think we ought to take up her propositions, amend and perfect them if need be, and then adopt or reject them. To avoid all misconstruction as to my individual opinions or position, I have reduced my views to writing, which, with the leave of the Conference, I will now read.

No objection being made, Mr. SEDDON proceeded to read the following:

REPORT OF MR. SEDDON.

The undersigned, acting on the recommendation of the Commissioners from the State of Virginia, as a member of the committee appointed by this Convention to consider and recommend propositions of adjustment, has not been so happy as to accord with the report submitted by the majority; and as he more widely dissents from the opinions entertained by the other dissenting members, he feels constrained, in vindication of his position and opinions, to present on his part this brief report, recommending, as a substitute for the report of the majority, a proposition subjoined. To this course he feels the more impelled, by deference to the resolutions of the General Assembly of his State, inviting the assemblage of this Convention, and suggesting a basis of adjustment.

These resolutions declare, that "in the opinion of the General Assembly of Virginia the propositions embraced in the resolutions presented to the Senate of the United States by the Hon. JOHN J. CRITTENDEN, so modified as that the first article proposed as an amendment to the Constitution of the United States shall apply to all the territory of the United States now held or hereafter acquired south of latitude 36° 30′, and provided that slavery of the African race shall be effectually protected as property therein during the continuance of the territorial government, and the fourth article shall secure to the owners of slaves the right of transit with their slaves between and through the non-slaveholding States or Territories, constitute the basis of such an adjustment of the unhappy controversy which now divides the States of this Confederacy, as would be accepted by the people of this Commonwealth."

From this resolution, it is clear that the General Assembly, in its declared opinion of what would be acceptable to the people of Virginia, not only required the Crittenden propositions as a basis, but also held the modifications suggested in addition essential. In this the undersigned fully concurs. But, in his opinion, the propositions reported by the majority do not give, but materially weaken the Crittenden propositions themselves, and fail to accord the modifications suggested. The undersigned therefore, feels it his duty to submit and recommend, as a substitute, the resolutions referred to, as proposed by the Hon. JOHN J. CRITTENDEN, with the incorporation of the modifications suggested by Virginia explicitly expressed, and with some alterations on points which, he is assured, would make them more acceptable to that State, and, as he hopes, to the whole Union. The propositions submitted are appended, marked No. 1.

The undersigned, while contenting himself, in the spirit of the action taken by the General Assembly of his State, with the proposal of that substitute for the majority report, would be untrue to his own convictions, shared, as he believes, by the majority of the commissioners from Virginia, and to his sense of duty, if he did not emphatically declare, as his settled and deliberate judgment, that for permanent safety in this Union, to the slaveholding States, and the restoration of integrity to the Union and harmony and peace to the country, a guarantee of actual power in the Constitution and in the working of the Government to the slaveholding and minority section is *indispensable.* How such guarantee might be most wisely contrived and judiciously adjusted to the frame of the Government, the undersigned forbears now to inquire. He is not exclusively addicted to any special plan, but believing that such guarantee might be adequately afforded by a partition of power in the Senate between the two sections, and by a recognition that *ours* is a Union of freedom and consent, not constraint and force, he respectfully submits, for consideration by members of the Convention, the plan hereto appended, marked No. 2.

Whether he shall feel bound to invoke the action of the Convention upon it, may depend on the future manifestations of sentiment in this body.

All which is respectfully submitted,

JAMES A. SEDDON.
Commissioner from Virginia.

February 15*th*, 1861.

No 1.

Joint Resolutions proposing certain amendments to the Constitution of the United States.

Whereas, serious and alarming dissensions have arisen between the Northern and Southern States, concerning the rights and security of the rights of the slaveholding States, and especially their rights in the common territory of the United States; and *whereas*, it is eminently desirable and proper that those dissensions, which now threaten the very existence of this Union, should be permanently quieted and settled by constitutional provisions, which shall do equal justice to all sections, and thereby restore to the people that peace and good will which ought to prevail between all the citizens of the United States: Therefore,

Resolved, by this Convention, that the following articles are hereby approved and submitted to the Congress of the United States, with the request that they may, by the requisite constitutional majority of two-thirds, be recommended to the respective States of the Union, to be, when ratified by Conventions of three-fourths of the States, valid and operative as amendments of the Constitution of the Union.

ARTICLE 1. In all the territory of the United States, now held or hereafter acquired, situate north of latitude thirty-six degrees and thirty minutes, slavery or involuntary servitude, except as a punishment for crime, is prohibited, while such territory shall remain under territorial government. In all the territory south of said line of latitude, slavery of the African race is hereby recognized as existing, and shall not be interfered with by Congress, but shall be protected as property by all the departments of the territorial government during its continuance; and when any territory, north or south of said line, within such boundaries as Congress may prescribe, shall contain the population requisite for a member of Congress, according to the then federal ratio of representation of the people of the United States, it shall, if its form of government be republican, be admitted into the Union on an equal footing with the original States, with or without slavery, as the Constitution of such new State may provide.

ARTICLE 2. Congress shall have no power to abolish slavery in places under its exclusive jurisdiction, and situate within the limits of States that permit the holding of slaves.

ARTICLE 3. Congress shall have no power to abolish slavery within the District of Columbia, so long as it exists in the adjoining States of Virginia and Maryland, or either, nor without the consent of the free white inhabitants, nor without just compensation first made to such owners of slaves as do not consent to such abolishment. Nor shall Congress at any time prohibit officers of the Federal Government, or members of Congress, whose duties require them to be in said District, from bringing with them their slaves, and holding them as such during the time their duties may require them to remain there, and afterwards taking them from the District.

ARTICLE 4. Congress shall have no power to prohibit or hinder the transportation of slaves from one State to another, or to a Territory in which slaves are by law permitted to be held, whether that transportation be by land, navigable rivers, or by the sea. And if such transportation be by sea, the slaves shall be protected as property by the Federal Government. And the right of transit by the owners with their slaves, in passing to or from one slaveholding State or Territory to another, between and through the non-slaveholding States and Territories, shall be protected. And in imposing direct taxes pursuant to the Constitution, Congress shall have no power to impose on slaves a higher rate of tax than on land, according to their just value.

ARTICLE 5. That, in addition to the provisions of the third paragraph of the second section of the fourth article of the Constitution of the United States, Congress shall provide by law, that the United States shall pay to the owner who shall apply for it, the full value of his fugitive slave, in all cases, when the marshal, or other officer, whose duty it was to arrest said fugitive, was prevented from so doing by violence or intimidation, or when, after arrest, said fugitive was rescued by force, and the owner thereby prevented and obstructed in the pursuit of his remedy for the recovery of his fugitive slave, under the said clause of the Constitution and the laws made in pursuance thereof. And in all such cases, when the United States shall pay for such fugitive, they shall reimburse themselves by imposing and collecting a tax on the county or city in which said violence, intimidation, or rescue was committed, equal in amount to the sum paid by them, with the addition of interest and the costs of collection; and the said county or city, after it has paid said amount to the United States, may, for its indemnity, sue and recover from the wrong-doers, or rescuers, by whom the owner was prevented from the recovery of his fugitive slave, in like manner as the owner himself might have sued and recovered.

ARTICLE 6. No future amendment of the Constitution shall affect the five preceding articles, nor the third paragraph of the second section of the first article of the Constitution, nor the third paragraph of the second section of the fourth article of said Constitution, and no amendment shall be made to the Constitution which will authorize or give to Congress any power to abolish or interfere with slavery in any of the States, by whose laws it is or may be allowed or permitted.

ARTICLE 7, Sec. 1. The elective franchise and the right to hold office, whether federal, State, territorial, or municipal, shall not be exercised by persons who are, in whole or in part, of the African race.

And *whereas*, also, besides those causes of dissension embraced in the foregoing amendments proposed to the Constitution of the United States, there are others which come within the jurisdiction of Congress, and may be remedied by its legislative power: and *whereas* it is the desire of this Convention, as far its influence may extend, to remove all just cause for the popular discontent and agitation which now disturb the peace of the country, and threaten the stability of its institutions: Therefore,

1. *Resolved*, That the laws now in force for the recovery of fugitive slaves are in strict pursuance of the plain and mandatory provisions of the Constitution, and have been sanctioned as valid and constitutional by the judgment of the Supreme Court of the United States; that the slaveholding States are entitled to the faithful observance and execution of those laws, and that they ought not to be repealed, or so modified or changed as to impair their efficiency; and that laws ought to be made for the punishment of those who attempt, by rescue of the slave or other illegal means, to hinder or defeat the due execution of said laws.

2. That all State laws which conflict with the fugitive slave acts, or any other constitutional acts of Congress, or which in their operation impede,

hinder, or delay the free course and due execution of any of said acts, are null and void by the plain provisions of the Constitution of the United States. Yet those State laws, void as they are, have given color to practices, and led to consequences which have obstructed the due administration and execution of acts of Congress, and especially the acts for the delivery of fugitive slaves, and have thereby contributed much to the discord and commotion now prevailing. This Convention, therefore, in the present perilous juncture, does not deem it improper, respectfully and earnestly to recommend the repeal of those laws to the several States which have enacted them, or such legislative corrections or explanations of them as may prevent their being used or perverted to such mischievous purposes.

3. That the act of the 18th of September, 1850, commonly called the Fugitive Slave Law, ought to be so amended as to make the fee of the Commissioner, mentioned in the eighth section of the act, equal in amount, in the cases decided by him, whether his decision be in favor of or against the claimant. And to avoid misconstructions, the last clause of the fifth section of said act, which authorizes the person holding a warrant for the arrest or detention of a fugitive slave, to summon to his aid the *posse comitatus*, and which declares it to be the duty of all good citizens to assist him in its execution, ought to be so amended as to expressly limit the authority and duty to cases in which there shall be resistance, or danger of resistance or rescue.

4. That the laws for the suppression of the African slave-trade, and especially those prohibiting the importation of slaves into the United States, ought to be made effectual, and ought to be thoroughly executed, and all further enactments necessary to those ends ought to be promptly made.

No. 2.

Proposed Amendments by Mr. Seddon.

To secure concert and promote harmony between the slaveholding and non-slaveholding sections of the Union, the assent of the majority of the Senators from the slaveholding States, and of the majority of the Senators from the non-slaveholding States, shall be requisite to the validity of all action of the Senate, on which the ayes and noes may be called by five Senators.

And on a written declaration, signed and presented for record on the Journal of the Senate by a majority of Senators from either the non-slaveholding or slaveholding States, of their want of confidence in any officer or appointee of the Executive, exercising functions exclusively or continuously within the class of States, or any of them, which the signers represent, then such officer shall be removed by the Executive; and if not removed at the expiration of ten days from the presentation of such declaration, the office shall be deemed vacant and open to new appointment.

The connection of every State with the Union is recognized as depending on the continuing assent of its people, and compulsion shall in no case, nor under any form, be attempted by the Government of the Union against a

State acting in its collective or organic capacity. Any State, by the action of a convention of its people, assembled pursuant to a law of its Legislature, is held entitled to dissolve its relation to the Federal Government, and withdraw from the Union; and, on due notice given of such withdrawal to the Executive of the Union, he shall appoint two Commissioners, to meet two Commissioners to be appointed by the Governor of the State, who, with the aid, if needed from the disagreement of the Commissioners, of an umpire, to be selected by a majority of them, shall equitably adjudicate and determine finally a partition of the rights and obligations of the withdrawing State; and such adjudication and partition being accomplished, the withdrawal of such State shall be recognized by the Executive, and announced by public proclamation to the world.

But such withdrawing State shall not afterwards be readmitted into the Union without the assent of two-thirds of the States constituting the Union at the time of the proposed readmission.

Mr. COALTER:—It is proper that I should say a word in relation to the position of Missouri in this Conference. It is expressly referred to in the resolution under which we hold our appointment, passed by the Senate and House of Representatives. It is believed by the people of Missouri that the rights and privileges of the slaveholding States are in danger, and that the time has arrived when they should be secured by additional guarantees. Those guarantees must be such as will secure the honor and equal rights of the slaveholding States.

I wish to say, further, that we, as Commissioners, must act at all times under the control of the General Assembly or the State Convention of our State. Before we can act definitely upon either of the propositions submitted, I think it will be our duty to transmit them to the General Assembly for instructions.

Mr. WICKLIFFE:—The several reports are now before the Conference. I presume it will be the desire of every member to give them a careful examination. In order to prevent all unnecessary delay, I move that the several reports be laid upon the table, that they be printed at once and distributed to the members, and made the special order of the Conference for 12 o'clock to-morrow.

The motion of Mr. Wickliffe was agreed to.

Mr. WICKLIFFE:—I have drawn up a preamble and a resolution which I wish to offer for the consideration of the Conference. I shall not press action upon them to-day, but desire to have them laid on the table and printed. I shall call them up after the report of the General Committee is disposed of. It would gratify me much, and I think greatly tend to the peace and harmony of the country, if they could be adopted at once, and published. It is well known to most of you that there is nothing in all the legislation or action of the Free States, which has created so much excitement and alarm among the people of the slaveholding States, as the passage of the so called "personal liberty" acts. They are regarded as deliberate infractions and breaches of the Constitution, and as attempts to nullify the operation of a constitutional enactment of Congress. But I do not wish to invite discussion upon the subject now; I hope my motion will not meet with objection.

The motion of Mr. WICKLIFFE was adopted, and the preamble and resolution were presented as follows:

MR. WICKLIFFE'S PREAMBLE AND RESOLUTION.

Whereas, the second section of the fourth article of the Constitution of the United States declares, "that no person held to service or labor in one State, under the laws thereof, escaping into another, shall in consequence of any law or regulation therein, be discharged from such service or labor, but shall be delivered up on claim of the party to whom such service or labor may be due."

This clause is one of the compromises without which no Constitution would have been adopted. It was a guarantee to the States in which such labor and service existed by law, that their rights should be respected and regarded by all the States; and it is not within the competency of any State to disregard the obligation it imposes, or to render it valueless by legislative enactments. And *whereas*, the House of Representatives of the United States did, on the —— day of February, by unanimous vote, declare that neither the Congress of the United States nor the people or government of any non-slaveholding State, has the constitutional right to legislate upon, or to interfere with slavery in any slaveholding State in the Union.

This declaration is regarded by this Convention as an admission that the statutes of those States, passed for the purpose of defeating the provision of the Constitution aforesaid, and the laws of Congress made to enforce the just and proper execution of this constitutional guarantee, are in violation of the supreme law of the land.

The provisions of the statutes in many of the non-slaveholding States, commonly known and called "personal liberty bills," amount in their consequences to a practical nullification of the acts of Congress of February 12th, 1793, and September 18th, 1850, and are in violation of the second section of the fourth article of the Constitution, as before stated. That the spirit of those statutes appears to be repugnant to the principles of compromise and mutual and liberal concessions which dictated the section of the Constitution in question, and which pervades every part of that instrument. It is, therefore, respectfully requested by this Convention that the several States abrogate all such obnoxious enactments.

That the spirit of comity between the States, and the spirit of unity and fraternity which should actuate all the people of these United States, require that complete right and security of transit with all persons who owe them service or labor should be allowed to the citizens of each State by the laws of every other State.

Resolved, That a copy of the foregoing be sent by the President of this Convention to the Governors of each of the free States, as the deliberate judgment and opinion of this Convention, and that he request the same be laid before their respective Legislatures.

Mr. CHASE:—I move that all the resolutions, of the States, under which Commissioners have been appointed, or relating to subjects to come before this Conference, be printed. I think this course convenient and necessary, and one reason that I may assign is this: The opinion of the Legislature of the State of Ohio, as expressed in one of the resolutions adopted by that body, is, that it would have been wiser and better if the time for holding this Conference had been deferred until a later period. Ohio has expressly said in her resolutions that she is not prepared to assent to the terms of settlement proposed by Virginia, and has expressed the opinion that the Constitution as it now stands, if fairly interpreted and obeyed, contains ample provision for the correction of all the evils which are claimed to exist. Nevertheless she is willing to meet in a friendly spirit and consult with her sister States. But the opinion extensively prevails that this Conference ought not to have been called upon so short a notice and before the inauguration of the incoming administration. We, the Commissioners from that State, are instructed in the resolutions, to which I have referred, to use our influence to procure an adjournment of this Conference, before final action is taken, to the 4th of April next. I shall feel it my duty, at some future time, to make a motion to that effect. The extent to which I shall urge its adoption will depend in some measure upon the course of events and the opinions of my colleagues. In the mean time I wish to see all the resolutions printed.

The motion of Mr. CHASE was agreed to. The resolutions as printed will be found in the appendix.

Mr. ALLEN, of Massachusetts:—Before the adjournment today I desire to know what will be the order of business when these various reports come up for discussion. By the general rules governing parliamentary proceedings, to which I suppose we are subject, I understand the first question will be upon the substitution of the minority report presented by the gentleman from Connecticut (Mr. BALDWIN) for the report of the majority; and that, upon that question, amendments may be offered, and either accepted or rejected, both to the reports of the majority and the minority. I think it would be well to have this matter understood. Am I right in this?

The PRESIDENT:—The Chair understands that the gentleman from Massachusetts has correctly pointed out the manner of proceeding.

On motion of Mr. HACKLEMAN, the Conference then adjourned until 12 o'clock to-morrow.

TENTH DAY.

WASHINGTON, SATURDAY, *February* 16*th*, 1861.

THE Conference was called to order by the PRESIDENT at 12 o'clock M.

Prayer was offered by Rev. Dr. SUNDERLAND.

The Journal was read by the Assistant Secretary, Mr. PULESTON, and, being corrected, was approved.

The PRESIDENT:—I have received a communication from Mr. W. C. JEWETT, which I am requested to lay before the Conference. Should any member desire to have it read, it will be presented upon motion. I am not inclined to occupy the time of the Conference by reading it, unless some member specially requests that it be read.

Mr. SEDDON:—Let it be laid on the table without reading.

The PRESIDENT:—That disposition will be made of it.

Mr. WICKLIFFE:—I am instructed, by the Committee on Rules and Organization, to propose an amendment to the Eleventh Rule which has been adopted. As the Rule now stands, no appeal is allowed from the decision of the Chair upon questions of order. It is not probable that either the Chair or the Conference would wish to be bound in that way. The purpose of the resolution is to assimilate the Rule in this respect to the practice in parliamentary bodies, and to allow an appeal from the decision of the Chair to the Conference itself. I offer the following resolution:

"*Resolved*, That the Eleventh Rule of this Convention be so amended as to allow an appeal from the decision of the PRESIDENT, which appeal shall be decided without debate."

On the passage of this resolution a division was called for, and upon a count by the Secretaries, the PRESIDENT declared it adopted.

Mr. WICKLIFFE:—I now offer another resolution—the following:

"*Resolved*, That in the discussions which may take place in this Convention, no member shall be allowed to speak longer than thirty minutes."

We must all by this time be impressed with the necessity of prompt, immediate, and efficient action. I do not charge any member of the body with any purpose unnecessarily to consume the time of the Convention in making speeches. I have no reason to believe that any such purpose exists. But the present Congress is rapidly drawing to a close. If any plan is adopted it will be nugatory, unless recommended by Congress. If we are to sit here until each member of the Conference has spoken upon each question presented, as many times and as long as he pleases, I fear the Congress will close its labors before we do ours.

Mr. DAVIS:—I think thirty minutes quite too long. Our opinions are formed. Before this time probably every member has determined his course of action, and it will not be changed by debate. I move to strike out the word "thirty," and insert the word "ten."

Mr. HITCHCOCK:—I am altogether opposed to this attempt in advance to cut off or limit debate. I am sure it cannot meet with favor from the Conference, for reasons so obvious that I will not occupy time in stating them. I move to lay the resolution on the table.

Several gentlemen here interposed and appealed to Mr. HITCHCOCK to withdraw his motion, as it would cut off all debate upon the merits of the resolution. Mr. HITCHCOCK accordingly withdrew it.

Mr. SEDDON:—We have one rule already which prohibits any member from speaking more than twice upon any question without special leave, and a member cannot speak a second time until every other, who desires to speak, has spoken. This was the rule, I believe, in the Convention that formed our present Constitution, and no one complained of its operation there. I am as much impressed with the necessity of expediting our action as any one can be, and should be among the last to protract our sessions. But this resolution looks too much like suppressing discussion—like cutting off debate. I desire at the proper time to be heard upon the report which I have submitted. It will be impossible to discuss the grave questions involved in it in the space of a brief half hour.

Mr. CHASE:—I hope Governor WICKLIFFE will consent to a postponement of his resolution for the present. It is anticipating a necessity that may not arise. As yet no one has abused the privileges of debate. It is not well to assume in advance that any one will do so.

Mr. WICKLIFFE:—I have no wish to press this resolution upon the Convention, and it may be as well to postpone it for the present. I will move its postponement until Tuesday morning next.

The motion to postpone was unanimously agreed to.

Mr. CRISFIELD:—I move that the hour of meeting hereafter be ten o'clock in the morning.

Mr. JOHNSON, of Maryland:—I am sure that we shall all agree that this hour is quite too early. I wish to make all reasonable progress, but I think we shall find it difficult to secure a quorum at that hour. I move to amend by inserting *eleven* o'clock.

Mr. EWING:—I think we had better let the hour of meeting remain where our rules leave it. We shall find our labors severe enough if we commence at twelve o'clock.

Mr. CRISFIELD:—I will accept the amendment of my colleague. Let the time of meeting be eleven o'clock.

The motion of Mr. CRISFIELD as amended was agreed to without a division.

Mr. CHASE:—I have a motion which I desire to make, and as I do not wish to press it to a vote at the present time, I will move to lay it on the table. But I wish to have it before the Conference. It is apparent to me that we ought to pass it at some time, in order to give members who may belong to delegations in which differences of opinion exist, an opportunity of appearing on the record as they personally wish to vote. I move to amend the first rule by inserting after the word "representing," the words, "The yeas and nays of the delegates from each State, on any question, shall be entered on the Journal when it is desired by any delegate."

On motion of Mr CHASE, the amendment was laid upon the table.

The PRESIDENT:—The Conference will now proceed to the order of the day, the question being upon the several reports presented by the General Committee of one from each State.

The chair was taken, at the request of the PRESIDENT, by Mr. ALEXANDER, of New Jersey.

Mr. BALDWIN:—I move to substitute the report presented by myself for the report of the majority of the Committee. I will consent to strike out that part of it which relates to—

Mr TURNER:—Before the gentleman from Connecticut proceeds with his argument I trust he will give way for the introduction of a resolution. I am sure the time has come when we ought to pass such a resolution as I now offer. I am unwilling to sit here longer unless some means are taken to secure a report of our proceedings.

The PRESIDENT:—A resolution is not now in order.

Mr. TURNER:—I ask that the resolution may be read for the information of the Conference, and also ask the leave of the Conference for its introduction.

The resolution was read. It provided for the appointment of a stenographer.

The question was taken, and upon a division the leave to introduce it was refused.

Mr. BALDWIN:—I rise for the purpose of supporting my motion to substitute the report presented by myself for that presented by the majority of the committee. As I was about to remark, when the resolution just disposed of was introduced, I will consent to strike out all that portion of my report which precedes the words "whereas unhappy differences," &c., in order that the substitute offered may conform more nearly in substance to the proposition of the majority. It seems desirable on all hands that whatever we adopt here should be presented to Congress; and if it receives the sanction of that body, should be by it presented to the States for their approval. My report when thus amended will be in a proper form for such a disposition.

My report, it will be noticed, is based mainly upon the action of the Legislature of Kentucky. I have adopted those resolutions of Kentucky as the basis of my recommendation, on account of the short time which remains for any action at all, and because it appears to me that the kind of proceeding indicated in them is best calculated to meet with favor in the States which must approve any action taken here before it can be made effectual.

The resolutions of Virginia, under which this Convention is called, were adopted on the 19th of January last. The resolutions of Kentucky to which I have referred were adopted on the 25th of the same month. It is not only the necessary presumption that the latter were passed with a full knowledge of the action of Virginia, but I understand from their reading that they were adopted in consequence of the proposition of the latter State. I am disposed to favor the line of policy initiated in the resolutions of the State of Kentucky.

There are two ways of presenting amendments to the Constitution provided in that instrument. By the first, by Congress whenever two-thirds of both Houses shall deem such amendments necessary: or by the second, the same body, upon the application of the Legislatures of two-thirds of the States, may call a convention for the purpose of proposing amendments. These two are the *only* modes in which, under that instrument, amendments can be proposed to the Constitution. Either of these is adequate, and it was the manifest intention of its framers to secure due consideration of any changes which might be proposed to the fundamental law of our Government.

It is conceded on all hands that our action here will amount to nothing, unless it meets the approval of Congress, and such proposals of amendment as we shall agree upon are recommended by that body to the States for adoption. The session of the present Congress is drawing to a close. There remain only fifteen or sixteen days during which it can transact business. Can any one suppose that in the present state of the country, with the large number of important measures before Congress and awaiting its action, any proposition of real importance emanating from this Conference could be properly considered by either House in this short time? I am assuming just now that this is a Convention which has the right, under the Constitution or by precedent, to make such propositions. But if we do not remember, most certainly Congress will, that however respectable this body may be, however large may be the constituency which it represents, it is, after all, one which has no existence under, and is not recognized by the Constitution. In a recent speech in the Senate, Judge COLLAMER, of Vermont, one of the ablest lawyers in that body, has more than intimated a doubt whether Congress could, under the Constitution, entertain proposals of amendment presented to it by such a body as this. But, waving all technicalities, the substantial objection which influences my mind is, that the course of action proposed by the majority of the committee is contrary to the spirit of the Constitution. When the people adopted that instrument and subjected themselves to its operation, they intended and had a right to understand that it should be amended only in the manner provided by the Constitution itself. They did not intend that amendments should be proposed under, or the existence of the Constitution endangered by any extraneous pressure whatever. They wisely provided a way in which amendments might be proposed, or rather two ways. Under either of them, due examination and consideration was secured. They would not have consented to any other way of proposing amendments. The General Government, on the adoption of the Constitution, for all national purposes, took the place of the State Governments. The people of the United States from that time, in the language of a distinguished Senator from Kentucky, owed a paramount allegiance to the General Government, and a subordinate allegiance only to the State Governments. Changes in the Constitution, then, can only be *properly* made in the manner provided by the Constitution. Propositions for changes in it must come from the people, or their representatives in Congress. Any attempt to coerce Congress, or to influence its action in a manner not provided by the Constitution, is a disregard of the rights of the people.

Why are we assembled here to urge these amendments upon

Congress? to induce Congress to recommend them to the people for adoption? Are we the representatives of the people of the United States? Are we acting for them, and as their authorized agents, in this endeavor to press amendments upon the attention of Congress? Because, if our action is to have any effect at all, it must be to induce Congress to conform to our wishes—to propose the very amendments which we prepare.

The members of the House of Representatives were elected by the people. They were selected to perform, and they do perform, their duties and functions under the obligations of their official oaths. There is no question about their agency, or their right to act in the premises. The Constitution makes them the agents of the people. The Legislature of the State of Kentucky, well understanding and appreciating the only true method in which constitutional amendments should be proposed, with all the formality of a legislative act approved by the Executive of that State, has applied to Congress for the call of a convention for proposing amendments to the Constitution of the United States, and has requested the President to lay those resolutions immediately before Congress. She wishes other States to unite with her in the preparing and proposing of amendments to the Constitution. This is the correct, the legal, the patriotic course. This was what Kentucky had the right to ask, and this is all she has asked.

Mr. BALDWIN here read the Kentucky resolutions, as follows:

Resolutions recommending a call for a Convention of the United States.

Whereas, The people of some of the States feel themselves deeply aggrieved by the policy and measures which have been adopted by some of the people of the other States; and *whereas* an amendment of the Constitution of the United States is deemed indispensably necessary to secure them against similar grievances in the future: Therefore,

Resolved, by the General Assembly of the Commonwealth of Kentucky, that application to Congress to call a Convention for proposing amendments to the Constitution of the United States, pursuant to the fifth article thereof, be, and the same is hereby, now made by this General Assembly of Kentucky; and we hereby invite our sister States to unite with us, without delay, in a similar application to Congress.

Resolved, That the Governor of this State forthwith communicate the foregoing resolution to the President of the United States, with the request that he immediately place the same before Congress and the Executives of the several States, with a request that they lay them before their respective Legislatures.

Resolved, If the Convention be called in accordance with the provisions of the foregoing resolutions, the Legislature of the Commonwealth of Kentucky suggest for the consideration of that Convention, as a basis for settling existing difficulties, the adoption, by way of amendments to the Constitution, of the resolutions offered in the Senate of the United State by the Hon. JOHN J. CRITTENDEN.

DAVID MERIWETHER,
Speaker of the House of Representatives.
THOMAS P. PORTER,
Speaker of the Senate.

Approved January 25, 1861.
B. MAGOFFIN.

By the Governor:
THOMAS B. MONROE, JR.,
Secretary of State.

Mr. BALDWIN continued:—Now, what are we asked to do by the majority of the committee? It is not to unite with Kentucky or to accede to her wishes for a convention of the States, under the Constitution, but to thwart the wishes of Kentucky, and to induce Congress itself to originate and propose amendments, or to propose those which we may originate. Kentucky asks that the people of the States themselves might elect delegates to a convention, who should carefully consider the whole subject. The Kentucky resolutions were transmitted to the President, who sent them to Congress, as he said, with great pleasure. Kentucky stated that she was in favor of the so-called Crittenden resolutions, but she did not request Congress to propose them as amendments to the Constitution.

How is this body constituted? Do we, its members, represent the people of the several States? Have they had an opportunity to elect delegates, to select those in whom they had confidence and whom they could trust? Not at all. Why should we assemble here and express our wishes to Congress in reference to the Constitution without permitting California, Oregon, or many other States not here represented, to unite in our deliberations? I cannot assent to such an unfair proceeding toward other States.

Suppose one-half the States should request Congress to propose amendments, will Congress agree to it? No, sir. The Constitution provides that Congress shall not propose amendments without the consent of two-thirds of the States. Congress has not deemed any amendments necessary, so far as we know, and yet a majority of the committee of this body ask Congress to propose the amendments on our responsibility alone. It appears to me, then, that this proceeding must be regarded not as one known to the Constitution, but as a revolutionary proceeding. All the States are not represented here, nor have all had an opportunity to be so represented. Some of us are acting under the appointment of the Legislatures of our States; other delegates are simply appointed by the Executives of their States and are acting without any legal authority. We are not standing upon equal ground; some are only acting upon their own judgment; others are acting under instructions from their several Legislatures. If the Virginia Legislature itself were here, its action would differ materially from the present views of the delegates from that State.

But how is this? The Resolutions of the Legislature of Virginia make the statement that unless these questions are settled, and settled soon, there is danger of the disruption of the Union. Admit this to be so, and it furnishes no reason for changing the mode of proposing constitutional amendments. The Constitution knows no such danger. It is a self-sustaining Constitution, and was supposed to contain within itself the power to secure its own preservation. The Constitution ought not to be amended without the deliberate action of the people themselves. I cannot and I will not disregard their rights. I cannot recognize the claim that the secession of a State, by an ordinance of its Convention, can carry either the State or its people out of the Union. There is no such thing as *legal* secession, for there is no power anywhere to take the people out of the protecting care of the Government, or to relieve them from their obligations to it.

And where is the clause in the Constitution that authorizes the call upon Congress to do what Congress is asked to do here? The Constitution was adopted "to form a more perfect Union." The people were not to be allowed to alter it, except in the two modes prescribed in it. The Convention which adopted it did not propose that changes should be made in it without ample time for deliberation and discussion. We are here, then, simply as conferees from States expressing our individual opinions. We are now asked to recommend to Congress amendments to our fundamental law; we have no more right to do so than members of the so-called Southern Confederacy. We, a mere fraction of the people, propose to unite in bringing a pressure upon Congress, which shall induce it to propose these amendments. This was not one of the modes contemplated or provided by the framers of that sacred instrument.

General WASHINGTON presided over the Convention which prepared our Constitution. None knew better than he the reasons which made its adoption necessary to the preservation of the Government—none knew better the dangers which would probably surround it in after years. In that last counsel of his to the American people—his Farewell Address—a paper drawn up with the greatest deliberation, embodying opinions which he entertained as the result of a long life of active study and reflection, he warns us against all such proceedings as those contemplated by the majority of the committee. I am sure the delegates from Virginia will not now refuse to listen to the words of that illustrious man, uttered upon the most solemn and momentous occasion of his life. Hear his words:

"Here, perhaps, I ought to stop. But a solicitude for your welfare, which cannot end but with my life, and the apprehension of danger natural to that solicitude, urge me on an occasion like the present to offer to your solemn contemplation, and to recommend to your frequent review, some sentiments which are the result of much reflection, of no inconsiderable observation, and which appear to me all-important to the permanency of your felicity as a people. These will be offered to you with more freedom, as you can only see in them the disinterested warnings of a parting friend, who can possibly have no personal motive to bias his counsel."

Again:

"But as it is easy to foresee, that from different causes and from different quarters much pains will be taken, many artifices employed, to weaken in your minds the conviction of this truth; as this is the point in your political fortress, against which the batteries of internal and external enemies will be most constantly and actively (though often covertly and insidiously) directed, it is of infinite moment that you should properly estimate the immense value of your national union to your collective and individual happiness; that you should cherish a cordial, habitual, and immovable attachment to it; accustoming yourselves to think and speak of it as the Palladium of your political safety and prosperity; watching for its preservation with jealous anxiety; discountenancing whatever may suggest even a suspicion that it can in any event be abandoned; and indignantly frowning upon the first dawning of every attempt to alienate any portion of our country from the rest, or to enfeeble the sacred ties which now link together the various parts."

Are not these admonitions at the present moment peculiarly worthy of our attention? And with them before us, can we invoke the action of Congress for the alteration of the fundamental law of the Government in any other ways than those provided in the Constitution? I earnestly hope not. If we act at all, let us act in that regular method which gives time for consultation, for consideration, and for action among the people of all the States. It appears to me, that in adopting the line of policy proposed by the majority of the committee, we are doing the very thing which WASHINGTON warned us not to do.

He said further:

"To the efficacy and permanency of your Union, a government for the whole is indispensable. No alliances, however strict, between the parts, can be an adequate substitute; they must inevitably experience the infractions and interruptions which all alliances in all times have experienced. Sensible of this momentous truth, you have improved upon your first essay, by the adoption of a Constitution of Government better calculated than your former for an intimate union, and for the efficacious management of your common concerns. This Government, the offspring of our own choice, uninfluenced and unmoved, adopted upon full investigation and mature deliberation, completely free in its principles, in the distribution of its powers, uniting security with energy, and *containing within itself a provision for its own amendment*, has a just claim to your confidence and your support. Respect for its authority, compliance with its laws, acquiescence in its measures, are duties enjoined by the fundamental maxims of true liberty. The basis of our political systems is the right of the people to make and to alter their Constitutions of Government. But the Constitution which at any time exists, *till changed by an explicit and authentic act of the whole* people, is sacredly obligatory upon all."

And again:

"Toward the preservation of your Government, and the permanency of your present happy state, it is requisite, not only that you should steadily discountenance irregular oppositions to its acknowledged authority, but also that you resist with care the spirit of innovation upon its principles, however specious the pretexts. One method of assault may be to affect in the forms of the Constitution alterations which will impair the energy of the system, and thus to undermine what cannot be directly overthrown. In all the changes to which you may be invited, remember that time and habit are at least as necessary to fix the true character of governments, as of other human institutions."

And still further:

"If, in the opinion of the people, the distribution or modification of the constitutional powers be in any particular wrong, let it be corrected by an amendment in the way which the Constitution designates. But let there be no change by usurpation; for though this in one instance may be the instrument of good, it is the customary weapon by which free governments are destroyed. The precedent must always greatly overbalance in permanent evil any partial or transient benefit which the use can at any time yield."

If we adopt the majority report here, we attempt to correct the Constitution by an amendment in a way which the Constitution does *not* designate. WASHINGTON says if there is any thing wrong, let it be corrected in a constitutional way; and that, sir, is just what Kentucky has said, and that is what every loyal State will say. Kentucky has inaugurated this proceeding, and it is one eminently worthy of her—true as she has always been to the Union. I cannot disregard this action of her Legislature. I do not think any exigency exists which requires us to disregard it. I am ready, and my State is ready, to confer with other States in reference to the Constitution, when asked to do so in any of the modes pointed out by that instrument.

Entertaining these opinions, and with these convictions, I should be untrue to my sense of duty to the Government and the State I represent, and to the people of the United States, if I should consent to disregard the Constitution and my obligations to it.

I have stated these considerations because they are powerful enough to influence and control my course. Others must act upon their own convictions. I have come to the conclusion that I ought to submit this minority report with distrust, and with distrust only, because so many of the able statesmen composing the majority of the committee have seen fit to adopt different views. My report leaves every thing to the people, where I think every such question should be left. When they consult together and decide in the constitutional way I shall bow to their decision, whatever it may be.

Mr. GUTHRIE:—I do not propose to follow the gentleman (Mr. BALDWIN) through all the ramifications of his speech. I have made the Constitution my study for many years, and I have looked at the causes which give it strength and the causes which give it weakness. I believe that our fathers organized this

Government in great wisdom. Its strength was in the affections of the people. It never had any other strength, and it was never intended it should have. It was not intended to be sustained by standing armies. Its strength was intended to be placed in the affections of the people, and I had hoped it would endure forever. Without the affections of the people it is the weakest Government ever established. The people! What a spectacle do we witness now! One portion of the people has lost confidence in the Government, and now seven States have left it. The Government cannot realize that they are gone. We have established the right of revolution, and that right gave to the world this splendid Government. This was the first precedent; it will stand for all time. It will always be acted upon when the people have lost confidence in the Government. I *hate* that word secession, because it is a cheat! Call things by their right names! The Southern States have framed another Government; they have originated a *revolution*. There is no warrant for it in the Constitution, but it is like the right of self-defence, which every man may exercise. The gentleman from Connecticut has forgotten that the Government made Congress the recipient of petitions. Why was this? It was that Congress might be influenced by the wishes of the people and act upon them.

We are twenty States assembled here. Congress has been in session more than two months. The Government is falling to pieces. Congress has not had the sagacity to give the necessary guarantees, the proper assurances to the slaveholding States. This session will make a shameful chapter in the history of this Government, to be hereafter written. Why should this Congress refuse to give the people guarantees? The proudest Governments in the world have been compelled to give their people guarantees.

We are assembled here to consult, and see what can be done; to consult as representatives of the States. Is there any impropriety in our stating what would restore confidence, to our putting this in writing, and to our proposing the plan of restoration we think should be adopted to Congress, and asking Congress to submit that plan to the people? Are we not the representatives of the people, sent here to do what we think ought to be done, and to ask Congress by way of petition to repair the foundations of the Government? It is all legitimate, and legitimate in the most technical sense.

Suppose we ask Congress to act on this proposition. We come directly from the people. We ask Congress to submit a plan which we think will save the Government, to the people. Is this taking any advantage of the States? *They* can take all the time they wish for deliberation, and we can bring no pressure to bear on them. In these times of great peril and trouble, we ask Congress, backed by the moral force of the States we represent, to act and save the country.

Two or three years hence will not answer. The foundations of the Government are undermined and growing weaker every day, and if the people who may give to it the necessary repair and strength do not do so, they will be called to a fearful account. When the building is on fire, it is no time to inquire who set it on fire. The North say the South did it, and the South say the North did it.

We are all interested in this Government; we love the Constitution; we love the Union; we want to repair it—we want to lay the foundation for bringing back the States who have left us, by reason and not by the sword. The delay which the gentleman proposes is too long; the Constitution has provided a shorter way. In adopting that we are only recognizing the right of petition.

I, sir, will answer to Kentucky; I don't want the gentleman to come between me and the people of Kentucky. He has no right to speak for the people of that State—her representatives here have that right and will exercise it. Why were these resolutions passed? Because Congress had failed to provide the means needful to our safety. The resolutions under which the Kentucky delegation came here were passed on the 29th, not the 25th of January. They were passed after the resolutions to which the gentleman refers. They ought to be regarded, as they are in fact, as the deliberate expression of the Legislature of Kentucky in favor of this Conference. In them it is stated that Kentucky heartily accepts the invitation of her old mother Virginia. She acts in no unwilling spirit, she hastens to avail herself of any opportunity to save the Government. She believes a favorable opportunity is offered by this Conference. I repeat again: Adopt the report of the majority of the committee and I will answer to Kentucky. I will go farther. I will answer that Kentucky herself will adopt the very proposals of amendment to the Constitution contained in the committee's report.

But the gentleman insists that the action proposed is not only improper but that it is *revolutionary*. I deny that it is revolutionary. It is no more revolutionary than any other form of petition. It is a petition sustained by the moral force of twenty States—a petition which Congress will not disregard.

But if the report of the majority is revolutionary, what of the gentleman's report? Is that provided for by the Constitution? Is that according to the forms of the Constitution? No, sir. Every argument he has brought against the report of the majority, applies with equal force to his own. His views will answer for those who are willing to stand by and see this Government drift toward destruction—to see this country involved in civil war. It will answer for those who will oppose all action, and who wish to do nothing at all. His report is a new excuse for inaction. It will not answer for us.

Sir, we are acting under a fearful responsibility. The eyes of every true patriot in the nation are turned toward this body. The people are awaiting our action, with anxious and painful solicitude. They know and we know that, unless the wisdom of this Conference shall devise some plan to satisfy the people of the slaveholding States—to quiet their apprehensions, a disruption of the Government is inevitable. If we adopt the gentleman's views, go home and do nothing, we take the responsibility of breaking up the Government.

I do not propose to discuss the merits of the majority report at the present time. I have only sought to answer the arguments of the gentleman against our acting at all. But I claim that this way of proceeding is entirely irregular. The report of the gentleman is not in order. The report of the majority was first presented, and should be first acted upon. I move to lay the report of the gentleman from Connecticut upon the table.

Mr. LOGAN:—I would ask Mr. GUTHRIE to withdraw his motion. If the motion were adopted it would prevent discussion. It was expected that we were to discuss the subject to-day. It is not of much consequence which report is first acted upon. They are all before the Conference, and the merits of all of them are under discussion.

Mr. GUTHRIE withdrew the motion to lay on the table.

Mr. MOREHEAD, of Kentucky, took the chair.

Mr. CURTIS:—I am a member of the present Congress; I have faithfully attended its deliberations, and have anxiously watched its course. Mr. GUTHRIE will find that there are other and different objections to the line of policy he proposes, to which he has not alluded, and which he does not understand. But they are objections which have determined, and will determine, the action of Congress. I would ask Mr. GUTHRIE if the adoption of his propositions, previous to their action, would have prevented the States which have already seceded from going out.

Mr. GUTHRIE:—I think it would have prevented them; all but South Carolina. I did not intend to assail Congress, or any member of it, personally.

Mr. CURTIS:—I do not agree with the gentleman. We know, and the gentleman knows, that there has been for a long time a purpose, a great conspiracy in this country, to begin and carry out a revolution. That has been avowed over and over again in the halls of Congress. Can you expect a member of Congress to do more than reflect the will of his constituents, the will of his people? Would you have him do any thing different? There were forty or fifty different propositions before the Congressional Committee of Thirty-three. There are many here. There are many difficulties attending the solution of this question in every respect. But we may as well speak plainly. I cannot go for the majority report of the committee, and among other reasons, for this reason: Their proposition makes all territory we may hereafter acquire slave territory.

Mr. JOHNSON:—No; such is not the fact.

Mr. CURTIS:—I have read it, and such is my construction.

Mr. JOHNSON:—Such is not the intention.

Mr. CURTIS:—Any future territory which we acquire must be from the south; we have extended as far as we can to the north and the northwest.

Mr. WICKLIFFE:—Will you agree to divide all future territory?

Mr. CURTIS:—I will do almost any thing to save the Union.

I will reflect the will of my constituents. I think it ought not to be divided equally, but the South ought to have its share. There is another trouble. Look at the difficulty of getting any proposition through Congress. Congress has only fifteen days of life. I ask you, even with general unanimity, if you can hope to pass at this session any new proposals of amendments? If you do, you will get along faster than is generally the case. There is one proposition before Congress that I believe can pass. It is the Adams proposition, to admit all the territories south at once. It is already slave territory. It is now applying for admission. If this is acceptable to the South, I will go for it. We are bound to admit it under the ordinance of 1789.

Mr. GOODRICH:—Do I understand my friend to claim that the ordinance of 1789 involves a proposition to divide the territory?

Mr. CURTIS:—I understand that in connection with the subsequent legislation it does.

Mr. GOODRICH:—The concession of territory from North Carolina contains a prohibition from acting on the subject of slavery in the territory ceded.

Mr. CURTIS:—I agree entirely with the gentleman. I am opposed to slavery, but we must divide the territory. Let us leave slavery where it is, and admit the territory for the purpose of settling the question. I do not agree with Mr. GUTHRIE that this Government depends on the will of the people. It is a self-supporting government; it will support itself. There is no justification for the action of the seceded States, and I cannot agree that Congress is responsible for their action. The secession plot was formed before Congress assembled. There *was* a power to check it. If our President had acted as Jackson did, there would have been an end of it. The day for hanging for treason has gone by. We must look at things as they are. Even in battle the white flag must be respected. Let this subject be frankly discussed in a conciliatory manner. If any State has the right to go out of the Union at its own volition, then this Government, in my opinion, is not worth the trouble of preserving. The President is sworn to protect and uphold the Government. So long as there is a navy, an army, and a militia, it is his sworn duty to uphold it—to uphold it as well against an attack from States as from individuals. The Government is one of love and affection, it is true, but it is also one of strength and power. Where was there ever a more indulgent people than ours? Our forts have been taken, our flag has been fired upon, our property seized, and as yet nothing has been done. But they will not be indulgent forever. Beware, gentlemen, how you force them further. Gentlemen talk about the inefficiency of Congress; I wish there was some efficiency in the Executive. If there was, or had been, our present troubles would have been avoided.

Mr. TURNER:—I do not understand that the report of the majority is applicable to future territory. I move the recommitment of the report, to have that question settled.

Mr. JOHNSON:—It is true there are different constructions which may be placed on the report. I think if it had been understood to apply to future territory, it could not have received the support of a majority of the committee. Mr. CRITTENDEN'S proposition applies to future territory. I submitted a proposition to the committee also intended to apply to future territory. A majority of the committee was opposed to it. Mr. EWING drew this part of the amendment, and there is some difference of opinion about it. In my opinion the amendment would not apply to future territory, and I intended at the proper time to offer an amendment which should make it plain, and not leave it open to construction. Personally, I should be glad to apply it to future territory, but I shall yield. I think if we can settle the question now, there will be no further trouble. I do not believe any territory will be acquired hereafter without great unanimity. It is not quite true, although it may be probable, that the future territory will be south of the line proposed.

Mr. TURNER:—I am still more confirmed that it was the intention of the committee to have the amendment only apply to existing territory. If this is settled now, it will shorten the debate. If the gentleman will move to amend now, I will withdraw my motion.

Mr. JOHNSON:—I move to amend by inserting the word *present* before the word *territory* in the first line of Section I., with such other verbal amendments as may make the sense conform, and to adopt that amendment now. This covers the whole ground. I wish to discuss these amendments, but am physically unable to speak to-day, and would prefer to have the discussion deferred.

Mr. JOHNSON then moved an adjournment, which was carried on a division, and the Convention adjourned at two o'clock and fifty minutes.

ELEVENTH DAY.

WASHINGTON, MONDAY, *February* 18*th*, 1861.

THE Convention was opened with prayer by Rev. P. D. GURLEY.

The Journal of yesterday was read and approved.

Mr. CHITTENDEN offered the following resolution:

Resolved, That the rules of this Convention be so far modified as to require the Secretary to employ a competent stenographer, who shall write down and preserve accurate notes of the debates and other proceedings of this body, which notes shall not be communicated to any person, nor shall copies thereof be taken, nor shall the same be made public until after the final adjournment of this Convention, except in pursuance of a vote authorizing their publication.

Mr. CHITTENDEN:—I have no desire to occupy time in debating this resolution, much less to waste it in a fruitless attempt to oppose what seems to be the settled purpose of a majority of this Convention. But if this body will consider the purpose which the resolution seeks to attain, it may, perhaps, be found less objectionable than other similar ones which have been defeated. The objection heretofore made is, that a publication of what transpires here would lead to an excited criticism in the country, which would be unfavorable to the calmness and ultimate success which should attend our deliberations. While I entertain no such apprehensions, permit me to observe that this resolution contemplates no present publication of our debates, but a publication at such a time, and in such a manner, as will be unobjectionable. That time may not come till after our adjournment. I am free to say, that when we are dealing with the important issues now before us, I prefer to have our action, our words, our whole conduct, all that we do and say, open and public. We should fear no criticism when we are right; we ought to be held to account when we are wrong. But if gentlemen will not consent to this, at least let the daily record of each of us be made up now: let it be full and perfect. When a question comes up hereafter which concerns the sentiments or the action of a member, let its decision depend upon no uncertain recollection, a recollection which must fade and grow dim with each one of us, as the time of this Convention recedes into the past. Such a record can injure no one; it may be of infinite service hereafter. I could not justify myself to my conscience, or to those who have a right to hold me responsible for my acts here, if I failed to do all that lays in my power to have the true history of this Convention laid before the country. A naked journal amounts to nothing. It is a skeleton. Our discussions alone will give it form and comeliness. I have prepared this resolution upon consultation with many members, whose ideas of what should be done here agree with mine. They concur with me in the propriety of offering it. If it fails, the responsibility of keeping our discussions from the people will not rest with us.

Mr. POLLOCK:—I move to lay the resolution on the table.

Mr. CHITTENDEN:—Let the vote be taken by States.

The vote was so taken, and the following States voted in the affirmative: Connecticut, Rhode Island, New Jersey, Delaware, Maryland, Kentucky, Tennessee, North Carolina, Missouri, Virginia, and Pennsylvania—11.

The following States voted in the negative: Maine, Vermont, New Hampshire, Massachusetts, Indiana, Illinois, Iowa, and New York—8.

So the motion to lay on the table prevailed.

When the State of Ohio was called, a member of her delegation stated that it was equally divided.

Mr. TUCK:—I ask the unanimous consent of the Conference to introduce a proposition in the form of an address to the people of the United States. I do so after having consulted a considerable number of members; and having found that it meets their approval, I desire to read it, and will then move that it be laid on the table and printed.

Mr. RANDOLPH:—Is the gentleman's motion in order?

Mr. EWING:—I object to the reading.

Mr. CLAY:—Certainly; I object also.

Mr. TUCK:—I will acquiesce with a single word. I certainly hoped no curt objection would be made to the reading of *any* proposition which any member might deem it his duty to offer. As gentlemen differ from me in this respect, I will hand the paper to the Chair. I hope at least it may be permitted to lay on the table.

The PRESIDENT:—I hold it the gentleman's undoubted right to read the paper if he chooses.

Mr. TUCK:—Very well.

He commenced reading when he was interrupted by

Mr. WICKLIFFE:—I hope Mr. TUCK will withdraw this paper. If the Convention agrees to any result, I shall favor its submission to the people with an address. I will pledge myself to suggest the gentleman's name as one of a committee to prepare the address at the proper time.

The PRESIDENT:—The gentleman from New Hampshire has the floor.

Mr. TUCK then completed the reading of the paper, as follows:

TO THE PEOPLE OF THE UNITED STATES:

This Convention of Conference, composed in part of Commissioners appointed in accordance with the legislative action of sundry States, and in part of Commissioners appointed by the Governors of sundry other States, in compliance with an invitation by the General Assembly of Virginia, met in Washington on the 4th of February, 1861. Although constituting a body unknown to the Constitution and laws, yet being delegated for the purpose, and having carefully considered the existing dangers and dissensions, and having brought their proceedings to a close, publish this address, and the accompanying resolutions, as the result of their deliberations.

We recognize and deplore the divisions and distractions which now afflict our country, interrupt its prosperity, disturb its peace, and endanger the Union of the States; but we repel the conclusion, that any alienations or dissensions exist which are irreconcilable, which justify attempts at revolution, or which the patriotism and fraternal sentiments of the people, and the interests and honor of the whole nation, will not overcome.

In a country embracing the central and most important portion of a continent, among a people now numbering over thirty millions, diversities of opinion inevitably exist; and rivalries, intensified at times by local interests and sectional attachments, must often occur; yet we do not doubt that the theory of our Government is the best which is possible for this nation, that the Union of the States is of vital importance, and that the Constitution, which expresses the combined wisdom of the illustrious founders of the Government, is still the palladium of our liberties, adequate to every emergency, and justly entitled to the support of every good citizen.

It embraces, in its provisions and spirit, all the defence and protection which any section of the country can rightfully demand, or honorably concede.

Adopted with primary reference to the wants of five millions of people, but with the wisest reference to future expansion and development, it has carried us onward with a rapid increase of numbers, an accumulation of wealth, and a degree of happiness and general prosperity never attained by any nation.

Whatever branch of industry, or whatever staple production, shall become, in the possible changes of the future, the leading interest of the country, thereby creating unforeseen complications or new conflicts of opinion and interest, the Constitution of the United States, properly understood and fairly enforced, is equal to every exigency, a shield and defence to all, in every time of need. If, however, by reason of a change in circumstances, or for any cause, a portion of the people believe they ought to have their rights more exactly defined or more fully explained in the Constitution, it is their duty, in accordance with its provisions, to seek a remedy by way of amendment to that instrument; and it is the duty of all the States to concur in such amendments as may be found necessary to insure equal and exact justice to all.

In order, therefore, to announce to the country the sentiments of this Convention, respecting not only the remedy which should be sought for existing discontents, but also to communicate to the public what we believe to be the patriotic sentiment of the country, we adopt the following resolutions:

1st. *Resolved*, That this Convention recognize the well-understood proposition that the Constitution of the United States gives no power to Congress, or any branch of the Federal Government, to interfere in any manner with slavery in any of the States; and we are assured by abundant testimony, that neither of the great political organizations existing in the country contemplates a violation of the spirit of the Constitution in this regard, or the procuring of any amendment thereof, by which Congress, or any department of the General Government, shall ever have jurisdiction over slavery in any of the States.

2d. *Resolved*, That the Constitution was ordained and established, as set forth in the preamble, by the people of the United States, in order to form a more perfect Union, establish justice, insure domestic tranquillity, provide for the common defence, promote the general welfare, and secure the blessings of liberty to themselves and their posterity; and when the people of any State are not in full enjoyment of all the benefits intended to be secured to them by the Constitution, or their rights under it are disregarded, their tranquillity disturbed, their prosperity retarded, or their liberty imperilled by the people of any State, full and adequate redress can and ought to be provided for such grievances.

3d. *Resolved*, That this Convention recommend to the Legislatures of the

States of the Union to follow the example of the Legislatures of the States of Kentucky and of Illinois, in applying to Congress to call a Convention for the proposing of amendments to the Constitution of the United States, pursuant to the fifth article thereof.

Mr. GUTHRIE:—I object to printing this paper. If that course is taken, every member may offer his disquisitions on the Constitution, and they will be printed at our expense.

Mr. TUCK:—Unanimous consent was given that it be read, laid on the table, and printed.

The PRESIDENT:—There were three motions involved in one. Now the question is upon laying the paper on the table and printing it.

Mr. ALEXANDER:—I call for a division of the question.

The PRESIDENT:—The question will be on the motion to lay it on the table.

Mr. TUCK:—Are we not entitled to have the question taken on the motion to print? I supposed all these questions would be taken in a spirit of conciliation. But if not, I will withdraw the motion to lay on the table, and move that the paper be printed.

Mr. MOREHEAD, of Kentucky:—I came here in a spirit of conciliation, and I shall act in that spirit. Let us all do so. I disagree entirely with Mr. Tuck and his proposition, but I am in favor of receiving every proposition that is offered, of printing them all, and at the proper time of considering them all. I trust that unanimous consent will be given to printing this paper.

The President then put the motion upon printing the address, and it was carried upon a division.

Mr. Guthrie offered the following resolution, which was adopted unanimously:

Resolved, That if the President shall choose to speak on any question, he may, for the occasion, call any member to preside.

Mr. MEREDITH:—I wish to offer a proposition, and hope for the present it may lie on the table, and be considered hereafter. I do not desire to move it as an amendment to the report of the committee, but think it better to present it as a direct and independent proposition. I present it now only for the purpose of having it before the Convention. It is as follows:

Article.—That Congress shall divide all the territory of the United States into convenient portions, each containing not less than sixty thousand square miles, and shall establish in each a territorial government; the several territorial legislatures, whether heretofore constituted, or hereafter to be constituted, shall have all the legislative powers now vested in the respective States of this Union; and whenever any territory having a population sufficient, according to the ratio existing at the time, to entitle it to one member of Congress, shall form a republican constitution, and apply to Congress for admission as a State, Congress shall admit the same as a State accordingly.

The proposition of Mr. MEREDITH was laid on the table without objection.

Mr. WICKLIFFE:—There appears to be a misunderstanding between the Secretary and myself upon the question of printing the Journal. To avoid question, I move that the Journal be printed up to and including to-day.

Mr. GOODRICH:—I move to amend by adding "and from day to day during the session."

The amendment and the motion were adopted without objection.

Mr. ALEXANDER, of New Jersey, took the chair.

The PRESIDENT:—The Convention will now proceed to the order of the day—the consideration of the report of the committee.

Mr. REID, of North Carolina:—I wish to move an amendment to the amendment offered by Mr. JOHNSON. It is to add to his the words "and future." If adopted, the language will be "present and future territory."

Mr. EWING:—This will render a division of the question necessary. The gentleman had better withdraw his amendment for the time.

Mr. REID:—I am instructed by the Legislature of North Carolina to offer it, and I think best to do so in this regular manner.

Mr. CLEVELAND:—I think the motion of Mr. REID is out of order. I suggest that if adopted, with Mr. JOHNSON'S amendment, the sense of the proposition as it now stands will not be changed.

Mr. RUFFIN:—I rise merely to make a suggestion to my colleague. This motion must be made at some time, by some one, so that we may have a regular vote upon it. Now, as it is not certain how the report of the majority of the committee is to be construed, I propose at a suitable time to move an amendment which will make the proposition applicable to territory hereafter acquired. If this will suit my colleague, I hope he will withdraw his motion.

Mr. REID :—I came here not to deceive the North or the South. I intend to be plain and unambiguous. Why should we send forth a proposition that is uncertain, vague, and, as gentlemen admit, open to different constructions? If we are to pour oil upon the troubled waters, let us do so to some purpose; above all, let us be definite, plain, and certain. I cannot consent to withdraw my motion. I must insist upon its consideration.

Mr. LOGAN :—I had hoped the question on Mr. JOHNSON's amendments would have been taken on Saturday. It is an important one, and one which must be met. I would suggest that it would be best to let the question be taken on Mr. JOHNSON's amendments now. The subject presents itself to my mind in this way: The proposition of the majority, as it now stands, is uncertain. The friends of the proposition ought to be allowed to perfect it, to make it satisfactory to themselves. If there is a doubt about it, let us make it clear that it applies only to the present territory. Then we can have a clear and decisive vote upon it. The substance of the proposition is what I wish to arrive at, and it will be more in order if the vote is not taken till we know what that substance is. I shall not object to its application to future territory. I hope the gentleman from North Carolina will withdraw his amendment, and let the question be taken on that of Mr. JOHNSON.

Mr. SEDDON :—One word only. I fear we are being placed in an awkward position. I am desirous to have the language of the proposition clear and not delusive. The amendment of Mr. JOHNSON embarrasses me; I hardly know how to vote upon it. If I vote for Mr. JOHNSON's motion, I shall have the semblance of favoring the limitation of the proposition to present territory. Mr. RUFFIN and myself both want the same thing, but on Mr. JOHNSON's motion he will vote one way and I the other.

Mr. RUFFIN :—Will the gentleman allow me to explain? I voted against the proposition in committee because, as it now stands, it applies only to existing territory. I wish to carry this proposition, but not by the vote of the South alone. I want

Northern votes, and assurances that the people of the North will vote for the proposition and adopt it.

Mr. SEDDON :—I shall feel disposed to vote against Mr. JOHNSON'S motion.

The question was here stated by the President as follows:

The vote will be taken upon the motion of Mr. REID to amend the amendment offered by Mr. JOHNSON.

Mr. REID :—It strikes me that the question is this: My proposition is to add the words "and future," but Mr. JOHNSON'S amendment is to add the word "present." Can this be treated as an amendment to his motion? I must say that my duty to my country and State will prevent my voting for the proposition as he proposes to limit it.

Mr. COALTER:—I think the committee ought to be permitted to amend and complete their report. Let us, by general consent, agree to have the word "present" inserted.

Mr. REID :—I object to that all the time.

Mr. TURNER:—I move that the report be recommitted for amendment.

Mr. COALTER :—Shall we adjourn over simply for this? That will use up another day.

Mr. GUTHRIE :—I hope it will not be recommitted. We can settle the question here in a moment.

The PRESIDENT :—The vote will now be taken.

Mr. McCURDY :—I call for the individual names of members voting.

The PRESIDENT :—The call is not in order.

The question was then taken on the amendment of Mr. REID, and resulted as follows:

AYES—New Jersey, Delaware, Maryland, Kentucky, Tennessee, North Carolina, Missouri, and Virginia—8.

NAYS—Vermont, Maine, New Hampshire, Massachusetts, Connecticut, Rhode Island, Ohio, Indiana, Illinois, Pennsylvania, New York, and Iowa—12.

So the amendment failed.

The PRESIDENT :—The question now recurs on the motion of the gentleman from Maryland.

Mr. JOHNSON :—I trust that I shall not trespass upon the time of the Conference, but the subject now before it is one of great importance, and it involves the consideration of many important questions. The amendment which I offer is for the purpose of making the proposition of the committee clear and plain. I was aware that a construction might be placed upon it different from that which the committee intended; and it is due to the frankness which is manifested here, that the purposes of the committee should be made plain. There ought to be no ambiguity in a constitutional provision. Some of the most important constitutional questions decided by the Supreme Court have been questions of construction. Lawyers would differ about the construction to be given the committee's proposition. I think the Supreme Court has placed a construction upon the terms used here, which would be conclusive. A similar question arose in the Dred Scott case. There the question was upon that article in the Constitution which confers on Congress the power "to dispose of and to make all needful rules and regulations respecting the *territories* or other property belonging to the United States." The Court in that case decided that the provision had no bearing on the controversy in that case, because the power given by that provision, whatever it might be, was confined, and was intended to be confined, to the territory which, upon the adoption of the Constitution, belonged to or was claimed by the United States, and was within their boundaries, as settled by the treaty with Great Britain. With this clause in the Constitution, therefore, it could have no influence upon the territory afterward acquired from a foreign government. I think this decision conclusive, and that the proposition, if incorporated into the Constitution, would refer only to the territory now owned by the United States.

It was the wish of the representatives of some States in the committee that the word "future" should be inserted in the report. I was opposed to it: it was so odious to me to put words into the Constitution, or to propose to do so, which should go forth to the world as an indication that this Government proposes to acquire new territory in any way. I have said that the Supreme Court in the Dred Scott case decided that the words "the territories" in the Constitution only applied to the then existing territory. I think they decided wrong in this respect, though I agree to the correctness of the decision in that case in the main;

but such as it is, the decision is binding upon this Conference and the people.

Mr. JOHNSON here read a portion of the opinion of Judge TANEY delivered in the Dred Scott case, and continued:

You perceive that Judge TANEY turns the question upon the construction of the word "the." Had the word "any" been used in its place, he must have held that the provision applied to future, as well as the then existing territory.

Knowing that it was the purpose of the majority of the committee to exclude future territory from the operation of this proposition, and that it was due to the committee and the Convention that their purposes should be carried out, I offer my amendment as applicable to the sixth line of the proposition as well as the first.

In discussing the merits of this report, in its application to the existing condition of the country, I have to say a word to my Southern friends. You have sought to extend this provision to territory which shall be hereafter acquired. You have had a decisive vote and have been beaten in this Conference. The fight has been a fair one; the question has been thoroughly understood. We ought to acquiesce in the decision of the majority. We cannot change this decision if we would; and if we could change it, the proposition amended as you would prefer to have it, would never pass Congress. The repeated action of that body, during its present session, shows this conclusively. Accepting this decision then, as definitive, can we not settle the question with reference to existing territory? Shall we settle it? Settle it fairly—recognizing and acknowledging the rights of all, and remain brethren forever with the Free States! From my very heart, I say yes. (Applause.) The proposition as it now stands covers all the territory we have. The whole ground, the whole trouble, which has brought this country into its present lamentable condition—has arisen over this question. I believe if it had been disposed of or settled in some way before, many States would have been kept in the Union that have now gone out. And why should we not settle it?

We have now a territory extensive enough to sustain two hundred millions of people—embracing almost every climate, fruitful in almost every species of production—rich in all the elements of national wealth, and governed by a Constitution that has raised us to an elevation of grandeur that the world has never before witnessed. That we should separate to the destruction of such a Government, on account of territory we have not got, and territory that we do not want, is not, I believe, the patriotic sense of the South.

But this proposition does not stand by itself alone. It is connected, and must be construed, with the provision relating to the acquisition of future territory. The second section of the committee's proposition provides that territory shall not be acquired by the United States, unless by treaty, nor, with unimportant exceptions, unless such treaty shall be ratified by four-fifths of all the members of the Senate. Is not that guaranty enough for us? Should we not act unreasonably if we required further guaranty in this respect? For myself, I should have preferred that the consent of two-thirds of the Senate only should be required, and that that two-thirds should comprise a majority both from the free and slave States.

Mr. RUFFIN:—At the proper time I shall move such an amendment.

Mr. JOHNSON:—If such an amendment is proposed I shall vote for it. I know there will be objections raised to it, but they will be far outweighed by the advantages it will give to the South.

But the objection of Mr. Baldwin is opposed here, and it is one which must be answered. He says this is the wrong way to propose amendments to the Constitution—that our action is inconsistent with that instrument. He does not claim that it is prohibited by the letter, but by the spirit of the Constitution. Where does he get the spirit but from the letter? There are two methods of proposing amendments to the Constitution provided by that instrument. Let us see what they are.

Mr. Johnson here read the article of the Constitution providing for amendments, and continued:

One is where two-thirds of Congress deem it advisable to propose amendments; the other is where the States themselves propose them. My learned brother would have us believe that the members of Congress, acting under their official oaths, must each be satisfied that each amendment proposed is proper to be incorporated in the instrument, before they should propose them; and he maintains that there is a difference, in fact, in the two methods prescribed. What right has this body, if there is any force in this objection, to submit *his* proposition to the States? If what we propose is revolutionary, then what he proposes is revolutionary. I reply to him, with all respect for his legal ability, and with all the humility which becomes me, and insist that he is wrong. He refers to the opinion of Judge COLLAMER. I hold Judge COLLAMER in much respect, and his opinion in great honor here, but his statements are at war with the objections made by the gentleman from Connecticut. Judge COLLAMER maintains that it is the duty of Congress *to propose* amendments, not to *recommend* them. It would be entirely proper, according to his opinion, for Congress to propose amendments which they would not adopt themselves. I go somewhat farther, and insist that it is the duty of Congress to propose amendments whenever desired by any State or any considerable section of the Union. If we have no right to suggest a line of action to Congress, no right to petition Congress, no right to ask Congress to propose amendments, as the gentleman insists, we had better go home, or rather, I should say, we should never have come here.

There are twenty States represented in this Conference. I have no doubt other States would have been here, but for the shortness of the time. But how and why are we here? We have come here on the invitation of Virginia; her resolutions are our constitution. We have come here at her instance. For what purpose did she ask us to come here? under what circumstances did she pass these resolutions? Virginia saw that the country was going to ruin—that one State had already seceded, and several others were about to follow. She saw there were circumstances affecting the condition of the South which aroused her to frenzy—not madness, but the frenzy which falls on every patriotic mind when it witnesses a country going to destruction. She saw the country was going to ruin with rapid steps, and that its ruin must be accomplished unless her friends in the free States would come forward, and consent to put into the Constitution additional guarantees which would satisfy the people of the slave States that their rights were secure. See what she did—what she said. She expresses it as her deliberate opinion, "that unless the unhappy controversy which now divides the States of this Confederacy shall be satisfactorily adjusted, a permanent dissolution of the Union is inevitable; and the General Assembly, representing the wishes of the people of the Commonwealth, is desirous of employing every reasonable means to avert so dire a calamity, and determined to make a final effort to restore the Union and the Constitution, in the spirit in which they were established by the fathers of the Republic."

Therefore she invites all States, whether slaveholding or non-slaveholding, who were willing to unite with her in an earnest effort to adjust the unhappy controversies in the spirit of the Constitution, to come together to secure that adjustment. She asks us to agree to some suitable adjustment. She does not leave us to suggest what that adjustment shall be. She tells us herself. She requests us to adopt it, and to submit it to Congress. She does not ask that Congress should call a convention, for Congress could not. Try, if we can, says Virginia, to come to some settlement of these unhappy controversies, and send that settlement to Congress, that Congress may submit it to the country.

Virginia invited you here. She told you just what she wanted. She says if you cannot consent to that, then let her commissioners come home and report the result. If this cannot be done, if the mode of adjustment indicated by her cannot be substantially carried out, then our whole authority is at an end.

This matter of amending the Constitution is not as intricate and difficult a work as gentlemen imagine. Are there not twelve amendments to the Constitution already? Were they submitted to the people by each member of Congress acting under his official oath? Or were they submitted in the very way the gentleman would avoid? Were they not brought into the Constitution by outside pressure?

The Constitution has been amended. I wish to mark how it was done, and then note why it was done.

There was a time when fears were entertained that wrongs might be done to different sections of the Union under the Constitution as it then stood. Congress listened to those fears, and did not hesitate to propose amendments suggested from outside its own body—to submit them to the people for adoption. It was necessary, in the judgment of Congress, to do this, in order to restore confidence. It was done, and confidence was restored. Is not that precisely our case now? Is not confidence lost in the North and in the South?—not exactly lost, perhaps, but shaken. The credit of the Government is gone. Even our naval commanders are unable to negotiate Government bills abroad—are reduced to the degrading alternative of asking the endorsement of foreign States, in order to such negotiation. Some brilliant individuals have suggested that we have already become so poor that our widows and wives must bring out their stockings.

Our last loan was negotiated at twelve per cent. discount. The present loan is not to be taken at any rate, unless the Government descends to the humiliating alternative of securing State endorsements. Our credit is going lower and lower every day, and it will soon come to the point where our bonds will be worth no more than Continental money was.

Suppose we do nothing here. Are gentlemen blind to the consequences? Gentlemen, honest and patriotic as I know you are, have you no love for this Union?—have you no care for the preservation of this Government? God forbid that I should say you have none! I know you too well. My relations have been too intimate with you, and have existed too long, for me to suppose it. You do love the Union. I speak for the South and to the South. I know that we can still labor to keep this Government together. If we follow the plain dictates of our judgment, any other course would be impossible.

The Virginia Convention is even now in session, and what a convention it is! Disguise as we may, deceive ourselves as we will, it is a convention which proposes to consider the question of withdrawing the State from the Union. Kentucky and Missouri, if we do nothing, will soon follow. If there ever was a time in the history of the Government for conciliation, for patriotic concession, that time is now. The time has come when parties must be forgotten. Let not the word party be mentioned here. It is not worthy of us. Representatives of the States, you are above party—high above. The cords that bind you together are a hundred times as strong as those which ever bound any party. Unless we do something, and something very quickly, before the incoming President is inaugurated, in all human probability he will have only the States north of Mason and Dixon to govern—that is, if he is to govern them in peace.

I think there is no right of secession; such is my individual opinion. But there is a right higher than all these—the right of self-defence, the right of revolution. It is recognized by the Constitution itself. The Constitution was adopted by nine of the States only. What right had those nine States to separate from the other four?

Mr. SEDDON:—The right of secession.

Mr. JOHNSON:—I won't dispute about terms. In all such discussions, Heaven save me from a Virginia politician!

The opinions of Mr. MADISON upon the Constitution are certainly entitled to value. He had more to do with making it than any other statesman of the time. I desire to read an opinion of his, which will be found in number forty-two of the Federalist:

> "Two questions of a very delicate nature present themselves on this occasion:—1. On what principle the Confederation, which stands in the solemn form of a compact among the States, can be superseded without the unanimous consent of the parties to it? 2. What relation is to subsist between the nine or more States ratifying the Constitution, and the remaining few who do not become parties to it?
>
> "The first question is answered at once by recurring to the absolute necessity of the case, to the great principle of self-preservation, to the transcendent law of nature and of nature's God, which declares that the safety and happiness of society are the objects at which all political institutions aim, and to which all such institutions must be sacrificed."

Now, apply these principles to the present condition of the country. The cases are exactly parallel. Mr. MADISON says in substance, that if one section of the Union refuses to recognize and protect the rights of another—in other words, if the free States now refuse to guarantee the rights of the South, that there is a right of self-preservation, a law of nature and nature's God, which is above all Constitutions. I am not here to inquire whether the South has a right to go out if these guarantees are not given. That is a question which I will not argue. Some of the States have already gone. I hold that to be a fact established.

Now, I put it to my friends of the North: Do you want us to go out? You are a great people, a great country—a powerful people, a rich country. No threat or intimidation shall ever come from me to such a people. I ask you in all sadness whether, in the light of all our glory, of all our happiness and prosperity, whether you will, by withholding a thing that it will not harm you to grant, suffer us, compel us to depart? Let me read what was said by the same great man of Virginia, in anticipation of the existence of the present state of things:

"I submit to you, my fellow-citizens, these considerations, in full confidence that the good sense which has so often marked your decisions will allow them their due weight and effect; and that you will never suffer difficulties, however formidable in appearance, or however fashionable the error on which they may be founded, to drive you into the gloomy and perilous scene into which the advocates for disunion would conduct you. Hearken not to the unnatural voice, which tells you that the people of America, knit together as they are by so many cords of affection, can no longer live together as members of the same family; can no longer continue the mutual guardians of their mutual happiness; can no longer be fellow-citizens of one great, respectable, and flourishing empire. Hearken not to the voice which petulantly tells you that the form of government recommended for your adoption is a novelty in the political world; that it has never yet had a place in the theories of the wildest projectors; that it rashly attempts what it is impossible to accomplish. No, my countrymen, shut your ears against this unhallowed language. Shut your hearts against the poison which it conveys. The kindred blood which flows in the veins of American citizens, the mingled blood which they have shed in defence of their sacred rights, consecrate their Union, and excite horror at the idea of their becoming aliens, rivals, enemies. And if novelties are to be shunned, believe me, the most alarming of all novelties, the most wild of all projects, the most rash of all attempts, is that of rending us in pieces, in order to preserve our liberties, and promote our happiness."

Grant us then, gentlemen of the North, what we are willing to stand upon—what we will try to stand upon, and what we believe we can. At least, this will save the rest of the States to yourselves and to us. The States that are now in the Union will continue there.

What is it we ask you to do? It is to settle this question as to our present territory. To settle it—how? By dividing it. And how by dividing it? By the line of 36° 30′. Apparently, you think we are asking the North to yield something. I tell you it is we who are yielding. By the decision of the Supreme Court we have the right to go North of this line with our slaves. Now, all we ask you to give us here is the territory south of that line; and even as to that, we give you the right to destroy slavery there whenever a State organized out of it chooses to do so. We are, in fact, yielding to you. We abandon our rights North. Will you not let us retain what is already ours, South?

Is it quite certain that the territory south of the line will be slave territory? Those who repealed the Missouri Compromise, believed that Kansas would be a slave State. It did not turn out so. All we ask is, that you should leave the territory south of the line where it has been left by the decision of the Supreme Court. We freely yield you all the rest.

I do not propose to discuss all the amendments proposed. I confine myself to the single one which, if satisfactorily disposed of, will settle all our troubles.

In conclusion, I ask, oppressed by a consciousness which almost overmasters me—which renders me unfit to do any thing but feel —will you not settle this question here? I feel, and I cannot escape the feeling, that on your decision hangs the question, whether we shall be preserved an united people, or be broken to atoms. The States now remaining in the Union may possibly get on for a few years with something like prosperity; but if this question is not settled in some way, man must change his nature or *war* in the end will come. War! What a word to be used here! War between whom? There is not a family at the South which has not its associations with the North—not a Northern family which has not its Southern ties! War in the midst of such a people! God grant that the future, that the events which must inevitably follow dissension here, may at least spare this agony to ourselves, our families, and our posterity.

Mr. SEDDON:—It is very clear to me that I ought not to make a prolonged address upon a question which I favor. The only question now before us is: Shall this amendment be made plain? We should deal honestly among ourselves; there should be no cheat—no uncertainty—no delusion here. Our language should be so clear that it will breed no new nests of trouble.

But the address of the gentleman from Maryland requires a brief notice from me. I listened with sadness to many parts of it. I bemoan that tones so patriotic could not rise to the level of the high ground of equality and right upon which we all ought to stand.

I appeal not to forbearance—I ask not for pity. I feel proud to represent the grand old commonwealth of Virginia here, and prouder still that I only come here to demand right and justice in her behalf. Aye! and it is more complimentary to you to have it so. I ask for such guarantees only as Virginia needs, and as she has the right to demand. It is far more complimentary to you to appeal to your sense of justice, to your sense of right, than to your forbearance or pity.

Virginia comes forward in a great national crisis. When support after support of this glorious temple of our Government has been torn away, she comes—proud of her memories of the past—happy in the part she had in the construction of this great system—she comes to present to you, calmly and plainly, the question, whether new and additional guarantees are not needed for her rights; and she tells you what those guarantees ought to be.

Nor does she stand alone. She is supported by all her border sisters. The propositions she makes are familiar to the country. They were made by a patriot of the olden time, a time near to that of the foundation of our Government. They were such as he thought suited to the exigencies of his time. They have since then received a larger meed of approval, north and south, than any other plan of arrangement.

My State offers these resolutions of her Legislature as a basis for our action here, with certain modifications acceptable to her people. One of these modifications has since been accepted by the mover of these resolutions himself. Most important among them is the provision as to future territory. The gentleman seems to think that Virginia would not insist on this provision as applicable to territory we may never have. It behooves not me to answer such a momentous question. I am only the mouthpiece of Virginia. She insists on the provision for future territory. She and her sister States plant themselves upon it. What right have I to strike out a clause which she makes specific? What right have I to esteem it of so little weight that it may be thrown aside and disregarded? I do not propose to give my reasons, though they would not be troublesome to give. It was an element in the Missouri Compromise that it should apply to future as well as to existing territory.

Does not the gentleman assert that under the laws as they now stand, we have the right to go north of the compromise line with our slaves? What, then, is our position? Under the decision of the Supreme Court we are entitled to participate in *all* the territory of the United States. We are offering to give up the great part and the best part of it, and in payment we are to take the naked chance of getting a little piece of the worthless territory south of the proposed line! Such an idea was never entertained by those who made the Compromise. The idea which governed their action was, beyond all doubt, not that present territory alone should be thus divided, but that the question should be removed from doubt and difficulty for all time, and to give us at the South a chance whatever change might come.

Shall we be rewarded for all we give up, and find full compensation in a clause which itself prevents the acquisition of future territory? The statement is in itself a sufficient answer to the question.

But there was another element in the propositions of the Legislature of Virginia. That, was security against the principles of the North, and her great and now dominant party; it was intended to put an end to the discussions that have convulsed the country and jeopardized our institutions.

It was the policy of our fathers to settle these questions. They determined to make a final and decisive line of demarkation, and to let that be conclusive. But this young people could not be restrained, and when new territory was acquired the same question arose again. It now comes up once more. Virginia early saw the seeds of trouble in it, because she saw that the tide of emigration would continue to press toward the fertile lands of the South. She saw and she acted. In consequence of her action we are here. Would it not be wise and well as statesmen and as patriots, that you should do what you can for adjustment? do what you can to bring back your sisters of the South who have departed? It is the part of wisdom to settle. Virginia was wise to ask it.

There is another thing. A great and mighty party has arisen at the North that is determined to exclude the institution of slavery, not only from all future, but from all *present* territory. We know that in all ways this party has declared that it would not consent to let slavery go where it does not now exist. More heated zealots, also animated and sustained by this same party, have determined that this natural and patriarchal institution of the South should be surrounded by a cordon of free States, and in the end be extinguished altogether.

Is it not wise in Virginia, that she should see that this project of surrounding the South with free States should be guarded against—most effectually guarded against now and in time to come, and so preserve her dignity and power?

This amendment adopted, and the proposition to Virginia will be a farce. Gentlemen, we hold that as the soul is to man, so is honor to a nation. Honor is the soul of nations. Without it, no nation can have a place in history or among the nations. We of Virginia must have in this Confederation the position of an equal. Equal in dignity—equal in right. In the Congress of the States of this Union, we insist on this as our right. We must have the same protection as the States of the North. Otherwise we are a dishonored people. We might live for a time otherwise, but we should be unworthy a place among the nations. We hold our *property*, yes, *our property in slaves*, as rightful and as honorable as any property to be found in the broad expanse between ocean and ocean.

We feel that in the existence, the perpetuity, the protection of the African race, we have a mission to perform, and not a mission only, but a right and a duty.

Upon this subject I have a word to say in all seriousness. Think not, gentlemen of the North, that we propose to deceive or mislead you. We of the South are earnest in what we say. This is a question which we answer to ourselves. We hold that these colored barbarians have been withdrawn from a country of native barbarism, and under the benignant influence of a Christian rule, of a Christian civilization, have been elevated, yes, *elevated* to a standing and position which they could never have otherwise secured. In respect to the colored race we challenge comparison with San Domingo, with the freed regions of Jamaica, with those who have been transferred to the coast of Africa. Ask the travellers who have visited those distant shores to contrast the condition of the colored people there with that of those on our Southern plantations, and they will give you but one answer—they will say, we have redeemed and kept well our high and our holy trust.

But this is a matter with our own consciences, not with yours. We appeal to you to leave it where it is, to leave the colored people where they are. Why should you undertake to interfere with the policy of a neighboring State concerning a people about which you know nothing? We feel, we know that we have done that race no wrong. Deep into the Southern heart has this feeling penetrated. For scores of years we have been laboring earnestly in our mission. In all this time we have contributed far more to the greatness of the North than to our own. Yet all this time we have been assailed, attacked, vilified and defamed, by the people of the North, from the cradle to the grave, and you have educated your children to believe us monsters of brutality, lust and iniquity.

I tell you, that from the time the abolition societies aroused the latent anti-slavery spirit of the North until now, nothing but evil has come of the excitement and discussion. It has spread a horrid influence far and wide; it has for years distilled, and is now distilling its poison and venom all over the land.

It was under English, yes, British, Anglo-Saxon instigation that it first commenced. By this instigation it has been fed, been given life, continuity and power. Think you the English authors of this instigation had any purpose but to disrupt this Republic? They professed to regard slavery as an evil and a sin. The fruits of their action were first manifested in religious societies—first in the largest churches in New England, in the Presbyterian or Congregational churches, next the Methodist, then the Baptist, and finally, the venom spread so widely, its influence separated other churches. What has the moral influence of this power done? It has made the abstraction of our slaves a virtue. Societies have been formed for that very purpose, inciting their members and others, by the vilest motives, to steal our slaves, to destroy our property.

Nor have they been sufficiently modest to cloak their designs under the veil of secrecy. These people advocated their pernicious doctrines openly in your leading cities, even within the consecrated walls of Fanueil Hall.

Openly among your people, in the very light of day, these efforts were carried on for the destruction of your sister States. There has not been an effort of the law nor an exertion of public opinion to put them down.

These efforts culminated in the actual invasion of my own old honored State, and your people thought they were doing GOD service in signing a petition to our authorities for mercy to John Brown and his ruffian invaders of our soil. And when these men met the just reward of their crime, there was, throughout the North, in your meetings and your public prints, expressions of sympathy for these robbers and murderers. They were looked upon as the victims of oppression, as martyrs to a holy and righteous cause. Gentlemen, consider these things, and tell me, is there not to-day reason for suspicion; on the part of the South for grave apprehension?

But the half is yet to be told; I have looked only at the moral aspect of the question. Dangerous enough hitherto, it becomes far more dangerous when it culminates on the arena of politics, and asks, with the powerful aid of a majority, the interference and the aid of the Government.

As soon as it became the party of one idea it began to draw to it, first the support of one, then another political party. It went on securing the assistance of one after another until it demoralized, until it brought each to ruin. It destroyed the grand old Whig party. Fanatic enough before, when it had brought that party to its grave, it thrust upon the arena of politics this question of slavery in the territories. Then for the first time it raised the cry of "Free Soil," and brought to its support the hearts of a majority of the people of the northern States.

The people of the North and Northwest have long been noted for their acquisitive disposition, especially for the acquisition of lands. This has been manifested in every form. Carried into effect it has made them powerful, until, not long since, they thought they might get entire dominion at no distant day. Then arose in their hearts a desire greater than the greed of land—the greed of office and power. They then saw that perhaps the North alone might control the national government, and with it the South. Then, too, the great class of protected interests at the North—always greater at the North than at the South—joined with them. All these protected classes, whose advantages had been diverted from other classes to which they belonged, joined with landseekers to secure power. Influence after influence of this sort combined, until it produced your great Republican party; in other words, your great Sectional party, which has at length come to majority and power.

I do not wish to dwell upon the principles of that party, or to discuss them; I simply assert that their principles involve all the sentiments of abolitionism. They may be summed up in this: you determine to oppose the admission of slave States in the future.

You say that the whole power of the country, the whole

power of the administration, shall be used in future for the final extinction of slavery.

This, now, is the ruling idea of your great sectional party. It is simply the rule of one portion of the country over another. There is no difference between attacking slavery in the States and keeping it out of the territories. It is only drawing a parallel around the citadel at a more remote point.

Now, see how the South is placed. The South has forborne as long as it can, just as long as party organization existed, and as long as the South could keep it in existence. It was only when we saw that the whole united Government was to be turned against us, that we began to think of taking the subject into our own hands.

What are we to expect now, when the power, direct and indirect, of this great Government is to be used in the most effective manner against us? A power which claims that we shall not exercise the rights of States even, a power which seeks to coerce us, when we propose to protect ourselves against this lowering and impending danger. You of the North are descended from men who honored the scaffold for the very rights we now seek to exercise. So are we. You would deserve to be spurned by the maids and matrons among you, if you refused to protect yourselves against the dangers thus drawing around you. Can you expect less of us?

Do you tell me that this is an artificial crisis? Would seven States have abandoned all the grand interest they possessed in a glorious and happy Confederacy like ours, but for more serious and vital interests, the interests of safety, security, and honor? Think well of these things, gentlemen!

I have hastily endeavored to show you where I conceive we of the South stand. The feelings which I express are entertained likewise by the border States, by all the citizens of the South, by every householder of my State in a greater or less degree.

The State to which I refer, Virginia, is now met in solemn convocation to consider whether she shall remain in the Union or go out of it; and with the most earnest desire to secure to herself a longer connection with the American Union, a Union of so much honor and pride, and with an equally earnest desire to bring back the wandering States of the South which have already left us, she, my own, my native State, comes here to ask for these guarantees. In my deliberate judgment, the Union and the Constitution, as they now stand, are unsafe for the people of the South, unsafe without other guarantees which will give them actual power instead of mere paper rights. Her stake in this controversy is too deep. In my judgment she has asked too little; I think fuller and greater guarantees ought to be required, and that this Convention should not stand upon ceremony, but in a free and liberal spirit of concession should yield to us all that we ask. Be assured we shall ask none but adequate guarantees.

But I am told that Virginia is content with the Crittenden Resolutions—I say this because I am instructed to say so—that is, if we are to treat these resolutions, not as the principles of the man who offers them, but as the principles of the great party just come into power.

Gentlemen, remember that we of the South are already stripped of one-half our sister States; our system is dislocated; the Union is disrupted.

How can you expect now to retain Virginia, to retain the border States, when they stand in the face of such a great, such an immense party? How can you expect Virginia to remain in the Union without these added guarantees?

I told you I would make no appeals to your pity. If we are not entitled to the guarantees we ask, according to the principles of sound philosophy, of right and justice, then we do not ask them at all.

Mr. BOUTWELL:—I have not been at all clear in my own mind as to when, and to what extent, Massachusetts should raise her voice in this Convention. She heard the voice of Virginia, expressed through her resolutions in this crisis of our country's history. Massachusetts hesitated, not because she was unwilling to respond to the call of Virginia, but because she thought her honor touched by the manner of that call and the circumstances attending it. She had taken part in the election of the sixth of November. She knew the result. It accorded well with her wishes. She knew that the Government whose political head for the next four years was then chosen, was based upon a Constitution which she supposed still had an existence. She saw that State after State had left that Government—seceded is the word used; had gone out from this great Confederacy, and were defying the Constitution and the Union.

Charge after charge has been vaguely made against the North. It is attempted here to put the North on trial. I have listened with grave attention to the gentleman from Virginia to-day, but I have heard no specification of these charges. Massachusetts hesitated I say; she has her own opinions of the Government and the Union. I know Massachusetts; I have been into every one of her more than three hundred towns. I have seen and conversed with her men and her women, and I know there is not a man within her borders who would not to-day gladly lay down his life for the preservation of the Union.

Massachusetts has made war upon slavery wherever she had the right to do it; but much as she *abhors* the institution, she would sacrifice every thing rather than assail it where she has not the right to assail it.

Can it be denied, gentlemen, that we have elected a President in a legal and constitutional way? It cannot; and yet you tell us in tones that cannot be misunderstood, that as a precedent condition of his inauguration we must give you these guarantees.

Massachusetts hesitated, not because her blood was not stirred, but because she insisted that the Government and the inauguration should go on, in the same manner they would have done had Mr. Lincoln been defeated. She felt that she was touched in a tender point when invited here under such circumstances.

It is true, and I confess it frankly, that there are a few men at the North who have not yielded that support to the grand idea upon which this confederated Union stands, that they should have done; who have been disposed to infringe upon, to attack certain rights which the entire North, with these exceptions, accords to you. But are you of the South free from the like imputations? The John Brown invasion was never justified at the North. If, in the excitement of the time, there were those to be found who did not denounce it as gentlemen think they should, it was because they knew it was a matter wholly outside the Constitution—that it was a crime to which Virginia would give adequate punishment.

Gentlemen, I believe, yes, I know, that the people of the North are as true to the Government and the Union of the States

now, as our fathers were when they stood shoulder to shoulder upon the field, fighting for the principles upon which that Union rests. If I thought the time had come when it would be fit or proper to consider amendments to the Constitution at all, I should believe that we would have no trouble with you except upon this question of slavery in the territories. You cannot demand of us at the North any thing that we will not grant, unless it involves a sacrifice of our principles. These we shall not sacrifice—these you must not ask us to abandon. I believe further, and I speak in all frankness, for I wish to delude no one, that if the Constitution and the Union cannot be preserved and effectually maintained without these new guarantees for slavery, that the Union is not worth preserving.

The people of the North have always submitted to the decisions of the proper constituted powers. This obedience has been unpleasant enough when they thought these powers were exercised for sectional purposes; but it has always been implicitly yielded. I am ready, even now, to go home and say that, by the decision of the Supreme Court, slavery exists in all the territories of the United States. We submit to the decision and accept its consequences. But in view of all the circumstances attending that decision, was it quite fair—was it quite generous for the gentleman from Maryland to say that, under it, by the adoption of these propositions, the South was giving up every thing, the North giving up nothing? Does he suppose the South is yielding the point in relation to any territory, which by any probability would become slave territory? Something more than the decision of the Supreme Court is necessary to establish slavery anywhere. The decision may give the *right* to establish it, other influences must control the question of its actual establishment.

I am opposed, further, to any restrictions on the acquisition of territory. They are unnecessary. The time may come when they would be troublesome. We may want the Canadas. The time may come when the Canadas may wish to unite with us. Shall we tie up our hands so that we cannot receive them, or make it forever your interest to oppose their annexation? Such a restriction would be, by the common consent of the people, disregarded.

There are seven States out of the Union already. They have organized what they claim is an independent Government. They are not to be coerced back, you say. Are the prospects very favorable that they will return of their own accord? But *they* will annex territory. They are already looking to Mexico. If left to themselves they would annex her and all her neighbors, and we should lose our highway to the Pacific coast. They would acquire it, and to us it would be lost forever.

The North will consider well before she consents to this—before she even permits it. Ever since 1820 we have pursued, in this respect, a uniform policy. The North will hesitate long before, by accepting the condition you propose, she deprives the nation of the valuable privilege, the unquestionable right, of acquiring new territory in an honorable way.

I have tried to look upon these propositions of the majority of the committee, as true measures of pacification. I have listened patiently to all that has been said in their favor. But I am still unconvinced, or rather I am convinced that they will do nothing for the Union. They will prove totally inadequate; may, perhaps, be positively mischievous. The North, the free States, will not adopt them—will not consent to these new endorsements of an institution which they do not like, which they believe to be injurious to the best interests of the Republic; and if they did adopt them, as they could only do by a sacrifice of principles which you should not expect, the South would not be satisfied; she would not fail to find pretexts for a course of action upon which I think she has already determined. I see in these propositions any thing but true measures of pacification.

But the North will never consent to the separation of the States. If the South persists in the course on which she has entered we shall march our armies to the Gulf of Mexico, or you will march yours to the Great Lakes. There can be no peaceful separation. There is one way by which war may be avoided and the Union preserved. It is a plain and a constitutional way. If the slave States will abandon the design, which we must infer from the remarks of the gentleman from Virginia they have already formed, will faithfully abide by their constitutional obligations, and remain in the Union until their rights are in *fact* invaded, all will be well. But if they take the responsibility of involving the country in a civil war; of breaking up the Government which our fathers founded and our people love, but one course remains to those who are true to that Government. They must and will defend it at every sacrifice—if necessary, to the sacrifice of their lives.

Mr. GUTHRIE:—I came here with my colleagues representing a Southern State. I have had full and free communication with the people of all portions of the South, before, during, and since the election of the sixth of November, and I state here, that I have never dreamed that there was the slightest objection anywhere to the inauguration of Mr. LINCOLN. To-day is the first time I ever heard the question raised, and yet I do not believe that any such objection now exists.

It is said that this is not a fit time to hold such a conference—not a suitable time to consider the questions now before us. Is there any reason why we should not consider the rights of any section of the country, whether a President is going out or coming in? As one delegate I will not consent to postpone the action necessary to secure our rights for any such reason as this.

Now, as to this question of slavery in the Territories. It is true that the Supreme Court has decided it in favor of the South. It is equally true that parties have repudiated that decision both in platforms and on the stump.

When territory has been acquired by the blood and treasure of the common Union, you cannot exclude one portion of the *cestuis que trust* from its rights. The Supreme Court so decided, and its decision was just and equitable.

At the South, we ask for our rights *under the Constitution.* We say, let all questions which affect or concern them be decided. The gentleman from Massachusetts says he will not give them up, that his State will not yield. Well, if this is so, let us go to the ballot box. If the question is decided in the gentleman's favor there, *we know how to take care of ourselves.*

The gentleman from Massachusetts does not understand this question. He does not understand why we of the South want it—why we must have it settled. There *was* a time when the embargo law threw our slaves out of employment. The North then contemplated a dissolution of the Union. Why? Because she thought the Government wanted power—was inefficient.

Now, there is a sense of insecurity felt throughout the South. Our property is depreciating, going down every day. We feel this want of security very deeply, this want of faith in the Government under which we live. The South is in agitation.

Suppose some event should in some way strike down the value of your property at the North. Would you not wish to have its security restored? Would you not call for guarantees? If you would not, you are not men. This is all we want; all we ask for, is security. There is nothing in the territorial question that we may not settle by a fair compromise.

The commonwealth of Virginia called this Conference in high patriotism. I have an earnest faith in her sincerity and her purity in doing so. She hoped to meet her sisters animated by the same patriotism—that they would join with her in granting the assurances, in giving the securities we need. Gentlemen, you can give us these securities—these assurances. We shall then go home and tell our people that we can still live on together, in security. Will it do to say that this cannot be done before the inaguration of Mr. LINCOLN? No! No such answer should go to the people of any of the States—no such answer will satisfy them. Give us the guarantees *here.* We will satisfy the people of the whole nation as to the appropriateness of the time.

There is no truth in the assertions of the gentleman from Massachusetts. We are willing to go before the old commonwealth of Massachusetts with all her glorious memories, willing to go before New York with her half million of voters, confident that both will do us justice. Why stand between us and the people? At least, let us ask their judgment upon our propositions.

We come here to confer, to propitiate, not to awaken old troubles and differences. If there are such existing and which must be settled, why should we not settle them here? We all wish to bring back the seven States which have left us; we have a common interest in them. I think they should not have deserted us; that they should have consulted us first, and then there would have been no necessity. If they were here, their presence surely would not have weakened us, nor would their presence have disturbed the North. We come not here to widen our separation—to drive them further off. We come to consult together, to give and receive justice.

I confess I am not much in favor of the second proposition of amendment. We must regard this as a progressive country. From four millions of people we have risen to thirty millions! Where will we be in eighty years more? There will be in that time a great population in our now unsettled territory—perhaps greater than all our present population. I thought the amendment unwise, but I consented to it, for if we would agree we must all yield something.

And now I hope, and hope most earnestly, that without crimination or recrimination we shall vote in good temper and in good time, so that our proposals may in due time go before Congress and before the people.

Do not let us give up to revolution anywhere, in any section of the Union! Do not you of the North impose upon us the necessity of fleeing our country! God knows this same necessity may come to you of the North, and sooner than you expect it. If disruption—if war must come, one-half your merchants, one-half your mechanics will become bankrupt. You are marching that way with hasty steps. Not one man, North or South, but must suffer if the sad conclusion comes. Our products will depreciate. Next year not one-half the fields now whitened by the rich growth of cotton will be cultivated if this unhappy contest goes on.

The people of my section, the people of the South, are restless and impatient. They are already in the way of revolution—all these influences are leading them on. Can they remain quiet when the fortunes of one-half of them are struck down? Can you at the North remain quiet under like provocations? And yet harmony may even yet be restored. All these differences may be settled harmoniously. We believe they may be settled now.

Mr. TUCK:—If we should agree to all your propositions, and Congress still should not act upon them, would not these difficulties be still more complicated?

Mr. GUTHRIE:—No, sir! No! We would then tell our people that this Conference would, but Congress would not do any thing to save the country. In such an event we would wait for the ballot box and a new Congress.

Mr. GOODRICH :—Permit me one question to the gentleman from Kentucky. Would this Convention, in his opinion, have been called by Virginia, if either Mr. DOUGLAS or Mr. BRECKENRIDGE had been elected?

Mr. GUTHRIE :—I do not think it would have been called in that event. Let me say, however, one thing which escaped me. It is not a divided Democracy—not the existence of a Whig party, but it is the union of all discordant elements combined, which have brought the abolitionists into power, which has produced this sense of insecurity in the South. It is their combined power which the people of the South feel, and which they wish to guard against.

Mr. CLEVELAND :—I feel bound to say to all here present, that unless this debate stops now, we might as well go home. I have pondered much upon the remark of my worthy friend from Kentucky, that if we could not do good here, at least we ought not to do harm. Why should we do any thing to aggravate these unhappy circumstances? Let us not widen our dissensions; let us do nothing to postpone or destroy the only hope we have for the settlement of our troubles.

Let us be gentle and pleasant. Let us love one another. Let us not try to find out who is the smartest or the keenest. Let us vote soon, and without any feeling or any quarrelling.

Mr. SEDDON :—I fear from some remarks that have been made during this discussion, that not only my motives, but the terms in which I have expressed them, have been misapprehended. I have been untrue to every purpose of my mind, if I have spoken with any bitterness or acrimony. I thought it was my duty to be plain—at the same time temperate though emphatic. I thought I had been so. Nothing is farther from my purpose than the irritation of any section, much less of any member here. Most assuredly I did not intend to create dissension or to give the slightest occasion for personal feeling or recrimination.

The PRESIDENT finding it necessary to leave the Conference, now called Mr. ALEXANDER to the chair.

Mr. CLEVELAND :—I did not mean to stir up anybody. I want to settle these unhappy points of difference here. I want to settle them to-day, now, this very hour. Suppose we do not settle them! Does not border war follow? does not civil war come? I speak to all of you, both North and South. What becomes of your property in such a case? Who wants to stake it all on such a hazard? We settled this question once fairly, and, as everybody thought, finally. That was in 1850. Why was not that settlement permitted to stand? Nothing but the ambition that has sent so many angels down to hell could have ever brought it up again.

It is too late to bring charges against either section now—too late to bring charges against individuals. The question now before us is,—Which is the way to lead the country out of her present danger? We want faith and good works—these alone will do it. If these fail, we have no hope elsewhere. I am in favor of the propositions of amendment submitted. These we can stand upon throughout the land. The people will adopt them. In the name of all that is good and holy let us settle these differences here.

Why talk about territory to be acquired hereafter? We have just the same title to it that the devil had to the territory he offered our Saviour on a certain remarkable occasion—just the same title, at all events, no better. For Heaven's sake, gentlemen, let us act for the good of the country! let us give to every section its rights—to every man his rights, and let this be remembered through all time as the Convention of Patriots which sacrificed every selfish and personal consideration to save the country!

Mr. GOODRICH:—I wish to make one remark to the Conference, and especially to the gentleman from Kentucky. Much is said here about equal rights. We have always believed in that doctrine. We believe this to be a country of equals. We went into the last Presidential contest as equals—and as such we elected Mr. LINCOLN. Now, when we have the right to do so, we wish to come into power as equals—with that superiority only which our majority gives us. When we are in power and disturb or threaten to disturb the rights of any portion of the Union, then ask us for security, for guarantees, and if need be you shall have both. How would you have treated us if we had come to you with such a request at the commencement of any Democratic administration?

Mr. LOGAN:—I want to refer the report of the majority,

and the substitute proposed by the minority, back to the committee. I believe that it is better to have action upon all these questions at the earliest possible moment. The question now is, not which section of the Union is suffering most—all sections are suffering; all are feeling the influence of this agitation; all look with fear and trembling to the future; all desire a speedy and a peaceful conclusion of our differences. If we cannot settle them here—if we cannot induce Congress to submit our propositions of amendment to the people, then I pray from my heart, I hope and believe, that our friends in every section will wait patiently until these propositions can go before the State Legislatures and receive proper consideration there.

The PRESIDENT here stated the proposition, to refer the reports of the majority and the minority of the committee back to the committee, with instructions.

Several members objected to the motion, declaring it not in order.

The motion was thereupon withdrawn.

The PRESIDENT:—The question recurs upon the amendment offered by the gentleman from Maryland, to insert the word "present" before the word territories, in the first line and the fifth line of the propositions of the amendment to the Constitution submitted by the majority of the committee.

The amendment was adopted without a count of the yeas and nays, and the first section of the majority report, after the adoption of the amendment, is as follows:

ARTICLE 1. In all the present territory of the United States, not embraced within the limits of the Cherokee treaty grant, north of a line from east to west on the parallel of 36° 30′ north latitude, involuntary servitude, except in punishment of crime, is prohibited whilst it shall be under a Territorial Government; and in all the present territory south of said line, the status of persons owing service or labor as it now exists, shall not be changed by law while such territory shall be under a Territorial Government; and neither Congress nor the Territorial Government shall have power to hinder or prevent the taking to said territory of persons held to labor or involuntary service, within the United States, according to the laws or usages of the State from which such persons may be taken, nor to impair the rights arising out of said relations, which shall be subject to judicial cognizance in the Federal Courts, according to the common law; and when any territory north or south of said line, within such boundary as Congress may prescribe, shall contain a population required for a member of Congress, according to the then Federal ratio of representation, it shall, if its form of government be republican, be admitted into the Union on an equal footing with the original States, with or without involuntary service or labor, as the Constitution of such new State may provide.

Mr. ROMAN :—I move that when this Conference adjourn, it adjourn to meet at seven o'clock this evening.

Mr. CHITTENDEN :—I move an adjournment of the Conference.

Mr. ROMAN :—Is not my motion first in order?

The PRESIDENT :—The question is on the motion of the gentleman from Vermont.

The motion to adjourn was put and carried.

TWELFTH DAY.

WASHINGTON, TUESDAY, *February* 19*th*, 1861.

THE Conference was called to order by the PRESIDENT at eleven o'clock.

The proceedings were opened with prayer.

The Journal was read by Assistant Secretary PULESTON, and, after sundry amendments, was approved.

Mr. SUMMERS:—The Committee on Credentials have received and considered the credentials of Mr. FRANCIS GRANGER, of New York, appointed to fill a vacancy in the delegation from that State, occasioned by the resignation of Mr. ADDISON GARDINER. They are satisfactory, and if no objection is made, the list of delegates from New York will be altered accordingly.

No objection was made, and Mr GRANGER's name was added to the list of delegates from New York.

Mr. WICKLIFFE:—I ask now that the resolution limiting the time to be occupied by each member in debate be taken up. I have become satisfied that unless we place some restrictions, in this respect, upon the discussions, we shall occupy much more time than we wish to have expended in that way. The session of the present Congress will soon terminate. Our labors will be useless, unless we submit the result of them to Congress in time to secure the approval of that body. The propositions will be debated there, and that debate must necessarily occupy time. I am sure no gentleman wishes to defeat the main purpose of the Conference by delay. The resolution is as follows:

Resolved, That in the discussions which may take place in this Convention upon any question, no member shall be allowed to speak more than thirty minutes.

Mr. DAVIS:—I move to amend the resolution by inserting *ten* minutes instead of *thirty* minutes.

Mr. FIELD:—Is it seriously contemplated now, after gentlemen upon one side have spoken two or three times, and at great length—after the questions involved in the committee's reports have been thoroughly and exhaustively discussed on the part of the South—and when only one gentleman from the North has been heard upon the general subject, to cut us off from all opportunity of expressing our views? Such a course will not help your propositions.

Mr. BOUTWELL:—Massachusetts will never consent to this.

Mr. WICKLIFFE:—If we cannot get Massachusetts to help us, we will help ourselves. We got along without her in the war of 1812; we can get on without her again. The disease exists in the nation now. It is of no use, or rather it is too late to talk about the cause, we had much better try to cure the disease.

Mr. FIELD:—New York has not occupied the time of the Conference for three minutes. Kentucky has been heard twice, her representative speaking as long as he wished. I insist upon the same right for New York. I insist upon the discussion of these questions without restriction or limitation.

Mr. DODGE:—I wish to speak for the commercial interests of the country. I cannot do them justice in ten minutes.

Mr. MOREHEAD, of North Carolina:—I am very desirous to reach an early decision, and yet I do not quite like to restrict debate in this way. Suppose, after holding one morning session, we have another commencing at half-past seven in the evening?

Mr. CARRUTHERS:—We have come here for the purpose of *acting;* not to hear speeches. There is no use in talking over these things; our minds are all made up, and talking will not change them. I want to make an end of these discussions. I move that all debate shall close at three o'clock to-day, and that the Conference then proceed to vote upon the propositions before it.

Mr. ALLEN:—The object which brought us together I presume we shall not disagree about. We came here for the purpose of consultation over the condition of the country. If this is true, nothing but harm can come from these limitations upon the liberty of speech. The questions before us are the most important that could possibly arise. Before our present Constitution was adopted it was discussed and examined in Convention for more than three months. We are now practically making a new Constitution. Though we as members differed widely when we came here, I think progress has been made toward our ultimate agreement. I think the general effect of our discussions is to bring us nearer together. I think our acquaintance and our association as members lead to the same end.

The gentleman from Kentucky says that we have come here to heal disease. I don't quite agree with him as to the disease. I differ widely from him as to the proper method of treating it. He seems disposed to apply a plaster to the foot, to cure a disease in the head. If these debates should continue for a week, the time would not be lost, the effect would be favorable. We should have more faith in each other, a more kindly feeling would be produced. Do not let us hurry. You may *force* a vote to-day, but the result will satisfy none. Such a course will give good ground for dissatisfaction. You may even carry your propositions by a majority, but what weight will such a vote have in Congress or with the people?

Mr. CHITTENDEN:—We who represent smaller States intend to be very modest here, but you will need our votes when you seek to place new and important limitations upon a Constitution with which we are now satisfied. I will answer for one State, and tell you that she will not listen to a proposition that comes to her with a taint of suspicion about it. If you will not allow her representatives to participate in the examination and discussion of these propositions here, her people will reject them without discussion, if they are ever called to act on them. She has not occupied the time of this Conference for one minute upon the general subject. She may not wish to do so. I submit whether it is wise for you to cut off her right to be heard here, if she chooses to exercise it.

Mr. RANDOLPH:—I agree with the gentleman from Tennessee, that we came here to act and not to talk. We have had talking enough, perhaps too much already. I have drawn up a resolution which I think covers the whole subject, I move its adoption. The resolution was read as follows:

Resolved, That this Convention will hold two sessions daily, viz., from ten o'clock, A. M., to four o'clock, P. M.; and from eight to ten o'clock, P. M.; and that no motion to adjourn prior to said hours of four and ten, P. M., shall be in order, if objection be made; and that on Thursday next, at twelve o'clock, noon, all debate shall cease, and the Convention proceed to vote upon the questions or propositions before them in their order.

The PRESIDENT commenced a statement of the various propositions relating to the subject now pending, when Mr. ALEXANDER moved to lay the whole subject on the table.

The motion to lay on the table was negatived by the following vote:—ayes, 48; nays, 54.

Mr. GOODRICH:—I call for the division of the question.

The PRESIDENT:—So many motions have been made that it is somewhat difficult to decide, by the rules of Parliamentary law, which is in order.

I will divide the questions as follows:

1st. Will the Conference hold two sessions daily?

2d. Shall the debate be closed on Thursday at twelve o'clock?

3d. Shall each member be limited to ten minutes in the discussion?

Mr. JOHNSON, of Missouri:—I hope the questions will be decided affirmatively.

Mr. CHASE:—It appears to me that we can arrange this whole subject without serious difficulty. If Mr. WICKLIFFE will adhere to his resolution, and the other proposals are withdrawn, we can then proceed. If any gentleman finds it necessary to ask for an extension of his time, it will no doubt be granted to him. Mr. RANDOLPH's proposition exacts too much labor. I think the Conference had better limit the time of each member. I am opposed to fixing a time for terminating the discussion. It will not be agreeable to many who may be cut off. It is contrary to the spirit of the rules we have already adopted. I hope we shall not be compelled to vote on the questions one by one, and I will suggest to Mr. RANDOLPH whether it would not be better that his resolution should be withdrawn.

Mr. HOPPIN:—I hope the resolution will pass as it is. We have come here to act. We are all ready to take the vote now. The sooner we vote the better. There is every necessity for prompt action.

Mr. MOREHEAD:—If the proposition had emanated from another quarter, I should feel at liberty to urge its adoption. As it is, I would pay the highest respect to it. I regret extremely to hear the talk about *sides* in this Conference. I came here to act for the Union—the whole Union. I recognize no sides—no party. If any come here for a different purpose I do not wish to act with them; they are wrong. I hope from my heart that we can all yet live together in peace; but if we are to do so we must act, and act speedily.

Mr. CHASE again stated his proposition.

Mr. CRISFIELD:—If I understand rightly, the question should be on striking out the latter clause of the resolution, so as to perfect it and make it meet the case. I make the point and—

Mr. RANDOLPH:—I think the gentleman from Maryland is right.

Mr. ALEXANDER:—I desire to ask whether a resolution to supersede the motion to adjourn is in order?

The PRESIDENT:—I think the question should first be taken on the motion to strike out the last clause in the resolution.

Mr. STOCKTON:—If the Conference felt as I do, it would at once establish such peremptory orders as would bring a speedy termination to this whole business. Upon what, let me ask gentlemen, does the salvation of the Union depend at this moment? What is it alone that prevents civil war now? I answer, it is the session of this Convention—this august Convention! We stand in the presence of an awful danger! We feel the throes of an earthquake which threatens to bring down ruin on the whole magnificent fabric of our Government! Is it possible that we should suffer this ruin to take place? Would it not impeach the wisdom and good sense of our day and generation to permit the edifice which our fathers constructed—to crumble to pieces? No! fellow countrymen, it is necessary that we, by trusting in God, who guided our ancestors through the stormy vicissitudes of the Revolution, should this day resolve that the Union shall be preserved!

In the execution of that resolve let us unfold a new leaf in our national history, and write thereon words of peace. Peace or war is in our hands—an awful alternative! Peace alone is the object of our mission; to restore peace to a distracted country. I have spent my whole life in the service of my country. I love the people of every State in it. They have been under my command and I have been under theirs. I know them, and I know that this Union can never be dissolved without a struggle. Will you hasten the time when we shall begin to shed each other's blood? No! gentlemen, no!

There seems to be but one question which gives us any difficulty in adjusting. That is, about the right of the South to take their slaves into the territories. Is it possible that we can permit this Union to be broken up because of any difference on such a question as this? Better that the territories were buried in the deep sea beyond the plummet's reach, than that they should be the cause of such a deplorable result.

But it is not the value of the territories which is in dispute; it is not whether the North or the South shall colonize them, because, as the gentleman from New York has said, that though the territory south of 36° 30′ had been ten years open to Southern colonization, only twenty-four slaves had been introduced into it. No, the real question is, whether pride of opinion shall succumb to the necessities of the crisis.

The Premier of the incoming administration has declared that parties and platforms are subordinate to, and must disappear in the presence of the great question of the Union. This gives me hope. Let him and his friends act upon that, and this Conference can in six hours, in conjunction with a committee of his political friends, adjust such terms of settlement as will save the Union.

The Roman Curtius offered himself as a sacrifice to save Rome, when informed by the oracle that the loss of his life would save his country. We are now in greater danger than Rome was then; but is there no Curtius for our salvation? We are not called upon to give up life, property, or honor, but to concede justice and equal rights to our Southern brethren. We only want the courage to yield extreme opinions. What power, after victory, refuses to lower the lofty terms which were asserted on the eve of the battle for the sake of peace? But the Republicans say, shall we surrender the fruits of victory to the vanquished? I answer, how are you to enjoy your fruits without pacification? You expected to govern the whole country. You aspired to the control of the whole empire. Without peace you will not succeed in establishing possession of that magnificent country which your predecessors governed, but you will govern a little more than half of it, and with that you have to provide for war.

It is easy to dispose of the threatening attitude of the South by denouncing it as a rebellion—as treason. It is idle to disguise the danger. The revolt of a whole people, covering a territory equal to half of Europe, is a revolution. You cannot dwarf the movement by stigmatizing it as treason. Its magnitude and proportions make the sword, and not the law, its arbiter. Is it possible that people can be so infatuated as to contemplate the use of the sword to conquer secession? Will you hasten the time when we shall begin to shed each other's blood? Coerce! force fifteen States! Why, you cannot force New Jersey alone! Force the South? They won't stop to count forces—neither side can be frightened. Don't think of it. You cannot frighten either, no more than the hero could be frightened whom the Roman poet has immortalized. Suppose after the expenditure of a thousand millions you shall have stopped dismemberment and subjugated the South, what is to become of the country then? what is to become of the army and its chiefs who have conquered? When the Long Parliament had murdered Charles, subdued Ireland and Scotland, and compelled the deference of all Europe, they supposed they would enjoy the fruits of their victories. They began to discuss the expenses of the army, and the expediency of its reduction. They had hardly commenced when Cromwell entered Westminster Hall and turned out the Republican party of that day. The whole country, tired of war, crouched under the iron heel of the Puritan soldier. The Republican party of England succumbed; Cromwell died; his son resigned the Protectorate, and the Republican party of England rose to the surface and made its last struggle for its power. General Monk and his army approached London, and Parliament with servility waited the pleasure of the army. The army declared for the King, and the King was restored.

When men meet to save the country, they must be prepared to give up every thing—to give their lives if necessary. How can men stop for party platforms when their country is in danger? But will the country consent to be dragged into civil war to maintain the Chicago Platform? It will not. That Platform was erected upon a perishable foundation. In the language of the New York Senator, it must "disappear."

I appeal to the brotherhood, to the fraternity of the North. My friends, peace or war is in your hands. You hold the keys of peace or war. You tell us not to hasten in this matter. But you do not realize the facts—no one does. It is said that the South challenges and invites war. No such thing. The mad action of South Carolina does not truly represent the South. There are disunionists South as well as North. It is the duty of patriotic men to checkmate the disunionists of both sections. By a proclamation of war, we shall effectually play into the hands and gratify the disunionists of both extremes. Civil war consolidates the South as a unit for disunion. The gallant southern men who have so nobly battled for the Union against great odds, will then be overpowered and forced into the ranks of the defenders of the South. While the South will thus be undivided and stand in solid phalanx, what will be our condition here at the North?

Can it be supposed that the Union men of the Democracy of of the North will stand by and see the country plunged into civil war to maintain the Chicago Platform? Will they acquiesce in the demolition of this Union by these means, when it can be preserved by peace? No, sir! Do you talk here about regiments for invasion, for coercion—you, gentlemen of the North? You know better; I know better. For every regiment raised there for coercion, there will be another raised for resistance to coercion. If no other State will raise them, remember New Jersey. The Republican leaders of the North, with hot haste, have worked through the Legislatures of the several States resolutions of a belligerent character, offering the military power of those States to the Government to subdue the South. Did the people of the North authorize those Legislatures to make any such tenders? Would the people of the North sanction any such nefarious policy? I know well the enormous bribe with which the Republican leaders would seduce the North into fratricidal war. The expenditure of uncounted millions, the distribution of epaulets and military commissions for an army of half a million of men, the immense patronage involved in the letting of army contracts, the inflation of prices and the rise of property which would follow the excessive issue of paper money, made necessary by the lavish expenditure;—these, indeed, are the enormous bribes which the Republican party offers.

How arrogant it is for the Republican leaders to tender the military power of their States! Who gave them or their States authority to raise armies? For national purposes the whole militia of the Union is subject to Congress. Congress alone has power to declare war and to call out the militia, and Congress can only call upon the militia to suppress insurrection or repel invasion. Pause, gentlemen! Stop where you are! You will bring strife to your own doors, to your very hearthstones—bloody, disheartening strife. War will be in your own homes, among your own families. Under ordinary circumstances you would hesitate. If the question was about tariff, you would hesitate and look at the awful consequences. That there is a diversity between us is very true. What of it? It lies in a nutshell. We can fix it in a minute, if you will be calm and act like brothers.

The only question, as I understand it, for I have thought and studied upon it, is this: You of the North will not yield to the South the small privilege of taking their slaves into the territories of the common Union. You will not give them a fair chance with you, even in the Government property—the territories. When the territories become States they will have to take care of themselves. You cannot theorize slave soil into free soil, nor *vice versâ*. Am I not right? Does the South ask any control or power over these territories after they have become States? No, gentlemen; the South demands no such thing. It is not demanded by her, and never will be. All I ask for the South, and all she asks for herself, is this: Let us be free to come with our slaves into all your territories, and hold them there until the territory is made up into States.

I have shown that if peace be not secured, the uprising of the South would be a revolution, and cannot be treated as mere insurrection. The bravado, therefore, of offering armies to the Government, can only have the effect, at this crisis, of preventing a peaceful adjustment. Against all such demonstrations we must fix our faces like flint. Peace we must have. The Union can only be preserved by peace. The South asks no more than the North will concede, if the people of the North can express their sentiments. The South only asks for equal rights, and to be let alone. For thirty years she has asked no more. The South will soon present its cause in an authoritative shape. Their conventions will soon declare their propositions. Let the North be prepared to consider them in conventions representing their people fairly. If this is done, there is no doubt the present crisis will pass without danger. Until time for these results can be taken, let warlike demonstrations be resisted. Let the Government abstain from collision, even with South Carolina. There is as much of loyalty to the Union at the South as anywhere. It has only disappeared in the presence of danger which threatened their domestic tranquillity, their safety, and their honor. Let the hostile attitude which the North assumed at Chicago give place to the recognition of the rights of the South, and we shall see an outburst of loyalty to the Union throughout the entire South, like that which welcomed to old England its constitutional sovereign after a long and bloody civil war, forced upon the English people by the Puritans. It is the spirit of the same fanatic intolerance which has caused our present troubles.

Intelligent citizens should abandon platforms and stand up for peace. Peace with all nations has been the master policy. It has elevated our country to its present condition of power and prosperity. Do not let us sacrifice peace, and suffer violence and discord to usurp its reign. We have a magnificent future if we can only preserve the Union as our fathers constructed it. While it lasts there is a great light in the firmament in which all may walk in security, hope, and happiness. It is a light reaching far down the depths of futurity cheering and guiding the steps of our children. It is a light shining to the remotest corner of the earth—raising up the down-trodden and illuminating the homes of the victims of oppression. But let that light be now eclipsed, go out in blood and darkness, and the hopes of mankind are forever blasted.

Gentlemen, will you not consider? Shall we not settle the question here, and not trouble the rest of the Union with it? We will settle it fairly and squarely. It is too small a matter to get mad about—to set about destroying the Union. Why quarrel over such a simple question? No, gentlemen, you shall not do it. I am going to talk to you as individuals—as men—as patriots. I know too many of you and too much about you. You love your country too well to destroy her for such a cause. You are too patriotic. The North will never dissolve this Union on any such pretexts. You cannot destroy your country for that. You love it too much. I call on you, WADSWORTH and KING, FIELD and CHASE and MORRILL—as able men, as brothers—as good patriots—to give up every thing else if it is necessary, to save your country. But we don't ask you to give up any thing in the way of principles.

Now that Chicago Platform of yours is a nice paper. It has many good things in it. But it must not control this question. You can keep that platform and save your country: but you must save your country. Shall we go into war upon this little question about the Territories. No! No!!

Under the most favorable circumstances possible for the experiment of self-government, with every possible inducement to preserve our country, we must not give it up. The years of civil war which will succeed dismemberment of the Union will cause true men to seek refuge and security, from military despotism, in some other country. Some Cæsar or Napoleon will spring from the vortex of revolution and war, and with his sword cleave his way to supreme command. If all history is not a failure, and if mankind are now what they have always been, such will be the fate of free government in the United States, in the event of war. Shall we bring such a catastrophe upon us to vindicate the Chicago Platform? No! the American people will rise in their omnipotence and trample into dust the man who dared to put in jeopardy this Union, in order to maintain such demagogism. Away with parties and platforms and every thing else which would obstruct the free and patriotic efforts now making for the salvation of the Union. It shall not be destroyed. I tell you, friends, I am going to stand right in the way. You shall not go home; you shall never see your wives and families again, until you have settled these matters, and saved your good old country, if I can help it. Spread aloft the banner of stripes and stars, let the whole country rally beneath its glorious folds, with no other slogan on their lips but the unanimous cry, THE UNION, IT MUST BE PRESERVED!

Mr. GRANGER:—New Jersey has addressed New York as though she supposed the delegation from that State to be united in its opinions, and its action. Let me set the gentleman himself and the Conference right on that point at the commencement. The members composing that delegation do not agree; very far from it. The vote of that delegation hitherto has been determined by a majority only; a majority reduced to the very smallest point possible now, since the delegation is full. It may be said that New York voted at the last Presidential election against us by a majority of fifty thousand; but let me assure you that if the noble propositions of the majority of your committee, which I read for the first time yesterday, could be submitted to them, the people of New York would adopt them by even a larger majority.

These *are* noble propositions; they are worthy the eminent and patriotic committee from which they have emanated. They present a fair and equitable basis for the adjustment of our difficulties; they are a shield and a sure defence against the dangers which threaten us. They are such as the people expect and such as they want. They know that the politicians who have brought the country to the verge of ruin can be trusted no longer. The time has come when they must act for themselves. Be assured, gentlemen, they will do so.

I wish to say a few words about the last election in New York, for it has been widely misrepresented and misunderstood. How did we go into that canvass? Upon what principles was it conducted? What representations were made? I am one of the men who have struggled to meet and oppose this Republican party from the outset—to avert, if possible, the adoption of its pernicious principles by the people of New York. I took my stand upon the Compromise of 1850, and separated myself politically from all men who could not stand with me on that platform. We struggled on until that Compromise was adopted by the Baltimore Convention.

The Kansas bill was introduced at a most fatal hour. It was distasteful to the whole country; satisfactory nowhere. In due time the Charleston Convention was assembled, and the Democratic party was broken up forever.

What next? Next came the Chicago Convention. It may have been conducted with dignity, and it nominated a candidate. I differ widely from that candidate in my principles and my policy. And yet I believe in him although I opposed his election. I would trust his Kentucky blood to the end, if all else failed. I think he is honest. I have no idea that he will permit the policy of his administration to be controlled by the hot-headed zealots who have been so conspicuous in the last canvass. I expect to see him call to his council board, cool, dispassionate, and conservative men; not men who are driven to the verge of insanity upon this question of slavery.

What next? The Baltimore Convention was held. The tragedy was consummated; the contest was ended. The mere scuffle to secure the control of the Convention which ended in its division, has brought the country into all its present difficulties. If that Convention had presented to the people a good conservative Democrat, there were seventy-five thousand good old line Whigs who would have buckled on their armor and would have won the battle for him.

When the Southern papers began to threaten disunion because LINCOLN did not suit the South, I was not one who abused or denounced them. I knew the temper of some of the politicians in the free States. I knew the action of the South was not impulsive. I knew there was a reason for it. They said their capital was to be rendered worthless—their property to be destroyed, and their country made desolate. God forbid that I should chide them for thinking so!

The Northern mind is in some respects very different from the Southern. It is not started by slight scratches, but strike the rowel deep, and there is a purpose in it that nothing can conquer or restrain. The people of the North will carry that purpose into execution, with a power as fierce as that of the maddest chivalry of South Carolina. The rowel *was* struck deep and the consequences were not considered.

Subjects have been introduced into this discussion which I should have been glad to have avoided, which it would have been better every way to have avoided. The gentleman from

Virginia has referred to the JOHN BROWN invasion. That is one of those subjects. He spoke of the feeling at the North regarding insurrections. I assure you that the North regarded the invader in that case as a foe in your homes—uncurbed and unrestrained—a terrible enemy. I would say to the gentleman from Virginia, that although too many instances among extreme men may have been found of attempts to justify that invasion, such was not the general feeling at the North. Those instances were rare exceptions; and because they were so few and so exceptional, acquired a degree of notoriety and received a degree of attention to which they were never entitled. Such instances as these have always served to prejudice the South improperly against the North. Men are too much given to forming opinions of us from the intemperate acts of a few meddling men.

How do we stand at the present moment in this respect. You will find a few men among us, even now, rash enough to say, "Let these Southern slaveholders go. The 'nigger' will rise upon them and cut their throats!" The action of such men, I admit, gives some color and justification to your charges and prejudices against the whole Northern people.

I agree with you, gentlemen, that this is now a question of peace or war. I believe it to be so from my very soul. The North has been much to blame in bringing it upon us. What has been the language used at the North? Men have used such expressions as this, "The South secede? Why, you can't kick out the South." And men who knew no better believed the statement to be true. I appeal to northern men to say whether this has not been so. I myself thought four States would go, but I believed secession would stop there. We had more to hope from Louisiana than from any other Gulf State. She has gone, and has now taken up a most offensive and threatening position. Virginia to-day is in more danger of immediate secession than Louisiana was a few short months ago.

My friend from New Jersey says that if this Convention does not prevent it, there must be war. I agree with him. War! what a fearful alternative to contemplate? War is a fearful calamity at best, sometimes necessary I admit, but always terrible. It cannot come to this country without a fearful expenditure of blood and treasure. It will leave us, if it leaves us a nation at all, with an awful legacy of widows' tears—of the blighted hopes of orphans—with a catalogue of suffering, misery, and woe, too long to be enumerated and too painful to be contemplated. For God's sake! let such a fate be averted at any cost, from the country. If it comes at all, it will be such a war as the world never saw. War is commonly, and almost universally, between nations foreign to each other—whose individuals are strangers to each other, and whose interests are widely separated. But we are a nation of brothers, of a common ancestry, and bound together by a thousand memories of the past—a thousand ties of interest and blood. It will be a war between brothers—between you who come to us in summer, and we who visit you in winter. It will be a war between those who have been connected in business—associated in pleasures, and who have met as brothers in the halls of legislation and the marts of commerce. Save us from such a war! Let not the mad anger of such a people be aroused. And, gentlemen, if war comes it must be long and terrible. You will see both parties rise in their majesty at both ends of the line. They will slough off every other consideration and devote themselves, with terrible energy, to the work of death. Oh ye! who bring such a calamity as this upon this once happy country! Pause, gentlemen, before you do it, and think of the fearfu laccountability that awaits you in time and in eternity.

But I am here to answer for the State of New York; the Empire State and the people of the Empire State. I have never been classed with the rash men of that State who have aided in bringing about this condition of things. I will not be classed with those who now thrust themselves between the Empire State and those glorious propositions of your committee. They are in the smallest possible majority even in our delegation. All I ask is, that we may have the judgment of the people upon these propositions, and I will be answerable for the rest; and these gentlemen who rely upon the fifty thousand (50,000) majority of last November, will have a fearful waiting for of judgment. Fifty thousand majority! Who does not know how that majority was made up? It was not a majority upon the question of slavery at all. It came in this wise: The opposite party was divided and distracted. The Republican party united all sorts of discordant elements; men voted for Mr. LINCOLN from a great variety of motives. Some, because they wanted the Homestead law; some because they wanted a change in the Tariff; and, gentlemen, let me assure you, there were more men who voted for Mr. LINCOLN—solely on account of the Tariff—than would have made up this fifty thousand majority. I know the people of New York, and I know I can answer for them when I say, Give us these fair and noble propositions and we will accept them with an unanimity that will gratefully surprise the nation.

How does the nation stand to-day? Look at Kansas! She is a State and yet in beggary. She is stretching out her hands to us for relief. We have relieved her for the time, but she will need more aid again. The whole country is excited and agitated. The press, North and South, is full of misrepresentation and vituperation. Sections are arrayed against each other. Men fear to trust each other. The very air is full of anxiety and apprehension. Such, gentlemen, is the miserable condition of the country. The nation is in great peril. Its interests, its institutions, its property, are all in great and common peril. Paralysis has seized upon the whole country. In vain now shall we argue about causes. The effect is upon us. Business is stagnated. Those who have capital do not dare to move it. But we here must do something. Mr. LINCOLN is coming, and all along the route the people are doing him honor. But that triumphal march is insignificant compared with the anxiety felt throughout the country that this Convention should agree upon some plan that will save the Government and the Union.

In one thing, under other circumstances, I would agree with the gentleman (Mr. BOUTWELL) from Massachusetts. Had the border States elected their members of Congress, I would wait. But the elections in the border States are yet to be held. And upon what idea? Why, sir, upon the idea that their whole interests and their whole property are in danger. Aspiring and dangerous men will go before an excited people full of anxiety and uncertainty for the future, and by them be elected instead of the sound, wise, and conservative gentlemen usually selected to represent those States. Those elections would be a mad scene of aspersion and vituperation. I cannot, I will not trust them. Rather give me in those States the glorious results of years gone by.

I say, and I am proud to declare here, that I had no association with the dominant party in the old Empire State at the last election. I struck every other name from the ticket, except those who voted for Bell and Everett. Glorious names! which received the triumphant endorsement of the mother of Presidents—the grand old commonwealth of Virginia.

Sometimes I meet with men who tell me what is going to be done. They talk of retaking forts now held by seceded States by force, of restoring things to their former condition, as they would about sending a vessel for a cargo of oranges to Havana. But they forget that the next administration, like the philosopher who would move the world with a lever, has no holding spot—no place whereon to stand. It is one thing to hold a fort where you have it, but quite another thing to take it when held by the enemy.

Who can magnify the importance of this Conference to all the nation? It is the most important ever held in this country. It holds the key of peace or war. The eyes of the whole people are turned hopefully upon it. By every consideration that should move a patriot, let us agree. Let us act for the salvation of our common country. I came here very unexpectedly to myself. Long withdrawn from political circles, living in comparative retirement, at peace with the world and myself, I would have preferred to remain there; but when I heard of my appointment as a delegate to this Conference, I felt it my duty to come here and say these few things to you.

And now let me close by again assuring you, that if all you ask of New York is the adoption of the propositions which I heard here yesterday as the propositions of a majority of your committee, New York will do you justice. She will answer "YES" by a most triumphant majority—a majority compared with which any heretofore given will seem insignificant! I will occupy time no farther. There is much which I would add, but this is a time for action and not for words.

Mr. RUFFIN:—There are few members of this Conference who attend its sessions with greater interest than myself. I presume that we have come together influenced by various considerations. There are some, I have no doubt, who do not desire the preservation of the Union—who do not care for the safety of the Government which our fathers founded. They may not avow their purposes, they may even conceal them under specious words, but their purpose will be disclosed when we see them arrayed against all projects of settlement—all measures to quiet the existing excitement. Others may think there is no necessity for any action at all, may think so honestly. But let me assure them they are mistaken—sadly mistaken.

Now, I do not care what motives influence others. It is of no consequence to me what their designs or purposes may be, I have no concealment and no deception. I came here for a purpose which I openly and distinctly avow. I proclaim it here and everywhere. I will labor to carry it into execution with all the strength and ability which my advanced years and enfeebled health have left me. *I came to maintain and preserve this glorious Government! I came here for Union and peace!* (Applause.)

My health is such that if I could avoid it, I would not mingle in this discussion. I would not say one word, if I did not know perfectly well that life or death to my part of the country was involved in the action of this Conference. If gentlemen felt as as deeply as I do, they would deprecate as I do the introduction of party or politics into this discussion, or the slightest reference to them. Of what importance is party, compared with the great questions involved here? Parties or men may go up or down, and yet our country is safe. But such Conferences as this, in such emergencies as the present, must act, if our country is to be saved. Let us discard politics and party—let us be brethren and friends.

A gentlemen asked yesterday whether the Convention would have been called, if a Democrat had been elected President. Certainly not. But considerations of a party character would not have prevented it. The true necessity that called us here, is that a President has been elected by a large majority, and a new and strong party is coming into power, which our people believe entertain views and designs hostile to our institutions. Do not understand me as charging the fact upon the new Government. Perhaps I might say that I do not believe it myself.

But that will not answer. Our people are agitated and excited, and we have come here to tell you all, with sorrow in our hearts, that if you will not do something to restore a confidence that is shaken, we are ruined, and we must see this noble Government go down.

We ask you for new constitutional guarantees; and what are the propositions we make? Is there any thing in them which you cannot grant? Is there any thing which it would be dishonorable for you to yield? You reply to us, that you will consent to call a convention to discuss and adjust matters. That will not do. We must act on the existing state of facts. Seven States are already in rebellion—in revolution! I don't care which you call it; either word is bad enough. Tennessee and North Carolina already form fourteen hundred miles of what is virtually a frontier. We are now the border States; we are to be the theatre of war, if it comes. The slave property we speak of will be in still greater peril than it is now. Now think of these things, and tell us whether we can wait for all this complicated machinery of a convention to be put into operation. At the very shortest, it will take three or four years to accomplish any thing.

But my friend from Massachusetts says he does not wish to do any thing at all; that the North is under duress, and her people would despise themselves if they acted under duress. No! no! This is not true in any sense. We respect the people of the North too much to attempt to drive them, or to secure what we need by threats or intimidation. We want the aid of the people of Massachusetts, and we will appeal to their sense of right and justice.

I believe that these propositions, if adopted, will not only satisfy and quiet the loyal States of the South, but that they will bring back the seven States which have gone out. I must be frank and outspoken here. We cannot answer for these States. We cannot say whether they will be satisfied. But we can even stand their absence. We can get on without them, if you will give us what will quiet our people, and what at the same time will not injure you.

Gentlemen, we of North Carolina are not hostile to you; we are your friends—brothers in a common cause—citizens of a common country. We are loyal to our country and to our Constitution. We lose both of them, unless you will aid us now.

As for me, I am an old man. My heart is very full when I look upon the present unhappy and distracted condition of our affairs. I was born before the present Constitution was adopted. May God grant that I do not outlive it. I cannot address you on this subject without manifesting a feeling which fills my heart. Let me assure you, in terms as strong as I can make them, that we cannot stand as we are; that unless you will do something for us, our people will be drawn into that mad career of open defiance, which is now opening so widely against the Government. All I ask of you is to let these propositions go to the people—to submit them at once to their conventions, and not wait the action of the Legislatures of all the States. We want the popular voice—the decision of the people, and the whole people; and if it is to avail us at all, we must have it at once and speedily.

Mr. NOYES :—I did not design to trespass upon the time of the Conference at this stage of the debate. But statements have been made upon this floor to-day which I cannot permit for a single hour to remain unanswered. I should be recreant to my conscience, and especially to my State, if I did not answer them here and now.

I came here for peace, prepared to do that justice to every section of the Union which would secure peace—prepared to go to the farthest limit which propriety and principle, and my obligations to the Constitution, would permit me, to satisfy our southern friends. I did not wish to commit myself to any thing, until I had patiently seen and heard all that was to be said and proposed. Even now I regret that this incidental discussion upon a subject entirely collateral has arisen. How thoroughly it shows the idleness and folly of attempting to limit, or trammel, or hamper discussion upon the general questions which are presented for our action!

Sir, I speak for New York! Not New York of a time gone by! Not New York of an old fossiliferous era, remembered only in some chapter of her ancient history, but young, breathing, living New York, as she exists to-day. Full of enterprise, patriotism, energy—her living self, with her four millions of people, among whom there is scarcely to be found a heart not beating with loyalty to the Constitution and the Government.

In behalf of that New York, the one and only one alive now, I propose to reply to some of the statements made here by one of her representatives.

In the name of the popular voice of that State, recently uttered in tones that I supposed any one could understand, I tell you, gentlemen of this Convention, beware of false prophets. *This day*, the Scripture is fulfilled among you. [Pointing to Mr. GRANGER.] "A prophet is not-without honor save in his own country, and in his own house!"

New York must stand upon this floor, and upon every other floor, as the peer of every other State. Her representatives must have the same rights as any other—and they must be treated like any other. If, in her judgment, New York ought not to give her assent to these propositions, that assent shall not be given; it can never be secured by threats or intimidations. She must have the same rights as any other State, certainly the same rights as New Jersey.

Mr. STOCKTON:—I am sure the gentleman is mistaken; I said nothing intended as a threat or an intimidation.

Mr. NOYES:—Well, let me say it once for all, New York will yield nothing to intimidation.

Now, what is the question which has led to this most extraordinary discussion? It is simply whether debate shall be hampered, or practically cut off, by short limitations as to time, after one section has had an opportunity of expressing its views.

Virginia has called this Conference together. We thought she had no right to do so, and that no possible good could come from her doing it. But we waived all considerations of that kind, and upon her invitation we came here.

She asks us to consider new and important amendments to the Constitution, alterations of our fundamental law; and in the same breath we are told that we must not discuss them—that we must take them as they are offered to us, without change or alteration.

We take time to make treaties. We do not even enter into private contracts without taking time for consideration and reflection. We have been here a little more than a week. The greater part of that time has been occupied by the committee in preparing these propositions. The discussion has scarcely commenced. I submit to the Conference, is it kind, is it generous, is it proper to stop here? Is it *best* to do so?

Mr. WICKLIFFE:—The gentleman seems to think my resolution was aimed at the delegation from New York. That is not true in any sense. I did not wish to cut off debate at all. I thought we might economize time and still have debate enough to satisfy everybody.

Mr. NOYES :—I believe I perfectly understand your proposition.

Mr. CHASE :—I have agreed to support the resolution, and must adhere to my agreement.

Mr. NOYES :—Personally I might be in favor of the adoption of the half-hour rule, for I think I could say all I desire to say in relation to these propositions within that time. I have certainly no desire that this discussion should be unreasonably protracted. But such limitations are always embarrassing. Other gentlemen do not wish to have them imposed. Mr. Field objects to them; and if gentlemen really think they need more time, I think it ungenerous not to yield to their wishes. And I insist that such a course is least calculated to promote conciliation. The more free and full you make this discussion, the more will your results find favor elsewhere. It has been my belief from the beginning, that by careful comparison of our views, by a discussion of all our points of difference, we should, in the end, come to an agreement. I had hoped that such sentiments would have universally prevailed, and that no desire would be shown to force the action of any delegation. I am willing to say for myself that if the thirty minute rule be adopted I will give way at once.

But I must proceed to notice some statements which have been urged here as reasons why we must adopt—

Mr. FIELD :—Will my colleague yield to me for one moment? I have a communication to make which I think will make every lover of his country in this Conference rejoice. It is news from a slaveholding State. It shows that her heart beats true to the Union.

Missouri has just elected delegates to a convention to consider the questions now agitating the Country. I hold in my hands a telegram, stating that a very large proportion of the delegates elected are *true Union men.*

The PRESIDENT :—I will assume it to be the pleasure of the Conference that the telegram be read.

Mr. FIELD then read the telegram announcing that Union

delegates to the Convention in Missouri had been elected by heavy majorities. The announcement was received with much applause.

Mr. NOYES :—This news is indeed cheering. It is an additional evidence of the depth to which love for our country has struck into the hearts of its people—another inducement to make us agree—another reason why we should not be led off upon false issues.

The Constitution has provided the only proper way in which amendments may be made to it. If these methods are followed, amendments will be thoroughly discussed and considered, and they will not be adopted unless the interests of the nation shall be found to require their adoption.

The State of Virginia seeks to precipitate action; to secure these vital changes in our fundamental law in a manner unknown to it, and in a manner which, in my judgment, it is not advisable to adopt. I make no complaint of Virginia. It is the right and privilege of any State to make such a request, but it is none the less unconstitutional.

Shall we be told that Virginia cannot wait, that her people are so impatient that they will not give the country time to consider these important changes in its form of Government? Why should there be such indecent haste? Why not wait a week—a month, and even six months, if that time is necessary? Be assured, gentlemen, that no substantial alteration of the fundamental law of this Government will ever be made until it has been discussed and considered by the Press and the people in all its details. The thing is impossible!

I have a few words to say for New York, as I said in the commencement—for the New York of the present day. Where, I ask, is the gentleman's (Mr. Granger) warrant of attorney to speak for the people of that State? Where is the evidence upon which he founds the assertion which he makes on this floor that New York will adopt the propositions to which he refers? Let me assure you, gentlemen, that the political principles of the people of New York do not sit thus lightly upon their consciences. They gave a heavy republican majority at the last Presidential election, not because they were carried away upon collateral issues, but because the principles of the Chicago Platform met their approval—because they thought the time had come when the destinies of this nation should no longer be left in the hands of men who would use them only to promote the interests of one section of the Union. Do not mistake, sir, the effect of that great demonstration! The people of New York were in earnest; they went into the election with a strong, determined purpose, and it is too late now to misconstrue or misunderstand that purpose. They were not influenced by collateral issues. Their action was upon the great principles involved. They believed that the platform of the Republican party embodied the true principles upon which the Government should be conducted, and they said so. You will find that their minds are to-day unchanged.

But the gentleman says, the result of recent elections shows that a change in their minds has taken place; that it indicates a strong wish on their part for conciliation and peace. Sir, I deny that such a change has taken place. There may have been slight changes in a few cities where the whole power and strength of the Democratic party has been put forth. But the country, upon the great issues before it, is unchanged. The county of St. Lawrence has just elected every Republican candidates for supervisor. In other counties, nearly the same unanimity prevails. The great heart of the country is still loyal and Republican.

And, sir, these threats of dissolution will all react against you. They operated in the Presidential election only in one way. I have no doubt that these threats gave Mr. LINCOLN five thousand votes in New York City alone. The people are sick of them. They know that if they once yielded to them, they would be forced to do so again. They do not like these insinuations against the Government involved in the propositions made here. If you wish them to be considered favorably by the people of New York, you must send them out free from all suspicion of duress or intimidation; you must permit them to be examined, discussed, and dissected here, by the representatives of New York and of every other State. I am opposed decidedly to cutting off or limiting these discussions. Let all parties be heard; give them time, and time enough, to deliberate, and the result will be peace and harmony to the country.

Mr. RIVES:—I rise for the purpose of answering some of the observations of the gentleman from New York; and first of all I wish to say a word about the motives and purposes of Virginia in calling this Convention. She has called this Convention together because she believed it would exert a powerful influence for the safety and honor of the country, and the perpetuity of its institutions. She is met *in limine* with the reproach that her action is unconstitutional. How unconstitutional?

Is not our Government based upon the sovereignty of the people? Is not that the idea upon which this Government rests? And when the people act, are they to be told that their action is unconstitutional or improper? Cannot Virginia and her people, acting through their representatives, suggest the means of amendment or improvement in our Constitution to Congress?—the Congress which represents the people, and whose members are servants only of the people? Can she not call together a convention of this kind and suggest measures to be considered by it for the purpose of saving an imperilled country? Virginia knew well that this was to be an advisory Conference merely. She invited commissioners from all the States to come here and present their views, to compare and discuss them, to devise measures for the benefit of the country, in the same way that any assemblage of the people may lawfully do. Has the gentleman looked into the history of our present Constitution? Virginia did the same thing previous to the adoption of that Constitution, which she is doing now.

Some State must invite a Conference, if one is to be had. If it was proper that Virginia should do it before the adoption of our present Constitution, it is eminently proper that she should do it now. There are occasions, sir, in the history of nations, when men should rise far above the rules of special pleading. This is one of them. Let the gentleman look into the history of the old articles of Confederation; let him read the debates which arose upon their adoption. Virginia originated measures then, far more important than any before us now; and there were gentlemen then, who took the same ground that gentlemen do now, who sought by the use of dilatory pleas, by interposing objections, temporary in their nature, to prevent and delay action upon the great national questions then under consideration. Now, in a time of great peril, when the whole country is convulsed, when the existence and perpetuity of the Government is in danger, Virginia has invoked her sister States to come here and see whether they cannot devise some method to avoid the danger and save the country.

In the preamble to the first ten articles of Confederation, there is to be found an express reference to the action of the State Legislatures in initiating proposals of amendment. Every amendment that has hitherto been made to our Constitution originated with the people, and directly or indirectly through the action of State Legislatures. What purpose can gentlemen have in interposing these dilatory pleas, objections merely for delay, when we all know that Congress is now waiting for—actually inviting the action of this Conference?

Senator COLLAMER, in his speech already referred to, makes the distinct proposition, that when any considerable portion of the people (certainly a much smaller portion than is here represented) desire to have amendments submitted, it is the duty of Congress to propose them, and to do so without committing that body either for or against them. Governor CORWIN, also of the Congressional Committee of Thirty-three, having this subject in charge, is understood to have stated that the committee desire to consider the propositions which may here be adopted.

Now, as I said, these dilatory objections were interposed previous to the adoption of our present Constitution.

Mr. NOYES:—Are we to understand that Virginia then asked for a General Convention to consider amendments to the Constitution?

Mr. RIVES:—No! The Annapolis Convention met. The invitation under which that body was convened was addressed to all the States. Five only responded, and they proposed a General Convention of all the States, to meet at Philadelphia. Virginia was the first to act and to appoint her delegates. I repeat, that the same objection was then urged, that Congress *or* the States should propose the amendments. The first Convention was just as unconstitutional as this. The two cases were perfectly alike. The crisis is infinitely more important now than it was then. Then, there was no disintegration of the States. They still held firmly together. How are we now? Seven States are out of the Union. *The Union is dissolved!* Virginia loves the

Union. She cherishes all its glorious memories. She is proud of its history and of her own connection with it. But Virginia has no apprehension as to her future destiny. She can live in the Union or out of it. She can stand in her own strength and power if necessary. Her delegates come here in no spirit of supplication, nor do they propose to offer any intimidation. She has called you here as brothers, as friends, as patriots. If the future has suffering in store for Virginia, be assured all her sister States must suffer equally.

Mr. PRESIDENT, the position of Virginia must be understood and appreciated. She is just now the neutral ground between two embattled legions, between two angry, excited, and hostile portions of the Union. To expect that her people are not to participate in the excitement by which they are surrounded; to expect that they should not share in the apprehensions which pervade the country; to expect that they should not begin to look after the safety of their interests and their institutions, were to expect something superhuman. Something must be done to save the country, to allay these apprehensions, to restore a broken confidence. Virginia steps in to arrest the progress of the country on its road to ruin. She steps in to save the country. I am here in part to represent her. I utter no menace; intimidation would be unworthy of Virginia, but if I perform my duty I must speak freely. The danger is imminent, *very* imminent.

Our national affairs cannot longer remain in their present condition; it is impossible, absolutely impossible that they should. My Republican friends, will you not take warning? Were there not pretended prophets of old, who cried, "Peace! Peace! when there was no peace"? Political prophets to-day say there is no danger. Have their counsels been wise heretofore? Can you not see that there is danger, and imminent danger in them, now?

Look, sir, at our position! I mean the position of the loyal South. By the secession of these States we are reduced to an utterly helpless minority; a minority of seven or eight States to stand in your national councils against an united North! It is not in the nature of the Anglo-Saxon race thus to stand in the face of a dominant and opposition party. Were the case reversed, you would not do it yourselves. We cannot hold our rights by mere sufferance, and we will not; we do not ask you to hold yours in that way. If the other States had kept on with us—had remained in the Union—we might have secured our rights in a fair contest. Now other paths are open to us, and one of these we must follow.

I desire to say a word in answer to the propositions of my honorable friend from Connecticut. What did he tell us? He said that this was a self-sustaining Government; a Government that possessed the power of securing its own perpetuity, and one that must not yield or make concessions. Sir, let me say that ideas, that principles, that statements of that kind have led to the downfall of every Government on earth which has ever fallen. What but ideas and language of this kind, forced our colonies into rebellion, and lost America to the British crown?

Sir, I have had some experience in revolutions in another hemisphere—in revolutions produced by the same causes that are now operating among us. What causes but these led to the two revolutions in France? One of them I saw myself, where interest was arrayed against interest, friend against friend, brother against brother. I have seen the pavements of Paris covered, and her gutters running with fraternal blood! God forbid that I should see this horrid picture repeated in my own country; and yet it will be, sir, if we listen to the counsels urged here!

It is too late to theorize, too late to differ theoretically. I do not believe in the constitutional right of secession. I proclaimed *that*, thirty years ago in Congress. I have always adhered to my opinions since. But we are not now discussing theories; we are in the presence of a great fact. The South is in danger; her institutions are in danger. If other excuses were necessary, she might justify her action in the eyes of the world upon the ground of self-defence alone.

I condemn the secession of States. I am not here to justify it. I detest it. But the great fact is still before us. Seven States have gone out from among us, and a President is actually inaugurated to govern the new Confederation.

With this fact the nation must deal. Right or wrong, it exists. The country is divided. Wide dissensions exist. A people have separated from another people. Force will never bring them together. Coercion is not a word to be used in this connection. There must be negotiation. Virginia presents herself as a mediator to bring back those who have left us.

The border States are not in revolt; and by border States I mean States on both sides of the border. They are here, and they came here to unite with you in measures that will reunite the country, and save it from irredeemable ruin.

There was one observation of the gentleman from Massachusetts that surprised me. He complained of Virginia for thrusting herself between the Republican party and its victory. It is not so.

Mr. BOUTWELL:—I said that Massachusetts thought her action had that appearance.

Mr. RIVES:—Let me say to you, Republican gentlemen, we wish to make your victory worthy of you. We wish to inaugurate your power and your administration over the *whole* Union. We wish to give you a nation worth governing. Do us at least the justice of supposing we are in earnest in this. We are laboring to relieve you from the difficulties that hang over you. War is impending. Do you wish to govern a country convulsed by civil war? The country is divided. Do you wish to govern a fraction of the country? Behold the difficulties that you must encounter. You cannot carry on your Government without money. Where is the capitalist who will advance you money under existing circumstances?

Gentlemen, believe me, as one who has given no small amount of time and careful reflection to this subject, when I tell you that you cannot coerce sovereign States. It is impossible. Mr. HAMILTON's great foresight made him assert that our strength lay in the Government of the States—of the undivided States. Look at New York. She herself is a match for the whole army of the United States. Look at the South. She stands now almost upon an equality with you. You may spend millions of treasure, you may shed oceans of blood, but you cannot conquer any five or seven States of this Union. The proposition is an utter absurdity. You must find some other way to deal with them. In the wisdom of the country some other way must be found.

Several gentlemen have referred to our army and our navy. As a citizen of the United States, I am proud of both. I am proud of the country they serve. I have enjoyed at times her honors, at others endured her chastisements. I respect the power which our army and our navy give to our nation, but our army and navy are impotent in such a crisis as this.

Mr. PRESIDENT, even England herself has been shaken to her centre by rebellions in her North with which she has been forced to contend. In Paris, too, I have myself seen regiment after regiment throw down their arms and rush into the arms of the people, of their fellow-citizens, and thus oppose, by military strength, the government under which their organization was formed. Will you repeat such occurrences here? Will you 'destroy the imperishable renown of this nation'? No! I answer for you all —you will not. Now, we, representatives of the South and of Virginia, ask of this Convention, the only body under heaven that can do it, to interpose and save us from a repetition of the scenes of blood which some of us have witnessed.

Our patriotic committee have labored for two weeks—have labored earnestly and zealously. Their report, though not satisfactory to Virginia in all respects, will yet receive her sanction, and the sanction of the border States. The representatives of Virginia know they are yielding much, when they tell you that they will support these propositions. We will do it because they will give peace to the country. Now, sir, when we are just in sight of land, when we are just entering a safe harbor, shall we turn about and circumnavigate the ocean to find an unknown shore? No, sir! no! Let us enter the harbor of safety now opened before us.

Mr. PRESIDENT, I know Massachusetts well. She is a powerful Commonwealth. She has added largely to the wealth, the power, and glory of this Union. I respect the gentleman who has addressed this Convention in her behalf; but when he went out of his way and stated that he abhorred slavery, the statement grated harshly on my ears. We of the South, we of Virginia, may not and do not like many of the institutions of Massachusetts, but we cannot and we will not say that we abhor them.

Let me recall to the gentleman from Massachusetts who has addressed us, a fact from history. Let me show him that his own State was powerful in colonial times in extending the time for the importation of slaves! Let me tell him that his State has helped to fasten the institution of slavery upon a portion of this nation. Is it for a son of Massachusetts now to complain of the result of the acts of his own State? Is it for him to use these reproaches, which, if not ungrateful, are at least wanting in charity? It was a representative of Massachusetts, Mr. GORHAM, through whose motion and influence the time for the importation of slaves was extended in that period of our colonial history. Virginia ever, in every period of her colonial existence, exerted herself to close her ports against the importation of slaves. It was the veto of her Royal Master alone that rendered her efforts nugatory. It was New England that fastened this institution upon us. Shall she reproach us for its existence now?

Mr. BALDWIN:—At the time of the adoption of our present Constitution, it was well understood that Georgia and South Carolina would not enter the Union without slavery. The only question then was, should slavery have an existence inside the Union or out of it.

Mr. RIVES:—No, sir! The gentleman is mistaken. In the Constitution, as first proposed to the Convention, an unlimited right was given to import slaves. Mr. ELLSWORTH declared that it would be an infraction of *State rights* to prohibit this importation. New England, engaged in commerce, found an advantage in the right of importation, and she endeavored to force it upon the South.

I regard the present course of New England as very unfair. She is herself responsible for the existence of slavery—she is now our fiercest opponent; and yet New Jersey and Pennsylvania, who have not this responsibility, have always stood by the South, and I believe they always will.

It is not by *abhorring* slavery that you can put an end to the institution. You must let it alone. We are responsible for it now, and we are willing to stand responsible for it before the world. We understand the subject better than you do. It has occupied the attention of the wisest men of our time. In fact, it is not a question of slavery at all. It is a question of race. We know that the very best position for the African race to occupy is one of unmitigated legal subjection. We have the negroes with us; you have not. We must deal with them as our experience and wisdom dictate; with that you have nothing to do. The gentleman from Massachusetts may congratulate himself that there are no negroes in that Commonwealth. I ask him what he would do, if he had the race to deal with in Massachusetts as we have it in Virginia?

I said, twenty years ago, in the Senate of the United States, and my whole experience since having confirmed the truth of the statement I repeat it now, that candid minds cannot differ upon this proposition, that the present position of the negroes of the United States is the best one they could occupy, both for the superior and inferior race.

And to the people of New England I have this to say: Your ancestors were most powerful and influential in fastening slavery upon us. You are the very last who ought to reproach us for its existence now. We do not indulge reproaches toward you. It is unpleasant for us to receive them from you. Their use by either can only serve to widen the unhappy differences existing between us. Let us all drop them, and, so far as we can, let us close up every avenue through which dissensions may come. We call upon you to make no sacrifices for us. It will cost you nothing to yield what we ask. Say, and let it be said in the Constitution, that you will not interfere with slavery in the District, or in the States, or in the Territories. Permit the free transit of our slaves from one State to another, and in the language of the patriarch, "let there be peace between you and me."

Let us all agree that there shall be landmarks between us; the same which our fathers erected. Let us say that they shall never be removed. I think upon this point I can cite an authority that will command universal respect. I discovered it in my researches into the history of the very Constitution we are now considering.

Mr. RIVES here read an extract from a letter written by Mr. MADISON after his retirement from public life. I have not a copy of this letter, but the substance of the portion read by Mr. RIVES was a statement by Mr. MADISON, that upon the passage of the Missouri Compromise, President MONROE was much embarrassed with the question of the constitutionality of the prohibition clause; that he took counsel with Mr. MARTIN, who declared that, in his judgment, Congress had no power over the subject of slavery in the territories.

Mr. JAMES:—Will you leave that question just where the Constitution leaves it, upon your construction of that instrument?

If so, we will agree to give you all necessary guarantees against interference.

Mr. RIVES:—No! I will not leave it there, for it would always remain a question of construction. I prefer to put the prohibition into the Constitution.

The gentleman from Massachusetts speaks for the North. Massachusetts does not constitute the North. I venerate the Commonwealth of Massachusetts. I have many friends there. I look with pride upon her connection with the Revolution; upon her public men, her manufactures, her public institutions. Her people who have accomplished so much, will not turn a deaf ear to our wants now. We wish to go to her people and obtain their judgment upon our propositions. But Massachusetts is not all the North. Rhode Island constitutes a part of it. She has always spoken for us. She will speak for us to-day. What does New Jersey say? What does the great State of Pennsylvania and the greater Northwest say? Surely they do not echo the sentiments of the gentleman from Massachusetts. They are with us, and we will trust to them.

I dislike this way of answering for sections of the country. I have heard similar language from Mr. CALHOUN. He was fond of saying, "The South says—The South thinks—The South will do," this or that. I did not like it then. It stirred up all the rebellious sentiments of my nature; for I knew the statement was not true. I do not like such language better now. Let the *people* of Massachusetts speak. I know they will not refuse to fulfil the compact of their fathers.

We are brothers. I feel we can settle this important question which portends over us like an eclipse; we can leave this glorious country to our posterity. Once more let me refer to the noble and eloquent counsels of MADISON, and I am done. As children of the same family, as fellow-citizens of a great, glorious, and proud Republic, he invoked the kindred blood of our people to consecrate our common Union, and to banish forever the thought of our becoming aliens.

Mr. EWING:—I have never in any manner countenanced the discussions of slavery and the questions connected with it, at the North. I have always, so far as possible, discouraged those discussions. No good can possibly come from them. Is the

North the *censor morum* of the South? We have faults enough ourselves; let us consider and try to correct them, before we interest ourselves so much in those of our neighbors.

If there was any danger that slavery would be extended at the North, I would oppose its extension there, and I would teach my sons to oppose it. But this danger has never existed. Does any one fear that slavery will go into New York or Massachusetts? No sane man thinks or ever thought so.

But it exists, and we must deal with it as it is. As one northern man, I do not want the negroes distributed throughout the North. We have got enough of them now. I have watched the operation of this emigration of slaves to the North. Ten negroes will commit more petty thefts than one thousand white men. We cannot permit them to come into Ohio. Wherever they have been permitted to come, it has almost cost us a rebellion. Before we begin to preach abolition I think we had better see what is to be done with the negroes.

Thirty years ago the subject of abolishing slavery was agitated in Virginia. Some of the most eloquent speeches were made in favor of the abolition movement that I ever read. The act providing for gradual abolition, was, I believe, lost by a single vote. I thought then that the result was an unfortunate one. But there is something to be said on both sides of the question. Had the act passed, the negroes would have been sent South, and we should have had plantation slavery, instead of the humane form which now exists in Virginia. But Virginia would have had one great, one powerful advantage. Her power would have increased tenfold. Free labor would have come in to take the place of slave labor, and the banks of the Potomac and the James would have blossomed as the rose.

The North has taken the business of abolition into its own hands, and from the day she did so, we hear no more of abolition in Virginia. This was but the natural effect of the cause. Now, we can never coerce the Southern States into abolitionism. It is not the way to convert them to our views by saying that we *abhor* their institutions. But these northern men will not listen to reason. They keep on making eloquent speeches—their pulpits thunder against the sin of slaveholding. All grades of speech and thought are made use of, and the sickening sentimentalism of some of them is disgusting. They repeat poetry. They say:

> "I would not have a slave to till my ground,
> To watch me when I wake—to fan me when I sleep;"

and much more of the same stuff!

In this way false ideas are inculcated throughout the North. The whole scheme is full of falsehood. It would be far better for each man to look for the beam in his own eyes before he troubles himself about the mote in his neighbor's.

England, also, has been very fierce in denouncing slavery in this country, and yet we have no slavery or misery to be compared with that existing in the India provinces. It is said that in a single season two hundred thousand of her subjects were starved to death in one province of Hindostan.

I might say the same thing almost of Ireland. Two millions have died there from famine, and God knows how many more would have perished but for the relief sent from this country. I say, and I have abundant reason for saying, that I never have, and I never will, favor any of these denunciations of southern slaveholders and slavery.

Let us rather look at this subject as members of a common family—let us acknowledge our mutual faults. The slave trade was once fostered by the North. That was when it was profitable, and when large fortunes were made in that trade by northern men. When it became unprofitable the North began to denounce it, and to call it sinful. Now, we fastened this institution upon the South, cannot we permit her to deal with it as she chooses?

I do not say that there is a necessary conflict between the white and the black races, but I assert that they cannot unite—that they cannot occupy the same country upon an equality. Our free laborers of the North will not work with slaves or with blacks. I have had experience in this matter, and I know I am right. The only way we can do, is to divide the common territory—divide it fairly, honestly.

Suppose there were two sons who succeeded to a joint inheritance of lands. One says to the other, "Your family is not so moral as mine, therefore your sons shall have none of the lands." Would this be right or honest? Would any one attempt to justify it? And yet this is what extreme men of the North are practically saying to the citizens of the South.

The Missouri Compromise was intended to settle the rights of the respective sections in the territories. The line adopted was not unfair to the North. The same line will answer now. I am for adopting it and arranging this difficult subject finally.

But one and another says, "Don't let us extend slavery." To that I answer, that our action will not make one slave more or less. There is no question of humanity involved in our propositions. I cannot see what question is involved so far as the North is concerned. We need no more territory. We do not want New Mexico. We have territory enough now for one hundred and fifty millions of people, and enough for the expansion of our people for one hundred and fifty years.

If gentlemen are found here who wish to make trouble, who cannot see the peril we are in, and how easily we can avoid the danger which threatens us, I shall be much pained, but not half so much as I shall be, to see this Union broken up and the Government destroyed.

I was surprised to hear the assertion of the gentleman from Connecticut, that this was an unconstitutional assembly. I hear to-day the statement made that it is a revolutionary assembly. If these assertions were true I would not be a member of it for one moment. If revolutionary, it is either treasonable or seditious. But it is neither. These gentlemen forget the constitutional right of petition. We have the right to meet here. We have the right to do just what we are proposing to do, and the right is to be found in the Constitution.

I am surprised, too, at the assertion, that there is a wish here to limit or cut off debate—that this resolution would cut off New York. Would it not cut off Ohio? I have no intention of depriving any gentleman or any State of any right. I do not believe such an intention exists in the Conference.

Mr. MORRILL:—In my judgment many subjects have been considered here, and many things said to the North especially, that are superfluous, and much more that is useless. I have listened to the gentleman from Ohio and to some gentlemen who have preceded him. They have all referred, in terms which I do not choose to characterize, to the action and the opinions of the North.

The gentleman from Ohio refers in strong terms to what he calls the sentimentalism of the North. He has recited poetry which he says is popular there.

Now, once for all, let me ask those gentlemen who are proposing various methods of settling our differences; Do you propose to make war upon the *sentiments*, the *principles* of the North? If you do, we may as well drop the discussion here. Our people, and we, their representatives, cannot meet you upon that ground. Our principles cannot be interfered with; we carry them with us always. Our consciences approve them. We can negotiate with you, and treat with you upon subjects which do not involve their sacrifice. If it is your purpose to attack them, you may abandon all other purposes so far as this body is concerned. The people of the North will never sacrifice their principles. It is useless for you to ask them to do so. It is entirely useless for you to urge war upon the sentiments or opinions of the North.

Again; let me tell you there is no disloyalty in the free States. The word dissolution has not been thought of there during the last half century. In all your discussions, in all your action, remember that we are loyal to the Constitution and the Union.

Strong appeals are made here to the free States. You call them by the general name of the Northern States. Gentlemen undertake to pledge different sections to this or that policy. We are told that New York—that Massachusetts—that Pennsylvania will adopt or will not adopt various propositions that are made here.

Sir, in my judgment all such questions are unworthy of our consideration. We spend time to little purpose upon them. The true question here is, "What will Virginia do? How does Virginia stand?" She to-day holds the keys of peace or war. She stands in the gateway threatening the progress of the Government in its attempts to assert its legal authority. Evade it as you may—cover it as you will—the true question is, "What will Virginia do? She undertakes to dictate the terms upon which the Union is to be preserved. What will satisfy her?

Mr. CLAY:—Has not Virginia spoken? Has she not already told us what she wants?

Mr. MORRILL:—I am coming to that point very soon. I assert again that Virginia must not be misunderstood in this matter.

The peril of the time is *Secession.* Six States are already in revolution. A distinct confederacy, a new government, has been organized within the limits of the United States.

Does Virginia to-day, frown upon this atrocious proceeding? No! so far from that she affirms that these States have a right to do what they have done. She boasts that she has armed her people, that she has raised five millions of money, and that she will use both to prevent the interference of the National Government with these States, now in revolution. Whether her course will conciliate the free States—whether under such circumstances the free States will negotiate with Virginia or others in her position, I leave for others to consider. It is my opinion that the people of this country will first of all *demand the recognition of the supremacy of the Government.*

Mr. RUFFIN:—No! I do not understand such to be the position of Virginia. She appeals to both sides to refrain from violence while these negotiations are pending.

Mr. SEDDON:—No! A little farther than that. Virginia *will not permit coercion.* She has plainly declared she will not. But in the very highest spirit of patriotism, she has asked for this Convention, and she proposes to exhaust the very last means of restoring peace to the Union. This is exactly her position. She hopes, and I hope, that this Convention will interpose to preserve the peace and to save this country from war.

Mr. MORRILL:—I thought I did not misunderstand the position of Virginia. She is armed to the teeth, and she now proposes to step in between the Government and the States. I understand her attitude. It is an attitude of menace. It gives aid and comfort to those who trample upon the laws and defy the authority of this Government.

No action of the Conference can be consummated for months: I might almost say for years. Any propositions we may make must go to the people. They must and will take time for consideration. Endeavor to force their action and you will secure the rejection of the terms proposed. While the people are acting you will have a Government and it must operate. It must operate not upon a section only, but upon the whole country. During this time, does Virginia propose to maintain the position she has assumed? To prevent by force of arms the execution of the laws of the Union in the seceded States? Yes, and we are told that her position is one exhibiting the highest patriotism. In my judgment her position is one of menace, and not of pacification. If I rightly understand her, nothing that is here proposed to be done will satisfy her even if adopted.

And now I wish to ask the gentleman from Virginia (Mr. SEDDON) a plain question, and I wish to receive a frank answer. If this Conference agrees to the amendments proposed by the majority of the committee, will Virginia sustain the Government and maintain its integrity, while the people are considering and acting on the new proposals of amendment to the Constitution? If she will not do this, if this proposition does not meet the heart of Virginia, there is no use—

Mr. SEDDON:—I can let Virginia speak for herself. She has spoken for herself in most emphatic language. She has told you what will satisfy her in the resolutions under which this body is convened. I have no right whatever to suppose that she will accept less. She is solemnly pledged to resist coercion. She will resist it to the very last extremity. She arrived at that conclusion after grave deliberation, and it was attended with every manifestation of concurrence on the part of the people. I have no reason to suppose there was any hesitation at the time, or that there has been any change since, or that there is any hesitation in her purpose now.

Now, if the gentleman wants my private opinion, I will tell him that whether the propositions of the majority of the committee or her own be adopted here, or by the people, the purpose of Virginia to resist coercion is *unchanged* and *unchangeable.*

Mr. HITCHCOCK:—I rise to a point of order. It appears to me that this discussion is very foreign to the subject before the Conference. It is so long since that subject has been named, that many have doubtless forgotten it. The question is upon the adoption of the resolution limiting the debate. I think we had better keep to the question.

The PRESIDENT :—The gentleman is undoubtedly correct in his statement of the question, but the discussion of the general subject has been permitted to go on without objection by the Convention, and I do not think it would be right to stop it now.

Mr. SEDDON :—I said the position of Virginia was unchanged. She considers this a Government of love and not of force. She thinks there should be no force or coercion used toward any sovereign State acting in its collective capacity. She does not propose to permit such coercion to be used.

And now, having answered the gentleman frankly, as he desired, I wish to ask him a question, and I wish also an explicit and frank answer. My question is this: Is it the purpose or is it the policy of the incoming administration to attempt to execute the laws of the United States in the seceded States by an armed force? The answer to this question involves information of the utmost importance to my State and others whose interests are involved with hers. It should be at once communicated, and especially to my part of the country. I now ask the gentleman, if he knows what the purpose of the incoming administration is in this respect, to state it here, and now. His relations to some of the officers elected will entitle his opinions to grave consideration. I invite a full and frank answer to my question.

Mr. MORRILL :—There is a point in the gentleman's answer which may as well be met, but I will not be diverted from the question I was discussing. I will show him in a moment why I cannot answer his inquiry from any personal knowledge of my own.

Sir, I was endeavoring to ascertain what was the present position of Virginia; to find out what she would accept and be contented. I wanted her to speak emphatically. She has done so. I now understand from Mr. SEDDON, that he has no assurances to give that Virginia will accept the propositions of the committee, and that while any propositions are pending she will resist the enforcement of the laws in the seceded States.

Then let it be understood that Virginia *has* spoken. That she makes the Crittenden resolutions her *ultimatum*, that she must have them and all of them, that nothing less will satisfy her. As I said at the beginning of my remarks, it is idle for us to stay here, useless for us to discuss the various propositions which are made here, unless we expect to satisfy Virginia.

It is important for us to understand her position. I do not under-estimate her influence. When the propositions of this Conference are presented to the people of the free States, the first question they will ask is, "Will Virginia adopt them? Will she be satisfied with them?" If she will not, there will be no action upon them. If she will, her position will exercise a powerful influence upon the people of the North in favor of their adoption.

But if Virginia puts her ancient Commonwealth across the path of the Government, if she stands between the administration and the enforcement of the laws, the execution of its official duty, its positive obligations—if this is the manner in which she proposes to mediate, her mediation will be accepted nowhere. Such I understand to be the position she assumes. It is a position of menace.

Mr. STOCKTON:—If the gentleman from Maine wants to get up a row, we are ready for him. He shall have enough of it right here! I should like to know why he makes such charges against Virginia? They are unfounded; we don't wish to hear them.

(There was at this point considerable confusion in the Conference, which was promptly suppressed by the PRESIDENT.)

Mr. MORRILL:—Gentlemen need not be disturbed or excited. I have accomplished my object. I know now what to expect from Virginia; the North will know what the course of Virginia is to be, and we can all act understandingly. I do not propose to waste valuable time in idle discussions in this hall, when we can come to the true point at once. I do not propose to talk around this question, nor to deceive or mislead the Conference. Other gentlemen may think differently, but I now understand Virginia to say, that the Federal authority shall not be reëstablished by the ordinary means, (where it is resisted) in certain of the States comprised in the Federal Union.

I will now answer the question of the gentleman from Virginia, in relation to the proposed policy of the incoming administration. I have no personal knowledge upon this subject. Mr. LINCOLN I never saw in my life. I know nothing of his opinions, except from his speeches; but I will say, that if he and his administration do not use every means which the Constitution has given them to assert the authority of the Government in all the States—to preserve the Union, and the Union in all its integrity, the people will be disappointed. I have felt and now feel the importance of the action of Virginia, and I have done what I could to learn here what we may expect from her.

In conclusion, let me say, that unless we can have the earnest concurrence of the slave States in whatever we do, and especially unless we have the heart of Virginia with us, our action will give no peace to the country.

Mr. Zollicoffer moved that the Conference adjourn. The motion was lost by a *viva voce* vote.

Mr. BROWNE:—I think we have debated these matters long enough. Let us come back to the question before us. Personally I am in favor of limiting debate to the shortest time, for I feel the necessity for prompt action. I think if Mr. Randolph would strike out the latter clause of his resolution, requiring the final vote to be taken on Thursday next, we should have no difficulty in agreeing to it. Its adoption in its present form might cut off some delegation or some gentlemen from speaking at all. I would not do this. Let every one speak, but let the speeches be short. I move to strike out the last clause of the resolution.

Mr. WICKLIFFE:—I did not expect to raise such a storm by introducing this resolution. I now ask to withdraw it and stop the debate.

Mr. MOREHEAD, of North Carolina:—The gentleman cannot do that, as several motions are involved. I object to his proposal to withdraw the resolution. I move to lay the whole subject on the table, and to make it the special order for ten o'clock to-morrow.

The motion of Mr. Morehead was carried.

Mr. SUMMERS:—I move that when the present session of the Conference adjourn, its next meeting be at seven o'clock this evening.

A Member:—Say eight o'clock.

Mr. SUMMERS:—Well, then, let it be eight o'clock. But let me ask you, gentlemen, not to protract or unnecessarily delay our action here.

Mr. PRESIDENT, my heart is full! I cannot approach the great issues with which we are dealing with becoming coolness and deliberation! Sir, I love this Union. The man does not live who entertains a higher respect for this Government than I do. I know its history—I know how it was established. There is not an incident in its history that is not precious to me. I do not wish to survive its dissolution. My hand or voice was never raised against it. They never will be. The Union is as dear to me as to any living man; and it would be pleasant, indeed, if my mind to-day could be as free from fear and anxiety about it, as the minds of other gentlemen appear to be. But, Sir, I cannot shut my eyes to events which are daily transpiring among a people who are excited and anxious, who are apprehensive that their rights are in danger—who are solicitous for—who will do as much to preserve their rights as any people. They must be calmed and quieted. It is useless now to tell them they have no cause for fear. They are looking to this Conference. This Conference must act. If it does not, I almost fear to contemplate the prospect that will open before us.

Sir! this Conference has now been in session fifteen days. While I have felt reluctant to do any thing which should have the appearance of precipitating our action, of cutting off or limiting debate, I have all the time been pressed with this conviction; that if we are to save this country we must act speedily. I have been in constant communication with the people of Virginia since I have been here. I know that this feeling of apprehension which existed when I came away, has been constantly increasing in my State since; and even last night I received letters from members of the Convention now in session in Richmond; gentlemen who are as true to this Union as the needle to the pole, informing me that every hour of *delay* in this Conference was an hour of *danger*.

I do not agree with some of my colleagues in their construction of the resolutions of the Virginia Legislature inviting this Conference. I understand that she suggests the resolutions of Mr. CRITTENDEN as *one* acceptable way of settling our present difficulties. She says that she will be satisfied with a settlement on the basis of those resolutions. But she has not made them her *ultimatum*. She has not said she will not consent to any other plan of arrangement. Her purpose was not to draw up certain articles of pacification; to call her sister States together, and say to them, "These or nothing! We have dictated the terms upon which the matter between us may be arranged. We will have these or we will not arrange at all!" I understand her as offering no restrictions whatever. She invites a conference—she asks the States to *confer* together. She expects reasonable concessions, reasonable guarantees, and with these she will be satisfied.

Nor do I know why the gentleman from Maine places Virginia in the position he described, nor upon what authority. I reply to him that he makes a grave assumption when he attributes to Virginia a dictatorial position. I have come here, and I trust my colleagues have also, animated by a single purpose:—that purpose is to save the Union. Virginia claims no greater rights than any other State. She would not take them if they were offered.

Let me say here, that it is my purpose to carry out the wishes of the people of Virginia; that exercising the best judgment I have I shall try to ascertain what that purpose is, and shall do all I can to accomplish it. When the proper time comes I shall cast my vote for the proposals of amendment offered by my colleague (Mr. SEDDON); I shall do so for several reasons. The first and most important of them all is this: The Union is our inheritance—it is our pride. To preserve it, what sacrifice should we not make? Its preservation is the one single desire that animates me. Can I not be understood by my Northern friends? Will you not yield something to our necessities—to our condition? Will you not do something which will enable us to go back to our excited people and say to them, "The North is treating us fairly. See what she will do to make our Union perpetual!"

Again; I shall vote cheerfully for Mr. SEDDON'S propositions, because the Legislature of my State has said that such amendments will satisfy the people of Virginia. I think the Legislature is right. I think in this respect it reflects the will of the people of Virginia. Remember, sir, that these propositions have been for some time before the country, that they have been discussed and commented upon by the public Press—that they will probably settle our difficulties, now and forever. They were introduced into Congress by a distinguished and an able man—a statesman, whose integrity and fidelity no one has ever questioned, and no one will question. It is my firm belief that the States can adopt them without any material sacrifice, and that they will adopt them if they have the opportunity.

But if the CRITTENDEN resolutions—if the propositions of my colleague cannot be recommended by this Conference—do not find favor with the majority here? What then? Shall we dissolve this body, and go home? Shall we risk all the fearful consequences which must follow? No, sir! No! We came here for *peace*. Virginia came here for *peace*. We will not be impracticable. You, representatives of the free States, will not be impracticable. Therefore, I tell you that it is my firm belief that the people of Virginia WILL accept the proposals of amendment to the Constitution as reported by the majority of the committee. I believe these propositions would be acceptable to our people. I believe if we should pass them here, that the Convention now in session in Richmond would at once adopt them and recommend them to the people of that honored member of the Federal Union. Can you not? Will you not give us one chance to satisfy our people, and to save us from that other alternative which I almost fear to contemplate?

I feared when the result was announced, that the late election in Virginia of the delegates to the Convention now in session, would be misapprehended and misunderstood at the North: that the North would regard it as a triumph of the Union sentiment in Virginia. In one sense it was such a triumph. The advocates of immediate and unconditional secession were defeated, were defeated by a heavy majority.

But the members comprising that Convention represent the true feeling of the people who elected them, and they represent the present feeling of Virginia. The people of that State are full of anxiety. They fear that the new administration has designs which it will carry into execution, fatal to their rights and interests. They are for the Union, *provided* their rights can be secured; provided, they can have proper and honorable guarantees. It is useless to discuss now whether they are right or wrong. Such is the condition of affairs now, and it is too late to enter into the causes which produced it. We must deal with things as they are.

I have known many gentlemen who have represented the interests of New England long and well. I know what sentiments filled their hearts years ago, and I do not believe those sentiments are changed now. I appeal to Vermont. Among her representatives here, I see a gentleman with whom, for a long time, I was upon terms of peculiar intimacy. In the whole course of that intimacy I cannot recall a single occurrence which did not impress me with his integrity, his ability, his justice. I appeal to him. I appeal to him by every consideration which can move a friend, which can influence a patriot, which can govern the action of a statesman. I appeal to Massachusetts, to all New England, which I know possesses many like himself; and I ask you to consider our circumstances, to consider our dangers, and not to refuse us the little boon we ask, when the consequences of that refusal must be so awful. Can you not afford to make a little sacrifice, when we make one so great? Can you not yield to us what is a mere matter of opinion with you, but what is so vital with us? Will you not put us in a position where we can stand with our people, and let us and you stand together in the Union? I have no delicacy here. The importance of our action with me, transcends all other considerations. I do not hesitate to appeal to New England for help in this crisis.

If New England refuses to come to our aid, it will not alter my course or change my conviction. In no possible contingency which can now be foreseen shall these convictions be changed. *I will never give up the Union!* Clouds may hang over it, storms and tempest may assail it, the waves of dissolution may dash against it, but so far as my feeble hand can support it, that support shall be given to it while I live!

When the dark days come over this Republic, and there is nothing in the future but gloom and despondency, I will do as WASHINGTON once said he would do in similar circumstances: I will gather the last handful of faithful men, carry them to the mountains of Western Virginia, and there set up the flag of the Union. It shall be defended there against all assailants until the friends of freedom and liberty from all parts of the civilized world shall rally around it, and again establish it in triumph and glory over every portion of a restored and united country.

Sir, the questions which now agitate and alarm the country do not affect the interests of all sections of the Union, or if they do affect all sections, certainly not in the same proportion. The farther sections are removed from each other, the less do the interests and the principles of their people assimilate. Maine and Louisiana, far distant from each other, differ widely. Approaching the line between the slave and free States all these differences grow less. This is shown by the action of this Conference. The border States can settle these questions. They will settle them if you will let them alone. Pennsylvania and Virginia, Maryland and New Jersey, States along the line, whose people are most vitally interested, can have no difficulty in coming to an agreement. With all the possible political interests which you may have, not only are the relations of society, of business, and commerce, to be interrupted, but these States are to form the long frontier between two foreign nations, if that fearful contingency is to happen, so often and so confidently referred to here.

Why, then, should remote sections interfere to prevent this adjustment? If they cannot aid us, why not let us alone? Let them look along the valley of the Ohio River, one of the most fertile sections of the continent, in itself great enough and fruitful enough to support a nation. It has already a large population, and that population is increasing every day. The people are attached to each other by every tie that binds society together. They now live in harmony and friendship; their property is secure. They are prosperous and happy. Such a people *cannot be, must not be divided.*

And therefore, I say, that if we are driven to that alternative; if the representatives of the two extremes will not give us the benefit of their counsel and assistance, the Central States, and the great Northwest, must take the matter into their own hands. North Carolina, Virginia, Kentucky, Tennessee, with Pennsylvania, New Jersey, and other States near them, must unite with Ohio and the Northwest to save the country. They have the power to do it—they must do it.

Remember, sir, that I only refer to this as a last alternative. It is one to which I hope and pray we may never be driven. I cannot yet give up the hope, that all we need here is patient and thorough discussion and examination of the subject; that when the true condition is understood, we shall unite together to restore confidence to the country. It must be so. The consequences of farther disagreement are too great, the crisis is too important to permit mere sectional differences, mere pride of opinion, party shackles or party platforms to control the action of any gentleman here. The Republic shall not be divided. The nation shall not be destroyed. The patriotism of the people will yet save the country against all its enemies.

Mr. RUFFIN gave notice, that at the proper time he wished to offer two amendments to the second section of the propositions reported by the committee.*

Mr. FIELD and Mr. DODGE rose and made motions at the same time.

The floor was given to Mr. DODGE, who moved, that when the Conference adjourn, it adjourn to meet at ten o'clock to-morrow.

Mr. RANDOLPH moved to amend, by inserting half-past ten o'clock.

Several motions were made by different members, and much confusion arose, which was suppressed.

Mr. CHITTENDEN:—We all, no doubt, wish to economize time as much as possible. The prevailing wish seems to be to meet about eleven o'clock to-morrow. That can be accomplished by a simple motion to adjourn, which I make, and which should take precedence of all others.

The PRESIDENT put the motion to adjourn, and declared it not carried.

A MEMBER:—I move to amend Mr. DODGE's motion, by inserting seven o'clock this evening.

This motion did not prevail, and the question was taken upon Mr. DODGE's motion, which was adopted, and the Conference then adjourned.

* Mr. RUFFIN stated the substance of the amendments he proposed in a voice so low, as not to be audible to the greater part of the Conference. They are not to be found in the Journal, nor in the documents printed by order of the Conference, nor were they heard by me.

THIRTEENTH DAY.

WASHINGTON, WEDNESDAY, *February 20th*, 1861.

THE Conference was called to order by President TYLER at ten o'clock, and after prayer by the Rev. Dr. SAMPSON, the Journal of yesterday was read and approved.

Mr. HARRIS :—I desire to call the attention of the Conference to the fact, that the time has not yet arrived when the Conference, by its rules, should commence business. The rule is, that the daily session shall commence at eleven o'clock.

The PRESIDENT :—The Conference, previous to its adjournment yesterday, adopted the motion of Mr. DODGE, fixing this hour for the commencement of the present session.

Mr. WICKLIFFE :—I wish to call attention to the 9th rule in the printed list. It has not been adopted by the Conference. It is in here by mistake. The Committee on Rules did not intend to recommend it. I ask now that it be stricken from the record.

Mr. FIELD :—I rise to debate that motion.

Mr. WICKLIFFE :—Then I withdraw it.

Mr. HARRIS :—I wish to offer a preamble and resolutions, and would like to have them read for the information of the Conference. I ask to have them printed and laid upon the table, so that I can move them as an amendment at the proper time.

The resolutions were laid upon the table and ordered to be printed, and are as follows:

Whereas, The Federal Constitution and the laws made in pursuance thereof, are the supreme law of the land, and should command the willing obedience of all good citizens; and *whereas* it is alleged that sundry States have enacted laws repugnant thereto. Therefore,

Resolved. That this Convention respectfully requests the several States to revise their respective enactments, and to modify or repeal any laws which may be found to be in conflict with the Constitution and laws of the United States.

Resolved, That the President of this Convention is requested to send a copy of the foregoing preamble and resolutions to the Governor of each of the States, with the request that the same be communicated to the Legislature thereof.

Mr. RANDOLPH:—I must now insist upon having my resolution, offered yesterday, considered. Congress is about adjourning, and, if we do not close our labors to-day, we cannot have our propositions acted upon under the rules of the Senate and House of Representatives. They can be kept out on the objection of any member. I do not wish to debate the resolution, and I hope the debate will not be continued in the general manner it was yesterday.

Mr. FIELD:—There seems to be a disposition to stop debate now, after nearly the whole time has been occupied by the other side. Yesterday the whole session was occupied by a general discussion of this question. It is my right to debate it as generally as other gentlemen have done. I shall avail myself of that right. I may not speak thirty minutes, but I will not submit to the imposition of a different rule upon me, if I can avoid it, from that which has been imposed upon others. The first question is on striking out the last clause of the resolution. On that I have nothing to say except that I ask for a vote by States.

A vote by States was then taken, and resulted as follows:

AYES.—Connecticut, Illinois, Indiana, Iowa, Maine, Massachusetts, Maryland, New York, New Hampshire, Ohio, Pennsylvania, and Vermont—12.

NOES.—Delaware, Kentucky, Missouri, New Jersey, North Carolina, Rhode Island, Tennessee, and Virginia—8.

Mr. CLAY:—I move to lay the whole subject upon the table. It is useless to attempt to stop discussion in this way.

Mr. CHASE—I call for a vote by States.

The motion of Mr. Clay prevailed by the following vote.

AYES.—Connecticut, Illinois, Indiana, Iowa, Maine, Massachusetts, New York, Vermont, Virginia, and New Hampshire—10.

NOES.—Delaware, Maryland, Missouri, New Jersey, North Carolina, Ohio, Pensylvania, Rhode Island, and Tennessee—9.

Mr. McCURDY:—There is really but one question that ought to engage the attention of this Conference. All others may be settled in half an hour. This question is a great one, and assumes a variety of forms. I wish to vote upon it understandingly, and I want some information from the committee which has had it in charge.

I ask that committee whether they are not proposing a change in the Constitution, which, if adopted, will operate as a direct and effectual protection of slavery in all the territories of the United States? This appears to me to be the true question for our consideration. I wish to know what meaning is attached by its friends to one part of the proposed article.

It states that "the *status* of persons owing service or labor as it now exists shall not be changed by law," &c.; and again, "that the rights arising out of said relations shall be subject to judicial cognizance in the Federal courts according to the *common law*." The *status*, then, shall not be changed. By that term I suppose condition is intended. I understand that perfectly. There shall be no law to change the condition, to *impair* the rights of the slaveholder; but shall there be no law to *protect* these rights? Now, what is intended by this? Why not make this provision plain, and not leave it open to any question of construction? The ghost of the old trouble rises here, and will not down at the bidding of any man. I believe under this article the institution of slavery is to be protected by a most ingenious contrivance. The *common law*, administered according to the pro-slavery view, is to be called in for its protection.

Now I ask the chairman of the committee reporting these propositions what he means by the *common law?* The common law, as we understand it, is the law of freedom—not of slavery. But I do not here propose to discuss that question. I wish to know how the truth really is. How does the committee, how do the friends of this proposition understand it?

By the *common law* a slave is still a man: a person, and not a personal chattel. He may owe service, as a child to its parent, an apprentice to his master, but he is still a *person* owing service. He is all the time recognized as a *man*. As such he may own and hold property, take it by inheritance and dispose of it at pleasure, by will or by contract. All these rights, all the principles on which they are founded, are in direct antagonism to slavery. The argument may be carried much farther, but this is far enough for my purpose. By the slave law, all this is reversed. The master owns the *body* of the slave, may sell or otherwise dispose of him, may make him the subject of inheritance. The slave loses all the attributes of a person, and becomes property as much as the horse or the ox that feeds at his master's crib. These, in a condition of slavery are the rights of the master over the slave. These rights the common law, under this proposition, is to recognize, protect, and enforce. I believe I am not mistaken in this. What other construction can you give the article? It is a distinct proposal to engraft slavery upon the common law: to declare in the Constitution that slavery is recognized and protected by the common law.

Now, the North has always protested against this. She will never consent to it. She understands all the consequences as well as you. No doubt it would be a great point gained for you, to have the Constitution recognize the institution of slavery as part of the common law. For then slavery goes wherever the common law goes. Its rights under this provision are not confined to the territories. Once established, these may be enforced in a free State just as well. It is the old proposition over again, which has come before the American people so many times under so many different guises. It makes slavery national, freedom sectional. If this is so, if such is the construction which it is intended this section shall receive, why not state it openly? why leave it as a question of construction?

This construction involves other considerations. This new kind of common law is to be substituted for the old. The latter has been understood for centuries almost. Its principles have been discussed and settled. It is a system founded by experience, and adapted to the wants of the people subject to it. Its very name implies that it was not created by legislative authority. A strange common law indeed that would be which is *created by the Constitution.*

But this is not all. Other principles of the common law are subject to change. They are adapted to the advance of civilization, to the wants of communities. Change is the universal law of nature. This new kind of common law is alone to be perpetual.

It is not my purpose to enter into a general discussion of the subject. This point struck me as important, as needing elucidation. If I am wrong in this construction, the committee will correct me.

Mr. EWING:—The proposition contained in the first article of the proposed amendment, is copied from the CRITTENDEN resolutions in substance. It is true that the language is somewhat changed, but the legal effect is identical in both the propositions. The term "*status*," &c., as there used is not applicable to all the territory of the United States. It only extends to that portion of the territory south of 36° 30′. It crushes out liberty nowhere. It changes nothing—no rights whatever. Again, whatever may be the *status* of the person in the State from which he comes, *that* is preserved in the territory, and that alone. It is precisely similar to the case of a contract to which the *lex loci* gives the construction, and the *lex fori* its execution.

I like the common law. I have made it my study. I like the use of this term here. It was a good system when not as perfect as it is now. The common law of England even tolerated slavery until it was abolished. The colliers of the North of England were once, to all intents and purposes, as much slaves as any negro on the Southern plantations, except in the matter of separation of families. I can refer you to a precedent on this subject, which you will find in a book of no very high authority. I mean the novel, *Red Gauntlet.*

The general principle applicable here is this: Whenever you establish the right—no matter how, if you *establish* it—the common law asserts the remedy. There is no crushing out about it. The simple proposition is this: Slavery exists already in that little worthless territory we own below the proposed line. Will we agree that it shall remain there just as it is now, so long as the territorial condition continues? That is all. There is no mystery or question of construction about it.

Mr. FIELD:—The questions now before the Conference I suppose arise upon the report presented by the majority of the committee, and upon the motion to substitute for that report the propositions of the minority of the same committee.

I propose to add to this report the three following propositions; and I will read them for the information of the Conference.

I. "Each State has the sole and exclusive right, according to its own judgment, to order and direct its domestic institutions, and to determine for itself what shall be the relation to each other of all persons residing or being within its limits.

II. "Congress shall provide by law for securing to the citizens of each State the privileges and immunities of citizens in the several States.

III. "The union of the States under the Constitution is indissoluble; and no State can secede from the Union, or nullify an act of Congress, or absolve its citizens from their paramount obligations of obedience to the Constitution and laws of the United States."

These additions would render the majority report much more acceptable to the northern people than it is in its present shape, though even then, I am bound to declare, I could not support it. I prefer the substitute. In what I have now to say, I shall not confine myself to a discussion of these propositions, but availing myself of the latitude of debate hitherto allowed to gentlemen who have addressed the Conference in favor of the report of the majority of the committee, I shall endeavor to bring to the notice of this body, more fully than I have yet done, my views upon the general question presented for our consideration.

For myself, I state at the outset that I am indisposed to the adoption, at the present time, of any amendment of the Constitution. To change the organic law of thirty millions of people is a measure of the greatest importance. Such a measure should never be undertaken in any case, or under any circumstances, without great deliberation and the highest moral certainty that the country will be benefited by the change. In this case, as yet, there has been no deliberation; certainly not so far as the delegates from New York are concerned. The resolutions of Virginia were passed on the 19th of January. New York (her Legislature being in session) appointed her delegates on the 5th of February. We came here on the 8th. Our delegation was not full for a week. The amendments proposed were submitted on the 15th. It is now the 20th of the month. We are urged to act at once without further deliberation or delay.

To found an empire, or to make a constitution for a people, on which so much of their happiness depends, requires the sublimest effort of the human intellect, the greatest impartiality in weighing opposing interests, the utmost calmness in judgment, the highest prudence in decision. It is proposed that we shall proceed to amend in essential particulars a Constitution which, since its adoption by the people of this country, has answered all its needs; with a haste which to my mind is unnecessary, not to say indecent.

Have any defects been discovered in this Constitution? I have listened most attentively to hear those defects mentioned, if any such have been found to exist. I have heard none. No change in the Judicial Department is suggested. The exercise of judicial powers under the Constitution has been satisfactory enough to the South. The Judicial Department is to be left untouched, as I think it should be. You propose no change in the form of the Executive or Legislative Departments. These you leave as they were before. What you do propose is, to place certain limitations upon the Legislative power, to prohibit legislation upon certain important subjects, to give new guarantees to slavery, and this, as you admit, before any person has been injured, before any right has been infringed.

There is high authority which ought to be satisfactory to you, that of the President of the United States, now in office, for the statement that Congress never undertook to pass an unconstitutional law affecting the interests of slavery except the Missouri Compromise. Well, you have repealed that. You have also every assurance that can be given, that the administration about coming into power proposes no interference with your institutions within State limits. Can you not be satisfied with that? No. You propose these amendments in advance. You insist upon them, and you declare that you must and will have them or certain consequences must follow. But, gentlemen of the South, what reasons do you give for entering upon this hasty, this precipitate action? You say it is the prevailing sense of insecurity, the anxiety, the apprehension you feel lest something unlawful, something unconstitutional, may be done. Yet the gentleman from Virginia (Mr. SEDDON) tells us that Virginia is able to protect all who reside within her limits, and that she will do so at all hazards. Why not tell us the truth outright? It is not action under the Constitution or in Congress that you would prevent. What is it, then? You are determined to prevent the agitation of the subject. Let us understand each other. You have called us here to prevent future discussion of the subject of slavery. It is *that* you fear—

it is *that* you would avoid—discussion in Congress—in the State Legislatures—in the newspapers—in popular assemblies.

But will the plan you propose, the course you have marked out, accomplish your purpose? Will it stop discussion? Will it lessen it in the slightest degree? Can you not profit by the experience of the past? Can you prevent an agitation of this subject, or any other, by any constitutional provisions? No! Look at the details of your scheme. You propose through the Constitution to require payment for fugitive slaves: to make the North pay for them. You are thus throwing a lighted firebrand not only into Congress, but into every State Legislature, into every county, city, and village in the land.

This one proposition to pay for fugitive slaves, will prove a subject for almost irrepressible agitation. You say to the State Legislatures, you shall not obstruct the rendition of fugitives from service, but you may legislate in aid of their rendition, thereby implying that the latter kind of legislation will be their duty. You thus provide a new subject of discussion and agitation for all these Legislatures. In the Border States especially, such as Ohio and Pennsylvania, you will find this agitation fiercer than any you have hitherto witnessed; of which you complain so much. You will add to the flame until it becomes a consuming fire.

You propose to stop the discussion of these questions by the press. Do you really believe that in this age of the world you can accomplish that? You know little of history if such is your belief. Free speech is stronger than constitutions or dynasties. You might as well put your hands over the crater of a burning volcano, and seek thus to extinguish its flames, as to attempt to stop discussion by such an amendment of the Constitution. Stop discussion of the great questions affecting the policy, strength, and prosperity of the Government! You cannot do it! You ought not to attempt to do it!

I wish to speak kindly upon this subject. I entertain no unfriendly feelings toward any section. But while you are thus complaining of us in the free States, because we agitate and discuss the question of slavery, are you not, in a great degree, responsible for this agitation yourselves? Do you not discuss it, and agitate it? Do you not make slavery the subject of your speeches in the South, and in the presence of your slaves? Do you not make charges against us, which in your cooler moments you know to be unfounded? Do you not charge us in the hearing of your slaves with the design of interfering with slavery in the States, with a design to free them if we succeed?

You have done all this and more, and if discontent, anxiety, and mistrust exist among your people, let me say that such discussion has contributed more to produce them, than all the agitation of the slavery question at the North. But your amendments are not pointed at your discussions. That kind of agitation may go on as before. It is only the discussion on the other side you would repress!

If the condition of affairs among you is as you represent it, have you no duties to perform; is there nothing for you to do? Should you not tell your people what we have assured you upon every proper occasion, that the Republican Party has always repudiated all intention of interfering with slavery, or any other Southern institution within the States? This you all know. Have you told your people this? If you would explain it to them now, would they not be quieted? Do not reply that they *believe* we have such a purpose. Who is reponsible for that belief? Have you not continually asserted before your people, notwithstanding every assurance we could give you to the contrary, that we are determined to interfere with your rights? It is thus the responsibility rests with you.

Although such is my conviction, supported, as I think, by all the evidence, I am still for peace. Show me now any proposition that will secure peace, and I will go for it if I can. We came here to take each other by the hand, to compare views, explain, consult. We meet you in the most reasonable spirit. Any thing that honorable men *may* do, we *will* do.

We will go back to 1845 when you admitted Texas; back to the Missouri Compromise of 1820. You certainly can complain of nothing previous to that time. If, since then, there has been any law of Congress passed which is unjust toward you, which infringes upon your rights, which operates unfairly upon your interests, we will join you in securing its repeal. We will go farther. If you will point out any act of the Republican Party which has given you just cause for apprehension, we will give you all security against it. We will do any thing but amend the fundamental law of Government. Before we do that we must be convinced of its necessity.

When you propose essential changes in the Constitution you must expect that they will be subjected to a critical examination; if not here, certainly elsewhere. I object to those proposed by the majority of the committee—

1st. For what they *do* contain.

2d. For what they *do not* contain.

I do not propose to criticize the language used in your propositions of amendment. That would be trifling. I think the language very infelicitous, and if I supposed those propositions were to become part of the Constitution, I should think many verbal changes indispensable. But I pass by all that, and come at once to the substance.

I object to the propositions, sir, because they would put into the Constitution new expressions relating to slavery, which were sedulously kept out of it by the framers of that instrument; left out of it, not accidentally, but because, as MADISON said, they did not wish posterity to know from the Constitution that the institution existed.

But I object further, because the propositions contain guarantees for slavery which our fathers did not and would not give. In 1787 the convention was held at Philadelphia to establish our form of Government. WASHINGTON was its presiding officer, whose name was in itself a bond of union. It was soon after the close of a long and bloody war. Shoulder to shoulder—through winter snows and beneath summer suns—through such sufferings and sacrifices as the world had scarcely ever witnessed—the people of these States, under Providence, had fought and achieved their independence. Fresh from the field, their hearts full of patriotism, determined to perpetuate the liberties they had achieved, the people sent their delegates into the convention to frame a Constitution which would preserve to their posterity the blessings they had won.

These delegates, under the presidence of WASHINGTON, aided by the counsels of MADISON and FRANKLIN, considered the very questions with which we are now dealing, and they refused to put into the Constitution which they were making, such guarantees to slavery as you now ask from their descendants. That is my interpretation of their action. Either these guarantees are in the Constitution, or they are not. If they are there, let them remain there. If they are not there, I can conceive of no possible state of circumstances under which I would consent to admit them.

Mr. MOREHEAD :—Not to save the Union?

Mr. FIELD :—No, sir, no! That is my comprehensive answer.

Mr. MOREHEAD :—Then you will let the Union slide.

Mr. FIELD :—No, never! I would let slavery slide, and save the Union. Greater things than this have been done. This year has seen slavery abolished in all the Russias.

Mr. ROMAN :—Do you think it better to have the free and slave States separated, and to have the Union dissolved?

Mr. FIELD :—I would sacrifice all I have; lay down my life for the Union. But I will not give these guarantees to slavery. If the Union cannot be preserved without them, it cannot long be preserved with them. Let me ask you, if you will recommend to the people of the southern States, in case these guarantees are conceded, to accept them, and abide by their obligations to the Union? You answer, Yes! Do you suppose you can induce the seceded States to return? You answer: We do not know! What will you yourselves do if, after all, they refuse? Your answer is, "*We will go with them!*"

We are to understand, then, that this is the language of the slave States, which have not seceded, toward the free States: "If you will support our amendments, we will try to induce the seceded States to return to the Union. We rather think we can induce them to return; but if we cannot, then we will go with them."

What is to be done by the Government of the United States while you are trying this experiment? The seceded States are organizing a Government with all its departments. They are levying taxes, raising military forces, and engaging in commerce with foreign nations, in plain violation of the provisions of the Constitution. If this condition of affairs lasts six months longer, France and England will recognize theirs as a Government *de facto*. Do you suppose we will submit to this, that we can submit to it?

I speak only for myself. I undertake to commit no one but myself; but I here assert, that an administration which fails to assert by force its authority over the whole country will be a disgrace to the nation. There is no middle ground; we must keep this country unbroken, or we give it up to ruin!

We are told that one State has an hundred thousand men ready for the field, and that if we do not assent to these propositions she will fight us. If I believed this to be true, I would not consent to treat on any terms.

From the ports of these seceded States have sailed all the fillibustering expeditions which have heretofore disgraced this land. There, have those enterprises been conceived and fitted out. Their new government will enter upon a new career of conquest unless prevented. Even if these propositions of amendment are received and submitted to the people, I see nothing but war in the future, unless those States are quickly brought back to their allegiance.

I do not propose to use harsh language. I will not stigmatize this Convention as a political body, or assert that this is a movement toward a revolution counter to a political revolution just accomplished by the elections. Nor will I speak of personal liberty bills, or of northern State legislation, about which so much complaint has been made. If I went into those questions, much might be said on both sides. We might ask you whether you had not thrown stones at us?

Did not the Governor of Louisiana, in his message to the Legislature of his State, recommend special legislation against the supporters of Mr. LINCOLN? Is there not on the statute books of Maryland a law which prohibits a "black Republican" from holding certain offices in that State?

Mr. JOHNSON:—There was a police bill before the Legislature of Maryland, in which some provision of that kind was inserted by one who wished to defeat it. Its friends were compelled to accept the provision in order to save the bill. The courts at once held the provision unconstitutional. All that is so.

Mr. FIELD:—I am answered. It is admitted that the Legislature of that ancient State did place upon her statute book an act passed with all the forms of law, containing a provision so insulting to millions of American citizens.

Mr. HOWARD:—Will Mr. FIELD permit me a single question? I ask it for information, and because I am unable to answer it myself. I therefore rely upon his superior judgment and better means of knowledge. It appears to me that Massachusetts, Maine, and New York have gone much farther. The charge is a serious one. Maryland has never refused to submit to the decisions of the proper judicial tribunals. The Constitution has provided for the erection of a tribunal which should finally decide all questions of constitutional law. That tribunal has decided that the people of the slave States have a legal right to go into the territories with their property. The gentleman from New York tells us he is in favor of free territory, and his people are also.

Now, I wish to ask, where in the Constitution he finds the right to appeal from the decision of the Supreme Court to the popular voice? In what clause of the Constitution is this power lodged? Where does he find this right of appeal to the people, a right which he insists the North will not give up?

Mr. FIELD:—I am happy to answer the question of the gentleman from Maryland, and I reply that when once the Supreme Court has decided a question, I know of no way in which the decision can be reversed, except through an amendment of the Constitution. I have the greatest respect for the authority of the Supreme Court. I would take up arms, if necessary, to execute its decisions. I say that States, as well as persons, should respect and conform to its judgments, and I would say they must. But I am bound in candor to add, that in my view the Supreme Court has never adjudged the point to which the gentlemen refers; it gave opinions, but no decision.

I was about to state, when I was first interrupted, that the majority report altogether omits those guarantees, which, if the Constitution is to be amended, ought to be there before any others that have been suggested. I mean those which will secure protection in the South to the citizens of the free States, and those which will protect the Union against future attempts at secession; guarantees which are contained in the propositions that I have submitted as proper to be added to the report of the majority.

But, sir, I must insist, that if amendments to the Constitution are required at all, it is better that they should be proposed and considered in a General Convention. Although I do not regard this Conference as exactly unconstitutional, it is certainly a bad precedent. It is a body nominally composed of representatives of the States, and is called to urge upon Congress propositions of amendment to the Constitution. Its recommendations will have something of force in them; it will undoubtedly be claimed for them in Congress that they possess such force. I do not like to see an irregular body sitting by the side of a legislative body and attempting to influence its action.

Again, all the States are not here. Oregon and California—the great Pacific dominions with all their wealth and power, present and prospective—have not been consulted at all. Will it be replied that all the States can vote upon the amendments? That is a very different thing from proposing them. California and Oregon may have interests of their own to protect, propositions of their own to make. Is it right for us to act without consulting them? I will go for a convention, because I believe it is the best way to avoid civil war.

Mr. WICKLIFFE:—If a General Convention is held, what amendments will you propose?

Mr. FIELD:—I have already said that I have none to propose. I am satisfied with the Constitution as it is.

Mr. WICKLIFFE:—Then, for God's sake, let us have no General Convention.

Mr. FIELD:—I think the gentleman's observation is not logical. He wants amendments, I do not. But I say if we are to have them, let us have them through a General Convention.

And I say farther, that this is the quickest way to secure them. If a General Convention is to be called, let it be held at once, just as soon as possible. If gentlemen from eight of the States in this Conference represent truly the public sentiment of their people, as I will assume they do, there is no other alternative. We must have either the arbitrament of reason or the arbitrament of the sword. The gloomy future alone can tell whether the latter is to be the one adopted. I greatly fear it is. The conviction presses upon me in my waking and my sleeping hours. Only last night I dreamed of marching armies and news from the seat of war. [A laugh from the Kentucky and Virginia benches.]

The gentlemen laugh. I thought they, too, had fears of war. I thought their threats and prophecies were sincere. God grant that I may not hereafter have to say, "I had a dream that was not all a dream."

Sir, I have but little more to trouble you with. In what I have said I trust there has been no expression that will be taken in ill part. I have spoken what I sincerely felt. If there has been an unkind word in my remarks I did not intend it, and am sorry for having uttered it.

For my own State and for the North I have only to say that they are devoted to the Union. We have been reminded of

HAMILTON's opinion, that the States are stronger than the Union, and that when the collision comes the Union must fall. This is a mistake. In the North the love for the Union is the strongest of political affections. New York will stand by the flag of the country while there is a star left in its folds. If the Union should be reduced to thirteen States—if it should be reduced to three States—if all should fall away but herself, she will stand alone to bear and uphold that honored flag, and recover the Union of which it is the pledge and symbol. God grant that time may never come, but that New York may stand side by side with Kentucky and Virginia to the end. That we may all stand by the Union, negotiate for it, fight for it, if the necessity comes, is my wish, my hope, my prayer. The Constitution made for us by WASHINGTON, FRANKLIN, MADISON, and HAMILTON, and the wise and patriotic men who labored with them, is good enough for us. We stand for the country, for the Union, for the Constitution.

I found yesterday upon my table a pamphlet bearing the title of "The Governing Race." It contains a sublime passage from LONGFELLOW's poem of "The Ship," which, as it closes the pamphlet, shall also close my observations:

"Thou, too, sail on, O Ship of State!
Sail on, O UNION, strong and great!
Humanity with all its fears,
With all the hopes of future years,
Is hanging breathless on thy fate!
We know what Master laid thy keel,
What Workmen wrought thy ribs of steel,
Who made each mast, and sail, and rope,
What anvils rang, what hammers beat,
In what a forge and what a heat
Were shaped the anchors of thy hope!
Fear not each sudden sound and shock,
'Tis of the wave and not the rock;
'Tis but the flapping of the sail,
And not a rent made by the gale!
In spite of rock and tempest's roar,
In spite of false lights on the shore,
Sail on, nor fear to breast the sea!
Our hearts, our hopes, are all with thee,
Our hearts, our hopes, our prayers, our tears,
Our faith triumphant o'er our fears,
Are all with thee,—are all with thee."

Mr. WHITE:—I shall not occupy much of the time of the Conference. All the speeches that have been made, and all the declamation that has been uttered on this floor, have not made a single convert. Last of all would I wish to follow the gentleman who has just taken his seat. He proposes to postpone action, asserts that we are acting without consideration, in haste, and without due deliberation. I look upon this subject from a different point of view. I believe the motive of Pennsylvania in first responding to the invitation of Virginia was to induce the States to meet here in council, and remove that peril which now threatens our common country.

Pennsylvania had another reason. She is a border State; she has a deeper and more vital interest in the present unhappy differences than New York or the North. If there is to be war; civil, unnatural war, whose country is to be devastated, whose fields laid waste and trampled down? They are those of the border States—of Ohio, Pennsylvania, Illinois, Indiana, and possibly New Jersey. These are the States that are to suffer. Gentlemen from New York and the North East, in the bosom of their families, their towns and cities not in the least danger, may be as impassive as the granite rocks that bind their shores. We have a deeper, a more vital interest; therefore we feel and speak. When Pennsylvania received the invitation of Virginia, South Carolina, Georgia, and other States had seceded. Dangers were accumulating. Then it was that the old conservative Keystone State threw herself into the breach. She sent her delegation here to save the country and not to change the Constitution—not to alter it, but to explain it and to give our Southern sisters the guarantees they once did not ask and did not need. We believed that the great majority of the people of the Southern States were Union loving men, who choose to sail under the flag of the Union, rather than under any piratical and treasonable banner. We knew there were rebels within those States, as there is a faction at the North composed of men as much rebels as they are. We knew, also, that there was a large body of men at the South, who, though loyal at heart, were in a state of great anxiety and apprehension, and who might be stirred up by demagogues, through appeals to their State pride and other influences, to take a stand against the Union.

The Republicans denied that they wished to interfere in any manner with the institution of slavery. We have come here to give the slave States a declaratory exposition of our views. We have come bearing the olive branch. We are met by the South in a spirit of conciliation. The delegates tell us that they hope to be able to bring back their erring sister States into the fold of the Union, if they can go to them bearing satisfactory guarantees from us. Pennsylvania is willing that we should give them that opportunity. We have lived in harmony with them: we wish to live in peace with them. If the seceded States will not come back, if the other Southern States cannot bring them back, then, are we in any worse position? No, sir! we are not. We desire to place ourselves right before the world. Then, if some States will not stay in the Union, on their heads be the responsibility. Then, if any wrong has been done, if any right has been violated, Pennsylvania will not be responsible. We shall have done our duty, on them will the responsibility rest. They must answer for it before the world and before the judgment-seat.

What will be the consequence of postponing action on this subject? We are strengthening the position of the seceded States. We

> "Keep the word of promise to the ear,
> And break it to the hope."

Every rebel will rejoice at our inaction.

The continuance of Virginia in the Union depends upon the action of a convention now in session in Richmond. If we send her commissioners home to say to that convention, "The North will wait two years and then consider your propositions," what will the convention say to that? The seceded States have at this moment commissioners at Richmond entreating Virginia to join their Confederacy, and to detach herself from the free States. If we fail to act, who can fail to foresee the consequences? Maryland is about calling a convention. She, too, will act, and she will go where her associations and her interests carry her.

From this you can infer some of the reasons why Pennsylvania has sent her commissioners here. Her object was not delay. Her wish was for action—speedy action. She wishes to do all she can to accelerate action. She wishes to have some plan laid before the country at once—something fair to all sections—and then, with the alternatives before them, let the people decide. She wishes to pour oil on the troubled waters.

We are told by our friend from New York, that the amendments are badly drawn. If so, let him help us to correct them. No one can do it better. Surely there is talent enough in this Conference to remedy such defects as are suggested by him.

Gentlemen say they do not wish to convert free territory into slave territory. Neither do I. We are not doing that. All the territory south of the line proposed is slave territory already. The adoption of these propositions does not extend slavery at all.

The first advantage the Republican party ever obtained in Pennsylvania, was on account of the repeal of the Missouri Compromise, followed by the decision of the Supreme Court, declaring that the normal condition of the territory was a condition of slavery, and on that ground holding the Missouri Compromise unconstitutional. Such being the state of the matter, do we lose any thing by the prohibition of slavery north of 36° 30′? No! All that vast territory north of the line will be dedicated to freedom. The South asks that faith shall be kept; that slavery in the territory south of the line shall not be interfered with. This is the only material averment in the declaration.

The second article contains a modification of the Constitution which was not intended. This I understand it is proper to amend.

Another proposition is to put a barrier into the Constitution, which will prevent the acquisition of territory in future by joint resolution. To this I am sure the gentleman from New York will not object.

Sir, I have read and carefully considered all the proposed amendments. To my mind they present no essential changes, or modifications, or constructions, of that instrument. I can see no injury in them to the interests of the North. I think they are rather to the advantage of the North. I believe the people of the North will hasten cheerfully to adopt them.

Now, if we can adopt them—if we can make them a part of our organic law, and thus settle these differences, who will not be glad? There is still a deep and abiding love of the Union in the hearts of all the people. They will hail with joy any action of yours which tends to strengthen it.

Mr. TUCK:—I should not address the Conference at this time if I did not discover early signs of closing the debate, and I prefer to be clearly understood upon the subject of discussion before it closes.

I well understand the appeals of the border slave States. They think that one-half their number are already out of the Union. They deem themselves weakened by their defection. I well understand the inquiry of the eloquent gentleman from Virginia, when he asked, on the second day of the session, "Can't you understand our position?"

I have listened to appeals stronger and more eloquent than I ever expect to hear again. The representatives from the South on this floor are skilful in debate and eloquent in speech. Were there no view of the case but the one they present, I might become a convert myself.

They have seen half of the slave States, acting on the theory of right claimed by the South, undertake to go out of the Union. If they love the States they represent, and the Union of all the States, they should be filled with apprehension and alarm. The venerable gentleman from North Carolina (Judge RUFFIN) has appealed to us with an ardor, patriotism, and eloquence which has produced an indelible impression upon my mind, while the gentleman (Mr. SEDDON) from Virginia, in describing parallels of attack which the North, as he said, were constructing, in the course of events, about the institution of slavery, commanded my undivided attention. Yet gentlemen greatly err in assuming that we of the North are acting under some wizard influence, and, out of pure malignity, are plotting the overthrow of slavery. There is no plot or general concert in the action of the North on this subject. We are, like the South, subject to general laws affecting mind and morals, as well as pecuniary concerns, which laws cannot be disregarded. We cannot act otherwise than we do. Ideas and principles control, and we and those whom we represent will act in accordance with them, whatever be the consequences.

Much is said here about saving to the Union the slave States not yet gone. All I have to say on this point is, I wish to save them, and I trust we shall have less trouble with the seven than with the fifteen.

The chair was here taken by Mr. ALEXANDER.

The people of this country, North and South alike, obey the laws of interest and morality. There is no disposition at the North to destroy slavery. Let these accusations and criminations be heard no more. What I am about to say may weigh but little, but I know something of the North, and a little of the South. I fully believe that the institution of slavery within the States should be left with them exclusively—that such is the prevailing sentiment of the North. I say so because there is no disposition at the North to interfere with it. Do we believe that we can manage slavery better than you? No, sir! I believe that we could not manage it so well. If we had been reared on your soil in the midst of slavery, we could manage it just as well. It is a mistake and a pernicious error, for the South to believe that either party at the North proposes to raise any question relating to slavery within State limits. There is not a man at the North who could stand up long enough to fall down, if he should take such a position.

There are problems connected with slavery which we cannot solve; we do not wish to undertake their solution. We will leave them with you.

What, then, should we do? My answer is, live along as we have done before. We will live with you in the Union, under a Constitution that requires us to help you keep the peace. Where you dwell, we will dwell. Your people shall be our people, and where you die, we will die. Our Constitution is good enough for a people who are wise enough to live under it. With such a Constitution, Virginia proposes to leave the Union.

Will you leave the Union because the Constitution has not been rightly construed? No; for it has been construed to your entire satisfaction. It has been made to speak your views. The judges of our Supreme Courts represent your opinions. There has never been a construction of the Constitution adverse to your interests. The Dred Scott decision protects slavery in all the territories according to your desire, though against our strong conviction of law and right. Will you leave the Union because you have not had the Government your share of the time? You have had possession and control of it for fifty years out of seventy-two; and during a large portion of the twenty-two years, when we have had the President from the free States, the administration has been under the control of southern sentiments, and southern interests have been in the ascendency, through the servility of northern men. Do you leave the Union in order to secure the protection of a better Constitution? No; for they who have left us have said that the Constitution was well enough, if the people were sufficiently enlightened to live under it. Why is it, then, with all these facts before you, that you propose to turn away from the Government of our fathers, from all the glories of the past, the blessings of the present, and the hopes of the future, to hunt for new and better things under a new Government?

You are going out of the Union because you say we propose to immolate you—to turn you over to the mercies of a Government of slaves set free. How unfounded is such a belief! Are we not brothers still? I doubt whether there was a better feeling between the masses of the North toward you ten or seventy years ago than there is to-day. Can you find better fortunes elsewhere? Where do you propose to go? To the doubtful fortunes of a Southern Confederacy? You certainly are not acting with your accustomed prudence and forethought. You know what the teachings of history are in relation to nations in that belt of latitude. You know how they have always compared with northern nations. Together the two sections may be prosperous and powerful; separated you can judge where the advantage must fall. Had we not better try and get along as we are?

This Conference presents some singular scenes. Although made up, so far as the North is concerned, of members of both political parties, yet, by a majority, it supports southern views of southern interests as earnestly and emphatically as any southern man has done. In all conflicts of the past and present you have carried your points, and you have reason to think you may do so in future. Yet you insist upon separation. Be assured, you will experience as bitter feuds among yourselves as you do in the fellowship of those you leave. You cannot be reconciled to even the existence of a minority against you, but you will find you cannot escape the minorities, and may fall into one yourselves. You propose to join the fortunes of the Southern Confederacy, in which there is a contention already. You turn your backs upon the Government of the Father of his Country, whose portrait is before us, and join your fortunes to a mere southern nationality. Beware of the act. Look back over the last two thousand years, and contrast the stability of governments in southern latitudes with those more northern, under latitudes which you leave. Mexico, Central America, and South America, furnish valuable lessons on this Continent, while the Eastern Hemisphere is, in this respect, full of instruction. Will you leave a people whose character and habits are like those which have produced the permanence and power of Russia, France, and England, and ally yourselves to those more southern people who have not hitherto enjoyed stability, power, or happiness? Is it not wiser to stay where you are, to scorn the pernicious doctrines of new teachers, and to live and die under the flag of our fathers?

The annexation of Texas opened a Pandora's box of evil. Had not that taken place, the Missouri Compromise would not have been repealed. Had not that Compromise been repealed, the shadow of our present troubles would not have arisen.

You speak of the opposition of the North to slavery. Believe us or not, it is true, nevertheless, that slavery is regarded at the North as strictly a State institution; as such, we are content to let it remain; we desire to let it remain such. But let not the North be misunderstood in its position. The North is willing to let slavery remain where it is—where our fathers left it; but against its extension into the territories, the North is inflexibly and unalterably opposed.

If there is any thing to pacificate I am in favor of pacification, but in favor of it according to the Constitution. The Constitution embraces all that any State can reasonably ask or honorably concede. But if from change of circumstances or other causes, the men of the South are of the opinion that their interests are overlooked or ill-defined, I, for one, will favor a call of a convention to consider amendments to the Constitution, and I will vote for such amendments as shall give as substantial protection to the South as the North ought to ask for, in the change of circumstances.

I submitted an address and resolutions a few days since for adoption in this Convention, which I hope may be carefully read before being rejected. They contemplated a convention, and their design is to give assurance of justice to the public. I oppose the proposition for an address by the committee, to be issued to the public after our adjournment. We wish to know beforehand what we adopt, and to weigh every word. There is a northern sentiment to be regarded as well as a southern sentiment.

We of the North have heard much said in denunciation of us, and have thought it political clap-trap and gasconade. But if we are made to believe in your hostility to us and the Government, we may conclude it is best to let you leave us. We have no fears in trusting ourselves, if necessary, to our industry, our habits, and enterprise, separate from the slaveholding States. Opinions are changing rapidly. I do not like the idea of maintaining the Union by force of arms. It is not in accordance with the theory of our Government.

A Virginian stated only a few days ago, that there was nothing which the South could ask or that the North could give, that was not found in the Constitution. But you say that we do not understand it alike—that the two sections differ in their construction of it. Well, if that is so, we are willing to submit to the courts.

You have always fared well enough there. If that is not enough we will leave the whole subject, amendments and all, to a General Convention. That we now propose. We propose it fairly, not for any purpose of delay or postponement. Call the convention as early as it can be done. We will aid you. We will go home and in good faith urge our people to go into the convention, and there patiently and fairly consider all your claims, all your complaints. We would urge them to concede all they can without a sacrifice of principle. We will do this as a party, and with all our strength. Now, this does not quite come up to what you want, but is it best for you to insist upon breaking up the Government on that ground? That is neither sensible nor safe. We are like two lobes in the same skull; one cannot outlive the other. Destroy one and you destroy the other. I do not believe this Republic can stand without the Union which our fathers made. But it will stand—it must stand. Wise counsels will yet prevail. You will yet believe us sincere in our desires to relieve you. The end of the Union has not come—it is not coming. The Union will yet outlive us and our posterity.

Mr. FRELINGHUYSEN:—In rising to express briefly my views, I feel oppressed and embarrassed in view of the magnitude of the subjects we are discussing, and in the presence of this distinguished auditory. I cannot claim to represent an Empire State with its four millions of people, nor a Bay State, which we are told, with its wealth, its enterprise, and its commerce, can settle a new State every year. But with my colleagues, I represent a State which performed her part in the dark night of the Revolution—her share in that great struggle for our priceless institutions—a State which has ever since been faithful in the discharge of all her constitutional obligations. In that bloody conflict, upon her own soil, New Jersey joined hands with the North and South. There is scarcely a church spire within her borders beneath whose shadows does not lay the remains of some of the entombed patriots in that great conflict from both these sections, commingled with those of her own sons!

New Jersey was true to the Union in that great struggle—she has always since been true; and under the favor of Providence she always will be faithful to the Union and its memories, so inseparably connected with the glory and honor of her sons. Other States may have done as much, may have as good a record, may be entitled to equal credit with her. But in all her past history, I can point to her fidelity to the Union and her sister States with no blush of shame upon my brow. Other States might be wanting! New Jersey never! She has always been true to her constitutional obligations; she has always kept—never sought to avoid them.

With a narrow stream separating her from a slaveholding State, there were never any underground railroads in New Jersey; she never rescued a fugitive slave from the custody of the law; no *personal liberty* bill ever disgraced the pages of her statutes, nor ever will disgrace them. In 1793 she enacted a statute providing for the prompt return of fugitive slaves found within her limits. She subjected any judge required to act under it, to imprisonment, if he neglected to perform his duties. That law has ever since been in force. It was reënacted in 1836, and again in 1846, when some of its defects were amended. Courteous as just, she provided by another law, passed in 1820, that any southern gentleman visiting her territory, might bring with him his household slaves, travel in, through, and out of the State, or even take up his temporary residence as securely in this respect as at home. This law was reënacted in 1847, and again in 1855; one of my worthy colleagues here was associated, upon the commission which revised this act, with that distinguished New Jersey Republican, WILLIAM L. DAYTON.

In the recent unhappy political contest, New Jersey, ever anxious to do justice to all sections of the Union, and injustice to none, as if hesitating and doubtful toward which of the two parties in that struggle she ought to incline, extended her fraternal hands to North and South, by giving one-half her electoral vote to each; thus showing that she still retains her unselfish spirit, which leads her to sacrifice her own preferences to her duty to the Union.

In the same spirit to-day she bears her full share of the heavy sorrow that rests, like a pall, over the people of the whole country as they witness this glorious fabric, which our fathers erected and cemented with their blood and their prayers—trembling, shattered, and dismembered. In the conciliatory spirit of my State, I, as a Jerseyman, proud of the title and every thing connected with it, wish to say a word to the South in all frankness and candor. I freely tell you that, in my opinion, you have a right to guarantees, and to constitutional guarantees. It is no answer to say that the Constitution has not been broken. That is not the question now. Reference has been made to the fact that WASHINGTON signed the present Constitution. Yes, but when he did so we had a population of but three millions, and now we have a population of upward of thirty millions. Is it surprising that some change should be required in that instrument with this great change in the nation? The balance of power so long fluctuating between the free and the slaveholding States has at length entirely changed. It has now come to us of the free States, and therefore we are bound to respect the claims of the South, and quiet the apprehensions of its people.

It is of little use to make patriotic speeches here. The South demands guarantees, and I feel under obligations to respond to that demand. I assert as a general principle, that whoever has a right is entitled to have it guaranteed. I believe there is not a gentleman here, who, in his heart, does not think so. If it is right for them to have these guarantees at all, they should have them to-day. I do not care whether Virginia occupies a menacing attitude or not, my moral code is still the same; it is not effected by any thing that has been done or can be done by Virginia or any other State. It is my belief that nineteen-twentieths of the people of the North to-day are in favor of giving to the South all the guarantees it asks against all interference with slavery in the territories. Some say, "We admit this, but we will do nothing until the Republican President is inaugurated on the 4th of March." I am ready to do it now; and my obligations to do right will not be changed by the 4th of March rolling over my head.

Gentlemen have made eloquent and patriotic speeches asserting their determination not to interfere with the rights of the South. That is very pleasant and very proper. But those speeches are the expressions of individuals, and they pass away. Where is the man who will consent to hold any political right at the will of any man or class of men, no matter how kindly disposed? We all require security. The highest and grandest aim and object of government is not the stability and peace of society, but a well-grounded confidence in the minds of the people of the perpetuity of that stability and peace.

The South asks the right to use and occupy a portion of the common territory of the country. As a northern man I will accept the compromise, and I believe a large majority of the people will agree with me. You, gentlemen of the South, have asked that the arrangement may be extended to territory hereafter to be acquired. New Jersey has voted in this Convention against interference with slavery in the territory, present or future, and she is the only northern State that has cast her vote in favor of your demand. Her representatives have been told somewhat sneeringly, that while slaveholding States voted against this proposition, New Jersey was the only free State that voted for it. Well, we accept the responsibility, and will bear it. New Jersey has made up her record. There it stands, and there let it stand forever. We are proud of it. If civil war is to come, if this land is to be deluged with fraternal blood, when that time comes there will not be a northern State represented here that would not give untold millions to be placed upon that record by the side of New Jersey.

The fact is, sir, we have acquired our liberties too cheaply. Had we purchased them at the cost our fathers did, by coloring the snows of winter by our blood tracks, and by passing the summers in the unhealthy morass, we should have learned to prize them more highly; we should be more patriotic and less proud, more sensible and less sensitive.

A word further on the subject of extending this provision to territory hereafter acquired. Gentlemen, you do not want that provision; you do not need any provision as to future acquisitions. You are better off without it. No present rights are involved in it. You are providing for a contingency which may never, and probably never will happen. Would it not be inconsistent for a nation to commit suicide because a constitution is not made to meet an improbable contingency? You have territory enough for the next two hundred years. You say you require it to maintain your honor, to preserve your fair equality, to maintain your lawful rights. Permit me to say you have no rights in territory which we never owned, and I hope never may. This is no question of honor or equality. But if we should acquire territory and should then exclude you from it, will it not then be time enough to resort to the expedient of national suicide as a remedy for the wrong? Nor do you require it for any particular purpose. You have within your States room for all the increase of a century. Your interest is to retain your sons at home and develop the wealth and advance the prosperity of your States, and not to send them to the western wilderness where one-half die in the process of acclimation. The fact that you are all in favor of placing in the Constitution new *restrictions* as to the *acquisition* of territory, proves you do not consider you need more territory. I heard it said, the other day, by a gentleman from Virginia, that the South wanted the provision for a finality, to end forever this dispute about slavery. With all my heart I sympathize with him in his desire to end this discussion forever. You think you have suffered from these discussions at the South; so have we at the North. It has separated families and neighborhoods; it has broken up and scattered

Christian churches; it has severed every benevolent society of the land; it has destroyed parties; it broke up the good old Whig party, and more recently sapped the strength and vigor from the Herculean Democracy. It now threatens the dissolution of the Union. Let us crush the head of the monster forever. Let us do it by restricting and defining its limits in existing territory.

Suppose the word "future" had been inserted. You do not wish to destroy all probability of the adoption of this proposition at the North. These proposals could not pass Congress, with the word "future," by the requisite vote; and if it passed Congress, there is no hope that twenty-five out of twenty-eight States would have adopted it. With it you would have given great strength to the opposition at the North. It would have created a more powerful anti-slavery party than ever before existed. No, you are better off by confining the provisions of this compromise to present territory—you having, as well as the North, in the contemplated amendment a veto on the acquisition of territory.

The North will want new territory before you will desire it. They will demand Mexico and Cuba for the advantages of trade. You then, having the veto power, can say to them—No, gentlemen, we will not agree to it unless our particular institution is there respected; or, if you please, you may go further and say, We will not acquiesce unless this territory comes in as a slave State so as to restore measurably the balance of power in the Government. With this veto power you would have the North in your hands, and could make your own terms. You make the provision more of a finality by letting it stand as it is.

But gentlemen say, they want the amendment for another purpose, in order that they may induce States that have gone out to return. Here, again, I sympathize with you. I had rather bring back South Carolina than to secure the annexation of both the Canadas. I would give more for one American than for a regiment of John Bulls. Ungenerous as South Carolina has been, I would receive her home again. I desire the States to return. Let their place at the Federal Board remain vacant for them. Let the stars of their sovereignty on our nation's ensign remain unobliterated and without further dishonor. We are ready to receive them. But this provision as to future territory is not necessary for their return. The same considerations to which I have alluded, and which will satisfy you that such provision is not requisite, will satisfy them. The guarantees which the North are ready to give as to the representation, taxation, and return of property, and the compromise as to the existing territory, will do much to satisfy them. To effect a compromise, you of the South must demand as little as you can render satisfactory to your people, and we of the North must give as much as our people will approve, and both parties must consent to avoid all objectionable phraseology.

Now, a few words to my friends of the North. There is resting upon us a grave responsibility. We are bound to settle this question finally in this Convention. Talk about a convention of the people! We who have no constitution, we who are tied up to no technicalities, must settle it. We of the North may meet political death; but let political death come, it is enough to have lived for, if we can settle this question.

But one asks, Will you strike hands with treason, and enter into compacts with rebels and traitors? Yes, sir! I will strike hands with just such rebels and traitors as I see around me; and I would give them what they ask as cheerfully and as freely as I would give a glass of water to a soldier returning wounded and weary from the field of battle.

But it is said we must first see whether we have a Government. We must try the strength of the Government. We must know whether the Government can assert its supremacy and compel obedience to its laws. Sir, that is just what I do not want to try. What, try the strength of the Government! and do so at the end of an administration in which corruption and treason and every evil principle have been contending for the mastery, when our ships are all away beyond sea, when our arms and our fortifications are out of our hands, when our treasury is bankrupt, our people divided, insolvency and ruin threatening our country, and all the Gulf States defying the authority of the Government? No, sir! this is no time to try the strength of the Government. When we do that, let us select some more auspicious period.

But another says these proposals of amendment contravene the Chicago platform. What if they do? Is the Chicago platform a law to us? Is it a law to any one? It was passed upon ten minutes' consideration in a convention of five thousand people.

If it was a law, the convention should have been perpetual and never dissolved, in order that the law might have been subject to requisite modifications without a change of circumstances. A strange manner in which to enact such a law! But things have changed since the Chicago Convention. In fifty days, fifty years of history have transpired. This is enough to release us from the obligation, if any existed. It is not a law; it is a doctrine, the spirit, the policy of the party that it undertakes to enunciate. It is not a law, because a majority of the people have never given it their sanction. Mr. Lincoln was elected by less than a majority. And in his vote how many old Whigs and Democrats may be counted who did not support him *because* he stood upon the Chicago platform, but because they preferred him to either of the opposing candidates. And even if it is a law, I call upon the North to support the proposals of amendment here submitted. Let us, as Republicans, be honest, and when the opportunity offers are we not bound so to change the Constitution that three-fourths of all our present territory, now open to slavery, shall be consecrated to freedom? Yes, we are bound to relieve that three-fourths from slavery. All we need to do to secure this, is not to carry slavery where it is not, but to secure it where it is. I can go home to the Republicans of New Jersey with a clear conscience and say to them, that by our action here we have not carried slavery one inch farther than it was before. If they are not satisfied with that, they must be dissatisfied.

But there is one plank in the Chicago platform to which I will call the attention of my Republican friends. It must not be forgotten. I read from a genuine copy which I brought from Chicago myself.

"*Resolved*, That to the Union of the States, this nation owes its unprecedented increase in population, its surpassing development of internal resources, its rapid augmentation of wealth, its happiness at home and its honor abroad, and we hold in abhorrence all schemes of disunion, come from whatever source they may."

It is a rule of construction, that all parts of an instrument must be construed together; that due regard and effect must be given to all parts of it, unless they are clearly repugnant. Will any gentleman tell me how the Union can be more effectually preserved than by controlling disunion? It is by granting what is asked to those who might disturb its tranquillity, when they ask nothing unreasonable. This resolution every patriot can subscribe to; and I hold that it can be as effectually violated by the neglect to do all we can to turn aside disunion, as by affirmative action against the Government. And let me say that the party in this country which goes between the people and the preservation of the Union, will sink so low, eventually, that a bubble will not return to mark the spot where it went down. But I cannot understand how any one who is honestly opposed to the extension of slavery, as a political institution, can refuse the compromise proposed. The federal courts, to which we have committed the power, have decided that slavery, of right, goes into all the territories. The distinguished Republican from Massachusetts has told us that the court cannot be so organized, even if we keep the power, as to change that decision in twenty-five years. In that time the whole question will be determined. Now we have an opportunity, at once and forever, by constitutional enactment, to prohibit slavery from going into three-fourths of the territory, by simply agreeing that as to the other one-fourth, while it remains a territory, the *status* of slavery shall not be changed. I confess I have not the ingenuity to contrive how I should apologize to an audience of Republicans for refusing such a contract.

Now, what can we of the North, we Republicans, do? By a settlement here we can retain the Border States, and, in my opinion, that is equivalent to saving the Union. Retain the Border States and the seceding States must come back. If the Border States go, I believe war is inevitable. How can two sections exist with only an imaginary line between them. I do not believe the South will ever consent to give up the Capital, claimed to be within her borders, and the North could never surrender it. Sir, I shrink from the prospect of civil war. The picture of civil war has often been painted, and by abler hands than mine. Its calamities and miseries, the sufferings that attend it, strike a chill of horror to the soul. But such a picture as a civil war in this country would be, has never been drawn. History would be searched in vain for its parallel. A civil war between the members of a family, between brother and brother, father and son, who have all enjoyed the same blessings which their fathers made early and bloody sacrifices to secure! Shall it be said that such a people, for such a cause, risked their interests, their country, their all, and rushed blindly into the calamities of a civil war? He has read history to little account who has not learned that such a warfare is, in its nature, not only cruel, but protracted. It is like letting loose the hurricane. Passion and poverty, carnage and crime, desolation and death, become the condition of a hitherto happy people. For thirty years Germany was ravaged, and millions slain by a contest occasioned by a difference in religious opinions. For more than thirty years the war of the Roses devastated England. The French Revolution, including the "Reign of Terror"—originating in a question of taxation and terminating with the supremacy of Napoleon—lasted nearly ten years. For a like decade civil war raged between England and Scotland, originating in a question of authority between the King and Commons, and ending in Cromwell's protectorate. Why, I ask, if we admit this fiendish visitant to our borders, should we anticipate that our fate would be more favorable? No! war is to be averted, and a nation still covered with glory is to be preserved by holding the Border States in the Union.

If I am asked what I would do; I answer, Compromise—compromise! Two gentlemen cannot live in a parlor together a single day without reciprocal compromises. I would not be "stiff in the back and firm in the knees." There is such a thing as too much "backbone." I say I would "back down" to save the country. I am not ashamed of the expression. Our Government itself was a compromise, and in nothing more so than as to the slavery question. HENRY CLAY was the great compromiser. The Missouri Compromise was his. Resigning his office as Speaker, on the floor of Congress by irresistible argument, and eloquence unequalled—though twice defeated, he succeeded in establishing the compromise line of 36° 30′—and thereby erected a barrier which severed the angry currents of opinion on this distracting theme, and which was as valuable to this nation as the isthmus at the equator, holding in check the mighty ocean on either side. The North has compromised before; let her do it again. Let our friends at the South take as little as they can, and let the North yield as little as she can, but let us come together. The party that stands between the people and the preservation of the Government will be crushed to atoms. It will be remembered in history only with curses and indignation.

We all love this Union, and we mean to preserve it. There is no one here who, as he has witnessed the freedom, the comfort, the prosperity, and the pure religion disseminated among the people, has not hoped this nation was to accomplish great social and moral good for our whole race. Yes, in fond conception we have seen her the Liberator and Equalizer of the world—walking like an angel of light in the dark portions of the earth. These sacred anticipations may not be disappointed without a fearful accountability somewhere. And, sir, suffer me to say that this whole people have a strong regard for each other, notwithstanding the petulant differences which have arisen between us. Kindred blood flows in our veins, and that of our fathers mingles on the same field; and even now, in the day of our country's peril, our affections meet at the hallowed grounds of Mt. Vernon, of Marshfield, and of Ashland.

We have our history. WASHINGTON and FRANKLIN, and HENRY and SUMTER, as well as Bunker Hill, and Yorktown, and Trenton, are yours, and they are all ours.

We have our religion—and with every diurnal revolution of this sphere, from North and South, through the efficacy of a common faith, a goodly company are ascending to that realm of peace where their harmonious union shall never more be severed. And to-day, from a thousand hearthstones in the sunny South, and in the more rigid North, the family prayer ascends to the Father of us all, for a blessing on our common country and for the preservation of this Union. Those prayers will be heard, and this priceless Union will be preserved.

Mr. WICKLIFFE:—I wish to call the attention of the Conference for a moment to another subject, in order that members may give it their consideration. I shall call up my motion to terminate the debate upon the report of the committee early to-morrow, and ask to have the discussion closed on the 21st instant. I am sure that I shall be sustained in this by every member who wishes to have this body come to any agreement. I wish to have the vote taken on the *twenty-second day of February*, that we may see whether the same day that gave a WASHINGTON to our Fathers, may not give PEACE to their posterity.

Mr. DODGE:—I have listened with intense interest to the addresses which have recently been made to the Conference. I respect the ability which they have exhibited—I honor the patriotism which has produced them. They have presented the important principles involved in the action of this Conference in a much more interesting and forcible manner than I could; and I would not occupy the attention of this body with a single observation, if I had the good fortune to be associated with a delegation in which unanimity of opinion and feeling prevailed. But I am not so fortunate. In that delegation I find many shades of opinion. I respect the views of my brother delegates. It is not for me to assume to sit in judgment upon them. I give each one of them credit for the same honesty and integrity which I claim for myself; and if I happen to differ from them, I claim that such difference honestly arises from the different paths in life which we pursue, which may lead us to take different views of the same subjects as they are here presented.

The Conference has heard the ideas of political and professional men expressed upon the important questions now presented for its consideration. These ideas have been well expressed, and we have all been interested in hearing them. Will you now hear a few words from a body of men who have hitherto been silent here, but who have a deep and abiding interest in the happiness and prosperity of the country and in the preservation and perpetuity of the American Union?

Sir! I am here as a plain merchant, out of place, I very well know, in such a Conference as this; but accident has brought me here, and I will tell you how and why I came. Three weeks ago I left my business—which in times like these certainly deserves all my attention—to come to the city of Washington on business of a public character. I came at the suggestion and request of the Chamber of Commerce of New York, hoping, in my humble way, to serve the public interests in this crisis. Inconvenient though it was, and involving personal sacrifices of no ordinary character, when others thought my country had need of my poor services, I did not hesitate to respond to her call. And I hope I may never hesitate under such circumstances.

I came here to visit Congress, as a member of a committee, bearing a petition to that body signed by more than thirty-nine thousand of my fellow-citizens, all interested in the welfare and permanence of this Government. This number included more than twenty thousand business men and firms. This petition was earnest and emphatic. In it, we asked and prayed that Congress would adopt some plan that would settle our present sectional troubles; that would relieve the country from the anxiety and apprehension which pervaded it, and permit business and commerce to resume their accustomed channels, with assurances of safety in the future. We knew that the time had arrived when patriotic men must act; that commercial and financial ruin was impending. Our petition set forth, that in the opinion of the signers, the plan contained in what were called the "Border State Resolutions" was best calculated to secure the end desired. We thought those resolutions ought to be satisfactory to the reasonable and true Union men of the South, and that they ought not to be obnoxious to the prejudices or objections of the people of the free States. Still we were not strenuous—we were not committed to any particular plan. All we desired, was to secure such action on the part of Congress and the Executive, as would satisfy the country; such action as would give the country peace.

When we came to Washington we met *seventy* republican members of the Senate and House of Representatives. We had with them a most satisfactory and delightful interview. It gave me renewed hope for my country and her interests when I heard the expressions of conciliation and good will which these gentlemen used; I felt my confidence renewed.

Besides these gentlemen, who met and heartily coöperated with us, there were several members from the Border States whose expressions were not less friendly, although they did not think it expedient to act with us. Our committee made all the representations and explanations which were deemed necessary; and having performed my duty in that connection, in the earnest hope that we had influenced the action of Congress in the right direction, I was about to return home with my colleagues, when I received a telegraphic despatch requesting me to attend the meeting of this Conference. I obeyed the summons; and since I received it, I have been laboring with all the ability, strength, and power with which GOD has blessed me, to secure the adoption of some plan here, that would settle our difficulties and avert from our beloved country the evils with which she is now threatened.

Sir, there has not one moment passed since I came here, during which I have not felt a deep and overpowering sense of the grave responsibility which rests upon myself and the other members of this Conference. I am accustomed to the trials, vexations, cares, and responsibilities of business; I know how to meet and grapple with them calmly. But I do not feel so here. My days are anxious and excited—my nights are wakeful and sleepless. In all the weary watches of last night, I could not close my eyes in slumber. The reason was, because I saw from a point of view which you do not, the certain and inevitable ruin that is threatening the business, commercial interests of this country, and which is sure to fall with crushing force upon those interests, unless we come to some arrangement here.

I speak to you now as a business man—as a merchant of New York, the commercial metropolis of the nation. I am no politician, I have no interest except such as is common to the people. But let me assure you, that even I can scarcely realize, much less describe, the stagnation whhic has now settled upon the business and commerce of that great city, caused solely by the unsettled and uncertain condition of the questions which we are endeavoring to arrange and settle here.

I tell you what I do not get from second hands, but what I know myself, when I assure you that had not Divine Providence poured out its blessings upon the great West in an abundant harvest, and at the same time opened a new market for that harvest in foreign lands, bringing it through New York in its transit, our city would now present the silence and the quiet of the Sabbath day. Why is this? It is because we, who have lived together in harmony with each other, a powerful and a happy people, are breaking up—are preparing to separate and go out from one another!

The merchants of our great commercial cities of Baltimore, Philadelphia, New York, and Boston, are not listless or unenterprising men. They are accustomed to the interests, the bustle, the excitement of business. They have heretofore seen their stores crowded with buyers. During the day the interiors of their places of business were like busy hives. Not unfrequently have their clerks been obliged to labor all through the night to secure and send off the goods which they had sold to reliable customers during the day. When business is good and driving throughout our commorcial cities, wealth and comfort are secured to merchants and agents engaged in commerce in those cities, and it indicates general prosperity in the country to which the goods purchased are transmitted. It shows a healthy condition of affairs both in city and country.

How stands the matter in those cities to-day? Now, just when the spring trade should be commencing, go to the extensive and magnificent establishments for the sale of goods in any of the cities I have named, where goods are sold which in prosperous times found their way into almost every family to a greater or less amount in this great country. What will you see in those cities now? The heavy stocks of goods imported last autumn, or laid in from our own manufactories, remain undisturbed and untouched upon the shelves. The customers are not there—they have not made their appearance. The few who have come at all, come not as buyers, but as debtors who cannot pay, and whose business is not to make purchases but to arrange for extensions. The merchants, in despair, are poring over their ledgers; checking off the names of their insolvent debtors, a new list of whom comes by each day's mail. Their clerks sit around in idleness reading the newspapers, or thinking mournfully of the wives and children at home, who will go unclad and hungry if they are discharged from their places, as they know they must be, if this condition of things shall continue. All alike, employers and employed, with all dependent upon them, are looking anxiously, and I wish I could say hopefully, to the Congress of the United States, or to this Conference, as the only sources from which help may come.

There are thousands and tens of thousands belonging to these classes all over the country who must have relief, or their ruin is inevitable. And then look at that other class, numerically larger, perhaps, certainly not less worthy of our regard, who are dependent upon these; I mean the mechanics, the day laborers, and those in turn dependent upon them. What are they to do? If some change does not come, if something is not done again to start the wheels of commerce and business, what is to become of them?

13

And look, too, at New England! She has latterly been the workshop of the South and the West. She has furnished their people with her manufactures—they have been her market. An excellent market, too, have they furnished her; she has grown rich through their consumption. How stands the matter with New England to-day? True, some of her shops are running, but many more are still. The noise of the loom, the rattle of the shuttle, have ceased in many of her factories, while others are gradually discharging their operatives and closing their business. But I will pursue this branch of the subject no farther. No one acquainted with the facts, will deny that the whole country is upon the eve of such a financial crisis as it has never seen—that this crisis will come as sure as that the sun will rise, unless we do something to avert it!

What is it that has thus stopped the wheels of manufactures and arrested the ordinary movements of commerce? What is it that has produced this unusual and uncommon stagnation of business? What is it that has driven away from the markets of the North those hitherto so welcome to them? I do not propose to go into the history of these questions. I will not attempt to enlarge upon the answers to them. I can condense the answer into few words. It is because anxiety, distrust, and apprehension, are universally prevailing. Confidence is lost. The North misunderstands the South—the South misunderstands the North. Neither will trust the other, and the consequences to which I have adverted necessarily follow.

I am a merchant. I am unused to public discussions or arguments, but I am a business man, and I take a business view of this subject. I can see as clearly as I can see the sun at noonday the causes of our present embarrassment. I believe I can see equally clear how those causes may be removed.

We have come here for a grand and lofty purpose. What nobler work can engage the mind of a true patriot than that of devising the means of saving his country when it is in peril? That work is ours. In performing it, are we not acting under a grave and solemn responsibility? We are, sir! The *people* will hold us responsible for the manner in which we perform this great trust. I know the people of this country. They value this Union. They will make great sacrifices to save it. They will disregard politics and parties—they will cast platforms to the winds of heaven, before they will place the Union in peril.

The delegates from New England in this Conference seem to be the most obstinate and uncompromising. They aver that they cannot agree to these propositions because their adoption involves a sacrifice of principles—that New England is opposed to slavery, and will not consent to put it into the Constitution, nor to its extension. They say the people hate slavery, and will not for that reason accept these proposals.

I do not believe one word of this. I know the people of New England well; they are true Yankees; they know how to get the dollars, and how to hold on to them when they have got them. They are a shrewd and calculating as well as an enterprising people; they understand their interests and will protect them. They will not sit quietly by and see their property sacrificed or reduced in value. Once show them that it is necessary to adopt these propositions of amendment in order to secure the permanence of the Government, and to keep up the property and other material interests of the country, and they will adopt them readily. You will hear no more said about slavery or platforms. They will never permit this Government, which has contributed so much to their wealth and prosperity, to be sacrificed to a technicality, a chimera. The people of New England know how to take care of themselves. Give them a chance, and they will settle all these points of difference in some peaceful way.

I am not here to argue or discuss constitutional questions. That duty belongs to gentlemen of the legal profession. I have lived under the Constitution. I venerate it and its authors as highly as any man here. But I do not venerate it so highly as to induce me to witness the destruction of the Government rather than see the Constitution amended or improved.

I regret that the gentlemen composing the committee did not approach these questions more in the manner of merchants or commercial men. We would not have sacrificed our principles, but we would have agreed—have brought our minds together as far as we could; we would have left open as few questions as possible. These we would have arranged by mutual concessions.

Mr. President, I speak as a merchant; I have a deep and

abiding interest in my country and its Government. I love my country; my heart is filled with sorrow as I witness the dangers by which it is surrounded. But I came here for *peace*. The country longs for peace; and if these proposals of amendment will give us peace, the prayer of my heart is, that they may be adopted. Believing such will be their effect, I will vote for them. I would like to say much more, but I will not occupy time that is now so valuable. Let us approach these questions in a spirit of conciliation. Above all, let us agree upon something. Let us do the best we can, and then let us go home and ask the people to approve our action. The people will approve it, and their approval will give us *peace!*

Mr. SMITH, of New York:—I did not propose to take any part in this debate. The Conference is made up of men, many of whose names are historical, and are intimately connected with the history of the country. I preferred to leave the whole discussion to them.

But as we are all seeking a common end, there are some views which have occurred to me that I thought should be presented, inasmuch as they appear not to have engaged the attention of others. New York, I am aware, has occupied considerable time, and I owe an apology on her part for trespassing farther upon your time.

We are here in a family meeting. On one side Virginia thought the parent was so ill that the family ought to be called together. I thought yesterday that we were undergoing some family discipline—that New York had in some way disgraced herself, and needed correction. I did not know what she had done; but I supposed the reproof was administered to her in a kindly spirit, though it was uncalled for.

The work proposed to us is, to be sure, a work of conciliation. But call it by whatever name you may, nothing less is proposed than an alteration of the Constitution. When we are asked to alter a Constitution that was made by WASHINGTON and MADISON, under which the country has grown to wealth and happiness, we certainly ought to approach the subject with the utmost deliberation. If we were settling family differences only, we would deliberate.. How much more should we do so when we are dealing with the great principles which uphold our Government!

It is by great principles that nations are governed and their destinies are shaped. The world is governed by ideas and not by material interests. These facts must be kept distinctly in view by those who take upon themselves the business of making constitutions.

It is stated that we are called here to settle the terms upon which certain sectional differences are to be arranged. We ought, then, first to ascertain what is the extent—what the limit of these differences.

In the first place, it is agreed that no constitutional rights have yet been invaded. The occasion for fear is not what *has been*, but what *may be* done. I suppose we are all alike tenacious of our rights, whether we derive them from the Constitution or from any other source. The rights of the State are just as important to New York as to Virginia. But it is said that appearances exist that indicate an intention on our part to interfere with some of the institutions of the South. We ask for the proof. None is forthcoming—nothing but the most vague and indefinite suspicion.

We propose to give the most satisfactory and absolute guarantees on that subject—the subject of interference with Southern institutions—even to put those guarantees into the Constitution. But that is not satisfactory—we are told that we cannot be trusted. I should hope that no Northern State could ever be truthfully required to admit that it had given cause for such an apprehension. But it is evident that this is not the real occasion of calling us together. What, then, is the occasion?

It is said, that certain sectional rights in the Territories must be secured and guaranteed. In that view I desire to call the attention of the Conference to two or three points in the plan of the proposed security.

As I understand the scheme, it is this: It is proposed to divide our present territory by the line of 36° 30′, with a view to have emigration from the free States go north, and from the slave States go south of that line. This is made in connection with a limitation preventing the acquisition of future territory. Now the first thing that impresses me is the objection to placing any such restraints upon emigration.

Mr. CLAY:—I think the gentleman misunderstands the

report. I have seen no proposition that proposes to confine or restrain emigration.

Mr. SMITH:—I concede that there is no express provision restricting emigration, but such I think will be the effect of the amendments.

By the third section, Congress is prohibited, forever, from interfering with the subject of slaves, and the sixth section makes the others, with certain provisions of the Constitution as it now stands, irrepealable and unchangeable. No matter how much the condition of the country may change; no matter if all but the most inconsiderable fraction of the people may desire to change them; these propositions must stand as long as this country stands, a part of its fundamental law.

These are the general provisions which the scheme contains. It is offered as a measure of peace; of conciliation; to calm and quiet the existing excitement.

I think I am right in saying that when you are making a constitution you should consider all the conditions of the people who are to be governed by it; that you should keep in view all sections and opinions. It is my belief that instead of calming the excitement these propositions will aggravate it—will arouse it to a pitch it has never yet attained. I believe this, because the entire proposition goes counter to the fundamental ideas upon which our Government is based.

It proposes to *establish* slavery South. Is not this the first time in the history of the Constitution that it has ever been proposed, by affixing an article to that instrument, to *establish*—to *plant* slavery in territory which was free when it was acquired? The ordinance of 1787 prohibited slavery from going into the territory which was acquired by it.

In similar language the article proposes to abolish slavery in the territory north of the line. It is well to consider what is the legal condition of that territory now. New Mexico and Arizona were free when we first acquired them. Is not this provision wholly unnecessary? Mr. CLAY left such language out of the Missouri Compromise, as he avowed, on the ground that slavery could not legally go into territory free when it was acquired, without the aid of affirmative legislation. Previous and up to the year 1850, there was no difference of opinion among lawyers on this question. All agreed with Mr. CLAY.

Now, slavery has gone into a portion of this territory; violently too; without such legislation. Limits are prescribed to it, it is true, but *it is there*, and in this way. *That* is the *status* which is to be recognized, constitutionalized by these articles. I am áware that there is a law of the territory that authorizes slavery, but slavery went there without law, in spite of the opinions and opposition of Mr. CLAY.

This is shown by the debate of 1850. It is proposed now to convert the territory south of the line of 36° 30′ into slave territory, and to make that conversion irrevocable. Suppose these propositions had been applied at the moment the territory was acquired. Then certainly slavery would have been carried there by force of these articles alone. The principle would have been the same; one case being no stronger than the other.

Mr. PRESIDENT, I shall not enter into any discussion of the merits or demerits of the question in any other than its political aspects. I have nothing to say respecting the morals of slavery. If there is virtue in the institution, you have the credit of it; if there is sin, you must answer for it. And here let me say that you discuss the moral aspect of slavery much more than we do. We hold it to be strictly a State institution. So long as it is kept there, we have nothing to do with it. It is only when it thrusts itself outside of State limits, and seeks to acquire power and strength by spreading itself over new ground, that we insist upon our objections.

Whatever the consequences may be, we should not conceal from each other the true condition of public opinion in our respective sections. A correct knowledge of this is essential and indispensable. It is in view of this opinion that our proposals should be framed, if they are ever to be adopted. The settled convictions of a people formed upon mature examination and experience, cannot be easily changed. This should be understood at the outset.

Now, I respectfully submit that no sentiment, no opinion ever took a firmer hold of the Northern mind—ever struck more deeply into it—ever became more pervading, or was ever adopted after maturer consideration, than this: That it is impolitic and wrong to convert free territory into slave territory. With such convictions the North will never consent to such conversion. Never! never!

This was the view of Mr. Clay. His opinion always had great weight at the North. Mr. Clayton, of Delaware, declared to the same purpose, and avowed that Northern men could not be expected to consent to this. We, at least, know how this opinion is consecrated in the hearts of the people of the North, and how idle it is for statesmen to run counter to it.

We are told by the gentleman from Maryland, that all the South wants is to have the force of the decision of the Supreme Court acknowledged as to that part of the territory south of the line, in consideration of which the South will yield what she gains by that decision in the territory north; and also that we must do this, or the slave States will be driven to join those States that have seceded. Now, it is due to frankness to say, that the North does not acquiesce in that statement; that the point as made by the gentleman from Maryland, has been *decided* by the Supreme Court. We know that the Chief Justice of that court has expressed his own opinion that way; but we don't know that it has been *decided* by that court. But if it has been so decided, the very ground of the decision is a misapprehension. If I rightly understand the language of Chief Justice Taney, he insists that the Constitution expressly affirms the right of property in slaves. I think it does not. The North thinks it does not.

Mr. Smith then proceeded to discuss the facts in the Dred Scott case, and the various opinions declared by the judges, showing that the decision did not extend so far as claimed by Mr. Johnson, and that the question of the *right* to hold slaves in the Territories was not presented by the record in that case.

Mr. WICKLIFFE:—There were two questions involved in the Dred Scott case. One was, the authority of Scott to sue; the other was, upon the constitutionality of the Missouri Compromise. Both these were decided in that case, and both were decided by the Supreme Court years ago.

Mr. SMITH:—I am aware of the views taken by the gentleman from Kentucky. I am stating as a matter of fact how this decision is regarded by a large portion of the people of the

North. I am aware that the Southern construction of the decision is different, and some at the North concur in it. I am trying to see how the majority propositions will suit the people who agree with the Northern view.

I understand it is claimed that the court decided that slaves were property, and that the Constitution did not permit any restraint to be laid upon the owners of that property in the Territories. Yes, the court did decide that the owner had the right to take his slaves into the Territory and hold them there; and to that extent they were property. It is a prevalent idea at the North that the Southern construction of this decision is not fair, and that it would be dangerous to adopt it.

We do not subscribe to the doctrine that the Constitution expressly affirms the right of property in slaves. We may be wrong; it may be a mere misapprehension. But with their present opinions, the people of the North will hesitate long before they make this express affirmation a part of the organic *law*.

Again; if the Constitution affirms this right, and was understood to do so by its framers, what was the need of the rendition clause? The Constitution is the supreme law in the free States as well as in the slave States. Under this construction the rights of the owner could have been enforced like any other right of property in the courts of law, without any provision for the rendition of slaves.

These are some of the opinions that are entertained at the North. They may be right or they may be wrong, but they have been deliberately adopted, and they prevail extensively. They cannot be changed by our action here. In all we do they must be respected. They are *constitutionally* entertained.

This proposition to carry slavery into the Territories, opens the discussion of the merits of that institution. Gentlemen say they wish to stop the discussion; that there has been too much of it already; that such a discussion would be especially unfortunate now. I do not propose to enter upon it here. But I desire to know in what manner you could more effectually invite discussion than by placing your proposed amendments before the people?

You must not forget that the people of the North believe

slavery is both a moral and a political evil. They recognize the right of the States to have it, to regulate it as they please, without interference, direct or indirect; but when it is proposed to extend it into territory where it did not before exist, it becomes a political question, in which they are interested, in which they have a right to interfere, and in which they will interfere. Such an attempt they consider it their duty to resist by all constitutional means.

The establishing of slavery in the Territories is the practical exclusion of free labor in them. True, there is no direct provision for the exclusion of free labor in your propositions, but such will certainly be their effect. I appeal to gentlemen from the South to say from their own experience whether free labor *can* be employed side by side with slave labor. This presents another consideration. You of the South ask us to guarantee a right which you say is very important and very dear to you. You ask that your children may enter into and possess these new Territories. We know it. But the North asks the same privilege. We want our children to go there, and live on the labor of their own free hands. They are excluded if slavery goes there before us.

Mr. President, the people of the North do understand that we are in a contest—a great and important contest. Yet it is one that can be carried on without trampling upon each other's rights—without attempting to secure any unfair advantage. That is the way the North proposes to carry on this contest in relation to the *extension* of slavery. This contest is between the owners of slaves on the one side, and all the *free men* of this great nation on the other.

There is another fact that should be kept in view. The Territories are the property not of the individual States, but of the General Government. They are held by the Government in trust, I grant. But in trust for whom? For the whole *people* of the Union; not in trust for thirty-four distinct States. The idea that these Territories are subject to partition—that South Carolina has the right to demand her thirty-fourth part of them in severalty, is one that by the North cannot be entertained. It is this idea which has produced that other more mischievous one—that an equilibrium must be maintained between the free and the slave States; in other words, between freedom and slavery.

Where did this idea creep into the Constitution? It never has found, and it never will find, favor with the people of the North.

We may talk around this question—we may discuss its incidents, its history, and its effects, as much and as long as we please. And after all is said—disguise it as we may—it is a contest between the great opposing elements of civilization—whether the country shall be possessed and developed and ruled by the labor of slaves or of freemen.

Leave it where it is, and all is well. We can live in peace while it is a State institution; extend it, and who can answer for the consequences? Leave it where it is! I humbly suggest that in that direction lays the only path of peace. So long as the Territories are common property, so long will the people insist upon protecting their interests in them. In a Government like ours, conflicts will ensue. The Constitution provides the proper and peaceful way of settling them; and it is not by a partition of every subject in which a mutual interest exists.

Mr. SEDDON:—Does the gentleman consider this a nation, or a federal union of States?

Mr. SMITH:—If I did not consider this a nation I should certainly not be here.

Mr. SEDDON:—Is not the whole machinery of the Government federative? Is not its whole action that of a confederation? Is not the recent election of Mr. LINCOLN a proof of the fact? He was elected by less than a majority of the people.

Mr. SMITH:—In all the action of the Government with other governments, we are a nation as much as France or England. In every thing pertaining to the acquisition of territory we are a nation. The rights of the States are preserved in the Constitution, I admit, but their power is to be exercised subject to the powers reserved by the Constitution to the General Government. In all that respects these powers the Government is supreme.

I have only sought to state some of the opinions which are conscientiously entertained at the North upon subjects connected with these propositions. They *are* entertained there, and they must be respected by the Conference.

This doctrine of the preservation of the balance of power is a new doctrine. It was unknown to the framers of our Constitution. In my opinion it is a most mischievous doctrine to the country, and can only produce the most pernicious results. It is closely akin to the doctrine once broached in the Senate of a *duality* of the Executive, which, extended, would require a President for every sectional interest. Such ideas were never popular at the North. I do not think they would operate very well in practice at the South.

Mr. CLEVELAND:—Will the gentleman give way for a motion to adjourn?

Mr. SMITH:—Certainly.

On motion of Mr. CLEVELAND the Conference adjourned to ten o'clock to-morrow.

FOURTEENTH DAY.

WASHINGTON, THURSDAY, *February 21st*, 1861.

THE Conference was called to order by the President, at ten o'clock and fifteen minutes A.M., and prayer was offered by Rev. Dr. STOCKTON.

The Journal of yesterday was read and approved.

Mr. WICKLIFFE:—As I stated yesterday, I now wish to call up my resolutions relating to the termination of the debate, and to have a vote taken upon them.

Mr. CHASE:—Will Governor WICKLIFFE permit me to make a formal motion, which cannot give rise to discussion? It is this: The resolutions passed by the Legislature of Ohio, under which myself and my colleagues hold our seats, make it my duty to lay before the Conference the resolves I now offer. I ask to have them read, laid upon the table, and printed.

The resolutions were read, and the motion of Mr. CHASE concurred in.

The resolutions are as follow:—

Resolved, That it is inexpedient to proceed to final action on the grave and important matters involved in the resolutions of the State of Virginia, in compliance with which this Convention has assembled, and in the several reports of the majority and minority of the committee to which said resolutions were referred, until opportunity has been given to all of the States to participate in deliberation and action under them, and ample time has been allowed for such deliberation and action.

Resolved, therefore, That this Convention adjourn to meet in the city of Washington, on the 4th day of April next; and that the President be requested to address a letter to the Governors of the several States not now represented in this body, urging the appointment and attendance of Commissioners.

Mr. EWING :—I wish to state here that I do not concur in these resolutions.

Mr. WICKLIFFE :—I now offer two resolutions, one providing that debate shall cease upon the report of the committee, at 10 o'clock to-morrow. The other, that five minutes shall be allowed to the mover of an amendment to explain it, with five minutes to the committee to reply. Upon reflection, I will offer a third: That a motion to strike out and insert shall not be divided. If desired, a vote may be taken on the resolutions separately, as I wish to have each stand upon its own merits. I will not discuss these resolutions, for I think all must be impressed with the necessity for passing them now.

The resolutions were as follow :—

Resolved, 1st, That at 10 o'clock, the 22d February, 1861, all debate upon the report of the Committee of one from each State shall cease, and the Convention will proceed to vote, and continue to vote until the whole subject shall have been disposed of.

2d. If an amendment be offered by the Commissioners of any State, or the minority of such Commissioners, five minutes is allowed for explanation, and the like time is allowed to the committee to resist the amendment, if they desire to do so; and the mover of the amendment, or any member of the same State, may have five minutes for reply.

3d. A motion to strike out and insert shall not be divided.

Mr. CHITTENDEN :—I shall not debate these resolutions. As I am engaged in taking notes of the discussion, I cannot enter into a contest for the floor, and I would not if I could. My State has not occupied a moment of time on the general subject, nor are her delegates very anxious to address the Convention at all.

Whether the Conference will give one of us a few minutes or not, is simply a question of policy, of which I am not a disinterested judge. It is possible that some suggestions might be made which would be worthy of attention.

Mr. GOODRICH :—I move to amend by inserting Saturday, instead of to-morrow, in the first resolution.

Mr. RANDOLPH :—There is force in the remark of the gentleman from Vermont. No State should be cut off. I suggest that the States whose delegates have not addressed the Conference, should have the preference.

Mr. JOHNSON, of Missouri :—I represent a youthful State.

She is not the daughter of any particular State or section, but of the Union. We Missourians love the Union, but we have fully arrived at the conclusion that the time has come when something must be done to prevent our entire separation. We have hitherto remained silent. We came here to preserve the Union. Not that we love the Union less, but we love our rights more. We love our rights more than the Union, our property, or our lives. We desire to come to a speedy adjustment. Ten days of Congress only remain. It will be difficult even to introduce our propositions, still more to get them considered. I sustain the motion of the gentleman from Kentucky; and Missouri will vote for it.

Mr. WICKLIFFE:—I will make the proposition as acceptable as possible. I will insert one o'clock instead of ten.

Exclamations were heard from several members of, "Let us agree," and the question being taken on the first resolution as amended, it was adopted.

Mr. BACKUS:—I move to insert in the second resolution, ten minutes instead of five, wherever the word occurs. That time is none too long to state the purpose of an amendment properly.

Mr. NOYES:—Is this resolution designed to exclude all discussion upon an amendment, except by the member moving it and the committee?

Mr. WICKLIFFE:—No! Such is not the intention. Any one can speak five minutes. I rely on our sense of propriety not to abuse this construction of the resolution.

The amendment of Mr. BACKUS was decided in the negative by a vote *viva voce*.

The resolution was then adopted, together with the resolution relating to motions to strike out and insert.

Mr. BROWNE:—I move that when the Convention adjourn, it adjourn to meet at half-past seven o'clock this evening.

Mr. CHASE:—I hope the Conference will not hold night sessions. Our day sessions are protracted and very laborious. I agree with Commodore STOCKTON, that night sessions are dangerous.

Mr. MOREHEAD, of Kentucky:—I do not agree with Mr. CHASE. I have particularly observed the demeanor of all the gentlemen in the Conference, and know that they are as well fitted for business at five o'clock in the afternoon as at ten o'clock in the morning.

A vote by the States was called for, which resulted as follows:

Ayes:—Delaware, Illinois, Kentucky, Maryland, Missouri, New Jersey, New York, North Carolina, New Hampshire, Pennsylvania, Rhode Island, Tennessee, and Virginia—13.

Noes:—Connecticut, Indiana, Iowa, Maine, Massachusetts, Ohio, and Vermont—7.

Mr. WILMOT:—In pursuance of the instructions of the Legislature of Pennsylvania, I offer the following. I wish to have it laid on the table, and printed, that I may move it as an amendment to the committee's report at the proper time.

The motion of Mr. Wilmot was agreed to, and the amendment is as follows:

"And Congress shall further provide by law, that the United States shall make full compensation to a citizen of any State, who in any other State shall suffer, by reason of violence or intimidation from mobs and riotous assemblies, in his person or property, or in deprivation, by violence, of his rights secured by this Constitution."

Mr. DENT:—I ask that the following may be adopted as an additional rule:

"When the vote on any question is taken by States, any Commissioner dissenting from the vote of his State, may have his dissent entered on the Journal."

Mr. CHASE:—I suggest whether it would not be better to call the yeas and nays, on the motion of any Commissioner. I have heretofore introduced a resolution to that effect, which, with the gentleman's permission, I will now call up.

Mr. DENT:—I won't insist.

Mr. Chase's resolution was taken up as follows:

"The yeas and nays of the Commissioner of each State, upon any question, shall be entered upon the Journal when it is desired by any Commissioner, and the vote of each State shall be determined by the majority of Commissioners present from each State."

Mr. GUTHRIE:—I hope the gentleman will waive the first part of the resolution. I think it is the best way not to disclose our divisions any farther than is indispensably necessary.

Mr. CHASE:—I copied the rule *verbatim* from the one

adopted by the Congress of the Confederation. I think it right and fair. But I have no objection to modifying it, so as to have the yeas and nays called on the motion of any entire delegation.

Mr. DENT:—I did not withdraw my motion. I think it will accomplish all we need. It will be taken, of course, that those who do not dissent vote with the delegation.

Mr. REID:—I think it is entirely too late to talk about saving time. How long will it take to have the names of dissenting delegates called? For one, I desire to exercise my rights under the authority of the State I represent. I will not consent to waive them. When the vote of my State is cast, I wish to have the record show who is responsible for it.

The question was taken on the resolution offered by Mr. CHASE, and it was rejected, and the additional rule proposed by Mr. DENT was adopted.

Mr. COALTER:—I offer the following, which I shall move as an amendment to the report. I ask that it be laid on the table, and printed:

"The term of office of all Presidents and Vice-Presidents of the United States, hereafter elected, shall be six years; and any person once elected to either of said offices, shall ever after be ineligible to the same office."

The above motion to lay on the table and print was agreed to.

Mr. BRONSON:—I also have an amendment, of which I ask to have the same disposition made. It is as follows:

"Congress shall have no power to legislate in respect to persons held to service or labor in any case, except to provide for the rendition of fugitives from such service or labor, and to suppress the foreign slave trade; and the existing *status* or condition of all the Territories of the United States, in respect to persons held to service or labor, shall remain unchanged during their territorial condition; and whenever any Territory, with suitable boundaries, shall contain the population requisite for a representative in Congress, according to the then federal ratio of representation, it shall be entitled to admission into the Union on an equal footing with the original States, with or without persons held to service or labor, as the Constitution of such new State may prescribe."

Mr. BRONSON'S motion was agreed to.

Mr GUTHRIE:—I call for the order of the day.

The PRESIDENT:—The order of the day is called for, and the gentleman from New York has the floor.

Mr. SMITH:—At the adjournment yesterday, I had proceeded to state two or three grounds upon which I think the proposals of amendment to the Constitution reported by the majority of the committee would be unacceptable to the North, and I had also stated some special objections to action in this way and at the present time.

The next consideration to which I would invite attention is this: Is it necessary or wise for the Conference, composed as it is of friends of the Union, or is it *expedient* thus to encounter the settled sentiments and convictions of the people of so large a section of the country? It is not necessary, for various reasons. This territorial question is, after all, a question to be looked at in a prospective view. Why is it necessary to disturb the Constitution by inserting such a provision as you propose? Why is it necessary for gentlemen from the South to have it in, in order to enable them to stand with their people at home?

Slavery is now in New Mexico. That must be acknowledged as a fact. The South think it rightfully there—the North believe it is there wrongfully. But its existence in the territories is a fact nevertheless. President LINCOLN cannot help it if he would. The Supreme Court will affirm its rightful existence there, whenever the question comes before that body. That Court cannot be changed before these territories are admitted as States, if the disposition exists to change it. You claim that the question is already decided. How, then, can it be important to you to press the adoption of these sections as a part of the Constitution? My judgment is, that it is best to leave this subject alone—that that is the true way to save the Union.

Gentlemen of the South, remember that if you must stand at home with your people, so also must we. There is a *North* as well as a *South!*—a northern people as well as southern people. You press us hard on these subjects. But can men who are rational ask us to abandon our own people, to go counter to their convictions and sentiments? We cannot do it! You would not respect us if we did! I am very sure that if this Conference is to attain any beneficial result, it must abandon all idea of coercion or intimidation as applied to the friends of the Union.

It is said we are contending for a party platform—that we are letting party stand between us and the Union. I could trample parties and platforms under foot to preserve the Union, but I cannot understand how honest men can abandon principles because a party has adopted them into its platform. Do not tell us that by adhering to the Union and the Constitution, we are simply adhering to a party platform. Our principles are at least as dear to us, as yours are to you; you must not expect us to sacrifice them either to promote our own material interests or to promote yours.

Let us then sink the question of slavery in the Territories. Let the courts take care of it if need be, or let it be dealt with when it properly comes up. "Sufficient unto the day is the evil thereof." In that direction lays the path of peace.

But perhaps it may be suggested that such a course would really leave no plan to be adopted. Perhaps so. Is it, then, not true that we are having all this trouble over a contingency that may or may not arise? That the Constitution is sufficient for all purposes but this, you aver; and yet you say in the same breath that the Court has settled this question entirely and finally in your favor. Why not be satisfied, then, with the settlement? Can you make it more of a finality in the way you propose? No, gentlemen; believe me when I tell you that the true remedy does not consist in endeavoring to humiliate the people of one section for the benefit of another. Remember we are dealing with the *American* people; I would not throw the Constitution into the vortex of disunion that is opening before us; I would preserve it rather as a rock on which we can all safely stand. Do not throw away the compass by which alone we can safely be guided!

If I were to suggest a suitable remedy, what I think a wise plan, it would be the one adopted on a similar occasion, when one of the States set itself up in opposition to the General Government, with such very beneficial results; and that would be, to have the Government appeal to the people for support—to throw itself into the arms of the people. The result then has become historical. It is remembered with pride and pleasure by all. I would have a similar course pursued now. The result would be equally grand, equally gratifying. It would rally every patriot, every friend of the Union from every section, to its support. You, gentlemen of the South, now friends of the Union, still give it the strength of your support, the favor of your countenance, and you shall be supported and sustained as you can be in no other way. You shall have the support of the power of the Government and of every friend of the Union in the country.

You remember how those patriotic statesmen, CLAY and WEBSTER—differing from the Executive, opposing his election with all the strength of their gigantic intellects—when the authority of the Government was questioned, and South Carolina, under the lead of Mr. CALHOUN, undertook to set herself up in opposition to it—how they waived all former differences, and instead of encouraging secession by their delay and timidity, without asking for new guarantees or for amendments of the Constitution, came voluntarily and earnestly to the support of the Executive and the administration, because the Executive was right, and was the chosen instrument of the people to preserve the integrity of the Union.

Mr. BARRINGER:—If the gentleman will excuse me, I will state that the course of the Executive against South Carolina was universally acquiesced in except in that State. And yet the opinion that President JACKSON far exceeded his powers, was equally unanimous. That precedent has been greatly misinterpreted.

Mr. SMITH:—I thank the gentleman from North Carolina. He entertains his opinions, I do mine, as to what then saved the Union. I should not probably be able to make him think with me; but I feel sure that the idea prevails quite extensively, that South Carolina returned to the path of duty then, because the power of the Government was wielded by an honest and energetic Executive. She came to the conclusion that any other course would probably be attended with danger.

Our present differences had no very remote origin. They belong to our own generation, and we ought to be compelled to deal with them. I think the so-called compromise of 1850 was the cause of all our troubles—that instead of saving the country it brought it into greater danger than it ever was before.

Mr. BARRINGER:—I wish to make a suggestion on that point.

Mr. SMITH:—I hope the gentleman will not forget that he will have a full opportunity to answer me. I am nearly through, and generally no good comes of interruptions. They only consume time.

I was about to say, that I do not propose to go into the question of who was to blame for that repeal. I agree with gentlemen from the South, that there is no profit now in discussing the origin of our troubles—in inquiring who set the house on fire before we put on the water.

Mr. CLAY:—Does the gentleman do justice to Mr. CLAY, when at one moment he says that Mr. CLAY held up the arms of the administration, strengthened the Executive, and aided the Government in putting down secession, and in the next, states that the compromise of 1850 was the cause of all our troubles, when it is well known that Mr. CLAY strongly favored that compromise?

Mr. SMITH:—When I speak of the unhappy effect of the compromise measures of 1850, I ascribe no wrong motives to Mr. CLAY or any one else. If he approved that compromise, I have no doubt he did it in the full belief that it would be beneficial to the country. Experience has shown that he was mistaken. Saying this is doing no injustice to Mr. CLAY. I spoke only of effects. I spoke of the zeal and the energy with which the patriots and eminent statesmen of all parties of this country have been accustomed to come forward and sustain the administration when any necessity existed for doing so. Now let this Conference—let all true friends of the Union everywhere, with one voice, without attempting to place any section or any man in a false or disagreeable position, unite in one determined effort in behalf of the Union, and in an attempt to bring the rash and dangerous men who would seek the destruction of the Government back to a sense of duty. Let us address the country, let us show that we are devoted to the Union, far beyond any considerations of party or self; let us invoke the aid of all true and patriotic men; let us ask them to lay aside for the time all other considerations, and give themselves for the present to the country! The spirit of the old time is yet alive. We can call it out in more than its old strength and vigor, and it will save the country. Our private interests may suffer, but the great interests of the Union will be strengthened and preserved, and the Constitution, which has been our pride and strength, will not be dragged down into the great whirlpool of disunion. I appeal to the venerable and able men around me, who bear historic names—who have been themselves long connected with the Union and its Government, to join us in our struggle to save the Constitution.

The views I have expressed may be chimerical. I have advanced them with no little diffidence, but I felt called upon to state them in the discharge of a duty I owe to a people who love and will make great sacrifices to save the Constitution and the Union.

A majority vote, one way or the other here, would be of little consequence. It would carry no weight with it. But if the members of this Conference would all unite in such an appeal to the country, the response would be instantaneous and effective. The heart of the country is loyal; the heart of the South is loyal, I believe. We have abundant evidence that it is not too late to rely upon the Union men in Missouri and Tennessee!

Mr. CARUTHERS:—The vote of Tennessee is entirely misunderstood.

Mr. SMITH:—Perhaps so. I have no acquaintance with the people of Tennessee. But I will not occupy the time of the Conference farther. I have spoken plainly, but I have spoken what I believe to be the honest convictions of a large majority of the people of this Union. Once more I say, let us not destroy the Constitution!

Mr. CLEVELAND:—I have not got up to make a speech. We have had too much speech-making here. It may be very well for gentlemen to get up and make long arguments and eloquent appeals, and show their abilities and powers, but it all does no sort of good—nobody is benefited, and no opinions are changed. I shall take no such course. I want to see whether this little handful of men who meet every day in this hall, cannot get together and fix up this matter which has been so much talked about. Let us pay no attention to the great men or the politicians. They have interests of their own. Some of them have interests which are superior to those of their country.

In the common affairs of life there are always a great many differences of opinion. Some treat these differences one way—some another. Foolish men go to law, and always come out worse off than when they started. Sensible men get together, and talk matters over; one gives up a little, the other gives up a little, and finally they get together. Now, friends, that is just what I want to see done here.

We are all friends—friends of the Union and of each other. Nobody wants to give up the Union, or hurt Mr. LINCOLN. The South has got frightened—not exactly frightened, but she thinks the Republicans, since they have got the power, are going to trample upon her rights. She wants the North to agree not to do so. Now I should like to know what objection there was to that? Who is afraid to do that? If we could go to work at this thing like sensible men, we could settle the whole matter in two hours.

Now about these propositions. I do not see any thing alarming in them. I have not set to work to pick flaws in them. Leave that to the lawyers. I don't care much about them, nor does the North care about them. If the South will take them and be satisfied—if they will stop this clamor about slavery and slavery extension, I think she had better have them. For one, I am sick of the whole subject.

Let us then go about the work like sensible men; let us stop making long speeches and picking flaws in each other. It is a matter of business, and pretty important business. Let us consider it as such, and from this moment let us throw aside all feeling, and set about coming to some understanding. We can do it to-day as well as next week. I do not know that these propositions are the best that can be made; but if they are not, let us talk the matter over like good Union men, and see what is best. When we can find that out, let us agree. If we stay here and make speeches until doomsday, we shall be no better off. I am for action, and coming to an immediate decision.

Mr. COALTER:—If the vote of Missouri is to be taken as an evidence of her devotion to the Union, it must also be understood with this qualification: Her interests and her sympathies unite her closely with the South. She feels, in common with others, her share of anxiety for the future. She is devoted to the Union, and at the same time she insists that it is fair and right that these guarantees should be given.

It has been distinctly avowed on this floor that the people of certain sections of the North *abhor* slavery. Ought we not to be distrustful when a party entertaining such sentiments comes into supreme power? If Massachusetts abhors *slavery*, how long will it be before she will abhor *slaveholders?*

Ignorance is the source of all our difficulties. The people of the North know little of the condition of the negro in a state of slavery. We know that the four millions of blacks in the South are better off in all respects than any similar number of laborers anywhere.

But I rise only to correct a false impression in regard to Missouri. I have only besides to express my full conviction that if the North will not give us these guarantees, we are henceforth a divided people.

Mr. GOODRICH:—Mr. President, the object of this Convention, assembled on the call or invitation of Virginia, is, as set forth in the preamble and resolutions of her General Assembly,

> "To restore the Union and Constitution in the spirit in which they were established by the fathers of the Republic;" or, as otherwise expressed, "to adjust the present unhappy controversies in the spirit in which the Constitution was originally made, and consistently with its principles."

This agrees, in substance, with the purpose of the Republican party, which, in the words of the Philadelphia platform, is declared to be that of "restoring the action of the Federal Government to the principles of WASHINGTON and JEFFERSON."

Virginia announces to the other States that she "is desirous of employing every reasonable means," and is "willing to unite" with them "in an earnest effort" for the accomplishment of this common end and object of that State and the Republican party; and she is moved to make this her "final effort," by "the deliberate opinion of her General Assembly, that unless the unhappy controversy which now divides the States of this Confederacy shall be satisfactorily adjusted, a permanent dissolution of the Union is inevitable," and by a desire to "avert so dire a calamity."

Massachusetts, equally willing to unite with the other States in an earnest effort to further the same end, accepted the invitation of Virginia, and sent Commissioners here to represent her.

The honorable Chairman (Mr. GUTHRIE) of the committee to report a plan of adjustment, in his opening speech, advocated with earnestness and eloquence a restoration of the Constitution to the principles of the fathers. The distinguished gentleman

(Mr. RIVES) from Virginia demands a "restoration of the Constitution to the landmarks of our fathers," and his colleague (Mr. SEDDON) urges a return to the "policy of our fathers in 1787."

This assumes that we have departed from the principles and landmarks of our fathers, and from the policy of 1787. The call of the Convention assumes this; the platform of the Republican party assumes it, and the gentlemen whose remarks I have quoted assume it, and it is true.

The particular object of a return to the principles and landmarks of the policy of 1787, as stated in the preamble and resolutions of the General Assembly of Virginia, is, "to afford to the people of the slaveholding States adequate guarantees for the security of their rights." This implies that such a return will afford these adequate guarantees. I agree that it will; and I am ready, and Massachusetts is ready, to adjust this unhappy controversy, and to give the guarantees demanded in exactly this way.

Stated in these general terms, there is a perfect agreement between us. But we find a wide difference when we go one step farther, and learn precisely what Virginia claims would be a restoration of the Constitution to the principles of the fathers, and a return to the policy of 1787. This she has told us in one of the resolutions sent out with the call for this Convention. That resolution is as follows:

"*Resolved*, That in the opinion of the General Assembly of Virginia, the propositions embraced in the resolutions presented to the Senate of the United States by Hon. JOHN J. CRITTENDEN, so modified as that the first article proposed as an amendment to the Constitution of the United States shall apply to all the territory of the United States, now held or hereafter acquired south of latitude 36° 30′, and provide that slavery of the African race shall be effectually protected as property therein during the continuance of the territorial government, and the fourth article shall secure to the owners of slaves the right of transit with their slaves between and through the non-slaveholding States and territories, constitute the basis of such an adjustment of the unhappy controversy which now divides the States of this Confederacy, as would be accepted by the people of this Commonwealth."

It was in reference to these propositions that the gentleman (Mr. SEDDON) from Virginia, has asked us the question, "Are we not entitled to these added guarantees according to the spirit of the compact of our fathers?"

The true answer to this question is the pivot on which this whole controversy must turn. If the slave States are not entitled to these added guarantees, "according to the spirit of the compact of our fathers," then Virginia, as I understand her Commissioners, and the resolutions of her General Assembly, does not claim them. She stands upon her rights according to that compact. And all such rights Massachusetts is ready to accord to her, fairly and fully.

By the spirit of the compact of our fathers is meant, the Constitution as they understood it, and as the people of that day understood it. And this is what is meant by the "landmarks of the fathers." All admit that the Federal Government should be administered now, as it was administered by its framers. This is what gentlemen from the slave States, in giving utterance to their intense devotion to the Union, say.

Then, what is the Constitution, as understood by those who framed it? What does it mean when interpreted by the light of the policy of 1787? and what is the spirit of the compact which they made? This is the question we are called to consider. In my remarks I do not mean to wander from it.

So far as the Constitution touches the question out of which the present unhappy controversy has arisen, I say it means this: That slavery, as it existed or might exist within the limits of the original States, should not be interfered with to the injury of the lawful rights of slaveholders under State authority; on the contrary, that it should have the right of recaption, and a qualified protection; but that outside of those limits, otherwise than in this right of recaption, it should never exist, neither in the territories nor in the new States.

And let me say here, that when I speak of the original States, I mean the territory of those States as then bounded. Alabama and Mississippi belonged to Georgia, Tennessee belonged to North Carolina, Kentucky belonged to Virginia, Vermont belonged to New York, and Maine belonged to Massachusetts, and were parts of the thirteen original States, at the time the Constitution was adopted. When, therefore, I speak of territory outside the original States, I do not refer to territory within any of the States named.

Mr. BOUTWELL:—I trust my colleague does not claim to

speak for Massachusetts, when he denies the right of any State of this Union to establish and maintain slavery within its jurisdiction, or to prohibit it altogether, according to its discretion. This right was reserved to the States; and States in this Union, whether original or new, stand on a footing of perfect equality.

Mr. GOODRICH:—I certainly do not claim to speak for Massachusetts, though I believe the opinion of the great majority of her people agrees with my own on this subject. However, what I claim is, that Ohio and the other States of the northwestern territory have no constitutional power to legalize slavery within their limits; that they were admitted into the Union without any such power, and that every other new State formed from territory outside the limits of the original States, according to the "spirit of the compact of our fathers," should have been admitted without that power, or the right to acquire it. This I will now proceed to show.

On the first day of March, 1784, the northwest territory, constituting the present States of Ohio, Indiana, Illinois, Michigan, and Wisconsin, was ceded by Virginia to the United States. The jurisdiction of the United States was then exclusive and paramount, or soon became so—such other States as had claimed any right of jurisdiction having ceded it. The cession of Virginia was made by THOMAS JEFFERSON, SAMUEL HARDY, ARTHUR LEE, and JAMES MONROE, who were delegates in Congress from that State, and had been appointed Commissioners for this purpose. On the same day the cession was made, Mr. JEFFERSON, in behalf of a committee, reported a plan for temporary governments in the United States territory then and afterwards to be ceded, and for forming therein permanent governments.

That plan provided, "that so much of the territory ceded, or to be ceded, by individual States to the United States, shall be divided into distinct States." It is obvious that this plan contemplated the possession of territory in no other way than by cession from the States. It was expected that Georgia and North Carolina would cede their western lands, now the States of Alabama, Mississippi, and Tennessee, as they did some years later; and Mr. JEFFERSON's plan was intended to embrace those lands or territories to be ceded. Consequently, the following provisions, which were part of the plan reported, were intended by him to apply to Alabama, Mississippi, and Tennessee, viz.:

"After the year 1800 of the Christian era, there shall be neither slavery nor involuntary servitude in the said States, otherwise that in the punishment of crimes."

Here the States were evidently those to be formed in United States territory. And farther on in the plan it is stated,

"That the preceding articles shall be formed into a charter of compact, and shall stand as fundamental Constitutions between the thirteen original States, and each of the several States now newly described, unalterable * * * but by the joint consent of the United States in Congress assembled, and of the particular State within which such alteration is proposed to be made."

This was a proposition to exclude slavery forever after 1800, not only from the territories which had been, and might afterwards be, ceded, but from the States to be formed in them, and to make it a fundamental Constitution between the original States and each new State. It excited a short discussion, and was postponed from time to time to the 19th of April, when Mr. SPEIGHT, of North Carolina, moved to strike it out. The motion was seconded by Mr. REED, of South Carolina. The vote by States, on the motion to strike out, was:

YEAS.—Maryland, Virginia, and South Carolina—3.

NAYS.—New Hampshire, Massachusetts, Rhode Island, Connecticut, New York, and Pennsylvania—6.

This was under the Confederation articles, which provided that the vote on all questions should be taken by States, each State casting one vote; that no proposition could be adopted without the vote of seven States in favor of it, and that the vote of no State could be counted unless two members, at least, were present. As there were but six States in favor of the proposition to prohibit slavery after 1800, it was stricken out.

There was but one member present from New Jersey, and the vote of that State was not counted. The member present voted for Mr. JEFFERSON'S proposition. Another vote from that State would have made the required number, and carried the measure.

In North Carolina, WILLIAMSON voted for prohibition, and SPEIGHT against it. One more vote from that State would have made seven States for the proposition, and it would have been carried.

JEFFERSON voted for his own proposition to prohibit; and if one of the other two members present from Virginia had voted with him, that, too, would have made the required number of seven States.

The vote North and South, by members, was in favor of prohibition: North, 14; South, 2—total, 16. Against prohibition, South, 7.

The majority was more than two-thirds; enough to carry it over an executive veto under the present Constitution, and yet it was defeated. And this vote was given in favor of absolute and unconditional prohibition, and that alone, without the right of reclaiming fugitive slaves, or any proposition, or any expectation to confer it. Under the Confederation, no such right existed, nor was it agreed to till more than three years afterwards, and then with the greatest reluctance, and as a matter of compromise, as I will presently show.

Such was the action of the American Congress in 1784—a unanimous vote from the North, and two in nine from the South—in favor of excluding slavery forever after 1800, in all new States to be formed, in territory ceded or to be ceded, embracing Tennessee, Alabama, and Mississippi, in the extreme South. Nothing can be clearer than that the interdiction was to apply to all such States, and to constitute a fundamental Constitution between them and the original States, unalterable without the consent of Congress. The new State was to be deprived of all power to admit slavery. This proposition was made and voted for by JEFFERSON. But how many votes would such a proposition receive in this Convention? Not many, I fear, even from the free States. My friend and colleague, though strongly anti-slavery, and earnestly devoted to freedom in the Territories, is afraid I shall commit Massachusetts to this old Jeffersonian doctrine of no slavery, and no right to establish it in the new States.

From this time till July, 1787, the question of slavery in the Territories and new States remained open and unsettled. In 1785, RUFUS KING renewed Mr. JEFFERSON's proposition to prohibit, and it was referred to a committee by the vote of eight States; but it never became a law, a few from the South always preventing it.

The Federal Convention to revise the old, or frame a new

Constitution, assembled in Philadelphia on the second Monday of May, 1787. And here let me read a single paragraph from a lecture by Mr. TOOMBS, of Georgia, delivered in Boston in 1856. It is as follows:

"The history of the times and the debates in the Convention which framed the Constitution, show that the whole subject of slavery was much considered by them, and perplexed them in the extreme, and that those provisions which relate to it were earnestly considered by the State Conventions which adopted it. Incipient legislation providing for emancipation had already been adopted by some of the States. Massachusetts had declared that slavery was extinguished by her Bill of Rights. The African slave trade had already been legislated against in many of the States, including Virginia, Maryland, and North Carolina, the largest slaveholding States. The public mind was unquestionably tending toward emancipation. This feeling displayed itself in the South as well as in the North. Some of the present slaveholding States thought that the power to abolish, not only the African slave trade, but slavery in the States, ought to be given to the Federal Government; and that the Constitution did not take this shape, was made one of the most prominent objections to it by LUTHER MARTIN, a distinguished member of the Convention from Maryland; and Mr. MASON, of Virginia, was not far behind him in his emancipation principles. Mr. MADISON sympathized to a great extent. Anti-slavery feelings were extensively indulged in by many members of the Convention, both from the slaveholding and the non-slaveholding States."

Mr. MADISON'S testimony is important here. He was a member of the old Congress in New York, until the assembling of the Constitutional Convention, and took his seat as a member of that body.

The History of the Ordinance of 1787, by Hon. EDWARD COLES, contains the following statement, as made to him by Mr. MADISON:

"The old Congress held its sessions, in 1787, in New York, while at the same time the Convention which framed the Constitution of the United States held its sessions in Philadelphia. Many individuals were members of both bodies, and thus were enabled to know what was passing in each—both sitting with closed doors and in secret sessions. The distracting question of slavery was agitating and retarding the labors of both, and led to conferences of intercommunications of the members."

I quote this testimony now, to show that Conferences were held between the members of Congress and the Federal Convention, upon the subject of slavery. I shall quote farther from it on another point, after turning for a moment to the proceedings of Congress.

On the 9th July, 1787, the Convention having been in session about two months, the ordinance for the government of the Western Territory, which had been reported in a new draft on the 26th of the preceding April, and ordered to a third reading on the 10th May, and then postponed, was referred to a new committee, consisting of Messrs. CARRINGTON, of Virginia; DANE, of Massachusetts; R. H. LEE, of Virginia; KEAN, of North Carolina; and SMITH, of New York. Two days afterwards, July 11th, Mr. CARRINGTON reported what has since been known as the "Ordinance of 1787," with the exception of the 6th article of compact, prohibiting slavery. When it came up the next day, the 12th, for a second reading, Mr. DANE rose and stated as follows:

"In the committee, as ever before, since the day when JEFFERSON first introduced the proposal to prohibit slavery in the territory, it was found impossible to come to any arrangement; that the committee desired to report only so far as they were unanimous; that they, therefore, had omitted altogether the subject of slavery; but that it was understood that any member of the committee might, consistently with his having concurred in the report, move in the house to amend it in the particular of slavery. He therefore moved as an amendment, to add a prohibition of slavery in the following words:

"That there shall be neither slavery nor involuntary servitude in the said territory, otherwise than in the punishment of crimes, whereof the party shall have been duly convicted."

And as a compromise, Mr. DAVIS proposed to add the following proviso:

"Provided always, that any person escaping into the same, from whom labor-service is lawfully claimed in any one of the original States, such fugitive may be lawfully retained and conveyed to the person claiming his or her labor or service as aforesaid."

This was at once unanimously accepted by the slave States. The next day, the 13th, the ordinance was passed, every slave State present, viz.: Delaware, Virginia, North Carolina, South Carolina, and Georgia, and every member from those States voting for it. The same prohibition—which a large majority of the South had resisted when presented alone—was now, when accompanied with the proviso, unanimously agreed to.

Here was a sudden change. But the proviso giving the right of reclamation in the said territory, only partially explains it. For a full explanation we must turn again to the Convention.

And the first thing is a further extract from Mr. MADISON, respecting a letter, before quoted, as follows:

"The distracting question of slavery was agitating and retarding the labors of both bodies—Congress and the Convention; and led to conferences and intercommunications of the members, which resulted in a Compromise, by which the Northern, or anti-slavery portion of the country, agreed to incorporate into the ordinance and Constitution, the provision to restore fugitive slaves; and this mutual and concurrent action was the cause of the similarity of the provisions contained in both, and had its influence in creating the great unanimity by which the ordinance passed, and also in making the Constitution the more acceptable to the slaveholders."

Mr. MADISON, also, in the Virginia Convention, urged the ratification of the Constitution for the following among other reasons, viz.:

"At present, if any slave escape to any of those States where slaves are free, he becomes emancipated by their laws; for the laws of the States are uncharitable to one another in this respect. This clause was expressly inserted to enable owners of slaves to retain them. This is a better security than any that now exists."

General PINCKNEY, one of the delegates in the Federal Convention, from South Carolina, in a debate in the House of Representatives of that State on the Constitution, said:

"We have obtained a right to remove our slaves in whatever part of America they may take refuge, which is a right we had not before. In short, considering all the circumstances, we have made the best terms we could, and on the whole I do not think them bad."

In the speech made by Mr. WEBSTER on the 7th of March, 1850, he remarked that:

"So far as we can now learn, there was a perfect concurrence of opinion between those respective bodies—the Congress and the Constitution—and it resulted in this ordinance of 1787."

When Mr. WEBSTER had closed his speech, Mr. CALHOUN arose, and among other things, said:

"He, Mr. WEBSTER, states very correctly that the ordinance commenced under the old confederation; that Congress was sitting in New York at the time, while the Convention sat in Philadelphia; and that there was concert of action. * * * When the ordinance was passed, as I have good reason to believe, it was upon a principle of compromise; first, that this ordinance should contain a provision similar to the one put in the Constitution, with respect to fugitive slaves; and next, that it should be inserted in the Constitution; and this was the compromise upon which the prohibition was inserted in the ordinance of 1787."

This agrees with Mr. MADISON. The idea he conveys could scarcely have been more identical with Mr. MADISON if he had used MADISON'S words. When the Southern members of Congress voted unanimously for the 6th Article, or anti-slavery clause in the ordinance, with the proviso in respect to slaves escaping into the Territory, it was with the understanding that the Convention would insert a similar provision in the Constitution respecting slaves escaping from one State to another; and this—its insertion in both—was the compromise upon which the prohibition was inserted in the ordinance. Such is the concurrent testimony of Mr. MADISON and Mr. CALHOUN.

We will now turn to the ordinance of 1787, and see whether it applies, as the one proposed by Mr. JEFFERSON in 1784 did, to the new States as well as to the Territories, and is the basis of State as well as Territorial Governments, and was so intended. It declares as follows:

"For extending the fundamental principles of civil and religious liberty, which form the basis whereon these republics, their laws and constitutions, are erected; to fix and establish these principles as the basis of all laws, constitutions, and governments, which forever hereafter shall be formed in the said Territory; to provide also for the establishment of States and permanent governments therein, and for their admission to a share in the Federal councils, on an equal footing with the original States, at as early periods as may be consistent with the general interest.

"It is hereby ordained and declared by the authority aforesaid: That the following articles shall be considered as articles of compact between the original States and the people and States in the said Territory, and forever remain unalterable, unless by the common consent."

Then follows six articles of compact. Part of the fifth and the sixth are in these words:

"ART. 5. * * * Whenever any of the said States shall have sixty thousand free inhabitants therein, such State shall be admitted, by its delegates, into the Congress of the United States, on an equal footing with the original States, in all respects whatever; and shall be at liberty to form a permanent Constitution and State Government; *provided* the Constitutional Government, so to be formed, shall be republican and in conformity to the principles contained in these articles."

"ART. 6. There shall be neither slavery nor involuntary servitude in the said Territory, otherwise than in the punishment of crimes, whereof the party shall have been duly convicted; *Provided, always*, That any person escaping into the same from whom labor or service is lawfully claimed in any one of

15

the original States, such fugitive may be lawfully reclaimed, and conveyed to the person claiming his or her labor or service as aforesaid."

Such is so much of the ordinance as bears directly upon the point I am discussing. And the Convention, as if for the very purpose of giving the unequivocal sanction of the Constitution and of the country to this compromise, and of establishing it as the permanent policy of the Government, expressly provided that the "engagements entered into before the adoption of this Constitution shall be as valid against the United States under this Constitution, as under the Confederation."

This ordinance, then, which was an unalterable compact, prohibiting slavery, and fixing and establishing freedom as the basis of all laws, constitutions, and governments in the Territory forever — State Constitutions and Governments of course included — was made valid by the Constitution itself. And on this point I refer to the highest Southern authority, the late Judge BERRIEN, who was thoroughly pro-slavery in his views, and should certainly be ranked among the ablest lawyers and statesmen Georgia has ever produced, who spoke to this precise point during the compromise discussion in the United States Senate in 1850, as follows:

"Validity was given to their act by the clause in the Constitution, which declares that contracts and engagements entered into by the Government of the Confederation, should be obligatory upon the Government of the United States established by the Constitution."

It is the "act" of Congress in passing the ordinance referred to here. This being so, it was the same in effect as though the ordinance had been written word for word in the Constitution itself. A contract can be made valid, only by making it binding and obligatory upon the parties to it, according to its terms and meaning. To make an unalterable compact valid is to make it perpetually binding.

Having shown that the articles of compact in the ordinance were unalterable; that validity was given to them by the Constitution itself; that in express terms they applied to States as well as to Territories, and must, therefore, being made valid by the Constitution, necessarily have been understood and intended by Congress and the Convention to prohibit slavery as effectually in one as the other, I will now show very briefly that they were also so understood in all parts of the country.

Mr. WILSON, of Pennsylvania, a prominent member of the Federal Convention, and also of the State Convention for ratifying the Constitution, remarked in the latter as follows:

"I consider this clause as laying the foundation for banishing slavery out of the land. * * * The new States which are to be formed will be under the control of Congress in this particular, and slavery will never be introduced among them."

Mr. WILSON speaks of the clause authorizing the prohibition of the African slave trade.

In the Massachusetts Convention to adopt the Constitution, Gen. HEATH said:

"Slavery cannot be extended. By their ordinance Congress has declared that the new States shall be republican States, and have no slavery."

Colonel BLAND, a member of the Convention from Virginia, said he "wished slavery had never been introduced into America," and that "he was willing to join in any measure that would prevent its extending farther." To allow it in new States would not prevent its extending farther, and therefore it was prohibited in such States.

Doctor RAMSAY, a member of the Convention of South Carolina, in his History of the United States, says:

"Under these liberal principles, Congress, in organizing colonies, bound themselves to impart to their inhabitants all the privileges of coequal States. * * * These privileges are not confined to any particular country or complexion. They are communicable to the emancipated slave, for in the new State of Ohio, slavery is altogether prohibited."

This compact, then, applies to State as well as Territorial governments, and was so understood in all sections of the country—northern, central, and southern—when the Constitution was ratified.

Let me now call attention to the very significant proviso to the sixth article. What does the word original mean, and what does the whole article mean with that word in the proviso?

"There shall be neither slavery nor involuntary servitude in the said Territory, otherwise than in the punishment of crimes, &c.; *Provided, always*, That any person escaping into the same, from whom labor or service is lawfully claimed in any one of the original States, such fugitive may be lawfully reclaimed, and conveyed to the person claiming his or her labor or service as aforesaid."

This means that there shall be neither slavery nor involuntary servitude, except for the purpose of reclaiming such fugitives—and I admit that slaves were intended—as are lawfully claimed in any one of the original States. The very fact of the proviso implies that Congress understood that the right of reclamation could not exist, unless it was excepted.

And of course it could only exist for the purpose excepted. The intention was to grant the right to the original States, but to limit it to them. It is impossible to conceive of a measure for framing the proviso as it is, if that had not been the intention. As the ordinance itself made provision for the formation of new States, such States must have been in the minds of members when acting upon it. If the object had been to authorize the reclamation of slaves escaping to this territory from other States than original States, it is certain the word "original" would have been omitted. It was intended for the purpose of limiting the right.

Now observe that this article, proviso and all, is part of an unalterable compact to which the Constitution has given validity. Nobody pretends Congress has ever had the power to alter it. Mr. Toombs denies any such power in express terms. A law which Congress cannot alter has substantially the force and effect of a constitutional proviso. This, then, is the only law for the reclamation of fugitive slaves in the five States of the north-west territory; and there can be no other, the Constitution having made it perpetually valid.

Such obviously is the meaning and legal effect of the fugitive slave provision in the ordinance. And the meaning of that, derived as it is not merely from the consent of the Federal and State conventions, but from their concurrent action, necessarily fixes the meaning of the provision on the same subject in the Constitution, and shows how it must have been understood. As the two were parts of the same compromise, of course neither was understood to be inconsistent with the other. The provision in the Constitution is in these words:

"No person held to service or labor in one State, under the laws thereof, escaping into another, shall, in consequence of any law or regulation therein, be discharged from such service or labor, but shall be delivered up on claim of the party to whom such service or labor may be due."

So far as this describes, or was understood to describe, persons held to service or labor as slaves, it necessarily must also have been understood to apply only to the original States. This follows from what has already been shown. And it must have been so understood for another reason, because it was only "in" and "under" the laws of those States that persons could be held to service or labor as slaves. Under the laws of the Territories and new States, their being so held was forever prohibited. Hence, none but those escaped from one of the original States could ever be legally liable to reclamation, according to the understanding and intention of the original parties to this compact. This manifestly was the meaning of "the fathers," when the ordinance and Constitution were framed and ratified.

The two provisions must be construed together. That in the ordinance was intended for the Territories and new States, and that in the Constitution for the original States. If that in the Constitution had been intended for the Territories, it would have read, "escaping into another State or into the Territory," and that in the ordinance would have been entirely omitted. The proviso to the prohibition in the Missouri Compromise in 1820 is a striking confirmation of this. That was copied, word for word, from the ordinance of 1787, or original compromise, except substituting for the words "in any one of the States," the words "in any State or Territory of the United States," as follows:

"*Provided, always*, That any person escaping into the same, from whom labor or service is lawfully claimed in any one of the original States, such fugitive," &c. And in the compromise of 1820:

"*Provided, always*, That any person escaping into the same from whom labor or service is lawfully claimed in any State or Territory of the United States, such fugitive," &c.

Why say "in any State or Territory of the United States," instead of "in any one of the original States," as in the ordinance of 1787, unless the Congress of 1820 understood the latter to limit the right of recovering fugitive slaves to the original States, and meant by the Missouri bill to extend it to all the States and Territories? They did extend it, but in palpable violation of the "spirit of the compact of the fathers," and of the "policy of 1787."

Originally the Southern States committed themselves to the policy of slavery restriction, by a compact in the nature of a contract for a consideration. By their own votes, they relinquished all pretence of right to any slaves beyond the jurisdiction of the original States. Slaveholders, as such, voluntarily shut themselves out of the new States, in consideration of the right of recovering their fugitive slaves in whatever part of America they might take refuge. The object, as I have clearly shown, was to secure to slavery in the original States the right of recovering fugitives, whether their escape should be from one of those States to another, or to the Territories and new States; but to make that the limit, both of the right of recovery on one side, and of the obligation to permit or allow it, on the other.

It follows, then:

First: That as between the new States of Ohio, Indiana, Illinois, Michigan, and Wisconsin, no right of reclamation exists, or can exist, there being no power in Congress, as the South admit, to alter the compact in the ordinance of 1787, which denies this right.

Second: That no person, escaping from those States into any other State or Territory, can be reclaimed as a fugitive slave, because no person can be held as a slave under their laws.

Third: That no slave escaping from the slave States of Missouri, Arkansas, Texas, Louisiana, or Florida, into Ohio, Indiana, Illinois, Michigan, or Missouri, can be lawfully reclaimed as a fugitive slave, because Missouri, Arkansas, Texas, Louisiana, and Florida are not *original* States.

Fourth: If slaves escape from any State or Territory other than the original States, into the States of the northwestern territory, no lawful power can touch them. The moment they reach those States they become free, because labor or service cannot lawfully be claimed of them in an original State.

Fifth: After the Missouri Compromise of 1820, slaves escaping from Arkansas and Missouri, for example to Kansas, Nebraska, Iowa, and Minnesota, could be reclaimed, but escaping to Illinois, Wisconsin, Michigan, Indiana, and Ohio, they could not be. And the Congress of 1820 so understood it. The particular in which the Missouri proviso was altered in copying from the ordinance of 1787, is proof enough of this.

But did the framers of the Government intend to distinguish in this manner between new and original slave States? Certainly not; and the reason is, they did not mean to have any new slave States. Otherwise they certainly did mean to make this distinction, for nothing can be clearer than that Louisiana and Missouri cannot go to Ohio to recover fugitive slaves within the meaning of this "compact of the fathers;" while Georgia can. Manifestly we have departed from the system devised by the fathers in allowing Missouri, Texas, Arkansas, Louisiana, and Florida to be admitted with slavery, which explains, and nothing else can, this anomalous condition of things.

There can be no escape from these conclusions, but to deny that the ordinance has ever had any validity under the Constitution; which would be scarcely less than to deny that the Constitution itself had ever been a valid instrument. Having the like unequivocal sanction of national authority, and expressing alike in the words of Mr. Toombs, "the collective will of the whole," they must stand or fall together.

Originally the territory was not divided by the line of 36° 30′, or by any other line giving part to freedom and part to slavery. It was all secured, and by consent of the South, to freedom. There is nothing, therefore, in the original compromise, to justify the remark of the Editor of the Boston *Courier* in a recent number of that paper, that "below the line of 36° 30′, the South have the right of prescription." Freedom has an older prescriptive right to all the Territories. The line established by the compromise, between slavery permitted and slavery prohibited, was the boundary line between the then existing States and the Territory of the United States; or the line between exclusive national jurisdiction and the jurisdiction of the States. It is an erroneous assumption, therefore, that the free States, by the introduction of slavery south of 36° 30′, as well as north of it, would receive more than a fair share or moiety of rights and privileges, as between States or parties entitled to equal privileges. The idea that the extension of slavery under the Federal Government can be claimed by anybody south or north as a right, is wholly inadmissible. The *Courier* will hold the following declarations from Mr. WEBSTER to be good authority, if others do not:

"Wherever there is a foot of land to be staid back from becoming slave territory, I am ready to assert the principle of excluding slavery." "We are to use the first and last, and every occasion which offers, to oppose the extension of slave power."

"I have to say, that while I hold with as much integrity, I trust, and faithfulness, as any citizen of this country, to all the original amendments and compromises in which the Constitution under which we now live was adopted, I never could, and never can persuade myself to be in favor of the admission of other States into this Union as slave States with the inequalities which were allowed and accorded to the slaveholding States then in existence by the Constitution. I do not think that the free States ever expected, or could expect, that they would be called upon to admit further slave States. * * * I think they have the clearest right to require that the State coming into the Union, shall come in upon an equality; and if the existence of slavery be an impediment to coming in on an equality, then the State proposing to come in should be required to remove that inequality by abolishing slavery or take the alternative of being excluded. I put my opposition on the political ground that it deranges the balance of the Constitution."

Wherever there is a foot of land to be staid back from slavery! Every occasion to be used to oppose the extension of the slave power! New States to abolish the inequality of slavery, or be excluded! I suppose Northern conservatives of the class referred to have endorsed those doctrines and declarations of Mr. WEBSTER a thousand times, as sound, national, conservative, and constitutional. But no Republican, so far as I know, has ever proposed to go an inch beyond the line of policy they indicated. The Chicago, or Republican Platform, certainly does not. And yet that same line of policy, when advocated by Republicans, is denounced as unsound, sectional, radical, and unconstitutional.

We have a great deal said about the equality of the States; of the new with the original States. This is said to be a fundamental doctrine of the Constitution.

It is claimed that citizens of the slaveholding States have an equal right in the Territories with the citizens of the non-slaveholding States; and I admit they have. But it is also claimed that they have the same right to the protection of property in slaves as property in cotton. This I deny. There is no such doctrine of State equality in the Constitution, nor was any thing like it contemplated by its framers. On the contrary, the Constitution denied this doctrine by clear implication, certainly for the first twenty years. It withheld from Congress the power to prohibit the importation of slaves into the "existing" States till 1808, while their importation into the Territories and new States might be prohibited at once. Ohio was admitted in 1802. Congress had power to prohibit the importation of slaves into that State from that time, and did do it in effect by the very terms and conditions of her admission, which required that her Constitution and Government should not be repugnant to the ordinance of the 13th of July, 1787, which interdicted slavery. But Congress had no power to prohibit the importation of slaves into Georgia till after 1808. Georgia and Ohio, therefore, in this respect, were not political equals from 1802 to 1808.

Nor have the States been all political equals in the sense claimed, since 1808. It will surprise many to be told that there is nothing in the Constitution about State equality, and especially nothing that affirms the equality of the new with the original States, even after 1808. And yet this is true. The only passages which refer to the new States, except impliedly in the importation clause, are these: "New States may be admitted by Congress into the Union; but no new State shall be formed or erected within the jurisdiction of any other State." There is nothing, certainly, in this language to show that the new States were to be admitted on an equality, or an equal footing with the original States.

And yet provision was made, when the Constitution was framed, for the admission of all the new States to be formed in United States Territory then possessed, "on an equal footing with the original States." But it was a footing of equality which was in nowise inconsistent with an absolute denial of the right to establish the inequality of slavery. And this is proved by the only compact in the English language contemporaneous with the Constitution which touches the subject, namely, that part of the fifth article of compact in the ordinance of 1787 which I have already quoted. There can be no shadow of claim that any thing else secured, or pretended to secure, the right of new States to admission into the Union on an equal footing with the original States. That, I admit, did. It is, to repeat it, in these words:

"Whenever any of said States shall have sixty thousand free inhabitants therein, such State shall be admitted, by its delegates, into the Congress of the United States, on an equal footing with the original States in all respects whatever, and shall be at liberty to form a permanent Constitution and State Government; *provided* the Constitution and Government so to be formed, shall be republican in conformity to the principles of these articles," the 6th, which prohibited slavery, included.

And this is all there is, contemporaneous with the Constitution, on the subject of the equality of the States. The very instrument, then, which secured the admission of new States, on an equal footing with the original States, itself provided that they were never to tolerate slavery.

The new States, then, neither were to have, nor have they, any political equality which the prohibition violates, as Southern gentlemen contend. Certainly those formed and admitted under the plan of Government devised by the fathers, have not. In this sense they are not political equals. The original States were, from the beginning, and have ever been, political equals in this and every sense. Not, however, because the Constitution says they are, for it says nothing on the subject; but because they were independent sovereignties, and as such, made a compact which united them under one Federal Government, with discriminating restrictions upon the subject of slavery, or upon any other subject. But the fact that the evil and inequality of slavery existed in the original States, and was tolerated from necessity, was no reason why it should be allowed in the Territories and new States, where it did not and need never exist. So the power of the Territories and new States was sufficiently restricted to secure equality in personal rights and freedom to all the "inhabitants." Of course it cannot be pretended that the mere fact that one or more States had established, and had power to perpetuate slavery, secured to new States the right to establish and perpetuate the same enormity, as a necessary result of State equality. That would make the right or power of one State, resulting from State equality, necessarily coextensive with tolerated evil in another. Manifestly "the fathers" had no such idea as this. Theirs was the common sense and rational idea that a moral and political evil which existed in the old States, and could not be removed, need not for that reason be tolerated in new States.

The Constitution guarantees to each State a republican form

of Government merely; but the ordinance of 1787 provides that the "Constitution and Government of each new State shall be republican." Why this difference? In the original States slavery existed, or in most of them; and so far they were anti-republican in fact and practice, though republican in form. The framers of the Constitution, having no power to abolish this anti-republican institution of slavery in those States, did nothing more than guarantee them Governments republican in form. But having the power to exclude it from the new States, they did exclude it, and provided that their constitutions and governments should be republican. That this was the reason for the difference may be inferred from the remark of LUTHER MARTIN, a distinguished member of the Federal Convention, that "slavery is inconsistent with the genius of republicanism," and of General HEATH in the Massachusetts Convention, that "Congress has declared that the new States shall be republican and have no slavery." No other reason can be given. Thus republicanism in fact, and not in form merely, was made a condition of admitting new States. This is part of the unalterable compact to which validity was given by the Constitution. The Constitution, therefore, while it guarantees a republican form of government, does in fact, by giving validity to the ordinance, guarantee republican governments to the new States. This is another very significant fact harmonizing perfectly with all the other facts in the original plan for extending the Union by admitting States from Territories.

The States are all equals, or not, according to the terms of their admission. The original States became members of the Union upon the single condition of ratifying the Constitution, which left them at liberty to tolerate slavery or not. But the States formed in the only Territory which belonged to the United States at the time the Constitution was framed, were admitted on condition that slavery should be perpetually interdicted within their limits, and as parties to an unalterable compact to that effect.

Slavery was regarded, South as well as North, when the Constitution was adopted, as a moral and political evil. This had been the general sentiment of the country many years before, and continued to be long after that period. The representatives of the extensive district of Darien in Georgia, on the 12th of January, 1775, spoke of slavery as "founded in injustice and cruelty, and highly dangerous to our liberties." JEFFERSON pronounced it "an injustice and enormity." The present Chief Justice of the United States, Mr. TANEY, who acted many years ago as counsel of Rev. Mr. GRUBER, who was indicted in the State of Maryland for preaching a sermon on the evils of slavery, spoke as follows in his defence:

> "Mr. GRUBER did quote the language of our great act of National Independence, and insisted on the principles contained in that venerated instrument. He did rebuke those masters who, in the exercise of power, are deaf to the call of humanity, and he warned them of the evils they might bring upon themselves. He did speak in abhorrence of those who live by trading in human flesh, and enrich themselves by tearing the husband from the wife, the infant from the bosom of the mother, and this was the head and front of his offending. So far is he from being the object of punishment in any form of proceeding, that we are prepared to maintain the same principles, and to use, if necessary, the same language here in the Temple of Justice, and in the presence of those who are the ministers of the law."
>
> "A hard necessity, indeed, compels us to endure the evils of slavery for a time. While it continues it is a blot on our national character; and every real lover of freedom confidently hopes that it will be effectually, though it must be gradually, wiped away, and earnestly looks for the means by which the necessary object may be best obtained. And until it shall be accomplished, until the time shall come when we can point, without a blush, to the language held in the Declaration of Independence, every part of humanity will seek to lighten the galling chain of slavery, and better, to the utmost of his power, the wretched condition of the slave."

Mr. JOHNSON, of Maryland:—Where did you get that?

Mr. GOODRICH:—I got it from a printed sermon recently preached by Dr. ORVILLE DEWEY, of Boston.

And Mr. CALHOUN, in the United States Senate, in 1838, said that "many in the South once believed that slavery was a moral and political evil;" and Mr. BUTLER, late a United States Senator from South Carolina, said in the Senate in 1850, that he "remembered the time when slavery was regarded as a moral evil, even in South Carolina."

In such a state of public sentiment, it is certainly no marvel that slavery was not allowed to extend into the Territories and new States. It was not prohibited in the northwest territory, because it was supposed to be, or would become, an evil in that territory particularly, or a greater evil there than anywhere else; but because it was regarded as an evil everywhere, and therefore wrong to permit its extension anywhere, when there was power to prevent it. There can be no doubt it would have been prohibited in the Territories and new States of Alabama, Mississippi, and Tennessee, if Georgia and North Carolina, previous to the Federal Convention, had ceded them to the United States upon the same conditions Virginia had ceded the northwest territory. Proof of this is found in the fact that the plan of territorial governments interdicting slavery forever after 1800, embraced all territory ceded, or to be ceded by individual States; and still further proof is in the fact, that the cessions by Georgia and North Carolina, after the adoption of the Constitution, were upon the express condition that slavery should not be prohibited; thereby showing that the policy of the Federal Government, as they understood it, was restrictive of slavery in the far southern latitudes as well as in the more northern, and that they expected the power to restrict would be exercised, if not withheld in the deeds of cession. A proposition was, in fact, made to apply the anti-slavery clause of 1787, to all the southern part of the Mississippi territory, now the southern parts of Alabama and Mississippi, by the act of April 7th, 1798, it being supposed at one time that it belonged to the United States; but the debate shows that the proposition was withdrawn because the jurisdiction was in Georgia, or because not five members of Congress, after the question was examined, believed otherwise. Georgia claimed absolute title and right of jurisdiction, and denied all right on the part of the United States to interfere with slavery. Congress did, however, prohibit the importation of slaves into the territory, and declare every slave so imported to be entitled to his freedom. This was probably wholly unauthorized, as it was six years before Georgia ceded it to the United States, and ten years before Congress had power to prohibit the importation of slaves into that State. But these facts show a strong disposition on the part of "the fathers" to curtail and circumscribe slavery, even in the far south, and at the hazard, too, of exercising doubtful power.

Nothing can be clearer than that the original States had a right to form a Federal Government on such terms as to themselves as they could mutually agree upon, and to fix the terms upon which they would permit new members to be admitted. The Northern States were under no obligation to protect slavery at all, not even by permitting fugitives to be reclaimed within their limits. If, then, they were willing to concede that right to the original States, only upon condition that slavery should not be allowed to extend, who will say they had not a right to make that condition, or that, if agreed to, it would not be valid and binding? With their views of slavery, believing it to be a moral and political evil, it was certainly their first and highest duty to make effectual provision against its extension, before undertaking, for any reason, to give the least protection to it. Such provision they supposed they had made, and it was this that justified them, if any thing could, in conceding the right of reclamation.

The free, or northern States, in the exercise of their admitted right in deciding upon the terms of Union, insisted on making it a fundamental and ever-binding condition that no obligation to protect slavery in Illinois should ever exist; and this was done for reasons which render it morally certain that they would have insisted on the same condition in reference to Missouri, if Missouri had been part of the original territory. It would be preposterous to suppose that while they would not consent to guarantee slavery in any manner in Illinois, because they believed it to be a moral and political evil, they meant at the same time to make a Government that could obligate them to guarantee it in the adjoining Territory or State of Missouri, either by the return of fugitive slaves, or in any other manner. They meant no such thing, nor can an honest interpretation of the terms of union bind them to such guarantee now. The right to recapture fugitive slaves could not exist without the consent of the free States; and as that consent was given upon conditions and with limitations, by necessary implication and every sound principle of construction, they reserved the right to say whether it should exist upon other conditions and with other limitations, or without either condition or limitation.

Mr. WICKLIFFE:—No one from Kentucky or Virginia wishes to alter the ordinance of 1787. For GOD'S sake spare us the argument.

Mr. GOODRICH:—I understand no alteration is proposed in the ordinance; nor am I arguing against any such proposition. I am showing what the policy of 1787 was, and what the compact of the fathers was. And I am doing this because it is in the spirit of that policy and compact that Kentucky and Virginia tell us they wish to have this controversy adjusted. Massachusetts and the other Northern States meant to fix, and supposed they had fixed, a limit to their connection with, and responsibility for slavery. By consenting to the clause which secured the right of reclamation, they did become responsible for it to a certain extent. So far as it was supposed, when that clause was agreed to, that its effect would be the recapture of fugitive slaves, and their return to bondage, and so far as the purpose was to make such recapture and return lawful, so far the responsibility of adding to the security of slavery was voluntarily assumed. But this was limited to the existing States by excluding slavery from all United States territory. If any part of such territory had been left for slavery—enough for a single slave State—it might be said that its extension from a part was for reasons applicable only to a part, and so could not be considered as establishing the principle of non-extension. But now this cannot be said. Not a foot was left for slavery.

We thus see what the state of things would have been to-day if foreign territory had not been acquired. Such acquisitions were not originally contemplated, and of course not provided for. The first—Louisiana—was deemed unconstitutional by Mr. JEFFERSON, and yet it was made while he was President; but with no right, "according to the spirit of the compact of the fathers," to place the Federal Government or the States under any other relation to slavery in subsequently acquired territory than that which they sustained to it—the only one they would consent to sustain—in the Territories possessed at the time that compact was made.

A great deal is said about State rights. But the doctrine of State rights proves too much. Massachusetts had a clear and undoubted right originally to limit her obligations upon this subject. And she did limit them. The original compromise was "better security" to slavery in the original States, with no extension of it to the Territories and new States. This better security was the accepted consideration for waiving the right to extend, and Massachusetts may rightfully insist on this waived right to extend, so long as this "better security" is demanded of her.

Southern gentlemen in this Convention propose to be governed by the principles of the founders of the Government, and by the Constitution, or compact of union, as those founders understood it. By that they say they are willing to do as the fathers did, and adjust the present unhappy controversy by applying to new territory the same principles which the fathers applied to the old. Let me assure gentlemen from the slave States that if they are really in earnest in offering these terms of adjustment, this unhappy controversy can be settled in less than an hour's time. Having always claimed the right to recapture fugitive slaves in territory acquired since, as well as in that acquired before the adoption of the Constitution, the slave States have ever been bound, upon every principle of honor and fair dealing, to concede the original consideration for it, that is, prohibition. A purpose secretly entertained when that compromise was made, to use the Government in the manner it has actually been used, to enlarge the area of slavery and the obliga tion to guarantee it, would have been dishonest and fraudulent; but the fact that this purpose was conceived afterward, as it doubtless was, does not alter the case a whit. No man possessed of the facts can honestly claim that the bargain between the North and South, interpreted according to the true interest and meaning of both parties at the time of making it, can justify the extension of slavery a rod beyond the original States, or a particle of protection to it beyond the right to recover fugitives from such States.

Having thus shown, as I think I have, that an essential element in the basis of the "more perfect Union" on the question of slavery, was the principle of non-extension, we find the first failure to assert this principle was in the omission to apply it to the Louisiana purchase. The importation of slaves into that territory was immediately prohibited. That probably cut off the only source of supply from which danger of extension was then apprehended. The policy of the Government was well understood, and no apprehension of a practical departure from it existed. There was nothing in the circumstance of the purchase, or the reasons for making it, to excite such apprehension. But it was seen on the application of Missouri for admission, that the ordinance of 1787 should have been applied to it at the time of the purchase. If it had been, Louisiana, Missouri, and Arkansas would never have become slave States (the few slaves in New Orleans and vicinity being emancipated, as they should have been, upon some equitable principle), and the Missouri Compromise, which was the second departure from the original policy, would never have been made. The third was the annexation of Texas as a slave State, and the argument to divide it into three or four more. Annexation led to the war with Mexico, and the acquisition of a large part of her territory, and to the compromise of 1850, by which it was Congressionally agreed that the States formed in that territory might be admitted with slavery, if their Constitutions should so prescribe. This was the fourth departure from the original policy of prohibition. The fifth was the repeal of the Missouri Compromise in 1850, and the attempts to subjugate and enslave Kansas. That repeal made the change from the original policy radical and total. Certainly it is high time "to restore the Union and Constitution in the spirit in which they were established by the fathers."

And now, sir, I propose to begin the work of "restoring the policy of 1787," by applying the ordinance of 1787 to every foot of organized and unorganized territory, wherever situated, which now belongs to the United States, precisely as the fathers applied it to every foot of such territory at the time the Constitution was made; and I ask, in all earnestness and seriousness, what any member of the Convention can have to say against this, who sincerely desires to "restore the Union and Constitution in the spirit in which they were established by the fathers of the Republic," and is "ready to adjust the present unhappy controversy" in the same spirit? What, I beg to know, can be said against this mode of adjustment by those who are in favor of a "restoration of the Constitution to the principles and landmarks of our fathers," and of a "return to the policy of 1787"? Can any man doubt that that ordinance would have been extended over all these territories in 1787, if they had belonged to the United States at that time? Let slavery, then, be prohibited now precisely as the fathers prohibited it then. Copy that old ordinance word for word, and give it legal force and effect, and make it the basis of all laws, and all constitutions, and all governments in these Territories forever, because the fathers gave it such force and effect, and made it the basis of all laws, and all constitutions and all governments forever in all the Territories of the Union, in 1787. If that would not be a return to the "principles and landmarks of the fathers," and to the "policy of 1787," then I beg to know what would be? How is it possible —I put it to you, gentlemen of the South—how is it possible to persuade yourselves that the principles and policy of 1787 can be restored by adopting the resolutions of the General Assembly of Virginia? By what process is it that the gentleman (Mr. SEDDON) from Virginia, has come to believe that the South is entitled, according to the spirit of the compact of the fathers, "to the added guarantees" of which he speaks? According to the spirit of that compact it is manifest the slave States are entitled to no added guarantees.

But another of the Virginia Commissioners (Mr. RIVES) tells us that this question of slavery in nowise concerns the free States. On this point I will quote from a very high authority, which Virginia, certainly, will respect. Mr. MADISON was a member of the first Congress under the Constitution. A colleague of his, Mr. PARKER, proposed a duty on the importation of slaves, and said he "hoped Congress would do all that lay in their power to restore to human nature its inherent privileges, and, if possible, wipe off the stigma under which America labors." Mr. MADISON, in remarking on that proposition, among other things said:

> "Every addition the States receive to their number of slaves tends to weaken and render them less capable of self-defence. In case of hostilities with foreign nations, they will be the means of inviting attack instead of repelling invasion. It is a necessary duty of the General Government to protect every part of their confines against danger, as well internal as external. Every thing, therefore, which tends to increase danger, though it be a local affair, yet, if it involve national expense and safety, becomes of concern to every part of the Union, and is a proper subject for the consideration of those charged with the general administration of the Government."

And we hear, too, a great deal about war, civil war, if this unhappy controversy is not satisfactorily adjusted, which means upon the terms proposed by the slave States. But do gentlemen mean that an appeal will be made to the sword, unless the Constitution shall be so amended as to "provide that slavery of the African race shall be effectually protected as property in all the territory of the United States, now held or hereafter acquired south of latitude 36° 30′"?—which is the proposition of Virginia. If that is what is meant, then let me, before I close, read an extract from one of the last speeches made by HENRY CLAY in the Senate of the United States. It is as follows:

> "If, unhappily, we should be involved in war, civil war, between the two portions of this Confederacy, in which the effort upon the one side should be to restrain the introduction of slavery into the new Territories, and upon the other side to force its introduction there, what a spectacle should we present to the astonishment of mankind, in an effort, not to propagate rights, but—I must say it, though I trust it will be understood to be said with no design to excite feeling—a war to propagate wrongs!"

Mr. HOWARD moved an adjournment.

Mr. BRONSON objected, raising the question of order. He claimed that the Conference, by adopting the resolutions of Mr. RANDOLPH, had fixed the limits of the sessions, from 10 o'clock A. M., to 4 o'clock P. M.

The motion of Mr. HOWARD was not concurred in.

Mr. LOOMIS:—I feel that this is an important crisis in the affairs of the country. Perhaps it is the most important that ever occurred in American history. The first Convention of thirteen scattered States was earnestly engaged in protecting the liberties which had been won in the Revolution. It gave us a Constitution under which, for more than seventy years, we have lived prosperously and happily. Now political contests have taken place. New questions have arisen, and one portion of the Union believes the Constitution inadequate to protect its interests. The question which we are obliged to consider is: How shall we save the country? Disguise it as we may, deceive ourselves as we may, the country is in danger—in great and imminent danger. A solemn duty is imposed upon each one of us. How shall we save the country?

Virginia has invited this conference of her sister States. Pennsylvania responded to her call with all activity. Pennsylvania has responded because she understood and appreciated Virginia. There is great misapprehension in the North concerning this venerated State, as well in regard to her motives as in regard to the principles and feelings that influence her people in their intercourse with and their action toward other States of the Union. I know Virginia well. I have associated with her people. I have practiced before her judicial tribunals.

Some years ago I was greatly pressed by an abolitionist who was indicted in Virginia, to undertake his defence. He was very fearful that he would not receive an impartial trial, that the court and jury would participate in the public excitement. I told him that he need indulge in no such misapprehensions. I knew Virginia too well for that. I told him, however, that if he desired it, I would go; but it was simply to defend him, and secure him a fair trial—to act as his counsel. I could not represent his sentiments, for I am not and never was an abolitionist. I assumed his defence. I told him I would go, and I went. I did find great excitement there, but it did not surprise me. Many valuable slaves had shortly before escaped, some of them through the assistance and instrumentality of my client. Judge Fry was the presiding judge of the court. His liberality, and that of all his officers, was great—as great as I ever enjoyed in my own State. The sheriff of the county drew thirty-six jurymen. Of these, twelve were slaveholders, twelve were abolitionists, and twelve were non-slaveholders. When the jury was finally empannelled it consisted of nine abolitionists and three non-slaveholders.

I never saw in my whole professional life a trial conducted with greater fairness or justice. The whole of it was entirely satisfactory to myself, and I believe to my client.

I have ever since entertained a feeling of the highest respect for Virginia. Her abstractions I confess I could never understand, nor did I ever wish to. They are her exclusive property, and she never uses them to the injury of her neighbors. If she chooses to make the resolutions of '98 a matter of importance, I do not know that anybody is injured.

I regretted to hear the imputations upon Virginia which some gentlemen have seen fit to make. Menace is not the habit of that ancient commonwealth. She does not indulge in it, and it would not become her. The gentleman from New York intimated that if a State came to him with a menace he would meet it with a menace. In this I agree with him. If Virginia came here with a menace I should meet her with defiance. But happily for us we have no occasion to consider the question in this light. If ever a State came to meet her sisters, to consult for the common good in a proper spirit, Virginia does so now.

A military chieftain once, when approaching his death, lamented that he had no children to transmit his name and his qualities to posterity. Virginia will never need to take up such a lamentation. She has children enough. She is the mother of WASHINGTON and JEFFERSON, of MADISON, MARSHALL, and CLAY. Rightly and justly she has been called the mother of States. She is the mother of States, and of millions of freemen.

I honor and respect Virginia, for she deserves it. She was among the foremost in the Revolutionary struggle; and since it was terminated, she has exhibited a continued example of patriotism and loyalty. Her sons have been among the ablest in our legislative councils, and even to-day she sets a noble example before the country, for the emulation of her sister States. Our interests are inseparably connected with her own. We will acknowledge the fact, and act in view of it. Let her remember, also, that she has a common interest with us. She will do so because she will be faithful to her old traditions as well as to her present duty.

I cannot believe that the time has come when it is necessary for us to contemplate a dissolution of the Union. The people are not prepared for such an awful event. We do not yet know how heavy sacrifices they will make to avoid it. Some States have left us I know, but I believe their absence is but temporary. We must have them back, and we will. As for the Border States leaving us in the present condition of affairs, with the present feeling of friendship for them, *that* I regard as an impossibility. Why should the Border States go out of the Union when three-fourths of the present Congress are ready to give them all the guarantees they ask?

But let not Pennsylvania be misunderstood in her position. She will yield a vast deal for peace. She will examine and recognize the rights of every section of the country. She believes that when this is done, it is the duty of all to stand by the Union. She believes that the Border States cannot connect themselves with a so-called Southern Confederacy without involving themselves in a vortex of ruin. The President of the Southern Confederacy already talks about the smell of gunpowder, and about battles at the North. Well! he is a brave man no doubt, but if he will invade Pennsylvania we will resist him. Pennsylvania has gold enough to calm her friends; she has iron enough to cool her enemies.

But Pennsylvania desires no war. She will do all that an honorable State can do to avoid war. In that temper she sends her delegates here, and they will do all that honorable men can do to carry out her wishes. She has no desire to be a frontier State with her four hundred miles of border, which she must guard and protect if disunion takes place on the terms suggested. She will do all she can to avoid disunion. She is now a central State—the keystone of the arch. She wants no imaginary line drawn along her border, with herself on one side of it and enemies upon the other.

Pennsylvania has always kept faith with the Union. She has always performed all her duties toward the Federal Government with cheerfulness and fidelity. Her three millions of people are true to all their obligations now—to the Government as well as to her sister States. Her voice is for peace. She would at all hazards avoid disunion. She would make many sacrifices to avoid civil war. Last of all, she would do all she could to save the Union; she would never permit the destruction of the country. My own position is easily defined. I fully sympathize with and endorse the position of Pennsylvania.

Mr. LOOMIS referred to the election, installation, and message of the Governor of Pennsylvania, also to various resolutions of political conventions in Pennsylvania, in confirmation of his own views of the sentiments of the people of that State, and continued:

I shall dwell but a short time upon the provisions of the proposed amendments. I can live under the Constitution as it is, or as it will be if these amendments are adopted. I shall uphold the Constitution. I shall commit myself to no opposite course. The whole amendment is connected with and concerns the question of slavery in the Territories. This has always been a fruitful source of trouble.

The character of the relation of the Government to the Territories, and the interests of the States in them, were questions raised in most of the States when the Constitution was adopted.

The compromise of 1820, it was hoped, settled one question concerning them—the question of slavery. But upon the repeal of the compromise the difficulty was opened again. Pennsylvania never took as ultra ground respecting this subject as many other States. She thought its importance was magnified. It is magnified now. If the South secured the amendment proposed it would not avail her much. The granting of it would not injure the North. The territory is unfitted for the profitable employment of slave labor. That is shown by experience. In ten years scarcely ten slaves had found their way into New Mexico and Arizona.

This is a question of sectional interest, and may be one, to some extent, of political power. Examine, for a moment, the true interests of both the North and South, in the question as it is now presented. I mean the interest of the extremes, for the Border States certainly cannot have a very deep interest in it. They lay between the two sections, and to some extent sympathize with both. The valuable portion of our present territory is north of the line proposed. It is rich in agricultural and mineral resources. It will be changed in time into a number of powerful and wealthy States. Is it not desirable now to exclude slavery from them forever? Then as to the territory south. It is smaller in extent, and almost infinitely less valuable. Much of it is barren desert which can never be cultivated. Considered as a material interest, the South is asking but little. The North is giving up almost nothing, by agreeing to give the South the control of this section while it remains a territory. But the South does not ask even that. She simply asks to have those rights guaranteed, the existence of which are already practically conceded.

As to future territory, I would raise no question about it. We want no more territory north or south. Its acquisition would only be attended with new troubles. New questions would be raised to threaten the quiet of the country and the stability of our institutions. Why should we trouble ourselves about the acquisition of new territory when we have already enough for one hundred millions of people?

We may form a Constitution which will be entirely satisfactory to the nation now. We may extend our territory in such a way as to render a change indispensable. Considerations of climate and race will be constantly occurring, which will require new changes. The Federal Constitution may have been well enough adapted to the four millions of people to whom it was first applied, and it is not strange that the growth of the nation, and the new interests which have since arisen, should require some changes now. I say that we need no more territory.

What objection, then, can there be to compromising this matter, to arranging it to the satisfaction of all parties, if the rights of all can be regarded and secured? The course which I would follow in such a case, would be that indicated by traditional policy of statesmen in whom our people have had confidence—the policy of such men as HARRISON and HENRY CLAY.

I do not regard the provisions relating to slavery in the District of Columbia as of any practical consequence to the North. Pennsylvania cares little about it. There would seem to be a propriety in countenancing slavery here so long as it exists in the adjoining States.

The Border States ask us now for these guarantees. They ask them earnestly and in a spirit of loyalty to the Union. My answer to such a request, urged in such a spirit, is, that I would give them any guarantees I could within the limits of the Constitution.

Pennsylvania forms one of the brotherhood of States. She is in the Union, and she will remain there. She is bound to it by all the memories and associations of the past, and by all the hopes of the future. She will discharge, as she always has discharged, all her duties, all her obligations to the Union. No State exceeds her in devotion to it. But, at the same time, she will not be unmindful of her duties and her obligations to the other States. She would discharge these obligations as she can afford to discharge them, in a spirit of generosity and conciliation. In that spirit she will give her assent to these propositions of amendment. I believe I have fairly represented the opinions of Pennsylvania in what I have said, and I rely upon her people —my constituents—for my justification.

Mr. CHITTENDEN:—I will consult the pleasure of the

Conference whether I shall proceed with my observations now, or during the evening session?

Mr. MOREHEAD:—I think the Conference had better adjourn. I make the motion.

The motion was adopted, and the Conference adjourned to meet at half-past seven o'clock this evening.

EVENING SESSION—FOURTEENTH DAY.

WASHINGTON, THURSDAY, *February* 21*st*, 1861.

THE Conference was called to order at half-past seven o'clock, Mr. ALEXANDER in the chair.

Mr. CHITTENDEN:—I feel gratified by the kindness which has given me an opportunity of making a few observations to the Conference, and I shall not abuse it.

The delegates from Vermont have acted throughout the session under great embarrassment. We hold our appointments from the Executive of that State. Her Legislature was not in session when the Virginia Resolutions were adopted, and the day fixed for the meeting of the Conference was so early that no time was given to the Governor of Vermont for consultation, or for taking any other means of ascertaining the temper of the State in relation to the Virginia plan. We were summoned by telegraph—myself upon an hour's notice—to come here, and we obeyed the summons.

By the rules of the Conference we are prohibited from correspondence with our constituents upon the subject of its action, and we are entirely without recent information concerning their views and wishes. But one course remains to us, and that we must inflexibly pursue. That is, to apply the propositions upon which we are called to vote, to the known and established opinions of our people upon the principles involved in them; and if these principles coincide with their opinions, to give our assent; if they do not, to withhold it. We hold it our duty to respect and obey the opinions of our constituents; and in our action here, such obedience is a pleasure.

First of all, before referring to the merits or demerits of these propositions, I wish to be informed distinctly upon one point. One section of the Union requires guarantees; the other does not. Here are two parties having different interests, proposing to themselves different courses of action. One of them proposes these guarantees in the form of what it calls a compromise. There are many subjects which, in the experience of life, we are obliged to compromise. All of us understand the meaning of the term. It implies that when two parties differ upon a subject of common interest, each is to yield something to the other, until both reach an agreement upon a middle ground, and the difference is settled. But one consequence always follows, always must follow, or it is in nowise a compromise: *Both parties are bound by the agreement.*

There is another way in which compromises are effected. When opposing parties cannot come to an understanding, they agree to submit the matters in difference to some tribunal that can decide between them. A like consequence always follows from such a proceeding. The parties agree to *submit* to the decision, to be *bound* by it, and mutually undertake to carry it into effect, whatever the decision may be.

There is still another way in which a *political* compromise may be made. Its terms may be agreed upon, and then it may be submitted to the people for adoption. When adopted, it becomes the law of the land—equally binding upon all sections of the country. If it is rejected, the party which proposed it has secured its submission to the proper tribunal—it has been considered, and that party should, upon every principle of law or morality, acquiesce in the result.

Except in one of these three methods I know of no way in which a *compromise* can be made. Let us apply these methods to the questions before us. One of them must be adopted if we *compromise* at all.

In fact there is one principle which forms the very foundation of our Government, and it should be kept constantly in mind. We cannot negotiate, we cannot legislate, we cannot *compromise,* unless all parties will acknowledge its binding force. If there is a party that does not acknowledge this, in my judgment that party has no right to be here. It is not a Republican party. I do not use this term in a party sense, but in the sense which is used in the fourth article in the Constitution, where the United States are required to guarantee to every State a *republican* form of Government. The principle to which I refer is this: That the will of the majority, constitutionally expressed, must control the Government, and all questions relating to it; and that will must be respected and obeyed by the minority.

Now, if the members representing the free States will accept these propositions of amendment in good faith—will agree to submit them through Congress to the people of the States, and to be bound by the decision of the majority, whatever that decision may be—will you, gentlemen of the slave States, do the same? I do not refer to the States which have undertaken to withdraw from the Union. I only call upon the members for the States here represented. You have the right to speak for your respective States. You are sent here for that purpose. You ask us to give our votes for proposals which are certainly unpleasant, not to say offensive to us, and to use such influence as we possess to induce Congress to submit these to the people. You express the highest degree of confidence in the result. This is *your* plan of compromise. If we resist it, you charge us with standing between the people and your plan—of sacrificing the Union to our platform. Very well. If we will submit your propositions to the people, and agree to be bound by and to acquiesce in their decision, will you do the same? If you will, it may be of service to protract this discussion, to make these propositions as acceptable as possible. If you will not, we are wasting time. We may as well stop here. Believe me, sir, Vermont, as well as every other free State, will have too much self-respect to agree to the terms of a compromise which will bind one party and will not bind the other.

There is one thing farther which we must understand. It has been frequently referred to in debate, and I shall not enlarge upon it. Time must elapse before these propositions can be acted upon. The free States expect faithfully to observe all their duties to the General Government—to keep faith with it as they always have. Will the slave States do the same? Will they not only *not obstruct* the Government in the execution of the laws, but will they *aid* the Government in executing the laws? The answer to this inquiry is as important as the other.

Now, it is useless to tell the people of the free States, that such is the present condition of the South, such is the apprehension and distrust prevailing there, that we must give them these guarantees at once, without any longer delay or discussion—that if we do not they will secede. Such an argument as that, sir, is an unworthy argument; it is unfit to be used in an assembly of men met to confer upon the Constitution. This is not the way in which good constitutions are made, for one of the several parties to present its ultimatum, and then insist upon its adoption, under the threat that if it is not adopted they will go no farther. If such is the true condition of affairs in some of the States, and the gentlemen representing them are the best judges, then before proceeding to amend the Constitution to satisfy them, I think we had better try to put them into a frame of mind suitable for negotiation. A Constitution adopted in that way would be good for nothing. Let it once be understood that such claims will be recognized, and we shall have amendments to the Constitution proposed as often as any section can find a pretext for proposing them. The agreeable course to us all would be to yield to your pressing appeals. But you ask us to compromise upon most extraordinary terms. You will not give us the slightest assurance that the people of the slave States will acquiesce in the vote of the whole people upon your propositions. You even say, you will not acquiesce, if the decision is adverse. You are in doubt if they will be satisfied if the decision is in their favor; and some gentlemen frankly avow that these propositions in themselves are not satisfactory. The gentleman from Virginia, with an openness and a frankness which seems a part of his nature, tells us in substance that Virginia will not be satisfied with these; that Virginia is settled in her determination that slave property shall be respected; that it has as high a right to protection as any other property, and in some respects higher; that Virginia will have these rights acknowledged and secured *under* the Constitution, or she will not be satisfied. The statement that she will *not be satisfied*, has a very peculiar and expressive signification.

Such being our present condition, I have little hope that good can come of our deliberations. We have started wrong. We should have settled the questions first, that the Union must be preserved, the laws enforced, and the duty of every State toward the Union performed, in every contingency and under all circumstances. Having resolved this, we could then go on, carefully consider the wants of every section, and we could afford to be generous in meeting the views of our Southern friends.

I feel more diffidence than I can well express in being obliged to differ so widely from the opinions of the gentlemen who have introduced the proposals contained in the majority report, and who have advocated them with such signal ability. I have less hesitation in expressing my unqualified dissent from the representatives of the free States, who pledge the people of those States so unreservedly to the support of these propositions, if Congress will submit them to their constituents. I object to these pledges, because I know they are deceptive, that they are made without authority, and that they will never be fulfilled. The South may as well understand this now, as hereafter.

The Union is precious to the people of the free States. They look upon it with a feeling closely approaching to reverence. They have looked upon its dissolution as the greatest national calamity possible. They have been taught to regard the idea of dissolution as a sin. Now, when the subject is forced upon their attention, when Conventions are called throughout the South to discuss it, when in some of the States the process has already commenced, I am well aware they will make heavy sacrifices to preserve the Union. They will sacrifice their prosperity, political influence, friendship, social relations, yes, their lives, to secure its perpetuity. But they will not sacrifice their principles which they have conscientiously adopted. No, not even to save the Union.

But let me not be misunderstood. A Government that cannot be maintained without the sacrifice of those principles upon which all good governments are founded, is not worth preserving. Such is not the case with *ours*. Its preservation requires no such sacrifice; and if we made it, the sacrifice would be useless. The habit once commenced, we should be called upon to repeat it over and over again, until at length we should have a Government destitute of principle.

The people of the slave States believe that slavery is a desirable institution, that a Goverment founded upon it would be most desirable. It has been declared here, that it is even a missionary institution, and that the North, in attempting to overthrow it, interposes between the slaveholder and his Maker, thereby preventing him from performing a duty toward the African race which his ownership imposes upon his conscience. Well, that is a question between yourselves and your consciences. We do not wish to interfere. Keep the institution within your own State limits, and we are content that you should have all the credit, and honor, and glory that pertains to it. Over and over again the truth has been asserted here, that there never has been, and is not now, any party, or any considerable number of men in the free States, who entertain the idea of interfering with slavery in the States. The opinions of a few rash men who entertain other views, are no more respected among us than among yourselves.

But the growth and extension of slavery outside of State limits, in the Territories which are our common property, present a very different question. If the North permits it there, to that extent it becomes responsible for slavery. I do not care what term you use to describe the feeling of the North in relation to slavery. One gentleman says that the North *abhors* it, and the use of the term has excited much comment. I may be still more unfortunate, but it is my duty to say that you cannot present an idea more repulsive to the northern mind or the northern conscience, than that of making the North responsible for the existence, expansion, growth, extension, or any thing else relating to slavery. Right or wrong, this sentiment has taken a firm hold of the northern mind. There it is, and it must be taken into account in every proposition which depends for its success upon the action of the North. Sneering at it will do no good; abuse will only make it stronger. You cannot legislate it out of existence. From this time forward, as long as the nation has an existence, you must expect the determined opposition of the North to the extension of slavery into free territory. If your proposals of amendment involve *that*, we may accept them, Congress may propose them, the South may adopt them; but the answer of the North to them all will be an emphatic, a determined, *No!*

Mr. GRANGER:—If you Republicans will let us go to the

people, we will show you what they will do. I think I understand the wishes and feelings of the people of the North.

Mr. CHITTENDEN:—No doubt. The gentleman says he supported the BELL and EVERETT ticket. The record of his State shows to what extent his opinions are in sympathy with those of the people of the North.

Mr. President, for a time I did expect profitable results from this Conference. As I watched it from day to day, it seemed to me that generally the States had been very fortunate in the selection of their representatives; that few of extreme opinions had been selected; and that such a body, animated by common love for the Union, and by a common desire to secure a perpetuity of its blessings, must finally come to an agreement which would satisfy all; or if not, to an agreement in which all would acquiesce. In that belief I had determined to give my assent to the most extreme propositions which might be made here, that did not run counter to the position of my State upon the question of slavery extension, if those propositions would quiet the country and settle our present difficulties.

But when I heard it announced on this floor that the propositions contained in the majority report even, which do provide for the extension of slavery into the Territories, which involve a direct constitutional recognition of slavery for the first time, which place it above and beyond legislation, which take it out of the hands of posterity, which compel the North to pay for fugitives; and when I heard it stated that even these were not enough to satisfy the South, that Virginia must have something more, that she was "solemnly pledged against coercion, that she would not agree to abide by the decision of the people upon these propositions," then hope went out from my heart! I have not since had any expectation that much good would come from our deliberations.

I have refrained from entering into the merits or demerits of slavery. I have refrained, so far as I could, from repeating what has been better said by others than I could say it. The point which I wish to press upon the Conference is this: Speaking for one State, we frankly tell you that she will not enter upon a compromise which is not fair and mutual, which does not bind both parties.

But, sir, although I have thus expressed myself, I do not at all despair of the Republic. I do not believe that a dissolution or destruction of this Government is to take place. Its origin and its existence have been characterized by too many signal interpositions of Providential favor. We cannot look into the future. I have no desire to do so. If we all conscientiously perform our prescribed duties, if we are faithful to ourselves, to our people and our Constitution, HE who rules the nations will take care of the rest. It may be that the clouds which now cover our horizon will be swept away, carrying with them all these subjects of difficulty and danger, which alone have troubled the quiet and the prosperity of the American Union.

Mr. LOGAN :—Instead of dreaming, like Mr. FIELD, of news from the seat of war, and of marching armies, I have thought of a country through which armies *have* marched, leaving in their track the desolation of a desert. I have thought of harvests trampled down—of towns and villages once the seat of happiness and prosperity, reduced to heaps of smoking ruins—of battle-fields red with blood which has been shed by those who ought to have been brothers—of families broken up, or reduced to poverty; of widowed wives, of orphan children, and all the other misfortunes which are inseparably connected with war. This is the picture which presents itself to my mind every day and every hour. It is a picture which we are doomed soon to witness in our own country, unless we place a restraint upon our passions, forget our selfish interests, and do something to save our country.

We feel these things deeply in the Border States. The people of these States bear the most intimate relations to each other. They are closely connected in business. They associate in their recreations and their pleasures. The members of a large number of their families have intermarried. State lines, except for legislative purposes, are scarcely thought of. The people of Kentucky, Ohio, Indiana, and Illinois, are one people, having an identity of sympathy, of feeling, and of interest.

We have in the West a section of country known as the dark and bloody ground. The historical incidents connected with it are of the most sad and mournful character. There is buried under it an ancestor of almost every family descended from the early settlers of the West. But this ground is limited in extent. If we are to plunge this country into civil war—if we are to go on exasperating the sections until they take up arms against each other, then shall we make a dark and bloody ground of all the Border States. We shall desolate all their fields, and carry sorrow and mourning into every family within their limits.

Should we not have a deep interest in avoiding war? Should we not labor with, and entreat the people of all sections to help us avoid it? If it comes, we are to be the sufferers. Upon *our* heads the ruin must fall. We cannot and will not talk about abstractions now. We are impelled by every consideration to do all we can to settle our differences, and keep off the evil day that brings civil war upon our happy and prosperous country, and to prevent the devastation of that country.

I wish to say a few earnest words to my brother Republicans. You object to these propositions because they are pressed just now when the new administration is coming into power. You say that there is no need of them, and that they involve submission on your part, as a condition of your enjoying the fruits of the victory you have won. Let me assure you that no one labored harder for the triumph of Mr. LINCOLN than myself; I exerted what little influence I had; I paid my money to secure his election; I now wish to give him an honorable administration. I believe he will make a good President, and I wish to give him a united country to rule. This can only be done by a settlement of our troubles. No one will rejoice over that settlement more than Mr. LINCOLN.

Fellow Republicans, the only way that opens before us now to settle them is, by adopting the report of the committee; by permitting the people to adopt it. Can you, dare you, refuse to let these propositions go to the people? Dare you stand between the people and these propositions?

I would appeal to you on another ground. Remember that it is the minority that is asking for these guarantees. You are just coming into power. The country has approved of your action in the election of Mr. LINCOLN. You can afford to be liberal. Liberality is a noble trait in any character, whether it be that of an individual or political party.

There are reasons why the South should be apprehensive

now. The organizations of the old Whig and Democratic parties had nothing sectional in them. There were no resolutions in their platforms which could give the South any cause of alarm. The contest between these parties did not involve any sectional interests whatever. Now, it is undeniable that the organization of the Republican party was brought about by the agitation of the slavery question in its various forms.

It is not strange to me that the success of that party in the late election should be misconstrued and misunderstood by the South, and that the people there should be apprehensive for the result.

If the Missouri Compromise had not been repealed we should not have found ourselves in our present condition. It was the repeal of that compromise that brought the Republican party into power. The masses of the people do not sympathize with extremists on either side. The Republican party took the middle ground, and thus rendered itself acceptable to them.

After the repeal of the Missouri Compromise came the Kansas agitation. In this the North was right and the South was wrong. Slavery was attempted to be forced upon an unwilling people. They resisted—the American people always will resist injustice. The excitement pervaded the whole country. Sympathy was excited for Kansas, and properly enough. This excitement benefited the Republican party—it injured all others. It overwhelmed all other considerations. The aspect of the slavery question was remembered in Kansas; elsewhere it was forgotten.

In this way, was the Republican party brought into power. I say now that if the Union is dissolved, that party will be responsible; responsible, as that party has now the power to prevent it.

The gentleman from Vermont, who has put his argument in a very ingenious way, insists that before the North is called upon to act on these propositions, that the South ought to declare whether she will be satisfied with them. I do not think so. I am perfectly aware of the difficulties under which the Representatives of the slave States are laboring. They cannot answer this question. Let the gentleman remember, when he presses this point so hard, and with such apparent candor, that even he will not undertake to answer for New England. More than that, he denies the authority of those who undertake to answer for the North. I do not believe the gentleman is very extreme in his opinions; but let him remember that the South should be treated fairly, and that she is placed in circumstances of peculiar embarrassment. It raised the hair upon Republican heads when they were told that Virginia had presented her ultimatum. Now complaint is made that she has not done so, and that she will not say what will satisfy her.

I feel that I have no interest in this question, except the interest of a citizen. I have no special interest in it. I ask nothing of politics, but I do feel for my country. I may be wrong. I do not claim infallibility; but I cannot bring my mind to the conclusion that we ought not to adopt these proposals. I cannot see any practical injury to the North in them, and I can see much benefit to the South.

The North is vitally interested in the preservation of peace, in the preservation of her commerce, and other relations with the South. These relations cannot be broken up without great injury to the Northern people. My heart would rejoice if we could think alike upon these propositions, and adopt them with a degree of unanimity that would give them weight with the country.

I would not assail the motives of gentlemen. Doubtless there are men who honestly believe that such a proposition ought only to be considered in a General Convention. In my judgment such a Convention would be utterly useless. It would lead to endless discussion, which would not be conducted with the decorum that characterizes these proceedings. It would amount to nothing.

No, gentlemen, there is a better way than that. Let us have no General Convention, but let us induce Congress to submit our propositions at once to the people. In no other way, in my judgment, can we avoid the disunion that threatens us. In no other way can the country be saved in her present peril.

Mr. DAVIS, of North Carolina:—*

* The speech of Mr. Davis is, I believe, the only one delivered in the Conference which I did not hear, and of which I did not preserve minutes more or less full. The reason for the omission was this: The morning session was protracted until a late hour, and the labor of reporting the remarks of the members had been very severe. The evening session commenced with some observations of my own; and after report-

Mr. ORTH:—Mr. President, I have thus far avoided any participation in the general discussion of questions which have claimed the attention of this Conference. My purpose has been to give a calm and careful attention to whatever may be offered for our consideration; to hear with unbiassed judgment the grievances which are the subject of complaint, and to afford redress, if redress be necessary.

Virginia, rich in her patriotism of the past, rich in her historic treasures, has called upon her sisters to convene and consult with reference to the condition of the Union, and the matters which are supposed to threaten our future peace and welfare. Indiana heard and heeded that call. To her it was as the voice of a mother to her child. It was a voice which none of the States of the great Northwest—carved out of that vast domain which Virginia granted to the United States as the common property of all—could fail to hear with favor. If dangers threaten the common welfare, if the future peace of this land is to be disturbed, it was well for Virginia, as in other days of danger, to sound the alarm, and invite a general council. In pursuance of that call, Indiana is here, and here to listen. She feels conscious that she has by no act of hers infringed upon the rights of any of her sister States; that she has been faithful to her constitutional obligations—seeking for nothing but what was right, and ever ready to remedy any wrong. Occupying this position, her representatives on this floor would be derelict in their duty if they

ing the remarks of Mr. Logan, which followed mine, I found myself in such a condition of physical exhaustion that I was obliged to retire to my room. It was during this temporary absence that the remarks of Mr. Davis were made. I was informed that his speech was very animated and in excellent temper—that he took the position that North Carolina was loyal to the Union, but that he fully concurred with the Southern States in the necessity of demanding constitutional guarantees; and that if these were not given, her relations were such with South Carolina and the Gulf States that, however much she might regret the necessity, she could not do otherwise than to leave the Union and unite her future with those of the seceded States.

I have been unable to communicate by letter with any of the members representing the States now in insurrection. As Mr. Davis was the only representative from North Carolina who entered into a general discussion of the reports of the majority and minority of the Committee of One from each State, I was the more desirous of securing some report of his remarks. But in all the material which has been furnished me, by the many members with whom I have corresponded, I find that none of them preserved notes of his speech.

attempted to assume any other, or to pursue any course of action inconsistent therewith.

What, then, in all candor, are the grievances of some of our sister States, as presented by their delegated authority to this Conference? Nothing of a tangible nature calling for practical and definite action. A deliberative body ought not to act upon the fears or imaginations of those desiring such action. The mere election of President of the United States by the votes of the northern portion of this Union, affords no just ground of complaint. That election is valid, being in strict conformity with all the requirements of the Constitution. The peculiar notions or political opinions of that President cannot be the ground of a just complaint, so long as these opinions in their practical operations do not interfere with or contravene the provisions of that Constitution. The opinions and principles of the President elect, however obnoxious they may be to any portion of the people of this Union, are harmless so long as his political opponents have in their control the legislative and judicial departments of the Government. The question of slavery in the Territories, if ever any real cause of grievance to any portion of the Union, is in process of final settlement, and will be settled before the close of the present Congress in a manner acceptable to a large majority of the American people. What, then, is left? "Personal Liberty bills" in some of the States; and these are being repealed as rapidly as possible; and so far as practical results are concerned, they have been a dead letter on the statute books ever since their enactment.

The non-enforcement of the fugitive slave law. The history of the country since the year of its enactment clearly shows that no law among the national statutes has received more prompt and vigorous execution, notwithstanding its exceedingly odious features. Here, then, is the list of grievances, or I might more properly say supposed grievances; and for a failure to redress them, this Government is threatened with civil war. To justify this unnatural and diabolical resort to arms, the chimera of "State sovereignty" is invoked. And what is State sovereignty? The gentleman from North Carolina has endeavored to enforce this doctrine, and deduce from certain premises, the right of a State, when she feels herself aggrieved, to secede from her sister

States, and assume an independent position and a separate nationality. The fallacy of the gentleman's position, in fact the fallacy of the doctrine of "State rights," and the deductions made therefrom by the school of politicians and statesmen to which the gentleman belongs, arises from confounding the terms State rights and State sovereignty, and using these as though they were convertible terms. The several States of this Union possess certain rights clearly defined, and known and understood by the reader of American political history. Subject to the restrictions of the national Constitution, they have the right to establish, regulate, and control their internal police and entire polity so far as it affects the persons and property subject to their jurisdiction; to regulate trade, commerce, contracts, marriage, the acquisition, possession, control, and disposal of real and personal property; also the assessing and collecting of taxes, and disbursement of the public revenue.

These are some of the main rights belonging to the States as such, but these do not in any just sense constitute sovereignty. The several States of the Union are not now and never have been sovereign States. They never possessed the right to declare war, to make peace, to coin money, to enter into treaty with nations, and none of them ever endeavored or attempted to exercise any such rights as these. These are attributes of sovereignty, as laid down by writers upon the laws of nations, and recognized as such by the civilized world. Examine the history of your several States, and tell me whether in any one of them any act or fact can be found which would entitle either of them at any time, past or present, to be recognized as sovereign independent nations?

Mr. RUFFIN:—Will the gentleman from Indiana permit me to inform him that during the Revolutionary War, the State of North Carolina had laid the foundation of a navy, and at the close of hostilities she transferred her vessels to the United States.

Mr. ORTH:—I thank the gentleman from North Carolina for the interruption, and for the allusion to the local history of his State, of which I was not before aware.

There, then, we have a single instance of one of the States taking one step toward sovereignty, by the establishing of a navy.

I believe this is the only instance now remembered, and this instance affords the strongest argument in favor of the position I assume and am endeavoring to enforce. North Carolina, it seems, had taken one step toward sovereignty; and yet upon the adoption of our national Constitution, upon the creation of the only sovereign Government in this Union, the *Government of the Union*, she transfers to that sovereign her infant navy; she relinquishes her only attribute of sovereignty—if such it be—to the United States, and merges herself with her sister States into that Union of States which has hitherto been our boast and pride, as well as the admiration of the world.

The several propositions now pending before us do not meet my approbation, and cannot receive my support. They are in the shape of amendments to the Constitution, and are all in the interest of slavery, seeking to strengthen that institution, and to give it an importance far beyond what the fathers were willing to concede. While the North is willing to recognize and enforce the requirements of the Constitution touching the various aspects of the slavery question, so nominated in the bond, they feel unwilling to grant new guarantees to a system which the civilized world is beginning to hold in detestation, and which is inimical to free institutions, and the only subject of contention that will ever seriously disturb the peace and prosperity of the Union. I am opposed to the proposition before us: First, because the grievances complained of are not of that serious character requiring any amendment of our fundamental laws. Secondly, because I am in favor of the Constitution as it is, firmly believing that no good reason exists for its change, and that an honest adherence to its wise provisions is our surest guarantee for real or supposed grievances, and that the present of all times is the most unpropitious moment to attempt any change or modification. Party politics in all their embittered madness rule the hour, but calm times and cool heads will be required whenever the American people desire to enter upon so hazardous an experiment. Let the Constitution remain; it has hitherto been, and will continue to be, the palladium of our rights, the sheet anchor of our safety. Thirdly, under no state of circumstances that can possibly arise among us as a people, will I ever consent, by word, thought, or deed, to do any thing to strengthen the institution of slavery. I regard it as an evil which all good men should desire to see totally eradicated; and I hope for the day to dawn speedily when, throughout the length and breadth of the land, freedom shall be enjoyed by every human being, without reference to caste, color, or nationality. While I am willing to tolerate its existence where it now is, I am unwilling to extend its boundaries a single inch, and will not give it any guarantee, protection, or encouragement, save what it can exact by the strict letter of the fundamental law. Beyond that I will never go; beyond that Indiana will never go; and to this, gentlemen from the other side had as well become reconciled. It is the *ne plus ultra* of the American people, and to that they will adhere through all coming time. If, in consequence of this position, the foundations of society are to be broken up, civil war inaugurated, and the destruction of the Government attempted, you must remember we are standing upon the Constitution, in favor of sustaining the laws of the land, denying the existence of any real grievance; and standing thus with that consciousness of strength which integrity imparts, you must strike the first blow, cross the Rubicon, commit the foul and damning crime of treason, and bring upon your people ruin, devastation, and destruction, and call down upon your guilty heads the curses of your children and the disapprobation of the civilized world!

Mr. BRONSON:—For what purpose was this Conference called? Why have we come here? I suppose we are here to do something, to accomplish something. If we are only here to make speeches, and not to arrive at conclusions, our mission is useless. The greater portion of the debate hitherto has been made up of set speeches, all like the circumlocution office in one of Dickens' novels, showing "how not to do it." I am not in favor of pursuing this course any longer. Let us talk the subject over like business men, in a sensible way, and then come to a vote. I think we may do something which will prove effectual, and I hope we shall. My political opinions are well known. For more than forty years I have belonged to one political party. I did not come here to speak. I did not intend to speak at all, and shall now only submit a few observations.

I hail from the old Democratic party. The most of you are members of the opposition. I do not know how or why I was selected as one of the delegates from New York. I do not even know how the vote of that delegation will stand on these proposals of amendment. I suppose the dominant party has taken care to send a majority of its members. If I was a mere politician, I do not know but I should be in favor of breaking up the Conference, and of doing nothing; but being only a Democrat, I desire to transmit to posterity the blessings of a good Constitution and a good Government.

The country has become disquieted. Its peace has been disturbed by the acts of politicians. Many have become disgusted with the present condition of affairs, and are unwilling to act or vote. A large portion of our people have become alarmed. They think their rights have been invaded. Some of the States have gone. GOD knows whether they will ever come back again. If we act wisely, perhaps they may. But there is occasion enough for alarm. I have felt alarmed for a long time. One way suggested to get these States back is by conquest. But what are we to do with a conquered State? Shall we establish a military despotism over it?

We all have the right to express our opinions, and I will express mine. There are eight other slave States whose condition is to be considered. If we do not act here, will they not leave us and join their sisters? I hope they will not. I would not raise my voice in this Conference, if it were not for the purpose of inducing them to stay.

Virginia, that noble old Commonwealth, has invited us together. She proposes the CRITTENDEN resolutions, and asks us to consider them. Now she is charged with standing in the way of the Government. This is not true. Blessed are the peacemakers, and the position of Virginia in this matter is that of a peace-maker. I thank her for bringing us together.

Two-thirds of the speeches here have been made by those of a political party to which I never belonged. I do not understand either their purposes or wishes. Perhaps I may be behind the times. I have not been actually engaged in politics for more than twenty-five years. During a large part of that time I have been engaged, in my humble way, in the administration of justice in the State I here in part represent. I do not know but I may be falling into the common fault of making a speech. If I do, you must check me. Again I say, I thank Virginia for her invitation. Why should we not confer together? Six or seven States—no matter which—are gone. If nothing is done, eight or nine others will follow, and other divisions will come as a matter of necessity. Rhode Island—patriotic Rhode Island—will not go with New England in this Conference. She will not separate from her southern sisters. Connecticut, I think, will not stay, and New York, I believe, will stand with the South.

How is it, or why is it, that we should do nothing? Why should we break up and go home? Have not all the States asked us to come here and do this work? Why did their legislatures take the trouble to send us here? All this circumlocution might have better been done at home.

Will a Convention answer the purpose, when another Confederacy has been formed in our very midst? It would be two years at least before any thing could be accomplished by a Convention, and then it would be too late. We all know how delegates to such a Convention are elected. We all know how much time would be consumed before the Convention could meet. I say we cannot bear the delay. I ask the gentleman (Mr. Baldwin) of Connecticut whether he thinks it would be safe to delay.

Mr. BALDWIN:—I think it is always safe to follow the Constitution. I think we can follow the example of Kentucky.

Mr. CLAY:—I would suggest to the gentleman from Connecticut that the representatives of Kentucky are here to speak for her.

Mr. BRONSON:—Kentucky has sent delegates to this Convention since she passed the resolutions to which the gentleman refers. I think we cannot stand upon the ground taken in these resolutions. I do not believe Kentucky herself would be satisfied with them now.

It is strange to see gentlemen so cool and apathetic under such circumstances. Is no one alarmed for the safety of the old flag about which so much is said? Can the Border States stay with us when their brethren are gone? If the action of the North in relation to slavery is such as to drive out South Carolina, can Delaware and the other Border States remain?

For one, I do not wish to put this Constitution into the hands of a General Convention. Who can tell what such a convention would do with the Constitution; what it would do with the decisions of the Supreme Court, under which so many of the vexatious questions have been settled? It would be worse than attempting to settle our differences in a town meeting. I would hesitate long before I would submit such questions to a convention. Before they could be settled in that way, the Union would be gone forever. The process would be too slow. I have nothing to gain in this matter. My only wish is to spend my few remaining days in the United States, and to transmit the blessings of our Government to my children.

Some of the Republican members here subordinate their platform to their country. I commend them for it; these are noble sentiments. Men should abandon platforms when they tend to destroy the country. I concur in the sentiments of the gentleman from Illinois, uttered this morning. They also are noble sentiments.

I venerate our Constitution. When made, it was equal to any ever framed. Nothing short of Almighty Wisdom could have framed a better. But was it given to human wisdom, to WASHINGTON and MADISON, to foresee all the events of the future? The Constitution has held us together for three-fourths of a century; that is a wonder in itself; but its makers did not foresee this day—a day when Freedom itself was in danger of perishing.

Why this hesitation about amending the Constitution? New York accepted it reluctantly, and only ratified it upon the assurance that it should be amended as she proposed. It is not so holy a thing now, that it may not be amended. WASHINGTON, you must remember, signed the Fugitive Slave Law of 1793, as well as the Constitution.

We are told by gentlemen from New York and Connecticut (Mr. NOYES and Mr. BALDWIN), that the action proposed here is unconstitutional. It does not become these gentlemen to raise this objection. There was never an amendment of the State Constitutions, in either of the States they represent, adopted, that was not brought before the people in substantially the same way.

Much has been said here about modern civilization and the spirit of the age. It is said that these are hostile to slavery.

Suppose they are? What have we to do with them? The example of England, also, has been referred to, as well as that of France. True, they have abolished slavery by name, but they have imported apprentices from Africa, and Coolies from Asia, and have placed them under the worst form of slavery ever known. England tolerates slavery in her mining districts to-day in a worse form than that existing in the Southern States. She has millions in India worse off than slaves. She has been the greatest land robber on the earth. She has contributed to the support of the Juggernaut, and has forced the Chinese at the point of the bayonet to eat opium. Do you forget that she ruined the capitol in this city, and blew it up, in 1814? I do not deny her virtues, but I do not care to follow her example.

Our fathers said slavery was strictly a State institution, and they would not meddle with it by the Constitution. Their doctrine is true now. The Union cannot be preserved if we interfere with the institutions of the States.

I will not stop to refer to the Missouri Compromise, or the compromises of 1850 and 1854. I will only say that the North understood these to settle the slavery question, and professed to agree not to meddle with slavery hereafter in the States. But the cry of freedom was raised, and its new apostles, during the last campaign, went through the land preaching destruction to slavery. What did they mean but that slavery was to be assailed at every possible point? This doctrine was involved in their platforms, and advocated in their speeches. They collected all the bad things ever said about slavery, whether true or untrue, and published them. The purpose to assail the institution was everywhere owned.

I wish to say a word about the Territories. What great harm would be done if all the Territories were thrown open to slavery? By the decision of the Supreme Court in the Dred Scott case, they are open already. But in the greater part of them slavery cannot exist at all. New Mexico has a slave code. So have the Cherokee and other Indian tribes; and yet slavery does not and cannot flourish among them. It cannot make head against the obstacles which oppose it, and yet you will attack it even there. If you do so, civil war is inevitable.

But what mischief is done if slavery does go into the Territories? It will not add another to the degraded race of Africans. It is a blessing to the slave if he may be permitted to go with his master into these new Territories. In the old slave States he is compelled to work in gangs under the whip of a driver, with no one to look after his health or comfort. Take him into one of these new Territories, and there are one hundred white men and women to protect each individual of his race, and to see that he suffers no wrong. It is a blessing to take him out of the plantation gangs, and to place him in a new country. Then why not let him go there and live in peace? Your zeal to exclude slavery from the Territories only injures the African race. If there is a good substantial reason for this exclusion I shall be glad to hear it. Up to this time I have heard no good reason stated. Although I have declared myself a Democrat, in this Conference I am no party man. Show me any good reason for not adopting these proposals of amendment and I will oppose them. But until that reason is shown they will receive my support. So far as I can judge, no argument has been proposed here against these propositions which is not of a partisan character.

The rights which the slave States now ask to have us recognize, are guaranteed to them by the Constitution as it now stands. We are giving them nothing new. Every lawyer is familiar with the rule of constitutional construction, that all the rights not expressly granted to the General Government are reserved to the States. Let us carry this principle into effect now. It is all that we are asked to do. Let us do something. Let us amend these propositions; make them as unobjectionable as we can, and send them to Congress. Let us urge Congress and the country to adopt them. In their adoption there is safety; there is great danger in their rejection.

Mr. Pollock obtained the floor, and at twelve o'clock the Conference adjourned to ten o'clock to-morrow.

FIFTEENTH DAY.

WASHINGTON, FRIDAY, *February 22d*, 1861.

THE Conference was called to order by President TYLER, at 10 o'clock A. M., and prayer was offered by Rev. Dr. SUNDERLAND.

The Journal of yesterday was read, corrected, and approved.

Mr. WICKLIFFE:—It will be necessary that some plan be adopted to defray the expenses of the Conference, and of printing the Journal. I move the appointment, by the President, of a committee of three to take those subjects into consideration.

The motion was adopted, and the President appointed Mr. JOHNSON, of Maryland, Mr. POLLOCK, and Mr. GRANGER as such committee.

Mr. HITCHCOCK:—I have an amendment in three sections which I shall offer to the report of the committee. I ask that it may be read, laid on the table, and printed.

The motion was agreed to, and the amendment read as follows:

Strike out Section 3, and insert the three following:

SEC. 3. Congress shall have no power to regulate, abolish, or control within any State the relations established or recognized by the laws thereof, touching persons held to service or labor therein.

SEC. 4. Congress shall have no power to discharge any person held to service or labor in the District of Columbia, under the laws thereof, from such service or labor, or to impair any rights pertaining to that relation under the laws now in force within the said District, while such relation shall exist in the State of Maryland, without the consent of said State, and of those to whom the service or labor is due, or making to them just compensation therefor; nor the power to interfere with or prohibit members of Congress, and officers of the Federal Government whose duties require them to be in said District, from bringing with them, retaining, and taking away persons so held to service or labor; nor the power to impair or abolish the relations of persons owing service or labor in places under the exclusive jurisdiction of the United States, within those States and Territories where such relations are established or recognized by law.

SEC. 5. Congress shall have no power to prohibit the removal or transportation of persons held to labor or service in any State or Territory of the United States, to any State or Territory thereof, where the same obligation or liability to labor or service is established or recognized by law; and the right during such transportation, by sea or river, of touching at ports, shores, and landings, and of landing in case of distress, shall exist; nor shall Congress have power to authorize any higher rate of taxation on persons held to service or labor than on land.

Strike out Section 7, and insert:

SEC. 9. Congress shall provide by law, that in all cases where the marshal, or other officer whose duty it shall be to arrest any fugitive from service or labor, shall be prevented from so doing by violence of a mob or riotous assemblage, or where, after arrest, such fugitive shall be rescued by like violence, and the party to whom such service or labor is due shall thereby be deprived of the same, the United States shall pay to such party the full value of such service or labor.

Mr. TURNER:—I offer the following resolution:

Resolved, That the time fixed upon to commence voting upon the questions before this Convention, be postponed until Monday, February 25th, at 12 o'clock M.

I am as desirous as any member of the Conference can be for action. Illinois is a Border State, and she feels, in common with the Border States, a deep interest in the questions we are discussing here. But I think a false issue has arisen, and that it ought to be corrected. This issue has been forced upon us, and it will go to the country unless corrected. Very little time has yet been occupied by Indiana, Illinois, and Ohio, but we wish and we ought to be heard.

Mr. JOHNSON, of Missouri, moved to lay the resolution upon the table.

The vote was taken by States, with the following result:

AYES.—Delaware, Kentucky, Maryland, Missouri, New Jersey, North Carolina, Pennsylvania, Rhode Island, Tennessee, and Virginia—10.

NOES.—Connecticut, Illinois, Indiana, Iowa, Maine, Massachusetts, New York, New Hampshire, Ohio and Vermont—10.

Mr. TURNER:—I see the resolution does not meet with favor. I will withdraw it.

Mr. CHASE:—I offer the resolution again. I wish to appeal to this Conference in the name of peace, not to press this vote to-day. We have been discussing general questions. There has been little or no discussion touching the merits of the proposed amendments to the Constitution. Do gentlemen suppose that if it is pressed through in this way, it will meet with favor when it comes before the country? Let me assure you, gentlemen, that you will not give the country peace by such a course.

There is a prospect that all sections of the Union may yet be induced to agree to a General Convention. The floor is so parcelled out that the Western States cannot be heard. Why do you force the vote in this manner? Two-thirds of Congress must concur, or these propositions cannot go to the people. The same two-thirds can suspend the rule at any time. There is no necessity for passing these propositions to-day. I regret that the proposition of Mr. WICKLIFFE, limiting the speeches to thirty minutes, has not prevailed. It was withdrawn.

Mr. WICKLIFFE:—No! It was laid on the table by enemies.

Mr. POLLOCK:—I have the floor. I will occupy it only thirty minutes, with the understanding that those who follow will do the same. We still have time for six speeches.

Mr. CHASE:—I have but little more to say. When we have a rule, we know what it is. A general understanding will amount to nothing. I have insisted that it was inexpedient to press these matters to a decision before the inauguration of Mr. LINCOLN; but when overruled I have cheerfully submitted. I now appeal to gentlemen to yield, and let us take the final vote on Monday.

One word now as to a General Convention. I have faith in that, and believe we can agree to call one. The idea was started by Kentucky, and promptly followed by Illinois. I have seen a copy of the "Louisville Journal," which strongly advocates it. It is practicable, and the country will assent to it.

Mr. HOUSTON:—The delegates from Delaware desire that the vote should be taken to-day. We have not discussed these propositions, and do not wish to discuss them. We want action.

Mr. BACKUS:—I concur in the views of the gentleman from Delaware. Discussion, so far, has tended very little toward harmony or unanimity. I am in favor of closing the general debate to-day. But I do protest against that part of the resolution we have adopted, which limits the discussion of an amendment to five minutes, and confines the reply to the committee. We ought not thus to be restricted and choked down. I will not move to amend the resolution now under discussion. It will answer my purpose to give notice that I shall move to amend the five-minute rule.

Mr. COOK:—We ought to have an opportunity to present the views of Illinois. As yet we have had none. We cannot justify ourselves to our people unless we do.

Mr. WICKLIFFE:—I move to lay the whole subject on the table. I want to test the question. Debate and discussion change the mind of no one. We have now been here eighteen days, and the country is expecting a decision.

The vote upon Mr. WICKLIFFE's motion was called by States, and resulted as follows:

AYES.—Delaware, Kentucky, Maryland, Missouri, New Jersey, North Carolina, Rhode Island, Tennessee, and Virginia—9.

NOES.—Connecticut, Illinois, Indiana, Iowa, Maine, Massachusetts, New York, New Hampshire, Ohio, Pennsylvania, and Vermont—11.

Mr. BACKUS:—I now offer my proposition as a substitute for Mr. CHASE's resolution, as follows:

Resolved, That the resolution heretofore passed, limiting debate on amendments that shall be offered to the report of the Grand Committee, be so amended as to allow the delegates who may desire, to speak not exceeding ten minutes on each amendment.

Mr. CHASE:—I do not wish to seem unreasonable. As my resolution meets with objection, I will withdraw it in favor of the one adopted by my colleague.

Mr. WICKLIFFE:—Have gentlemen calculated how many hours this will take? It will amount to a total defeat of all action. We could not get through by the middle of next month.

Mr. EWING:—I favor the resolution. All should have a fair chance.

Mr. HOUSTON:—I move to amend, giving each delegate ten minutes.

Mr. WILMOT:—I object to that very strenuously. Many delegations are divided. I hope the resolution will pass as it is.

Mr. HECKLEMAN:—I approve of the rule as it now stands. Practically, it gives ten minutes.

Mr. RANDOLPH:—I move to lay the resolution on the table. We adopted the rule unanimously.

Mr. WILMOT:—The motion is not in order. We have once voted not to table the resolutions.

Mr. HOUSTON:—I will withdraw my motion, at the instance of the gentlemen around me.

Mr. CHASE:—The question is upon the adoption of the resolution offered by Mr. BACKUS. I have accepted it in place of the one offered by myself.

The PRESIDENT:—It is subject, at any time, to a motion to lay on the table.

Mr. RANDOLPH:—That is my motion.

The motion to lay the resolution of Mr. BACKUS on the table was lost by the following vote—the vote by States being requested by Mr. CHASE:

AYES.—Delaware, Kentucky, Maryland, Missouri, New Jersey, North Carolina, Pennsylvania, Rhode Island, Tennessee, and Virginia—10.

NOES.—Connecticut, Indiana, Illinois, Iowa, Maine, Massachusetts, New Hampshire, New York, Ohio, and Vermont—10.

Mr. GUTHRIE:—I presume we all desire to know the result of our labors. I regret to see so much feeling manifested. Perhaps some of us had better take the benefit of the prayers of the church on Sunday. Some of us wish to get our propositions to Congress at an early hour. Those who oppose us—those determined to defeat action, can speak on until the fourth of March. I hope such is not their intention.

Mr. TUCK:—If the rule is abused, the Convention will stop the abuse.

At this point there were loud calls of "question," and the PRESIDENT put the question to vote, *viva voce*.

The PRESIDENT:—I think the Noes clearly have it.

Mr. CHASE:—A vote by States was called for by several members.

Mr. BARRINGER:—Is this resolution intended to give the right of reply? If so, we shall have a half-hour speech upon every amendment.

Mr. BACKUS:—If any member wishes to divide his time, he can do so; but he can only occupy ten minutes in all. We are called to deliberate, as well as to act. We are asked if we wish to stave off final action? I answer, No. I want speedy action. But at the same time let us have deliberation. I wish to give a vote that my constituents will approve.

The PRESIDENT:—The vote will be taken by States.

The resolution was adopted by the following vote:

AYES.—Connecticut, Illinois, Indiana, Iowa, Maine, Massachusetts, New York, New Hampshire, Ohio, Pennsylvania, and Vermont—11.

NOES.—Delaware, Kentucky, Maryland, Missouri, New Jersey, North Carolina, Rhode Island, Tennessee, and Virginia—9.

Mr. HALL offered the following, which was read, laid on the table, and ordered to be printed:

Amendment to Section 8 of the Committee's Report, to come in after the words "retaining and taking away persons so bound to labor:"—"but the bringing into said District of persons held to service for the purpose of being sold, or placed in depot to be afterwards transferred to any other place to be sold as merchandise, is forever prohibited, and Congress may pass all necessary laws to make this prohibition effectual; nor shall Congress have," &c.

The PRESIDENT:—The Conference will proceed to the order of the day, and Mr. POLLOCK has the floor:

Mr. POLLOCK:—Brevity is always a virtue. I intend to practice that virtue now. I would not make a single observation, if I did not feel that by keeping silence I should neglect my duty. As it is, I do not intend to occupy the time of the Conference more than twenty minutes.

When the committee upon the subject invited Pennsylvania to furnish a block for the Washington Monument in this city, they asked also for a motto, to be inscribed upon it, which should express some idea characteristic of Pennsylvania. What was the motto selected in behalf of that great State? Did we go to Germantown and invoke the memories of the mighty dead? Did we ask the motto of Valley Forge? No, brothers, no! Pennsylvania stood by the side of the grave of Penn, the man of peace, and in his example she found her motto, and it stands inscribed upon her contribution to that monument to the Father of his Country to-day. There may it stand forever. "*Pennsylvania was founded by deeds of Peace.*" How noble the sentiment! How characteristic of that Commonwealth!

Animated by the same sentiment, filled with the same spirit, herself asking nothing, requiring nothing, Pennsylvania comes into this Conference and says to every delegate here, "*Peace, Brothers, Peace.*" She is not for war. She believes that the power of kindness is far greater than that of the sword; that in the affection of brother toward brother there is greater strength than in all the iron contained in all her thousand hills and mountains. She comes here at the instance of a sister. She heard the voice of that sister asking for consultation, and she obeyed it. She is here, and in the right spirit.

A word now as to the motive of Virginia in calling the States together. Some object that Virginia comes bearing the olive branch on the point of the bayonet. Not so, sir. She is placed in a peculiar position, and I appreciate it. She does not make use of threats. These exist only in the imagination of gentlemen. I am willing to meet her here upon the very ground she takes, and unite with her in saying, "Our Union as it is, now and forever." We are here taking counsel, not with traitors, not with secessionists, but with lovers of the Union.

The people love the Union; they will not give it up. They are true. My heart almost leapt from my bosom when that telegraph message was read from Missouri a few days ago. Tennessee has taken up the cry, "Union for ever." The nation is troubled. All nations are, at times. But our troubles are not insurmountable. We are all here together to settle them. Why not settle them, and give peace to the Union, and joy to the hearts of the people?

We can settle our difficulties. The right feeling animates gentlemen from both sections. Where was the heart in this Conference that did not start with emotion, when, some days ago, that glorious old patriot from North Carolina (Mr. RUFFIN) told us of his devotion to the Union? Who did not honor and respect him? Old men and young men wept as they listened. Friends! Countrymen! I come here from a Border State. These States have a vital interest in the result, therefore we speak earnestly. Let us say to the angry passions of the country, "Peace, be still!"

The Border States are united; they have common interests. Beside the hearthstones of each, sit wives, and children, and families, connected with each other by ties of blood, of interest, of social intercourse. We are one. Is Maryland or Delaware ready to say that either will part company from Pennsylvania? No! We are brethren—come weal, come wo, we will stand by each other, and we will stand by the Union.

Gentlemen say there will not be war, if we do not agree. I wish I could think so, but I cannot. But if war should come, let me ask the gentlemen from New York who think principles are standing in their way, will you take the risk? Will you see the soil of Pennsylvania drenched with blood? Can you risk all this hereafter, when you can avoid it by accepting a proposition that involves no sacrifice of principles? Never in my whole life have I felt the weight of official responsibility as I feel it now. God grant that war may be averted from the country!

Let the lightning this day flash to the extreme limits of the Union, the glad tidings that we have settled these questions. The message would be received with gratitude and thanksgiving. Our friends in the Border States say, "We love the Union, we wish to stay in it; we do not wish to be driven out." Can you not, will you not, do something for them? Let us trust this matter to the people. I am not afraid to trust the people of Pennsylvania. New York and Massachusetts, trust yours!

We talk calmly of war, but we forget its calamities. Let us remember that we should not sacrifice one life for this paltry abstraction. Let us remember how great are the miseries of war. Let us think of the rush of angry armies, of the widows and orphans, of the sorrow and desolation that war always leaves in its path.

Christian men! remember that our great Saviour was a Prince of Peace—that he came to conquer with peace, not with the sword. "The Lord God omnipotent reigneth."

Disunion is a crime against every thing. Above all, it is a crime against God. Christians, pause and reflect. Let me entreat you to help us save this country from disunion.

I speak earnestly. We Pennsylvanians are upon the border. Our soil must be the battle ground. Upon us will the heavy trouble fall. Once more I say, let us trust the people. They are always right. They will do something; and honest men, sincere men, tell us that unless something is done, the border slave States cannot be retained in the Union.

I am not here as a party man, but as an American citizen, and a citizen of Pennsylvania. I am here to perform my duty to the whole country, if I can find out what that duty is.

Our friends say there is great apprehension at the South that the Republican party meditates unconditional interference with Southern rights. I do not believe for a moment that there is any ground for such an apprehension. But, nevertheless, it exists. Acting upon it, several States have withdrawn from the Union. We must deal with it in the best way we can. If we can satisfy our southern brethren, in the name of peace let us do it. I labored for the election of Mr. LINCOLN, but I never understood that hostility to slavery was the leading idea in the platform of his party. Pennsylvania had other interests—other reasons very powerful, for supporting him. There was the repeal of the Missouri Compromise—ruinous discriminations in the Tariff—the corruption of the Government—the villanous conduct of its high officers; these and other considerations gave Mr. LINCOLN more strength in Pennsylvania than the slavery question.

There are sentiments and opinions at the North that must be respected. There are sentiments and opinions at the South that must be respected; but there are no differences that cannot be honorably adjusted. The only practicable way that I can discover is to adopt the plan reported by the committee, and secure its submission to the people.

How can we do greater honor to this glorious day, which gave the immortal WASHINGTON to his country and to the world, than by marking it on the calendar as the day that secured the safety and perpetuity of the American Union?

Mr. SUMMERS:—The Committee on Credentials have examined the case of Mr. J. C. STONE, who is commissioned as a delegate from Kansas, and are of opinion that he is duly accredited.

Mr. FIELD:—I understand that he was appointed by Mr. BEEBE, the Secretary of the Territorial Government.

Mr. CLAY:—There is a provision in the Kansas Act authorizing the Secretary to perform all the duties of the Governor in his absence.

Mr. BROCKENBROUGH:—I represent an old and honored Commonwealth. I speak, remembering the maxing that "a soft answer turneth away wrath." But I should disregard my duty if I did not reply to what was said a few days ago, in arraignment—in unfair and improper arraignment, of Virginia.

Virginia occupies no menacing position, no attitude of hostility toward the Union or her sister States. Virginia knows that "eternal vigilance is the price of liberty." She knows, too, that there is good policy in the maxim, "in peace prepare for war." Her action is only such as is dictated by a prudent foresight. How unkind, then, are such taunts against Virginia, the mother of us all. She comes here in a paternal spirit; she desires to preserve the Union; she disdains to employ a menace; she knows that she never can secure the coöperation of brave men by employing menaces. No! She wishes to use all her efforts to perpetuate the reign of peace.

Another says we are seeking to secure an amendment of the Constitution by the employment of unconstitutional means, and that this meeting is a revolutionary mob—that these eminent men of the country assembled here, constitute a mob. No, sir! No!

Mr. BALDWIN :—If the gentleman from Virginia refers to me, he quite misunderstood me. I said only that the action proposed here was not contemplated by the Constitution, and was revolutionary in its tendency.

Mr. BROCKENBROUGH :—I cannot for my life so consider it. This is merely an advisory body. We are here to devise an adjustment, and to lay it before Congress. We are exercising the right of petition, and that is a sacred right. Is this revolutionary? No, sir! You would insist that Congress should *receive* a petition, although that body had no right to act upon it. If so, how much more should our petition be received, when we seek to preserve the Union, and when the Constitution expressly authorizes Congress to act in such a case.

The gentleman from Vermont said last evening, that a pledge from the South to abide by the result would be a condition precedent to the submission of the proposition at all, and yet he says he cannot pledge Vermont. Why, then, does he ask us to pledge Virginia?

Mr. CHITTENDEN :—I am not willing to be misunderstood. I thought my language was plain. What I said was, that no one could pledge the free States for or against these propositions; but I did say we could pledge them *to abide by the Union, whatever* the result might be. *That* is the pledge we ask from the South.

Mr. BROCKENBROUGH:—Well, that is a pledge we have no authority to give. We cannot accept these propositions as a boon from any section. We must have them as a right, or not at all.

But let me address myself at once to the momentous question. It seems that we can agree upon every thing but this question of slavery in the Territories. So far as that subject is concerned, Virginia has declared that she will accept the Crittenden resolutions. She and her southern sisters will stand upon and abide by them. If gentlemen will come up to this basis of adjustment with manly firmness, the electric wires will flash a thrill of joy to the hearts of the people this very hour. Why not come up to it like men?

The Supreme Court has already established the rights of the South, so far as this question is concerned, upon a basis which is satisfactory. Under the Dred Scott decision, the people of the South have the right to go into any portion of the Territory with their slaves. You, gentlemen of the North, will not abide by that decision. You have declared in your platform that it is a miserable dogma. How can we be satisfied with such a guarantee for our rights as that?

But it is said that this part of the Dred Scott decision is only an *obiter dictum;* that the question was not presented by the record. This is not so. As was said by Governor WICKLIFFE, the other day, there were two questions in that case. The judgment of the court was upon them both, and both were presented by the record.

We know that the dominant party has elected a President on a purely sectional issue, and in deadly hostility to our institutions. We believe, from all the indications of the times, that our institutions are utterly insecure. Therefore we ask these guarantees. Give them to us, and from that time you will restore peace and quiet to the country. You at once attach the Border States firmly to you forever. I hope you will do so; but I tell you that the Border States cannot be retained unless you will consent to give such guarantees as will bring back the seceded States, and unite us all in a glorious confederation.

Sentiments have been uttered here that grate harshly on the minds of Southern gentlemen. It is said that this is a war of ideas. If so, then there is certainly that irrepressible conflict about which we have heard so much. But it is not true that slaves exclude free labor. Come to the harvest homes of Western Virginia. There you will see the union of white and black labor—see the two races working harmoniously together. The mechanics are white, the field hands are black. Those only make such assertions who know nothing about it.

You insist at the North that slavery is a sin. If it is as you claim it to be, a sin, the sum of all villanies, then we may as well separate. We cannot live together longer.

If we cannot have the aid of other sections, the Border States must take the subject into their own hands, and settle it for themselves. These States, with one exception, have shown a most excellent spirit. Let them all come up to the work to-day; on this natal day of WASHINGTON, of whom it was said that nature had denied him children, in order that he might be indeed the Father of his Country. New Jersey has most nobly responded, through her distinguished sons, but especially through the voice of that eloquent man, who swept with a master hand the chords of the human heart, in his remarks here, and tones of heavenly music responded to the touch.

The whole nation stands on tiptoe awaiting the final result of the action of this Conference. All sections are ready to make sacrifices, but sacrifices are not required. Let us act, and then go home. A grateful people will bind the wreath of victory around your brows, for "Peace hath her victories not less than War."

We make no appeal to the sympathies of gentlemen. We ask you to do justice, simple justice to the South. Do it, and you will do honor to yourselves. Give us the guarantees we ask, and my word for it, you will see the seceded States coming back one by one, and we shall see ourselves once more a happy and a united people!

Mr. WILMOT:—It is not my purpose to enter upon the wide field that has been opened in this debate. I did not intend to speak at all. I know well the position I occupy before the country. I am regarded by those who do not know me as an extreme man. I am, if I know myself, a man of moderation, and, I trust, of firmness. I make these remarks because the time has come when I must separate from my delegation. I concede every thing to their patriotism, good intentions, and integrity. But I must separate from them in the votes they are about to give.

We are called here to consider the condition of the country. It is said that condition requires our interference—that such interference is necessary. The country has just passed through one of those conflicts which are incidental to our form of Government. It has borne the trial, and I think it is safe.

Those who insist that certain things shall be done, place us in a delicate position. You say that you do not object to the inauguration of Mr. LINCOLN, but you refuse to permit his principles to be carried into effect. We say that we have not merely elected Mr. LINCOLN, but we have decided the principles upon which his administration shall be conducted. You refuse to permit this, and say that you will leave us and revolutionize, unless we consent to a counter resolution.

The contest in which we are now engaged is not a new one. It is of twelve or fifteen years' standing. It assumed new proportions when we acquired Texas. Texas, under the laws of Mexico, was then free. We insisted that slavery should not be recognized there. You claimed that it should—that slavery should go into all the common Territories of the Union. You succeeded. You procured what you claim is a decision of the court in your favor. But the people would not give the question up. The issue was formed—Slavery or Freedom; and on that issue we went into the late election. It was well understood in all its bearings. It was discussed and argued upon both sides and all sides, and the people determined the question against the South. In my section of the country there was no change. In all the excitement of a Presidential contest, I do not know of twenty votes that were changed. The opinions of the people were formed before; now they have declared them.

My first allegiance is to the principles of truth and justice. Convince me that your propositions are right, that they are just and true, and I will accept them. I will sustain them to the end. If they are wrong—and I now believe them to be—I will never sustain them, and I will show my faith in GOD by leaving the consequences with Him.

Any substantial change in the fundamental principles of government is revolutionary. Yours may be a peaceable one, but it is still a revolution. The seceded States are in armed revolution. You are in direct alliance with them. You say the Government shall not retake the forts, collect the revenue, and you ask us to aid you in preventing the Government from doing its duty.

Permit this, and the judgment of the world will be that we have submitted to the inauguration of your principles as the principles of the Government. It would exhibit a weakness from which the country could never hope to recover. These are reasons satisfactory enough to me. I cannot vote for the first article.

Mr. WICKLIFFE:—Do you wish to get the seceded States back?

Mr. WILMOT:—Certainly I do.

Mr. WICKLIFFE:—How do you propose to do it?

Mr. WILMOT:—I cannot say that I have any special way. It is their duty to return. There are better methods of coercing them than to march our army on to their soil. Now I understand it is your purpose to intrench slavery behind the Constitution.

Mr. RUFFIN:—Certainly. That is true—in a certain portion of the Territories.

Mr. WILMOT:—I thought I was not mistaken. The Government has long been administered in the interest of slavery. The fixed determination of the North is, that this shall be no longer.

Mr. HOUSTON:—Will the gentleman hazard the assertion that such has been the policy of Tennessee, Maryland, or Delaware?

Mr. WILMOT:—I did not intend to say more than that such has been the general policy of the Government. Another objection to the proposed amendment is its ambiguity. Its construction is doubtful, when it should be plain. Don't let us differ when we go home. If we do we shall settle nothing. Some will claim that the first article does not furnish a slave code. Others will claim that it does, and such I think is a fact. I am also opposed to the second article. I do not think it is right thus to bind posterity. I am opposed to the third article, except the first clause. If you think there is really a purpose at the North to interfere with slavery in the States, I am willing a declaratory amendment should be adopted prohibiting such interference. I like that of Mr. FIELD much better. I can go for that with all my heart.

As to the foreign slave trade we ask nothing. The laws are well enough as they are, if properly enforced. Besides, you make too much of it. You will claim hereafter that this formed one part of the compromise. It will amount to nothing.

Mr. BARRINGER:—But the South wants the foreign slave trade prohibited.

Mr. WILMOT:—Do not the statutes prohibit it? Why not enforce them?

Mr. BARRINGER:—We had rather have the prohibition in the Constitution.

Mr. WILMOT:—I am opposed also to abrogating the power of Congress over the District of Columbia. I hope to see slavery abolished in the District.

Mr. WICKLIFFE:—Will the gentleman from Pennsylvania abide by the decision in the Dred Scott case?

Mr. WILMOT:—Certainly, so far as it decides what is in the record.

Mr. SEDDON:—You will not permit it to settle the principle?

Mr. WILMOT:—I will not, any more than Virginia would accede to the decision upon the Alien and Sedition Laws. I will be frank and go farther. If the Court had undertaken to settle the principle, I would do all I reasonably could to overthrow the decision.

Mr. SEDDON:—My voice has failed me to-day, and I do not know that I can speak in audible tones, but I will try.

I understand the gentleman who last addressed us to say, that there are to be incorporated into the administration of the Government two new principles: one is, that there shall be no slavery in the territories; the other is, that the action of the Government shall be on the side of freedom. And furthermore, that slavery is to be regarded as a purely local institution, and that slaves are not to be regarded as property anywhere except in the slave States. Now, that was just the way in which I interpreted the action of the North in the last election, and it is precisely this view which has led to the secession of the States. The gentleman well understands that a different view of their rights under the Constitution prevails among the Southern people. Will he also understand and recognize the fact, that the Supreme Court has clearly given the sanction of its opinion to the Southern construction?

Mr. WILMOT:—Ought not the action of the Government under WASHINGTON to be a precedent of some weight in our favor?

Mr. SEDDON:—I cannot accede to that. Now the North has inaugurated this policy. We of the South say it is a subversion of the Constitution. The gentleman must as freely admit that the party just coming into power must of necessity be a Northern party. It can have no affiliation with any party at the South. Now I ask, can we, as a matter of policy or justice, whose rights are so vitally involved, sit by and see this done? Slavery is with us a democratic and a social interest, a political institution, the grandest item of our prosperity. Can we in safety or justice sit quietly by and allow the North thus to array all the powers of the Government against us?

The hour of one o'clock having arrived, the PRESIDENT announced that under the resolutions adopted by the Conference, general debate must cease, and the Conference would proceed to vote upon the report of the General Committee, and various amendments proposed thereto.

Mr. FIELD:—I rise to a question of privilege. What was done by the Conference with the credentials of the gentleman from Kansas?

The SECRETARY:—The practice heretofore has been, to consider a gentleman a member, when the Committee on Credentials report in his favor.

Mr. FIELD:—Then I move to reconsider the action of the Conference in this case.

Mr. PRICE :—I rise to a question of order. The committee have reported in favor of Mr. STONE, and that is conclusive.

The PRESIDENT :—I think the Conference has a right to pass upon the credentials.

Mr. FIELD :—I have a serious objection to the admission of the gentleman from Kansas. He holds the commission of the Secretary of the Territory alone, from a man who has never been appointed Governor. It is very irregular. It looks as though the gentleman was sent here only for the purpose of giving the vote of Kansas to certain propositions.

Mr. JOHNSON, of Missouri :—The delegate comes here with an appointment under the seal of the State of Kansas. The act admitting Kansas provides that all the territorial officers shall exercise jurisdiction until others are elected. I think it is in very bad taste for the gentleman from New York to question the regularity of the appointment.

Mr. WICKLIFFE :—I make a point of order. We have decided to proceed to the vote at this time.

The PRESIDENT :—I think this is a privileged question.

Mr. HOUSTON :—I respectfully appeal from the decision of the PRESIDENT.

Mr. MOREHEAD :—I move to lay the whole subject on the table.

Mr. FIELD :—I ask for a vote by States.

The PRESIDENT :—It is somewhat difficult to decide what motion has precedence. What was the motion of the gentleman from New York?

Mr. FIELD :—I moved a reconsideration of the action of the Convention admitting Mr. STONE. Let us have a vote on that motion. It is as good a test as any.

Mr. MOREHEAD :—I insist that the question is upon my motion to lay the whole subject on the table.

The question was taken upon the motion of Mr. MOREHEAD, with the following result:

AYES.—Delaware, Kentucky, Maryland, Missouri, New Jersey, North Carolina, Pennsylvania, Rhode Island, Tennessee and Virginia—10.

NOES.—Connecticut, Illinois, Indiana, Maine, Massachusetts, New York, New Hampshire, Ohio, and Vermont—9.

Mr. CLAY :—I would ask, as a matter of courtesy, not to say

of common decency, that Mr. STONE may be permitted to state how and why he came here.

Mr. STONE, of Kansas:—I understand that I was appointed by the Secretary of Kansas, who was at the time the Acting Governor. I understand that the appointment was made in accordance with the Enabling Act of Kansas. I am not inclined to argue my right to a seat in the Conference.

Mr. FIELD:—I wish to ask the gentleman only one question. Was not Governor ROBINSON actually in possession of his office before the delegate received his appointment, and is he not in such possession now?

Mr. STONE:—He was, and is.

Mr. ALEXANDER:—I call for the reading of the fourth Rule.

The fourth Rule was read by the Secretary, as follows:

4TH RULE.—A member shall not speak oftener than twice, without special leave, upon the same question; and not a second time, before every other who has been silent shall have been heard, if he chooses to speak upon the subject.

Mr. FIELD:—In order to bring the subject fairly before the Conference, I will put my motion in the form of a resolution, as follows:

Resolved, That the credentials of Mr. STONE, who desires to act as a Commissioner from Kansas, be referred back to the Committee on Credentials, with instructions to that committee to report the facts concerning his appointment, and whether it proceeded from the Territorial Secretary.

Mr. SUMMERS:—I wish the Committee on Credentials to stand right with the Conference. We accepted the commission of the Acting Governor as *prima facia* correct.

Mr. VANDEVER:—I wish to offer a resolution.

Mr. GUTHRIE:—All resolutions are out of order.

The PRESIDENT:—I think resolutions under the ruling of the Conference cannot now be considered.

Mr. CURTIS:—I ask leave for the State of Iowa to vote on the motion to lay the subject of the admission of the delegate from Kansas on the table.

The motion was granted, and Iowa being called, voted No; and the vote stood: Ayes, 10; Noes, 10. And so the motion was lost.

Much discussion here ensued on the subject of the admission of the delegate from Kansas, which was participated in by Messrs. STOCKTON, CLEVELAND, COALTER, and others, when

Mr. STONE observed that he had no desire to force himself into the Conference, and until the question was settled he thought it proper to withdraw.

The resolution offered by Mr. FIELD was adopted without a division.

VOTE ON THE PROPOSITIONS AND AMENDMENTS.

The PRESIDENT:—The Conference will now proceed to the consideration of the report of the General Committee, and the amendments thereto. The question will be taken on the adoption of the first section reported by the Committee of One from each State, which the SECRETARY will now read.

The SECRETARY read the report as follows:

SECTION 1. In all the present territory of the United States, not embraced within the limits of the Cherokee treaty grant, north of a line from east to west on the parallel of 36° 30′ north latitude, involuntary servitude, except in punishment of crime, is prohibited whilst it shall be under a territorial government; and in all the present territory south of said line, the status of persons owing service or labor as it now exists shall not be changed by law while such territory shall be under a territorial government; and neither Congress nor the territorial government shall have power to hinder or prevent the taking to said territory of persons held to labor or involuntary service, within the United States, according to the laws or usages of the State from which such persons may be taken, nor to impair the rights arising out of said relations, which shall be subject to judicial cognizance in the Federal Courts, according to the common law; and when any territory north or south of said line, within such boundary as Congress may prescribe, shall contain a population required for a member of Congress, according to the then Federal ratio of representation, it shall, if its form of Government be republican, be admitted into the Union on an equal footing with the original States, with or without involuntary service or labor, as the constitution of such new State may provide.

SECTION 2. Territory shall not be acquired by the United States, unless by treaty; nor, except for naval and commercial stations and depots, unless such treaty shall be ratified by four-fifths of all the members of the Senate.

SECTION 3. Neither the Constitution nor any amendment thereof shall be construed to give Congress power to regulate, abolish, or control, within any State or Territory of the United States, the relation established or recognized by the laws thereof touching persons bound to labor or involuntary service therein; nor to interfere with or abolish involuntary service in the District of Columbia, without the consent of Maryland, and without the consent of the owners, or making the owners who do not consent just compensation; nor the power to interfere with or prohibit representatives and others from bringing with them to the city of Washington, retaining and taking away, persons so bound to labor; nor the power to interfere with or abolish involuntary service in places under the exclusive jurisdiction of the United States within those States and Territories where the same is established or recognized; nor the power to prohibit the removal or transportation, by land, sea, or river, of persons held to labor or involuntary service in any State or Territory of the United States to any other State or Territory thereof where it is established or recognized by law or usage; and the right during transportation of touching at ports, shores, and landings, and of landing in case of distress, shall exist. Nor shall Congress have power to authorize any higher rate of taxation on persons bound to labor, than on land.

SECTION 4. The third paragraph of the second section of the fourth article of the Constitution shall not be construed to prevent any of the States, by appropriate legislation, and through the action of their judicial and ministerial officers, from enforcing the delivery of fugitives from labor to the person to whom such service or labor is due.

SECTION 5. The foreign slave trade, and the importation of slaves into the United States and their Territories, from places beyond the present limits thereof, are forever prohibited.

SECTION 6. The first, third, and fifth sections, together with this section six of these amendments, and the third paragraph of the second section of the first article of the Constitution, and the third paragraph of the second section of the fourth article thereof, shall not be amended or abolished without the consent of all the States.

SECTION 7. Congress shall provide by law that the United States shall pay to the owner the full value of his fugitive from labor, in all cases where the marshal, or other officer, whose duty it was to arrest such fugitive, was prevented from so doing by violence or intimidation from mobs or riotous assemblages, or when, after arrest, such fugitive was rescued by force, and the owner thereby prevented and obstructed in the pursuit of his remedy for the recovery of such fugitive.

Mr. GUTHRIE:—I hope now the Conference will proceed in the regular way, and that the majority report will be first perfected so far as amendments are concerned, and that then it may be adopted.

Mr. SEDDON:—I move to amend the first section by inserting, after the words "in all the present territory south of said line," the words "including the Cherokee grant," and I call for a vote by States on the adoption of the amendment I propose. My object is to carry out the instruction of the committee. A small part of the grant lies north of the line. It is better to include the whole.

Mr. BACKUS:—I move to amend the amendment proposed by the gentleman from Virginia, by substituting the word "excluding" for the word "including," and on my motion ask a vote by States.

Mr. RUFFIN:—I think the gentleman does not understand the effect of his amendment.

Mr. BACKUS:—I do not think we ought to regard the Cherokee grant at all.

Mr. FRANKLIN:—I think both the amendments important.

Mr. SEDDON:—We must recognize the Cherokee Territory, and not divide it. Upon mature reflection, I think the amendment is important.

The vote was taken upon the motion of Mr. BACKUS, and resulted as follows:

AYES.—Connecticut, Illinois, Indiana, Iowa, Maine, Massachusetts, New York, New Hampshire, Ohio, Pennsylvania, and Vermont—11.

NOES.—Delaware, Kentucky, Maryland, Missouri, New Jersey, North Carolina, Rhode Island, Tennessee, and Virginia—9.

The PRESIDENT:—The question is now upon the amendment offered by the gentleman from Virginia, as amended by the Conference.

Mr. GUTHRIE:—I hope the amendment will not be adopted. It is not necessary to the sense of the article. It is cumulative in its effect. We have expressly excluded the Cherokee grant, lest we might seem to overrule the Cherokee treaty by a provision of the Constitution.

The vote was taken by States, on the adoption of the amendment proposed by Mr. SEDDON, as amended, with the following result:

AYES.—Connecticut, Illinois, Indiana, Iowa, Maine, Massachusetts, New York, New Hampshire, Ohio, and Vermont—10.

NOES.—Delaware, Kentucky, Maryland, Missouri, New Jersey, North Carolina, Pennsylvania, Rhode Island, Tennessee, and Virginia—10.

Thus the amendment was lost.

Mr. PRATT:—I wish to enter my dissent from the vote of Connecticut.

Mr. FRANKLIN:—I now offer as a substitute for the first section, as reported, the following:

Strike out after the words "United States," in the first line, and insert as follows:

"Not embraced by the Cherokee treaty, north of the parallel of 36° 30′ of north latitude, involuntary servitude, except in punishment of crime, is prohibited. In all the present territory south of that line, the *status* of persons held to service or labor, as it now exists, shall not be changed; nor shall any law be passed to hinder or prevent the taking of such persons to said territory, nor to impair the rights arising from said relation; but the same shall be subject to judicial cognizance in the Federal courts, according to the common law. When any territory north or south of said line, within such boundary as Congress may prescribe, shall contain a population equal to that required for a member of Congress, it shall, if its form of government be republican, be admitted into the Union on an equal footing with the original States, with or without involuntary servitude, as the constitution of such State may provide."

Mr. FOWLER:—Let us first perfect the original. I move to amend by inserting after the word "prevent," in the first section, the words "or facilitate."

Mr. REID:—I think we ought to perfect the section before we vote on a substitute. I move to amend it by inserting after the word "line," after the words "territory south of said line," the following words: "involuntary servitude is recognized, and property in those of the African race held to service or labor in any of the States of the Union, when removed to such territory, shall be protected and"—

I have not expressed my views at large upon the subject of the committee's report. I have earnestly wished to settle the perplexing questions which now distract the country. I do not rise to make a speech. I have not come here to exact more than the North can honorably grant, nor to deceive the North in the result, if the rights of the South are not protected. Our property is involved in your action. You can afford to be liberal. If you intend to recognize property in slaves, write it down in the bond. If the North wants any protection, name it, and we will put it into the bond. If you fear that slavery may go north of the proposed line, we will give you any assurance to the contrary. But I tell you that on the other side we require reciprocal terms. Nothing else will satisfy the public sentiment. Twelve months hence and we will not take what we now offer to take.

What are we talking about? Every one knows that the African race is better off at the South than it could be elsewhere. We do not wish to disrupt the Union. You are doing it on a mere Northern abstraction. Suppose a foreign power asked you what you were fighting about, what would be your answer?

But I was saying that the only way is for the North to be liberal; to be reciprocal; to make us entirely safe. Our security must be put into the bond and be faithfully preserved. The present *status* of the States in the Union is deceptive. If I am to remain in the Union, it don't suit me. If I am to go into a southern confederacy, it is just what I should want. Beware, gentlemen of the North! You are cutting yourselves off from future glory and expansion.

Mr. VANDEVER:—The gentleman from North Carolina wants the distinct recognition of slavery in the bond. I would like to refer him to the condition of this question when the Constitution was adopted. The men of that time would not assert such a position. They did not think it proper or necessary. If we adopt his views we attempt to sit in judgment on the men of that day. Mr. Calhoun understood this matter perfectly, and in one of his speeches refers to the unwillingness of the Convention to recognize slavery specifically. The sentiment of Iowa is that no such recognition ought to be made now. I am opposed to the amendment.

Mr. SEDDON:—I consider this an important amendment, and a very just one. The principle upon which we are proceeding is that of partition. We, with our property are prohibited from going north of the line. The exact correlative of that would be, that you should be prohibited from going south with your institutions. That we do not ask. On one side involuntary servitude is prohibited. On the other we simply ask that it may be recognized. We give up two-thirds of the territory altogether. All we ask is protection in the remaining one-third.

What is the meaning of this proposition as it now stands? Who does not see that its meaning is ambiguous? It requires us to give up territorial protection, and leaves us with nothing but the shred of a right protected by the Federal courts. Once more let me tell you, that in my opinion the South will never consider this a satisfactory adjustment. You say we are protected by the principles of the common law. Who can tell what this will amount to? Assuming the territorial government to be favorable, it could do nothing. You leave it powerless. Suppose a citizen of Virginia emigrates to the territory south of the line with his property. He would have no earthly right except under the laws of Virginia. The power to enforce those laws is a thousand miles away. If we are to make a partition, let it be a partition. As the provision stands, it is the unfairest bargain ever made. It is all on the side of the North. In common fairness and honesty, I submit that the North ought to vote for this amendment.

Mr. ORTH:—There is much that is worthy of consideration in the remarks of the gentleman from Virginia. I hope earnestly that we shall not adopt a proposal of amendment that admits of two interpretations. If I could vote for the report of the majority at all, I would throw around it all the protection it needs. This is a new and peculiar species of property which we are now making the Constitution recognize and protect. If the South is entitled to the proposition itself, I think they are entitled to this amendment. After all, it is only making the amendment express just what we know its friends claim it implies.

Mr. GUTHRIE:—I would have preferred the direct recognition by express terms of slavery south of the line proposed, and I voted that way in the committee. I suppose, however, that the clause as it stands recognizes the *status* there, as it now exists—that it prevents all interference with the *status*. Would you prefer to put into the proposition certain express terms which would destroy all chance of its adoption by the people? I do not think the world is governed by ideas alone. It is governed by ideas and material interests. The Constitution of 1787 secured the interests of the slaveholder in the States. This clause does the same in the Territories. No man can be cheated by it unless he cheats himself. Gentlemen favoring the amendment must know that at least it will not improve the prospects of the proposition with the people. Do you wish to break up the Conference? This is an effectual way of doing it.

We ask for this proposition substantially as it stands. The North can give it to us if it chooses. If it will not, then we shall go home and tell our constituents. They must decide for themselves what they will do. This will settle the Territorial question effectually. What more do we want? The additional guarantees? These are provided for in the other clauses.

Mr. CHITTENDEN:—I call for a vote by States on Mr. REID's amendment.

Mr. BARRINGER:—I shall vote for the amendment of my colleague. I have occupied no time in the general debate, but now I do desire to say a few words about this amendment, and the proposition to which it is offered. The amendment brings up the very *gist* of the matter. Differences of opinion exist as to the effect of the clause. The amendment settles them. This is no place to talk about devotion to the Union. To be a Union at all it must be one that recognizes and protects the rights of all. Any other Union is not worth the name; is not worth preserving. We came here, it is true, to save the Union. We came here to devise the means of saving it. Practically the Union is already dissolved. If not dissolved it is disintegrated.

We ask first, additional guarantees for our rights—for Southern rights. They must be such as will satisfy our people, and bring back the States that have left the Union. Short of this they will amount to nothing. I know the public opinion of the South on these important questions. I have closely watched its growth. My own convictions as to what it will require are decided. Unless you use language and adopt terms in your proposals of amendment which will satisfy the seceded States—which will induce them to return to the Union—your labors will have been in vain.

What is our claim? It is this, in short: We claim that every Southern man has the right to go into the Territories with his property, wherever these Territories may be. The Territories belong to both; to the South as well as to the North. We want equality. We have no wish to propagate slavery, but every man at the South does wish to insist upon his right to enter the Territories upon terms of perfect equality with the North, if he chooses to do so. He may not exercise the right, but he will not give it up.

We want a division of the Territories. We want to set up landmarks so that neither we nor our posterity shall dispute hereafter about the line.

North Carolina has instructed us to say to this Conference, that if the CRITTENDEN amendment can be adopted here, we can carry it almost with unanimity. There will be a struggle even with our own people, but we can induce them to adopt it.

We have three hundred miles of border in common with South Carolina. Our trade and our associations are in that direction. It is useless to deny that South Carolina has sympathizers among us in her recent movement. You must consider these things, and give us a chance. We must base our argument on principle; we must stand upon terms of perfect equality.

The proposition needs this amendment. As it stands it is ambiguous. It is worse than that, for its construction will depend on the opinion of a Territorial Judge.

Mr. CRISFIELD:—I come from a State that is deeply interested in the subject of slavery. Nevertheless, I shall vote against the amendment of the gentleman from North Carolina.

I belong to that class of politicians which believes that the people of every section of the Union have a right to go into all the Territories of the Union, and take with them their property and hold it in safety. But we ought not, in our proposals of amendment to the Constitution, to insist upon what will be repulsive to any section of the Union. I think the amendment is unnecessary—that the right we claim is sufficiently protected without it. As it stands, neither Congress nor the Territorial Government has the right to impair the *status* of the slave. What farther protection do we need? What other can we have? Why should we insist upon the adoption of a new style of language? We ought not to be unreasonable; we ought to content ourselves with the proposition as it stands, and not put expressions into it which will make the whole repulsive to a large section of the country, and which, in all probability, will defeat the whole amendment when it comes before the country. I am not even sure that we could get it there. I doubt whether it would pass Congress.

This is a very serious and important question. We wish to stay the hands of extremists on both sides. We wish to stand by the Union. If war comes, our soil is to be the battle ground. I wish to avoid war. I will insist upon this, and I will consent to no extreme opinions.

Mr. VANDEVER:—I do not see why Mr. GUTHRIE cannot accept the proposed amendment. He and the gentleman from North Carolina are both aiming at the same thing. The amendment is certainly the clearest. Do you suppose the people are not going to understand the subject thoroughly? Do you suppose that they will be deceived by any such transparent disguise of words? You do not pay them a very high compliment by such a supposition.

I must vote against the amendment, because I am opposed to the *principle* of protecting slavery in the Territories. Such is the sentiment of the North. If it was not, I should vote for the amendment.

Mr. MOREHEAD, of Kentucky:—As I intend to vote against the amendment, it is due to the Convention that I should state the reasons for my vote. I am in favor of a clear recognition of all the rights of the South, especially of our rights in the Territories. I voted for the CRITTENDEN amendment in the committee. I thought the North ought, in justice to us, to adopt that amendment. We, in this Conference, have selected a Committee of One from each State—a committee of able men, and we have placed this subject in their charge. They have consulted together. They have ascertained the views and feeling of the different sections of the country; they have embodied the result of their labors in this report. The question now presented appears to my mind to be this: After all the time and ability they have given to their report in the present distracted and perilous condition of the country, shall I consent to put words into the amendment of the Constitution which they recommend, that will ensure its defeat when it comes before the people?

I know as certainly as that GOD rules in heaven, that unless we come to some satisfactory adjustment in this Conference, a convulsion will ensue such as the world has never seen.

I have been travelling for nearly two months in the seceded States. I believe I understand the temper of their people. I have found there an all-pervading dissatisfaction with the existing state of things, but I have also found great devotion to the Union. I think we can yet save the seceded States. But at least let us save Texas and Arkansas. As it is, black ruin sits nursing the earthquake which threatens to level this Government to its foundations. Can you not feel it, while there is yet time to prepare for the shock? If this giant frenzy of disunion raises its crested head—if red battle stamps his foot, the North will feel the shock as severely as the South.

Such is the prospect before us, and near to us, and yet gentlemen say that they will not give *one* guarantee to avert such dire calamities. Will not the gentleman from New York do one thing to save that Ship of State of which he spoke so eloquently, when she is already among the breakers, and driving so rapidly toward that rocky shore against which her ribs of steel cannot long protect her? We are patriots all—we are bound to act together—to do something—to do our duty, and our whole duty—to do what will ultimately preserve the Union.

Mr. PALMER:—A few days ago the Conference listened to a deliberate defence of the institution of slavery by its friends from the slave States, in which at least one gentleman from a free State (Mr. Ewing) participated. That defence could have had but one object. That object was to place us who do not believe in slavery in such a position that we could not agree to a compromise without endorsing the views then expressed. Gentlemen expect us to give up our opinions and concur with them. I have but one remark to make to all such suggestions. We entertain our opinions on the subject of slavery; we cannot, we will not surrender them.

We are told that this contest must cease, or the Union must perish. I am inclined to think so myself. We stand ready to make any reasonable compromise to save the Union, short of sacrificing our opinions. You, gentlemen of the South, cannot be satisfied unless our capitulation is complete.

I do not assent to much that is said here about the Border States. If the Union is not dissolved until the Border States go to fighting each other, it will last forever.

Mr. REID:—If we all mean the same thing, let us put it into the bond. Then there will be no room for misunderstanding or controversy. If you leave this article open to construction, nothing will be settled. The gentleman is mistaken if he supposes that I wish him to adopt my arguments. I do not. If this provision, as it stands, protects slavery in the Territories south of 36° and 30′, why not say so in express terms? I question whether the article, as reported, recognizes property in slaves at all. I wish to settle the question now and forever. I do not wish to have my purpose perverted. I wish to carry home to North Carolina a reasonable story. We have given up all our rights in the territory north of the line. Let the North be reciprocal. What shall I tell my people at home? That I have given away their rights in more than one-half the territory, and have not even secured a provision protecting property in slaves in the remainder?

The vote, on the request of Mr. CHITTENDEN, was taken by States, and resulted as follows:—

AYES.—Virginia, North Carolina, and Missouri—3.

NOES.—Maine, New Hampshire, Vermont, Massachusetts, Rhode Island, Connecticut, New York, New Jersey, Pennsylvania, Delaware, Maryland, Tennessee, Kentucky, Ohio, Indiana, Illinois, and Iowa—17.

So the amendment was lost.

Mr. CARRUTHERS:—Tennessee approves the sentiment of the amendment, but she thinks the requisite security is already given.

Messrs. BUTLER and CLAY, of Kentucky, and Mr. DENT, of Maryland, asked to have their dissent recorded from the votes of their respective States.

Mr. BARRINGER:—I wish to make a suggestion in relation to Mr. FRANKLIN's substitute. I think it is not in order. The Conference has already determined to perfect the committee's report, before substitutes are to be considered.

Mr. CURTIS:—I now move to amend Mr. FRANKLIN's substitute, by striking out all after the word "prohibit," in the third line, down to and including the words "common law," and inserting instead thereof the words, "but this restriction shall not apply to territory south of said line."

My proposition is offered in good faith, and to show that Iowa is disposed to compromise. I do not say that this is as far as she will go. I have inserted the very words used by our fathers. They prohibited slavery north and tolerated it south of the line. This was the original proposition of Virginia. If there is any thing in its ethics, they are Virginia ethics. Slavery now exists in these Territories. Let it be there. There is slavery in Kansas, Utah, and Nebraska. We cannot help it. It appears to me that the South ought to accept this amendment. It recognizes the opinions of our fathers. This was JEFFERSON'S idea when he drew the ordinance of 1787.

The Constitution does recognize the relation of master and slave, in my opinion. I do not like it, I confess. You in the South do not regard your blacks as slaves in the absolute sense of the term. You have a right in their services, not in their bodies. You recognize them as *men* in various ways.

Again I say, I do not offer this amendment to embarrass the action of the Conference. It secures slavery south of 36° 30′.

Mr. GUTHRIE :—This amendment would not be satisfactory either to the South or myself. In my judgment, it ought not to be adopted. We claim the right under the Constitution as it is, to go into all the Territories of the Union with our property. This right is confirmed to us by the decision of the Supreme Court. There will be no compromise, if we cannot go home to our people and tell them that you concede this right south of 36° 30′. Otherwise, they would throw the propositions in our faces. As it stands, the article gives you security, North. As it would be when this amendment is adopted, it would give the South law and litigation. We want peace. We cannot take this amendment.

Pending the consideration of the amendment offered by Mr. CURTIS, on motion of Mr. JAMES, the Conference adjourned to ten o'clock to-morrow morning.

SIXTEENTH DAY.

WASHINGTON, SATURDAY, *February 23d*, 1861.

THE Conference was called to order at ten o'clock A. M., by President TYLER, and its proceedings commenced with prayer from Rev. Dr. BUTLER.

The Journal of yesterday, in part, was read. The Secretary stated that he had not found time to complete it.

Mr. ALEXANDER:—I move to rescind the resolution adopted yesterday allowing ten minutes to a member proposing an amendment, and ten minutes for the reply. I do not propose to discuss the motion. I think all will agree upon the necessity of rescinding the resolution. This will leave the five minutes' rule in full force.

A vote by States was asked by several members.

Mr. SEDDON:—I wish to call the attention of the Conference to this subject for a moment. I hope the present rule will not be changed. The debate up to yesterday was upon general questions. We have not yet gone into detail. We tried the operation of the ten minutes' rule yesterday. I am sure that it will not be claimed that any gentleman abused it.

Mr. JAMES:—We have scarcely discussed a question of detail connected with an article in the committee's report.

Mr. ALEXANDER:—I will withdraw my motion.

Mr. VANDEVER:—I tried to offer a resolution yesterday which I deemed important. It was then ruled out of order. I am sure it is in order now. It reads as follows:

Resolved, That whatever may be the ultimate determination upon the amendment of the Federal Constitution, or other propositions for adjustment approved by this Convention, we, the members, do recommend our respective States and constituencies to faithfully abide in the Union.

Mr. BRONSON:—I rise to a question of order. The report of the committee and the amendments thereto, are the special order of business. We ought not to permit collateral questions to be brought in. We adjourned yesterday with the amendment proposed by Mr. FRANKLIN as a substitute for the first article of the committee's report before us. To that Mr. CURTIS, of Iowa, had offered an amendment, which was under discussion. Let us keep to our rules.

The PRESIDENT:—I think the resolution of the gentleman from Iowa is in order now.

Mr. VANDEVER:—I hope the question will be taken upon my resolution at the present time. All the questions we have been discussing are, in my judgment, secondary to another which ought to be first decided. Is this Conference true to the Union—true under all circumstances? If so, I regard it as highly important that the Conference should give some expression to that effect. Even if we should settle this great contention about slavery to-day, other questions might afterward arise. I am quite prepared to see a claim set up, to what is called the right of peaceful secession. I would guard against all such claims. The passage of this resolution would have a beneficial effect upon the public mind. I think we still have a Government which can protect itself and the nation. My constituents believe this preliminary question quite as important as that of protecting slavery in the Territories.

Mr. RANDOLPH:—I move to lay the resolution introduced by the gentleman from Iowa, on the table.

Mr. BUTLER:—I want the resolution read again.

Mr. VANDEVER:—Let us all go on to the record. I ask a vote by States.

The resolution was read, and the vote being taken by States, resulted as follows:

AYES.—Rhode Island, New Jersey, Pennsylvania, Delaware, Maryland, Virginia, North Carolina, Tennessee, Kentucky, Missouri, and Ohio—11.

NOES.—Maine, New Hampshire, Vermont, Massachusetts, Connecticut, New York, Indiana, Illinois, and Iowa—9.

So the motion to lay the resolution on the table prevailed.

The PRESIDENT:—The Conference will now proceed to the consideration of the order of the day. The question is upon the amendment offered by the gentleman from Iowa, to the substitute for the first section of the report of the committee, offered by the gentleman from Pennsylvania.

Mr. HITCHCOCK:—I came into this Conference with the honest and single purpose of healing the unfortunate differences which now distract the country, having no sinister ends to answer. That purpose has hitherto remained unchanged. To accomplish it, there is nothing I will not sacrifice except principle and honor. I think the amendment of the gentleman from Iowa is, in substance, just the same as Mr. FRANKLIN's substitute. In the one, a fact is implied; in the other, the same fact is expressed. I understand that neither proposition can command the support of those gentlemen in the Conference who favor a National Convention. Neither can the amendment command the approval of the border slave States. Certainly not all, if it can any of them. The adoption, then, of this amendment, will operate as a defeat of the first section of the proposed amendment of the Constitution. Neither party in this Conference will accept it. While, therefore, I believe it ought to be accepted—while I believe it amounts to nearly the same as the original proposition, I will not peril the Union upon a mere question of form.

I did not come here to inquire into causes. Our differences exist, and I do not think they were occasioned by the success of the Republican party in the last Presidential election. The plotters against the Union have seized upon the occasion to accomplish their designs.

By no fault of their own, several of the Border States are placed in a very unfortunate position. They wish to remain in the Union, but their people insist that certain of their rights shall be previously secured; in other words, guaranteed.

It is my firm belief that if the inauguration of President LINCOLN was over, if his administration had been for a few months in operation, we should all be at peace. Now, we must act upon the facts as they are presented to us.

I must vote against the amendment of the gentleman from Iowa in order to give the original proposition a fair chance. I wish to have it distinctly understood that this is the reason why I cast my vote against his amendment.

Mr. JAMES:—I do not rise to debate the question at length,

now before the Conference. I think that this amendment brings us at once to the true issue which the case presents. We have hitherto been talking about abstractions. Now we come directly to the point. As this is a Conference to settle disputed questions, the sooner we come to the true points in issue, the better.

What is the cause of our present differences? It is not found in any action of the North. No Northern State proposes to disrupt the Union or to threaten its stability. But certain of the Southern slave States come here and say to us that certain alleged rights of theirs must be secured, or they cannot induce their people to consent to remain in the Union.

I have heard a great deal said in this Conference about civil war. Now, civil war is not a pleasant subject to consider; but, gentlemen, I pray you to remember that the North proposes no civil war. She declines to consider the subject at all, now. If civil war is brought upon the country, it will be your work, not ours. The North will do all she can to stay your hands—to prevent you from plunging the country into civil war. She will not enter upon it until you force her to do so. When you begin it, and force her into war in order to defend the Government and the Union, I have no doubt she will enter the field and carry on civil war until the Union is restored and its enemies put down. Let me ask you, gentlemen, who have so much to say about war, whether you had not better leave that question where it is?

It has been assumed, and very often stated here, that the present Constitution gives the right to the Southern slave owner to take his negroes into any of the Territories of the United States, and hold them there as slaves. I think it would be well for you not to act so entirely upon that assumption. A different view prevails quite extensively at the North. It will be a long time before that view is changed.

Now, you gentlemen of the South propose to restore the Missouri Compromise line. To induce us to adopt it, you say that the territory south of it is a barren, worthless desert—that slavery can never obtain a substantial foothold there. Why, then, do you make the subject one of so much importance? Why do you risk all the calamities of civil war and a disruption of the Union for such a poor reward? We should distrust all your statements, we should disbelieve all your professions of patriotism, if we could for a moment credit the assertion that you would break up the Union on such a worthless pretext.

You ring the changes in our ears upon the decision of the Supreme Court in your favor. Let me tell you plainly that there is no section of the Union in which the decisions of that court have been so fully and fairly respected and observed as in the free States of the North. With that you should be satisfied.

You are in trouble; that is evident. Your troubles have been caused by the repeal of the Missouri Compromise. That, again, was your work, not ours. We opposed the repeal to the end. You had the power and you carried it. Now the North is indifferent about the restoration of that compromise; but if that will satisfy you, restore the *status quo*, and the North will stand by you. But you must not expect now, that the North will do any thing better for you than to extend the provisions of the Missouri Compromise to the Pacific Ocean.

Mr. CARRUTHERS:—The gentleman from New York who has last addressed the Conference, appeals to us to accept the amendment now proposed, upon the grounds of justice and equity. What is the present state of the case? We claim the right to go into all the Territories with our southern property. The Supreme Court has confirmed this right to us. With this advantage in our favor, we have met here to compromise. What is the proposition now? It is to give the North all the territory north of 36° 30′, and to leave all questions concerning the territory south of that line without any adjustment at all! That gentleman favors no compromise at all. He proposes that we should go home without any adjustment. Shall we go back to our excited people and say this: "The North will make no adjustment with you"? Is this the way to settle the important questions that now distract the country?

We have not come here for war; we have come here for peace. We have come to settle all the questions between us upon a fair and equitable basis. How are we met? Gentlemen from the North say they will give us nothing. All we ask is right and justice—that right which the Constitution and the Court has given us in *all* the territory, *secured in one-third of it*. With that we will be content.

Some gentlemen object to the phraseology of the article.

Let them have all that their own way. They stop here to quarrel about words? Settle those as you like, but we ask all the friends of the Union to stand by, and reject all amendments which affect the substance of the article. Such a course will end all contention.

We read in Sacred History that the Israelites were once so conscientious that they would not fight on Sunday. They were attacked and overthrown. They finally agreed to compromise the question of conscience so far as to fight in self-defence on Sunday. They were attacked then, and the enemy was overthrown.

The report is not such as we could wish it might be, but, such as it is, we will accept it and stand by it. We will adopt it, and we ask the North to adopt it, in the true spirit of compromise.

Mr. LOGAN:—I am under the necessity of believing that the gentleman from Iowa is in earnest, in offering this amendment; but if I were to present it, I should not expect any one to believe I was in earnest. What is the compromise which this amendment proposes? It is, in substance, that the North will take three-fourths of the Territory under the Constitution, and the rest by force. If gentlemen entertain such views, we might as well come to a direct vote at once, and see whether any thing can be done.

The gentleman from Iowa says this is the Missouri Compromise; but it lacks much of it. Besides, circumstances have greatly changed since 1820, when the compromise was adopted. Now, seven States have left us and gone out of the Union, and we are acting in view of that fact. There is a contest between the North and the remaining Southern States, and the latter have no better chance in that contest alone, than Turkey had in the grasp of the rugged Russian Bear. The gentlemen from these States do not threaten. All they say is, "If we cannot agree longer together, let us go in peace. We will fight only in self-defence."

They ask us further, "If we stay with you, how do you intend to treat us? As equals, or as inferiors?" If as inferiors, we cannot sustain ourselves with our people, saying nothing of our own self-respect. I acknowledge the force of these inquiries.

A civil revolution terminated at the last election. The power to wield the Government came into the hands of the Republicans. The circumstances suddenly change. Political power leaves the South. What now shall we give them in place of that? Shall we leave these States at our mercy? This is an earnest time. We should act as if the fate of a great nation depended on our action. If we intend to say we will do nothing, let us say so plainly, and not by indirection.

Mr. MOREHEAD, of North Carolina:—I thank GOD I hear a voice such as I have just heard from *that* section of the country (Iowa)! I have been a member of a recent Legislature of North Carolina, in which there was a majority of secessionists. I have been jeered at in that body for the opinions I have expressed, for I have told those gentlemen repeatedly that if we could once get the ear of the North, the North would do us justice. They pointed me to the raid of John Brown—to the meeting in Boston, where the gallows of John Brown was carried with solemn ceremonies into the Cradle of Liberty. They pointed me to the man who presided over that meeting, since elevated to the high and honorable position of Governor of Massachusetts. Notwithstanding all this, I have replied that the masses of the northern people would deal fairly by us. I have told these secessionists to their teeth that Mr. Lincoln was properly elected under the Constitution, and that he ought to be inaugurated. Their reply was, "Kansas, and the John Brown raid!"

Now, I ask this Conference to look for one moment at the effect of the amendment which is proposed. It withdraws all constitutional protection from us north of 36° 30′. Adopt it, and what has Massachusetts to do but to import her foreigners into the country south, and take possession of it. New York will back her, and we shall be swept from the face of the earth.

If the gentleman from New York means to say that the nation can put its foot on to the neck of the States and crush them into submission, let him go into Virginia and join in another John Brown raid. Virginia will treat him as she did John Brown. No! the gentleman has not studied the motto of the Union. There is the *E pluribus* as well as the *unum*. If the new President proposes to come down to the South and conquer us, he will find that the whole temple shall fall. We can be crushed, perhaps, but conquered, *never!*

Mr. BRADFORD:—Maryland has, under the lead of her constitutional Chief Magistrate, determined to preserve her position of neutrality, and not by any action of hers to add to the prevailing excitement on either side. She has done what she could to allay the existing irritation, and will continue to pursue the same policy she has hitherto adopted.

Here is a large file of amendments. Almost every delegation has given notice of an intention to offer one or more. If we begin to adopt them, I feel sure that we shall destroy all hope of an ultimate agreement.

Mr. President, I desire to make an emphatic declaration to this Conference. It is this: Give us the report as it came from the committee, without substantial alteration, and there is no power on earth that can draw the State of Maryland out of the Union! Maryland has been called the heart of the Union. The day she leaves the Union, that heart is broken! I am now inclined to set my face against all amendments. I think that is the better course.

In the populous section of the State where I reside, the universal cry is, "For God's sake, settle these questions!" Why can we not settle them? The committee inform us that the members of which it is composed, were nearly unanimous upon all points except the territorial question. Will reasonable men not yield a little to each other in order to settle that?

Then let us look calmly at the consequences which must follow our disagreement. I will enter into no panegyric of the Union. To use an often repeated expression, it needs none. It is enshrined in the hearts of the people with all the glories of the past, with all the glorious hopes of the future. It has given us a position in the front rank of the nations. There is every prospect that it will make us in the end the most powerful among the nations. Who can look unmoved upon the spectacle of such a Union about to fall into fragments? What sacrifice too great to avert such a ruin?

We all understand, we all agree that we can save the Union by settling this miserable question of slavery in the Territories. We should be unworthy of ourselves and our trusts, if we set our division upon this question above the preservation of the Union. How can it be possible that Union men, or even politicians, can hesitate as to which path ought to be taken? One leads to ruin, the other to a haven of safety.

It will be a world-wonder hereafter, if we do not agree. The people—the whole country, will stand aghast at the spectacle of folly we present. I would not, for all the wealth and honors the nation could bestow, be remembered hereafter as a man who stood between these measures of pacification and the people who should finally decide upon them. I would not have the priceless blessing of the Union put in peril for a single hour, when its safety can be purchased at so small a cost.

Mr. HACKLEMAN:—The civilized world is amazed at the present condition of one of the greatest Governments on the face of the earth. I participate in that amazement myself. What is that condition? In a time of profound peace, of great prosperity, with the Government itself in the hands of southern men, State after State has dared to attempt to sever its connection with the Union. Even Florida, which has cost us so many millions, which ever since we had her has been a constant slough of expenditure, says we cannot even have the national property which happens to be within her territorial limits!

I am not so strong a believer in the effect of legislative action as many others. I have looked at the main points of our differences in the light of history, and it is my belief that the laws of soil and climate will settle this question of slavery in the Territories, much more effectually than we can settle it by any legislative or constitutional provisions.

The Missouri Compromise once settled this Territorial question in a manner satisfactory to the South. Through the influence of the South it was repealed. Now the South desires to have its provisions restored. As I understand the amendment of the gentleman from Iowa, it exactly restores the *status quo*.

We are told, farther, that the natural allies of the border slave States have left them; that, reduced in numbers, they cannot maintain their position against the North. This assumes that the North is hostile to the South. I deny it. I say that my state is the natural ally of Kentucky, a more powerful ally than she ever had South.

Parties are governed by certain natural laws. A party which adopts a principle at war with the sentiments of the people may succeed for a time by the force of party drill, but in the end it will go down. The CALHOUN doctrine destroyed a party. Under the operation of the same law the Democratic party has gone done. But you cannot destroy a party before its time. The effort of Virginia now is to overthrow the Republican party. The effort will not succeed. It is equivalent to an attempt to overthrow the country.

I am not frightened at this idea of giving guarantees. I do not think them of much importance. I am willing to give such as are reasonable. We hold to a certain extent to your doctrine of State sovereignty, and would protect it.

Our people North and South are too much alike in many respects. We are all inclined to stand too much upon party abstractions. This is almost the only reason why we cannot agree.

We are told that some things stated here grate harshly upon the ears of gentlemen from the South. The converse of this is equally true. I can take a rebuke, I trust, in a good temper, but I do not like to be stabbed in the house of my friends. I do not like to have doctrines and opinions imputed to me and my party which are only entertained by a little knot of fanatical abolitionists in the neighborhood of Boston; a few men who will not vote under the present Constitution, and who are led and controlled by LLOYD GARRISON and WENDELL PHILLIPS.

Mr. HOUSTON:—I am strongly averse to the introduction of the subject of party into the deliberations of the Conference. I did not intend to allude to party at all; but since the subject has been referred to in such impassioned terms, I feel that I must say a word about it.

Many references have been made in this debate to the opinions of WASHINGTON. I wish his opinions were better observed and respected. I refer to his appeal to his countrymen not to form parties with reference to geographical lines, and asking them to frown indignantly upon every attempt to form such parties.

What WASHINGTON foresaw, at length has come to pass. Parties have been formed, and are now in existence, divided by geographical lines, having no interests or opinions in common.

But no such parties can long exist without threatening the stability of the Government.

So long as parties were national in their character; so long as they excluded sectional interests from their platforms, their existence was a benefit rather than an injury to the Union. Gradually they have all drifted toward sectionalism, until now we find ourselves in a position which taxes the ability and ingenuity of the ablest men to provide for the existence even of our Government.

Now, I see no chance of safety for us until we reëstablish political parties upon their old bases, excluding all sectional considerations. When this is accomplished, the country is safe. It can only be done by settling this territorial question, and removing all inducement to the formation of sectional parties.

The election of Mr. LINCOLN was a fair election. It afforded no just pretext for secession, much less for the formation of sectional parties, or for creating sectional issues.

The time has come when the advice, the counsels of WASHINGTON, become his most precious legacy to the country. Shall we not regard the solemn admonitions of the Father of his Country?

I would ask our friends from the North—for they are our friends and not our enemies—whether they will not listen to these counsels of WASHINGTON? He was always ready, always willing to submit to just compromises, when they were necessary to the peace and happiness of his country. Will they not emulate his example now?

Delaware does not feel any special interest in this question of slavery in the Territories. She would have it settled in that way which would promote the interests of the whole Union. Her present impression is, that the report of the committee presents the most practicable and equitable mode of adjustment. Long ago Delaware favored the abolition of the slave trade. She has been consistent in her course on that question ever since. It is not unlikely that she may soon favor the abolition of slavery within her limits. Her progress has been in that direction. When the present Constitution was adopted, Delaware had fifteen thousand slaves. Now she has not more than eighteen hundred.

Mr. TUCK:—I recognize the reason and propriety of the wishes of the gentleman from Maryland, to try the proposition now before the Conference upon its merits. I certainly do not desire to have time taken up in unnecessary delay. I do not think much of these statements about civil war. Nor is there any attempt here to defame or injure any section. No member here has any such intention. We seem to be divided into two parties. Both are willing to act; neither asks for delay. One desires action through Congress, the other through the people, acting in General Convention. We all have confidence in the people. What do you see in this Conference? One-half of the Republicans here, are ready to join hands with those who would invoke the action of Congress, and carry their propositions through, to send them at once to Congress. I am ready to carry your propositions directly to the people.

A word now to the Democrats in this Conference. You have always been our superiors in political address and management. You expect in four years to bring the Government back under your control. My strong bias is in favor of a General Convention. That bias I got from the old Democratic party. The first mention of such an idea I found in an article in the "National Intelligencer"—a paper which certainly does not advocate radical views. I am aware of the opposition which this idea will meet with here, and yet I have heard many gentlemen from the South say, that this idea carried out the question fairly submitted to the people, and decided by them, their decision would be satisfactory. And would not many of the Southern slave States be satisfied with a decision upon these questions by a General Convention? Would not Georgia, Kentucky, Maryland, and Tennessee be willing to submit their interests to such a tribunal?

Now, I wish to ask the members representing the Southern States in this Conference, whether, when we offer you a General Convention, fairly elected, which shall patiently hear and firmly decide all our points of difference, you had not better accept it? I assure you, gentlemen, in the most perfect good faith, that a convention is the best alternative the North can now offer you. It is a fair and an honorable alternative; and because it is so, the North will insist that it ought to be satisfactory to you. If you refuse it, I ask you whether, in the sight of GOD and Man, you will not have stood between the country and peace? We act in secret here, but in the end all our actions will be exposed to the world. It will be seen that we were ready to do justice to you, and to submit all your claims to the final verdict of the people. Should you not at least wait for their decision?

Mr. DONIPHAN:—Will the gentleman support these proposals of amendment in a convention of the people, and will he use his influence to elect members of such a convention who will do the same? If the North will give us such pledges as will secure that kind of action, perhaps we will go for a General Convention. Without such a pledge, a General Convention would be worse than useless.

Mr. WICKLIFFE:—I am glad I have obtained the floor for a few minutes. I feel that it will be very painful for me to address the Conference, on account of physical debility.

But I came here with the single purpose of accomplishing the settlement of one or two important questions. Permit me, once for all, and for the last time, to tell the gentlemen from New Hampshire and Connecticut, that they wholly misunderstand the import of the action of the Legislature of Kentucky, and the views of the "Louisville Journal." I have said, before, that in view of the fact that Congress could not settle our difficulties, the Legislature of Kentucky asked for a National Convention, as our only hope of making an adjustment. After this came the invitation of Virginia, like a bright beam of hope. Virginia invited you all, New York, New Hampshire, and Massachusetts, and the other States, to meet and consult for the public safety. If you did not wish to secure our common safety, you should not have accepted her invitation.

Mr. BOUTWELL:—Then we are to understand that if we do not favor the CRITTENDEN resolutions, we should not have come here at all.

Mr. WICKLIFFE:—I say nothing of the kind. But I insist that you should tell us now, what the conclusion is to which you have arrived. We want to know what you gentlemen, representing the Northern States, intend to do. Give us your votes. We have had enough of discussion, which amounts to nothing. If you will consent to no arrangement, let us know it now. We have a duty to perform toward our own people.

We wish to relieve them from suspense, so that they may determine what their future course shall be, in view of the fact that you will do nothing for them.

Mr. COOK:—If Illinois had understood that she was only to come here for the purpose of agreeing to the propositions of Virginia as announced in the resolutions which accompanied her invitation, the Conference may be assured that Illinois would not have appeared here at all. She understood that she was invited to a *Conference*, in which all the States were to meet upon a basis of perfect equality. The very resolutions of the Legislature of Illinois, under which we received our appointments, assert that their adoption is not to be regarded as an assent to the resolutions of Virginia.

We think we are not passing the limits of propriety, when we insist that we should be permitted to state the views and opinions of the people of Illinois, on the questions which this Conference proposes to decide. To state what we will and what we will not concede. There seems to be an unwillingness to give us this permission. If the people are now ready to give their sanction to the propositions contained in the Virginia resolutions, they would send delegates here who would accept these propositions without debate or discussion. They have not yet done so. If they intended to limit our right of private judgment, they have certainly not yet expressed any such intention. They understand, and we have not forgotten, that there is a broad distinction between the guaranty of old rights and the creation of new ones.

We now understand just what the South proposes. The question is plainly and distinctly presented to us, whether we will assent to a constitutional recognition of the right to hold slaves in a portion of the Territories of the United States. It is not a question of prohibition at all. We are required to assert the affirmative right of holding slaves independent of State laws, and under the Constitution.

Gentlemen present us this question, and coolly tell us we want no more discussion, no more arguments, no examination of our respective rights under or outside the Constitution. We wish you to tell us at once whether you will assent to our wishes or not. If you will not, then comes some dark insinuations about going home to their people, and certain consequences are to follow, of the precise nature of which we are not informed.

Gentlemen, when was the sanction of the American people ever secured to an important proposition in such a way as this? If we are not to exercise our judgment, and act according to its dictates, upon every proposal of amendment here presented, then, for one, I care not how soon our deliberations end. Until we better understand our relative positions than we seem to at present, I do not see much use in prolonging the discussion.

Mr. EWING:—Some concession must be expected from both sides, or we cannot agree. As a Northern man, I feel it to be my duty to get these propositions made as acceptable to the North as I can, and then to ensure their submission to the people. Even then, we are not committed to the support of these propositions, though I myself should feel so to some extent. A single question is now presented to us. Shall we accept these propositions when they are perfected as far as they can be, or shall we submit to a dissolution of the Union? I am willing to say that I will yield my personal opinions for the purpose of concession, and I do not think I show myself an inferior man by doing so. In all disputes, the firmest men are the first to yield. Let a man be firm as a rock in battle, but conciliatory in council; especially in such a council as this, where the lives of millions may be concerned. There is a firmness which is but another name for imprudence—for rashness. Take the case of a railroad collision. One engineer may have the right of track; it may be the duty of all others to recognize that right, and not interfere with his exercising it. But, if another gets on to it, he who has the right would not be justified, if, in its exercise, he ran blindly on, and produced a collision, destroying the lives of his passengers, when he could have avoided the collision. So it is here. We may be right—the North may be right; but we should not hazard the existence of the Union by a determination to exercise that right at all events, when, by some slight concessions, we could save the Union. Let us use our judgments—let us act in view of the facts here presented, with that prudence and discrimination which we apply to the ordinary affairs of life, and all will yet be well.

Mr. KING :—I have not spoken hitherto, and should not now say a word, but for the remark of the gentleman from Kentucky. I come here as one of the representatives of the State of New York. As such I am the equal—the peer of any representative of any other State on this floor. I do not intend to be lectured into or intimidated from doing any thing which my judgment tells me I should not do, or should do.

Speaking for New York, I say that she holds her allegiance to the Constitution and the Government of the United States above and beyond any other political duty or obligation. With this obligation always before them, her representatives have come here to consult with you upon the present condition of the country. I am as old as the gentleman from Kentucky. I recognize no right in him to lecture me on my political duties. I revere the Constitution of my country. I was educated to love it, and my own father helped to make it. I cannot sit still and hear such declarations as have been hourly repeated here for the last few days.

Mr. SEDDON :—Does the gentleman consider this a consolidated Government or a confederation of States?

Mr. KING :—I consider this a confederation of States under the Constitution, and that in all that respects the General Government, every good citizen owes an allegiance to it above and beyond that which he owes to his State or to any other political authority. And that statement comprises nearly all I wish to say. The State of New York at all times, in peace or war, has been loyal to the Constitution; and, although some of her representatives here may undertake to make you think differently, she always will be. Yes! loyal with all her strength and power! And as one of her representatives, I shall yield nothing on her part to threats, menaces, or intimidations. I believe the Constitution as it now stands gives you guarantees enough—all you ought to have.

Mr. GOODRICH :—I ought not to permit this vote to be taken, without a word of reply to the remarks of the gentleman from North Carolina. The impression would certainly be derived from his speech that Governor ANDREW, of Massachusetts, approved of the JOHN BROWN raid. This is not true. There is not a particle of truth in the assertion. There is a gentleman here, who heard Governor ANDREW state publicly when he first heard of that raid, that JOHN BROWN must be crazy. It is true that a meeting was held in Boston to raise funds to support the poverty-stricken family of JOHN BROWN. Governor ANDREW, I believe, presided; and a single paragraph taken from some remarks he made on that occasion, has been scattered broadcast over the country. In order to understand what he did say, both the context and what followed it are indispensable. Those were carefully suppressed. The opinions of Governor ANDREW are well known. They are in sympathy with those of the people of Massachusetts. Neither he nor they approved the JOHN BROWN invasion.

Mr. RANDOLPH :—I call the gentleman to order. He is discussing a subject which is strictly personal, having no connection with the report of the committee, or the amendments offered to that report.

The PRESIDENT :—I think the remarks of the gentleman from Massachusetts are not in order.

Mr. GOODRICH :—Well, I cannot proceed in order. I only desired to correct a misapprehension. I do not quite understand why these misrepresentations should be made, and then objections interposed to their correction.

Mr. HOPPIN :—I rise, Mr. President, to address the Conference with great reluctance. If there is a gentleman within the sound of my voice whose heart is full of anxious solicitude for the safety of the country, he will know how to sympathize with me. I do not represent a State containing four millions of people, but one of the smallest in the Union; and yet little Rhode Island has a heart which beats true to the Union. It so happened that she was one of the last to accept the Constitution; but when she did accept it—when she took upon herself its obligations—she became faithful to it, and she has ever since been true.

I feel that my position is peculiar. I cannot judge of other men as some gentlemen do. The North is full of men who do not concur in my opinions upon the question of slavery. I know they are honest and honorable men. I should do injustice to them and to myself, if I believed them to be either corrupt or enemies of the Union and of good government; and it is just the same in the South as in other sections. Looking around me upon these able and patriotic representatives, who come here with full hearts and tell us of their position—of the feelings of their people—of the anxiety and apprehension which is so deeply felt among them, can I believe that these men are dishonest? that they do not mean what they say? No, sir! Nobody can be so unjust and unfair as that.

I think of these questions which we are discussing earnestly and continually. My heart is torn by conflicting emotions. I wish to perform my duty toward all sections, and I do feel sure that something must be done for our southern friends. They wish to remain in the Union—they do not wish to be driven out; and they tell us in all sincerity that something must be done to satisfy their people, or they cannot keep them in the Union. I know that the questions presented here are very embarrassing to the North, but we must decide them. We must do the best we can, and the North will sustain us; our constituents will approve our action.

Rhode Island wishes to act fairly by all. She does not herself, need any amendments to the Constitution; but if her sisters need them, she will consider their necessities. Her delegation here acts unitedly, and its members are influenced by the same spirit. We have done all we could to bring ourselves to a rational conclusion; and we feel, my friends, as though this body ought never to separate until we come to an agreement—until we come to some compromise which will be satisfactory to all.

I cannot now, in the short time that remains, go into a minute examination of the various points presented. This has been done by abler men. But I do feel that although the questions may be difficult, there are none of them which, as sensible men, we cannot settle. Don't let us forget our great mission and descend into personal abuse. Do not let us forget our high duties. Let us perform them in a friendly and a Christian spirit. Let us look at the facts as they are. Let us not spend our time in trying to find out who struck the first blow, or who is responsible. Let us all unite together in one great, final effort to save the country and the Union.

As matters now stand, we who represent Rhode Island can see no way more desirable than to vote for and support the report of the committee. And yet we do not insist upon that report. Show us any thing better, and we will go for it. But we will do nothing to widen the breach—we will do all we can to heal it. My friends, I say once more, let us go to work earnestly, and do not let us separate and go to our homes, until we can carry with us the glorious news that we have healed up all dissensions and adopted a plan that will secure the Union and make it perpetual.

Mr. CROWNINSHIELD:—I understand that the proposition of the gentleman from Iowa is to restore the Missouri Compromise. If so, does not his proposition commend itself to the Conference as one that will command the respect and support of the country? I have asked, many others have asked, what is the cause of our present difficulties? The question meets no direct reply—no definite answer. The repeal of the Missouri Compromise is referred to, hinted at, as the principal cause. If an answer were extorted, I think it would be, the repeal of that Compromise.

The history of the Missouri Compromise is so simple that we all understand it. Southern men forced the measure upon the North. The few northern men who voted for it were swept out of their political existence at the election which followed its passage. Which section is responsible for its repeal—the North or the South? You say its repeal was moved by a northern man. Very true! But he was a northern man who had adopted southern principles, and who sought to secure the favor of the South by this act. Southern men supported his proposition and carried it through Congress against the votes and the remonstrances of the North.

The South, then, established and destroyed the Missouri Compromise. The South wishes to have its provisions restored. Why, then, are you not satisfied to have it put into the Constitution, and so make it permanent and perpetual, if the North will consent to it? Are the circumstances of the South so much changed? If it was equitable in 1820, *à fortiori* it ought to be equitable in 1861. Territory has been acquired since 1820, it is true, but it is all or nearly all, south of the compromise line. Restore the Missouri Compromise and this territory will be devoted to southern institutions. What territory has been acquired since? Will gentlemen reply, "Oregon"? I insist that

Oregon was virtually acquired before. It only required the final agreement upon a boundary line.

If there is any proposition in which the North can concur—any that will restore harmony between the North and the South—it is the restoration of the Missouri Compromise. If any other is proposed less favorable or just to the North, I do not believe the people will adopt it.

I am not insensible to the condition of the country. Neither are my colleagues, nor the constituents they represent. But you must not expect us here, in the worst emergency you can imagine, to forget or throw away the rights of our people. If we consent to support this amendment, it is as far as we can go. You ought not to ask us to go farther.

Mr. DENT:—I will only occupy one moment. Maryland has spoken in language which satisfies me. As I understand him, I concur in what my colleague has said.

Now the nut is to be cracked. The majority report proposes to give up three-fourths of our territory to the North absolutely, retaining the little balance for the South. The amendment proposes to pick the kernel out of the balance, and to leave the husks to us. To that we shall agree when we are compelled to; not before.

Mr. JOHNSON, of Missouri:—The Supreme Court has already decided, in terms which are not ambiguous, that Congress has no right, under the Constitution, to prohibit slavery in the Territories. Now, our brethren of the North propose to give us the Missouri Compromise. What do they mean? Do they intend to give us a substantial right—one that we can enforce and rely upon, or do they intend to keep it from us? They are shrewd as well as honorable men. They know that the effect of this amendment will be to leave the territory south of the line, without the slightest acknowledgment or guaranty, just where it is at the present time, so far as slavery is concerned.

The construction placed upon the Missouri Compromise was, that the prohibition of slavery north of the line which it established, implied the right of holding slaves south of the line. At the time of its adoption there was, in respect of this construction, no difference of opinion. Such was the construction of Mr. WEBSTER.

Now you propose to leave it still for Congress to legislate as to the territory south. You secure that north, by a prohibition in the Constitution; you will get that south, by the action of Congress.

The decision in the Dred Scott case may be reversed. It afforded no permanent protection. One of your leaders (Mr. WILMOT) says he will war against it. The gentleman from New York (Mr. SMITH) denies the force of the decision in this respect. Now, gentlemen, all we of the South want, is to have this question settled. You know well that the adoption of this amendment, so far from settling it, leaves it all open; or rather it settles the question North, and leaves it open South. The country is in danger—that all concede. Will you, because you do not agree in opinion with the Supreme Court, refuse to join us in one more effort to save the country?

Mr. CLAY:—I have not unnecessarily occupied a moment of the time of this Conference, and it is not now my intention to occupy the whole ten minutes to which I am entitled. But I do wish to express some of the opinions which I entertain upon the questions immediately under our consideration. "Red Gauntlet" has been cited as an authority in this body, but I think I might cite another of the same class which would be more in point. It is the "Bleak House," by Charles Dickens, in which the circumlocution office is so graphically described. It would be decidedly more appropriate to our present action.

Why have we come together? What brought us here? We have come to devise the means of saving a distracted and bleeding country. What the South asks you to do, is, to recognize the property which her citizens possess; and when they take that property to the Territories, to secure its protection there, or rather to protect it south of the line of 36° 30′. Will you do it? Are you going to do it? If you intend to recognize our property south of this line, write it down so plain that my constituents can understand it—so that they will not be cheated. If you intend to do nothing, let us know it at once. We will then know what to expect, and how to advise our people.

The question of slavery is but an incident to the great questions which are at the bottom of our divisions. Such differences have brought war after war upon Europe. It is, after all, the old question of the balance of power between the different sections and different interests. Who does not remember that in 1832 and 1833 the Tariff brought up the same questions? Why did South Carolina then threaten to nullify? Because nullification then, was one of the effects which the disregard of the rights of a section caused.

The South have always insisted upon terms of equality with the North. To this equality no one can deny she is justly entitled. So long as new States came in *pari passu*, North and South, she was satisfied. When this equilibrium was disturbed, she began to insist upon guarantees. Now, when you propose to put the point of equilibrium out of sight altogether, the South insists upon these guarantees, as not only necessary, but indispensable to her safety. This is right and fair. The North would insist upon the same thing, under like circumstances.

Gentlemen from the North have complained here that we have not stated exactly what would satisfy us. We have told you what we wanted over and over again. We want the CRITTENDEN resolutions. We told you that, when we first came here. We have now been here for nearly four weeks, and the CRITTENDEN amendment has never once been submitted to a vote. Since our difficulties first assumed importance, there has never been a measure of pacification suggested which has met with such a measure of acceptance as the CRITTENDEN resolutions. State after State has sent petitions to Congress asking for their adoption. Almost the entire South, with Virginia, the Mother of States, in the advance, tells you that these resolutions will be an acceptable measure of pacification, and yet you will not give us a vote upon them; you will scarcely consent to consider them. Even the committee, whose report is so unsatisfactory to the North (and a portion of the South also), does not appear to have given them much attention.

Mr. President, in behalf of the South, I think I know what to say. If our differences are to be settled at all, we must have our property in our slaves in the Territories recognized; and when that property is constitutionally recognized, it must be constitutionally protected. Such, I know, are the sentiments of the people of Kentucky.

Mr. ALLEN:—I wish to ask the attention of the Conference

for only one moment to the true aspect of the question now before us. We are asked if we will suffer the Union to be destroyed on account of the Territory of New Mexico. Let me ask these gentlemen who it is that proposes to break up and destroy the Union? It is the South—it is *not* the North. But all that I pass by.

If it were merely a question of who should have the beneficial possession of our present unoccupied territory, we would give that up at once to the South. But it is not a question of possession at all. It is *the* question which shall control and give direction to the policy of the country—the institutions of Slavery or the institutions of Freedom! You ask for a provision in the Constitution which will place that policy under the control of the institutions of slavery. This we cannot grant you.

We of the North stand where our fathers did, who resisted the Stamp Act; who threw overboard the tea in Boston harbor. We have been taught to resist the smallest beginnings of evil; that this is the true policy. *Obsta principii* was the motto of our fathers. It is ours. The debates of this Conference, and those of the Convention of 1787, will stand in a strange contrast to each other.

Mr. BALDWIN:—I now offer the minority report of the committee, with the accompanying resolutions as an amendment to—

The PRESIDENT:—The gentleman from Connecticut is not in order.

The vote was then taken by States, upon the amendment offered by Mr. Curtis, to the substitute proposed by Mr. Franklin, for the first article of the section reported by the General Committee, with the following result:

Ayes.—Maine, Vermont, Massachusetts, Connecticut, Iowa, and New York—6.

Noes.—New Hampshire, Rhode Island, New Jersey, Pennsylvania, Delaware, Maryland, Virginia, North Carolina, Tennessee, Kentucky, Missouri, and Ohio—12.

And the amendment was lost.

Mr. CORNING:—I dissent from the vote of New York.

Mr. WILMOT:—I wish to be recorded as voting Aye!

Mr. DODGE:—I dissent; I am against the amendment.

Mr. WOOD:—I wish my vote recorded in favor of the amendment.

Mr. COOK:—And so do I.

Mr. LOGAN:—I am the other way.

Mr. TUCK:—I dissent from the vote of New Hampshire.

Mr. GRANGER:—And I from that of New York.

Mr. WOLCOTT:—I dissent from the vote of Ohio. I notice that my colleague, Mr. CHASE, is not present at this moment.

Mr. BRONSON:—I also dissent from the vote of New York. My associate, GEN. WOOL, is confined to his room by a severe indisposition. For his benefit, and as I know he feels a deep interest in these votes, and desires to have his name appear upon the record, in his behalf I offer the following resolution:

Resolved, Whereas JOHN E. WOOL, a delegate from New York, is unable to attend the Convention, from sickness, therefore that he be permitted, when he does attend, or by communication in writing to the Secretary, to have his dissent recorded, as to any vote of his State.

This resolution was agreed to without a division.

The PRESIDENT:—The question now will be upon the adoption of the substitute proposed by the gentleman from Pennsylvania (Mr. FRANKLIN), to the first section of the article reported by the committee.

Mr. FRANKLIN:—Before that question is taken, I desire to accept certain verbal amendments which have been proposed by various members, which will, I think, improve the substitute which I offer. These amendments are as follows:

1st. In the fifth line, as printed, after the words "nor shall any law be passed," insert the words "by Congress or the Territorial Legislature."

2d. In the sixth line, after the words "the taking of such persons," insert "from any of the States of this Union."

3d. In the eighth line, before the words "according to the common law," insert the words "course of the."

4th. In the seventh line, after the words "prevent the taking of such persons," insert the words "from any State in the Union."

These amendments I adopt, and wish them to be treated as incorporated into my substitute.

The PRESIDENT:—Such will be assumed as the pleasure of the Conference, as no objection is made.

Mr. GUTHRIE:—I am content, on the part of the committee, that the substitute offered by the gentleman from Pennsylvania should be adopted in the place of the first section of the article reported by the committee. It amounts to the same thing, and is expressed in shorter and better language.

Mr. FRELINGHUYSEN :—I move to amend Mr. FRANKLIN's substitute as follows :* I think these words would be more acceptable to the people of the Northern States.

Mr. PALMER :—Does not the gentleman's amendment involve an Hibernicism ? I think if we are to adopt the report of the committee, the FRANKLIN amendment admits of no improvement. It had better stand as it is. If we undertake to change it we shall all get to sea.

Mr. FRELINGHUYSEN :—I withdraw my proposition.

Mr. JAMES :—It was moved yesterday to insert the words, "or facilitate" after the words "hinder or prevent," in that part of Mr. FRANKLIN's amendment which negatives the right to pass laws. What was done with that ?

Mr. FOWLER :—Nothing. I moved it, and I insist upon the motion.

Mr. GUTHRIE :—I submit to the Conference whether this amendment is necessary or proper. Suppose some new question arises relating to slavery which it may be greatly for the interest of the Territory to protect. Suppose mines are discovered, and the Territory should want slaves to work them. Shall we put it into the Constitution that no law shall be passed to encourage their emigration ?

Mr. BRONSON :—I see no need of it.

Mr. JAMES :—The point generally comes out. Now you say that you will have the right to go into the Territory with your slaves, and no law shall be passed to prevent you, no matter how much such a law would promote the material interests of the Territory. The converse of this you will not agree to. You are not content to let slavery stand by itself, you must have it nursed by the Territorial Legislatures. Does slavery always require such partiality ? I say the power of the Legislature should be exercised on both sides, or it should not be exercised at all. I am trying to perfect the article. If it is to pass, and go to the people as a measure of pacification, and if you expect them to adopt it, you must not have it so one-sided and unfair. The peo-

* This was a verbal amendment. I was not able to note it at the time, nor have I since been able to procure it.

ple will understand it—it will be our duty to explain it to them, and to give them its history.

Mr. GUTHRIE:—But your amendment would prohibit the passage of a law permitting the transit of a slaveholder through the Territory with his property. Remember, also, that the prohibition only continues so long as the territorial condition exists.

Mr. SMITH:—Before this vote is taken, I wish to call attention to the character of the prohibition. "Nor shall any law be passed to hinder or prevent the taking of such persons to said Territory, nor to impair the rights arising from said relation," &c. Now, this is very broad. Suppose a law giving the right of transit to the people of the free States, or any law for their protection in the Territory, as inhabitants, is held by the Territorial Judge to "impair the rights arising from said relation." He holds it unconstitutional. Where is the remedy? What views are entertained upon some of these points in some sections of the South we know. If you do not adopt this amendment it is quite in the power of the Legislature to exclude any person from the Territory whose presence there may be thought injurious to slavery. Did the committee intend this?

The question upon the adoption of Mr. FOWLER's amendment resulted as follows:

AYES.—Maine, New Hampshire, Vermont, Massachusetts, Rhode Island, Connecticut, New York, Indiana, Illinois, and Iowa—10.

NOES.—New Jersey, Pennsylvania, Delaware, Maryland, Virginia, North Carolina, Tennessee, Kentucky, Missouri, and Ohio—10.

So the amendment was rejected.

Mr. GROESBECK:—I move to amend the substitute offered by Mr. FRANKLIN, by inserting after the words "nor shall any law be passed," the words "by Congress or the Territorial Legislature." I think this is necessary to make our intention plain. Otherwise it might be said that the prohibition did not apply to Congress.

Mr. FRANKLIN:—I think the suggestion a very proper one. I will accept the amendment.

Mr. WILMOT:—I only wish to understand where we are. Have we disposed of the word "facilitate"?

The PRESIDENT:—That amendment was not adopted.

Mr. WILMOT:—Then I move to insert before the word "*status*," the word "legal."

Mr. RUFFIN:—That raises again every question we have been discussing. The word, as used in the substitute, only refers to the status *in fact.*

Mr. GUTHRIE:—This brings up all our old troubles. Let us reject it.

Mr. RANDOLPH:—I wish to understand this subject, and what will be the effect of adopting this amendment. I understand that the slave has what we call a *status.* The substitute of Mr. FRANKLIN is intended specifically to recognize and protect that *status* in the Territories as fully as it is protected and recognized in the States. I think it has that effect. Adopt the amendment, and the effect is precisely the opposite. The amendment rescinds the *status.*

Mr. PALMER:—I wish to make an inquiry of the mover. Does the amendment, after all, make any difference? Must not any *status*, not against law, be, of necessity, a *legal* status?

Mr. WILMOT:—No. I think there is a wide difference, and the South thinks so. One is a status in fact, the other, one in law.

Mr. LOGAN:—I hope we shall not adopt the amendment. We all want these questions settled. The amendment opens them all wider than before. If we intend to give the South the right she asks for, and, as I think, rightfully asks for, let us give it to her in plain and unequivocal language. Let us not give her a legacy of litigation, by using words which mean one thing or the opposite, according to the construction you place upon them. I wish to settle all these questions fairly. The amendment leaves the question as to what constitutes a *legal status*, to be decided by the Court. The North would claim that there cannot be such a thing as a legal status, a legal condition of slavery. The South would claim the opposite.

Mr. WILMOT:—If the amendment of the gentleman from North Carolina had been adopted, I would not have moved this. The section then would have been unambiguous and clear. Now it is all open to construction.

Mr. CHASE:—In my judgment it is unimportant whether the amendment is adopted or not. The condition of the slave in the Southern States is one arising out of law, established by legislative provisions. *Status in fact* must mean *status in law* as well as *status in fact.*

I have listened with attention to the appeals made by gentlemen who urge the interests of the South in favor of a settlement of these questions. But you are now prosecuting a plan which will be the subject of debate throughout the country. Adopt your article in either form, and the question, What does status mean? will still remain.

A majority of the people have adopted the opinion that under the Constitution slavery has not a legal existence in the Territories. The triumph of this opinion is not the result of any sudden impulse. A President has been elected, and a Government will soon be organized, whose duty it will be to respect and observe the opinions of the people. You are now seeking, by the adoption of a single section, to change these opinions and this policy. Do not deceive yourselves, gentlemen. You will never accomplish this result so easily. You are presenting such a subject for debate and excitement as the country never had before. It is best we deal frankly.

The vote was taken upon the adoption of the amendment, and resulted as follows:

AYES.—Maine, New Hampshire, Vermont, Massachusetts, Connecticut, New York, Indiana, Illinois, and Iowa—9.

NOES. Rhode Island, New Jersey, Pennsylvania, Delaware, Maryland, Virginia, North Carolina, Tennessee, Kentucky, Missouri, and Ohio—11.

And the amendment was rejected.

Mr. GOODRICH:—I move to insert in the substitute offered by Mr. FRANKLIN, after the words "south of that line," the words "not embraced by the Cherokee treaty."

A word of explanation. Do we intend to prohibit the Cherokee Nation from changing the status of persons within their Territory, if they think proper to do so? Would not this be a violation of our understanding, if not of our treaty stipulations with these Indians?

Mr. EWING:—I have looked into this subject, and I do not think the proposition would be improved by the amendment.

Mr. GOODRICH:—Then I will withdraw it for the present.

Mr. GUTHRIE:—I hope the vote on the main question will now be taken. It is evident that the sense of the majority is against accepting amendments.

Mr. GOODRICH:—That obliges me to renew my motion. I do renew it, and ask for a vote by States.

The vote upon the amendment offered by Mr. GOODRICH was taken, with the following result:

AYES.—Maine, New Hampshire, Vermont, Massachusetts, Connecticut, New York, Pennsylvania, Ohio, Indiana, Illinois, and Iowa—11.

NOES.—Rhode Island, New Jersey, Delaware, Maryland, Virginia, North Carolina, Tennessee, Kentucky, and Missouri—9.

So the amendment was adopted.

Mr. TURNER:—I move to amend the substitute offered by Mr. FRANKLIN, by inserting after the words "hinder or prevent," the words "or encourage."

I think there is a palpable difference between the word "encourage" and the word "facilitate." The former is broader and less restricted. If this measure is to be commended to the favor of the North, it should be deprived of this one-sided character.

Mr. GUTHRIE:—We have already decided this question. In every practical sense the words are synonymous.

The vote was taken upon the amendment offered by Mr. TURNER, and resulted as follows:

AYES.—Maine, New Hampshire, Vermont, Massachusetts, Rhode Island, Connecticut, New York, Indiana, Illinois, and Iowa—10.

NOES.—New Jersey, Pennsylvania, Delaware, Maryland, Virginia, North Carolina, Tennessee, Kentucky, Missouri, and Ohio—10.

And the amendment was lost.

Mr. GUTHRIE:—I ask the Conference now to let us have a vote.

Mr. SEDDON:—Not just yet. I move to amend the substitute offered by the gentleman from Pennsylvania, by the insertion after the clause providing for the division of the territory, of the following:

"All appointments to office in the Territories lying north of the line 36° 30′, as well before as after the establishment of Territorial governments in and over the same, or any part thereof, shall be made upon the recommendation of a majority of the Senators representing, at the time, the non-slaveholding States. And, in like manner, all appointments to office in the Territories which may lie south of said line of 36° 30′, shall be made upon the recommendation of a majority of the Senators representing, at the time, the slaveholding States. But nothing in this article shall be construed to restrain the President of the United States from removing, for actual incompetency or misdemeanor in office, any person thus appointed, and appointing a temporary agent, to be continued in office until the majority of Senators as aforesaid may present a new recommendation; or from filling any vacancy which may occur during the recess of the Senate; such appointment to continue *ad interim*. And to insure, on the part of the Senators, the selection of the most trustworthy agents, it is hereby directed that all the net proceeds arising from the sales of the public lands, shall be distributed annually among the several States, according to the combined ratio of representation and taxation; but the distribution aforesaid may be suspended by Congress, in case of actual war with a foreign nation, or imminent peril thereof."

Mr. SEDDON:—I invite the careful and deliberate attention of the Conference to the provisions of this amendment. It is commended by high authority. It is commended by nothing inferior to the wisdom and experience of our honored President. It is intended as a division of the territory between the North and the South.

Now, to insure a fair operation of the provisions of the Constitution, as they will stand in that instrument when amended as we propose, we deem it very essential that the rights of the southern section should be secured by such an amendment as this. It will be noticed that Mr. FRANKLIN's substitute precludes us from any appeal to Congress or the Territorial Legislatures for affirmative protection. The powers of those bodies will be negative only. We have nothing left, then, but the Federal Courts. We ask now that we may not be subjected to the government and power of Federal officers, whose opinions are against us—who will exercise those powers for our oppression. Congress or the President may send into a Territory in the southern section, a set of officers who are anti-slavery propagandists, who will exercise all their official powers to our injury. I hold this amendment to be eminently just and fair. We have no protection from Congress; none from the Legislature. Is there a chance, even, unless such a provision is adopted, that the South will ever be placed in the favorable possession or enjoyment of the rights you are willing to concede to us?

The latter portion of the amendment is equally just. The

Government holds the public lands in trust. It is better to divide their proceeds at short intervals, and thus remove the snbject from all danger of corrupting influences. But I shall leave this to be discussed by the mover.

Mr. PALMER:—I move to rescind the ten-minute rule adopted by the Conference, so far as the President is concerned.

The motion of Mr. PALMER was agreed to without a division.

President TYLER:—I am very grateful for the compliment which the Conference extends to me in the vote which has just passed. I will not abuse its kindness.

The amendment which is offered may, at first sight, appear to be extraordinary; but I wish to say, in all seriousness, that all my experience in public life leads me to favor its adoption. I wish to have the Conference understand fully its import and meaning.

That policy is the best, which reduces within the narrowest limits the patronage to be exercised by the Executive authority. Every party out of power has discovered that in the patronage of the President there is a voice of greater potency than is heard elsewhere in the Government. This amendment places a limitation upon the power of the President. It confers upon a majority of the Senators from each section the power to recommend appointments to office, and this will be found in practice equivalent to the power of appointment. It is the only practicable limitation of Executive patronage. The power of the Executive in this Government is very great. Limit it, abridge it as you may, and the President will have a power in the Government which is not possessed by any sovereign of any throne in Europe.

This is not a political question. Our warrant for the adoption of this plan will be found in the tranquillity it will give to the country—in the peace which will result from it. We are now settling differences between the States. Adopt this provision, and we secure unanimity forever. You will always find that dissatisfaction is confined to limited portions of the country. The North is content with the existing state of things—so is three-fourths of the South. Remove this power from the Executive, and those measures will be adopted which will promote the welfare of the greater number. Do you not see that you have in this way good security for the selection of the best men?

Suppose the Government should start to day on this new policy—that it should avoid all propagandism—should place honest, competent men, only, in office—should let all others understand that there was no chance for them—should permit both sides, all sides to be fairly represented. You would ensure peace, secure quiet in the country forever. You would thus heal the wound, not cicatrize it. How small would be the cost of so great a victory!

May I not go one step farther. I have heard with pleasure the feelings expressed, the references made, to the Cotton States. I have scarcely heard an unkind word said against them. We have come here to cement the Union—to make that Union, of which gentlemen have so eloquently spoken, permanent, noble, and glorious in the future as it has been in the past—not to be content with it as a maimed and crippled Republic.

Now, eight flourishing States are practically lost to us. The crest of the noble Mexican Gulf has separated from us. Let us exert every power we possess to bring them all back to the fold. Why should we not? Every motive of interest or patriotism should induce us to do so. Suppose the States were vacillating and in doubt where to go. Suppose they were set up for sale in market *overt*, and the States of Europe were to bid for them—for this, not only the richest portion of our own country, but of the world—because this portion of our land has an element of wealth and power which must be prized and valued wherever commerce is known. What would not one of the Powers of Europe give for this favored section? The treasures of the continent would be opened. Nations would unlock the caskets of their crown jewels to secure it. England would double her national debt to have it; so would France; so would Russia. And yet we stand here higgling over these little differences which alone have caused our separation. Is it not better that we should rise to the level of the occasion, and meet the requisition of the times, instead of expending precious hours in the discussion of these miserable abstractions?

We talk about the events of the Revolution and their consequences. Have we forgotten our revolutionary history? Have we forgotten the Marions, the Sumters, the Pickens, of those times? Has the spirit of sacrifice which animated those men wholly departed from their descendants? God forbid!

Our body politic is not free from disease. The disease should be treated properly and judiciously. Whenever disease shows itself we should apply a suitable remedy—one that is suggested by the pharmacy of mutual brotherhood, and yet powerful enough to reach every nerve in our political system.

It is to accomplish this purpose that we have come together. It is to secure this desirable result that I urge the adoption of this amendment. I press it because I feel that it will give peace to all sections. Adopt it, and from that moment you may date the beginning of the return of the seceded States into the fold of the Union. How heartily would we welcome their return! Do we not all desire it? Has not Virginia a heart large enough to give them their old place in the Union? Has not Rhode Island and New Jersey?

I say my proposition will accomplish this, and a single reason will disclose the ground of my faith. It preserves the equilibrium, the balance of power, between the sections. It enables each section to appoint its own officers, to protect its own interests, to regulate its own concerns. It is fair and equal in its operations. With it, no section can have any excuse for dissatisfaction. I pledge the united support of the South to the Union, if it is adopted.

The latter branch of the amendment looks to the annual distribution of the net proceeds of the sales of the public lands among the several States. This was one of the favorite ideas of HENRY CLAY. His argument upon this subject, to my mind, was always conclusive. Will the party which has adopted his principles repudiate this, or will its members put their feet down firmly and give it their support?

I have watched the operations of this Government with great interest and care, and I have noticed that every approach toward making each source of revenue or expenditure separate and independent of all others, tended to the profit and advantage of the Government, and increased the chances of securing honorable and honest agents to transact its business. A marked instance of this will be found in the administration of the affairs of the Post Office Department. And here I cannot refrain from relating an anecdote which is strongly in point, and which forms one of the pleasantest recollections of my own connection with the administration of the General Government.

Upon a certain occasion I called my cabinet together. Sad complaints had been made concerning the administration of several of the Departments, and the press had not failed to predict heavy losses to the Government through the dishonesty and the defalcations of its agents. I determined that I would know what the facts were, and I directed all the departments to furnish me, by a certain day, with a correct and accurate list of all their defaulting employés, and on the same day I summoned my cabinet to consider these reports. The lists came in from the several Departments, and I assure the Conference that they were formidable enough to give ample occasion for anxiety. But the list from the Department of the Post Office was not forthcoming. My friend, Governor WICKLIFFE, was at that time at the head of that Department. The day of the cabinet meeting arrived. We were all assembled but the Postmaster General. We waited for a long time for him and for his report. At length he came, bringing his report with him, but with the marks of great care and anxiety upon his brow. *He had discovered a defalcation* in his Department. He had been occupied for a long time in tracing it out, but he had at length succeeded. He came to announce to the President that the postmaster of a certain "Cross Roads" in Kentucky had absconded, and defrauded the Government out of the sum of *fifteen dollars!* and worst of all, his bail *had run away with him!!*

This is only one of the many proofs which my own experience would furnish of the propriety, if not the necessity of keeping each Department of the Government by itself—of not connecting it with others, and of making the agents of each Department responsible to itself alone. Carry this idea into practice in all the Departments of the Government, and a better class of agents would be secured, and the loss by defaulters would be much lessened.

The enormous increase of the expenditures of the General Government might, by the same process, be prevented. How does it happen that in a time of peace these expenses have risen from twenty-three millions of dollars up to seventy or eighty millions? In the same proportion, the sum to which they will reach in another decade will be frightful! It is high time that a stop was put to this lavish expenditure, and especially to the losses by dishonest agents. The plan here proposed will give you a starting point. The proceeds of the vast domain of the public lands are now so mingled with the other expenditures of the Government, that no one can tell what becomes of them. They are now common plunder. Divide them among the States, and they will be saved—they will be applied to some worthy object, and you will have adopted a principle which, after a little time, under any honest administration, will be applied to the other Departments of the Government. I trust the whole amendment may be adopted. As the amendment may be divided into two parts—one relating to appointments to office, and the other to the public domain—I would ask that the vote may be taken upon each proposition separately.

The vote was then taken upon the first portion of the amendment proposed by Mr. SEDDON, with the following result:

AYES.—Maryland, Virginia, North Carolina, Kentucky, and Missouri—5.

NOES.—Maine, New Hampshire, Vermont, Massachusetts, Connecticut, Rhode Island, New York, New Jersey, Pennsylvania, Tennessee, Ohio, Indiana, Illinois, and Iowa—14.

And the amendment was rejected.

Mr. JOHNSON:—I cannot concur in the vote just given by Maryland. I desire to have my dissent recorded.

Mr. CRISFIELD:—I dissent, also, from the vote of Maryland.

President TYLER:—The last part of the amendment will be considered as withdrawn.

Mr. McCURDY:—I move to amend the substitute proposed by Mr. FRANKLIN, by adding thereto the following words:

"*Provided*, That nothing in this article contained shall be so construed as to carry any law of involuntary servitude into such Territory."

Mr. GUTHRIE:—I hope we shall reject all such amendments. I consider this simply procrastination.

Mr. JOHNSON, of Missouri:—I wish to raise a point, a question of order. This conflicts directly with the sense of the substitute proposed. We ought not to entertain it.

The vote was taken upon the amendment proposed by Mr. McCURDY, with the following result:

AYES.—Maine, New Hampshire, Vermont, Massachusetts, Connecticut, New York, and Iowa—7.

NOES—Rhode Island, New Jersey, Pennsylvania, Delaware, Maryland, Virginia, North Carolina, Tennessee, Kentucky, Missouri, Ohio, Indiana, and Illinois—13.

And the amendment was rejected.

Mr. ORTH:—I dissent from the vote of Indiana.

Mr. RUFFIN:—I rise to inquire whether it will now be in order to offer a substitute? I have one which I wish at the proper time to present.

The PRESIDENT:—The question is now upon the adoption of a substitute—that offered by the gentleman from Pennsylvania—to the first section of the article reported by the committee. I do not think any other substitute is in order at the present time.

Mr. CHASE:—I hope that this vote may be postponed, and I will briefly state the reason why. I am informed that a delegation from the State of Kansas has arrived during the day, and that their credentials are now in the hands of the appropriate committee. That committee has not yet reported, and cannot until they have a meeting after our adjournment. The credentials of three of these delegates have been presented by myself but a few minutes since. The Committee on Credentials, I am informed, will not report until Monday. I wish the youngest State in the Union to express her opinion upon this motion. I therefore move an adjournment.

Mr. EWING:—I do not think any delay is necessary. We can let them vote on Monday.

Mr. SUMMERS:—I only wish to say a word of explanation in behalf of the Committee on Credentials. The delay in the case of Kansas is not the fault of that committee. The delegates themselves think it better that the report should not be made until all the delegates arrive who are expected. The committee can report at any time.

The vote was taken on the motion to adjourn, with the following result:

AYES.—Maine, Massachusetts, Connecticut, New York, and Indiana—5.

NOES.—New Hampshire, Vermont, Rhode Island, New Jersey, Pennsylvania, Delaware, Maryland, Virginia, North Carolina, Tennessee, Kentucky, and Missouri—12.

So the motion to adjourn was negatived.

The PRESIDENT:—The question will now be taken upon the substitute of the gentleman from Pennsylvania (Mr. FRANKLIN), offered for the first section of the article reported by the committee.

Which vote being taken, resulted as follows:

AYES.—Maine, New Hampshire, Vermont, Rhode Island, Connecticut, New York, New Jersey, Pennsylvania, Delaware, Maryland, Kentucky, Ohio, Indiana, and Illinois—14.

NOES.—Virginia, North Carolina, Tennessee, and Missouri—4.

And the substitute was agreed to.

Mr. FIELD:—There seems to be a misapprehension as to the proper time for offering substitutes for the whole report of the committee. I shall act upon the understanding that the proper time to offer them will be when we have gone through with the report of the committee. If I am wrong I wish to be corrected now.

Mr. LOGAN:—I am informed that Mr. LINCOLN, the President-elect, has arrived in this city. I feel certain that the Conference would desire to treat him with the same measure of respect which it has extended to the present incumbent of that high office. I therefore move that the President of this Convention be requested to call upon the President-elect of the United States, and inform him that its members would be pleased to wait upon him in a body at such time as will suit his convenience, and that this Convention be advised of the result.

The motion of Mr. LOGAN was agreed to unanimously.

Mr. WILMOT:—I move an adjournment to half-past seven o'clock this evening,

The motion was agreed to, and the Conference adjourned.

EVENING SESSION—SIXTEENTH DAY.

WASHINGTON, SATURDAY, *February 23d*, 1861.

THE Conference was called to order by the President, at half-past seven o'clock.

The PRESIDENT:—I have addressed a note to the President-elect, announcing the desire of the Conference to offer their respects to him in a body, at seven and one-half o'clock this evening, or at such other time as would be agreeable to him. I have received his reply, stating that he will be pleased to receive the members of this body at nine o'clock this evening, or at any other time which may suit their convenience.

The Conference then proceeded to the order of the day, being the consideration of the second article of the section reported by the committee.

Mr. GUTHRIE:—I move to strike out the second article, and to insert the following in its place:

> "Territory may be acquired for naval and commercial stations and transit routes, and by discovery, and for no other purposes, without the concurrence of four-fifths of the Senate."

It is generally conceded that under our present Constitution the United States have no power to acquire territory for coaling or naval stations, within the country of a foreign power. It was the committee's intention to remedy this defect by the present section. But as it stands, I do not like it. The idea is somewhat awkwardly expressed. I wish to have the enabling power conferred in direct terms.

Mr. SUMMERS:—I would ask to interrupt the order of business for a moment, in order to make a report from the Committee on Credentials, in the Kansas case. The defect adverted to in the case of Mr. STONE, has been supplied to the satisfaction of the committee, and Messrs. CONWAY, EWING, and ADAMS, have also presented themselves as delegates from the State of Kansas, with proper credentials. It has not been our practice heretofore to admit members by a formal vote, nor do I see any necessity for making the case of Kansas an exception. The committee would suggest that the clerk enter the names of these gentlemen upon the roll of delegates, unless objection is made.

The PRESIDENT:—The Secretary will make the entry, as no objection is made.

Mr. SUMMERS:—Some days ago I introduced into the Conference, and caused to be printed, a substitute which I proposed to offer for the second section of the committee's article. I offer it now, as follows:

"No territory shall be acquired by the United States without the concurrence of a majority of all the Senators from States which allow involuntary servitude, and a majority of all the Senators from States which prohibit that relation; nor shall territory be acquired by treaty, unless the votes of a majority of the Senators from each class of States hereinbefore mentioned, be cast as a part of the two-thirds majority necessary to the satisfaction of such treaty."

I do not propose to occupy time in discussing it, but I ask a minute or two to explain its provisions. The second section of the article proposed by the committee, requires that a treaty under which territory or commercial or naval stations is acquired, should require four-fifths of the Senate for its ratification. This, I think, is an unnecessary restriction upon the treaty-making power. Occasion may arise when it would not be advisable to wait for the exercise of this power at all. The question of acquiring territory may arise under circumstances when delay would be fatal. Suppose our title to an island in the Arctic Ocean, or a point upon the shore, by discovery or otherwise, which might be settled by prompt action! There might be no national authority with which we could treat for its acquisition. I think it would be hazardous to provide that in no event should territory be acquired except by treaty. The case I have supposed has no relation whatever to the case of an ordinary acquisition of territory by treaty with a recognized foreign power.

But the question of slavery always arises when the subject of acquiring territory is mentioned. This clause would fix the *status*, would put it in the power of either class of States to prevent the acquisition, but it would not permit a small number of States to do it. To leave it where a *majority* of the Senators of both sections could control the subject, would seem to me the mode of settlement least objectionable. The ratification would require two-thirds of the Senate, like all treaties, and these two-thirds would include a majority of both sections.

Objection will be made to this classification of the States. I do not like it myself, but there it no way to avoid it. I have adopted the language of the Ordinance of 1787. There can be no very sound objection to the use of these terms. The objection is rather sentimental than otherwise.

The amendment I offer ought to satisfy the South, and I think it will. The South asks for these provisions because they settle all questions about our present territory, and prevent questions arising over that we may acquire hereafter. They will give to both sides equality of power. But voting is far more important now than speaking. I will consume no more time.

Mr. GUTHRIE:—The gentleman from Virginia desires to try his motion. For the present, I will withdraw mine.

Mr. FIELD:—I have only a word to say on this subject. There are very grave objections to this classification of sections. I will not repeat them here. I supposed the sense of the Conference had been expressed against it.

But I wish to inquire why this second section is necessary at all? It came up in the committee rather by accident than otherwise. I do not think any one of the committee intended to make it one of the subjects of our action, and the section was finally presented by a small majority.

Let us leave this subject where the Constitution leaves it. We can now acquire territory by discovery or by treaty. So far the Constitution has operated satisfactorily. The country owes much of its greatness to this very provision of the Constitution. No grievance to the South, assuredly, has been caused by it. I am much averse to any alteration.

Mr. BARRINGER:—I think, after some reflection, that this amendment is of much more importance than many of us have supposed. I shall vote for it, because I do not wish to have too many limitations placed upon the power of the Government in relation to the acquisition of territory. We know how difficult it is to change our fundamental law. Very few amendments to the Constitution have been made since the death of WASHINGTON. We are now establishing our fundamental law for ages to come.

Is there upon the face of the civilized earth a nation with such a limitation upon the power of acquiring territory as this original article proposes? Its adoption would place us at the feet of foreign nations.

In war, conquest is one means of indemnity—often the best and only one. We must look to the acquisition of future territory; we must make our settlement with that in view.

Reference has been made here to the seceded States, and some hard words have been used toward them. This is not the place for such words. What is the condition of these States now? They say they are out of the Union. We say, No! The question between us may be decided by the Courts; it may be decided by the sword. But we all want them back; we would place no restrictions upon their return. They will only come back by treaty. Unless you adopt this amendment, the section proposed will be applicable to their case, and a mere fraction could keep them out of the Union forever.

In regard to the subject of slavery, what we want is security for the future. That we can arrange. In my opinion you will never get back the seceded States, without you give them some hope of the acquisition of future territory. They know that when slavery is gathered into a *cul-de-sac*, and surrounded by a wall of free States, it is destroyed. Slavery must have expansion. It must expand by the acquisition of territory which now we do not own. The seceded States will never yield this point—will never come back to a Government which gives no chance for the expansion of their principal institution. They will insist upon equity, upon the same rights with you in the common territory, and the same prospect, of acquiring foreign territory that you have. If you are not prepared to grant all this, do not waste your time in thought about the return of the seceded States.

Mr. RANDOLPH:—New Jersey voted to make the first section of the article reported applicable to future territory, not because she wishes to acquire new territory, but because she knows that it will be acquired; and she believes all questions raised here can be settled now, in regard to it, better than they can be hereafter. These questions have raised a ferment in the nation; we would settle them any way. We should have voted for these restrictions upon the power of acquiring territory; and still we cannot shut our eyes to the fact that in a few years new territory must be acquired. Look at Sonora, at all Mexico; they furnish the reason for our action. An effort will be made, perhaps, to secure the new territory by treaty. Better get it in that way than by conquest.

Personally, I would oppose any farther acquisitions. We need no more territory, and yet I know that more will be acquired. The North wishes it more than the South. In the end, the North will insist that we should have Cuba. What is the sentiment of our commercial cities now?

I think we ought to surround this power of acquisition by some judicious restrictions; not make them too strong, or the country will break over, and not regard them. What restriction would not have been broken down, when the question came up in relation to Texas? We must anticipate occasions of the same kind. I am inclined to vote for the substitute of the gentleman from Virginia. At all events let us adopt some limitations. If not these, then such as are contained in the original article.

Mr. JOHNSON, of Maryland:—I propose to amend the substitute offered by the gentleman from Virginia, by inserting after the words "United States," the words "except by discovery, and for naval and commercial depots and transit routes."

There is now a law, the constitutionality of which has not been doubted, providing for the acquisition of territory by discovery. But the Court, in the Dred Scott case, decided that territory could not be acquired, except as preliminary to the formation of a State. This difficulty should be obviated. I think the amendment I propose will do it. If we adopt the proposition of Mr. SUMMERS, we cut off the power of acquiring territory for transit routes, &c., except by treaty. I think my amendment will make the section more satisfactory to the South.

Mr. SUMMERS:—I will accept the amendment, and treat it as a part of my substitute.

Mr. BROCKENBROUGH:—I feel a deep solicitude in this subject. We are here for the purpose of settling a great difficulty. Instead of settling it, we shall add to it by placing these unnecessary obstructions in the way of acquiring territory in future. Would not the South be safer by the adoption of this guarantee? It is the only one, aside from the first section, which gives the

South a grain of power. We cannot go on with things as they are—only seven States to contend with all the rest of the nation. We must all desire that the seceded States should return to the Union. How are they to come back? By treaty, or by the sword? Who will not prefer to win them back by adopting principles in our amendments which will make it for their interest to return? If the amendment is adopted, no future territory will be acquired without the consent of a majority of Senators on both sides of the line. Reject this, and I have not the slightest hope of ever seeing the seceded States again in the Union. I believe this amendment will meet the wishes of a large majority of the people of Virginia.

The vote upon the adoption of the substitute proposed by Mr. Summers resulted as follows:

Ayes.—Rhode Island, New Jersey, Delaware, Maryland, Virginia, North Carolina, Tennessee, Kentucky, and Missouri—9.

Noes.—Maine, Vermont, Massachusetts, Connecticut, New York, Pennsylvania, Indiana, Illinois, Iowa, and Kansas—10.

And the amendment was lost.

Mr. GUTHRIE:—I will now renew my proposition, and ask a vote upon it by States.

The vote upon the substitute offered by Mr. Guthrie, for the section of the article reported by the committee, resulted as follows:

Ayes.—New Hampshire, Rhode Island, Connecticut, New Jersey, Pennsylvania, Delaware, Maryland, Tennessee, Kentucky, and Ohio—10.

Noes.—Maine, Vermont, Massachusetts, New York, Virginia, North Carolina, Missouri, Illinois, Indiana, and Iowa—10.

And the amendment was lost.

Mr. Price dissented from the vote of New Jersey, and Mr. Barringer from the vote of North Carolina.

Mr. WICKLIFFE:—As the hour named for the call upon the President-elect is approaching, I move that a committee of three members be appointed by the President to make arrangements for the introduction of the members of the Conference.

The motion of Mr. Wickliffe was agreed to, and the President appointed Messrs. Wickliffe, Field, and Chase, as the committee.

Mr. McKENNAN:—I move a reconsideration of the vote of the Conference rejecting the substitute offered by the gentleman from Virginia. I am not at all certain that we may not think it advisable to adopt that amendment.

The order of the day was now suspended, and the committee appointed to wait upon the President-elect, reported that they had performed that duty, and that the President-elect would be pleased to receive the members of the Conference in his parlors in Willard's Hotel, at the present time.

For the purpose of waiting on the President, on motion of Mr. Ewing, the Conference adjourned until the 25th inst., at ten o'clock A. M.

SEVENTEENTH DAY.

WASHINGTON, MONDAY, *February 25th*, 1861.

THE Convention was called to order at ten o'clock, pursuant to adjournment, by President TYLER, and prayer was offered by Rev. Dr. SMITH.

The Journal of Saturday was read.

Mr. HACKLEMAN:—The Delegates from the State of Indiana desire that the vote of that State upon the proposition of amendment offered by the gentleman from Iowa (Mr. CURTIS), on Friday last, may be recorded. The vote was taken on Saturday, and Indiana desires to record her vote against said proposition.

The Conference granted the leave asked, and the vote of Indiana was accordingly entered upon the Journal.

The PRESIDENT:—There have been transmitted to me the proceedings of a meeting of the Democrats of Pennsylvania, in which are contained certain resolutions relating to the matters now before us. I am informed that the meeting was one of the largest ever held in that State. The usual course would be to enter them upon the record, but in this instance I would suggest the propriety of having them read. However, the Conference will take such order upon them as it thinks proper.

Mr. POLLOCK:—The policy of the Conference from the beginning has been not to receive or consider resolutions of a partisan character. That decision was made on one of the early days of our session, upon a series of resolutions adopted by a convention held in New Haven, Connecticut, which were presented by Mr. Clay. I think we had better pass over the subject informally, and I would call for the order of the day.

Mr. MOREHEAD, of Kentucky:—I think the resolutions had better be referred to the Committee on Credentials.

Mr. CLAY:—I quite approved of the course taken by the Conference of the resolutions which were sent to me for presentation. I hope we will pursue the same course now. I move that these resolutions be entered upon the Journal as received, and that they be laid on the table.

The motion of Mr. Clay was agreed to, and the resolutions were laid on the table.

Mr. SMITH, of New York:—I would inquire whether any action has been taken under the order of the Conference for the printing of the Journal from day to day. It is very important that we have these Journals, that we may know exactly what has been done. No gentleman can carry all our proceedings in his memory.

The Secretary made a statement to the effect that he had not found time fully to complete the Journal, or to arrange for its being printed under the rule requiring that secrecy should be preserved; that the Mayor of Washington had proposed to have the printing done under a supervision which would secure its non-publication by the press, and that various reasons existed why the order of the Conference had not been complied with.

Mr. SMITH:—Then I hope the order will be complied with to-day. It is very important that each member should have a copy of our daily Journal. I certainly expected one this morning. I will not make a motion now, but if these copies are not furnished, I shall move the appointment of a committee to secure their future publication.

Mr. DENT:—There was a vote passed upon this subject. It may have been in the absence of the Secretary.

The PRESIDENT:—The Conference is informed that the Journal shall be published as soon as possible.

Mr. BROCKENBROUGH:—I have two amendments which I shall offer. At present I desire to have them laid on the table and printed.*

* I suppose these amendments offered by Mr. Brockenbrough were never printed; certainly no printed copy of them was ever distributed to the members of the Conference, and they were never inserted in the Journal. In preserving my notes, I naturally

The PRESIDENT :—The Conference will now proceed to the consideration of the order of the day, which is the motion to reconsider the vote rejecting the substitute offered by Mr. SUMMERS, for the second section of the articles of amendment reported by the committee.

Mr. McKENNAN :—At the request of one of my colleagues I would ask a postponement of the vote upon my motion of reconsideration for the present. It will produce no injurious result, and I think myself we had better hold this amendment subject to the future action of the Conference.

Mr. SUMMERS :—I will not withhold my consent to the postponement. But I hope the members of this Conference will consider my amendment, and give it their attention when it comes up again.

Mr. GUTHRIE :—If we pass Mr. SUMMERS' amendment, we should pass by the consideration of the whole section. I think that is the better way. Let us now proceed to the consideration of the third section in the article of amendment proposed by the committee.

The PRESIDENT :—Such will be taken as the pleasure of the Conference.

The third section was read.

The PRESIDENT :—The third section is open to propositions of amendment.

Mr. GUTHRIE :—I move to amend this section by striking out the words "by land, sea, or river," occurring after the words "or transportation."

Mr. GUTHRIE's motion was adopted without a division.

Mr. GUTHRIE :—I now move to insert after the words "during transportation," the words "by sea or river."

Which motion was also agreed to without a division.

Mr. HITCHCOCK :—I now move to amend the third section by striking out all after the word "give," in the second line thereof, and inserting as follows :

assumed that I could rely upon the printed copies distributed to the members, for the various amendments offered. At the period of writing out these notes communication with Mr. BROCKENBROUGH is impossible, and I am obliged to omit farther notice of his amendments. I am not even able to state the subjects to which they referred.

"to Congress power to regulate, abolish, or control, within any State, the relations established or recognized by the laws thereof, touching persons held to service or labor therein."

SECTION 4. Congress shall have no power to discharge any person held to service or labor in the District of Columbia, under the laws thereof, from such service or labor, or to impair any rights pertaining to that relation, under the laws now in force within the said District, while such relations shall exist in the State of Maryland, without the consent of said State, and of those to whom the service or labor is due, or making them just compensation therefor; nor the power to prohibit or interfere with members of Congress and officers of the Federal Government whose duties require them to be in said District, from bringing with them, for personal service only, retaining, and taking away persons so held to service or labor, nor the power to impair or abolish the relations of persons owing service or labor in places under the exclusive jurisdiction of the United States, within those States and Territories where such relations are established or recognized by law.

SECTION 5. Congress shall have no power to prohibit the removal or transportation of persons held to service or labor in any State or Territory of the United States to any State or Territory thereof where the same obligation or liability to labor or service is established or recognized by law; and the right during such transportation, by sea or river, of touching at ports, shores, or landings, and of landing in case of distress, shall exist; nor shall the Congress have power to authorize any higher rate of taxation on persons held to service or labor than on land.

Although it may not be strictly in order, yet, as a part of my plan, I wish to bring forward a substitute which I shall offer to the seventh section of the committee's article, which, if adopted, should be numbered

SECTION 9. Congress shall provide by law, that in all cases where the Marshal, or other officer whose duty it shall be to arrest any fugitive from service or labor, shall be prevented from so doing by violence of a mob or riotous assemblage; or where, after such arrest, such fugitive shall be rescued by like violence, and the party to whom such service or labor is due shall thereby be deprived of the same, the United States shall pay to such party the full value of such service or labor.

I offer these in separate sections, in order not only that the vote may be taken upon each one separately here, but also when the same questions come before the people. The first section of my amendment, as I understand from every quarter, sets all opposition at rest; all are willing to agree to it. This may be adopted and the others rejected, which could not be done if the original section was adopted. The other sections conform to the language of our present Constitution, and for that reason I think they will meet with more favor. Each subject is thus made to stand on its own merits.

The PRESIDENT :—The question will be taken upon each section of the substitute proposed.

Mr. JAMES :—I propose the following as a substitute for the first section of the amendment offered by Mr. HITCHCOCK. It is, I believe, the same as that proposed in Congress by the Committee of Thirteen. I understand, also, that the Committee of the House of Representatives are about to substitute it for what is known as the ADAMS Proposition. We all have the same purpose in view, to negative in express terms the right of Congress to interfere with the institution of slavery within the States. I present the amendment because I think it expresses the purpose in better language.

'SECTION 1. No amendment shall be made to the Constitution which will authorize or give to Congress the power to abolish or interfere, within any State, with the domestic institutions thereof, including that of persons held to labor or service by the laws of said State.

Mr. CHASE :—This amendment would be limited in its application to the States. Congress would still have power in this respect over Territories.

Mr. GUTHRIE :—The report of the committee has been agreed upon after much discussion, and printed. We all understand it, and I hope we shall adhere to it without any alteration. If we begin to adopt these amendments no one can tell where they will carry us.

Mr. JAMES :—My proposition is offered as an amendment to that offered by Mr. HITCHCOCK.

Mr. GUTHRIE :—So I understand; but his amendment is proposed as a substitute for the third section of the article reported by the committee. I object to the whole of it.

Mr. RANDOLPH :—Do I understand that the question now is upon substituting Mr. HITCHCOCK'S amendment for the committee's report.

Mr. JAMES :—No. It is upon substituting my proposition for the first section of Mr. HITCHCOCK'S amendment.

The vote upon the amendment offered by Mr. JAMES resulted as follows:

AYES.—Maine, New Hampshire, Vermont, Massachusetts, Connecticut, New York, and Indiana—7.

NOES.—Rhode Island, New Jersey, Pennsylvania, Delaware, Maryland, Virginia, North Carolina, Tennessee, Kentucky, Missouri, Ohio, Illinois, and Kansas—13.

And the amendment was lost.

Mr. WOOD :—I must enter my dissent from the vote of Illinois.

Mr. FOWLER :—I have an amendment which I offer to the substitute proposed by Mr. HITCHCOCK—

Mr. RANDOLPH :—I object to it as out of order. Let us take the vote upon the various sections of Mr. HITCHCOCK'S proposition. If they are rejected, then these amendments may all be moved to the committee's report.

The PRESIDENT :—I have already decided that the substitute is open to amendment.

Mr. RANDOLPH :—Then I will appeal from the decision of the Chair.

The PRESIDENT :—I will state the ground of my decision. It is true, as claimed by the gentleman from New Jersey, that if the propositions of Mr. HITCHCOCK are *rejected* these amendments may be moved to the sections reported by the committee. If, on the contrary, they are *adopted*, or either of them, so far as they are adopted they must stand as the order of the Conference, and are no longer subject to amendment. I understand the Parliamentary rule in such a case to be well settled.

A somewhat confused debate here arose, when Mr. RANDOLPH withdrew his appeal from the decision of the chair.

Mr. BALDWIN :—I move to amend the proposition of the gentleman from Ohio, by striking out the words "nor shall Congress have the power to authorize any higher rate of taxation on persons held to service or labor, than on land." I do not think these words are appropriate in a provision of the Constitution.

Mr. HITCHCOCK :—I supposed the Conference would understand my purpose. It was to substitute my three sections for the third section of the committee's report. I did not suppose this series of amendments would be offered. For the present, I will withdraw my amendments.

Mr. HARRIS :—The gentleman forgets that if we once adopt them, they are no longer subject to amendment.

Mr. BRONSON:—I wish to make a suggestion. I don't know but Parliamentarians would call it a point of order. Now let us go on and decide whether we will, or will not, adopt the third section as reported by the committee.

Mr. SEDDON:—I have several amendments which I am constrained to offer to this third section. My State would think me remiss if I did not offer them. I move, first, to insert after the words "State or Territory of the United States," the words "or obstruct, hinder, prevent, or abolish."

By the section as reported by the committee, Congress is prohibited from controlling or abolishing slavery in any State or Territory. This amendment which I propose will prevent any action in relation to it—in aid of it, or otherwise. The Territorial Legislature will always be the creature of Congress, and under the committee's section it might act upon the subject of slavery. I understand that the purpose of the committee was to prevent Congress from abolishing slavery in the Territories, but not to prevent the Territorial Legislature from acting in aid of it. My amendment will secure slavery from all interference. That is what we want.

Mr. GUTHRIE:—The first section of the report covers this. The amendment, I think, is unnecessary.

Mr. SEDDON:—I think the first section, properly construed, would prevent the Territorial Legislature from enacting a law in aid of slavery, even if the whole people of the Territory desired it.

Mr. GUTHRIE:—I do not desire to go over these questions again. If the Conference intends to come to any conclusion at all, I hope it will vote down all these amendments.

Mr. SEDDON:—I call for a vote by States.

Mr. WOOD:—I move that the amendment be laid on the table.

Mr. BALDWIN:—Which motion is in order—mine or that of the gentleman from Virginia?

The PRESIDENT:—The gentleman from Ohio having withdrawn his amendment, the proposal of the gentleman from Connecticut is no longer before the Conference. The question is upon the motion of the gentleman from Virginia to amend the third section of the article reported by the committee.

The vote upon the amendment proposed by Mr. SEDDON resulted as follows:

AYES.—Maryland, Virginia, North Carolina, Tennessee, Kentucky, and Missouri—6.

NOES.—Maine, New Hampshire, Vermont, Massachusetts, Rhode Island, Connecticut, New York, New Jersey, Pennsylvania, Delaware, Ohio, Indiana, Illinois, and Kentucky—14.

And the amendment was not adopted.

Mr. SEDDON:—I now move to amend the third section reported by the committee, by striking out the words "City of Washington," and inserting in their place the words "District of Columbia."

The motion of Mr. SEDDON was agreed to without a division.

Mr. WICKLIFFE:—I do not see why this privilege of bringing their slaves into the District should be limited to members of Congress.

Mr. GUTHRIE:—It is not. The expression is "representatives and *others*."

Mr. SEDDON:—I now propose to amend the same section by inserting after the words "without the consent of Maryland" the words "and Virginia." I think slavery ought not to be destroyed in the District of Columbia without the consent both of Maryland and Virginia. If there is any reason for requiring the consent of one State, the same reason exists as to the other. This amendment will make the section much more acceptable to the slaveholding States.

Mr. GUTHRIE:—The committee did not require the assent of Virginia, because no part of the present District came from Virginia. We thought it unnecessary.

Mr. DENT:—Maryland and Virginia originally joined in the cession of the District to the United States. Afterwards that portion which came from her was re-ceded to Virginia. But this question is not one of territory alone. The policy and interest of the two States are intimately connected. It would be far more satisfactory to both these States, and to the South, if the assent of Virginia was required before Congress could abolish slavery in the District. Still Maryland does not insist upon it.

Mr. EWING:—I can see no necessity for, or propriety in, the amendment. We might as well require the consent of North

Carolina or any of the other slave States. Virginia owns none of the District. She has no right to interfere.

The amendment proposed by Mr. SEDDON was rejected by the following vote:

AYES.—Maryland, Virginia, North Carolina, Tennessee, and Missouri—5.

NOES.—Maine, New Hampshire, Vermont, Massachusetts, Rhode Island, Connecticut, New York, New Jersey, Pennsylvania, Kentucky, Ohio, Indiana, Illinois, and Kansas—14.

Mr. SEDDON :—My next proposition is to amend the third section by inserting after the words "landing in case of distress, shall exist," the words "and if the transportation be by sea, the right of property in the person held to service or labor shall be protected by the Federal Government as other property."

We claim that our property in slaves shall be recognized by the Union just like any other property—that no unjust or improper distinction shall be made. When we trust it to the perils of the seas, we wish to have it protected by the Federal Government.

Mr. WICKLIFFE :—I would inquire of the gentleman from Virginia whether it has not already been decided that this species of property is as much entitled to Federal protection as any other. I refer to the "Creole" case. The British Government made compensation for this species of property in that case. This was done upon the award of the commissioners pursuant to the decision of the umpire.

Mr. SEDDON :—Yes! But on the express ground that slavery was recognized in the islands. Express notice was given, that when the emancipation policy was adopted, the same principles would not be recognized. We are now removing doubts. We wish to have these matters no longer involved in uncertainty. We insist upon having these provisions in the Constitution.

Mr. RUFFIN :—I wish to say a word on this subject, much as I regret the consumption of time. I am willing to leave this question where it is now; and my reason is this: If we put this into the Constitution, the question may be raised, whether if foreign nations should interfere with this kind of property on the high seas, the Government would not be bound to consider it a cause of war. We ought not to bind ourselves to go to war. War should always depend upon considerations of policy. We should raise a thousand troublesome questions by putting these words "shall be protected" into the Constitution. The matter is well enough as it is. Our rights in this respect are well enough protected by the ordinary course of national diplomacy. I would not be willing to put into the Constitution language which would embarrass us hereafter.

Mr. SEDDON:—I will frankly say that I think slave property upon every ground is as well entitled to the national protection as any other species of property.

Mr. BARRINGER:—This amendment brings up the very gist of the matter. The question of the right of our property to Federal protection is now an open one. In the case of the Creole it was settled by negotiation, and not by the courts. The question so often hinted at and suggested in this Conference is now fairly brought up for decision. Governor CHASE struck at the very root of the matter the other day, when he said that slavery was an *abnormal* condition. He laid down the opinion of the North. He is a statesman and a lawyer. He says that slavery cannot exist anywhere until it is established or authorized by law. This is the Northern idea, and it is a technical one. I hate technicalities almost as bad as I do sectionalism. The North deals in both. I regret to speak in these terms of the North, but I must if I speak truth. Now, I will lay down what is the opinion of the South upon the subject. We say that the right to hold and use slave property, always, everywhere, exists until it is prohibited by law. We say that it is a natural right, which grows out of the very necessities of society. We hold that the condition of slavery is a normal condition—not local at all; that it is found everywhere, except where it is forbidden by law. We claim that the right to hold slaves is a natural right, recognized by the law of nations, and of the world. I am quite aware that the North does not agree with our opinion.

Mr. VANDEVER:—I would ask whether this normal condition is confined to the blacks, or does it extend to all races?

Mr. BARRINGER:—Most assuredly it is not confined to a single race. It extends to all races. Slavery of all races exists even in Europe.

Mr. FIELD:—Not now!

Mr. BARRINGER:—Perhaps not now, and why? For the

reason that it has been abolished by law, as in the recent case of Russia. Slavery once existed in the Northern States. By law it was also abolished in those States. We say that when slave property is on the high seas it ought to be protected—the rights of the owner ought to be protected.

This question came up in the case of the "Amistead." Mr. ADAMS claimed that although these slaves were recognized by the laws of Spain as property, yet, when once upon the high seas, they were, by the law of nations, *free*, and these slaves have never been paid for to this day.

This amendment is highly important to the South. The concession we ask is no greater than has been made before. In the treaties of 1783 and 1815, slaves were to be protected as property.

Mr. WICKLIFFE:—I do not wish to nullify the action, or change the course of our Government on this question. Slaves upon the high seas have always been recognized as property. Look at the treaty of 1815. That recognized slaves as property, and those which were taken from the District were paid for. ADAMS, of Massachusetts, took the same ground now taken by the North. The Government took the opposite ground. The question was ultimately referred to the Emperor of Russia, who decided that property in slaves must be recognized by the law of nations, and sustained our view. Take the "Creole" case also. But I will not go over the ground. The "Amistead" case stood upon grounds which were entirely different.

But it is not necessary to put this amendment into the Constitution. The rights of the South in this respect are well enough protected now.

Mr. GRANGER:—I regret that the distinguished gentleman from Virginia has again raised a question which was decided against him by a large majority in the Conference a few days ago.

Mr. SEDDON:—The gentleman is quite correct. The principle must be the same whether applied to the Territories or to the high seas.

Mr. GRANGER:—It is claimed by the South that slaves are property everywhere. Why, then, name slave property more than any other species in the Constitution?

Mr. BARRINGER:—We say that slaves are *both* persons and property.

Mr. GRANGER:—It has always been the course of the Government to pay for slaves taken on the high seas. The gentleman has referred to the "Amistead" case as having been decided against the southern claim. I present the "Amistead" case as a perfect answer to the miserable calumnies which have been disseminated against that Court. The Judges in that case were unanimous with a single exception, and he was a Judge from a free State. We of the North upon these national questions are prepared to go with you to the extreme verge of right and loyalty.

Mr. MOREHEAD, of North Carolina:—I have no desire to complicate these questions of international law. The treaties of 1783 and 1815 were participated in by JAY and the elder ADAMS. They expressly provided for the payment for slaves like other property. This is plain English, and settles the question so far as the North is concerned. I am for letting it alone where it is.

Mr. CRISFIELD:—I am not able to support this proposition of the gentleman from Virginia. I consider the right of property in slaves, in the slave States, and in the territory south of 36° 30′, as fully recognized and established in the report of the majority of the committee. In this very clause this property is expressly admitted, and Congress is prohibited from interfering with it. This is enough—it is all that should be done. We have come here to settle our domestic troubles. The report of the committee recognizes and affirms these rights of the South which have heretofore been denied or doubted. I think their report gives us all the assurance we need. We were not sent here to engraft new principles into our foreign policy, and I will not consent to enter upon that business. We have got this right of property specifically recognized, and no administration hereafter will refuse to carry out the plain provisions of the Constitution.

Mr. SEDDON:—Where in the article do you find this right recognized? It simply prohibits Congress from interfering with slavery within certain limits. Nothing beyond that.

Mr. CRISFIELD:—I find the recognition pervading the whole report. The right of transportation, for instance, is secured. Does not that involve, of necessity, a recognition of the right of property? I am sure the South is safe in leaving this question where the report leaves it.

Mr. HOUSTON :—We feel disposed to adhere firmly to the report of the committee. We know the arduous labor they have bestowed upon the subject, and feel that we ought to be satisfied with the result. We do not wish to have our friends put us in a false position. We shall vote against the amendment of the gentleman from Virginia, not because we do not think it is right on principle, but because we think it is unnecessary. The right of property in slaves is protected now wherever that property goes.

Mr. BARRINGER :—I admit that the policy of the Government hitherto has been as the gentlemen claim. If the South could have been satisfied with that, we should never have been sent here—this Convention would never have been called. But we have come together for the reason that we fear the established policy of the Government will be changed by the party now coming into power. We ask for assurances that the old policy should be continued; and we wish to have the obligation to continue it, written down in the bond.

The Chair restated the question, and Mr. SEDDON called for a vote by States.

The vote upon Mr. SEDDON's amendment resulted as follows:

AYES.—Virginia, Tennessee, North Carolina, and Missouri—4.

NOES.—Maine, New Hampshire, Vermont, Massachusetts, Rhode Island, Connecticut, New York, New Jersey, Pennsylvania, Delaware, Maryland, Kentucky, Ohio, Indiana, Illinois, Iowa, and Kansas—17.

And the amendment was lost.

Messrs. BUTLER and CLAY, of Kentucky; Messrs. DONIPHAN and JOHNSON, of Missouri; Messrs. HOWARD and DENT, of Maryland, dissented from the votes of their respective States.

Mr. SEDDON :—I now move the following amendment of the same third section. After the words "in case of distress, shall exist," insert the following:

"And the rights of transit by persons holding those of the African race to labor or service, in and through the States not recognizing the relations of persons held to labor or service, in passing with them from one State or Territory recognizing such relation, to another, shall be secure."

I only wish to say in reference to this amendment that it secures a right specifically referred to in the resolutions of Virginia under which this Conference is called. On that account I feel bound to offer it, but I will not occupy time in its discussion.

Mr. GUTHRIE:—In the early years of our Government this right was extended by courtesy to the slaveholding States. Since these differences have sprung up, in some States it has been denied—in others, the courtesy still exists. We considered this question thoroughly in committee. We did not wish to put any thing into our report that would operate to excite the prejudices of any section against it, and so lessen the chances of its being adopted. We thought it best not to insert such a provision. I am opposed to the amendment.

Mr. SEDDON:—I call a vote by States.

The amendment proposed by Mr. SEDDON was rejected by the following vote:

AYES.—Virginia, North Carolina, Kentucky, and Missouri—4.

NOES.—Maine, New Hampshire, Vermont, Massachusetts, Rhode Island, Connecticut, New York, New Jersey, Pennsylvania, Delaware, Maryland, Tennessee, Ohio, Indiana, Illinois, Iowa, and Kansas—17.

Mr. SEDDON:—One more amendment. I move to amend the third section as follows: after the words "by the laws thereof touching," insert the words "the relations existing between master and slave or."

I shall not detain the Conference for five minutes in the discussion of this amendment. I wish, however, to have the words "master and slave" somewhere inserted in this article, in plain English language, so that the dangerous delusion so prevalent at the North, that the Constitution does not recognize slavery, may be thoroughly and forever removed; so that the Constitution shall, beyond any question, recognize the relation of master and slave; a duplex relation—a relation of person and property. I wish to meet that question fairly and squarely. Let it be thoroughly understood as a relation of person and property. This is what we ask, and this is what we insist upon. Put this into the Constitution, and you take the shortest and the most effective means of settling the question, and of promoting peace and tranquillity. You strike the axe to the very root of bitterness, whence has sprung all our trouble, all our difficulties. I ask a vote by States.

Mr. GUTHRIE:—What I have already said applies with equal force to this amendment. I will not repeat my objections.

The amendment offered by Mr. SEDDON was rejected by the following vote:

AYES.—Virginia, North Carolina, and Missouri—3.

NOES.—Maine, New Hampshire, Vermont, Massachusetts, Rhode Island, Connecticut, New York, New Jersey, Pennsylvania, Delaware, Maryland, Tennessee, Kentucky, Ohio, Indiana, Illinois, Iowa, and Kansas—18.

Mr. CRISFIELD—Maryland votes "No," not because she specially objects to the amendment, but she stands by the report of the committee.

Mr. DENT:—I dissent from the vote of Maryland.

Mr. CLAY:—And I from the vote of Kentucky.

Mr. ALEXANDER:—*

Mr. HALL, of Vermont:—I move to amend the third section by striking out the word "nor," immediately succeeding the words "persons so bound to labor," and inserting the following:

"But the bringing into said District of persons held to service, for the purpose of being sold, or placed in depot to be afterwards transferred to any other place to be sold as merchandise, is forever prohibited, and Congress may pass all necessary laws to make this prohibition effectual; nor shall Congress have."

It is well known that much of the agitation upon the question of slavery has formerly arisen from the existence of the slave-trade in the District of Columbia. Since the prohibition of 1850, the public mind has been much more quiet, so far as this subject is concerned. I suppose the committee did not intend to change the law of 1850, but I fear their action will not be so understood at the North. I propose to make the matter clear. [Mr. HALL here read the section of the Act of 1850 referring to this subject.] My amendment puts the language of this act into the Constitution. My only purpose is, to have this question left in exactly its present position. Without the amendment, I fear it will be claimed that the article restores the slave-trade in this District. Nothing would more effectually destroy the article at the North.

Mr. WHITE:—The language of the report is clear. It gives no right to sell slaves in the District.

* The published Journal states that Mr. ALEXANDER dissented from the vote of New Jersey. My notes do not show that he dissented, and I think the Journal may be erroneous in this particular.

Mr. HALL :—I wish to be understood. The article prohibits Congress from interfering with slavery. *Ergo*, it will be claimed they cannot prohibit the exercise of any of its functions. The construction, to say the very least, will be doubtful. It should not be left in doubt.

Mr. NOYES :—The slave-trade in the District of Columbia has always been a subject of great dissatisfaction. I don't know that it is considered of much importance in the South, but at the North it always has been. Ten years ago it was abolished by act of Congress. I fear that unless the amendment of the gentleman from Vermont is adopted, the effect of the committee's report will be to restore the slave-trade in the District. The section reported by the committee permits any person to bring his slaves into the District; to retain them there as long as he chooses, and to take them away. It recognizes the right of absolute dominion. It secures it effectually. It imposes upon the soil of the District the right of holding, retaining, and taking away the slaves by the owner himself, his agent or assignee. The slave-trade, in my judgment, is thus restored.

Mr. GUTHRIE :—I am satisfied that the article reported by the committee is not susceptible of misconstruction, and I hope we shall not mar the report by adopting the amendment. Our intention was only to permit public officers to bring their servants here.

Mr. AMES :—Two words will cure all this difficulty. The insertion of the words "for personal service only."

Mr. GUTHRIE :—We have no intention of reviving the slave-trade in the District. I have no more to say.

Mr. DODGE :—I hope this section will not be left in doubt. When I first read it I said to myself, "This thing will never do; it will bring the slave-trade back to the District."

Mr. AMES :—Will the gentleman from Vermont accept my amendment?

Mr. HALL :—No. I cannot accept it. I offer the amendment in good faith, for I believe it necessary.

Mr. MOREHEAD, of North Carolina :—Cannot we avoid the verbiage of the amendment?

Mr. EWING :—I shall vote against the amendment of the gentleman from Vermont, so that I can vote for that proposed by Mr. AMES.

The vote upon Mr. HALL'S amendment being taken by States, resulted as follows:

AYES.—Maine, New Hampshire, Vermont, Massachusetts, Connecticut, New York, Ohio, Indiana, Illinois, Iowa, and Kansas—11.

NOES.—Rhode Island, New Jersey, Pennsylvania, Delaware, Maryland, Virginia, North Carolina, Tennessee, Kentucky, and Missouri—10.

And the amendment was adopted.

Messrs. HOPPIN and BROWNE, of Rhode Island, dissented from the vote of that State.

Mr. McCURDY:—I move to amend the original article of the committee's report by the addition of this proviso. My object is to prevent the sale of slaves in the waters of New York or any other port:

"*Provided*, That nothing in this section shall be so construed as to prevent any States in which involuntary servitude is prohibited, from restraining by law the transfer of such persons, or of any right or interest in their services, from one individual to another, within the limits of such State."

Mr. GUTHRIE:—I insist there is not the slightest necessity for this amendment. I hope gentlemen will stop interposing these useless propositions; they confound the sense of the article, and we are guarding against questions which by no possibility can arise.

The vote was then taken on the amendment of Mr. McCURDY, and resulted as follows:

AYES.—Maine, New Hampshire, Vermont, Massachusetts, Connecticut, New York, Ohio, Indiana, Illinois, Iowa, and Kansas—11.

NOES.—Rhode Island, New Jersey, Pennsylvania, Delaware, Maryland, Virginia, North Carolina, Tennessee, Kentucky, and Missouri—10.

And the amendment was agreed to.

Messrs. LOGAN and PALMER, of Illinois, dissented from the vote of that State.

Mr. HOWARD:—I would ask the gentleman from Connecticut if he ever knew or heard of a case where a slave was sold in a free State?

Mr. McCURDY:—I do not intend to argue that question; but as I am appealed to, although the proviso is adopted, I will state the grounds on which it rests.

Mr. CLAY:—I wish to know whether the object of the

amendment is to prevent the making of contracts connected with the purchase or sale of slaves in the free States?

Mr. McCURDY:—My object is apparent from the amendment. It explains itself. I wish to prohibit any transactions concerning the purchase or sale of slaves, either within the free States or the navigable waters connected therewith, or under free State jurisdiction. If there were no such prohibition, a cargo of slaves might be brought from the coast of Africa into the port of New York, and transferred there to parties residing in the slave States. The free States have a right to direct what shall, and what shall not be a subject of commerce within their limits. I presume it is not intended that the Constitution shall prohibit the exercise of this right. I desire not to leave this open to construction, but to make the section declare that no such intention exists.

Mr. GUTHRIE:—I am now satisfied that we shall get nothing here that is satisfactory to the people of the south side of the river. We are continually waylaid by suspicions, which are unjust, unfounded, and ought not to exist. If this class of amendments is to be adopted, I cannot go on, with respect to myself or the Convention. I feel now, since this amendment is adopted, that my mission here is ended.

Mr. REID:—I move to insert at the end of the third article reported by the committee these words: "Persons of the African race shall not be deemed citizens, or permitted to exercise the right of suffrage, in the election of federal officers."

Mr. GUTHRIE:—This is worse than ever, and it comes from the South too.

Mr. REID:—I will withdraw it then.

Mr. WICKLIFFE:—I ask the unanimous consent of the Conference to move the adoption of the previous question. We may as well come to the point now as ever. There is no use of discussing this question any longer. I move the previous question upon the report.

Objections and cries of "No, no," were made by several members.

Mr. WICKLIFFE:—I will withdraw the motion.

Mr. TURNER:—I think it would be very unreasonable for any gentleman to expect that we were to get through with the questions presented by this report without the exercise of mutual forbearance. The adoption of an amendment implies no disrespect to the committee. No member of the committee should take it in that sense. I will move a reconsideration of the vote by which the last amendment was adopted. I do not think we had better take the vote now, but pass the subject for the present.

The PRESIDENT:—It can be passed by common consent.

The vote was reconsidered without a division, and the immediate consideration of the question passed.

Mr. HITCHCOCK:—I now renew the offer of my substitute for the third section of the article reported by the committee.

Mr. FIELD:—I thought when the motion to reconsider the vote upon Mr. McCurdy's amendment was agreed to, it was understood that the consideration of the whole section was to be passed for the present. My vote upon that amendment was given deliberately, and I have no idea that this Convention is to break up because a vote is passed in it which is distasteful to any man, State, or delegation.

Mr. HITCHCOCK:—I think I must insist upon the consideration of my substitute.

Mr. BROWNE:—I move to lay the substitute proposed by the gentleman from Ohio on the table. If that motion is carried, I do not understand that the effect of it is to lay the report of the committee on the table.

Mr. SMITH:—I rise to a question of order. I think the question now should be on Mr. McCurdy's amendment. I ask for information. I do not quite see how that amendment can be informally passed over without at the same time passing the consideration of the whole article.

The PRESIDENT:—It was passed by universal consent.

Mr. CHASE:—As I understand it, the gentleman from Illinois made the motion that the vote be reconsidered, and the consideration of the amendment passed for the present, and this was agreed to by the Conference unanimously.

The motion of Mr. Browne to lay the motion of Mr. Hitchcock on the table, was agreed to without a division.

Mr. BALDWIN:—I move to strike out these words in the third section: "Nor shall Congress have power to authorize any higher rate of taxation on persons bound to labor than on land." I have already stated that I think this language singularly inappropriate to a provision of the Constitution. The Constitution already prohibits such distinctions in the laying of taxes, and, therefore, there is no necessity for the adoption of this clause. But I have another and more important objection to it; it contains and proposes to place in the Constitution the distinct recognition of the right of property in slaves. This recognition was carefully avoided in the Convention which framed the Constitution, and the North always has been, and always will be, opposed to any such recognition. Place it there, and your article will never be adopted in any of the free States.

Mr. WICKLIFFE:—The first statutes passed by Congress on this subject recognized the right to tax slaves. This implied the right to hold slaves. This recognition of the right of taxation was made in express terms. The gentleman has forgotten the history of the legislation on this subject. The object of the committee is to prevent any possibility that those who come after us should make any distinction between these classes of property in levying taxes. We do not seek a recognition of the right of property in slaves in this; that right is already recognized to our satisfaction in the Constitution.

Mr. TUCK:—I understand the gentleman from Kentucky, and I think he is right. If we adopt the article at all we ought to retain this language.

The vote was taken by States on the amendment proposed by Mr. Baldwin, with the following result:

Ayes.—Maine, Massachusetts, and Connecticut—3.

Noes.—New Hampshire, Vermont, New York, Ohio, Indiana, Illinois, Iowa, Kansas, Rhode Island, New Jersey, Pennsylvania, Delaware, Maryland, Virginia, North Carolina, Tennessee, Kentucky, and Missouri—18.

Mr. Pratt dissented from the vote of Connecticut.

Messrs. Noyes and Smith also dissented from the vote of New York.

Mr. FOWLER:—I move to strike out the words "without the consent of Maryland," immediately following the words "service in the District of Columbia."

I can see no necessity for requiring the consent of Maryland to the abolition of slavery in the District. There is no more reason for it than for requiring the consent of Maine, or any other State. By the cession of the District to the United States Maryland has parted with all power over it, and the exclusive power of legislation is given to Congress. The District has become the common property of the Union as much as any of the Territories, and ought to be controlled in the same way.

Mr. CRISFIELD:—I hope this amendment will not prevail. The District is almost surrounded by the Territory of Maryland. The abolition of slavery in it would be very destructive to our interests and property. To convert the District into free territory would offer a direct invitation to our slaves to abscond and go into the District. Even if the rendition clause of the Constitution was faithfully observed and carried out, it would involve us in much expense and difficulty. If we are required to maintain faith with the Government, the Government must keep faith with us.

Mr. FOWLER:—I did not suppose my motion would meet with such serious objections. If they exist I will withdraw it.

Mr. BATES:—I have an amendment to propose, which I think will improve the language of the section, and make it more consonant with that used in the Constitution. I move to amend the third section by striking out the word "bound" wherever it occurs therein, and inserting in its place the word "held;" also to insert after the words "to labor" wherever they occur, the words "or service."

The amendments proposed by Mr. BATES were adopted without a division.

Mr. CARRUTHERS:—I propose to amend the section as it stands after the adoption of the amendments of Mr. BATES, by inserting between the words "or" and "service" where they occur in that connection, the word "involuntary."

Mr. EWING:—I had rather leave out the word "involuntary;" it would look better. As the section now stands, both voluntary and involuntary service are included.

Mr. CARRUTHERS:—By the insertion of the words "service" in Mr. BATES' amendment, one portion of my purpose is accomplished. I will withdraw my motion.

Mr. GROESBECK:—I would ask if it is now in order to move a substitute for the whole section. I have one which meets my wishes, and which, I think, will meet the views of, and be acceptable to, the Conference.

Mr. CRISFIELD:—I do not think it is in order to offer a substitute at the present time.

Mr. GROESBECK:—Then I will call it a motion to strike out and insert, which, certainly, is in order. I, therefore, move to strike out the whole of the third section and insert the following:

SECTION 3. Congress shall have no power to abolish or control within any State the relations established or recognized by the laws thereof respecting persons held to service or labor therein.

SECTION 4. Congress shall have no power to legislate respecting the relation of service or labor in places under its exclusive jurisdiction, but within States where that relation is established or recognized, and while it continues, without the consent of such States; nor abolish or impair such relation in the District of Columbia, without the consent of such States; nor abolish or impair such relation in the District of Columbia, without the consent of Maryland, and compensation to persons to whom such service or labor is due.

SECTION 5. Congress shall have no power to prohibit the removal from any State or Territory of persons held to service or labor therein, to any other State or Territory in which persons are so held; and the right during removal of touching at ports, shores, and landings, and of landing in case of distress, shall exist, but not the right of transit in or through any State or Territory without its consent. No higher rate of taxation shall be imposed on persons so held than on land.

Three objects are sought to be obtained by the third section as proposed by the committee: one is, the declaration that Congress has no power over slavery in the States; the second, that Congress shall not legislate respecting slavery in territory under its jurisdiction, but within the limits of States, without the consent of such States, nor abolish slavery in the District without the consent of Maryland; the third concerns the subject of the removal of slaves from place to place. It is desirable that these three subjects should be so presented that one or more of them may be adopted, and the others rejected; a purpose that cannot be accomplished if they are all embraced in the same section. My substitute is plain and simple, and I think covers the whole ground.

Mr. ROMAN:—Has not the gentleman entirely left out the

provision relative to bringing slaves into the District of Columbia?

Mr. GROESBECK:—I have, because I believe it entirely unnecessary. Cannot the South take a proposition that is fair? A slave within the District cannot be taken from the owner under any authority of Congress, unless the owner receives full compensation. Compensation would in all cases be an equivalent for the slave in the District, or elsewhere. Under the Constitution, slavery cannot be abolished without compensation, except by the consent of all parties interested in the subject. It is not pretended that Congress has a right to abolish slavery anywhere without making compensation to the owner.

Mr. SEDDON:—The owner should always have compensation, it is true; but his right in this respect is based upon the right of property in slaves. It is not true that compensation is in all cases an equivalent for the slave. An owner should be free to determine for himself the question whether he will part with his property upon receiving suitable compensation. Under the gentleman's proposition this right would be exercised by Congress and not by the owner. But there is a farther, and still greater objection to the proposition: The North denies the right of property in slaves, and would deny compensation also, unless compelled to make it under the Constitution. The North holding slavery to be unjust and unrighteous, would desire to abolish the institution without paying for it.

Mr. GROESBECK:—I am willing to amend Section 4 of the substitute I offer, by denying to Congress the power to abolish the relation without making compensation, and the section may be thus considered.

Mr. DODGE:—I wish to support the proposition of Mr. GROESBECK; and let me say one thing farther: our words should be plain and simple; we should use language which common men can understand, and which does not require to be construed by lawyers. Above all, let us have some confidence in each other.

Mr. BARRINGER:—There is another entire and important omission in Mr. GROESBECK'S proposition: there is no provision whatever for the Territories.

Mr. DENT:—I think the Conference had much better adhere

to the section reported by the committee as it has been already amended. We have all read and studied that section. We understand it. A State that will not adopt the whole of the section will not adopt any part of it, and so there is no use in severing the subjects provided for. I am opposed to the adoption of the substitute. We understand the original article better than we can any other.

Mr. WILMOT:—I think the original proposition the best; the word "regulate" has been struck out of it, leaving only the words "impair or abolish."

Mr. McCURDY:—I ask leave to revive my motion. I regret having withdrawn it. I think I have the right to renew it now.

The PRESIDENT (Mr. ALEXANDER in the chair):—The motion of the gentleman from Connecticut is out of order.

Mr. CRISFIELD:—I understand we are now considering the amendment offered by the gentleman from Ohio (Mr. GROESBECK). If so, I move to insert in his proposition after the word "abolish" the words "or impair."

Mr. GROESBECK:—I think the amendment improves it. I will accept it.

Mr. CHASE:—There is, certainly, a misunderstanding as to the effect of the vote laying the amendment offered by Mr. HITCHCOCK upon the table: it was offered as a substitute to the third section; if it did not carry the whole section to the table, then motions to amend that section are in order. In that view, I think Mr. McCURDY's motion is in order either way: to amend the article proposed by the committee, or to amend the amendment of Mr. GROESBECK.

Mr. RANDOLPH: I think Mr. McCURDY's motion is entirely out of order; it has once been passed by informally.

Mr. CLEVELAND:—Is it not in order at any time to make a motion which will render the proposed substitute more perfect?

Mr. McCURDY:—I do not wish my proposition ruled out upon any technical construction of rules. I will now move it as an addition to the third section.

Mr. FOWLER:—I move to reconsider the vote adopting the motion proposed by the gentleman from Vermont (Mr. HALL).

Mr. FIELD:—I oppose the motion. The amendment is

both proper and necessary. It can certainly do no harm to the South; and if the South wishes to be fair, it will not object to it.

Mr. CHITTENDEN:—I oppose the reconsideration of the vote adopting Mr. HALL's amendment, and I will state very shortly the reason why. If the doctrine is to be established here, that the report of the committee is too sacred to be touched—too perfect to be made subject to amendment—let us know it. It will relieve myself, and I think many others, from farther attendance here; and I wish to say now, that if we are to sit here, such considerations must not be presented in future.

Mr. FOWLER:—I will withdraw my motion.

Mr. FRELINGHUYSEN:—I certainly wish some one would renew the motion to reconsider the vote upon Mr. HALL's amendment. I do not like to do it myself, but I think if that amendment were reconsidered, we would fix upon some terms that would be satisfactory to all sides.

Mr. AMES:—I do not see the necessity for adopting Mr. McCURDY's proposition. I think it amounts to nothing. It is simply a prohibition in the Constitution against the exercise of a right which no one wishes to exercise. I oppose it because it is unnecessary.

Mr. McCURDY:—I certainly do not wish to insist upon an unnecessary amendment. If the third section, as reported by the committee, is adopted, it declares that the right of transportation, &c., *shall exist*. Under this, if no amendment is adopted, slaves may be bought and sold in any of the waters of the free States.

Mr. CRISFIELD:—What difficulty or damage does the gentleman propose to obviate by his amendment?

The PRESIDENT:—The Chair has already decided that the proposition of Mr. McCURDY is not in order.

Mr. CHASE appealed from the decision of the Chair, and upon the appeal the decision was sustained.

Mr. FIELD:—I understand this decision cuts off both the amendments offered by Mr. HALL and Mr. McCURDY; that compels us to vote against the proposition of Mr. GROESBECK.

Mr. CHITTENDEN:—The amendment offered by my colleague, Mr. HALL, has been accepted. It stands as the order of the Conference, and cannot be rescinded except by a vote. I sustain the decision of the Chair, because, by every rule of parliamentary law, it was correct. But one thing farther. It is now perfectly in order to move Mr. McCurdy's proposition, or any other, as an *addition*.

The PRESIDENT:—Most clearly so.

Mr. CRISFIELD:—I do not discover any particular objection to the amendment of Mr. Groesbeck. If it had been reported by the committee, I should have preferred it; but the South is willing to take the section as it stands, and prefers the original to any substitute.

Mr. NOYES:—I am against the substitute, for it destroys the effect of the amendments offered by Messrs. Hall and McCurdy.

The vote was then taken upon Mr. Groesbeck's amendment, and resulted as follows:

Ayes.—New Hampshire, Rhode Island, Connecticut, Pennsylvania, Delaware, Ohio, and Indiana—7.

Noes.—Maine, Vermont, Massachusetts, New York, New Jersey, Maryland, Virginia, North Carolina, Tennessee, Missouri, Illinois, and Kansas—12.

And it was rejected.

Mr. GUTHRIE:—I feel that my mission here is ended, and that I may as well withdraw from the Conference. I seem to be unable to impress gentlemen with the necessity of accomplishing any thing. The report of the committee is not satisfactory to the South; it is even doubtful whether they will adopt it; certainly they will not, if it is cut to pieces by amendments. I may be compelled to sacrifice my property, or go with the secessionists. At my time of life, I do not wish to do either.

Mr. McCURDY:—I regret that my amendment produces so much feeling, but I think, at all events, we should prevent the sale of slaves in the free States; it should be prevented beyond any possibility. I renew the offer of my amendment.

Mr. EWING:—If the laws of New York will permit the sale of slaves within the limits of that State, then we should prohibit the sale in the Constitution as proposed; but so long as that State has power to pass a law prohibiting it, there is no necessity for the amendment. The owner is only permitted to touch with his slaves, under certain circumstances, at the ports of free States.

Mr. RUFFIN:—It is impossible that slaves can be sold in a free State under the section reported by the committee. We propose to give the right of touching at those ports as a privilege, but we give no right of sale there. The laws of a free State could not be evaded in this way. Each State is supreme within its own limits; that supremacy would not be aided by this proviso.

Mr. TURNER:—Suppose a slave owner is compelled to stop at the port of Cairo, through stress of weather or any other cause, and he dies there, are his slaves set free by his death? Does not the law of actual domicil prevail? I think they will be regarded as slaves, and that under this provision they might be administered upon and sold as a part of his estate.

Mr. POLLOCK:—I think we may obviate all difficulty by inserting after the words "landing in case of distress," the words "but not for traffic or sale."

Mr. TUCK:—I am in favor of the amendment proposed by the gentleman from Pennsylvania. It is not proper or best to encumber these propositions with amendments that are not necessary.

Mr. LOGAN:—Every State has the right to regulate transit within its own limits to suit itself. The proposed amendment gives no rights except such as are expressly named: "a right, during transportation, of touching at the ports, and of landing in case of distress." The right of the State to regulate transit is left unimpaired.

Mr. HOWARD:—There is one principle of law which will settle this question at once: property that is held under State laws must be transferred by the operation of State laws alone. Slaves are held and transferred by the specific laws of the States in which they are held.

Mr. PALMER:—The right of sale cannot possibly arise out of the right to touch during transportation at a port, or the right to land in case of distress. I cannot see the slightest occasion or necessity for the adoption of Mr. McCurdy's amendment.

Mr. McCurdy's amendment was rejected by the following vote:

AYES.—Maine, Vermont, Massachusetts, Connecticut, New York, Indiana, and Iowa—7.

NOES.—New Hampshire, Rhode Island, New Jersey, Pennsylvania, Delaware, Maryland, Virginia, North Carolina, Tennessee, Kentucky, Missouri, Ohio, Illinois, and Kansas—14.

Mr. POLLOCK's amendment was then adopted without a division.

Mr. VANDEVER:—I wish to propose an amendment by way of proviso:

"*Provided* nothing herein contained shall be so construed as to prevent any State from prohibiting the introduction as merchandise of persons held to service or labor, or to prevent such State from prohibiting the transit of persons so held to service or labor through its limits."

Mr. FIELD:—This does not cover Mr. McCURDY's proposition at all. Is there any secret purpose here to bring into the Constitution a provision which will permit the sale of slaves in free States? If there is not, why not say plainly that the States shall have the exclusive right to determine who shall and who shall not cross its borders, and what shall be the subject of sale or traffic within them?

Mr. GUTHRIE:—The States have all the powers which are not expressly delegated under the Constitution to be exercised by Congress. Congress has no power, except such as are expressly conferred upon them. The power to prohibit the sale of slaves rests somewhere. It has not been conferred upon Congress; it must remain in the State.

Mr. SMITH:—The argument of the gentleman from Kentucky seems to me very inconsistent with his report in other respects.

Mr. HOWARD:—The Border States are trying to get back the seceded States. We hope they will come back. We expect the adoption of this report to offer a strong inducement to them to return to the Union. It will not offer such inducement if its general effect is ruined by amendments.

The vote upon Mr. VANDEVER's amendment resulted as follows:

AYES.—Maine, Vermont, Massachusetts, Connecticut, New York, Indiana, and Iowa—7.

NOES.—New Hampshire, Rhode Island, New Jersey, Pennsylvania. Delaware, Maryland, Virginia, North Carolina, Tennessee, Kentucky, Missouri, Ohio, Illinois, and Kansas—14.

So the amendment was not agreed to.

Mr. CLAY:—I have already stated that the State of Kentucky is prepared to adopt the CRITTENDEN amendment; that amendment will be satisfactory to the Border States. The longer we remain here the more I become satisfied that the CRITTENDEN amendment will meet with more general favor than any other; therefore I ask the consent of the Conference to introduce the CRITTENDEN amendment as a substitute for the committee's report.

The consent of the Conference was not given to Mr. CLAY's proposition.

Mr. GROESBECK:—I move to amend the third section by inserting after the words "in case of distress shall exist," the words "but not the right of transit in any other State or Territory without its consent."

We must certainly do something to cover this difficulty; if we omit the subject entirely, we shall leave much opportunity for cavil on this question when the question goes to the people.

Mr. RUFFIN:—I move to amend the amendment by substituting in place of the words "without its consent," the words "against its dissent."

Mr. GROESBECK:—I will accept the amendment.

The amendment of Mr. GROESBECK was agreed to by the following vote:

AYES.—Maine, New Hampshire, Vermont, Massachusetts, Rhode Island, Connecticut, New York, New Jersey, Pennsylvania, and Ohio—10.

NOES.—Delaware, Maryland, Virginia, North Carolina, Tennessee, Kentucky, Missouri, and Illinois—8.

Mr. ALEXANDER, of New Jersey, dissented from the vote of that State.

Mr. GRANGER moved that when the Conference adjourn it adjourn to half-past seven o'clock this evening.

The vote upon Mr. GRANGER's motion was taken by States, and resulted as follows:

AYES.—Maine, New Hampshire, Vermont, Massachusetts, Connecticut, New York, Pennsylvania, Tennessee, Ohio, Indiana, Illinois, Iowa, and Kansas—13.

NOES.—Rhode Island, New Jersey, Delaware, Maryland, Kentucky, and Missouri—6.

So the motion was adopted.

On motion of Mr. CHASE the Conference adjourned.

EVENING SESSION—SEVENTEENTH DAY.

WASHINGTON, MONDAY, *February 25th*, 1861.

THE Conference was called to order at half-past seven o'clock, Mr. ALEXANDER in the chair.

Mr. SMITH, of New York:—I move that a committee of two be appointed by the PRESIDENT to arrange for the printing of the Journal.

The motion of Mr. SMITH was adopted, and the PRESIDENT appointed as such committee, Mr. SMITH, of New York, and Mr. HOWARD, of Maryland.

The Conference then proceeded to the consideration of the order of the day, being the third section of the article reported by the committee.

Mr. HITCHCOCK:—I move to amend the third section by striking out the words "or Territory of the United States," occurring after the words "within any State."

I think we shall make the amendment more satisfactory by limiting the prohibition to States alone; still leaving the power in Congress to be exercised in conformity with the other provisions that regulate slavery in the Territories.

Mr. GUTHRIE:—I have the same objection to this as to other amendments. It may not be important, but I do not want to commence by adopting amendments at all.

The question was taken upon the amendment proposed by Mr. HITCHCOCK, and was agreed to by the following vote:

AYES.—Maine, New Hampshire, Vermont, Massachusetts, Connecticut, New York, Pennsylvania, Ohio, Indiana, and Kansas—10.

NOES.—Rhode Island, New Jersey, Delaware, Maryland, Virginia, North Carolina, Tennessee, Kentucky, and Missouri—9.

Mr. SUMMERS:—I now desire to call up for consideration the amendment proposed by myself on the evening of the 23d instant. The state of the case is this: Mr. JOHNSON, of Maryland, moved an amendment to my proposition, which was accepted; my amendment was then rejected by a vote of the Conference, and on the 25th the Conference reconsidered the vote by which the amendment was rejected. I will not now repeat what I said, when the amendment was offered, in favor of its adoption.

I would only call the attention of gentlemen to the remarks I then made, and say in addition, that I earnestly hope the Conference will now adopt the amendment. It will make the proposition much more acceptable to the South, and, certainly, not more objectionable to the North. The amendment is offered to the second section, and is as follows:

"No territory shall be acquired by the United States, except by discovery, and for naval and commercial stations, depots and transit routes, without the concurrence of a majority of all the Senators from States which allow involuntary servitude, and a majority of all the Senators from States which prohibit that relation; nor shall territory be acquired by treaty, unless the votes of a majority of the Senators from each class of States hereinbefore mentioned, be cast as a part of the two-thirds majority necessary to the ratification of such treaty."

The amendment of Mr. Summers was adopted by the following vote:

Ayes.—New Hampshire, Rhode Island, New Jersey, Pennsylvania, Delaware, Maryland, Virginia, North Carolina, Tennessee, Kentucky, Missouri, and Ohio—12.

Noes.—Maine, Massachusetts, Connecticut, Indiana, Illinois, and Kansas—6.

The PRESIDENT:—No further amendment being offered to the second and third sections, the Conference will proceed to the consideration of the fourth section of the report, or any amendments proposed to that section.

None being proposed, the Conference proceeded to the fifth section.

Mr. SEDDON:—I move to strike out the whole of the section. It has been heretofore stated, on behalf of the North, when this section was under consideration, that its adoption was not desirable, inasmuch as existing laws, properly enforced, amount to a sufficient prohibition of the slave-trade. If the North does not desire it, the South does not. I hope the Conference will consent to strike it out.

Mr. GUTHRIE:—I think it very important to retain this section; it can, certainly, do no harm. We all agree, North and South, that the foreign slave-trade should not be revived.

The amendment offered by Mr. Seddon was rejected by the following vote:

Ayes.—Virginia, North Carolina, Kentucky, and Missouri—4.

Noes.—Maine, New Hampshire, Vermont, Massachusetts, Rhode Island,

Connecticut, New York, New Jersey, Pennsylvania, Delaware, Maryland, Tennessee, Ohio, Indiana, Illinois, Iowa, and Kansas—17.

Mr. BRADFORD :—I move to amend the fifth section by inserting after the words "slave-trade," the words "by citizens of the United States."

In proposing amendments to the Constitution, it seems to me improper that we should attempt to bind any but our own citizens. The adoption of the section in this form would seem to imply that we undertook to prohibit the slave-trade in other countries and among citizens of other countries. I desire to see it prohibited, but wish to have the constitutional provision expressed in appropriate terms.

Mr. CROWNINSHIELD :—I object to this amendment. It would nullify the operation of the section entirely. There are in the United States thousands of persons who are not citizens, but who, under such a provision of the Constitution, would revive the slave-trade and infuse into it a vigor which it never before possessed. It would be better to have no section at all than to permit such an amendment as this. The amendment can bear but one construction. It is intended to prohibit the slave-trade by our own citizens, and expressly to permit it by those who are not citizens.

Mr. COALTER :—I am in favor of the amendment.

Mr. BRADFORD :—I do not desire to embarrass the action of the Conference, and I will withdraw the amendment.

Mr. JAMES :—I move to amend this section by striking out the following words : "from places beyond the limits thereof."

The object of this amendment is apparent, and does not need explanation.

The amendment of Mr. JAMES was agreed to by the following vote :

AYES.—Maine, New Hampshire, Vermont, Massachusetts, Rhode Island, Connecticut, New York, New Jersey, Pennsylvania, Delaware, Maryland, Tennessee, Kentucky, Ohio, Illinois, Indiana, and Kansas—17.

NOES.—Virginia, North Carolina, and Missouri—3.

Mr. MOREHEAD, of North Carolina :—I move that the vote just passed striking out the words "from places beyond the present limits thereof," be rescinded.

I think the action of the Convention in passing this vote was hasty, and not taken upon due consideration. It may be an important question to determine, what are "the present limits thereof." Upon one construction it might prohibit the bringing of slaves from the States which have seceded and left the Union; upon another construction, which assumes that these are still in the Union and does not recognize their secession, it would not cut off the trade between those States and the others. I do not like to have such a question raised.

Mr. BACKUS :—I am against this reconsideration. So far as I am concerned, I do not propose, in this Conference, to recognize the secession of the States at all. I deny the legal power of a State to withdraw itself from the Union without the consent of the others. And beyond this, I do not think the question is raised as the gentleman asserts.

Mr. RUFFIN :—I think the clause is better as it is. By striking out the words "from beyond the present limits thereof," we do not establish any territorial limitation. And whether these States come back or not, no question of territory is raised. But if this reconsideration is carried, and the seceding States do not return to the Union, they will retaliate upon us. In the event of their continued secession we cannot get back from those States those of our slaves who are now temporarily there. We may wish to bring back those slaves, and some of our people may wish to carry ours there.

Mr. GRANGER :—I hope this vote will not be reconsidered. The argument of Judge RUFFIN is conclusive.

Mr. COALTER :—This is likely to be a troublesome question any way. Why not leave it as we have to leave many others—to the discretion of Congress? We certainly do not wish to adopt a provision which will cut off the traffic in slaves between the Gulf States and the others. Nobody is in favor of that, and I am at a loss how to manage this question. The negroes are a portion of the families of Southern men. They are regarded as such in all the transactions of life. Those families may at times become separated. A portion of them may now be in the seceded States, and a portion farther North. Again, it often happens that during one season of the year the planter, with his family and slaves, lives upon the plantation in the Gulf States; and at another season, removes with his family and slaves to a plantation farther North. We do not wish to obstruct a relation or proceeding of this kind. This is not a mere matter of dollars and cents. It is one involving the happiness of families. The blacks themselves are interested in it. I think it better to let the section stand as it does, and to leave the whole matter to the discretion of Congress.

Mr. GRANGER :—I have always stood up against all the societies and organizations which have been established at the North to carry on crusades against slavery. My position in that respect is still unchanged. I hold that the people of the free States have nothing to do with slavery; that they are not responsible for it, and that it is their duty to let it alone. At the same time I have just as steadily opposed the slave-trade. I think it inhuman and atrocious, and I am the last man that would consent to its restoration. This section as it stands, in my judgment, cannot be improved. I think we had better leave it, and not raise these troublesome questions which will inevitably be suggested if these words are restored.

Mr. MOREHEAD :—This is a matter which requires some reflection, and, on the whole, I am inclined, for the present, to withdraw my proposition.

Mr. SEDDON :—I do not like this plan of legislating in the Constitution. The Constitution ought to be an instrument defining and limiting the powers of Congress. We had better leave to Congress, or rather, to assign to Congress the power to exercise this prohibition. I, therefore, move to amend by inserting at the commencement of the section these words: "The Congress shall have power to prohibit," and to strike out at the end of the section the words "are forever prohibited."

Mr. ALLEN :—This would be a most effectual way of reviving the slave-trade. It would remove the constitutional prohibition, and permit Congress to prohibit or permit it, as that body may choose. Would that ever hereafter be considered a crime which Congress had power to permit? No. I cannot conceive it possible that any State should seriously wish to see a traffic resumed which has been stigmatized by the whole civilized world as worse than piracy. This is a question which I would not leave to Congress. We know how immensely profitable this trade is—that fortunes are made by a single successful voyage.

Don't let such an inducement to corruption creep into our Constitution.

Mr. COALTER :—I am in favor of this amendment, not because I am in favor of the slave-trade, but because such a section is out of place in the Constitution. The Constitution is a bill of rights, an instrument which defines and settles the rights of citizens. It is not a law. I have no fear that if we leave this to Congress the slave-trade will be revived.

Mr. DONIPHAN :—I cannot agree with my colleague. I am opposed to the foreign slave-trade in every form. I would not even make a treaty with a nation or a State that would permit it. If the seceded States are to be regarded out of the Union, I would not treat with them; I would not invest Congress with such a dangerous power. Nothing will suit me but an unqualified prohibition of this trade in the Constitution itself.

Mr. HOUSTON :—The gentleman from Missouri has expressed the views of Delaware. His argument is conclusive.

Mr. HOWARD :—The intervention of Congress will be necessary whether this amendment passes or not. The section as adopted makes no provision for the punishment of any one who violates it. If a vessel should be seized while engaged in the trade, this section does not provide for her forfeiture or condemnation, or the punishment of her officers or owners. The section would be inoperative without the action of Congress. Why not let Congress have all the power?

Mr. DODGE :—Congress will declare the punishment.

Mr. SEDDON :—If you cut off the slave with the seceded States, they will do the same with you. I think the Border States should at all events adopt the amendment.

The Conference refused to agree to the amendment of Mr. SEDDON by the following vote:

AYES.—Maryland, Virginia, North Carolina, Tennessee, and Missouri—5.

NOES.—Maine, New Hampshire, Vermont, Massachusetts, Rhode Island, Connecticut, New York, New Jersey, Pennsylvania, Delaware, Kentucky, Ohio, Indiana, Illinois, Iowa, and Kansas—16.

Messrs. JOHNSON and DONIPHAN, of Missouri, dissented from the vote of that State.

Mr. MOREHEAD :—I move to strike out the whole of this section, and insert a new one of the following tenor: "The foreign slave-trade is hereby forever prohibited; and it shall be the duty of Congress to pass laws to prevent the importation of slaves into the United States and their Territories, from places beyond the limits thereof."

Mr. WICKLIFFE:—I like the amendment proposed better than the original, but I wish to suggest an amendment to it myself.

We are aware that certain countries which are much exercised over the criminality of slavery and the slave-trade, have recently adopted a system, the horrors of which are not surpassed by those of the middle passage. I refer to the importation of coolies and other persons from China and the East. In my judgment, this is the slave-trade in one of its worst forms. I think if we prevent the importation of slaves at all, the provision ought to be made to cover such a case. I therefore move to amend the proposition of Mr. MOREHEAD, by inserting after the words "importation of slaves," the words "or coolies, or persons held to service or labor."

Mr. MOREHEAD:—I accept the amendment of Mr. WICKLIFFE, and should have inserted it myself had it occurred to me. My proposition as it now stands, covers both the points here made; it declares the entire prohibition of the slave-trade, and it makes it also the duty of Congress to pass laws effectually to prevent it.

The amendment offered by Mr. MOREHEAD was agreed to by the following vote:

AYES.—Pennsylvania, Delaware, Maryland, Virginia, North Carolina, Tennessee, Kentucky, Missouri, Ohio, Indiana, and Illinois—11.

NOES.—Maine, New Hampshire, Vermont, Massachusetts, Rhode Island, New York, New Jersey, and Kansas—8.

Mr. HOPPIN, of Rhode Island, Messrs. ORTH and ELLIS, of Indiana, and Mr. STOCKTON, of New Jersey, dissented from the votes of their respective States.

Mr. CROWNINSHIELD:—I move to strike out the whole section. I had rather have no section at all, and no provision upon the subject, than such a one as we have now adopted. The requisition upon Congress making it their duty to enact laws, will be considered as a necessary one; the consequence which must result is, that until Congress legislates, there is no law against the importation of slaves.

The motion of Mr. CROWNINSHIELD was rejected by the following vote:

AYES.—Massachusetts, Virginia, and Tennessee—3.

NOES.—Maine, New Hampshire, Vermont, Rhode Island, Connecticut, New York, New Jersey, Pennsylvania, Delaware, Maryland, North Carolina, Kentucky, Missouri, Ohio, Illinois, Indiana, Iowa, and Kansas—18.

The PRESIDENT:—The Conference will now proceed to the consideration of the sixth section.

No amendment being offered thereto, the Conference proceeded to the seventh section.

Mr. TURNER:—I move to strike out the whole of the seventh section, and insert in lieu thereof the following:

"Congress shall provide by law for securing to the citizens of each State the privileges and immunities of citizens of the several States."

The seventh section, as it now stands, will encounter more serious objection at the North than all the remaining portion of the article. It is objectionable for many reasons: it looks to the actual exercise of violence and intimidation by mobs and unlawful assemblies at the North. Although such may have occurred in one or two sections only, generally the provisions of the fugitive slave law have been observed and carried out. The whole subject is very distasteful to the North. I think if we keep it out of the article, and in its place secure that respect for the privileges of citizens in the varions States, to which, indeed, under the Constitution, they are entitled, we shall do much better.

Mr. LOGAN:—There are various reasons peculiar to some of the free States why this provision should not be adopted. The laws of several of the Western States do not recognize negroes as citizens. I move to amend the amendment proposed by my colleague, by inserting the words "free white" before the word "citizens."

The amendment offered by Mr. LOGAN was adopted by the following vote:

AYES.—New Jersey, Pennsylvania, Delaware, Maryland, Virginia, North Carolina, Tennessee, Kentucky, Indiana, and Illinois—10.

NOES.—Maine, New Hampshire, Vermont, Massachusetts, Rhode Island, Connecticut, New York, and Iowa—8.

Mr. ORTH, of Indiana, dissented from the vote of his State.

Mr. TURNER:—I suppose the purpose of my colleague has been attained. If there is a delegation willing to make such a distinction in the Constitution, they will, of course, support the amendment as it is now amended.

The vote was then taken upon the amendment, as amended, with the following result:

AYES.—None.

NOES.—Maine, New Hampshire, Vermont, Massachusetts, Rhode Island, Connecticut, New York, New Jersey, Pennsylvania, Delaware, Maryland, Virginia, North Carolina, Tennessee, Kentucky, Missouri, Ohio, and Indiana—18.

Mr. WILMOT:—If the seventh section is adopted, I think the North should have some compensation therefor. I think citizens of the North have as much occasion for complaint on account of the action of mobs and riotous assemblies in the slave States, as the slave States have of the occurrence of those mobs and assemblies in the North. I therefore move the following as an addition to the seventh section:

"And Congress shall further provide by law, that the United States shall make full compensation to a citizen of any State, who, in any other State, shall suffer by reason of violence or intimidation from mobs and riotous assemblies, in his person or property, or in the deprivation, by violence, of his rights secured by this Constitution."

Mr. GUTHRIE:—I am opposed to this amendment upon the general principles I have so often stated. I oppose it for another reason. I am not in favor of an amendment which encourages mobs and riots at the North, and I will not consent to one which, like this, encourages seditious speeches at the South.

Mr. WILMOT:—Such is not the effect of my amendment. It does not protect a man in making seditious speeches in the slave States. It only secures to the citizen his rights without regard to the State to which he belongs. We have a provision of the Constitution on that subject now, but it is not effective.

Mr. COALTER:—I am in favor of the amendment. There is great necessity for it.

Mr. SEDDON:—I think gentlemen entirely misconstrue the intent and purpose of the present provision of the Constitution on that subject. It grows out of and rests upon that provision which requires the return of fugitive slaves. It imposes an obligation upon Congress to secure to the owner, when he pursues his slave into a free State, the right which he enjoys as a citizen of his own State. In all other respects it is unnecessary. If a man is injured in his person or his property, he has his redress in the State courts; or if he is a foreigner or a citizen of another State, he may go into the Federal courts and get his redress there. In this respect the citizens of both sections are amply protected.

Mr. STEPHENS:—I earnestly hope this amendment may be rejected. We have come here to arrange old difficulties, not to make new ones. Adopt this, and you lay the foundation stone of disunion. It is an encouragement to seditious speeches and purposes. The clause is well enough as it is. We do not wish to encourage men to come among us and excite discontent among our slaves. We will not permit them to do it. Our safety requires that we should not. Our own citizens do not connive at the escape of slaves. None do it who have any business in our States. We are here for peace. When half a dozen States are out, whose return we wish to secure, shall we put such a clause as this into the Constitution? Do it, and a half dozen others will follow. I am not at all sure that the report of the majority, if adopted, will satisfy my State. It certainly will not if it is mangled and frittered away. I have not occupied time in making speeches here. I say to you gentlemen, beware! If I thought the spirit of the North was truly represented in this Conference, I would go home and advise my State to secede; and if she did not, I would abandon her forever.

Mr. RUFFIN:—I am opposed to the amendment because I think it unnecessary, and because it opens a new and very serious controversy. The rights of Northern men are fully protected now. There is not a court in the South in which a Northern citizen cannot find a lawyer to advocate his cause. If he is poor, he may even sue *in forma pauperis*, and incur no liability even for costs.

Mr. WILMOT:—I am claiming no more than I have a right to claim under the decision of the Supreme Court. That court, in the case of Prigg *vs.* The State of Pennsylvania, decided that the Constitution imposes the duty upon Congress of carrying this provision into effect. I insist upon making it plain. Rights upon both sides are sought to be protected by this article. They are correlative.

Mr. LOGAN favored and Mr. EWING opposed the amendment, in a few brief remarks.

Mr. ORTH:—I do not think we shall accomplish much by protracting our present session longer. I move that the Conference adjourn, and ask a vote by States.

The Conference refused to adjourn, by the following vote:

AYES.—Maine, Connecticut, New York, Indiana, Illinois, Iowa, and Kansas—7.

NOES.—New Hampshire, Vermont, Massachusetts, Rhode Island, New Jersey, Pennsylvania, Delaware, Maryland, Virginia, North Carolina, Tennessee, Kentucky, Missouri, and Ohio—14.

The PRESIDENT:—The question recurs upon the amendment of the gentleman from Pennsylvania.

The vote upon the question of agreeing to the motion of Mr. WILMOT, resulted as follows:

AYES.—Maine, New York, Indiana, Vermont, Massachusetts, Pennsylvania, Illinois, and Iowa—8.

NOES.—Rhode Island, Connecticut, New Jersey, Delaware, Maryland, Virginia, North Carolina, Tennessee, Kentucky, Missouri, and Ohio—11.

And the motion was rejected.

Mr. BARRINGER:—I now move to amend the seventh section, by adding thereto the following words:

"And in all cases in which the United States shall pay for such fugitive, Congress shall also provide for the collection by the United States of the amount so paid, with interest, from the county, city, or town in which such arrest shall have been prevented, or rescue made."

I am certain that no objection can be made to the equity of this amendment. If a municipal corporation shall permit the rights of a slave owner to be disregarded by the rescue of a slave, it not only fails to perform its duty under the Constitution, but becomes an active participant in the crime. Shall the consequences of its own fault be visited upon the people of the whole country? Those who acknowledge and carry out their obligations under the Constitution, as well as those who do not? This would inflict a punishment upon the innocent for the crime of the guilty. It is not right to leave it in that way. It would present an inducement to these violations of law which the provision is intended to prevent. We ought to make the guilty party pay the penalty.

Mr. HACKLEMAN:—If such a proposition were to come from a free State, the mover would be charged with attempting to destroy all hope that the committee's report could be adopted by the people. However, if the friends of the report are willing to adopt it, I do not know that I ought to object. It places the Government in a position where it is bound under the Constitution to prosecute a municipal corporation for the acts of its individual members. It is certainly novel, and introduces a new system into the jurisprudence of the country. Is the mover serious in his proposition?

Mr. BARRINGER:—I am certainly serious. I would like to hear some substantial argument against my motion.

The question being taken on the amendment of Mr. BARRINGER, resulted as follows:

AYES.—Virginia, North Carolina, and Kansas—3.

NOES.—Maine, New Hampshire, Vermont, Massachusetts, Rhode Island, Connecticut, New York, New Jersey, Pennsylvania, Delaware, Maryland, Tennessee, Kentucky, Ohio, Indiana, Illinois, and Iowa—17.

And the amendment was rejected.

Mr. DENT:—I wish to enter my dissent from the vote of Maryland. I consider the amendment as eminently just and proper.

Mr. CLAY:—I dissent from the vote of Kentucky.

Mr. FRELINGHUYSEN:—I have an amendment which I intend to offer at some time, and I may as well propose it now. The people of the free States have complained, and not without good reason, that one clause in the Constitution is not carried into effect in some of the slaveholding States. Their complaints are similar to those made on the part of the South, which it is the purpose of the seventh section to remove. If there have been instances at the North where mobs and riotous assemblies have obstructed the administration of justice in the case of fugitive slaves, so there have been instances at the South where mobs and riots have disregarded the rights of citizens of Northern States. I propose to deal fairly by all sections. Let us remove both causes of complaint. I move to amend the seventh section by adding thereto the following words:

"Congress shall provide by law for securing to the citizens of each State the privileges and immunities of citizens in the several States."

Mr. GUTHRIE:—I repeat my objection to all these amendments. If our work here is to have any efficacy, we must adhere to the report. Why bring in another bone of contention?

Mr. ORTH:—Will you not extend the same protection to free citizens which you do to slaveholders?

The question was taken on the motion of Mr. FRELINGHUYSEN, with the following result:

AYES.—Connecticut, Delaware, Indiana, Illinois, Iowa, Maine, Massachusetts, Maryland, New Jersey, New York, New Hampshire, Ohio, Pennsylvania, Rhode Island, Vermont, and Kansas—16.

NOES.—Kentucky, Missouri, North Carolina, Tennessee, and Virginia—4.

So the amendment was adopted.

Mr. ROMAN dissented from the vote of Maryland.

Mr. AMES:—I move an amendment which will make the section more explicit. I move to strike out the word "force," and to insert instead thereof the words "violence or intimidation."

The motion was agreed to without objection.

Mr. ORTH:—I move to amend the seventh section by adding at the close thereof the following words:

"And such fugitives, after such payment, shall then be discharged from such service."

I am opposed to this whole business of making compensation for fugitive slaves; but if this section is to be adopted, and the Government pays the owner the whole value of the fugitive, upon every principle of equity and justice the fugitive should be discharged, and the master should have no right to reduce him again to slavery. You make the measure of the owner's damages in such a case the value of the slave. Do you intend, after he has secured that, he shall still have the right of capture—that after the damages have been fully paid, he may still call on the courts of law for the slave's surrender? This would be a double compensation indeed. I shall insist upon this amendment, and ask a vote by States.

Mr. ROMAN:—I have not hitherto addressed the Conference, but I should do myself injustice if I remained silent any longer. I came here in good faith, encouraged with the hope that this Conference would do something which would indicate a purpose to protect and acknowledge the rights of the slave-holding States. I have patiently attended your sittings, and little by little that hope has faded, until to-night it has almost passed away. What good can come of these deliberations, when upon every question which is presented the lines of sectionalism are tightly drawn, and with one or two exceptions every northern State is arrayed against us? Suppose these proposals of amendment as reported by the committee are adopted, there is evidently a purpose manifested here by a large delegation from the free States, to prevent their adoption by the people. I know the opposition which in any event will be arrayed against them. It is an opposition which nothing but unanimity among the moderate conservative men of the country can overcome. Believe it or not, gentlemen, I assure you we are in earnest, in our determination to have our rights under the Constitution defined and guaranteed. Our safety, as well as our self-respect, requires this. I have not been satisfied with the majority report, but if I had been disposed to accept it—if the South would accept it now, you will not concede even that. You insist upon weakening its provisions by amendments, and by amendments which are insulting to us.

It is now seriously proposed under the Constitution, by an express provision, to deprive us of our property in slaves against our consent, and to emancipate them by making compensation. What other effect can be given to such an amendment? One of our slaves escapes into a free State. He is arrested by the marshal and discharged by a mob. Does this act discharge him from his service? Does this lawless violence make him free? And if the town or city where the mob occurs is made to pay a slight penalty, does this also divest the owner of his right? This is nothing but an inducement to mobs and riots. Pass this provision, and no fugitive slave will ever again be returned from a free State. There will always be abolitionists enough to pay for a slave, and this payment will set the slave free, and will constitute the only penalty for this violence. For one, I would prefer to have no provision at all on the subject than to have one encumbered with such an amendment.

I have but little more to say. If the peace of this country

is to be hereafter established on a permanent basis, and the Union is to be preserved, you, gentlemen of the North, must recognize our rights, and cease to interfere with them. You have nothing to do with this question of slavery. It is an institution of our own. If it is a crime, we are responsible for it, and will bear the responsibility. We have never interfered with your institutions. You must now let us alone.

Mr. ORTH:—The objection of the gentleman from Maryland may be answered in a word. It is for the owner to elect whether or not to accept compensation and set his slave free. If he still chooses to pursue him, he need not accept compensation; but if he does not, and receives payment for him, the slave should go free. As to mobs and riots, we punish men at the North who engage in them.

Mr. CRISFIELD:—I entirely agree with my colleague in this respect. We could not accept the section if such an amendment was adopted. The report of the committee is the very least that will satisfy our people. Do not destroy it by such amendments as these.

The vote was then taken upon the amendment proposed by Mr. ORTH, with the following result:

AYES.—Illinois, Indiana, Iowa, Maine, Massachusetts, New York, New Hampshire, Ohio, Pennsylvania, and Kansas—10.

NOES.—Connecticut, Delaware, Kentucky, Maryland, Missouri, New Jersey, North Carolina, Rhode Island, Tennessee, Vermont, and Virginia—11.

And the amendment was rejected.

Mr. CLAY:—I move to amend the report by adding a section to be numbered Section 8, as follows:

"The second paragraph of the second section of fourth article of the Constitution shall be so construed that no State shall have the power to consider and determine what is treason, felony, or crime, in another State; but that a person charged in any State with treason, felony, or crime, who shall flee from justice and be found in another State, shall, on demand of the executive authority of the State from which he fled, be delivered up, to be removed to the State having jurisdiction of the crime."

I do not think discussion necessary upon such an amendment as this. It is well known to the Conference that great difficulties have been found to exist in carrying into effect this provision of the Constitution. So far as the slave States are concerned, it is a perfect nullity. Unless it is amended it may as well be stricken from the instrument. I believe the tenor of the decisions at the North has been to permit the executive upon whom the requisition is made, to determine whether the offence charged is a crime under the law of the State to which the person charged has fled. If it is a crime, the fugitive is delivered up. If not a crime in that sense, he is discharged. The decisions of the courts have been to the same effect; whenever the fugitive has been brought upon *habeas corpus*, the decision has been the same. It is obvious that under this construction of the Constitution no fugitive will be hereafter returned for an offence in which the question of slavery is involved. This is only one of the many evasions of the Constitution which have been practised in the free States. I deem the amendment very important.

Mr. BRONSON:—The gentleman from Kentucky is entirely mistaken in his statement of the decisions of the northern courts or northern governors. The decisions are uniform so far as I know, that where the offence charged is either a crime at common law, or under the statutes of the State from which the fugitive has fled, he has been delivered up.

Mr. CLAY:—Did not the Executive of New York refuse to deliver up a fugitive on the demand of the Governor of Virginia?

Mr. BRONSON:—In that case I think there was no evidence that the offence charged was a crime under the statutes of Virginia, and it certainly was not at common law.

The vote was taken upon Mr. CLAY's amendment, and resulted as follows:

AYES.—Kentucky, Missouri, North Carolina, Tennessee, and Virginia—5.

NOES.—Connecticut, Delaware, Illinois, Indiana, Iowa, Maine, Massachusetts, Maryland, New Jersey, New York, New Hampshire, Ohio, Pennsylvania, Rhode Island, Vermont, and Kansas—16.

And the amendment was rejected.

And on motion, at two o'clock A. M., the Conference adjourned.

EIGHTEENTH DAY.

WASHINGTON, TUESDAY, *February 26th*, 1861.

THE Conference, pursuant to adjournment, was called to order at eleven o'clock.

Prayer was offered by Rev. Dr. GURLEY.

The PRESIDENT informed the Conference that in consequence of the length of the Journal of yesterday, the Secretary had not been able to write it out, and that it would be necessary to omit the reading thereof this morning.

Mr. McCURDY:—There was a vote taken in the confusion near the close of the session last evening, in which Connecticut, according to the minutes of the Secretary, appears to have voted in the negative. It was upon the amendment of Mr. ORTH, declaring that the slave should be free whenever his master had accepted payment for him. On that amendment the vote of Connecticut was Yea. As the vote is recorded Nay by mistake, I move to reconsider the vote by which the amendment was rejected.

Mr. BRONSON:—The motion to reconsider is not necessary. Connecticut can record her vote as she wishes to have it stand. It will not change the result.

The PRESIDENT:—I think the motion is in order, if made by Connecticut.

Mr. BATTELL:—I will move to reconsider. I voted with the majority.

Mr. MOREHEAD, of North Carolina:—No individual delegate can make such a motion. States vote here, not individuals. I submit that the motion is out of order, unless made by a majority of the delegation.

Mr. BALDWIN :—The question is not complicated at all; neither is the motion out of order. A majority of the delegation from Connecticut cast the vote of that State in favor of Mr. ORTH's amendment. By mistake that vote was recorded against the amendment. The same majority whose vote is made to do them injustice by a mistake for which its members are not responsible, now moves to reconsider the vote.

The question was then taken upon Mr. McCURDY's motion, and resulted as follows:

AYES.—Connecticut, Illinois, Indiana, Iowa, Maine, Massachusetts, New York, New Hampshire, Ohio, Vermont and Kansas—11.

NOES.—Delaware, Kentucky, Maryland, Missouri, New Jersey, North Carolina, Pennsylvania, Rhode Island, Tennessee, and Virginia—10.

And the motion prevailed, and the vote was reconsidered.

The PRESIDENT :—The question now recurs upon the amendment offered by Mr. ORTH. On this amendment the vote will be taken by States.

Mr. WHITE :—I consider this amendment as entirely unnecessary. The result which it seeks to attain is only the announcement of a well-understood provision of the common law. By the common law, if an action is brought for a trespass, and judgment recovered for that trespass, and the damages under that judgment paid, the property which is the subject of the action, and which may have originally been wrongfully taken, becomes transferred; the damages take the place of the property, the defendant has paid for his wrongful act, or, in other words, has paid for the property. The same principle applies to the case of the fugitive slave who is rescued from the custody of the law, when his owner has consented to accept payment for him. The legal right of the owner in the slave is satisfied by such payment; the money takes the place of the slave. But if this were not so, we ought not to encumber the Constitution with such provisions. Congress will undoubtedly make the proper provision both for the protection of the slave and his master. Congress will not permit payment to be made for a slave, and then suffer him to go back to bondage. This would be both unlawful and unjust. I can see no necessity for adopting the amendment.

Mr. ORTH :—I understand there is some difference of opinion between members of the Conference as to the effect of the phraseology of my amendment. I will change that phraseology, and make the amendment read as follows:

"And such fugitive, after the master has been paid therefor, shall be discharged from such service."

Mr. MOREHEAD, of Kentucky:—I am opposed to this amendment upon every ground. I would rather see some direct scheme of emancipation adopted and inserted in the Constitution. Adopt this amendment, and the result is inevitable. It would amount to emancipation upon the largest possible scale. Our slaves would escape, you would rescue and pay for them, and that would be the end of them. Why not leave it to Congress to pass the necessary laws upon this subject? The adoption of this amendment would destroy all hope that our labors would be acceptable to the South. I say again, we had better establish emancipation at once.

Mr. DENT:—If this amendment is to be adopted, I hope we shall at the same time reconsider the vote by which we rejected the amendment of the gentleman from North Carolina, requiring the payment by the county, city, or town wherein the slave is rescued from the custody of the law. This provision would make the General Government pay for the crimes of a few citizens in one section. In that case the General Government ought to own the negro. It has paid for him, and the property in him ought to be transferred.

Mr. WILMOT:—There is nothing in this. We do not wish to have the Government own the negro. It is bad enough to have individuals own slaves. We do not propose to turn the Government into an extensive slave owner.

But let me ask the gentleman seriously, who is to own the negro, in such a case, after he has been paid for? Certainly not the former owner, because his right is gone. This amendment only states a conclusion of law; the right of the owner being gone, the negro is free.

Mr. CHASE:—I think a single word will settle this. By the Constitution as it now stands, the escaped fugitive is not discharged from service or labor. The original section, as proposed, requires that the slave should be paid for, when he is rescued. Now, he might be rescued three or four times. Shall he be paid for as often? Do gentlemen claim that his owner shall receive compensation more than once? I cannot see why gentlemen interested in slavery should object to this amendment.

Mr. RIVES:—I think if gentlemen would look at this proposition seriously, there would be no difference of opinion among us. Such a proposition would foist into the Constitution a most injurious, pernicious, and troublesome doctrine. By the most ultra abolitionists of the free States the power of emancipating our slaves has been disclaimed. From the organization of the Government, no such right has been claimed by any respectable party or body of men. The question arose in the first Congress, I think, upon the petition of the Quakers of Pennsylvania. It was decided almost unanimously against the power, even when exercised by Congress. But there is no need of multiplying or citing precedents. From that time to this, no political party has claimed the power of emancipation. Such is the universal doctrine now.

The right to abolish slavery in the District of Columbia is now claimed by some. I think that is the doctrine of Mr. CHASE. But upon what argument is it founded? Simply this: That the States, by the act of cession, have surrendered this power to Congress. This is the only argument I have ever heard in favor of the right, even in the District.

But this amendment proposes a most comprehensive scheme of emancipation. It accomplishes emancipation in every one of the slave States. It amounts to forcible emancipation upon the principle of compensation.

The point has been well stated by gentlemen who have preceded me. Place this in the Constitution, and there is an end of returning fugitives. The very courts will act upon it. They will say that if any one will come forward and pay the value of a slave when arrested, all the requirements of the Constitution are satisfied, and he shall go free.

What is the object of our Conference? Why are we here? We are here to bury out of sight all the causes of our difference and trouble. And yet you propose to insert a new principle into our fundamental law, which, however you may look upon it, will be regarded at the South as totally inconsistent with our independence. Our people will not consent to it.

There is another view which I would suggest. This is eminently a matter of legislative regulation. If the slave is paid for, Congress will at once recognize the impropriety and injustice of permitting the owner to receive payment for, and also receive his slave. Congress may say with great propriety that the owner shall give a bond to return the money upon the restoration of his slave. I hope no principle will be implanted in the Constitution which will be more troublesome—more productive of difficulties than any which has heretofore been made the subject of discussion.

Mr. EWING :—If we do any thing of this kind, perhaps we had better say that if the owner accepts compensation for his slave, he shall execute a deed of manumission. This will make it a matter of consent on the part of the owner. Put the amendment in that form and I will vote for it.

Mr. COALTER :—This amendment would offer a most powerful inducement to our slaves to run away. It would be dangerous in the extreme. When a fugitive has been paid for, and thus emancipated, he can come back and settle by the side of his master. What effect would that have upon the rest of his slaves? Would they not attempt the same thing? It may be said that the States can pass laws which will prevent their return. But this power will not be exercised. I know many free negroes in the slave States who are respectable persons, who own property, and have their social and domestic ties. These examples are bad. A fugitive who has been set free is not a safe man to return and settle as a free negro among those who were his co-slaves.

Mr. BROCKENBROUGH :—By this amendment you are inaugurating a system of covert emancipation to which the South can never submit. We protest against its adoption. The argument upon which you seek to sustain it is a false one. How can the owner receive the full value of his rescued slave when he himself, as a citizen and tax-payer, pays a part of the price?

Mr. MOREHEAD, of North Carolina :—I move to amend this amendment by adding thereto these words:

"And the negro when thus emancipated shall not be permitted to leave the State in which the emancipation takes place."

We know from past experience what the abolitionists of the free States would do under such a provision as this in the Constitution. There will be an underground railroad line along every principal route of travel. There will be depots all along these lines. Canoes will be furnished to ferry negroes over the Potomac and Ohio. JOHN BROWN & Co. will stand ready to kill the master the very moment he crosses the line in pursuit of his slave. What officer at the North will dare to arrest the slave when JOHN BROWN pikes are stacked up in every little village? If arrested, there will be organizations formed to rescue him, and you may as well let the "nigger" go free at once. You are opening up the greatest scheme of emancipation ever devised.

Mr. BACKUS:—I move to amend the amendment proposed by Mr. ORTH by the substitution of the following:

"And the acceptance of such payment shall preclude the owner from further claim to said fugitive."

It is claimed that this is a scheme of emancipation. It is nothing of the sort. It is not intended that the owner shall be obliged to accept compensation for his slave. That is left optional with him. He may take it or not as he likes. The effect of accepting compensation would be just the same as if he sold his slave to the North. The gentleman from Virginia raises a curious objection; that the owner does not receive a full compensation because he pays a portion of it himself. Well,.I suppose the owner would pay the one hundred and thirty-millionth part of the price! Does not the same objection lay against the payment of any tax whatever? It is asked, Does this payment transfer the legal title to the slave? Well, it probably goes to the party who pays for it. If the payment is made in a free State, where slavery is not tolerated, the title would not pass at all. I submit to our friends from the South, whether they wish to have the Government become a slave-trader, to set it up as a huckster of slaves in the shambles. My amendment imposes the responsibility upon Congress. I have no doubt Congress will legislate properly upon the subject.

Now let me say one word to gentlemen, friends of the South, in all kindness. I have appreciated your position, and it has influenced my action. I have not refused to give you any reasonable guarantees, and I shall not refuse them. But I submit to you, whether it is in good taste for you to declare that, if we do not yield all these little points to you, the Government is to be broken up; that that is the only alternative?

Mr. GUTHRIE:—I hope this amendment will be adopted. As a Southern man, I declare that it is acceptable to me. Let us adopt it, and end the matter. [Cries of "Agreed."]

Mr. JOHNSON, of Missouri:—I have a very serious objection to putting any bid in the Constitution to induce slaves to run away. I firmly believe that if this amendment should ever become a part of the Constitution, it would lead to the ultimate extinction of slavery. The State of Missouri is surrounded on three sides by free States. When one of our slaves escapes and crosses the border, he finds himself at once among a people, some of whom will vindicate his freedom with their lives. I am willing to leave this whole subject to Congress. Congress will not permit the owner to get his money, and also retain his slave. In the name of God I ask that no such provision may be put into the Constitution!

Mr. MOREHEAD:—I will agree to this. The difference between the two is as wide as the poles.

The vote was then taken upon the amendment as amended, and resulted as follows:

AYES.—Connecticut, Delaware, Illinois, Iowa, Kentucky, Maine, Massachusetts, Maryland, New Jersey, New York, North Carolina, New Hampshire, Ohio, Pennsylvania, Rhode Island, Tennessee, and Vermont—17.

NOES.—Indiana, Missouri, and Virginia—3.

So the amendment was agreed to.

Messrs. CLAY, of Kentucky, DENT and ROMAN, of Maryland, STEPHENS and TOTTEN, of Tennessee, dissented from the votes of their respective States.

Mr. BRONSON:—It is evident under the rules, as they now stand, that this debate is not to close within a month. I move to amend the rules as follows:

"Before reaching the final question on the plan to be submitted to Congress, no member shall be allowed to speak more than three minutes on any proposition."

Mr. SEDDON:—I rise to a question of order. I submit that the motion of the gentleman from New York is not in order.

Mr. GUTHRIE:—I move to lay the amendment on the table.

The motion of Mr. Guthrie prevailed without a division.

Mr. FIELD:—I move to add an additional section to the report, as follows:

Section 8. The Union of the States under the Constitution is indissoluble, and no State can secede from the Union, or nullify an act of Congress, or absolve its citizens from their paramount obligation of obedience to the Constitution and laws of the United States.

In offering this amendment as an additional section, I propose very briefly to state the reasons for its adoption. I shall not anticipate any of the objections that may be urged against it, for, as I understand the rule, I shall have the right to speak in reply. I will only state one or two arguments in favor of the article.

We have been discussing the means of removing the symptoms of the disease called secession. This amendment attacks the disease itself. The doctrines of Calhoun, originated and advocated by him, have now been taken up by his followers, who are striking at the very foundation of our Government. The doctrine of the North is, that no State can secede from the Union. This amendment asserts that doctrine. Before we begin to amend, we ought to know whether we have any Constitution to amend. The people of my section wish to know whether we can compel obedience of a State, if every man in it undertakes to refuse obedience. They believe that power to exist in the Constitution now. If there is any doubt about it, they wish that power distinctly asserted.

Mr. EWING:—I move to lay the amendment on the table at present, without affecting the section of the report under consideration.

Mr. FIELD:—This motion is debatable.

Mr. FRELINGHUYSEN:—I submit that the motion of the gentleman from New York is not an amendment; that it is an addition, and may be laid on the table without affecting the remainder of the report.

Mr. BRONSON:—We have now gone through with the propositions, and are ready to take a final vote upon them. Mr. Field's amendment is properly an addition, and relates entirely

to other subjects. Laying that on the table does not carry the whole subject there.

The motion of Mr. EWING prevailed by the following vote: Ayes, 11; Noes, 10.*

Messrs. MEREDITH, WILMOT, and CHASE dissented from the votes of their respective States.

Mr. FIELD:—I now offer it as an amendment to the 7th section.

Mr. BRONSON:—I rise to a point of order. My colleague has proposed this amendment as an additional section, and it has been laid upon the table. He now proposes to put the same thing in another place. That is certainly not in order.

Mr. FIELD:—I now offer it distinctly as an amendment to the 7th section, to avoid the quibbling by which a direct vote was avoided before. It may as well be understood that other than slave States have certain rights upon this floor, and that those rights will be asserted. I wish gentlemen to understand that I shall resist, as well as I may, every attempt to avoid or dodge this question.

The PRESIDENT:—In the opinion of the Chair it is not in order.

Mr. FIELD:—Then I offer one-half the amendment as follows: "The Union of the States, under the Constitution, is indissoluble."

Mr. WICKLIFFE:—Is it necessary to put this into the Constitution? Does not the gentleman think the Constitution prohibits secession now? If so, let him offer a resolution to that effect, and I will vote for it.

Mr. DENT:—I rise to a point of order. The amendment is not germane to the section.

The PRESIDENT:—That is entirely a matter of opinion. The Chair cannot rule out an amendment on that ground.

Mr. FIELD:—If gentlemen will give us a square vote on my proposition, I will not debate it.

Mr. GUTHRIE:—I believe every word that is stated in

* I relied upon the Journal for the individual list of the votes. In this respect the Journal is defective, and does not give the names of the States voting. My minutes show that the vote was taken by States with the fore going result.

that proposition. It is all in the Constitution now; but the South thinks differently, and this is one of the great obstructions in our path. There is not a man here who does not believe that this provision is already in the Constitution. I hope, therefore, that we shall vote at once, and vote it down.

Mr. EWING:—The amendment proposed, implies the existence of the right of secession, under the present Constitution. I do not believe in that, and shall therefore vote against it.

Mr. FIELD:—I desire to obtain a clear vote upon this question, and not have it pass off upon any technical points. I will withdraw my amendment, and now move to amend the 7th section by striking out the whole of it, and inserting in its place the following:

"No State shall withdraw from the Union without the consent of all the States, given in a Convention of the States, convened in pursuance of an act passed by two-thirds of each House of Congress."

Mr. GOODRICH:—I do not quite like the language of the amendment, for it might seem to give the implication of a right to secede. I move the following as a substitute:

"And no State can secede from the Union, or nullify an act of Congress, or absolve its citizens from their paramount obligations of obedience to the Constitution and laws of the United States."

Mr. MOREHEAD, of North Carolina:—There is no objection on my part against the gentleman from New York taking any course he pleases, and as much time as he likes; but I should regret extremely to have this amendment adopted, and to have the Constitution made practically to assert a right of secession. I have denied that right always in my State, in public and in private. I am aware that on this point I differ from the general sentiment of the South, and I hold there is no right of secession, and on the part of the General Government no right of coercion. I claim that a State has no right to secede, because that right is not found in the Constitution, and the theory of the Constitution is against it.

The PRESIDENT:—I think the amendment of Mr. GOODRICH is not in order.

Mr. FIELD:—As suggested by a friend, I will modify my motion, and state it in this way, which certainly will avoid all these objections:

"It is declared to be the true intent and meaning of the present Constitution, that the Union of the States under it is indissoluble."

Mr. COALTER:—Does the gentleman mean this as a substitute for the entire report of the committee, for all that we have hitherto done?

Mr. FIELD:—Certainly not.

Mr. COALTER:—We have not met here for any such purpose as that indicated in the present amendment. We are not here to discuss the question of secession. We are here because the Border States are alarmed for their own safety. We wish them to remain in the Union. The purpose of our consultations is to make an arrangement under which they can stay in the Union. If we do not confine ourselves to that purpose, and leave these questions alone, our differences may be submitted to a greater than any human judge. I hope, in Heaven's name, they will not be submitted to the arbitrament of battle. No practical good whatever can come from debating this amendment. I move to lay it on the table; but if that motion will have the effect to carry the whole report on the table, I will not make it.

Mr. CRISFIELD:—I shall vote against this amendment. I believe the Constitution is endowed with sufficient authority to accomplish its own preservation, and to carry into execution its own laws; and, believing so, I deny the right of secession, but the right of revolution is a natural right possessed by every people. They may revolutionize their governments when they become oppressive. The Constitution was adopted as the logical consequence of this idea. There is no use now in discussing the abstract question of secession. We must treat the present condition of the Gulf States as a revolution in fact accomplished. We must meet them fairly. I vote against this amendment, and wish to stand right upon the record. If the history of this Convention is to be written, I do not wish to be handed down to posterity as one who favors the right of secession, which I believe to be a radical error.

Mr. WILMOT:—Pennsylvania is agreed in principle upon the doctrine of this amendment. I believe the whole North agrees also that the right of secession cannot be conceded, but my colleagues and myself differ essentially as to the manner in which we shall make our doctrine most effective. I think the true way is, to vote for this plain proposition, and not vote against it.

Now, all the North agrees that there is no right under the Constitution to interfere with slavery where it exists. No one has ever asserted such right, or believed in it. We are now asked to give a declaratory provision on that subject—to give it in order to quiet the slave States. One of my colleagues—Mr. POLLOCK—was willing to give that declaratory clause, which was necessary. I went with him in that; I now ask him to go with me, not against a mere shadow, but against what is the doctrine of a large portion of the people of the slave States; a doctrine of that proportion which proposes to overthrow the Constitution of the country. It is a demoralizing doctrine. My colleague proposes to vote against it. Did my colleague believe that any one proposed to interfere with slavery in the States?

Mr. POLLOCK:—No, I do not believe there was any such intention entertained by any considerable party. But there was an apprehension upon this subject in the slave States, caused by the action of a few radical men at the North. I was willing to vote for a declaratory resolution to quiet that apprehension.

Mr. WILMOT:—This amendment points to something more than an apprehension. It deals with an existing fact. Seven States have already gone out of the Union, asserting that the principal allegiance of their people is to the State, and not to the General Government. I think it high time that the Constitution was made unequivocal upon this subject of secession.

Mr. PRICE:—I occupy even a few minutes of time with much reluctance. Time is precious to us—too precious to be used in debate. I believe in the doctrine of the gentleman from New York. That is the doctrine of my State; but I believe in a great many other things which it is not necessary to insert in the Constitution. We came here to treat a fact, a great fact. There is a Southern Confederacy—there is a President DAVIS—there is a Government organized within the Union hostile to the United States. I came here, as the gentleman from Illinois has said, to act as if I had never given a vote or united with a political party. I say, with my colleague, that when the country is in danger my political robes hang loosely upon my shoulders.

There is an element in this Conference which, from the first day of our session, has opposed any action. Its policy has been to distract and divide our counsels, to put off every thing, to prevent all action. How different this is from what I expected when I came here. Shall we sit here debating abstract questions when State after State is seceding? I hope not. I trust the patriotic spirit which animates a majority of this Conference will to-day send forth a proposition which will restore peace to the country. We all agree to the principle contained in this amendment; but if we adopt it and make it a part of the Constitution, we could never, under it, bring back the seceded States. They will not admit the principle. What is to be gained, then, by adopting it? Why will gentlemen insist upon propositions which will nullify our action? New Jersey occupies high constitutional ground. She is ready to do any thing that is fair, and she goes for these propositions of the majority because they are fair. She will adopt these, and I believe every State will adopt them—New York as quickly as any. I do not think the gentleman properly represents the wishes of his constituents. He misrepresents them. Let us act, then, promptly, and act now. Every moment is precious. I know the trembling anxiety with which the country is awaiting our action. Do not let us sit here like the great Belshazzar till the handwriting appears on the wall. Let us set our faces against delay. Let us put down with an indignant rebuke every attempt to demoralize our action or destroy its effect.

Mr. BUCKNER:—I move to amend the amendment of Mr. FIELD, by adding the following:

"But this declaration shall not be construed so as to give the Federal Government power or authority to coerce or to make war directly or indirectly upon a State, on account of a failure to comply with its obligations."

Mr. FRELINGHUYSEN:—I hope the gentleman from New York will withdraw his resolution. The view of this Convention is against secession, and we all know that the Union of the States under the Constitntion is indissoluble. We know just as well that it is not necessary to assert this principle now. It is not expedient to assert it. We want to get back the seceded States. If we are earnest in this, is it best to call them traitors? I ask the gentleman whether the rejection of his proposition will not tend to weaken the Government and the Union? It will stand as a naked vote of rejection; the reasons why we vote against it will not go before the world.

Mr. BRONSON:—With the exception of a few minutes between eleven and twelve o'clock, a few nights since, I have not occupied the time or attention of the Conference. I will not now occupy but a few minutes. I came here to do something. I supposed we could accomplish something. We learned very soon after our arrival here that my colleague was opposed to any amendment of the Constitution. The same is true of several of my colleagues; perhaps a majority of them are here to do nothing. I supposed that something ought to be done to quiet the country. Instead of that an amendment is now offered asserting that we do not believe in the right of secession, that we do believe that these States which have seceded have done wrong. Suppose we do not believe in secession, what relevance has that to the present subject? Such an amendment may be used to delay or embarrass our action. There are a good many ways to defeat the project, a good many ways to suppress secession. My colleague looks to force alone. He proposes to bring back the seceded States by force. I contemplate the use of force in this connection with horror. It can never be used successfully.

We are here to agree upon something which will give peace to the country. Our committee has submitted a report which they think will accomplish that. My colleagues are skilful; they know how many ways there are to accomplish their purposes. One way to defeat any action here is by making long speeches, by loading down the propositions of amendment to the Constitution with other amendments, which will make the whole thing offensive to the country.

I stand here for my country. I would leave politics and political parties in the back ground. I would vote for nothing here which is not pertinent to the Constitution, and which will not help us in our attempts to quiet the apprehensions of our fellow-citizens. My colleague now brings forward a proposition which may be true in itself, but it is not pertinent and amounts to nothing. I am sorry he is not in his seat to hear what I have to say. He shot his arrow, and, I understand, has left for New York.

I am ready to vote down his proposition. I wish to see it

voted down. I am prepared to take all the consequences of voting it down, here and elsewhere. But I have drawn an amendment myself which I offer in lieu of his. Permit me to read it:

"While we do not recognize the constitutional right of any State to secede from the Union, we are deeply impressed by the fact that this Government is not maintained by force, but by unity of origin and interest, inducing fraternal feelings between the people of different sections of the country; and our labors have been directed to the end of giving a new assurance to our brethren, North, South, East, and West, of our determination to stand firmly by all the compromises of the Constitution."

I think we can vote for this amendment. It denies the right of secession as explicitly as the amendment of my colleague. But it has no coercion about it, and it asserts, as I understand it, the true principle upon which our Government is founded. I offer it as an expression of my own views. I have sat here for eight or ten days and have voted, except in a few instances, with the delegation from my own State. There is a bare majority of that delegation against the propositions of the committee. That majority ordinarily casts the vote of our State. I cannot express my views by my votes, and for that reason I undertake to express them in this amendment.

Mr. KING:—Like my colleague, I have taken but little part in the discussions in this Conference. I cannot be justly charged with having occupied time unnecessarily, as I have spoken on but one occasion, and then very briefly. I would not speak now if I did not sincerely believe this amendment to be eminently proper for the consideration of this body.

Myself and the majority of my colleagues differ from the majority of the Conference. That difference is an honest difference of opinion. It is based upon principle. If we consulted policy only, it would give us pleasure to yield to the wishes of the majority. But our first duty is to our constituents, and we must represent their opinions here. We should do it because our opinions coincide with theirs; and it was because we entertained these opinions that we were selected to represent New York in this body. When we are called upon to vote, we shall vote to carry out those opinions; and even when we differ from some of our colleagues, we are entitled to the same consideration from this body that they are. We do not intend to be driven from our position by threats or by intimidation. We believe that it is eminently proper for this Conference to express its decided convictions upon the question of secession. We are told here that secession is a fact. Then let us deal with it as such. I go for the enforcement of the laws passed in pursuance of the Constitution. I will never give up the idea that this is a Government of the people, and possessing within itself the power of enforcing its own decrees. This I shall never do. This Conference could perform no nobler act than that of sending to the country the announcement that the union of the States under the Constitution is indissoluble, and that secession is but another term for rebellion.

The gentleman from New Jersey says we misrepresent our constituents. How does he know that? Who gave him the right to place himself between our constituents and ourselves—to sit in judgment upon us? He will find that statement a very adventurous one. I should know something about New York and the people of New York. I have lived in that State all my life. I have been honored by the confidence and support of my fellow-citizens. Let me assure the gentleman that I know the people of that State far better than he. We will undertake to answer to our constituents; let him answer to his.

I will occupy no farther time. I wish to live in peace and harmony with our brethren in the slave States. But I wish to put upon the record here a statement of the fact that this is a Government of the people, and not a compact of States.

Mr. PALMER:—It is no part of my business or duty to vindicate the motives or conduct of the gentleman from New York, who is charged by one of his colleagues with interposing his amendment only for the purpose of delay. But that amendment meets my approval, and will have my support without regard to such imputations. Of what consequence are the gentleman's motives to us if his motion is right and proper? Are we to be gravely told that secession and treason are not proper subjects for our consideration? To be told this when every mail that comes to us from the South is loaded with both these crimes? Sir, we have commenced wrong. The first thing we ought to have done was to declare that these were crimes, and that we would not negotiate with those who denied the authority of the

Government, and claimed to have thrown off their allegiance to it. Far better would it be for the country if, instead of debating the question of slavery in reference to our Territories, we had set to work to strengthen the hands of the Government, and to put down the treason which threatens its existence.

You, gentlemen of the slave States, say that we of the North use fair words, that we promise fairly, but you insist that you will not rely upon our promises, and you demand our bond as security that we will keep them. I return the statement to you with interest. You, gentlemen, talk fairly also—give us your bond! You have been talking fairly for the last dozen or twenty years, and yet this treason, black as night, has been plotted among you, and twelve years ago one of your statesmen predicted the very state of things which now exists. I am willing to give bonds, but I want our action in this respect to be reciprocal. I want your bond against secession, and I ask it because seven States in sympathy with you have undertaken to set up an independent Government—have placed over it a military chieftain who asserts that we, the people of the United States, are foreigners, and must be treated with as a foreign nation.

You charged John Brown with treason. You convicted and executed him; and yet among you are thousands of men guilty of treason, beside which that of John Brown was paltry and insignificant. If we are to act at all, gentlemen, we must act upon reciprocal terms. I am willing to make every reasonable concession. Will you do the same? Will you, gentlemen of the South, declare that you will stand by the Union, and brand secession as treasonable? If you will, you must vote for this amendment.

Mr. HOWARD:—I am sure no member of this Conference could have listened to the remarks of the two gentlemen who have last spoken without the deepest regret. It has been intimated here that Maryland will secede unless she secures these guarantees. I do not know whether she will or not. I know there is danger that she will.

I agree that there is no *right* of secession. I think that secession is revolution. But the right of revolution always exists. It has always been maintained by statesmen North and

South. It was admitted by WEBSTER in his reply to HAYNE. I would read a quotation from his speech if time was not so valuable.

Yes, gentlemen, we are all in danger. The storm is raging; Virginia has hung her flag at half-mast as a signal of distress. If Virginia secedes our State will go with her, hand in hand, with Providence as our guide. This is not intended as a threat. GOD forbid! It is a truth which we cannot and ought not to conceal.

Why will not New York and Massachusetts for once be magnanimous? Why will they not follow the glorious example of Rhode Island? If they will, I should still have hope. But if those two great States are against us, I can see nothing but gloom in the future.

Mr. SMITH:—I hope the true state of the question will not be lost sight of. The first question is on the motion of the gentleman from Missouri, to amend the proposition of my colleague. On that I rise to a point of order. The motion of the gentleman from Missouri is a distinct proposition, and inconsistent with that offered by Mr. FIELD.

The PRESIDENT:—I do not think the point of order is well taken.

The question upon agreeing to the amendment of Mr. BUCKNER was then taken by States, with the following result:

AYES.—Delaware, Maryland, Missouri, North Carolina, and Virginia—5.

NOES.—Connecticut, Illinois, Indiana, Iowa, Maine, Massachusetts, New Jersey, New York, New Hampshire, Ohio, Pennsylvania, Rhode Island, Tennessee, Vermont, and Kansas—15.

So the amendment was lost.

Mr. BRONSON:—My motion is now in order as an amendment. I insist that the question should be taken upon its adoption.

Mr. WICKLIFFE:—Does the gentleman propose to put this into the Constitution? If the gentleman wishes to publish it as his speech, I will agree to it.

The question on the adoption of Mr. BRONSON'S motion was taken *viva voce*, and the amendment was rejected.

The PRESIDENT:—The question now recurs on the amendment offered by the gentleman from New York—Mr. FIELD.

Mr. RIVES:—I hope the Conference will pardon me for saying a few words upon this motion. I feel so sensibly the gravity of the consequences involved in the result of this vote, that I ask for a few minutes only in which to beseech the Conference not to act now upon a mere abstraction.

Gentlemen, what have we come here for? We have come at a time when the Government of our country is in great peril; and after a long session of diligent labor, and when we are just upon the point of arriving at the satisfactory adjustment of our differences, we have these abstract questions thrust upon us. They do not belong here. They ought not to be considered here. They would better befit a debating society than an assembly of statesmen met to consider constitutional questions. The gentleman (Governor KING) of New York announces his theory that this is a Government of the people and not a compact of the States. While I should agree with him upon his conclusions, we should differ widely as to the premises from which they are derived. It is a compact. All the authorities say so; and like any other compact, it is one from which each independent party may withdraw.

Now, what is this proposed amendment but an abstraction? In theory, the union of the States under the Constitution is indissoluble. But how is it in fact? It is now a fact that the Union is disrupted, is dissolved, because certain of the States composing it have withdrawn. But this is no time to discuss these questions. While we are talking about abstractions, we are wasting our time. I do not propose to enlarge upon the observations I have already submitted. But I beseech you, one and all, recognizing every member of the Conference as a brother of a common family, that now, after the labor of three weeks, and upon the very verge of adjustment, you should not destroy all we have done by interposing questions of this kind. Do not let us be seen engaged in the idle labor of Sisyphus. Do not let us now, just as we are about placing on the top of the mountain the block of constitutional adjustment, suffer that block to rebound. Dismiss the amendment with, I pray you earnestly, all questions of this sort, and let us proceed to the practical matters involved in the report, and its adoption.

Mr. NOYES:—If my colleague who offered this amendment, was not at this time absent, I should not address the Conference at all. I should like, however, to know what possible dangerous consequence we may anticipate from the adoption of this clause. Whether this Union is a compact of the States or a Government of the people, is equally unimportant in this connection. In either case it is not to be broken up at pleasure. If it is claimed either that the right exists already—if it is apprehended that the people themselves may assert the right to overthrow the Constitution and destroy the Government at pleasure—we should not, by all means, pass this amendment.

The slave power has now had possession of the Government in all for more than fifty years. A President has been elected belonging to the opposing party. For that cause alone, and without claiming or assigning any other, the slave States, under the powerful protection of Virginia, have come here for guarantees. We are told, over and over again, that seven States have left the Union. There is a fact with which we have to deal. On our side, we are merely dealing with apprehensions. If you have a right to guarantees to quiet your apprehensions, have we not a right to insist that secession shall be put down and condemned by an explicit clause of the Constitution? It is this claim of the right of secession which has brought all the trouble upon the country. We are right in our claim that it should be dealt with in this Conference. If we, as delegates, should prove faithless to our trust, should yield you all the guarantees you ask, and should insist upon nothing on our side, such action would not avail you any thing.

The North and the people of the North must be satisfied upon this point. Much has been said here about the right of revolution. I do not propose to discuss that right. At all events that is not a right which depends upon the Constitution, or grows out of it. If it exists at all, it is higher than, and above all Constitutions. The statement in this amendment does not controvert the right of revolution. It is simply a statement that *the Union of the States, under the Constitution, is indissoluble.* I regard the adoption of this amendment as both expedient and essential.

Mr. TURNER, of Illinois:—I do not think this amendment very important either way. If this is intended as a mere declaration of the purposes of the Constitution, it may be well enough. But will the assertion that such is the purpose of the Constitution preserve that instrument and the Government under it? No, sir. We may call spirits from the vasty deep; but the question is, will they come?

If the right of secession exists at all, it is not confined to the South. If it is conceded at all, it must be conceded in much broader terms—in terms that are common to all the States. This amendment secures to the States no practical benefit. I protest against being bound to harmonize on all abstract questions. This is an abstraction. Gentlemen schooled in deduction could spend weeks in argument over it.

The vote was taken upon the amendment proposed by Mr. FIELD, and resulted as follows:

AYES.—Connecticut, Illinois, Indiana, Iowa, Maine, Massachusetts, New York, New Hampshire, Vermont, and Kansas—10.

NOES.—Delaware, Kentucky, Maryland, Missouri, New Jersey, North Carolina, Ohio, Pennsylvania, Rhode Island, Tennessee, and Virginia—11.

So the amendment was disagreed to.

Mr. GUTHRIE:—I now submit that we ought to take the vote on the substitute proposed by the gentleman from Connecticut. I trust we are through with speeches, and hope we shall now get to some result. We may as well vote upon all these propositions within the next hour.

Mr. SOMES:—I desire to move an amendment by adding the following, to be numbered

SECTION 8. "That the freedom of speech, or of the press, shall not be abridged; but that the people of any Territory of the United States shall be left perfectly free to discuss the subject of slavery."

Mr. BRONSON:—I move to lay that amendment on the table.

Mr. SOMES:—Is not that motion debatable?

The PRESIDENT:—It is not debatable.

The motion to lay the amendment offered by Mr. SOMES upon the table, prevailed by the following vote:

AYES.—Delaware, Indiana, Kentucky, Maryland, Missouri, New Jersey, North Carolina, Ohio, Pennsylvania, Rhode Island, Tennessee, Virginia, and Kansas—13.

NOES.—Connecticut, Illinois, Iowa, Maine, and Vermont—5.

Thus the amendment was laid upon the table.

Mr. VANDEVER:—I move to amend the report by the addition of the following section:

"The navigation of the Mississippi River shall remain free to the people of each and all the States; and Congress shall provide by law for the protection of commerce on said river against all interference, foreign or domestic."

The importance of this proposition can be seen at once. It is one in which the whole country is interested, especially that portion of it in which I reside, which is drained by the upper waters of the Mississippi and Missouri. On this subject we have our apprehensions, and they are better founded, too, than any which I have heard from the South. We believe that our right to the navigation of this great national highway is imperilled. I submit whether we are to be cavalierly treated in this matter, and whether a subject of so much importance is to be laid upon the table? We may at all events, with perfect propriety, go this far, and make it, under the Constitution, the duty of Congress to protect the free navigation of the Mississippi River by law. We want it understood that the navigation of that river should be free and unobstructed, and that the faith of the nation is pledged to enforce that right. HENRY CLAY once stated that nothing upon earth could induce him to agree to any thing that should impede the free navigation of that river. I assert and repeat his declaration. We of the Northwest ask that this right should be guaranteed to us.

Mr. CRISFIELD:—I am as anxious for the free navigation of the Mississippi River as the gentleman. I wish simply to say that it is made the duty of the people of Iowa, and of other States bounded by this river, to protect that right of navigation. But the amendment is not germane to the report of the committee. I move to lay it on the table.

The motion of Mr. CRISFIELD prevailed by the following vote:

AYES.—Delaware, Indiana, Kentucky, Maryland, Missouri, New Jersey, North Carolina, New Hampshire, Ohio, Pennsylvania, Rhode Island, Tennessee, Vermont, and Virginia—14.

NOES.—Connecticut, Illinois, Iowa, Maine, Massachusetts, and New York —6.

So the amendment was laid on the table.

Mr. BALDWIN :—I move that my substitute be taken up, and ask that it may be read.

It was read as follows:

Whereas unhappy differences exist, which have alienated from each other portions of the people of the United States, to such an extent as seriously to disturb the peace of the nation and impair the regular and efficient action of the Government within the sphere of its constitutional powers and duties;

And whereas, the Legislature of the State of Kentucky has made application to Congress to call a Convention for proposing amendments to the Constitution of the United States;

And whereas, it is believed to be the opinion of the people of other States that amendments to the Constitution are, or may become, necessary to secure to the people of the United States, of every section, the full and equal enjoyment of their rights and liberties, so far as the same may depend for their security and protection on the powers granted to or withheld from the General Government in pursuance of the national purposes for which it was ordained and established:

This Convention does therefore recommend to the several States to unite with Kentucky in her application to Congress to call a Convention for proposing amendments to the Constitution of the United States, to be submitted to the Legislatures of the several States, or to Conventions therein, for ratification, as the one or the other mode of ratification may be proposed by Congress, in accordance with the provision in the fifth article of the Constitution.

I propose to avail myself of the privilege of a short reply to the arguments against my proposition; and in order that I may occupy as little time as possible, I have reduced my reply to writing. At the risk of repeating some of the remarks I made at the opening of the discussion, I wish to recur to the facts on which my report is based.

The resolution which I have moved to substitute, recommends to the several States to unite with Kentucky in her application for the calling of a Convention for proposing amendments to the Constitution.

On the 28th day of January, seven days before the assembling of this Conference Convention, the Governor of Kentucky transmitted to the President of the United States the joint resolutions of the General Assembly of that Commonwealth, "recommending a call for a Convention of the United States," with a request that the President would lay the same before Congress; and on the 5th of February, the day after the assembling of this Convention, they were, by a special message of the President, communicated to Congress, with the expression of great satisfaction in the performance of that duty, and of confidence that Congress would bestow upon those resolutions the careful consideration due to the distinguished and patriotic source from which they proceeded, as well as to the great importance of the subject which they involve. The resolution requesting the call of a Convention I have already read to the Conference.

There are, sir, but two modes provided by the people of the United States for altering the fundamental law of their Government, both of which are specified in the fifth article of the Constitution:

1. Congress, whenever two-thirds of both houses *shall deem it necessary*, shall PROPOSE amendments to the Constitution; or,

2. On the application of the Legislatures of two-thirds of the several States, shall *call a Convention* for PROPOSING *amendments*, which, in either case, shall be valid as part of the Constitution, when *ratified* by the Legislatures, or by Conventions in *three-fourths* of the States.

The first mode is recommended by the majority of the committee, in the expectation that Congress, by a two-thirds vote of both houses, will propose, on the request of this Convention, for ratification by the States, the several amendments they have reported.

The second mode is the one proposed by the Legislature of Kentucky, and which, in accordance therewith, I have moved to substitute for the recommendation of the committee.

There are now but few days remaining before the termination of the functions of the present Congress. If it were within the fair scope and interest of the constitutional provision that Congress should act, in the proposing of amendments, on the recommendation of this Conference Convention, no one, I think, can reasonably expect them to consider and deliberately act on such recommendation during the few remaining days of the present Congress. Other questions, of engrossing interest, now pending before them, and the acts of necessary legislation at the close of the session, will prevent it. It must, therefore, go over to the next Congress. Assuming that during the term of that Congress the amendments recommended by this Convention shall, by two-thirds of both houses, be *deemed necessary*, and be proposed to the States for ratification; there would probably be no earlier final action by the requisite number of States, than in the mode proposed by Kentucky, and recommended by the resolution which 1 have moved to substitute for the mode of amendment reported by the committee. But the great objection, in my mind, to the mode of amendment contemplated by the majority report, is that it is not in accordance with either the letter or the spirit of the Constitution. The people of the United States intended, when they adopted the Constitution under which we have for more than seventy years enjoyed a higher degree of prosperity than has fallen to the lot of any other people, that it should remain in full force and unchanged, except in one of the two modes prescribed in that sacred instrument for its own amendment.

It is a Constitution which binds the people of every State, as the supreme law of the land, until it can be changed by the action, in the first instance, of those who are *sworn* to support it. No amendments can, consistently with the letter or the spirit of the Constitution, be *proposed* by Congress, unless two-thirds of both houses, acting under the responsibility of their official oaths, shall "*deem* them *necessary.*" No interference or pressure by any extraneous body unknown to the Constitution, was contemplated, or can be allowed with safety to the people, to impair the exercise of this function under all the responsibilities and official sanctions that properly appertain to it. The judgment of two-thirds of both houses of Congress in regard to the *necessity* of the amendments, must precede their proposal to the States for *ratification.*

The Government of the United States, in its sphere of duties, is supreme. The State Governments, when they consented to its formation by the people of the United States, surrendered so much of their separate sovereignties as was essential to its strength and efficiency. To that extent we became one people. This Government, for all *national* purposes, took the place of the State Governments, as well in regard to the *paramount allegiance* as to the duty of protection of the people of every State in the enjoyment of all their federal rights. It spowers can neither be enlarged nor diminished, except in the *constitutional* mode, without violating the rights of the States as well as of the people.

Any attempt from without, by combinations and associations not responsible to the people, to *coerce* or overawe Congress, or in any way to impair the free and *deliberate* exercise of its judgment in *proposing* amendments "as deemed *necessary*" by Congress, is a palpable violation of the privileges of the people. They elected the members of the House of Representatives with the intention that they should freely and deliberately, under their official oaths, propose amendments, or not, to the Constitution, as *they* might *deem necessary*, and not at the dictation of *States even*, who cannot themselves propose amendments, but can only require of Congress to call a Convention of *all the States* for that purpose. Much less can a convention of delegates from the Legislatures, or the Executive of a part only of the States—a body unknown to, and unauthorized by, the Constitution—assume to exercise, or dictate to Congress the exercise of this high prerogative.

WE do not represent the people of the United States. This Government, for every purpose for which it was established, is a separate, and in some sense a foreign government to the States. It operates directly on the people, and is itself their true protector in all their Federal rights.

Any number of States, less than two-thirds, have no more right to call into action the power of Congress either to call a Convention, or to propose amendments, than the individual members of their Legislatues in their private capacities; and Congress might as well, and probably would, treat our interference with their official duties as an *usurpation;* as much so as if we should seek to interfere with the appropriate duties of the Legislatures of Virginia or Massachusetts. And, sir, I cannot but regard it, so far as the *free* action of Congress should be influenced by the recommendations of this body, as in the nature of a *revolutionary proceeding* for which there is no sufficient cause or justification. Sir, all the States are not here represented. All have not even had an opportunity to be here. And yet we are endeavoring to influence the action of Congress in a manner which may deeply affect their interests. If, under any circumstances, a body so convened, would have a right to act upon Congress, by the expression of our opinions as a Convention of States, ought not all to have an opportunity to participate in our deliberations? Most certainly they ought.

But it is said some of the States are threatening to secede from the Union; others have seceded, and must be induced to come back, by the speedy action of Congress on the amendments recommended by the committee. Does the *Constitution* authorize amendments under such circumstances, with *less care* and deliberation than in time of peace and tranquillity?

This Government, sir, cannot recognize the fact that *States* have seceded. It is not a Government over *States*, but over the *people* of the United States, irrespective of the State in which they live. This Government, and not the States, protects them in their Federal rights, and requires allegiance and obedience from the people in every State, to the Constitution and laws of the United States as the supreme law of the land, any thing in the laws or ordinances of any State to the contrary notwithstanding. It is the *people* and not the States that are governed by that law, within the sphere of its constitutional operation.

I have said that the course proposed by the majority of the committee is, in my judgment, not only against the letter, but the spirit of the Constitution. The State of Kentucky, ever patriotic and conservative, must have so regarded it, when, instead of asking Congress to propose the amendments they desired, they requested their sister States to unite with them in an application in the mode prescribed by the Constitution to Congress to call a Convention for that purpose.

Our fathers, who framed that Constitution, and the people of the United States, who ratified it, set it forth in the preamble as their first great purpose "to form a more perfect Union." They intended to establish thereby a Government of perpetual obligation and of self-sustaining vigor. They did not contemplate the necessity of amendments for any other causes than such as, after calm, deliberate, undisturbed consideration should be judged necessary. They did not intend that it should be exposed to the danger of hasty action under the influence of excited passions or timid and groundless apprehension. They would not trust the entire people even with the right of amendment, except in the mode prescribed, with all the delays incident to that mode; and then only by the action, in every stage of the proceeding, of persons bound by solemn oath to support it.

The Constitution, in prescribing the modes of proposing amendments, endeavored to provide against irregular combination of a part only of the States to effect them. Hence it prohibited all agreements or compacts between the States; and it made no provision for the recognition of any action by a convention, except when called on the recommendation of two-thirds of the States applying to Congress, by separate action of their Legislatures, for that purpose.

Any interference with the duty of Congress by such a body as we are, representing only a portion of the States in any form, and some of us only the executives of the States from which we come, would be as much at variance with the Constitution as with the counsel of that illustrious American—I will not say Virginian—for WASHINGTON belonged to his whole country—in the Farewell Address which he dedicated to the people of the United States on his retirement from the public service, and which ought to be cherished in the heart of every patriot. In addition to what I have already read from that address let me read this passage:

"All obstructions to the execution of the laws, all *combinations* and *associations*, under whatever plausible character, with the *real design to direct, control, counteract*, or *awe* the regular deliberation and action of the *constituted authorities*, are destructive to this fundamental rule, and of fatal tendency."

Let me read it again. "All obstructions," &c. "All combinations," &c.

This address is replete with words of true wisdom. Let us heed them; for they are eminently adapted to the present occasion. There is no exigency which should be allowed to overawe Congress in the performance of its constitutional duties. No State intervention, no combination or association of representatives of States in a manner unknown to the Constitution, can be recognized as authoritative by those to whom, on their own responsibility, the people of the United States have conferred their national interests and the guardianship of their fundamental law. "We owe," in the language of the illustrious statesman of Kentucky, "*a paramount* allegiance to the Government of the United States—a subordinate one to our State."

Sir, while I am willing to perform all my constitutional duties—all my fraternal duties toward the people of every section of our common country, I, for one, feel bound to abstain from any encroachment on the duties which the Constitution of my country has delegated to others to be performed, in the modes, and with the responsibilities, which the *people* for their own security have deemed it proper to prescribe.

With these opinions, I should be unfaithful to my own convictions of duty, and recreant to the trust which has devolved on me as a citizen of the United States, and by inheritance from an ancestor who took a part in the deliberations of the Convention which framed our Constitution, and to whose public services, you, sir, so kindly alluded at the opening of the Conference, were I to unite with the majority of the committee in urging upon Congress the amendments they have proposed.

Entertaining as I do for the members of the committee who have concurred in that report a profound respect, it has been with a feeling of unaffected diffidence and self-distrust that I have ventured to express my sentiments on this occasion. But as I must act on my own convictions of duty, which are in harmony with those of my associates from Connecticut, so far as in the brief period which has elapsed since the report was submitted I have had opportunity to ascertain them, I felt bound to make known to the Convention the reasons which will govern my action.*

The vote was then taken by States on the substitute proposed by Mr. BALDWIN, and the substitute was rejected by the following vote:

AYES.—Connecticut, Illinois, Iowa, Maine, Massachusetts, New York, New Hampshire, and Vermont—8.

NOES.—Delaware, Indiana, Kentucky, Maryland, Missouri, New Jersey, North Carolina, Ohio, Pennsylvania, Rhode Island, Tennessee, Virginia, and Kansas—13.

So the amendment was not agreed to.

The following gentlemen disagreed to the vote of their respective States:

Mr. BRONSON, of New York; Mr. GRANGER, of New York; Mr. DODGE, of New York; Mr. CORNING, of New York; Mr. ORTH, of Indiana; Mr. HACKLEMAN, of Indiana.

Mr. SEDDON:—I suppose it is now in order for me to move my substitute for the report of the majority of the committee.

Mr. TUCK:—I also have a substitute to offer. I shall not discuss it.

* The closing remarks of Mr. BALDWIN were committed to writing. I am able through the kindness of a member of his family to avail myself of a copy.

Mr. SEDDON:—The substitute which I propose embodies the CRITTENDEN resolutions, with the modifications suggested by Virginia. These are principally confined to the first section, which is made to apply to our future as well as our present territory. I have modified the form of the substitute in several particulars, and now offer it without farther introduction. These are the amendments which I understand the delegation from Virginia is instructed to insist upon:

JOINT RESOLUTIONS

PROPOSING CERTAIN AMENDMENTS TO THE CONSTITUTION OF THE UNITED STATES.

WHEREAS, serious and alarming dissensions have arisen between the Northern and Southern States, concerning the rights and security of the rights of the slaveholding States, and especially their rights in the common territory of the United States; and whereas, it is eminently desirable and proper that those dissensions, which now threaten the very existence of this Union, should be permanently quieted and settled by constitutional provisions, which shall do equal justice to all sections, and thereby restore to the people that peace and good will which ought to prevail between all the citizens of the United States: therefore,

Resolved, by this Convention, that the following articles are hereby approved and submitted to the Congress of the United States, with the request that they may, by the requisite constitutional majority of two-thirds, be recommended to the respective States of the Union, to be, when ratified by conventions of three-fourths of the States, valid and operative as amendments of the Constitution of the Union.

ARTICLE 1. In all the territory of the United States now held or hereafter acquired, situate north of latitude 36° 30′, slavery or involuntary servitude, except as a punishment for crime, is prohibited, while such territory shall remain under territorial government. In all the territory now or hereafter acquired south of said line of latitude, slavery of the African race is hereby recognized as existing, and shall not be interfered with by Congress; but shall be protected as property by all the departments of the territorial government during its continuance; and when any territory, north or south of said line, within such boundaries as Congress may prescribe, shall contain the population requisite for a member of Congress, according to the then federal ratio of representation of the people of the United States, it shall, if its form of government be republican, be admitted into the Union on an equal footing with the original States, with or without slavery, as the constitution of such new State may provide.

ARTICLE 2. Congress shall have no power to abolish slavery in places under its exclusive jurisdiction, and situate within the limits of States that permit the holding of slaves.

ARTICLE 3. Congress shall have no power to abolish slavery within the

District of Columbia, so long as it exists in the adjoining States of Virginia and Maryland, or either, nor without the consent of the free white inhabitants, nor without just compensation first made to such owners of slaves as do not consent to such abolishment. Nor shall Congress at any time prohibit officers of the Federal Government or members of Congress, whose duties require them to be in said District, from bringing with them their slaves and holding them, as such, during the time their duties may require them to remain there, and afterwards taking them from the District.

ARTICLE 4. Congress shall have no power to prohibit or hinder the transportation of slaves from one State to another, or to a Territory in which slaves are by law permitted to be held, whether that transportation be by land, navigable rivers, or by the sea. And if such transportation be by sea, the slaves shall be protected as property by the Federal Government. And the right of transit by the owners with their slaves in passing to or from one slaveholding State or Territory to another, between and through the non-slaveholding States and Territories, shall be protected. And in imposing direct taxes pursuant to the Constitution, Congress shall have no power to impose on slaves a higher rate of tax than on land, according to their just value.

ARTICLE 5. That in addition to the provisions of the third paragraph of the second section of the fourth article of the Constitution of the United States, Congress shall provide by law, that the United States shall pay to the owner who shall apply for it, the full value of his fugitive slave, in all cases, when the marshal, or other officer, whose duty it was to arrest said fugitive, was prevented from so doing by violence or intimidation, or when, after arrest, said fugitive was rescued by force, and the owner thereby prevented and obstructed in the pursuit of his remedy for the recovery of his fugitive slave, under the said clause of the Constitution and the laws made in pursuance thereof. And in all such cases, when the United States shall pay for such fugitive, they shall reimburse themselves by imposing and collecting a tax on the county or city in which said violence, intimidation, or rescue was committed, equal in amount to the sum paid by them, with the addition of interest and the costs of collection; and the said county or city, after it has paid said amount to the United States, may, for its indemnity, sue and recover from the wrong-doers, or rescuers, by whom the owner was prevented from the recovery of his fugitive slave, in like manner as the owner himself might have sued and recovered.

ARTICLE 6. No future amendment of the Constitution shall affect the five preceding articles, nor the third paragraph of the second section of the first article of the Constitution, nor the third paragraph of the second section of the fourth article of said Constitution, and no amendment shall be made to the Constitution which will authorize or give to Congress any power to abolish or interfere with slavery in any of the States by whose laws it is or may be allowed or permitted.

ARTICLE 7. SEC. 1. The elective franchise and the right to hold office, whether Federal, State, territorial, or municipal, shall not be exercised by persons who are, in whole or in part, of the African race.

And whereas, also, besides those causes of dissension embraced in the foregoing amendments proposed to the Constitution of the United States, there are others which come within the jurisdiction of Congress, and may be remedied by its legislative power: and whereas it is the desire of this Convention, as far as its influence may extend, to remove all just cause for the popular discontent and agitation which now disturb the peace of the country, and threaten the stability of its institutions: Therefore,

1. *Resolved*, That the laws now in force for the recovery of fugitive slaves are in strict pursuance of the plain and mandatory provisions of the Constitution, and have been sanctioned as valid and constitutional by the judgment of the Supreme Court of the United States; that the slaveholding States are entitled to the faithful observance and execution of those laws, and that they ought not to be repealed or so modified or changed as to impair their efficiency; and that laws ought to be made for the punishment of those who attempt, by rescue of the slave or other illegal means, to hinder or defeat the due execution of said laws.

2. That all State laws which conflict with the fugitive slave acts, or any other constitutional acts of Congress, or which, in their operation, impede, hinder, or delay the free course and due execution of any of said acts, are null and void by the plain provisions of the Constitution of the United States. Yet those State laws, void as they are, have given color to practices, and led to consequences which have obstructed the due administration and execution of acts of Congress, and especially the acts for the delivery of fugitive slaves, and have thereby contributed much to the discord and commotion now prevailing. This Convention, therefore, in the present perilous juncture, does not deem it improper, respectfully and earnestly, to recommend the repeal of those laws to the several States which have enacted them, or such legislative corrections or explanations of them as may prevent their being used or perverted to such mischievous purposes.

3. That the act of the eighteenth of September, eighteen hundred and fifty, commonly called the fugitive slave law, ought to be so amended as to make the fee of the commissioner, mentioned in the eighth section of the act, equal in amount, in the cases decided by him, whether his decision be in favor of or against the claimant. And to avoid misconstruction, the last clause of the fifth section of said act, which authorizes the person holding a warrant for the arrest or detention of a fugitive slave to summon to his aid the *posse comitatus*, and which declares it to be the duty of all good citizens to assist him in its execution, ought to be so amended as to expressly limit the authority and duty to cases in which there shall be resistance, or danger of resistance or rescue.

4. That the laws for the suppression of the African slave-trade, and especially those prohibiting the importation of slaves into the United States, ought to be made effectual, and ought to be thoroughly executed, and all further enactments necessary to those ends ought to be promptly made.

The substitute offered by Mr. SEDDON was rejected by the following vote:

AYES.—Kentucky, Missouri, North Carolina, and Virginia—4.

NOES.—Connecticut, Delaware, Illinois, Indiana, Maine, Massachusetts, Maryland, New Jersey, New York, New Hampshire, Ohio, Pennsylvania, Rhode Island, Tennessee, Vermont, and Kansas—16.

Mr. DENT dissented from the vote of Maryland.

Mr. HOUSTON:—I wish to explain the vote of Delaware. She has endorsed the CRITTENDEN resolutions. She would accept the mode of adjustment proposed by the gentleman from Virginia. She has adhered to her opinions as long as she thinks it fit or expedient to do so. Under these circumstances Delaware feels it her duty to vote for the report of the majority. As we desire to harmonize conflicting opinions, and to arrive at a fair settlement, we have voted against Mr. SEDDON'S amendment.

Mr. CRISFIELD:—Like Delaware, Maryland prefers the CRITTENDEN plan of adjustment. That we think is now impossible. But that plan does not differ very widely from the report of the majority. Certainly not enough to warrant us in risking the Union, when we can get the one and cannot have the other. For this reason Maryland votes "No" on Mr. SEDDON'S proposition.

Mr. CLAY:—I gave notice some days ago that I should offer as a substitute the CRITTENDEN resolutions—pure and undefiled—without the crossing of a "t" or the dotting of an "i." I now offer them as follows, and demand a vote by States:

WHEREAS, the Union is in danger; and owing to the unhappy divisions existing in Congress, it would be difficult, if not impossible, for that body to concur, in both its branches, by the requisite majority, so as to enable it either to adopt such measures of legislation, or to recommend to the States such amendments to the Constitution as are deemed necessary and proper to avert that danger; and whereas, in so great an emergency, the opinion and judgment of the people ought to be heard, and would be the best and surest guide to their representatives: Therefore,

Resolved, That provision ought to be made by law, without delay, for taking the sense of the people, and submitting to their vote the following resolutions as the basis for the final and permanent settlement of those disputes that now disturb the peace of the country and threaten the existence of the Union.

And that whereas serious and alarming dissensions have arisen between the Northern and Southern States, concerning the rights and security of the rights of the slaveholding States, and especially their rights in the common territory of the United States; and whereas, it is eminently desirable and proper that those dissensions, which now threaten the very existence of this Union, should be permanently quieted and settled by constitutional provisions, which shall do equal justice to all sections, and thereby restore to the people that peace and good will which ought to prevail between all the citizens of the United States: Therefore,

Resolved, That the following articles be, and hereby are, proposed and submitted as amendments to the Constitution of the United States, which shall be valid to all intents and purposes as part of said Constitution, when ratified by conventions of three-fourths of the several States:

ARTICLE 1. In all the territory of the United States now held or hereafter acquired, situate north of latitude 36° 30′, slavery or involuntary servitude, except as a punishment for crime, is prohibited, while such territory shall remain under territorial government. In all the territory south of said line of latitude, slavery of the African race is hereby recognized as existing, and shall not be interfered with by Congress; but shall be protected as property by all the departments of the territorial government during its continuance; and when any Territory, north or south of said line, within such boundaries as Congress may prescribe, shall contain the population requisite for a member of Congress, according to the then Federal ratio of representation of the people of the United States, it shall, if its form of government be republican, be admitted into the Union on an equal footing with the original States, with or without slavery, as the constitution of such new States may provide.

ARTICLE 2. Congress shall have no power to abolish slavery in places under its exclusive jurisdiction, and situate within the limits of States that permit the holding of slaves.

ARTICLE 3. Congress shall have no power to abolish slavery within the District of Columbia, so long as it exists in the adjoining States of Virginia and Maryland, or either, nor without the consent of the inhabitants, nor without just compensation first made to such owners of slaves as do not consent to such abolishment. Nor shall Congress at any time prohibit officers of the Federal Government or members of Congress, whose duties require them to be in said District, from bringing with them their slaves, and holding them, as such, during the time their duties may require them to remain there, and afterwards taking them from the District.

ARTICLE 4. Congress shall have no power to prohibit or hinder the transportation of slaves from one State to another, or to a Territory in which slaves are by law permitted to be held, whether that transportation be by land, navigable rivers, or by the sea; and the right of transit by the owners with their slaves in passing to or from one slaveholding State or Territory to another, between and through the non-slaveholding States and Territories, shall be protected.

ARTICLE 5. That, in addition to the provisions of the third paragraph of the second section of the fourth article of the Constitution of the United States, Congress shall have power to provide by law, and it shall be its duty so to provide, that the United States shall pay to the owner who shall apply for it, the full value of his fugitive slave in all cases, when the marshal or other officer whose duty it was to arrest said fugitive was prevented from so doing by violence or intimidation, or when, after arrest, said fugitive was rescued by force, and the owner thereby prevented and obstructed in the pursuit of his remedy for the recovery of his fugitive slave, under the said clause of the Constitution and the laws made in pursuance thereof. And in all such cases, when the United States shall pay for such fugitive, they shall have the power to reimburse themselves by imposing and collecting a tax on the county or city in which said violence, intimidation, or rescue was committed, equal in amount to the sum paid by them, with the addition of interest and the costs of collection; and the said county or city, after it has paid said amount to the United States, may, for its indemnity, sue and recover from the wrong-doers, or rescuers, by whom the owner was prevented from the recovery of his fugitive slave, in like manner as the owner himself might have sued and recovered.

ARTICLE 6. No future amendment of the Constitution shall affect the five preceding articles, nor the third paragraph of the second section of the first article of the Constitution, nor the third paragraph of the second section of the fourth article of said Constitution; and no amendment shall be made to the Constitution which will authorize or give to Congress any power to abolish or interfere with slavery in any of the States by whose laws it is or may be allowed or permitted.

ARTICLE 7. SEC. 1. The elective franchise, and the right to hold office, whether federal, State, territorial, or municipal, shall not be exercised by persons who are, in whole or in part, of the African race.

SEC. 2. The United States shall have power to acquire, from time to time, districts of country in Africa and South America, for the colonization, at expense of the Federal Treasury, of such free negroes and mulattoes as the several States may wish to have removed from their limits and from the District of Columbia, and such other places as may be under the jurisdiction of Congress.

And whereas, also, besides those causes of dissension embraced in the foregoing amendments proposed to the Constitution of the United States, there are others which come within the jurisdiction of Congress, and may be remedied by its legitimate power; and whereas it is the desire of this Convention, as far as its influence may extend, to remove all just cause for the popular discontent and agitation which now disturb the peace of the country, and threaten the stability of its institutions: Therefore,

1. *Resolved*, That the laws now in force for the recovery of fugitive slaves are in strict pursuance of the plain and mandatory provisions of the Constitution, and have been sactioned as valid and constitutional by the judgment of the Supreme Court of the United States; that the slaveholding States are entitled to the faithful observance and execution of those laws, and that they ought not to be repealed or so modified or changed as to impair their efficiency; and that laws ought to be made for the punishment of those who attempt, by rescue of the slave or other illegal means, to hinder or defeat the due execution of said laws.

2. That all State laws which conflict with the fugitive slave acts, or any other constitutional acts of Congress, or which in their operation impede, hin-

der, or delay the free course and due execution of any of said acts, are null and void by the plain provisions of the Constitution of the United States. Yet those State laws, void as they are, have given color to practices, and led to consequences which have obstructed the due administration and execution of acts of Congress, and especially the acts for the delivery of fugitive slaves, and have thereby contributed much to the discord and commotion now prevailing. This Convention, therefore, in the present perilous juncture, does not deem it improper, respectfully and earnestly, to recommend the repeal of those laws to the several States which have enacted them, or such legislative corrections or explanations of them, as may prevent their being used or perverted to such mischievous purposes.

3. That the act of the eighteenth of September, eighteen hundred and fifty, commonly called the fugitive slave law, ought to be so amended as to make the fee of the commissioner, mentioned in the eighth section of the act, equal in amount, in the cases decided by him, whether his decision be in favor of or against the claimant. And to avoid misconstruction, the last clause of the fifth section of said act, which authorizes the person holding a warrant for the arrest or detention of a fugitive slave to summon to his aid the *posse comitatus*, and which declares it to be the duty of all good citizens to assist him in its execution, ought to be so amended as to expressly limit the authority and duty to cases in which there shall be resistance, or danger of resistance or rescue.

4. That the laws for the suppression of the African slave-trade, and especially those prohibiting the importation of slaves into the United States, ought to be made effectual, and ought to be thoroughly executed, and all further enactments necessary to those ends ought to be promptly made.

The question on agreeing to said amendment resulted in the following vote:

Ayes.—Kentucky, Missouri, North Carolina, Tennessee, and Virginia—5.

Noes.—Connecticut, Delaware, Illinois, Indiana, Maine, Massachusetts, Maryland, New Jersey, New York, New Hampshire, Ohio, Pennsylvania, Rhode Island, and Vermont—14.

So the amendment was not agreed to.

Mr. DENT :—I desire to dissent from the vote of Maryland.

Mr. EWING :—I desire to record the vote of Kansas in the negative.

The PRESIDENT :—Leave will be given unless objection is made.

Mr. TUCK :—I hold in my hand a substitute which I propose to offer for the report of the committee. I know all the delegates have made up their minds how to vote, and what to vote for. Argument now will amount to but little. But I submit this as indicating to a certain extent the views of the minority here. I shall make no farther remarks, but shall pass it to the Secretary, and I hope the Conference will be patient for five minutes while it is read.

The proposition of Mr. TUCK was read as follows:

TO THE PEOPLE OF THE UNITED STATES:

On the 4th day of February, 1861, in compliance with the invitation of the State of Virginia, commissioners from several other States met the commissioners of that State in Conference Convention, in the City of Washington. From time to time, commissioners from other States appeared, appointed as were those who first appeared, some by the Legislatures, and some by the Governors of their respective States, until, on the 23d instant, twenty-one States were then represented. The Convention thus constituted claims no authority under the Constitution and laws; but deeply impressed with a sense of existing dissensions and dangers, proceeded to a careful consideration of them and their appropriate remedies, and having brought their deliberations to a close, now submit the result to the judgment of their fellow-citizens.

We recognize and deplore the divisions and distractions which now afflict our country, interrupt its prosperity, disturb its peace, and endanger the Union of the States; but we repel the conclusion, that any alienations or dissensions exist which are irreconcilable, which justify attempts at revolution, or which the patriotism and fraternal sentiments of the people, and the interests and honor of the whole nation, will not overcome.

In a country embracing the central and most important portion of a continent, among a people now numbering over thirty millions, diversities of opinion inevitably exist; and rivalries, intensified at times by local interests and sectional attachments, must often occur; yet we do not doubt that the theory of our Government is the best which is possible for this nation, that the Union of the States is of vital importance, and that the Constitution, which expresses the combined wisdom of the illustrious founders of the Government, is still the palladium of our liberties, adequate to every emergency, and justly entitled to the support of every good citizen.

It embraces in its provisions and spirit, all the defence and protection which any section of the country can rightfully demand or honorably concede.

Adopted with primary reference to the wants of five millions of people, but with the wisest reference to future expansion and development, it has carried us onward with a rapid increase of numbers, an accumulation of wealth, and a degree of happiness and general prosperity never attained by any other nation.

Whatever branch of industry, or whatever staple production, shall become, in the possible changes of the future, the leading interests of the country, thereby creating unforeseen complications or new conflicts of opinion and interest, the Constitution of the United States, properly understood and fairly enforced, is equal to every exigency, a shield and defence to all, in every time of need. If, however, by reason of a change in circumstances, or for any cause, a portion of the people believe they ought to have their rights more exactly defined or more fully explained in the Constitution, it is their duty, in accordance with its provisions, to seek a remedy by way of amendment to that instrument; and it is the duty of all the States to concur in such amendments as may be found necessary to insure equal and exact justice to all.

In order, therefore, to announce to the country the sentiments of this Convention, respecting not only the remedy which should be sought for existing discontents, but also to communicate to the public what we believe to be the patriotic sentiment of the country, we adopt the following resolutions:

1st. *Resolved*, That this Convention recognize the well-understood proposition that the Constitution of the United States gives no power to Congress, or any branch of the Federal Government, to interfere in any manner with slavery in any of the States; and we are assured by abundant testimony, that neither of the great political organizations existing in the country contemplates a violation of the spirit of the Constitution in this regard, or the procuring of any amendment thereof, by which Congress, or any department of the General Government, shall ever have jurisdiction over slavery in any of the States.

2d. *Resolved*, That the Constitution was ordained and established, as set forth in the preamble, by the people of the United States, in order to form a more perfect Union, establish justice, insure domestic tranquillity, provide for the common defence, promote the general welfare, and secure the blessings of liberty to themselves and their posterity; and when the people of any State are not in full enjoyment of all the benefits intended to be secured to them by the Constitution, or their rights under it are disregarded, their tranquillity disturbed, their prosperity retarded, or their liberty imperilled by the people of any other State, full and adequate redress can and ought to be provided for such grievances.

3d. *Resolved*, That the Constitution of the United States, and the acts of Congress in pursuance thereof, are the supreme law of the land, to which every citizen owes faithful obedience; and it is therefore respectfully recommended to the Legislatures of the several States to consider impartially whatever complaints may be made of acts as inconsistent therewith, by sister States or their citizens, and carefully revise their statutes, in view of such complaints, and to repeal whatever provisions may be found to be in contravention of that supreme law.

4th. *Resolved*, That this Convention recommend to the Legislatures of the several States of the Union to follow the example of the Legislatures of the States of Kentucky and of Illinois, in applying to Congress to call a Convention for the proposing of amendments to the Constitution of the United States, pursuant to the fifth article thereof.

Mr. CHASE:—I have not thought it best to occupy much of the time of the Convention in discussing the propositions presented for its decision. I have indeed been impressed with an idea that a decision upon these propositions just now may be premature.

I have already stated to the Conference that the delegates from Ohio act under resolutions of the General Assembly of that State, one of which requires them to use their influence in procuring an adjournment of this body to the 4th of April next. It is the wish of that State that opportunity may be given for full consideration of any constitutional amendment that may be proposed here, and especially to avoid precipitate action under apprehensions of resistance to the inauguration of Mr. LINCOLN on the 4th of next month.

I have already submitted resolutions in accordance with the views of the Legislature, and intended, at the proper time, to ask a vote upon the proposed adjournment. On consultation with my colleagues, however, I find a majority of them averse to postponement; and, in view of the fact that the resolution of the Legislature is not imperative in its terms, and especially in consideration of the assurances constantly given here by delegates from slaveholding States that, whatever may be the result of our deliberations, no obstruction or hindrance will be opposed to the inauguration of Mr. LINCOLN, I have determined to forbear urging a vote.

Upon the respective merits of the propositions of the committee, and the proposed amendments, I have not much to say. But what I do say will be said in all seriousness.

I do not approve the confident pledges made here of favorable action by the people of either section, or of any State, upon whatever propositions may receive the sanction of this Conference. The people of the free States, so far as my observation goes, do not commit their right of judgment to anybody. They generally exercise it themselves, and be assured they will exercise it freely upon any proposition coming from this body. Whatever our actions may be here, every proposition to amend the Constitution must come before the people. They will discuss it, and must adopt it before it can become a part of the fundamental law. Dismiss, then, the idea that all that is necessary to secure amendments acceptable to a particular interest or section is to secure for them the sanction of a majority in this hall.

The result of the national canvass which recently terminated in the election of Mr. Lincoln has been spoken of by some as the effect of a sudden impulse, or of some irregular excitement of the popular mind; and it has been somewhat confidently asserted that, upon reflection and consideration, the hastily-formed opinions which brought about that election will be changed. It has been said, also, that subordinate questions of local and temporary character have augmented the Republican vote, and secured a majority which could not have been obtained upon the national questions involved in the respective platforms of the parties which divide the country.

I cannot take this view of the result of the Presidential election. I believe, and the belief amounts to absolute conviction, that the election must be regarded as the triumph of principles cherished in the hearts of the people of the free States. These principles, it is true, were originally asserted by a small party only. But, after years of discussion, they have, by their own value, their own intrinsic soundness, obtained the deliberate and unalterable sanction of the people's judgment.

Chief among these principles is the restriction of slavery within State limits; *not* war upon slavery within those limits, but fixed opposition to its extension beyond them. Mr. Lincoln was the candidate of the people opposed to the extension of slavery. We have elected him. After many years of earnest advocacy and of severe trial, we have achieved the triumph of that principle. By a fair and unquestionable majority we have secured that triumph. Do you think we, who represent this majority, will throw it away? Do you think the people would sustain us if we undertook to throw it away? I must speak to you plainly, gentlemen of the South; it is not in my heart to deceive you. I therefore tell you explicitly that if we of the North and West would consent to throw away all that has been gained in the recent triumph of our principles, the people would not sustain us, and so the consent would avail you nothing. And I must tell you farther, that under no inducements whatever will we consent to surrender a principle which we believe to be so sound and so important as that of restricting slavery within State limits.

There are some things, however, which I think the people are willing to do. In all my relations with them, and these relations have been somewhat intimate, I have never discovered any desire or inclination on the part of any considerable number, to interfere with the institution of slavery within the States where it exists. I do not believe that any such desire anywhere prevails. All your rights have been respected and enforced by the people of the free States. More than this: even your claims have been enforced, under repulsive circumstances, and, in my judgment, beyond right and beyond constitutional obligation. When and where have the people of the free States, in their representatives, refused you any right? When and where have they refused to confer with you frankly and candidly when you imagined your rights to be in danger? They have been, and still are, patient and forbearing. They do not believe that you need any new constitutional guarantees. You have guarantees enough in their voluntary action. But, since you think differently, they send us hither to meet you, to confer with you, to consider the questions which threaten the Union, to discuss them freely and decide them fairly.

Now, gentlemen, what do we ask of you? Do we ask any thing unreasonable in the amendment which has been submitted? We simply ask that you say to your people that we of the free States have no purpose, and never had any purpose, to infringe the rights of the slave States, or of any citizen of the slave States. And that our devotion to the Government and the Constitution is not inferior to that of any portion of the American people. By uniting with us in the declaration we propose, you tell your people at home that no considerable party, that no considerable number of persons, in the free States, has any wish or purpose to interfere with slavery in the States where it exists, or with any of your rights under the Constitution. You can say this with absolute truth, and with entire confidence. In all the action of the delegates who favor this amendment, in all our private consultations, every heart has been animated by a most anxious desire to maintain the Union and preserve the harmony of the Republic. No word has been uttered indicating the slightest wish to avoid any obligation of the Constitution, or to deprive you of any right under it. All concur in desiring to give effect to the Constitution and the laws passed in pursuance of it. The same sentiments animate the people of the free States. Congress has declared, with the almost unanimous concurrence of the members from the free States, against national interference with slavery in the slave States. The Chicago Convention most emphatically asserted the same doctrine. It has been reiterated over and over again by the Legislatures of the free States, and by great and small conventions of their people. Is it, then, too much to ask you to unite with us in a declaration that all fears of aggression entertained by your people are groundless? Such a declaration will go far to insure peace; why not make it?

You profess to be satisfied with slavery, as it is and where it is. You think the institution just and beneficial. The very able gentleman from Virginia (Mr. SEDDON), who commands the respect of all by the frankness and sincerity of his speech, has said that he believes slavery to be the condition in which the African is to be educated up to freedom. He does not believe in perpetual slavery. He believes the time will come when the slave, through the beneficent influences of the circumstances which surround him, will rise in intelligence, capacity, and character, to the dignity of a freeman, and will be free.

We cannot agree with you, and therefore do not propose to allow slavery where we are responsible for it, outside of your State limits, and under National jurisdiction. But we do not mean to interfere with it at all within State limits. So far as we are concerned, you can work out your experiment there in peace. We shall rejoice if no evil comes from it to you or yours. [Mr. CHASE's time having expired, he was unanimously invited to proceed.]

Aside from the Territorial question—the question of slavery outside of the slave States—I know of but one serious difficulty. I refer to the question concerning fugitives from service. The clause in the Constitution concerning this class of persons is regarded by almost all men, North and South, as a stipulation for the surrender to their masters of slaves escaping into free States. The people of the free States, however, who believe that slaveholding is wrong, cannot and will not aid in the reclamation, and the stipulation becomes therefore a dead letter. You complain of bad faith, and the complaint is retorted by denunciations of the cruelty which would drag back to bondage the poor slave who has escaped from it. You, thinking slavery right, claim the fulfilment of the stipulation; we, thinking slavery wrong, cannot fulfil the stipulation without consciousness of participation in wrong. Here is a real difficulty, but it seems to me not insuperable. It will not do for us to say to you, in justification of non-performance, "the stipulation is immoral, and therefore we cannot execute it;" for you deny the immorality, and we cannot assume to judge for you.

On the other hand, you ought not to exact from us the literal performance of the stipulation when you know that we cannot perform it without conscious culpability. A true solution of the difficulty seems to be attainable by regarding it as a simple case where a contract, from changed circumstances, cannot be fulfilled exactly as made. A court of equity in such a case decrees execution as near as may be. It requires the party who cannot perform to make compensation for non-performance. Why cannot the same principle be applied to the rendition of fugitives from service? We cannot surrender—but we can compensate. Why not, then, avoid all difficulties on all sides, and show respectively good faith and good will by providing and accepting compensation where masters reclaim escaping servants and prove their right of reclamation under the Constitution? Instead of a judgment for rendition, let there be a judgment for compensation, determined by the true value of the services, and let the same judgment assure freedom to the fugitive. The cost to the National Treasury would be as nothing in comparison with the evils of discord and strife. All parties would be gainers.

What I have just said is, indeed, not exactly to the point of the present discussion. But I refer to this matter to show how easily the greatest difficulties may be adjusted if approached in a truly just, generous, and patriotic spirit.

I refer to it also in order to show you that, if we do not concede all your wishes, it is because our ideas of justice, duty, and honor forbid, and not because we cherish any hostile or aggressive sentiments. We will go as far as we can to meet you—come you also as far as you can to meet us. Join at least in the declaration we propose. Your people have confidence in you. They will believe you. The declaration, made with substantial unanimity by this Conference, will tranquillize public sentiment, and give a chance for reason to resume its sway, and patriotic counsels to gain a hearing.

Do you say that after all what we propose embodies no substantial guarantees of immunity to slavery through the perversion of Federal powers? We reply that we think the Constitution as it stands, interpreted honestly and executed faithfully, is sufficient for all practical purposes; and that you will find all desirable security in the legislation or non-legislation of Congress. If you think otherwise, we are ready to join you in recommending a National Convention to propose amendments to the Constitution in the regular and legitimate way. Kentucky, a slave State, has proposed such a Convention; Illinois, a free State, has joined in the proposition. Join us, then, in recommending such a Convention, and assure us that you will abide by its decision. We will join you and give a similar assurance.

This, gentlemen, is the proposition we make you to-day. It is embodied in the amendment just submitted. Is it not a fair proposition? It is a plain declaration of facts which cannot reasonably be questioned, and a plain submission of all disputed questions to the only proper tribunal for the settlement of such questions—that of the American people, acting through a National Convention.

The only alternative to this proposition is the proposition that the present Congress be called upon to submit to the States a thirteenth article embodying the amendments recommended by the committee. In order to the submission of these amendments to the States by Congress, a two-thirds vote in each House is necessary. That, I venture to say, cannot be obtained. Were it otherwise, who can assure you that the new article will obtain the sanction of three-fourths of the States, without which it is a nullity? As a measure to defeat all adjustment, I can understand this proposition. As a measure of pacification, I do not understand it. There is, in my judgment, no peace in it. Gentlemen here, of patriotism and intelligence, think otherwise. I am sorry that I cannot agree with them.

Gentlemen say, if this proposition cannot prevail, every slave State will secede; or, as some prefer to phrase it, will resort to revolution. I forbear to discuss eventualities. I must say, however, and say plainly, that considerations such as these will not move me from my recognized duty to my country and its Constitution. And let me say for the people of the free States, that they are a thoughtful people, and are much in earnest in this business. They do not delegate their right of private judgment. They love their institutions and the Union. They will not surrender the one nor give up the other without great struggles and great sacrifices. Upon the question of the maintenance of an unbroken Union and a whole country they never were, and it is my firm conviction they never will be divided. Gentlemen who think they will be, even in the worst contingency, will, I think, be disappointed. If forced to the last extremity, the people will meet the issue as they best may; but be assured they will meet it with no discordant councils.

Gentlemen, Mr. LINCOLN will be inaugurated on the 4th of March. He will take an oath to protect and defend the Constitution of the United States—of the whole—of all the United States. That oath will bind him to take care that the laws be faithfully executed throughout the United States. Will secession absolve him from that oath? Will it diminish, by one jot or tittle, its awful obligation? Will attempted revolution do more than secession? And if not—and the oath and the obligation remain—and the President does his duty and undertakes to enforce the laws, and secession or revolution resists, what then? War! Civil war!

Mr. President, let us not rush headlong into that unfathomable gulf. Let us not tempt this unutterable woe. We offer you a plain and honorable mode of adjusting all difficulties. It is a mode which, we believe, will receive the sanction of the people. We pledge ourselves here that we will do all in our power to obtain their sanction for it. Is it too much to ask you, gentlemen of the South, to meet us on this honorable and practicable ground? Will you not, at least, concede this to the country?

The question on agreeing to said amendment resulted in the following vote:

AYES.—Connecticut, Illinois, Indiana, Iowa, Maine, Massachusetts, New York, New Hampshire, and Vermont—9.

NOES.—Delaware, Kentucky, Maryland, Missouri, New Jersey, North Carolina, Ohio, Pennsylvania, Rhode Island, Tennessee, and Virginia—11.

So the amendment was not agreed to.

Mr. WILMOT:—I wish now to offer an amendment which

embraces an unconditional proposition for the call of a Convention.

Mr. BRONSON:—This has been voted down already.

Mr. WICKLIFFE:—What changes do you gentlemen from Pennsylvania and Ohio wish to make in the report of the committee? Would you adopt that report in a General Convention?

The PRESIDENT:—The Chair rules that the amendment offered by the gentleman from Pennsylvania is not in order.

Messrs. Wilmot, Chase, Corning, and Bronson then entered their dissents from their respective States upon the substitute offered by Mr. Tuck.

Mr. WICKLIFFE:—I hope now that we may be permitted to take the vote at once upon the report of the majority.

Mr. REID:—Before this vote is taken, I deem it my duty to myself and my State to make a remark.

I came here disposed to agree upon terms that would be mutually satisfactory to both sections of the Union. I would agree to any fair terms now, but the propositions contained in the report of the majority, as that report now stands, can never receive my assent. I cannot recommend them to Congress or to the people of my own State. They do not settle the material questions involved; they contain no sufficient guarantees for the rights of the South. Therefore, in good faith to the Conference and to the country, I here state that I cannot and will not agree to them.

Mr. CLEVELAND:—If the gentlemen from the South, after we have yielded so much as we have, assert that these propositions will not be satisfactory to the slave States, I, for one, will not degrade myself by voting for them.

Mr. WICKLIFFE:—I insist now upon taking the vote.

The PRESIDENT:—The rules of the Conference do not require the vote to be taken upon this proposition by sections.

Mr. WICKLIFFE:—We have not heretofore adhered to the rules. Let us vote then on the whole as a proposition, and not by sections.

Mr. SEDDON:—I think we should take the vote by sections. It is certainly within the discretion of the President to rule that the vote may be so taken. The rules do not apply to an article which is composed of many sections. We certainly should vote upon them separately.

Mr. BROCKENBROUGH:—I desire now to get the amendment which I have proposed once more before the Conference. I move to amend by adding to the first section a clause which shall provide that

"The rights of the slave States shall be protected by all the departments of the territorial government during its continuance."

By the section as it now stands, the rights of the North are absolute; those of the South should be equally clear. It is true that the section contains a distinct recognition of the relation of master and slave, but this recognition is in negative terms. It is certainly the duty of the territorial legislature and government to protect these rights wherever they are invaded. If this is so, why not declare it in the provision?

Mr. WILMOT:—I desire to ask whether this proposition is in order.

Mr. BROCKENBROUGH:—I insist that it is. I assert the existence of certain rights, and I want these rights protected under the Constitution. Rights without remedies are anomalies of which the law knows nothing.

Mr. WILMOT:—I feel constrained to oppose any amendment of this kind.

The PRESIDENT:—The Chair is inclined to rule this amendment as not in order.

Mr. RUFFIN:—Before the final vote is taken, I wish to say a word by way of explanation. My colleague says he cannot vote for the report of the committee because he does not approve the whole of it. I do not like the first article, but the report as a whole is a great improvement upon the Constitution as it now stands. I think the report ought to go before the people. If we can secure what the report proposes, we are certainly no worse off. I wish to submit it to my people, and thus have them to judge for themselves whether they will adopt it.

Mr. MOREHEAD, of North Carolina:—I would not say a word were it not for the words that have fallen from my colleague—Governor REID. I came here to try to save the Union. I have labored hard to that end. I hope and believe the report of the majority, if adopted, will save the Union. I wish to carry these propositions before the people. I believe that the people of North Carolina and of the Union will adopt them. Give us an opportunity to appeal to the generosity of the people of the whole Union. Certainly no Southern man can object to submitting these propositions to the popular vote.

Mr. LOOMIS:—I am content to vote for the first article.

Mr. CARRUTHERS:—I only desire to say for my State that if you will give us these propositions, Tennessee will adopt them, and it will sink secession beyond any hope of resurection.

Mr. BARRINGER:—I cannot say that I am gratified with the display which I have just witnessed in these appeals from the Conference to the people. We come here to deal with facts, not theories. I do not speak with the confidence of some with respect to the action of some of the people. I know the people of the South, and I tell you this hollow compromise will never satisfy them, nor will it bring back the seceded States. We are acting for the people who are not here. We are their delegates that have come here, not to demand indemnity for the past, but security for the future. This is my opinion. You will see whether I am right or not. We could stand upon the CRITTENDEN proposition or the Virginia alternative. With Virginia in our favor we could have stood upon either. You, gentlemen of the North, might as well have consented to either as to the report which is now presented. I desire the preservation of the Union; I would go for this scheme if that would accomplish it. But it will not. There is great force in the statement of the gentleman from Ohio, Mr. CHASE, in which he says there is no importance to a scheme which goes from this Conference to the States only by a majority of one or two States. If one or two States only, which are here, reject this compromise, it will be rejected entirely. Once more I say it would have been better for all to have stood upon the Virginia alternative.

Mr. STOCKTON:—I have not much to say, sir. I rise with a sadness which almost prevents my utterance. I was born at Princeton. My heart has always beat for the Union. I have heard these discussions with pain from the commencement. Shall we deliberate over any proposition which shall save the Union? The country is in jeopardy. We are called upon to save it. New Jersey and Delaware came here for that purpose, and no other. They have laid aside every other motive; they have yielded every thing to the general good of the country.

The report of the majority of the committee meets their concurrence. Republicans and Democrats alike, have dropped their opinions, for politics should always disappear in the presence of a great question like this. Politics should not be thought of in view of the question of disunion. By what measure of execration will posterity judge a man who contributed toward the dissolution of the Union? Shall we stand here and higgle about terms when the roar of the tornado is heard that threatens to sweep our Government from the face of the earth? Believe me, sir, this is a question of peace or war.

In the days of Rome, Curtius threw himself into the chasm when told by the oracle that the sacrifice of his life would save his country. Alas! is there no Curtius here? The alternative is a dreadful one to contemplate if we cannot adopt these propositions and secure peace. It is useless to attempt to dwarf this movement of the South by the name of treason. Call it by what name you will, it is a revolution, and this is a right which the people of this country have derived in common from their ancestors.

Mr. GUTHRIE:—I now move that we proceed to take the vote, and propose to take it upon the first section of the report of the majority.

Mr. ELLIS:—I move so to amend the rule that when the report is taken up each section and each distinct proposition shall be voted on separately.

The PRESIDENT:—I think this motion is out of order, and the question will be taken on the motion of the gentleman from Kentucky for the adoption of the first section, which the Secretary will now read.

SECTION 1. In all the present territory of the United States north of the parallel of 36° 30′ of north latitude, involuntary servitude, except in punishment of crime, is prohibited. In all the present territory south of that line, the status of persons held to involuntary service or labor, as it now exists, shall not be changed; nor shall any law be passed by Congress or the Territorial Legislature to hinder or prevent the taking of such persons from any of the States of this Union to said territory, nor to impair the rights arising from said relation; but the same shall be subject to judicial cognizance in the Federal courts, according to the course of the common law. When any Territory north or south of said line, within such boundary as Congress may prescribe, shall contain a population equal to that required for a member of Congress, it shall, if its form of government be republican, be admitted into the Union on an equal footing with the original States, with or without involuntary servitude, as the Constitution of such State may provide.

The question on agreeing to said section resulted as follows—Indiana declining to vote:

AYES.—Delaware, Kentucky, Maryland, New Jersey, Ohio, Pennsylvania, Rhode Island, and Tennessee—8.

NOES.—Connecticut, Illinois, Iowa, Maine, Massachusetts, Missouri, New York, North Carolina, New Hampshire, Vermont, and Virginia—11.

And the section was not agreed to.

The following gentlemen dissented from the votes of their respective States: Mr. RUFFIN and Mr. MOREHEAD, of North Carolina; Mr. TOTTEN, of Tennessee; Mr. COALTER and Mr. HOUGH, of Missouri; Mr. BRONSON, Mr. CORNING, Mr. DODGE, Mr. WOOL, and Mr. GRANGER, of New York; Mr. MEREDITH and Mr. WILMOT, of Pennsylvania; Mr. RIVES and Mr. SUMMERS, of Virginia; Mr. CLAY and Mr. BUTLER, of Kentucky; and Mr. LOGAN, of Illinois.

The vote was taken in the midst of much partially suppressed excitement, and the announcement of the vote of different States occasioned many sharp remarks of dissent or approval. After the vote was announced, for some minutes no motion was made, and the delegates engaged in an informal conversation.

Mr. TURNER finally moved a reconsideration of the vote.

Mr. GRANGER:—To say that I am disappointed by the result of this vote, would fail to do justice to my feelings. I move that the Conference adjourn until half-past seven o'clock this evening. I think it well for those gentlemen from the slave States especially, who have by their votes defeated the compromise we have labored so long and so earnestly to secure, to take a little time for consideration. Gentlemen we have yielded much to your fears, much to your apprehensions; we have gone to the very verge of propriety in giving our assent to the committee's report. We have incurred the censure of some of our own people, but we were willing to take the risk of all this censure in order to allay your apprehensions. We expected you to meet us in the path of compromise. Instead of that you reject and spurn our propositions. Take time, gentlemen, for reflection. Beware how you spurn this report, and incur the awful responsibility which will follow. Reject it, and if the country is plunged in war, and the Union endangered, you are the men who will be held responsible.

Mr. President, I have been deeply pained at the manner in which some gentlemen have here spoken of the possible dissolution of this Government. When, perchance, the rude hand of violence shall here have seized upon the muniments and archives of our country's history; when all the monuments of art that time and treasure may here have gathered, shall be destroyed; when these proud domes shall totter to their fall, and the rank grass wave around their mouldering columns; when the very name of WASHINGTON, instead of stirring the blood to patriotic action, shall be a byeword and a reproach—then will this people feel what was the value of the Union!

The motion to reconsider was then adopted by a vote of 14 ayes to 5 noes, and the Conference adjourned to seven o'clock and thirty minutes this evening.

EVENING SESSION—EIGHTEENTH DAY.

WASHINGTON, TUESDAY, *February 26th*, 1861.

THE Conference was called to order pursuant to adjournment by the President.

Mr. WICKLIFFE:—I hope after some of the informal consultations which have been held since the adjournment of the Conference this afternoon, that we may yet be able to bring our minds together, and to adopt the propositions recommended by the committee. It is, however, certain that the vote had better not be taken this evening. I therefore move an adjournment until ten o'clock to morrow morning.

The motion to adjourn was agreed to; ayes 17, noes 3, and the Conference adjourned.

NINETEENTH DAY.

WASHINGTON, WEDNESDAY, *February 27th*, 1861.

THE Conference assembled pursuant to adjournment, and was called to order by President TYLER. Prayer was offered by Rev. Dr. GURLEY.

The PRESIDENT:—The Conference will now proceed to the consideration of the order of the day, the proposals of amendment to the Constitution reported by the majority of the committee.

Mr. GUTHRIE:—I suppose, under the rules which the Conference has adopted, discussion of these proposals is no longer in order. I hope now the Conference will proceed to the vote. The opinions of each delegation are undoubtedly fixed, and cannot be changed by farther argument.

I move you, sir, the adoption of the first section of the report as amended, which I ask to have read by the Secretary.

The section was read by the Secretary, as follows:

SECTION 1. In all the present territory of the United States north of the parallel of 36° 30′ of north latitude, involuntary servitude, except in punishment of crime, is prohibited. In all the present territory south of that line, the status of persons held to involuntary service or labor, as it now exists, shall not be changed; nor shall any law be passed by Congress or the Territorial Legislature to hinder or prevent the taking of such persons from any of the States of this Union to said territory, nor to impair the rights arising from said relation; but the same shall be subject to judicial cognizance in the Federal courts, according to the course of the common law. When any Territory north or south of said line, within such boundary as Congress may prescribe, shall contain a population equal to that required for a member of Congress, it shall, if its form of government be republican, be admitted into the Union on an equal footing with the original States, with or without involuntary servitude, as the Constitution of such State may provide.

The vote upon said section resulted as follows:

AYES.—Delaware, Illinois, Kentucky, Maryland, New Jersey, Ohio, Pennsylvania, Rhode Island, and Tennessee—9.

NOES.—Connecticut, Iowa, Maine, Massachusetts, North Carolina, New Hampshire, Vermont, and Virginia—8.

So the section was adopted.

The vote of New York being called, Mr. KING, temporary Chairman of the delegation, said:

The question arises concerning the vote of New York. Mr. FIELD, one of the delegates from this State, is necessarily absent from the Conference, having left to attend to the argument of a cause in the Supreme Court noted for argument this morning. It is his understanding, and with him that of a majority of the delegation, that the vote of New York is to be cast against this section, and the whole report. Under these circumstances I propose to give the vote of New York as it would be given if Mr. FIELD was present.

Mr. CORNING:—I object to this. The vote of that State should be given as the majority of the commissioners present decide. And I think this is a matter for the delegation, and that the Conference has nothing to do with it.

The PRESIDENT:—An absent member cannot participate in the control of a vote except by general leave of the Convention.

Mr. KING:—If Mr. FIELD is not to be taken into the account, the vote of New York upon this section is divided.*

* I have not heretofore expressed my own opinions upon the action of the Conference or of delegations; but as much has been said about the vote given by New York, or rather the division of the delegation, under which no vote was given, it is due to the parties concerned that I should state my own understanding of the practice of the Conference in this respect. After the rejection of the motion of Mr. CHASE (found on page 209), and the adoption of the proposition of Mr. DENT, so far as my own knowledge goes it was never deemed necessary that the entire delegation from a State should be present in order to cast its vote. I was present all the time, and frequently cast the vote of my own State upon previous consultation with my colleagues, when a majority of the delegation was absent. This was frequently done, to my personal knowledge, by other States: by none more frequently than Virginia. During several of the sessions the President himself was absent, and the chair was filled for the greater part of the time by Mr. ALEXANDER, or Mr. MOREHEAD, of Kentucky. I can recall to mind several occasions when the vote of Virginia was cast by Mr. SEDDON

Mr. EWING :—The vote of Kansas is also divided.

Mr. HACKLEMAN :—The vote of Indiana is divided. The commissioners of Indiana were appointed by virtue of resolutions passed by the Legislature of that State, which require them to report to the Legislature any proposition before voting for it finally, so as to commit the State either for or against it. It is impossible, under the circumstances, to submit this proposition of amendment to the Legislature of Indiana for approval or rejection. Indiana, therefore, declines to vote.

Mr. SLAUGHTER :—As the delegation from Indiana declines to cast its vote, I desire to have my individual vote entered in the affirmative upon this section.

Mr. ELLIS :—For the same reason I desire to have my vote entered in the negative.

The following gentlemen dissented from the vote of their respective States: Mr. Clay and Mr. Morehead, of Kentucky; Mr. Ruffin and Mr. Morehead, of North Carolina; Mr. Meredith and Mr. Wilmot, of Pennsylvania; Mr. Totten, of Tennessee; Mr. Cook, of Illinois; Mr. Rives and Mr. Summers, of Virginia; and Mr. Chase and Mr. Wolcott, of Ohio.

Mr. GUTHRIE :—I move the adoption of the second section of the report as amended, and ask that it may be read.

The Secretary read it as follows:

Section 2. No territory shall be acquired by the United States, except by discovery, and for naval and commercial stations, depots, and transit routes, without the concurrence of a majority of all the Senators from States which allow involuntary servitude, and a majority of all the Senators from States which prohibit that relation; nor shall territory be acquired by treaty, unless the votes of a majority of the Senators from each class of States hereinbefore mentioned be cast as a part of the two-thirds majority necessary to the ratification of such treaty.

The vote on the adoption of section two was taken, and resulted as follows:

Ayes.—Delaware, Indiana, Kentucky, Maryland, Missouri, New Jersey, Ohio, Pennsylvania, Rhode Island, Tennessee, and Virginia—11.

Noes.—Connecticut, Illinois, Iowa, Maine, Massachusetts, North Carolina, New Hampshire, and Vermont—8.

alone, no other member of his delegation being present. When the question arose upon the vote of New York, I was surprised that this point was not insisted upon; but deeming it a matter exclusively for the delegation from that State to settle, I did not think the case one in which others should interfere. L. E. C.

New York and Kansas were divided.

So the section was adopted.

The following gentlemen dissented from the vote of their States: Mr. MEREDITH and Mr. WILMOT, of Pennsylvania; Mr. RUFFIN and Mr. MOREHEAD, of North Carolina; Mr TYLER, of Virginia; Mr. CLAY, of Kentucky; and Mr. HACKLEMAN and Mr. ORTH, of Indiana.

Mr. GUTHRIE:—I now move the adoption of the third section of the report as amended, and request that it may be read.

The Secretary proceeded to read as follows:

SECTION 3. Neither the Constitution nor any amendment thereof shall be construed to give Congress power to regulate, abolish, or control, within any State, the relation established or recognized by the laws thereof touching persons held to labor or involuntary service therein, nor to interfere with or abolish involuntary service in the District of Columbia without the consent of Maryland and without the consent of the owners, or making the owners who do not consent just compensation; nor the power to interfere with or prohibit representatives and others from bringing with them to the District of Columbia, retaining and taking away, persons so held to labor or service; nor the power to interfere with or abolish involuntary service in places under the exclusive jurisdiction of the United States within those States and Territories where the same is established or recognized; nor the power to prohibit the removal or transportation of persons held to labor or involuntary service in any State or Territory of the United States to any other State or Territory thereof, where it is established or recognized by law or usage; and the right during transportation, by sea or river, of touching at ports, shores, and landings, and of landing in case of distress, shall exist; but not the right of transit in or through any State or Territory, or of sale or traffic, against the laws thereof. Nor shall Congress have power to authorize any higher rate of taxation on persons held to labor or service than on land.

The bringing into the District of Columbia of persons held to labor or service for sale, or placing them in depots to be afterwards transferred to other places for sale as merchandise, is prohibited.

The question on the adoption of said section resulted in the following vote:

AYES.—Delaware, Illinois, Kentucky, Maryland, Missouri, New Jersey, North Carolina, Ohio, Pennsylvania, Rhode Island, Tennessee, and Virginia—12.

NOES.—Connecticut, Indiana, Iowa, Maine, Massachusetts, New Hampshire, and Vermont—7.

New York and Kansas were divided.

So the section was adopted.

The following gentlemen dissented from the vote of their

States: Mr. Clay, of Kentucky; Mr. Cook, of Illinois; Mr. Slaughter, of Indiana; and Mr. Chase, and Mr. Wolcott, of Ohio.

Mr. GUTHRIE :—I move the adoption of the fourth section of the report as amended.

And the Secretary read it as follows:

Section 4. The third paragraph of the second section of the fourth article of the Constitution shall not be construed to prevent any of the States, by appropriate legislation, and through the action of their judicial and ministerial officers, from enforcing the delivery of fugitives from labor to the person to whom such service or labor is due.

The question on the adoption of said section resulted in the following vote:

Ayes.—Connecticut, Delaware, Illinois, Indiana, Kentucky, Maryland, Missouri, New Jersey, North Carolina, Ohio, Pennsylvania, Rhode Island, Tennessee, Vermont, and Virginia—15.

Noes.—Iowa, Maine, Massachusetts, and New Hampshire—4.

New York and Kansas were divided.

And the section was adopted.

The following gentlemen dissented from the vote of their respective States: Mr. Baldwin, of Connecticut; Mr. Hackleman and Mr. Orth, of Indiana; and Mr. Chase and Mr. Wolcott, of Ohio.

Mr. GUTHRIE :—I now move the adoption of the fifth section of the report as amended.

It was read by the Secretary as follows:

Section 5. The foreign slave-trade is hereby forever prohibited; and it shall be the duty of Congress to pass laws to prevent the importation of slaves, coolies, or persons held to service or labor, into the United States and the Territories from places beyond the limits thereof.

The vote on the adoption of this section resulted as follows:

Ayes.—Connecticut, Delaware, Illinois, Indiana, Kentucky, Maryland, Missouri, New Jersey, New York, New Hampshire, Ohio, Pennsylvania, Rhode Island, Tennessee, Vermont, and Kansas—16.

Noes.—Iowa, Maine, Massachusetts, North Carolina, and Virginia—5.

So this section was adopted.

The following gentlemen dissented from the vote of their respective States: Mr. Baldwin, of Connecticut; Mr. Clay, of Kentucky; Mr. Ruffin and Mr. Morehead, of North Carolina; Mr. Wolcott and Mr. Chase, of Ohio; and Mr. Hackleman and Mr. Orth, of Indiana.

Mr. GUTHRIE:—I move the adoption of the sixth section of the report as amended, and desire that the Secretary may read that also.

The Secretary read as follows:

SECTION 6. The first, third, and fifth sections, together with this section of these amendments, and the third paragraph of the second section of the first article of the Constitution, and the third paragraph of the second section of the fourth article thereof, shall not be amended or abolished without the consent of all the States.

The vote on the adoption of this section stood as follows:

AYES.—Delaware, Illinois, Kentucky, Maryland, Missouri, New Jersey, Ohio, Pennsylvania, Rhode Island, Tennessee, and Kansas—11.

NOES.—Connecticut, Indiana, Iowa, Maine, Massachusetts, North Carolina, New Hampshire, Vermont, and Virginia—9.

The State of New York was divided.

And this section was adopted.

The following gentlemen dissented from the vote of their States:—Mr. RUFFIN and Mr. MOREHEAD, of North Carolina; Mr. CHASE and Mr. WOLCOTT, of Ohio; Mr. COOK, of Illinois; and Mr. SUMMERS and Mr. RIVES, of Virginia.

Mr. GUTHRIE:—I move the adoption of the seventh section of the report, as amended.

The Secretary read as follows:

SECTION 7. Congress shall provide by law that the United States shall pay to the owner the full value of his fugitive from labor, in all cases where the marshal, or other officer, whose duty it was to arrest such fugitive, was prevented from so doing by violence or intimidation from mobs or riotous assemblages, or when, after arrest, such fugitive was rescued by like violence or intimidation, and the owner thereby deprived of the same; and the acceptance of such payment shall preclude the owner from further claim to such fugitive. Congress shall provide by law for securing to the citizens of each State the privileges and immunities of citizens in the several States.

The vote on the adoption of this section was as follows:

AYES.—Delaware, Illinois, Indiana, Kentucky, Maryland, New Jersey, New Hampshire, Ohio, Pennsylvania, Rhode Island, Tennessee, and Kansas—12.

NOES.—Connecticut, Iowa, Maine, Missouri, North Carolina, Vermont, and Virginia—7.

The vote of New York was divided.

So this last section was also adopted.

The following gentlemen dissented from the vote of their

respective States :—Mr. Ruffin and Mr. Morehead, of North Carolina; Mr. Totten, of Tennessee; Mr. Hackleman and Mr. Orth, of Indiana; and Mr. Chase and Mr. Wolcott, of Ohio.

Mr. CHASE :—The sections which have been adopted severally, as a whole may not be acceptable to a majority of the Conference. They have been adopted by different votes and different majorities. I think a vote should be taken upon them collectively, in order that we may know whether, as a single proposition, they meet the approbation of the Conference. I move that a vote be taken upon the several sections as a whole.

The PRESIDENT:—It is the opinion of the Chair that this motion is not in order. Each section, when once approved by a majority of votes, stands as the order of the Conference. These sections have been severally taken up, amended, and adopted, and no further vote is necessary or proper, except by way of reconsideration.

Mr. CHASE :—I think the motion an important one, and with all deference, appeal from the decision of the Chair to the Conference.

The PRESIDENT :—The question is, Shall the decision of the Chair stand as the order of the Conference?

Mr. CHASE :—As I have no wish except to secure a fair vote, and the opinion of the Chair may be technically correct, I will withdraw my appeal.

Mr. FRANKLIN :—Having adopted the report of the committee, I think now there should be an expression of the Conference upon the question of secession. I therefore move the adoption of the following resolution:

Resolved, As the sense of this Convention, that the highest political duty of every citizen of the United States is his allegiance to the Federal Government created by the Constitution of the United States, and that no State of this Union has any constitutional right to secede therefrom, or to absolve the citizens of such State from their allegiance to the Government of the United States.

Mr. BARRINGER :—I move to lay that resolution on the table. This is a Convention to propose amendments to the Constitution, not to make commentaries upon that instrument.

Mr. CLEVELAND :—I ask a vote by States.

The question was taken by States, and resulted as follows:

AYES.—Delaware, Kentucky, Maryland, Missouri, New Jersey, North Carolina, Ohio, Tennessee, and Virginia—9.

NOES.—Connecticut, Illinois, Indiana, Iowa, Maine, Massachusetts, New York, New Hampshire, Pennsylvania, Rhode Island, Vermont, and Kansas—12.

And the Convention refused to lay the resolution upon the table.

Mr. COALTER:—I offer the following amendment: strike out all after the word resolve, and insert as follows:

"The term of office of all Presidents and Vice-Presidents of the United States, hereafter elected, shall be six years; and any person once elected to either of said offices shall ever after be ineligible to the same office."

The amendment of Mr. COALTER was rejected by a *viva voce* vote.

Mr. SEDDON:—I now move to amend by striking out all after the word "resolved" in Mr. FRANKLIN's resolution, and insert a series of amendments hitherto proposed by myself, as follows:

To secure concert and promote harmony between the slaveholding and non-slaveholding sections of the Union, the assent of the majority of the Senators from the slaveholding States, and of the majority of the Senators from the non-slaveholding States, shall be requisite to the validity of all action of the Senate, on which the ayes and noes may be called by five Senators.

And on a written declaration, signed and presented for record on the Journal of the Senate by a majority of the Senators from either the non-slaveholding or slaveholding States, of their want of confidence in any officer or appointee of the Executive, exercising functions exclusively or continuously within the class of States, or any of them, which the signers represent, then such officer shall be removed by the Executive; and if not removed at the expiration of ten days from the presentation of such declaration, the office shall be deemed vacant, and open to new appointment.

The connection of every State with the Union is recognized as depending on the continuing assent of its people, and compulsion shall in no case, nor under any form, be attempted by the Government of the Union against a State acting in its collective or organic capacity. Any State, by the action of a convention of its people, assembled pursuant to a law of its legislature, is held entitled to dissolve its relation to the Federal Government, and withdraw from the Union; and, on due notice given of such withdrawal to the Executive of the Union, he shall appoint two commissioners, to meet two commissioners to be appointed by the Governor of the State, who, with the aid, if needed from the disagreement of the commissioners, of an umpire, to be selected by a majority of them, shall equitably adjudicate and determine finally a partition of the rights and obligations of the withdrawing State;

and such adjudication and partition being accomplished, the withdrawal of such State shall be recognized by the Executive, and announced by public proclamation to the world.

But such withdrawing State shall not afterwards be readmitted into the Union without the assent of two-thirds of the States constituting the Union at the time of the proposed readmission.

I desire to get these amendments on the Journal. It is my duty to offer them, and I wish the Journal to show that I have performed that duty.

Mr. FRANKLIN:—I then move to lay the amendment on the table, and to give the gentleman leave to have it inserted in the Journal. That will accomplish his purpose.

The question was taken on the motion to lay the amendment on the table, and resulted in an affirmative vote.

Mr. RUFFIN:—I regard the mission of this Convention as now performed, and I hope we shall take up no new questions, which can only distract and divide us. I therefore move to postpone the consideration of this resolution indefinitely.

The question was taken on Mr. RUFFIN's motion, with the following result:—

AYES.—Delaware, Kentucky, Maryland, Missouri, New Jersey, North Carolina, Ohio, Rhode Island, Tennessee, and Virginia—10.

NOES.—Connecticut, Illinois, Indiana, Iowa, Maine, Massachusetts, and Pennsylvania—7.

The vote of New York was divided.

Messrs. DUNCAN and AMES dissented from the vote of Rhode Island.

Mr. GUTHRIE:—It will be necessary that this proposition be presented to Congress in an authentic form, and I suppose it will not be necessary for the Convention to continue its sessions until this presentation is made. I therefore offer the following preamble:

TO THE CONGRESS OF THE UNITED STATES:

The Convention assembled upon the invitation of the State of Virginia to adjust the unhappy differences which now disturb the peace of the Union and threaten its continuance, make known to the Congress of the United States that their body convened in the city of Washington on the 4th instant, and continued in session until the 27th.

There were in the body, when action was taken upon that which is here submitted, one hundred and thirty-three commissioners, representing the following States: Maine, New Hampshire, Vermont, Massachusetts, Rhode

Island, Connecticut, New York, New Jersey, Pennsylvania, Delaware, Maryland, Virginia, North Carolina, Tennessee, Kentucky, Missouri, Ohio, Indiana, Illinois, Iowa, and Kansas.

They have approved what is herewith submitted, and respectfully request that your honorable body will submit it to conventions in the States as an article of amendment to the Constitution of the United States.

Mr. RANDOLPH:—I move the adoption of the preamble, and that the same, with the propositions already adopted, be authenticated by the present Secretary, and that all be presented by the President of this Convention to the Senate and House of Representatives, with a respectful request for their passage.

This motion was agreed to.

Mr. BARRINGER:—As the labors of the Convention are now closed, I presume there is no occasion for continuing the injunction of secrecy. As notes of the proceedings have been taken with a view, I presume, to publication, I now move that the injunction of secrecy against speaking of the action of the Convention, or the publication of its proceedings, be removed.

The motion of Mr. BARRINGER was agreed to by a *viva voce* vote.

Mr. JOHNSON:—I desire here to have printed in the Journal the following resolution.

Leave was granted to Mr. JOHNSON as requested, and his resolution was as follows:

Resolved, That while the adoption, by the States of South Carolina, Georgia, Florida, Alabama, Mississippi, Louisiana, and Texas, of ordinances declaring the dissolution of their relation with the Union, is an event deeply to be deplored; and while abstaining from any judgment on their conduct, we would express the earnest hope that they may soon see cause to resume their honored places in this Confederacy of States; yet to the end that such return may be facilitated, and from the conviction that the Union being formed by the assent of the people of the respective States, and being compatible only with freedom, and the republican institutions guaranteed to each, cannot and ought not to be maintained by force, we deprecate any effort by the Federal Government to coerce in any form the said States to reunion or submission, as tending to irreparable breach, and leading to incalculable ills; and we earnestly invoke the abstinence from all counsels or measures of compulsion toward them.

Mr. POLLOCK:—The Committee on Finance have made an examination of the expenses which have been incurred for printing, stationery, &c., by the Conference. It has been already stated that the expense of printing the Journal is met by the city of Washington. The additional expense incurred amounts to $735. If this is equally apportioned among the States represented it will amount to $35 each. It is for the Conference to decide in what manner the assessment shall be made.

Mr. BROWNE:—I offer the following resolution:

Resolved, That the report of the committee be received and accepted; that the committee be continued, and requested to make the necessary disbursements; and that the States now pay over the sum assessed to the chairman.

And the resolution was unanimously adopted.

Mr. LOOMIS:—I take great pleasure in presenting to the Conference the following letter, which has been addressed by the proprietors of the hall to the Secretary. I ask that the letter may be read, and I also offer the following resolution.

The letter was read, as follows:

CRAFTS J. WRIGHT, ESQ.,
Secretary Conference Convention:

SIR:—Please inform the Convention that we have tendered, free of charge, the use of our Hall and lights, which they have occupied. We hope the use may be sanctified by restoring peace to the Union.

We are, respectfully, &c.,
J. C. & H. A. WILLARD.

February 23*d*, 1861.

And the resolution, which was unanimously adopted, was as follows:

Resolved, That the thanks of this Convention are justly due, and are hereby given, to the Messrs. Willard, for the liberal and generous tender, free of charge, of the use of the Hall and the lights, for the purposes expressed in their letter to the Secretary; and that the Secretary be requested to communicate to them a copy of this resolution.

Mr. DODGE offered the following resolution, and that, too, was unanimously agreed to:

Resolved, That the thanks of this Convention are justly due and hereby given to the Mayor and Council of the city of Washington, for their kindness and liberality to the members of this Convention, in defraying so large an amount of their expenses for printing and stationery, and also for the officers to protect this hall and the members from intrusion whilst in session, and that the Secretary be requested to communicate the same to said parties.

On motion of Mr. RANDOLPH, the thanks of the Conference

were tendered to the clergymen of the city for their services during the Conference.

The thanks of the Conference were also presented to the Secretary and his assistants.

Mr. EWING:—I move the adoption of the following:

Resolved, That the thanks of this Convention be tendered to the President, for the dignified and impartial manner in which he has presided over the deliberations of this body.

The resolution being seconded by Mr. HACKLEMAN, it was unanimously adopted; whereupon President TYLER addressed the Conference as follows:

"GENTLEMEN OF THE CONFERENCE:

"The labors of this Convention are drawing to a close. Before we separate never in this world to meet again, I am much pleased that the resolution you have just adopted gives me an opportunity of uttering a few words of congratulation and farewell.

"We came together at a most important and critical time. One of the oldest members of the American Union, a commonwealth which had contributed its full share to the honor and glory of the nation—having as great interests at stake as any other member of the sisterhood of States—summoned you here to consider new additions to our Constitution, which the experience of near three-quarters of a century had taught us were required. I expected from the first that you would approach the consideration of the new and important questions which must arise here, with that patriotism and intelligence which belongs to the descendants of the patriots of the Revolution and the statesmen of the Convention of 1787. I have not been disappointed. In the whole course of a public life, much longer than usually falls to the lot of man, I have been associated with many bodies of my fellow-citizens, convened for legislative or other purposes, but I here declare that it has never been my good fortune to meet with an association of more intelligent, thoughtful, or patriotic men, than that over which I have been here called to preside. I cannot but hope and believe that the blessing of GOD will follow and rest upon the result of your labors, and that such result will bring to our country that quiet and peace which every patriotic heart so earnestly desires. I thank you most sincerely for that kindness and partiality on your part which induced you to call me to the honorable position of your presiding officer, and for the courtesy so uniformly extended in the discharge of the responsible duties of that position.

"Gentlemen, farewell! I go to finish the work you have assigned me, of presenting your recommendations to the two Houses of Congress, and to ask those bodies to lay your proposals of amendment before the people of the American Union. Although these proposals are not in all respects what I could have desired—although I should have preferred the adoption of those recommended by the Legislature of Virginia, because I know they would have been acceptable to my own constituents, still it is my duty to give them my official approval and support. It is not to be expected that entire unanimity of opinion should exist among the representatives of so large a population, and so many diversified interests, as now comprise the Republic of the United States. It is probable that the result to which you have arrived is the best that under all the circumstances could be expected. So far as in me lies, therefore, I shall recommend its adoption.

"May you have a happy and safe return to your constituents and your families! May you all inculcate among your people a spirit of mutual forbearance and concession; and may GOD protect our country and the Union of these States, which was committed to us as the blood-bought legacy of our heroic ancestors!"

Mr. WICKLIFFE:—I move that the Convention do now adjourn, its labors having come to an end; and I would suggest that the delegates meet informally and take leave of each other at three o'clock this afternoon.

Mr. Browne moved that the Conference adjourn without day, and his motion was adopted by the following vote:

Ayes.—Delaware, Illinois, Kentucky, Maryland, New Jersey, Ohio, Rhode Island, Tennessee, and Vermont—9.

Noes.—Connecticut, Indiana, Missouri, North Carolina, and Pennsylvania—5.

And the Conference adjourned without day.

APPENDIX.

No. I.

Before the final vote was taken upon the proposals of amendment to the Constitution of the United States, reported by the General Committee of which Mr. Guthrie was Chairman, and the votes upon the various substitutes offered for such proposals, there were *twenty-one* States represented in the Conference.

Maine and Iowa were represented by their respective Congressional delegations; Tennessee, Ohio, Kentucky, Indiana, Delaware, Illinois, New Jersey, New York, Pennsylvania, Massachusetts, Rhode Island, and Missouri, by delegates appointed by their respective Legislatures, under joint resolutions which are here inserted; New Hampshire, Vermont, Connecticut, Maryland, North Carolina, Indiana, and Kansas, by delegates appointed by their respective Governors.

The resolutions of Virginia originated the call for the Conference.

Michigan, Wisconsin, Minnesota, California, and Oregon were not represented. South Carolina, Florida, Georgia, Alabama, Mississippi, Arkansas, and Texas had passed ordinances of secession previous to the meeting of the Conference. Messrs. Benjamin and Slidell, the Senators from Louisiana, withdrew from the Senate of the United States before the proposed amendments to the Constitution were reported to the Conference.

The following resolutions of their respective States were presented by the delegates to the Committee on Credentials, and were ordered by the Conference to be printed, on the motion of Mr. Chase.*

* See page 54, Proceedings of the Conference.

TENNESSEE.

RESOLUTIONS *proposing amendments to the Constitution of the United States.*

Resolved by the General Assembly of the State of Tennessee, That a Convention of delegates from all the slaveholding States should assemble at Nashville, Tennessee, or such other place as a majority of the States coöperating may designate, on the fourth day of February, 1861, to digest and define a basis upon which, if possible, the Federal Union and the constitutional rights of the slave States may be perpetuated and preserved.

Resolved, That the General Assembly of the State of Tennessee appoint a number of delegates to said Convention, of our ablest and wisest men, equal to our whole delegation in Congress; and that the Governor of Tennessee immediately furnish copies of these resolutions to the Governors of the slaveholding States, and urge the participation of such States in said Convention.

Resolved, That in the opinion of this General Assembly, such plan of adjustment should embrace the following propositions as amendments to the Constitution of the United States:

1. A declaratory amendment that African slaves, as held under the institutions of the slaveholding States, shall be recognized as property, and entitled to the *status* of other property, in the States where slavery exists, in all places within the exclusive jurisdiction of Congress in the slave States, in all the Territories south of 36° 30′; in the District of Columbia; in transit; and whilst temporarily sojourning with the owner in the non-slaveholding States and Territories north of 36° 30′, and when fugitives from the owner, in the several places above named, as well as in all places in the exclusive jurisdiction of Congress in the non-slaveholding States.

2. That all the territory now owned, or which may be hereafter acquired by the United States south of the parallel of 36° 30′; African slavery shall be recognized as existing, and be protected by all the departments of the Federal and Territorial Governments, and in all north of that line, now owned, or to be acquired, it shall not be recognized as existing; and whenever States formed out of any of said territory south of said line, having a population equal to that of a congressional district, shall apply for admission into the Union, the same shall be admitted as slave States, whilst States north of the line, formed out of said territory, and having a population equal to a Congressional district, shall be admitted without slavery; but the States formed out of said territory north and south having been admitted as members of the Union, shall have all the powers over the institution of slavery possessed by the other States of the Union.

3. Congress shall have no power to abolish slavery in places under its exclusive jurisdiction, and situate within the limits of States that permit the holding of slaves.

4. Congress shall have no power to abolish slavery within the District of Columbia, as long as it exists in the adjoining States of Virginia and Maryland, or either, nor without the consent of the inhabitants, nor without just

compensation made to such owners of slaves as do not consent to such abolishment. Nor shall Congress at any time prohibit the officers of the Federal Government or members of Congress whose duties require them to be in said District, from bringing with them their slaves, and holding them as such, during the time their duties may require them to remain there, and afterwards take them from the District.

5. Congress shall have no power to prohibit or hinder the transportation of slaves from one State to another, or the Territory in which slaves are by law permitted to be held, whether that transportation be by land, navigable rivers, or by seas.

6. In addition to the fugitive slave clause, provide that when a slave has been demanded of the Executive authority of the State to which he has fled, if he is not delivered, and the owner permitted to carry him out of the State in peace, the State so failing to deliver, shall pay to the owner the value of such slave, and such damages as he may have sustained in attempting to reclaim his slave, and secure his right of action in the Supreme Court of the United States, with execution against the property of such State and the individuals thereof.

7. No future amendment of the Constitution shall affect the six preceding articles, nor the third paragraph of the second section of the first article of the Constitution, nor the third paragraph of the second section of the fourth article of the Constitution; and no amendments shall be made to the Constitution which will authorize or give to Congress any power to abolish or interfere with slavery in any of the States by whose laws it is, or may be allowed or permitted.

8. That slave property shall be rendered secure in transit through, or whilst temporarily sojourning in, non-slaveholding States or Territories, or in the District of Columbia.

9. An amendment to the effect that all fugitives are to be deemed those offending the laws within the jurisdiction of the State, and who escape therefrom to other States; and that it is the duty of each State to suppress armed invasion of another State.

Resolved, That said Convention of the slaveholding States having agreed upon a basis of adjustment satisfactory to themselves, should, in the opinion of this General Assembly, refer it to a Convention of all the States, slaveholding and non-slaveholding, in the manner following:

It should invite all States friendly to such plan of adjustment, to elect delegates in such manner as to reflect the popular will, to assemble in a Constitutional Convention of all the States North and South, to be held at Richmond, Virginia, on the —— day of February, 1861, to revise and perfect such plan of adjustment, for its reference for final ratification and adoption by a Convention of the States respectively.

Resolved, That should a plan of adjustment, satisfactory to the South, not be acceded to by a requisite number of States to perfect amendments to the Constitution of the United States, it is the opinion of this General Assembly that the slaveholding States should adopt for themselves the Constitution of the United States, with such amendments as may be satisfactory to the slaveholding States, and that they should invite into the Union with them all States of the North which are willing to abide such amended Constitution and frame of Government, severing at once all connections with States refusing such reasonable guarantees to our future safety; such renewed conditions of Federal Union being first submitted for ratification to Convention of all the States respectively.

Resolved, That the Governor of the State of Tennessee furnish copies of these resolutions immediately to the Governors of the non-slaveholding States.

OHIO.

JOINT RESOLUTIONS *of the General Assembly of the State of Ohio, relative to the appointment of Commissioners to the Convention to meet in Washington on the* 4*th of February, proximo. Passed January* 30, 1861.

WHEREAS, The Commonwealth of Virginia has appointed five Commissioners to meet in the City of Washington on the fourth day of February next, with similar Commissioners from other States, and after full and free conference to agree, if practicable, upon some adjustment of the unhappy difficulties now dividing our country, which may be alike satisfactory and honorable to the States concerned; therefore be it

Resolved, by the General Assembly of the State of Ohio, That the Governor, by and with the advice and consent of the Senate, be and he is hereby authorized and empowered to appoint five Commissioners to represent the State of Ohio in said Conference.

Resolved, That while we are not prepared to assent to the terms of settlement proposed by Virginia, and are fully satisfied that the Constitution of the United States as it is, if fairly interpreted and obeyed by all sections of our country, contains ample provisions within itself for the correction of all evils complained, yet a disposition to reciprocate the patriotic spirit of a sister State, and a sincere desire to have harmoniously adjusted all differences between us, induce us to favor the appointment of the Commission as requested.

Resolved, That the Governor be requested to transmit without delay a copy of these Resolutions to each of the Commissioners to be appointed as aforesaid, to the end that they may repair to the City of Washington, on the day hereinbefore named, to meet such Commissioners as may be appointed by any of the States in accordance with the aforesaid propositions of Virginia.

Resolved, That in the opinion of this General Assembly, it will be wise and expedient to adjourn the proposed Convention to a later day, and that the Commissioners to be appointed as aforesaid, are requested to use their influence in procuring an adjournment to the fourth day of April next.

KENTUCKY.

RESOLUTIONS *appointing Commissioners to attend a Conference at Washington City, February 4th, in accordance with the invitation of the Virginia Legislature.*

WHEREAS, The General Assembly of Virginia, with a view to make an effort to preserve the Union and the Constitution in the spirit in which they were established by the Fathers of the Republic, have, by resolution, invited all the States who are willing to unite with her in an earnest effort to adjust the present unhappy controversies, to appoint Commissioners to meet on the 4th of February next, to consider, and if practicable, agree upon some suitable adjustment—

Resolved, That we heartily accept the invitation of our Old Mother Virginia, and that the following six Commissioners, viz.: Wm. O. Butler, James B. Clay, Joshua F. Bell, C. S. Morehead, James Guthrie, and Chas. A. Wickliffe, be appointed to represent the State of Kentucky in the contemplated Convention, whose duty it shall be to repair to the City of Washington, on the day designated, to meet such Commissioners as may be appointed by any of the States in accordance with the foregoing invitation.

Resolved, That if said Commissioners shall agree upon any plan of adjustment requiring amendments to the Federal Constitution, they be requested to communicate the proposed amendments to Congress, for the purpose of having the same submitted by that body, according to the forms of the Constitution, to the several States for ratification.

Resolved, That if said Commissioners cannot agree on an adjustment, or if agreeing, Congress shall refuse to submit for ratification such amendments as they may propose, the Commissioners of this State shall immediately communicate the result to the Executive of this Commonwealth, to be by him laid before this General Assembly.

Resolved, That in the opinion of the General Assembly of Kentucky, the propositions embraced in the resolutions presented to the Senate of the United States by the Hon. JOHN J. CRITTENDEN, so construed, that the first article proposed as an amendment to the Constitution of the United States shall apply to all the territory of the United States now held or hereafter acquired south of latitude 36° 30′, and provide that slavery of the African race shall be effectually protected as property therein during the continuance of the Territorial Government; and the fourth article shall secure to the owners of slaves the right of transit with their slaves between and through the non-slaveholding States and Territories, constitute the basis of such an adjustment of the unhappy controversy which now divides the States of this Confederacy, as would be acceptable to the people of this Commonwealth.

Resolved, That the Governor be, and he is hereby requested to communicate information of the foregoing appointment to the Commissioners above named, at as early a day as practicable, and that he also communicate copies of the foregoing resolutions to the Executive of the respective States.

INDIANA.

A Joint Resolution *authorizing the Governor to appoint Commissioners to meet those sent by other States in Convention on the state of the Union.*

Whereas, The State of Virginia has transmitted to this State resolutions adopted by her General Assembly, inviting all such States as are willing to unite with her in an earnest effort to adjust the unhappy controversies, in the spirit in which the Constitution was originally formed, to send Commissioners to meet those appointed by that State in Convention, to be held in the City of Washington, on the fourth day of February next, to consider, and if possible, to agree upon some suitable adjustment.

And whereas, some of the States to which invitations were extended by the State of Virginia have already responded and appointed their Commissioners; therefore,

Resolved, by the General Assembly of the State of Indiana, That we accept the invitation of the State of Virginia, in the true spirit of fraternal feeling, and that the Governor of the State is hereby directed and empowered to appoint five Commissioners to meet the Commissioners appointed by our sister States, to consult upon the unhappy differences now dividing the country; but the said Commissioners shall take no action that will commit this State until *nineteen* of the States are represented, nor without first having communicated with this General Assembly in regard to such action, and having received the authority of the same so to commit the State.

Resolved, That while we are not prepared to assent to the terms of settlement proposed by the State of Virginia, and are fully satisfied that the Constitution, if fairly interpreted and obeyed, contains ample provisions within itself for the correction of the evils complained of; still, with a disposition to reciprocate the patriotic desire of the State of Virginia, and to have harmoniously adjusted all differences existing between the States of the Union, this General Assembly is induced to respond to the invitation of Virginia, by the appointment of the Commissioners herein provided for; but as the time fixed for the Convention to assemble is so near at hand that the States cannot all be represented, it is expected that the Commissioners on behalf of this State will insist that the Convention adjourn until such time as the States shall have an opportunity of being represented.

Resolved, That his Excellency, the Governor, be requested to transmit copies of these resolutions to the Executives of each of the States of the Union.

DELAWARE.

Joint Resolutions *appointing Commissioners.*

Whereas, The State of Virginia has recommended the holding of a Convention of Delegates from all the States of the Union, at the City of Washington, on the fourth day of February next, for the purpose of taking into consideration and perfecting some plan of adjusting the matters in controversy now so unhappily subsisting in the family of States, and has appointed five Commissioners to represent the people of that Commonwealth in said Convention; and

Whereas, the people of the State of Delaware regard the preservation of the Union as paramount to any political consideration, and are fixed in their determination that Delaware, the first to adopt the Federal Constitution, will be the last to do any act tending to destroy the integrity of the Union; therefore,

Be it resolved by the Senate and House of Representatives of the State of Delaware in General Assembly met, That the Hon. George B. Rodney, Daniel M. Bates, Esq., Dr. Henry Ridgley, Hon. John W. Houston, and William Cannon, Esq., be, and they are hereby appointed Commissioners, on behalf of the State of Delaware, to represent the people of said State in the Convention to be held at Washington, on the fourth day of February next.

Resolved, That in the opinion of this General Assembly, the people of Delaware are thoroughly devoted to the perpetuity of the Union, and that the Commissioners appointed by the foregoing resolution are expected to emulate the example set by the immortal patriots who framed the Federal Constitution, by sacrificing all minor considerations upon the altar of the Union.

Resolved, further, That it shall be the duty of the Secretary of State to furnish a copy of the above preamble and resolutions to each of the Commissioners herein and hereby appointed, duly attested under the great seal of the State.

Resolved, further, That immediately upon the adoption of the foregoing preamble and resolutions, it shall be the duty of the Clerk of the House to transmit to the Secretary of State a copy thereof, certified by him; and when the Secretary of State shall have received said copy so certified, it shall be evidence that said preamble and resolutions were duly adopted by this General Assembly.

ILLINOIS.

WHEREAS, resolutions of the State of Virginia have been communicated to the General Assembly of this State, proposing the appointment of Commissioners by the several States to meet in Convention, on the fourth day of February, A. D. 1861, at Washington.

Resolved by the Senate, the House of Representatives concurring herein, That with the earnest desire for the return of harmony and kind relations among all our sister States, and out of respect to the Commonwealth of Virginia, the Governor of this State be requested to appoint five Commissioners on the part of the State of Illinois, to confer and consult with the Commissioners of other States who shall meet at Washington: *Provided*, That said Commissioners shall at all times be subject to the control of the General Assembly of the State of Illinois.

Resolved, That the appointment of Commissioners by the State of Illinois, in response to the invitation of the State of Virginia, is *not* an expression of opinion on the part of this State that any amendment of the Federal Constitution is requisite to secure to the people of the slaveholding States adequate guarantees for the security of their rights, nor an approval of the basis of settlement of our difficulties proposed by the State of Virginia, but it is an expression of our willingness to unite with the State of Virginia in an earnest effort to adjust the present unhappy controversies in the spirit in which the Constitution was originally formed, and consistently with its principles.

Resolved, That while we are willing to appoint Commissioners to meet in convention with those of other States for consultation upon matters which at present distract our harmony as a nation, we also insist that the appropriate and constitutional method of considering and acting upon the grievances complained of by our sister States, would be by the call of a Convention for the amendment of the Constitution in the manner contemplated by the fifth article of that instrument; and if the States deeming themselves aggrieved, shall request Congress to call such Convention, the Legislature of Illinois will and does concur in such call.

NEW JERSEY.

JOINT RESOLUTIONS *in relation to the Union of the States.*

WHEREAS, the people of New Jersey, conforming to the opinion of "the Father of his Country," consider the unity of the Government, which constitutes the people of the United States one people, a main pillar in the edifice of their independence, the support of their tranquillity at home and peace abroad, of their prosperity, and of that liberty which they so highly prize; and properly estimating the immense value of their National Union to their individual happiness, they cherish a cordial, habitual, and immovable attachment to it as the palladium of their political safety and prosperity; therefore,

1. *Be it resolved by the Senate and General Assembly of the State of New Jersey*, That it is the duty of every good citizen, in all suitable and proper ways, to stand by and sustain the Union of the States as transmitted to us by our fathers.

2. *And be it resolved*, That the Government of the United States is a National Government, and the Union it was designed to perfect is not a mere compact or league; and that the Constitution was adopted in a spirit of mutual compromise and concession by the people of the United States, and can only be preserved by the constant recognition of that spirit.

3. *And be it resolved*, That however undoubted may be the right of the General Government to maintain its authority and enforce its laws over all parts of the country, it is equally certain that forbearance and compromise are indispensable at this crisis to the perpetuity of the Union, and that it is

the dictate of reason, wisdom, and patriotism, peacefully to adjust whatever differences exist between the different sections of the country.

4. *And be it resolved*, That the resolutions and propositions submitted to the Senate of the United States by the Honorable John J. Crittenden, of Kentucky, for the compromise of the questions in dispute between the people of the northern and of the southern States, or any other constitutional method that will permanently settle the question of slavery, will be acceptable to the people of the State of New Jersey, and the Senators and Representatives in Congress from New Jersey be requested and earnestly urged to support those resolutions and propositions.

5. *And be it resolved*, That as the Union of the States is in imminent danger unless the remedies before suggested be speedily adopted, then, as a last resort, the State of New Jersey hereby makes application, according to the terms of the Constitution, of the Congress of the United States, to call a Convention (of the United States) to propose amendments to said Constitution.

6. *And be it resolved*, That such of the States as have in force laws which interfere with the constitutional rights of citizens of the other States, either in regard to their persons or property, or which militate against the just construction of that part of the Constitution that provides that "the citizens of each State shall be entitled to all the privileges and immunities of citizens in the several States," are earnestly urged and requested, for the sake of peace and the Union, to repeal all such laws.

7. *And be it resolved*, That his Excellency Charles S. Olden, Peter D. Vroom, Robert F. Stockton, Benjamin Williamson, Joseph F. Randolph, Frederick T. Frelinghuysen, Rodman M. Price, William C. Alexander, and Thomas J. Stryker, be appointed Commissioners to confer with Congress and our sister States, and urge upon them the importance of carrying into effect the principles and objects of the foregoing resolutions.

8. *And be it resolved*, That the Commissioners above named, in addition to their other powers, be authorized to meet with those now or hereafter to be appointed by our sister State of Virginia, and such Commissioners of other States as have been, or may be hereafter appointed, to meet at Washington on the fourth day of February next.

9. *And be it resolved*, That copies of the foregoing resolutions be sent to the President of the Senate and Speaker of the House of Representatives of the United States, and to the Senators and Representatives in Congress from New Jersey, and to the Governors of the several States.

NEW YORK.

CONCURRENT RESOLUTIONS *appointing Commissioners from this State to meet Commissioners from other States at Washington, on invitation of Virginia.*

WHEREAS, the State of Virginia, by resolutions of her General Assembly, passed the 19th instant, has invited such of the slaveholding and non-slaveholding States as are willing to unite with her, to meet at Washington, on the fourth of February next, to consider, and, if practicable, agree on some suitable adjustment of our national difficulties; and whereas, the people of New York, while they hold the opinion that the Constitution of the United States, as it is, contains all needful guarantees for the rights of the States, are nevertheless ready, at all times, to confer with their brethren upon all alleged grievances; and to do all that can justly be required of them to allay discontent; therefore

Resolved, That David Dudley Field, William Curtis Noyes, James S. Wadsworth, James C. Smith, Amaziah B. James, Erastus Corning, Addison Gardiner, Greene C. Bronson, William E. Dodge, Ex-Governor John A. King, and Major-General John E. Wool, be and are hereby appointed Commissioners, on the part of this State, to meet Commissioners from other States, in the City of Washington, on the fourth day of February next, or so soon thereafter as Commissioners shall be appointed by a majority of the States of the Union, to confer with them upon the complaints of any part of the country, and to suggest such remedies therefor as to them shall seem fit and proper; but the said Commissioners shall at all times be subject to the control of this Legislature, and shall cast five votes to be determined by a majority of their number.

Resolved, That in thus acceding to the request of Virginia, it is not to be understood that this Legislature approves of the propositions submitted by the General Assembly of that State, or concedes the propriety of their adoption by the proposed Convention. But while adhering to the position she has heretofore occupied, New York will not reject an invitation to a conference, which, by bringing together the men of both sections, holds out the possibility of an honorable settlement of our national difficulties, and the restoration of peace and harmony to the country.

Resolved, That the Governor be requested to transmit a copy of the foregoing resolutions to the Executive of the several States, and also to the President of the United States, and to inform the Commissioners without delay of their appointment.

Resolved, That the foregoing resolutions be transmitted to the honorable the Senate, with a request that they concur therein.

PENNSYLVANIA.

RESOLUTIONS *to appoint Commissioners to a Convention of the States.*

WHEREAS, the Legislature of the State of Virginia has invited a meeting of Commissioners from the several States of this Union, to be held in the City of Washington, on the fourth day of February next, to consider, and if practicable, agree upon some suitable adjustment of the unhappy differences which now disturb the business of the country and threaten the dissolution of this Union:

And whereas, in the opinion of this Legislature, no reasonable cause exists for this extraordinary excitement which now pervades some of the States, in relation to their domestic institutions, and while Pennsylvania still adheres to, and cannot surrender the principles which she has always entertained on the subject of slavery, this Legislature is willing to accept the invitation of Virginia, and unite with her in an earnest effort to restore the peace of the country, by such means as may be consistent with the principles upon which the Constitution is founded; therefore,

Resolved by the Senate and House of Representatives of the Commonwealth of Pennsylvania in General Assembly met, That the invitation of the Legislature of Virginia to her sister States, for the appointment of Commissioners to meet in the City of Washington, on the fourth of February next, be and the same is hereby accepted; and that the Governor be, and he is hereby authorized to appoint seven Commissioners for the State of Pennsylvania, whose duty it shall be to repair to the City of Washington on the day designated, to meet such Commissioners as may be appointed by any other States which have not authorized or sanctioned the seizure of the forts, arsenals, or other property of the United States, to consider, and if possible, to agree upon suitable measures for the prompt and final settlement of the difficulties which now exist: *Provided*, That the said Commissioners shall be subject, in all their proceedings, to the instructions of this Legislature.

Resolved, That in the opinion of this Legislature, the people of Pennsylvania do not desire any alteration or amendment of the Constitution of the United States, and any recommendation from this body to that effect, while it does not come within its appropriate and legitimate duties, would not meet with their approval; that Pennsylvania will cordially unite with the other States of the Union in the adoption of any proper constitutional measures adequate to guarantee and secure a more strict and faithful observance of the second section of the fourth article of the Constitution of the United States, which provides, among other things, that "the citizens of each State shall be entitled to all privileges and immunities of citizens of the several States," and that no person held to service or labor in one State under the law thereof, escaping into another, shall in consequence of any law or regulation therein, be discharged from such service or labor, but shall be delivered up on the claim of the party to whom such service or labor may be due.

MASSACHUSETTS.

RESOLVE *for the appointment of Commissioners to attend a Convention to be held in the City of Washington.*

WHEREAS, the Commonwealth of Massachusetts is desirous of a full and free conference with the General Government, and with any or all of the other States of the Union, at any time and on every occasion when such conference may promote the welfare of the country; and whereas, questions of grave moment have arisen touching the powers of the Government and the relations between the different States of the Union; and whereas, the State of Virginia has expressed a desire to meet her sister States in Convention at Washington; therefore,

Resolved, That the Governor of this Commonwealth, by and with the advice and consent of the Council, be and he hereby is authorized to appoint seven persons as Commissioners, to proceed to Washington to confer with the General Government, or with the separate States, or with any association of delegates from such States, and to report their doings to the Legislature at its present session; it being expressly declared that their acts shall be at all times under the control, and subject to the approval or rejection of the Legislature.

RHODE ISLAND.

WHEREAS, the General Assembly of the Commonwealth of Virginia, on the 19th day of January inst., adopted resolutions inviting the sister States of this Union to appoint Commissioners to meet on the fourth day of February next, in the City of Washington, to consider the practicability of agreeing on terms of adjustment of our present national troubles:

Resolved, That the Governor be, and he is hereby authorized to appoint five Commissioners, on the part of this State, to meet such Commissioners as may be appointed by other States, in the City of Washington, on the fourth day of February next, to consider and, if practicable, agree upon some amicable adjustment of the present unhappy national difficulties, upon the basis and in the spirit of the Constitution of the United States.

MISSOURI.

JOINT RESOLUTION *to appoint Commissioners.*

Resolved by the House of Representatives, the Senate concurring therein, That Waldo P. Johnson, John D. Coalter, A. W. Doniphan, Harrison Hough, and A. H. Buckner be appointed Commissioners on the part of the State of Missouri, to meet Commissioners from Virginia, and other States, in Convention at Washington City, on the 4th of February, 1861, to endeavor to agree upon some plan of adjustment of existing difficulties, so as to preserve or to reconstruct the Union of these States, and to secure the honor and equal rights of the slaveholding States. Said Commissioners shall always be under the control of the General Assembly, except when the State Convention shall be in session, during which time they shall be under the control of the Convention.

No. II.

The following is a corrected list of the Delegates to the Conference, with their respective post office address.

MAINE.—William P. Fessenden, *Biddeford;* Lot M. Morrill; Daniel E. Somes, *Biddeford;* John J. Perry, *Oxford;* Ezra B. French, *Damariscotta;* Freeman H. Morse, *Bath;* Stephen Coburn; Stephen C. Foster, *Pembroke.*

NEW HAMPSHIRE.—Amos Tuck, *Exeter;* Levi Chamberlain; Asa Fowler, *Concord.*

VERMONT.—Hiland Hall, *North Bennington;* Levi Underwood, *Burlington;* H. Henry Baxter, *Rutland;* L. E. Chittenden, *Burlington;* B. D. Harris, *Brattleboro'.*

MASSACHUSETTS.—John Z. Goodrich, *Stockbridge;* Charles Allen, *Worcester;* George S. Boutwell, *Groton;* Theophilus P. Chandler, *Boston;* Francis B. Crowninshield, *Boston;* John M. Forbes, *Salem;* Richard P. Waters, *Salem.*

RHODE ISLAND.—Samuel Ames, *Providence;* Alexander Duncan, *Providence;* William W. Hoppin, *Providence;* George H. Browne, *Providence;* Samuel G. Arnold, *Providence.*

CONNECTICUT.—Roger S. Baldwin, *Windham;* Chauncey F. Cleveland; Charles J. McCurdy, *Lyme;* James T. Pratt; Robbins Battell; Amos S. Treat, *Bridgeport.*

NEW YORK.—David Dudley Field, *New York;* William Curtis Noyes, *New York;* James S. Wadsworth, *Geneseo;* James C. Smith, *Canandaigua;* Amaziah B. James, *Ogdensburg;* Erastus Corning, *Albany;* Francis Granger, *Canandaigua;* Greene C. Bronson, *New York;* William E. Dodge, *New York;* John A. King, *Jamaica;* John E. Wool, *Troy.*

NEW JERSEY.—Charles S. Olden, *Princeton;* Peter D. Vroom, *Trenton;* Robert F. Stockton, *Princeton;* Benjamin Williamson, *Elizabeth;* Joseph F. Randolph, *Trenton;* Frederick T. Frelinghuysen, *Newark;* Rodman M. Price, *Harrison, Hudson Co.;* William C. Alexander, *P. O.*, 92 *Broadway, N. Y.;* Thomas J. Stryker, *Trenton.*

PENNSYLVANIA.—James Pollock, *Milton;* William M. Meredith, *Philadelphia;* David Wilmot, *Towanda;* A. W. Loomis, *Pittsburg;* Thomas E. Franklin, *Lancaster;* William McKennan, *Washington;* Thomas White, *Indiana.*

DELAWARE.—George B. Rodney, *Newcastle;* Daniel M. Bates, *Wilmington;* Henry Ridgely, *Dover;* John W. Houston, *Milford;* William Cannon, *Bridgeville.*

MARYLAND.—John F. Dent, *Milestown;* Reverdy Johnson, *Baltimore;* John W. Crisfield, *Princess Ann;* Augustus W. Bradford, *Govanstown;* William T. Goldsborough, *Cambridge;* J. Dixon Roman, *Hagerstown;* Benjamin C. Howard, *Catonsville.*

VIRGINIA.—John Tyler, *Sherwood Forest;* William C. Rives; John W. Brockenbrough, *Lexington;* George W. Summers, *Kanawha C. H.;* James A. Seddon, *Goochland.*

NORTH CAROLINA.—George Davis, *Wilmington;* Thomas Ruffin, *Graham;* David S. Reid, *Pleasantville:* D. M. Barringer, *Raleigh;* J. M. Morehead, *Greenboro'.*

TENNESSEE.—Samuel Milligan, *Greenville;* Josiah M. Anderson, *Walnut Valley;* Robert L. Carruthers, *Lebanon;* Thomas Martin, *Pulaski;* Isaac R. Hawkins, *Huntington;* A. W. O. Totten, *Jackson;* R. J. McKinney, *Knoxville;* Alvin Cullom, *Livingston;* William P. Hickerson, *Manchester;* George W. Jones, *Fayetteville;* F. K. Zollicoffer, *Nashville;* William H. Stephens, *Jackson.*

KENTUCKY.—William O. Butler, *Carrollton;* James B. Clay, *Ashland;* Joshua F. Bell, *Danville;* Charles S. Morehead, *Louisville;* James Guthrie, *Louisville;* Charles A. Wickliffe, *Bardstown.*

MISSOURI.—John D. Coalter, *St. Louis;* Alexander W. Doniphan, *Liberty;* Waldo P. Johnson, *Osceolo;* Aylett H. Buckner, *Bowling Green;* Harrison Hough, *Charleston.*

OHIO.—Salmon P. Chase, *Columbus;* William S. Groesbeck, *Cincinnati;* Franklin T. Backus, *Cleveland;* Reuben Hitchcock, *Cleveland;* Thomas Ewing, *Lancaster;* V. B. Horton, *Pomeroy;* C. P. Wolcott, *Akron.*

INDIANA.—Caleb B. Smith, *Indianapolis;* Pleasant A. Hackleman, *Rushville;* Godlove S. Orth, *Lafayette;* E. W. H. Ellis, *Goshen;* Thomas C. Slaughter, *Corydon.*

ILLINOIS.—John Wood, *Quincy;* Stephen T. Logan, *Springfield;* John M. Palmer, *Carlinville;* Burton C. Cook, *Ottowa;* Thomas J. Turner, *Freeport.*

IOWA.—James Harlan, *Mt. Pleasant;* James W. Grimes, *Burlington;* Samuel H. Curtis, *Keokuk;* William Vandever, *Dubuque.*

KANSAS.—Thomas Ewing, jr., *Leavenworth;* J. C. Stone, *Leavenworth;* H. J. Adams, *Leavenworth;* M. F. Conway, *Lawrence.*

No. III.

In the United States Senate, February 27th, 1861, while the Army Appropriation bill was under consideration, proceedings relating to the Peace Conference were opened as follows:

Mr. POWELL:—Is it in order to move to postpone this bill and take up another?

The PRESIDING OFFICER:—The Chair believes it is in order.

Mr. POWELL:—I move to postpone the Army bill for the

purpose of taking up the resolutions to amend the Constitution proposed by my colleague. For several weeks Senators have declined to make an effort to call up the propositions of my colleague, for the reason that certain Peace Commissioners were in session in this capital, convened at the call of the State of Virginia. I am confident now that that Commission, or Peace Congress, or Conference, or whatever you may call it, will not accomplish any thing. Indeed, certain facts have fallen under my notice, that cause me to believe that it has been the fixed purpose of certain Republicans that that Conference should not accomplish any thing. I believe, sir, that certain commissioners from States of this Union have been brought into that Conference for the purpose of preventing them from agreeing on any thing. I have thought that for some time past. A friend sent to me yesterday the Detroit *Free Press*, containing two letters from the distinguished Senators from the State of Michigan to their Governor, which, I think, clearly and fully establish the fact that the Republicans, a portion of them at least, instead of sending commissioners to that Conference with a view to inaugurate something that would compromise the difficulties by which we are surrounded, and save this country from ruin, have absolutely been engaged in the work of sending delegates there to prevent that commission from doing any thing. I send this paper to the desk, and ask the Secretary to read these letters.

The Secretary read as follows:

WASHINGTON, *February* 15*th*, 1861.

DEAR SIR: When Virginia proposed a Convention in Washington, in reference to the disturbed condition of the country, I regarded it as another effort to debauch the public mind, and a step toward obtaining that concession which the imperious slave power so insolently demands. I have no doubt at present but that was the design. I was therefore pleased that the Legislature of Michigan was not disposed to put herself in a position to be controlled by such influences.

The Convention has met here, and within a few days the aspect of things has materially changed. Every free State, I think, except Michigan and Wisconsin, is represented; and we have been assured by friends upon whom we can rely, that if those two States should send delegations of true, unflinching men, there would probably be a majority in favor of the Constitution as it is, who would frown down rebellion by the enforcement of laws. These friends have urged us to recommend the appointment of delegates from our State; and, in compliance with their request, Mr. CHANDLER and myself telegraphed to you last night. It cannot be doubted that the recommendations of this Convention will have a very considerable influence upon the public mind, and upon the action of Congress.

I have a great disinclination to any interference with what should properly be submitted to the wisdom and discretion of the Legislature, in which I place great reliance; but I hope I shall be pardoned for suggesting that it may be justifiable and proper, by any honorable means, to avert the lasting disgrace which will attach to a free people who, by the peaceful exercise of the ballot, have just released themselves from the tyranny of slavery, if they should now succumb to treasonable threats, and again submit to a degrading thraldom. If it should be deemed proper to send delegates, I think, if they could be here by the 20th, it would be in time.

I have the honor, with much respect, to be truly yours,

K. S. BINGHAM.

To his Excellency Governor BLAIR.

Mr. FESSENDEN :—I submit whether it is in order to go into a discussion on this motion. If so, I suppose this must be regarded as a part of the speech.

The PRESIDING OFFICER :—The Chair understood the discussion to be in order. It was certainly not objected to at the time the Senator commenced.

Mr. FESSENDEN :—It is not too late to raise the point.

The PRESIDING OFFICER :—The motion is to lay aside one bill and take up other business; and the Chair understood the Senator from Kentucky to be giving his reasons why he wished that to be done.

Mr. FESSENDEN :—If it is in order, of course I cannot object to it; but I raise that question.

The PRESIDING OFFICER :—The Senator from Maine raises the question whether this debate is in order.

Mr. POWELL :—There was no objection to my proceeding, and I suppose I have a right to go on. I wish the letters read as part of my speech.

Mr. FESSENDEN :—There is no objection to reading them.

The PRESIDING OFFICER :—The Chair has decided that the Senator from Kentucky is in order.

Mr. POWELL :—I have not yielded, except for the purpose of reading these letters.

The PRESIDING OFFICER :—Is an appeal taken from the decision of the Chair?

Mr. FESSENDEN :—I take no appeal.

The Secretary read as follows:

WASHINGTON, *February* 11*th*, 1861.

MY DEAR GOVERNOR: Governor BINGHAM and myself telegraphed you on Saturday, at the request of Massachusetts and New York, to send delegates to the Peace or Compromise Congress. They admit that we were right and that they were wrong; that no Republican State should have sent delegates; but they are here and cannot get away. Ohio, Indiana, and Rhode Island are caving in, and there is danger of Illinois; and now they beg us, for God's sake, to come to their rescue, and save the Republican party from rupture. I hope you will send *stiff-backed* men, or none. The whole thing was gotten up against my judgment and advice, and will end in thin smoke. Still, I hope as a matter of courtesy to some of our erring brethren, that you will send the delegates.

Truly your friend,

Z. CHANDLER.

His Excellency Austin Blair.

P. S.—Some of the manufacturing States think that a fight would be awful. Without a little blood-letting this Union will not, in my estimation, be worth a rush.

Mr. POWELL:—I think it evident from these letters, that there is, and has been, a fixed purpose in certain quarters, that the Peace Conference should do nothing. Indeed, it seems, from the letter of the Senator from Michigan [Mr. Chandler], that while he opposed any Republican State going into this Conference, yet, as some of them were there, and Indiana, and Illinois, and Ohio, and Rhode Island were about to cave in, on the advice of Massachusetts and New York he asked Michigan to come in and relieve them, and save the Republican party from rupture. Is it possible that the Republican party is to be saved, even if the Union be destroyed? It is very evident that those "stiff-backed" gentlemen were to be sent here in order to prevent any compromise being presented. The object, then, as I stated, on the part of certain members on the other side of the Chamber, has been to send delegates to the Conference for the purpose of preventing any compromise measures being proposed by that body. They desire, in the language of these letters, to save their party from destruction. They say that if the Conference should agree on any thing, it would have a demoralizing effect upon the people, and upon the two Houses of Congress. In one word, it will have the effect to make a rupture in the Republican party, which, in the estimation of the Senators, is higher, holier, and better, it seems, than the Union.

In consequence of this fact being apparent, that it is not the design or the intention that the Peace Conference should do any thing, I think we should not wait for it any longer, but the Senate should proceed at once to the consideration of the amendments to the Constitution proposed by my colleague. I think we had better be engaged in that work—one that is calculated, if the propositions of my colleague should pass, in my opinion, to save the country from further disintegration. I think we had better be at that, than be appropriating money to support an Army that is to be engaged, it seems, in the work of blood-letting.

The Senator from Michigan thinks the Government is not worth a rush until it shall have drawn a little blood. I hope my motion will prevail, and that we shall lay this bill aside and proceed to the consideration of the measures proposed by my colleague.

Mr. CHANDLER:—The Senator from Kentucky has read what purports to be a short note that I sent the other day to the Governor of Michigan. Whether it is a correct copy or not, I cannot say; I kept no copy of it, nor do I care.

Mr. POWELL:—If the Senator will allow me one word, I will state to the Senate that, when I received this paper, yesterday—

Mr. CHANDLER:—I was about to state that.

Mr. POWELL:—I asked both the Senators if the letters were right. They told me they kept no copies, but they believed they were substantially so.

Mr. CHANDLER:—I was going to say that. Now, sir, I desire to answer the Senator from Kentucky, and to set myself right on this question—(my position from the first has been well known upon this question, and upon most others)—but, at the earnest solicitation of the Senator from Maine, who has charge of this bill, I will forego the response which I intended to make, and which I shall make to the Senator from Kentucky, for the present, for the purpose of going on and disposing of the Army appropriation bill. At another day I propose to give my views more at large upon these compromise measures, that the Senator from Kentucky seems so anxious to take up at this time. I am as anxious as he is to go into that discussion. I am anxious to go into it. It is a question that ought to be discussed. It is a question in which the people of Michigan take a deep interest. They are opposed to all compromises; they do not believe that any compromise is necessary; nor do I. They are prepared to stand by the Constitution of the United States as it is; to stand by the Government as it is; ay, sir, to stand by it to blood, if necessary.

Mr. POWELL:—I ask for the yeas and nays on my motion.

The yeas and nays were ordered.

Mr. MASON:—I ask the general permission of the Senate to give notice that at three o'clock I shall move to go into executive session; and if it is not agreed to, I shall then ask that the galleries may be cleared, for the purpose of disclosing what I consider ought to be passed on in executive session.

Mr. JOHNSON, of Tennessee:—If I can obtain the attention of the Senator from Kentucky, I wish to make a suggestion. Those resolutions, as I understood, went over until last Monday at one o'clock, and were then to be taken up and considered. I do not know whether the motion was made in that way, or whether it was an informal understanding that they should be taken up last Monday for consideration; but as the Army bill is now under consideration, and the time is growing short, would it not be better to have a night session, and postpone the subject until seven o'clock this evening, and let it be taken up at that time; and then let this other bill go on to-day? Those who want to make speeches on those resolutions could do it to-night; we should thus save time and expedite business.

Mr. FESSENDEN:—I think the Senator from Virginia has given an additional very good reason for taking up the Army bill, and going through with it; and not postponing it for speeches at the present time.

The question being taken by yeas and nays, resulted—yeas 17, nays 27; as follows:

YEAS.—Messrs. Bayard, Bigler, Bragg, Bright, Clingman, Douglas, Fitch, Gwin, Hunter, Johnson of Tennessee, Kennedy, Lane, Latham, Mason, Polk, Powell, and Rice—17.

NAYS.—Messrs. Anthony, Baker, Bingham, Cameron, Chandler, Clark, Collamer, Dixon, Doolittle, Durkee, Fessenden, Foot, Foster, Grimes, Hale, Harlan, King, Morrill, Pearce, Seward, Simmons, Sumner, Ten Eyck, Trumbull, Wade, Wilkinson, and Wilson—27.

So the motion to postpone the Army bill, in order to take up the resolutions of Mr. CRITTENDEN, was not agreed to.

Subsequently the following action, by the Senate, was taken on the report of the Peace Conference.

The VICE-PRESIDENT:—The Chair has received a communication from Ex-President TYLER, as President of the Conference which has been recently sitting in this city, which he will lay before the Senate; and also the proceedings of that body.

The Secretary read the communication, as follows:

To the Senate of the United States:

I am instructed, as the presiding officer of the Convention, composed of Commissioners appointed by twenty-one States, now in session in this city to deliberate upon the present unhappy condition of the country, to present to your honorable body the accompanying request and proposed amendment.

JOHN TYLER,
President of the Convention.

WASHINGTON, D. C., *February* 27, 1861.

To the Congress of the United States:

The Convention assembled, upon the invitation of the State of Virginia, to adjust the unhappy differences which now disturb the peace of the Union, and threaten its continuance, make known to the Congress of the United States that their body convened in the City of Washington on the fourth instant, and continued in session until the twenty-seventh.

There were in the body, when action was taken upon that which is here submitted, one hundred and thirty-three Commissioners, representing the following States: Maine, New Hampshire, Vermont, Massachusetts, Rhode Island, Connecticut, New York, New Jersey, Pennsylvania, Delaware, Maryland, Virginia, North Carolina, Tennessee, Kentucky, Missouri, Ohio, Indiana, Illinois, Iowa, *Wisconsin*, and Kansas. They have approved what is herewith submitted, and respectfully request that your honorable body will submit it to conventions in the States as article *thirteen* of the amendments to the Constitution of the United States.

Attest: J. HENRY PULESTON,
Secretary.

ARTICLE XIII.

SEC. 1. In all the present territory of the United States north of the parallel of 36° 30′ of north latitude, involuntary servitude, except in punishment of crime, is prohibited. In all the present territory south of that line, the *status* of persons held to involuntary service or labor, as it now exists, shall not be changed; nor shall any law be passed by Congress or the Territorial Legislature to hinder or prevent the taking of such persons from any of the States of this Union to said territory, nor to impair the rights arising from said relation; but the same shall be subject to judicial cognizance in the Federal courts, according to the course of the common law. When any Territory north or south of said line, within such boundary as Congress may prescribe, shall contain a population equal to that required for a member of Congress, it shall, if its form of government be republican, be admitted into the Union on an equal footing with the original States, with or without involuntary servitude, as the constitution of such State may provide.

SEC. 2. No territory shall be acquired by the United States, except by discovery and for naval and commercial stations, depots, and transit routes, without the concurrence of a majority of all the Senators from States which allow involuntary servitude, and a majority of all the Senators from States which prohibit that relation; nor shall territory be acquired by treaty, unless the votes of a majority of the Senators from each class of States hereinbefore mentioned be cast as a part of the two thirds majority necessary to the ratification of such treaty.

SEC. 3. Neither the constitution, nor any amendment thereof, shall be construed to give Congress power to regulate, abolish, or control, within any State, the relation established or recognized by the laws thereof touching persons held to labor or involuntary service therein, nor to interfere with or abolish involuntary service in the District of Columbia without the consent of Maryland and without the consent of the owners, or making the owners who do not consent just compensation; nor the power to interfere with or prohibit Representatives and others from bringing with them to the District of Columbia, retaining, and taking away, persons so held to labor or service; nor the power to interfere with or abolish involutary service in places under the exclusive jurisdiction of the United States within those States and Territories where the same is established or recognized; nor the power to prohibit the removal or transportation of persons held to labor or involuntary service in any State or Territory of the United States to any other State or Territory thereof where it is established or recognized by law or usage, and the right during transportion, by sea or river, of touching at ports, shores, and landings, and of landing in case of distress, shall exist; but not the right of transit in or through any State or Territory, or of sale or traffic, against the laws thereof. Nor shall Congress have power to authorize any higher rate of taxation on persons held to labor or service than on land. The bringing into the District of Columbia of persons held to labor or service, for sale, or placing them in depots to be afterwards transferred to other places for sale as merchandise, is prohibited.

SEC. 4. The third paragraph of the second section of the fourth article of the Constitution shall not be construed to prevent any of the States, by appropriate legislation, and through the action of their judicial and ministerial officers, from enforcing the delivery of fugitives from labor to the person to whom such service or labor is due.

SEC. 5. The foreign slave-trade is hereby forever prohibited; and it shall be the duty of Congress to pass laws to prevent the importation of slaves, coolies, or persons held to service or labor, into the United States and the Territories from places beyond the limits thereof.

SEC. 6. The first, third, and fifth sections, together with this section of those amendments, and the third paragraph of the second section of the first article of the Constitution, and the third paragraph of the second section of the fourth article thereof, shall not be amended or abolished without the consent of all the States.

SEC. 7. Congress shall provide by law that the United States shall pay to the owner the full value of his fugitive from labor, in all cases where the marshal, or other officer, whose duty it was to arrest such fugitive, was prevented from so doing by violence or intimidation from mobs or riotous assemblages, or when, after arrest, such fugitive was rescued by like violence or intimidation, and the owner thereby deprived of the same; and the acceptance of such payment shall preclude the owner from further claim to such fugitive. Congress shall provide by law for securing to the citizens of each State the privileges and immunities of citizens in the several States.

Mr. MASON:—I suppose the proper disposition is to have it printed.

Mr. CRITTENDEN:—There is nothing to print.

Mr. GREEN:—And refer it to the Committee for the District of Columbia. I think that is about right.

Mr. CRITTENDEN:—I move that it be referred to a select committee, with instructions to report to-morrow morning.

Mr. MASON:—We ought certainly to have it printed.

Mr. DOUGLAS:—It can be printed in the mean time.

Mr. FESSENDEN:—We should have time to look at it.

The VICE-PRESIDENT:—It is moved that the communication be printed and referred to a select committee, with instructions to report to-morrow morning.

Mr. BIGLER:—I would be glad to make a suggestion to the Senator from Kentucky, that he name in addition an hour to-morrow at which the consideration of the report shall be in order, or else a single objection will throw it over to the next day.

Mr. CRITTENDEN:—Well, to-morrow at twelve o'clock, I would say. ["One."] I move one o'clock.

Mr. BIGLER:—With instructions to the committee to report to-morrow morning, and that the report be the special order at one o'clock?

Mr. CRITTENDEN:—Yes, sir.

The VICE-PRESIDENT:—Does the Senator indicate the number of the committee?

Mr. GREEN:—Seventeen.

Mr. DOUGLAS:—Five is enough.

Mr. CRITTENDEN:—A committee of five; no more.

Mr. COLLAMER:—I would suggest to gentlemen not only that it be made the order of the day for twelve o'clock to-morrow, but that it be adopted by three-fourths of the States the next day. [Laughter.]

The VICE-PRESIDENT:—It is moved and seconded that the communication be printed and referred to a select committee of five members, to report to-morrow at one o'clock.

Mr. HALE:—I ask for a division of the question.

The VICE-PRESIDENT:—The first question will be on printing.

The motion to print was agreed to.

The VICE-PRESIDENT:—The next question is that the communication be referred to a select committee of five, with instructions to report to-morrow at one o'clock.

Mr. HALE:—I ask for a division of that.

The VICE-PRESIDENT:—How would it be divided?

Mr. HALE:—The motion to refer to a select committee is one proposition, and the instructions are another.

The VICE-PRESIDENT:—That is the form in which the Senator wants it divided?

Mr. HALE:—Yes, sir.

Mr. BIGLER:—As the Chair states the proposition, it does not reach the object which the Senator from Kentucky had in view. The instructions should be that the committee report to-morrow morning, and that the report shall be the special order at one o'clock. Unless that is done, one objection will put it over.

The VICE-PRESIDENT:—The Senator from New Hampshire asks for a division of the question, and it is susceptible of division. The first question is on referring the communication to a special committee of five.

The motion was agreed to.

The VICE-PRESIDENT:—The next branch of the proposition is that that committee be instructed to report to-morrow morning, and that their report be made the special order for to-morrow at one o'clock.

Mr. HALE:—On that, I should like to have the yeas and nays.

The yeas and nays were ordered.

The VICE-PRESIDENT:—The question is upon directing the committee to report to-morrow morning, and that the report be made the special order for to-morrow at one o'clock.

The Secretary proceeded to call the roll.

Mr. CLINGMAN:—Though I am utterly opposed to the proposition, I am willing to give it the direction its friends desire, and I vote "yea."

Mr. LATHAM:—I desire to change my vote. I have no confidence in this thing, and I fear it will be an unnecessary consumption of time; but I yield to the judgment of my political associates and I vote "yea."

The result was announced—yeas 26, nays 21; as follows:

YEAS.—Messrs. Anthony, Baker, Bayard, Bigler, Bragg, Bright, Clingman, Crittenden, Dixon, Douglas, Fitch, Foster, Gwin, Hunter, Johnson of Tennessee, Kennedy, Lane, Latham, Mason, Nicholson, Pearce, Polk, Powell, Rice, Sebastian, and Thomson—26.

NAYS.—Messrs. Bingham, Chandler, Clark, Collamer, Doolittle, Durkee, Fessenden, Foot, Green, Grimes, Hale, Harlan, King, Morrill, Seward, Simmons, Sumner, Ten Eyck, Trumbull, Wade, and Wilson—21.

So the motion was agreed to.

Mr. CRITTENDEN:—I move that the committee be appointed by the Chair.

The motion was agreed to; and Mr. CRITTENDEN, Mr. BIGLER, Mr. THOMSON, Mr. SEWARD, and Mr. TRUMBULL, were appointed the committee.

On the 28th of February the committee so appointed, presented to the Senate the following report, and the following action was taken thereon:

Mr. CRITTENDEN:—The select committee, to whom was referred the communication received yesterday from the Convention assembled in this place, commonly called the Peace Convention, with instructions to report by twelve o'clock to-day, have had the subject under consideration, and have directed me to make the following report—

Mr. HALE:—I object to its consideration to-day.

The PRESIDING OFFICER (Mr. FITCH in the chair):—Objection being made, it cannot be considered until one o'clock, but it will be read.

The Secretary read the joint resolution reported by Mr. CRITTENDEN (S. No. 70), proposing certain amendments to the Constitution of the United States, as follows:

JOINT RESOLUTION *proposing certain amendments to the Constitution of the United States.*

WHEREAS Commissioners, appointed on the invitation of the State of Virginia, by the following States, respectively: Maine, New Hampshire, Vermont, Massachusetts, Rhode Island, Connecticut, New York, New Jersey, Pennsylvania, Delaware, Maryland, Virginia, North Carolina, Tennessee, Kentucky, Missouri, Ohio, Indiana, Illinois, Iowa, Wisconsin, and Kansas, have met in Convention at the City of Washington, for the purpose of considering the distracted and perilous condition of the country, and proposing measures for the preservation of the peace, the safety of the people, and the security of the Union, and having performed that duty, and communicated to Congress the result of their deliberations, with a request and recommendation on the part and in the name of said States, that the following be proposed to the several States as amendments to the Constitution of the United States, according to the fifth article of said instrument, namely: [See article preceding.]

Mr. SEWARD:—Mr. President—

Mr. GWIN:—I think I am on the floor.

Mr. SEWARD:—I desire to speak a word from the committee touching the present report.

Mr. GWIN:—Certainly.

Mr. HALE:—I object to its present consideration.

Mr. SEWARD:—I am not proposing to consider it.

Mr. BIGLER:—The Senator from New Hampshire has no right to make the objection.

Mr. SEWARD:—I am not proposing to consider it at the present moment; but I am desirous of making an explanation from the committee, touching the report made by the Senator from Kentucky. The honorable Senator from Illinois [Mr. TRUMBULL], and myself, constituted a minority of the committee. We dissent from the report, and we proposed in committee to submit a substitute. The majority held that, for some reason, sufficient in their estimation, we were not entitled to submit a minority report. I therefore ask leave of the Senate to introduce a joint resolution in my own name, and in which the honorable Senator from Illinois authorized me to say that he concurs with me, and which I ask unanimous consent to have read and printed; and it will be the subject of consideration at such time hereafter as the Senate shall choose to hear it, either in connection with the other or not.

Mr. MASON:—Is it in the form of a report?

Mr. SEWARD:—No; it is not insisted on in that form; it is submitted on my own behalf. I desire that it may be read for information and printed, subject to the future action of the Senate.

The proposition of Mr. SEWARD was read, as follows:

A joint resolution concerning a National Convention to propose amendments to the Constitution of the United States.

WHEREAS, The Legislatures of the States of Kentucky, New Jersey, and Illinois, have applied to Congress to call a Convention for proposing amendments to the Constitution of the United States: Therefore,

Be it Resolved, &c., That the Legislatures of the other States be invited to take the subject into consideration, and to express their will on that subject to Congress, in pursuance of the fifth article of the Constitution.

Mr. BIGLER:—I desire to make—

The PRESIDING OFFICER:—The Senator from California was on the floor. No action is now requested on the paper just offered, only a motion to print. Shall the paper be printed?

Mr. HALE:—Was it read for information?

The PRESIDING OFFICER:—For information only.

Mr. SEWARD:—I move that it be printed.

The PRESIDING OFFICER:—The Chair hears no objection.

Mr. BIGLER:—I desire to make a remark in reference to the question of order made by the Senator from New Hampshire. The Senator objects to the consideration of the report to-day. Yesterday, when the Senator from Kentucky made the motion, I insisted on further moving that the report of the committee should be the special order at one o'clock to-day.

The PRESIDING OFFICER:—That is the record.

Mr. BIGLER:—That instruction was offered, and therefore the Senator's objection will not apply.

Mr. HALE:—Therefore it will.

Mr. SEWARD:—I insist on the motion to print.

The PRESIDING OFFICER:—The Senator from California is on the floor. The Senator from New Hampshire having objected to the present consideration of the resolution reported by the Senator from Kentucky, for the time being it cannot be considered.

Mr. SEWARD:—Will the Senator from California allow the question to be put on my motion to print?

The PRESIDING OFFICER:—The Chair heard no objection to that; and it was ordered.

Mr. DOOLITTLE:—The Senator from California will allow me to say a single word. I observe that, in this report, the State of Wisconsin is mentioned as having sent delegates to this Convention, commonly denominated the Peace Convention. That is a mistake. I desire, also, to give notice that when this subject shall come up for consideration, I shall offer as an amendment to the first section of article thirteen, as proposed, the following proviso:

Provided, however (and this section shall take effect upon the express condition), That no State, or any part thereof, heretofore admitted, or hereafter to be admitted, into the Union, shall have power to withdraw from the jurisdiction of the United States; and that this Constitution, and all laws passed in pursuance thereof, shall be the supreme law of the land therein, any thing contained in any constitution, act, or ordinance of any State Legislature or Convention to the contrary notwithstanding.

The section will then read as follows:

SEC. 1. In all the present territory of the United States north of the parallel of 36° 30′ of north latitude, involuntary servitude, except in punishment of crime, is prohibited. In all the present territory south of that line, the *status* of persons held to involuntary service or labor, as it now exists, shall not be changed; nor shall any law be passed by Congress or the Territorial Legislature to hinder or prevent the taking of such persons from any of the States of the Union to said territory, nor to impair the rights arising from the said relation; but the same shall be subject to judicial cognizance in the Federal courts, according to the course of the common law. When any Territory north or south of said line, within such boundary as Congress may prescribe, shall contain a population equal to that required for a member of Congress, it shall, if its form of government be republican, be admitted into the Union on an equal footing with the original States, with or without involuntary servitude, as the Constitution of such State may provide: *Provided, however* (and this section shall take effect upon the express condition), That no State, nor any part thereof, heretofore admitted, or hereafter to be admitted into the Union, shall have power to withdraw from the jurisdiction of the United States; and that the Constitution, and all laws passed in pursuance thereof, shall be the supreme law of the land therein, any thing contained in any constitution, act, or ordinance, of any State Legislature or Convention to the contrary notwithstanding.

And I desire that that amendment, which I now send to the Chair, may be printed.

The PRESIDING OFFICER:—Is there any objection to printing the paper which the Senator has just read? The Chair hears no objection.

The same day the Report of the Peace Conference was called up for consideration, when Senator HALE objected to the consideration of the report. Considerable discussion then ensued, in which Messrs. HALE, BIGLER, TRUMBULL, CRITTENDEN, and DIXON participated. This discussion related merely to the question, whether under the rules of the Senate the Report of the Peace Conference could at this time be taken up. The merits of the report were not considered, and for that reason it is not deemed necessary to report the proceedings of the Senate in this respect. The joint rules of the two Houses were suspended in order that another subject might be taken up, and no decision was had upon the question, whether the Report of the Peace Conference at this time should be considered.

The allotted time having been consumed in this discussion, the Senate proceeded to the consideration and disposal of several orders of the day. On the first of March it resumed action on the Report of the Peace Conference.

The PRESIDING OFFICER (Mr. FITCH):—It is the duty of the Chair to announce the special order of the day, being the joint resolution (S. No. 70) proposing certain amendments to the Constitution of the United States.

Mr. DOUGLAS:—I ask that the resolutions from the House of Representatives, in regard to amendments of the Constitution, be laid before the Senate, in order that they may be considered at the same time.

The PRESIDING OFFICER:—The Chair will lay before the Senate a joint resolution from the House of Representatives.

The joint resolution (H. R. No. 80) to amend the Constitution of the United States, was read the first time by its title.

Mr. DOUGLAS:—I ask that that be made the special order at the same time, in connection with the joint resolution reported by the Senator from Kentucky.

Mr. MASON:—I have looked at that joint resolution, and it certainly ought to be committed to a committee to correct its English. It is unintelligible.

Mr. DOUGLAS:—My object is merely to have it considered at the same time with the other.

The PRESIDING OFFICER:—The joint resolution will have its second reading.

The joint resolution (H. R. No. 80) was read a second time by its title.

The PRESIDING OFFICER:—It is now the subject of any motion that may be made in regard to it.

Mr. DOUGLAS:—I move that it be made the special order in connection with the joint resolution reported by the Senator from Kentucky.

Mr. CLARK:—How does that happen to be in order here when there is a special order called up?

The PRESIDING OFFICER:—It is not in order to consider it, except by unanimous consent.

Mr. CLARK, Mr. BINGHAM, and Mr. SUMNER:—I object.

The PRESIDING OFFICER:—The special order is before the Senate.

Mr. DOUGLAS:—I ask that the other resolutions which have come from the House of Representatives, be read. There are two of them, I believe.

The House joint resolutions (No. 64) declaratory of the opinion of Congress in regard to certain questions now agitating the country, and of measures calculated to reconcile existing differences, were read the first time by the title.

The PRESIDING OFFICER:—The second reading—

Mr. CHANDLER and others:—I object.

The PRESIDING OFFICER:—Is objection made?

Mr. CHANDLER:—I withdraw my objection.

Mr. SUMNER:—I object.

The PRESIDING OFFICER:—Objection being made, it cannot be read the second time.

Mr. SIMMONS:—It passed the other House unanimously. There can be no objection, I think.

Mr. CLARK:—We have another subject up.

The PRESIDING OFFICER:—The special order is before the Senate. The question is on the second reading.

The joint resolution (S. No. 70) proposing certain amendments to the Constitution of the United States, was read the second time, and considered as in Committee of the Whole.

Mr. PUGH:—Let the resolution be read, not the proposition itself, but the formal part, the introduction.

Mr. HUNTER:—Is that open to amendment now?

The PRESIDING OFFICER:—It is in Committee of the Whole, and open to amendment. The reading of the formal part of the joint resolution is called for.

The Secretary read it.

Mr. SEWARD:—I offer the following as a substitute:

Strike out all after the word "whereas," in the preamble, to the end of the resolution, and insert:

The Legislatures of the States of Kentucky, New Jersey, and Illinois, have applied to Congress to call a Convention for proposing amendments to the Constitution of the United States: Therefore,

Be it resolved by the Senate and House of Representatives of the United States of America in Congress assembled, That the Legislatures of the other States be invited to take the subject of such a Convention into consideration, and to express their will on that subject to Congress, in pursuance of the fifth article of the Constitution.

The PRESIDING OFFICER:—The Chair understands that a proviso was offered to the matter that the Senator from New York proposes to strike out. The vote will first be taken on the proviso offered by the Senator from Wisconsin [Mr. DOOLITTLE], to insert at the end of section one of article thirteen:

Provided, *however* (and this section shall take effect upon the express condition), That no State, nor any part thereof, heretofore admitted, or hereafter to be admitted into the Union, shall have power to withdraw from the jurisdiction of the United States; and that this Constitution, and all laws passed in pursuance thereof, shall be the supreme law of the land, any thing contained in any constitution, act, or ordinance of any State Legislature or Convention to the contrary notwithstanding.

Mr. HUNTER:—I believe that the amendment of the Senator from Wisconsin is not pending.

The PRESIDING OFFICER:—The Senator from Wisconsin proposes that as a proviso to the matter which the Senator from New York moves to strike out; and the question must first be taken on that.

Mr. HUNTER:—I did not know that that was before the Senate.

Mr. BIGLER:—He only gave notice of it.

Mr. HUNTER:—I thought the Senator from Wisconsin only gave notice that he would offer it.

The PRESIDING OFFICER:—The Chair may have misunderstood the Senator's motion at the time. He called for the printing of it; but if that is the understanding of the Senate—

Mr. SEWARD:—What does the record say?

The PRESIDING OFFICER:—The Chair understands that the record presents it as "intended to be offered."

Mr. SEWARD:—Then the question is on the substitute. I ask that the question be taken,

Mr. HUNTER:—I have an amendment to submit. I propose to amend the first section of the proposition before us, by inserting in lieu of it the first article of what are called the CRITTENDEN resolutions. I move to strike out the first article of the peace propositions, and to insert:

> That in all the territory of the United States now held, or hereafter acquired, situate north of latitude 36° 30′, slavery or involuntary servitude, except as a punishment for crime, is prohibited while such territory shall remain under territorial government. In all the territory south of said line of latitude, slavery of the African race is hereby recognized as existing, and shall not be interfered with by Congress; but shall be protected as property by all the departments of the territorial government during its continuance; and when any Territory, north or south of said line, within such boundaries as Congress may prescribe, shall contain the population requisite for a member of Congress, according to the then Federal ratio of representation of the people of the United States, it shall, if its form of government be republican, be admitted into the Union on an equal footing with the original States, with or without slavery, as the constitution of such new State may provide.

Mr. COLLAMER:—I rise to a question of order. It will be observed that this paper is before us under a recital that, whereas these propositions of amendment have been presented by the Commissioners, as they are called, from the several States—naming them—who have asked Congress to submit them, therefore we propose to submit them to the States. The whole proceeding is based and predicated on this recital. I say that it cannot be amended. If it were amended, it would cease to be the application of that body which the recital States. I therefore object to any amendments, except a substitute; perhaps a substitute may be offered striking out the recital and all; but an amendment to it is out of order, in my view.

Mr. HUNTER:—In regard to the question of order, I understand that the recital is the recital of the committee, and that the question before us is on these propositions for amending the Constitution of the United States, which are to be treated as a bill. If so, each section is subject to amendment as a bill would be subject to amendment. It was my purpose to offer the entire series of what are called the CRITTENDEN resolutions, as an amendment to these, and I still intend to offer them, section by section; but I was prevented from offering them in that form, because the Senator from New York got the floor first, and offered his proposition as a substitute. I therefore could not raise the question which I desired to raise, except by offering the amendments, section by section, in order to perfect the original proposition. I submit that it is in order.

Mr. COLLAMER:—I submit, still, my question of order, suggesting to gentlemen that if we make any amendment, we must strike out the recital.

Mr. BIGLER:—I do not see that any ordinary question of order can be raised in this case; but I do think there is a consideration much more grave, and that is the question whether we will treat the series of resolutions presented here by this Peace Congress as a proposition which we ought either to accept or reject. I was one of those in the select committee who took that position. It was manifestly intended that we should accept the entire programme, or reject it. Therefore I was unwilling; and we decided to consider no question of amendment—

Mr. HUNTER:—That is not a question of order, but of propriety. It would be an argument against any amendment.

Mr. BIGLER:—I have said it was no ordinary question of rules; but that there was a far graver question of propriety. I agree with the Senator in that view; and I rose for the purpose of alluding to the view taken of this subject by the select committee. The Senator from New York desired the leave of the committee to report his proposition as a substitute; but the majority of the committee held that the resolutions had not been committed to us for the purpose of considering them and changing them, or substituting something else, but simply to attach to them the formal resolution to present them as amendments to the Constitution for the ratification of the States. For that reason we proposed no amendment; and the Senator from New York yesterday offered his substitute on his own responsibility, because, as I understood him, of the view taken by the committee. Now, sir, I still entertain the view that, while the Senate have a clear right unquestionably to change these resolutions, and to change the resolution of submission to make it conform to any thing we may do, we ought to consider these resolutions sent here by this Peace Conference as a whole, and accept them or reject them; but there can be no question of ordinary rule raised as to the right to offer an amendment; there is a greater, a graver question of propriety as to how they shall be treated.

Mr. SEWARD:—It is not merely a question of form or order, but the proposition of the Senator from Virginia would change the whole character of the transaction. This joint resolution is one single, complete proposition. It is one act. It begins with a declaration by Congress, that "whereas Commissioners, appointed on the invitation of the

State of Virginia," have performed a certain duty confided to them, "and communicated to Congress the result of their deliberations, with a request and recommendation on the part and in the name of said States"—of Maine, New Hampshire, Vermont, Massachusetts, Rhode Island, and the rest of the States represented in the Convention—"the following"—nothing different, nothing originating in Congress, nothing originating anywhere else, but—"the following be proposed to the several States as amendments to the Constitution of the United States, according to the fifth article of said instrument." Now, if we should adopt this whole transaction, we should simply do this: we should submit these amendments to the people of the United States for their acceptance, for the reason that the Peace Convention, as it is called, has considered upon the subject, and thought it grave enough to solicit us to invest it with the legislative or congressional sanction, and so submit it to the Legislatures and conventions of the States; but whenever you have made a single alteration in it, such as is proposed now by the Senator from Virginia, it is not, then, the proposition of the States "of Maine, New Hampshire, Vermont, Massachusetts," or any other States; but it is a recommendation of the Congress of the United States. The whole character is changed. The Convention is swept out of existence in the history of Congress. The resolutions then adopted become the deliberate conviction of the majority of the Congress of the United States, who substitute their own judgment, and their own wisdom, and their own will, for the wishes, the opinions, respectfully submitted to them by the representatives of those States, and take the responsibility of saying that this is what the Peace Convention should have submitted, instead of the proposition which they have sent here.

Mr. HUNTER:—I wish to make a suggestion in regard to the real position of this question, as it now appears before us. The arguments that have been urged by the Senator from Pennsylvania and the Senator from New York might very well be brought up against the propriety of adopting the amendment; but, so far as the question itself stands, it is only brought before us by a report of our committee. The Peace Conference had no power to present questions or make communications to us; but they having made a communication, and we, having respect for that body, agreed to take it up, and we referred their proposition to a committee. The only authority which we have now for considering it in the Senate, is on the recommendation of our committee. This proposition stands here as a recommendation of that committee to alter the Constitution, as proposed by this Conference. It being their recommendation in regard to the alteration of the Constitution, under our rules it stands like a bill; and I have a right to move to amend it, section by section; and in doing so, I should be pursuing the method taken by the Peace Conference, as I understand, for I am told they never took a vote on it as a whole, but voted on it proposition by proposition; and in fact, the majority who passed the propositions were composed of different States, and they never did take a vote on the articles as a whole.

Now, I am proposing to amend this as it comes up, proposition by proposition; and if it would be in order for me to make such a motion, supposing that this proposition had originated with a committee of this body, who had made a report proposing such amendments to the Constitution, I should have a right to make it now, for it is only in that way that it appears legally before us. I say, then, so far as the question of order is concerned, it seems to me that I have clearly a right to do it. I would be willing, in order to get rid of the question of order, to move to strike out the preamble too; but in my opinion it stands before us as a bill would stand. I may amend the particular sections. I am not proposing by this amendment to perfect the whole proposition, but a part of it; and if I should succeed in that, I can then go back, and move to amend the preamble.

So far as the question of order is concerned, I cannot see how it is that I am out of order. There may be a question of propriety. Those who believe that this proposition is one that ought to be accepted as a whole, and ought to be accepted because it comes from this body, eminently respectable, as we all acknowledge it to be, may say that we ought not to amend it; not that we have not the power, but that we ought not to amend it. Those of us, however, who think as I do, that it is a proposition not to be accepted; that it is a proposition highly dangerous, and one which will give rise to great difficulties, on the other hand, may think it eminently proper to amend it. I, thinking in that way, avail myself of what I suppose my parliamentary right, to offer an amendment; and it is upon that question of parliamentary right alone, as I understand, that the Chair is to determine.

Mr. TRUMBULL:—Mr. President, it seems to me very clear that, as a question of order, this proposition does not stand in any respect different from any other. Suppose an individual Senator had thought proper to propose amendments to the Constitution; that they had been referred to a committee; and the committee had approved them: what would it have done? Precisely what this committee has done. It would have reported back the proposition, with a resolution in conformity with that clause of the Constitution which points out the mode of its amendment. The fact that this proposition was adopted by gentlemen from various States does not alter it at all. It comes here as a mere petition. However respectable and dignified the Convention may have been which arrived at these conclusions; however much weight their conclusions may be entitled to in the country, they come here simply as petitioners—in that light, and none other—asking Congress to submit certain resolutions to the States of the Union to be adopted or not as portions of the fundamental law, and, unquestionably, any Senator has a right to propose an amendment in the same way as if they were introduced by an individual Senator. Can it be possible that if I draw up a series of propositions as amendments to the Constitution of the United States, and a select committee thinks proper to recommend them to this body, the hands of the body are tied up, and it must take them, word for word, and letter for letter, as I have drawn them? The question is, whether it is proper to do this; whether the respect due the Peace Convention should not deter gentlemen from offering amendments, is a question we are not discussing. The point is one of order; and as a question of order, I was astonished when the Senator from Pennsylvania first suggested it.

Mr. BIGLER:—I suggested no question of order.

Mr. TRUMBULL:—I did understand the Senator from Pennsylvania to say, that that was the view he took in committee in response to what was said by the Senator from Vermont, and it was to that I alluded when I said I was astonished at the ground he took, that the committee could not amend these propositions, or that any other person could not move to amend them.

Mr. BIGLER:—The Senator from Vermont made a distinct point of order; but I did not sustain the Senator's views on the point of order. On the other hand, so far from that, I stated distinctly, that there could be no ordinary question of order under the rule; but a question of propriety, a question as to the consideration that was to be attached to this proposition of the Peace Convention; that the select committee, or a majority, at least, were under the impression that it was expected we would treat it as a whole, and accept it or reject it. That is what I said. I have no doubt whatever of the right of a Senator on this floor to move to amend this resolution. But, sir, I cannot agree with the Senator from Illinois by any means, that this proposition should be treated as the mere report of a committee or the proposition of an individual Senator. Who supposes that twenty States would have sent commissioners here to consider this great question and suggest to Congress—

Mr. TRUMBULL:—The Senator from Pennsylvania, I see, is misunderstanding me. I said, as a question of order, it was to be treated the same as if offered by an individual Senator; that however much respect we might have for it, as coming from the source it did, yet, as a question of order, there was no difference in the rules.

Mr. BIGLER:—I did not understand the Senator as placing entire stress on the question of order. I have been endeavoring to take this question away from the rules, to set it above the rules, and I say that we ought to consider it without reference to the rules. If it be that this programme is not acceptable to the Senate, let it be rejected. What I supposed was intended from the beginning was, that whatever they sent here was to be considered as an entirety—accepted or rejected. I was about to remark, who supposes that twenty States would have sent commissioners to prepare a programme of peace for the consideration of Congress, if they had supposed that immediately the peculiar views of each member of Congress would be set up in opposition to them?

Mr. President, a single remark in relation to what fell from the Senator from New York, and I shall have done. The Senator from New York alludes to the terms of the preamble, that, for the reason that these commissioners agreed, therefore these propositions are submitted as amendments to the Constitution. I do not wish to be understood as regarding it in that light. I do not think it is the right of Congress to submit propositions of amendment of the Constitution because they come from any source. The spirit of the Constitution is, that Congress will submit amendments to the Constitution; because Congress approves those amendments, and it would be a reason why I should vote for or against them, whether I approved them or not. If, as a whole, I could vote for them, I would vote for them; if, as a whole, I could not, I would vote against them. That does not affect the question whether, under all the circumstances, and solemn surroundings, the labor which has been bestowed, and the character of the men that have presented this paper, we should consider it as an entirety, or attempt to cut it up by piecemeal, by which neither they, nor the public, will ever ascertain what the judgment of Congress was on the results of their labor. That is what I say.

Mr. SEWARD:—The honorable Senator may very naturally and very properly take the ground that he would not vote, and that Congress ought not to vote, for submitting this proposition to the people, for the reason assigned in the paper before us. I have not any disposition to quarrel with him about it. I might take the same view, and say that I would not submit to the people a proposition which was futile, which was frivolous. That is not what I was speaking to. What I was speaking to was, the character of this proposition; and this is a proposition just to this effect, logically and technically expressed: that whereas these commissioners appointed by the States have met, consulted, considered, and adopted that resolution, therefore, for that reason, independent of every thing else, Congress submits it to the States.

Mr. PUGH:—I want to make an appeal to the friends of some proposition of peace. This is the last day of the session but one, and we have not made the progress of one line. We have gone into an eternal discussion about questions of order, and that, too, in defiance of the rule of the Senate. I insist that the question shall be decided without further debate.

The PRESIDING OFFICER (Mr. FITCH):—It is not for the Chair to decide any question of propriety, except as an individual Senator. As Presiding Officer, he does not deem the question of order, made by the Senator from Vermont, to be well taken. The joint resolution differs in no respect from other resolutions, and is open to amendment, and is before the Senate, as in Committee of the Whole, for that purpose. The question is on agreeing to the amendment which has been offered by the Senator from Virginia.

Mr. HUNTER:—Mr. President, I have offered this amendment, as the first of a series which I shall offer, for the purpose of carrying out the will of my State, as it has been expressed through its Legislature; and I might say there are other Senators similarly situated, for there are other States which have declared a disposition to settle upon the basis of what are called the CRITTENDEN resolutions. That is the first reason which prompts me; and to me it is imperative, because the Legislature of the State which I have the honor in part to represent, has declared that this is the basis upon which it would settle, and intimated that it would not take less than they propose by way of security for the South. I have also another reason. I have examined this proposition of the Peace Conference—

Mr. WADE:—Will the Senator let us hear it read? We do not understand what his proposition is.

Mr. HUNTER:—My proposition is the first article from the CRITTENDEN amendments, in regard to the territorial adjustment.

Mr. WADE:—We understand that.

Mr. HUNTER:—After as careful an examination as I have been able to give this proposition from the Peace Conference since it was printed, that is to say, within the last day or two, I have come to the conclusion that it would not only make a great many more difficulties than it would remove, if it should be adopted as an amendment to the Constitution, but that it would place the South—the slaveholding States—in a far worse position than they now occupy under the present Constitution, with the Dred Scott decision as its exposition.

Mr. CLARK:—Will the Senator from Virginia allow me to make a suggestion?

Mr. HUNTER:—Certainly.

Mr. CLARK:—I understand him to say he proposes to offer the several propositions of the CRITTENDEN amendment one after the other.

Mr. HUNTER:—Yes, sir.

Mr. CLARK:—Then I suggest, as that is the intention of the Senator, that unanimous consent be given to move them as one amendment, so that we may have them all up for discussion, if any one chooses to discuss them, at the same time.

Mr. HUNTER:—I have no objection to that, if it is the general wish. I was saying, Mr. President, when I was interrupted, that after as careful an examination as I was able to give this peace proposition, since it was printed, I came to the conclusion that it would put the southern States in a far worse position than they now occupy under the present Constitution, and with the Dred Scott decision. Under that Constitution, and with the Dred Scott decision, they had a right, as the court has decided, to carry their slaves into any Territory of the United States. That is a right which has been adjudicated to them by a solemn decision of the Supreme Court; and it is to be remembered that this right has not only been accorded to them by the decision of the court, but by the action of the several branches of the Federal Government. That is their present state of things under the present Constitution of the United States with regard to the territorial question. In what position, then, does this proposed territorial adjustment place them? Why, sir, it excludes them; it puts the WILMOT proviso on all territory north of 36° 30′; and south of 36° 30′ it gives them the privilege of another lawsuit, in order to try their right and title to enter the territory with their slaves. What are the words of this proposed amendment of the Constitution?

"In all the present territory south of that line, the *status* of persons held to involuntary service or labor, as it now exists, shall not be changed; nor shall any law be passed by Congress or the Territorial Legislature to hinder or prevent the taking of such persons from any of the States of this Union to said territory, nor to impair the rights arising from said relation; but the same shall be subject to judicial cognizance in the Federal courts, according to the course of the common law."

"In all the present territory south of that line, the *status* of persons held to involuntary servitude or labor, as it now exists, shall not be changed." What is the meaning of that word "*status*"? What is the *status?* The word *status* may be applied to different things; there may be a local *status* or a political *status*. In some countries a slave may hold property, and, in a certain form, sue; in others, he cannot. Or it may be the social and legal relation, that of the slave to his master, which constitutes the *status* that is referred to; and I presume it is that which it is declared shall not be changed. But, sir, shall not be changed by whom? By Congress? It does not say so. By the Territorial Legislature? It does not say so in terms. Does it mean that it shall not be changed by Congress or by the government of the Territory? Does it mean that it shall not be changed at all by anybody? Does it mean the master shall not emancipate him if he chooses? Is it an absolute prohibition of any change of the *status* of the slave, of any sort or description?

These are the terms which we are obliged to resort to in order to escape from the manly declaration of the CRITTENDEN resolution, that south of that line slavery shall be recognized and protected. It was eminently proper, as we excluded them north of it, that our institutions should be recognized and protected south of that line. That, sir, was plain English; that everybody could understand; but here we are interpolating law Latin into the Constitution; this word "*status*" is introduced; and who is to determine what the *status* was? I thought it had been considered a march forward, a step of progress, an evidence of improvement in English legislation, when it abandoned Norman French and law Latin, and resorted to the mother tongue; and especially it should be so, when we are making constitutions for American people of English descent, and who speak the English tongue. A constitution is for the millions, and the millions should be able to understand it.

But, Mr. President, let us proceed a little further. This whole matter is to be subject to judicial cognizance in the Federal courts, according to the course of common law. That embraces the right of the master to his slave as a matter of cognizance under the common law before the courts; because what do they mean by the *status* of all persons held to involuntary servitude or labor? They mean rightfully held. They do not mean if a man is kidnapped and held illegally to involuntary service or labor that he is always to be so held. It means that the *status* of persons who are rightfully and legally held shall not be changed; and who is to determine that? The courts are to determine it according to the common law. That is to be determined by judges who are to be appointed from a party, and by a party who believe that there cannot be property in man; by a party who believe that, in the Somerset case, Lord MANSFIELD has laid down the common law properly; by a party who will probably believe that the decision of the English courts, in regard to the slave ANDERSON, that it was no murder for a slave when escaping to kill his master, was a correct exposition of the common law.

How, then, do we stand? Why, sir, in relation to our right to slaves, we have to try that right before judges who are thus appointed, and appointed from a party who we know entertain these opinions. Why, sir, you might poll that party through the whole United States, and I would venture any thing upon the assertion that you cannot get one in a hundred thousand who would not deny that there could be property in man, especially under the common law. We thus lose the advantage of the Dred Scott decision. According to the Dred Scott decision, we can carry them into the territory of the United States and hold them, and it is decided that there is property in slaves—decided under the Constitution. The court maintain that the Constitution recognizes it. It is upon constitutional ground that we have made our claims, and so far, it is upon this that we have fought and won the battle, not upon common law; and now we are to abandon the advantages that we have got from that ground of title under the Dred Scott decision, and go into court and try a case that has been already decided in our favor; and under the common law, try it before judges who are to be selected by a party entertaining such opinions as I have just described; and I am sorry to say, without appeal to the Supreme Court; because, in the territorial bills which have been lately passed, that right has been taken from us. My friend from North Caroina will be kind enough to read an article in the Chicago platform, showing what is held on that subject by those who wield the power of this Government.

Mr. CLINGMAN read, as follows:

Eighth. "That the normal condition of all the territory of the United States is that of freedom; that as our republican fathers, when they had abolished slavery in all our national territory, ordained that 'no person should be deprived of life, liberty, or property, without due process of law,' it becomes our duty, by legislation, whenever such legislation is necessary, to maintain this provision of the Constitution against all attempts to violate it; and we deny the authority of Congress, of a Territorial Legislature, or of any individuals, to give legal existence to slavery in any Territory of the United States."

Mr. HUNTER:—Thus much, Mr. President, in regard to the *status;* and it is to be observed that the same word is used in reference to persons who are now held to involuntary servitude in the Territories and to those whom we are to have the right to take into the Territories from the States recognizing slavery. So that we submit this question of our right to slaves, when it reaches the Territories, to be tried under the common law, by courts appointed by the party entertaining the opinions I have described, and that without appeal. This is in regard to the Territories which we now own. What is the settlement provided for in regard to territory hereafter to be acquired? Here it is, in the third section:

SECTION 3. Neither the Constitution, nor any amendment thereof, shall be construed to give Congress power to regulate, abolish, or control, within any State, the relation established or recognized by the laws thereof touching persons held to labor or involuntary service therein, nor to interfere with or abolish involuntary service in the District of Columbia without the consent of Maryland, and without the consent of the owners, or making the owners who do not consent just compensation; nor the power to interfere with or prohibit Representatives and others from bringing with them, to the District of Columbia, retaining and taking away, persons so held to labor or service; nor the power to interfere with or abolish involuntary service in places under the exclusive jurisdiction of the United States within those States and Territories where the same is established or recognized.

That is, they shall not prohibit it as to future acquired territory, where it is established or recognized. Will not the inference be claimed from such an expression, that where it is not established and not recognized, they may prohibit it? Will it not be said that the expression of one exception to the power of Congress to prohibit slavery in the Territories excludes the idea of an exception to that power when slavery is not recognized in the Territories?

Mr. COLLAMER:—If the gentleman will indulge me a moment, I desire to say that is a section declaring that Congress shall not abolish slavery in the dock-yards, &c., in the States where it is recognized. There is nothing in it about future acquired territory.

Mr. HUNTER:—This third section applies not only to present but to future acquired territory. It is not confined, like the first section, to the territory at present acquired. It is not confined to dock-yards and arsenals in the Territories and States. If the Senator will examine it, he will find that it is applied to all places where the United States have exclusive jurisdiction. "Exclusive jurisdiction" is the word. Will it not be claimed that they have exclusive jurisdiction in the Territories of the United States? Will not those who have the power to construe, and carry out their construction, so construe it? Will they not say it is a prohibition to Congress to prohibit slavery where it is recognized in the Territories or States, but not a denial of the right to prohibit slavery in Territories where it is not recognized by law, although that Territory may be vacant and uninhabited?

Mr. COLLAMER:—That clause of the section is, that Congress shall not have power—

"To interfere with or abolish involuntary service in places under the exclusive jurisdiction of the United States within those States and Territories where the same is established or recognized."

That, so far as I have read, is confined only to where they have local jurisdiction in the States holding slaves.

Mr. HUNTER:—I thought so at first myself; but the Senator will find, on a further examination, I think, that he is mistaken. They shall not prohibit it wherever they have exclusive jurisdiction in places where slavery "is established or recognized." It is not confined to dock-yards, forts, and arsenals. Why should it be in the Territories? They have exclusive jurisdiction over the whole. There is reason for confining it to dock-yards in the States; but there is no reason for confining it to dock-yards, &c., in the Territories. But that is not the construction which will be given; the construction given to it will be, that they shall not prohibit it where they have exclusive jurisdiction, if it is recognized in such places; but if it be not recognized in such places, where they have exclusive jurisdiction, I say the inference will be drawn, plausibly, if not justly, that they shall have power to prohibit; and I say if this be so, then it is a power (so far as Mexican territories are concerned, if there should be any acquisition there) by which the South will be forever estopped; because there the Mexicans have abolished slavery, and there, under this clause giving in that territory exclusive jurisdiction, the party now controlling the Government would claim the right to prohibit it. And what a difference between our position then and our position now under the decision of the Supreme Court! Under the decision of that court, all the people of all the States have a right to go into the common territory with their institutions. It belongs to all in common, and Congress cannot prohibit them from taking their property there.

I say that those who have the power to carry out any construction they choose to give, would be interested in putting upon it the construction which I fear; and it would be difficult to raise an argument which they would deem conclusive against it. But take it the other way; suppose that the Senator from Vermont is right in his first supposition, that it was only meant to be applied to forts, arsenals, and dock-yards, then I ask what settlement does this proposition give us in regard to future acquired territories; what earthly settlement is it? We have all the old difficulties to encounter that we have to meet now, every one of them. We not only have all the old difficulties to encounter, but the slaveholder would have an additional obstacle which this first clause would put in his way. It requires that the right to slaves in the present territory shall be tried by the common law, and it might be said in court that the inferences drawn heretofore from those provisions of the Constitution recognizing slavery were to be overruled by the fact that the people in their latest action—by way of constitutional amendment—had introduced another rule in order to determine the *status* of those held to involuntary service or labor, and the consequence of that would be that the South never could acquire another foot of territory; that is, the few southern States who are left in the Union.

I am told that here is a provision that you cannot acquire territory except by the assent of a majority of the Senators from both sections. Does any man believe that the North, with its eighteen, soon to be twenty, or thirty, non-slaveholding States, would allow a majority of six, or seven, or eight slave States, that are now attached to them, to prevent them from acquiring any territory hereafter? Would they agree to such an amendment, in the first instance; and if they did, how long before they would change this restriction in the Constitution? Indeed, it is hardly to be supposed that they will agree to it in the first instance, so far as it regards the acquisition of territory; but of what avail would it be to the South? There is but one conceivable acquisition—I speak of possible things, and I hope gentlemen will not understand me as coveting my neighbor's goods, or desiring to lay violent hands on the property of any other States or nations—but, if things should so happen that we could rightfully acquire Cuba, under my view of the probable construction to be given to this clause, and because slavery there is recognized, Congress might be prevented from prohibiting it; but, everywhere else, the South would be shut out and excluded.

Then, sir, what would be its position? It would be prevented from acquiring any territory under this Government as an outlet for its slaves; and the only chance of securing that necessity of its condition would be to quit this Union and join the Southern Confederacy, which can acquire territory. It would be an inducement to disunion so strong as would almost force them to it.

Let us go a little further. Here is another clause holding out the same temptation:

"The foreign slave-trade is hereby forever prohibited, and it shall be the *duty* of Congress to pass laws to prevent the importation of slaves, coolies, or persons held to service or labor, into the United States and the Territories from places beyond the limits thereof."

This is to be the duty of Congress. As it now stands, it is in the power of Congress. When it was merely given as a power to Congress, was there a failure to execute that power? Do we not know that every State in the present Confederation has desired to suppress the African slave-trade? Some do it from sentiment and principle; some from interest; but there is a controlling motive with each and all of them. It is safe enough to leave it where it stood, giving Congress the power merely. Here you make it their duty. Suppose this case: the States that have left us have set up another Government, another Confederation; under this clause you forbid us to buy their slaves, to interchange and trade in slaves with them: what will be the consequence? They will exclude us from selling our slaves in their territory, and where then do we stand? If you should think it prudent, if you should think it politic, you would have no means, under this proposed amendment, of allowing that to be done between these two coterminous countries. Though it would be to the advantage of both Confederacies that there should be this interchange, you preclude Congress from allowing it; and then where would that place the border slave States? They would not be able to sell their slaves in the States further South; and if they carried them there, they would have to emigrate with them. You would thus prevent Congress from adopting a regulation which would make it possible for them to remain in this Union with safety, with advantage, to themselves. Why was this put in? Why not have left it where it stood, giving Congress the power, when we all know that there is no State in the present Confederation that would not exercise that power for the purpose of suppressing the slave-trade from Africa? This probably would constitute the only exception. Why shut ourselves out from allowing the exception?

But, Mr. President, my desire is to be brief; I do not want to consume the time of the Senate; I am merely endeavoring to state the points of objection as briefly as I can. Here is, at the close of it, another provision which, it seems to me, contains the seeds of civil war; and that is this: "Congress shall provide by law for securing to the citizens of each State the privileges and immunities of citizens in the several States;" that is to say, Congress shall have power to pass laws to force the States to receive those persons whom they have excluded from police considerations—considerations of domestic safety. Yes, sir, to force the States to receive persons who would be dangerous to their peace; to force upon them, if you will, abolition lecturers; to force upon them persons whom they regard as the most dangerous emissaries that could be sent among them; to enable Congress to obtrude, in fact, into all the business of the States. That was not intended when the Constitution was framed, and never ought to have been. The present provision in regard to the rights of citizens in the several States, I regard as in the nature of an inter-treaty stipulation. It is a duty imposed on each State, for the violation of which there is no remedy; no remedy, unless the State aggrieved may resort sometimes to retaliation.

There are various things of that sort in the Constitution. Duties imposed upon the States, but without a remedy for the failure to execute them. No State shall keep a standing army; but suppose it does: what are you to do? Congress cannot remedy it; and it would not be right to give Congress the power to remedy it. You have to trust something to the sense of right and duty of the States themselves; and so it should be in regard to this matter of citizens. Suppose one State should say that the citizens of another should not sue in its courts; how is Congress to enforce their right? Is Congress to say they shall be allowed to sue, and that the Sheriffs and officers of the State shall execute the process? Is it proposed to allow Congress, by law, to interpose in all these delicate matters? Is it not far better to leave it to the sense of justice of the States—to their sense of duty and of honor? Have we not got along very well while we left it there? If there be any instances in which there have been exceptions, they are instances in which persons have been excluded on account of police considerations, deemed to be dangerous to the safety of the people who excluded them. Is it proposed so to amend the Constitution as to take from the people of the States this right of self-defence?

If we once introduced this as an amendment to the Constitution, what would become of the feeble southern States, six or seven (for Delaware can hardly be considered as a slave State), that would be left? Arkansas may conclude to secede whon she shall determine finally upon her position in the Union. What would become of us in the hands of this powerful majority, who would pass what laws they pleased in regard to the introduction of their citizens among us, and the rights of those citizens to do as they pleased after they got there? Is it not obvious that these various changes would lead to endless discontents, to irreparable breaches between these States? Would you not certainly drive out the Border States? They would say, "If we go south, we ally ourselves to a homogeneous people; we shall have none of these difficulties; we have no reason to fear their citizens; we can grant all these privileges without the least difficulty or danger; we can send our slaves south from a country where they are not profitable, to one where they are; but if we stay here, we are forbidden to do any of these things; if we stay here, we are prevented from ever obtaining any outlet for our slave property." Will you not offer them the highest inducements, nay, will you not make it almost necessary for them to leave you, if you should adopt such a proposition as this?

Nor is that all, Mr. President. Our present Constitution—for I am comparing our position under it with that in which this would place us—in most of its difficult provisions has been expounded—expounded by the action of the State Governments, by the action of all the departments of the Federal Government. We have had legal interpretations in the decisions of the State and Federal courts. We have come almost to a point—indeed, I, who believe that the Dred Scott decision is law, think we have come to a point—where we have a legal exposition on the whole of these matters. Are we to be turned aside from that, to wander into a new sea of doubt and difficulty and ambiguity? No candid man can take this up and say it is not full of double constructions, full of ambiguities, giving ground for new quarrels between the sections, to new constructions of courts, to new lawsuits.

Mr. COLLAMER:—And to be perpetual.

Mr. HUNTER:—Yes, sir; and to be made perpetual. We cannot change them afterwards, if we want to do it. I can conceive nothing that would endanger what is left of this Union so much as the adoption of this proposition, although it has been produced by persons so eminent and so respectable as those who composed the Peace Congress.

I know that this measure does emanate from a body eminently patriotic and wise, entitled to the public deference and affection; and for their work I feel all possible respect. Against that work I will pronounce nothing except what the necessities of the occasion may require. But when the peace, the safety, the rights of the State which I seek to represent—when the peace of the whole country, as it seems to me, would be so seriously imperilled as it would be if this were adopted, I feel bound by a sense of what I owe to those who sent me here, bound by a sense of what I owe to those who have some respect for my opinions, to express them here on this occasion, and to give briefly the points and the heads upon which I differ from the conclusions of that Congress. Indeed, sir, before taking my seat, I may suggest a doubt whether I am in truth acting against any thing which they have really done. I was informed by a member of that Congress that they never did take a vote upon this proposed article, as a whole.

Mr. DOOLITTLE:—If the Senator will allow me, I beg leave to state that I was informed of the same fact by a distinguished member of the Convention; and I was further informed that the person who claims to be the secretary of the Convention was never elected as such. And there is another fact stated in the preamble that I know is not correctly stated: that the State of Wisconsin was in that Convention, or took any part in it. How many more mistakes there are in the preamble, I am unable to say.

Mr. HUNTER:—I believe it is certain that they never did take a vote on this article as a whole, but upon its separate sections. I think it equally probable that it could not have passed as a whole. That opinion was expressed to me by a member. As it did pass, I think there were three or four States not voting; and the States not voting were supposed to be against it. Under such circumstances, I do not know that this is to be taken as an expression of the will of that Congress. Further: I will say, in regard to myself, that a majority of the members from my own State voted against it, and were very decided in their opposition to it. They believed it was not such a proposition as the South could safely accept; and that majority, I believe, have returned home to express that opinion to the State Convention, and to give their reasons for it. Under all these circumstances, I have thought that I ought to present, as a counter proposition (believing that the people whom I represent cannot and ought not to accept these), resolutions upon which they have said they were willing to settle this controversy. I believe the State of Kentucky has declared the same thing. I understand the State of California has done likewise. I believe, though I may be mistaken, that Tennessee has said the same. The State of North Carolina has made the same declaration unanimously. To the last, I believe I may add Missouri.

Now, I am making a proposition to amend, by inserting the resolutions of the honorable Senator from Kentucky; upon which so many of the border slaveholding States have said they would settle the difference. Why not send them out to the States and the people? We know that some of them would settle on that. Why should we send out such a proposition as this, which there is every reason to believe they will not accept, and which will have the effect of dividing the conservative men of the North? Those northern men who are willing to settle on some proposition that would give satisfaction to the Border States, would just as soon vote for the CRITTENDEN resolutions as for these, and some probably would prefer to do so. They will waste all their strength, and efforts, and energies, in going for a proposition which the South in the end will not accept, or at least which I do not believe they will accept, as there is every reason to suppose they will not accept it. Then, when we know there are propositions upon which so many of the Border States have said they would be willing to settle existing difficulties, why not submit them? I think, under such circumstances, notwithstanding the respect which I feel for the members composing the Peace Congress, my duty to my own State, whose Legislature has spoken in regard to it, and my sympathy with so many of the Southern States who have declared the same opinion, should induce me to present the proposition which they desire instead of one to which none of them have as yet given their adhesion, and to which I have no idea they will ever agree.

Mr. CRITTENDEN:—I suppose, Mr. President, not only out of deference to the Presiding Officer of this body, but because it seems to me to be entirely reasonable, that the decision of the Chair on the question of order which was made as to the admissibility of these amendments, was correct. The question which these amendments present, I think, is a question of consistency or inconsistency with the proceeding in which we are engaged, with the resolutions offered by the Peace Conference; and each member, in deciding ultimately upon the question for or against the proposed amendment, will consider that question of consistency or inconsistency, and regulate his vote accordingly. It is not, perhaps, strictly a question of order, to be decided on the consistency or inconsistency of amendments. So I take it. I am willing it should be decided by this body. Now, what is it? The proposed amendment contravenes the whole nature of the transaction, and changes its character. The representatives of twenty-one or twenty-two States—we will not make any question about Kansas; whether it be in or not, is not material—the representatives and delegates of over twenty States of the Union have recommended to us the adoption of certain amendments to the Constitution, which they say will arrest the troubles of the country and adjust those great differences which now so much threaten us; and they ask Congress to propose these amendments to the several States, according to the fifth article of the Constitution, for their adoption. These amendments have been submitted to us, and the question is, whether we will submit them to the States or not? That I take to be the specific and solitary question. This imposes no obligation on us to sanction these constitutional amendments by proposing them to the people. We can do as we please upon that point; but what is the question and the only question? It is not whether we ourselves will propose amendments to the Constitution, but whether we will propose to the people the amendments which this Convention has proposed to us. Now, that whole character is effaced, and a new character is given to the transaction, if any one of the amendments proposed by Senators be adopted.

Suppose these same States, by their Legislatures, had respectively recommended to us these particular and specific constitutional amendments, asking us to propose them according to the Constitution: would it have been proper for us then to undertake to amend their resolutions? It would be a different transaction altogether. In the one instance, out of respect to the States, we are proposing their resolutions; in the other case, we are proposing our own to the States. Now, the question here is, whether the resolutions have come to us with a sufficient sanction to constitute in our minds a reason for referring to the States the amendments which the States themselves have asked. That is all. It seems to my mind to be a clear question. They have asked us, they have requested us, to submit their resolutions, and not any others, to the States; and the question is, will we comply with their request, not whether we will fabricate amendments of our own and refer them to the people. They have asked of us to submit their proposals; and the question is, whether we will do it.

This amendment implies, in the first instance, that we will not do that, because the moment we adopt the amendment of the Senator from Virginia, that moment we say in effect, "We will not propose your recommendations to the people; while proposing our own, which we will substitute for yours." That is passing by this Convention altogether; it is negativing the States represented in it.

If gentlemen take this view it will be a sufficient reason, I trust, in itself, for voting against the proposed amendment. These propositions which the Convention has recommended may be such as we may refuse; it is in our power to refuse; but the question is, whether a recommendation, coming so sanctioned to us, is not, in itself, a sufficient reason why Congress, if disposed to satisfy the people, shall do the small act of presenting this to the people themselves, for their adoption. We may reject it, if we please. The people, when it is sent to them, will, of course, have the power to reject or adopt it. The only question now is, whether we will give the States an opportunity of saying whether this proposition is satisfactory or not.

Sir, I do not wish to occupy time; but I cannot perceive the justice of the criticisms made upon these resolutions of the Convention. They seem to me to be perspicuous and intelligible in every part and in every sentence. I do not see where the difficulty is to arise. Gentlemen need not tell us here, in respect to these resolutions, that a member of the Convention told them thus and so. No matter what a member of the Convention told this one or that one about the votes that were given, it is certified to us, in a formal manner, by the President of the Convention—himself a Virginian, and once a President of the United States—that this is the result of the proceedings of the Convention.

Mr. HUNTER:—If the Senator will allow me, I will state to him how that occurred. It was decided, as it will be seen when we get the Journal, that, according to some rules of the old Convention, they should not vote upon a proposition as a whole, but upon each particular provision. That was the rule of the Convention; and therefore he certified it as the Convention had instructed. The vote was taken only section by section, and the vote was never taken on it as a whole. There is no inconsistency between what I have said, and the certificate of the President of the Convention, because, according to the rules adopted by them, he had to certify it if it was adopted by sections, though it was not voted upon as a whole.

Mr. CRITTENDEN:—I suppose this remark is intended to annul the Convention, and discredit all their proceedings, though the Senate have received the letter of the President and Secretary as authentic evidence that this does contain the result of the deliberations and the proceedings of the body. I take it so, whatever a discontented member here and there may have said to the contrary notwithstanding. He may have said it all truly, for aught I know, but we must regard this as the authentic act of the Convention; otherwise it was nothing; and it is certified to us by the proper authority as its act, by the President of the Convention, with the request that we shall adopt it. It must have had, in some form or shape, the sanction of a majority of the Convention, or it could not have been so certified to us. How they voted, whether upon parts or the whole, they gave such votes as they thought were necessary to ascertain the meaning of the body, and the expression of their will and opinion upon the subject. This is what they have done.

I do not stop to inquire whether I like these resolutions better than I do those proposed by myself, or the amendments now offered by the Senator from Virginia. We are near the close of our session. I have looked upon the proceedings of this great and eminent body of men as the best evidence of public opinion outside of this body, and of the wish and will of the States they represent. I am for peace. I am for compromise. I have not an opinion on the subject of what would be best that I would not be perfectly willing to sacrifice to obtain any reasonable measure of pacification that would satisfy the majority. I want to save the country and adjust our present difficulties. [Applause in the galleries.]

The PRESIDING OFFICER (Mr. BRIGHT in the chair) called to order.

Mr. CRITTENDEN:—That is what I want to do. That is the object I am aiming at. I attach no particular importance—I feel, at least, no selfish attachment—to any opinions I may have proclaimed on the subject heretofore. I proclaimed those opinions because I thought them right; but I am ready to sacrifice them, any and every one of them, to any more satisfactory proposition that can be offered. I look upon the resolutions proposed by this Convention as furnishing us, if not the last, the best hope of an adjustment; the best hope for the safety of the people and the preservation of the Government. I will not stop to cavil about the construction of these words; but I see none of the difficulties that suggest themselves to the mind of my friend from Virginia. Look at that third section, which has been the subject of his particular criticism. Every part and portion of it is a negation of power to Congress, and nothing else; and yet he has argued as if it gave Congress power; as if it conferred more power upon Congress. It leaves to the States all the rights they now have; all the remedies which they now have; and consists merely in a negation of power to Congress. How can that take away the rights of the people? How can that make our condition worse? I cannot possibly see. It is nothing but a negative from beginning to end; and therefore it cannot take away any thing from the people. It may take from Congress, but cannot take away from the States, or the people, any thing. It is a negative in its form and in its language, from beginning to end, that Congress shall have no power to do this, that, or the other. If they have that power under the present Constitution, it is taken away. That is all. It takes away no power from the States. It takes away no rights from individuals. Its simple office is the negation of power to Congress. That is all there is in it; and how, under that, can the gentleman find constructions which are to increase our difficulties and diminish our rights? He says the language will need construction. So does all language need construction. I do not see that this is particularly so.

Now, sir, the Senator offers my own proposition as an amendment to this. I shall vote against my own proposition here; I shall vote for this. [Applause in the galleries.]

Mr. MASON:—I shall be constrained to require that the galleries be cleared, if there be any further demonstrations in that quarter.

Mr. BAKER:—I hope the galleries will not be cleared. The admiration of a noble sentiment is never out of place.

The PRESIDING OFFICER:—There is no motion to clear the galleries.

Mr. CRITTENDEN:—I shall vote for the amendments proposed by the Convention, and there I shall stand. That is the weapon offered now, and placed in my hand, by which, as I suppose, the Union of these States may be preserved; and I will not, out of any selfish preference for my own original opinions on this subject, sacrifice one idea or one particle of that hope. I go for the country; not for this resolution or that resolution, but any resolution, any proposition, that will pacify the country. Therefore, I vote against my own, to give place to a proposition which comes from an authority much higher than mine—from one hundred and thirty of the most eminent men of this country, out of which number a Senate might be selected that might well compare in point of talent and intellect and ability even with this honorable body. They have recommended this on arduous, laborious consultation with one another; through many difficulties, through many diversities of opinion, they have at last arrived at these conclusions, and sent them to us. Shall any Senator stand upon the little consideration, "this changes my resolution," and shall he compare that little atom of his production with the great end and object proposed to be attained for a whole nation? No, sir; not a moment. I believe our best hope of preservation is in adopting the resolutions proposed by this Convention, and I adhere to them against all amendments.

Mr. President, the only material or substantial change in respect to the first section of this proposed amendment from my first proposition is, that it omits all reference to territory hereafter acquired, limiting our consideration and our settlement to territory which we now have. When I first offered my resolutions, I explained somewhat in reference to that particular provision which related to future territory. I said that I wanted no more territory. Our great trouble now is from the magnitude of the territory which we have already acquired. New Mexico is one of our acquisitions, and what a subject of dispute it has been! I want no more acquisitions. My country is big enough, and great enough. I say that further acquisitions are dangerous. We have found them to be so. Our experience and our reason, then, unite in teaching us "to beware of that sin, ambition." National aggrandizement! I want no more. I proposed that, however, as the idea then was, that we wanted a settlement that was to last forever; to be eternal; to embrace the present and to embrace the future, with all its acquisitions, all its changes. Reflection since, and the arguments of others, I will say, have changed my opinion on that point. If they had not changed it, however, I should be ready here to sacrifice it and give it up, if thereby I could obtain the assent of any respectable portion of my countrymen to the propositions for peace. If we can settle in respect to what we have, in God's name let us do it; and if we are to have future acquisitions, let us leave the troubles they may bring upon us to a future day. We have enough for to-day. I do not object, therefore, to the first section of the proposition of the Convention, that it is confined to the territory which we now have. The adjustment which they have made varies but little in substance in regard to the territorial question, and the question of slavery as connected with it, from my original proposition. South of the line which we propose to establish, 36° 30′, you have no foot of territory left, but what is embraced in the Territory of New Mexico. In New Mexico, by law of the Territory—a constitutional law, a valid law of the Territory—slavery exists as fully and completely as the law can establish it, or has established it.

Now, this proposition is, that the *status* of things shall continue as it is until that Territory becomes a State; and when it becomes a State, let it dispose of the question of slavery as it chooses. There is no ambiguity about this. In substance, though in a different form of words, the same is expressed in my proposition. The proposition of the Convention is the same in substance, only omitting the words—a very proper and a very timely omission—supposed to be offensive in certain parts of the country, and substituting others that are equally well understood in all parts of the country, and which were less offensive to some.

Sir, now is the time for mediation; now is the time for pacification; now is the time to omit every word that can give offence or add to the irritation under which the country is. I desire, by the most moderate terms, by the most unoffending language, to reach some mode of adjustment that can give satisfaction to the whole country and reunite us all.

My friend from Virginia seems to apprehend that under these amendments we shall be worse off in respect to territory hereafter acquired. That is supposed to be sufficiently provided for and secured in the provision, that no future acquisition shall be made, by purchase or by treaty, except that treaty or that purchase be ratified by a majority of the Senators from the slaveholding States, as well as a majority of Senators from the non-slaveholding States. Does not this give the South a safe assurance, an assurance to be relied upon? My friend from Virginia says, however, do we believe the North, with its superior number, would submit to this provision of the Constitution? Why, sir, the Convention have had the caution to make this provision, *if I understand them, irrepealable by any future amendment of the* Constitution. There it stands, then, in the most solemn form that men can enter into any compact, in the most formal language by any terms that Government can establish, that all are bound by that provision of the Constitution which requires a majority from each section. When the gentleman asks whether we can believe for a moment that this law will be acquiesced in and adhered to, I say we must to some extent have confidence in one another, or all human society must lose its basis, not merely of government, but its foundation, and all society would be torn up at once by the roots. That confidence is the root of society; it is the root of all the associations of men in public or private life; it is the root and foundation of all government. What more can you have, what better security can you have than written, solemn terms upon any subject which is to regulate government? There is nothing more solemn among men, unless you would require angels to come down and make responses for them. Here you have the very highest security that can be given; and when any gentleman shall say these are not to be relied upon, he says there is no Government that stands upon any foundation that can be relied upon. Such an assertion strikes not at this provision; it strikes at the root of all government. What further security can be had? If our brethren of the other section were willing to give the highest possible security they could, what can they give more? Nothing. This argument, then, can avail nothing.

Mr. President, I have gone perhaps a little further than I ought to have done. It is not now necessary that I should enter into a vindication of every provision of these amendments offered by the Convention. It is sufficient to speak to the amendment which the gentleman has offered. Excluding territory hereafter to be acquired, I think, in substance, we ought to be satisfied with that; I believe that will make peace; I believe that will give substantial security to our rights, and to the rights which the Southern States claim. With that I am satisfied. It is enough for the dreadful occasion. It is the dreadful occasion that I want to get rid of. Rid me of this, rid the nation of this, and I am willing to take my chance for the future and meet the perils of every day that may come. Now is the appointed time upon which our destiny depends. Now is the emergency and exigency upon us. Let us provide for them. Save ourselves now, and trust to posterity and that Providence which has so long and so benignly guided this nation, to keep us from the further difficulties which in our national career may be in our way.

I prefer the propositions which the Convention have made to my own propositions, because I have no hope for my propositions. They have not been so fortunate as to receive the favor of my colleagues of the Senate from the North, the men whose sanction of them was necessary to give them effect. I transfer all my hopes of peace to these propositions and terms proposed by the Convention representing twenty-odd of the States of this Union—a large majority of all the States. I will not go into particulars about it; but since gentlemen have made some allusion to the out-of-door rumors and reports and sayings in respect to this Convention, I believe that perhaps a majority of those who voted for these amendments were men representing non-slaveholding States. I do not know the fact, and I will not state it, but I am under that impression now, and that impression encourages my hopes that the Senate, rather than see the country fall into ruin, fall into dismemberment, limb from limb, and blood flowing at the plucking out of every limb, will supply the remedy which is proposed. It seems to me proper and just. But little is asked, and great is the reward, and mighty are the consequences that are to flow from it.

Sir, I have occupied more of the time of the Senate on this particular question than I ought to have done.

Mr. MASON:—Mr. President, there is a very grave duty devolving upon the Senate on the proposition which is now before us. We are called upon, pursuant to the Constitution, to propose amendments to the Constitution. The fifth article of the Constitution says this:

"The Congress, whenever two-thirds of both Houses shall deem it necessary, shall propose amendments to this Constitution."

Now, sir, I cannot agree, for one, to propose an amendment to this Constitution unless it has the sanction and the approbation of my judgment; and I suppose no other Senator will. I am bound, therefore, by every obligation of faith and honor to my State, when a proposition is submitted to the Senate as one that should be proposed to the States as an amendment to the Constitution, to examine it and understand it, and see it in all its bearings and effects, as far as my intellect will enable me, and to propose it or to withhold it by my vote, as I shall be guided by my judgment. I can see no other position of a Senator.

Now, sir, what are the facts? The country was convulsed by the success in the late presidential election of one of the political parties of the country. The tremor was evinced at once in all the Southern States, in a belief that their existence and their safety was imperilled by that election. Congress met. As was proper and necessary, the very first act in each House was to appoint a committee to take the condition of the country into consideration, and see if, by any mode of amendment to the Constitution, those perils could be avoided. A committee was raised in the collateral branch. A committee was raised in this Senate, I think upon the motion of the honorable Senator from Kentucky, actuated as he always is by principles of the highest patriotism. Those committees met. They remained in anxious deliberation for weeks. What was the result? They were unable to agree. I think the committee came before the Senate and admitted the fact. They could agree upon no form of amendment which they believed would remedy the evils and avert the perils under which the country suffered.

In that state of things, the Legislature of Virginia—my own honored State—having been called into special session on the 19th of January, passed a series of resolutions, one of which recites this:

> "That on behalf of the Commonwealth of Virginia, an invitation is hereby extended to all such States, whether slaveholding or non-slaveholding, as are willing to unite with Virginia in an earnest effort to adjust the present unhappy controversies in the spirit in which the Constitution was originally formed, and consistently with its principles, so as to afford to the people of the slaveholding States adequate guarantees for the security of their rights."

That is the recital of the resolution of the Legislature of Virginia: "to afford to the people of the slaveholding States adequate guarantees for the security of their rights;" and there was a further provision, that, if those States should meet and agree upon any form of adjustment, it should be submitted to Congress. A number of the States—some twenty or twenty-one, it seems—some by their Legislatures, some by their Executives—met the invitation of Virginia, and deputed their commissioners to the conference in Washington, to see if they could agree upon a mode of adjustment. We have the report of that Conference before us now, presented through a committee of this body; and they propose an additional article to the Constitution. Mr. President, the honorable Senator from Kentucky, who has pronounced so deserved a eulogium upon that body, does not exceed me in the respect which I bear to it. If there be one more than another Senator upon whom it would devolve to treat the work of that Convention with peculiar respect, it would devolve upon me and my colleague, because they met at the invitation of my State. I yield to none in the respect which I bear to those gentlemen or to the purity of their motives in the results which they have attained in that Conference; but, sir, I am bound by my obligations to the Constitution, by my honor as a man, by my faith to my own State, to understand what they have done, and to exhibit it either in recommendation or disapproval, as my judgment may dictate. *Nullius addictus jurare in verba magistri.*

I admit no authority to bind my judgment as a representative of one of the States of the Union. I yield my respect to what they have done; but I will scan it, and if, in my honest, unbiased judgment, I cannot recommend it as an amendment to the Constitution, I am bound to withhold that recommendation, and to give the reasons for it.

As I have said, sir, the State of Virginia, finding that Congress was at a loss for a mode of adjustment, invited the States to send commissioners here for this purpose:

"To agree upon something which would afford to the people of the slaveholding States adequate guarantees for the security of their rights."

Virginia knew that, under the Constitution as it was interpreted under the constituted authorities of the country as they have been elected, there was no security for their rights; and it was in the hope of obtaining such a security—Congress failing to agree upon it—that, at her invitation, these gentlemen from the different States met here in conference. I am to look, therefore, to their work, and to see if it affords that security for their rights; and if I am satisfied in my own judgment, as I honestly am—and the reasons for which I am now to announce to the world—that it not only affords no security for the rights of the South, but takes away what little they have, I should be a traitor if I would recommend it as an amendment to the Constitution of the United States.

Now, sir, let us look at it. It is presented as an entire article, to be the thirteenth article, if adopted, of the Constitution. The first section of it relates to the Territories—the great and difficult point of division between the two sections. If that could be overcome—if these rights that are spoken of in the resolutions of Virginia in the Territories could be guaranteed by adequate securities to the slaveholding States—I believe the rest of the path would be smooth. It embraces almost the whole controversy. What securities are provided in the Territories to the slaveholding States by this first section of the thirteenth article? It proposes to divide the present Territories—for it is confined to them—by an east and west line, a parallel of latitude. North of that line, there is a clear cut entirely, unsusceptible of misinterpretation. None can doubt what the condition of servitude is north of that line. It is a clear cut; it is prohibited, and prohibited forever. No interpretation can mistake it; no casuist can doubt upon it; it is a work well done. North of that line involuntary servitude, except for crime, is prohibited. How is it south? My honorable colleague, I think, has well said that, south of that line, for our rights, at best we are remitted to a lawsuit. I will read the language:

"Nor shall any law be passed by Congress or the Territorial Legislature to hinder or prevent the taking of such persons—"

That is, persons held to service—

"from any of the States of this Union to said Territories, nor to impair the rights arising from said relation."

Neither Congress nor the Territorial Legislature has power to interfere with the rights arising from the relation of master and servant, or master and slave. That is the meaning; that is clear. What next?

"But the same—"

The rights resulting from the relation of master and slave—

"shall be subject to judicial cognizance in the Federal courts, according to the course of the common law."

There is the security for the rights of the South. South of that line they are remitted to the courts under the common law. Now, sir, let us examine that. By this section, if it is adopted as an article of the Constitution, the common law, *eo nomine*, is made a part of the Constitution, so far as it affects the relations of master and slave. Now, what is the common law? Who is there upon this floor that will tell me what common law is meant by this section? With all my respect for the thorough knowledge and the legal acquirements of the honorable Senator from Kentucky, I know he cannot tell me what common law is meant by that first section. We know, as jurists, what is meant by the term common law, for it is a technical term. The common law is the law of England, the unwritten law of England, the *lex non scripta*. That is the common law in its legal acceptation. Is it, then, the law of England that is made a part of the Constitution, and to which the master is remitted for the security of his rights between him and his servant? Will any gentleman tell me that it is the common law of England that is to be made a part of the Constitution to which we are to be remitted? If it is the common law of England, is it the common law of England as it stands at this day, on the first of March, 1861?

Mr. CRITTENDEN:—If my friend will allow me, I take it that that term applies only to the remedies known to the common law. The laws of the Territories are to be enforced, and the remedies under them are to be administered according to common law. The master is to have his rights according to the law of the Territory, and to secure those rights according to the common law.

Mr. MASON:—The language of the section is, that neither Congress nor the Territorial Legislature shall interfere to impair the rights arising from this relation of master and slave; "but the same"—that is, this relation between master and slave—"shall be subject to judicial cognizance in the Federal courts, according to the course of the common law."

Now, the honorable Senator says that means only the remedy of the common law; that you are to take the law of the Territory, whatever it may be, and administer that, by confining it to the remedies known to the common law. I deny the interpretation. The Senator may be right, or I may be right. I say the text does not warrant the interpretation. The text refers to the rights in the relation of master and slave, and says they (those rights) shall be the subject of judicial cognizance, according to the course of common law. Now, I ask, what is the common law that is thus made a part of the Constitution for the subject to which it refers? Is it the law of England? There is no common law, that I am aware of, known to jurists as the law of England. There is no law in the State of Virginia, and, I presume, none in the State of Kentucky, known as common law. The State of Virginia, when it became independent as a colony of Great Britain, adopted and made its own that which before had been the common law of England, and therefore the common law of the colony. The State of Virginia (and I instance that only because I am familiar with it), when it became independent, adopted as its law the common law of England, as that common law stood at the commencement of the fourth year of James I.; and thereby, by statute, made that which had been the common law, the law of Virginia. Now, it is the law of Virginia, not because it is the common law, but because statutes made it the law of Virginia. But is the common law of Virginia, if you will call it by that name, the common law of Kentucky; or is the common law of Kentucky the common law of Missouri; or is the law of those three States, or any other State, now the common law of England? I demand to know, therefore, when we make the common law a part of the Constitution, if this enactment should prevail, what is meant by the common law? To that vague, grand residuum of judicial legislation we are to be remitted for our rights between master and slave, if this is enacted.

Now, sir, suppose it were so: my colleague has well said (and I will not repeat it after him, for I should only weaken it), that there is not one judicial interpreter or expounder of the common law, in any one of the free States, in reference to the relation of master and slave, that does not deny that the master has any property in his slave, at this day and this hour. Why, sir, what is the pending controversy between the State of Ohio, one of the free States, and the State of Kentucky, one of the slave States—a controversy depending here recently in the Supreme Court? The Governor of Kentucky demanded, under the Constitution, the rendition of a fugitive from justice, who had abducted a slave from Kentucky, and carried him into Ohio. The Governor of Ohio refused the demand, upon the ground that there could be no stealing of a man; that there could be no property in man; and that the slave, being a man, was not a subject of theft, of larceny; and he refused, and refuses up to this day, under the common law, to recognize the existence of property in man.

Now, take the common law of England at this day: here, within the last three or four weeks, the Queen's Bench, in England, has declared as the common law, that if a slave murders his master, or murders the agent of his master, in the attempt to recapture him, he is justified. That is the common law to which we are to be remitted for the rights resulting from the relations of master and slave. Sir, I have looked back a little to see what the common law was in England in this famous Somerset case. I find this in the argument of the counsel there, expounding the common law, which was afterwards sustained by Lord Mansfield in his decision:

"But it has been said by great authorities, though slavery, in its full extent, be incompatible with the natural rights of mankind, and the principles of good government, yet a moderate servitude may be tolerated, nay, sometimes must be maintained."

And again:

"There is now, at last, an attempt, and the first yet known, to introduce it [slavery] into England. Long and uninterrupted usage, from the origin of the common law, stands to oppose its revival."

And again:

"A new species has never arisen till now; for had it, remedies and powers there, would have been at law; therefore, the most violent presumption against it, is the silence of the laws, were there nothing more. It is very doubtful whether the laws of England will permit a man to bind himself by contract to serve for life; certainly will not suffer him to invest another man with despotism, nor prevent his own right to dispose of property."

And again:

"There are very few instances, few, indeed, of decisions as to slaves in this country. Two in Charles II., where it was adjudged trover would lie. Chamberlayne and Perrin, William III., trover brought for taking a negro slave; adjudged it would not lie. 4th Ann., action of trover; judgment by default. On arrest of judgment, resolved that trover would not lie. Such the determinations in all but two cases; and those the earliest, and disallowed by the subsequent decisions. Lord HOLT: 'As soon as a slave enters England he becomes free.'"

In the opinion of the court, of Lord MANSFIELD, as to these principles of common law, that very distinguished and able judge, who made the law, as I understand, for the occasion, but certainly ruled it as the common law, says this:

"The state of slavery is of such a nature that it is incapable of being introduced for any reasons, moral or political; but only by positive law, which preserves its force long after the reasons, occasion, and time itself from whence it was created, is erased from memory. It's so odious that nothing can be suffered to support it but positive law. Whatever inconveniences, therefore, may follow from a decision, I cannot say this case is allowed or approved by the law of England."

I need not go back to authority. We have it abundantly in our own country, in all the free States, so far as I know, without exception. They deny what the amendment of my honorable friend from Kentucky affirms. They deny that there is property in a slave. The amendment of the Senator affirms there is property in a slave. This section is silent, omniously silent, portentously and potentially silent. It is not only silent, Mr. President, but when it refers you to that code of law which is to protect the right of the master to the slave, it refers you to the common law, and the common law to be expounded by the Federal courts, and the common law, which is judicially and historically known to the whole country, to be expounded in all the free States as one that denies that very property which we say must be secured. That is our position under this section. Sir, the State of Virginia has said that we must have adequate guarantees; and I am asked here to vote away what little guarantees we have. I am asked, almost in the high ethics or morals of revealed religion, when my adversary takes away my cloak, that I shall give him my coat also. I am required to do that by this section. We believe that our rights are secured under the present Constitution; we know that they have been withheld by the political party which has now come into power; we believe that they are insecure unless there are further and adequate guarantees; but, so far from their being proposed by the section before us, in my judgment, what little we have is taken away. Sir, I cannot vote for these propositions.

I regret it. I was prepared, whether it had the approval of my judgment or not, to follow the instructions of my State, and to vote for the amendment offered by the honorable Senator from Kentucky after it had been modified, as was required by the resolutions of my State.

The amendment of the Senator from Kentucky was so modified, I do not know whether at the instance of Virginia or not; but it was modified by a vote of this Senate, so as to embrace what was required in the resolutions of Virginia. I am not at liberty to recommend, or, in the language of the Constitution, to propose to the States this section of the thirteenth article; because it not only withholds, but denies by withholding, any security, far less that security which the State of Virginia requires.

There are further provisions in this proposition that are objectionable, one of which was pointed out by my colleague: that which calls upon Congress to legislate on that clause of the Constitution which secures to the citizens of one State all the privileges and immunities of citizens of the several States. I need not say that any legislation on that subject by Congress would be any thing but the messenger of peace to which the honorable Senator from Kentucky looks. Why, sir, it has been found indispensable in slaveholding States, as a part of their police regulations, to punish all persons who were either of the State or otherwise, who tamper with the slaves, who have intercourse with them that is forbidden by law, far more those who preach to them sedition, or insurrection, or revolt; and yet, if we were to be controlled within the body of the State by Federal relations in our interior police, we should be completely at the mercy of the free States.

Mr. President, I should have been certainly gratified, if my honored State of Virginia had been successful in the mediation which she invited of all the States, with a view to agree upon an adjustment which would guaranty the rights of the South. I deeply deplore, and I doubt not my State will deplore, that that mediation has not been effected. So far from impugning any motives or purpose of that honorable and distinguished body, I doubt not that, in the short time that was allowed to them, they got together the best mode of adjustment which would satisfy their judgment, but which I am sure will not satisfy the judgment of the Southern States, but would place them in still greater peril, if they were to admit that to become a part of the Constitution. I did not intend to do more than state my objections to it as briefly as I could. I have done so temperately and without heat. I regret that I cannot, as one Senator, propose this as an amendment to the Constitution.

Mr. CRITTENDEN:—I wish only to reply for a single moment

to the material objection urged by the Senator from Virginia. The portion of the article to which the Senator from Virginia objects, declares that the *status* of persons bound to service and labor shall remain unchanged; that neither Congress nor the Territorial Legislature shall pass any law affecting the relation, or the rights growing out of the relation between master and servant—I do not pretend to recite the exact words; but that is the exact idea—well knowing that, according to the laws of the Territory, the *status* of slavery was fully established, and all the rights of the master in and to his servant established, as they exist in the State of Missouri, or the State of Virginia, by positive law of the Territory. It is therefore equivalent to saying that that law shall stand, when it says that the *status* shall continue unchanged. It then goes on to say (which I admit was altogether unnecessary) that the remedy for the violation of the rights of the master, whatever they might be, shall be had in the Federal courts, and according to the course of the common law. Now, sir, what right does this take away from any slaveholder? That law which secured and gave him a right, is declared to be unchangeable. That law acknowledges his property in any sense in which you please to take it, or in any sense in which it is applicable. It acknowledges it, and gives legal remedies for the violation of it; and in addition to all that, and, as I admit, by a sort of pleonasm of expression, it says that he shall have his remedy in the Federal court, according to the course of the common law.

Mr. MASON:—Will the Senator allow me a moment?

Mr. CRITTENDEN:—Certainly.

Mr. MASON:—With the permission of the Senator I will put this proposition to him: He says that the meaning of the language, "according to the course of the common law," is confined to the remedy. Now, admitting that to be the case, for the sake of the argument, suppose, in one of these Territories, a slave is purloined, seduced, got away; the slave of A gets into the possession of B, and he is there at work for him upon his farm, or in his house, and A brings an action of trover to recover him; that is an action known to the common law; and the decision of the Federal court is, that trover lies only to recover property, and a slave is not property: what is the remedy? That is the decision in England; and I presume it would be the decision in the free States, if the suit were brought.

Mr. CRITTENDEN:—It was to avoid going into definitions of that sort that this language was employed in the amendments of the Convention. They saw and had before them the law of New Mexico, which did acknowledge the existence of this right as fully as it is acknowledged by the law of Virginia. However it may be disputed here, however legal opinions may differ about it, the law of New Mexico established property in slaves; and there the law stands; and the Convention now comes and says that *status* shall remain unchanged.

Mr. BRAGG:—Oh, no.

Mr. CRITTENDEN:—That is the resolution.

Mr. BRAGG:—Will the honorable Senator allow me a word, for I am very anxious to understand it?

Mr. CRITTENDEN:—Certainly.

Mr. BRAGG:—The Senator says it provides that that law, the law of New Mexico, whatever it may be, shall remain unchanged, if I understand him, and that that fixes the *status* of slavery in the Territory. I call the attention of the Senator to the language. I think that only fixes the *status* of persons now in the Territory, and not those to be carried there hereafter—not the *status* of slavery, but the *status* of persons who are there now, held to service or labor, and not the *status* of those who are to be carried there in future. That is provided for in the language which it follows in another part.

Mr. CRITTENDEN:—Here it is, sir:

"In all the present territory south of that line"—

Which I have explained, and which gentlemen admit to be embraced in the Territory of New Mexico—

"the *status* of persons held to involuntary service or labor, as it now exists."

It is not as to such slaves as are now there, but such slavery as now exists.

Mr. BRAGG:—If it said that, I admit that it would cover the *status* of slavery.

Mr. CRITTENDEN:—It does say that. It seems to me that is the only construction that can be given to the language. It could not be intended to confine it to the twenty-six slaves that are now held there, especially when they provided, in a subsequent article, that it shall be lawful for any one to carry slaves there.

Mr. BRAGG:—Will the honorable Senator again allow me to interrupt him?

Mr. CRITTENDEN:—Certainly.

Mr. BRAGG:—I have not the slightest doubt that a great many who voted for the proposition consider it as the Senator does. I have equally as little doubt that others intended it to mean precisely what I have stated. I cannot see, for my life, while they were framing a constitutional provision, why they did not place this matter beyond any sort of doubt. If they intended to recognize slavery, they could have said so in one word. If they intended not to recognize it, they could have said it in another word. If they intended to mystify and leave in doubt, then they have been very successful in accomplishing their purpose.

Mr. CRITTENDEN :—" In all the present territory south of that line, the *status* of persons held to involuntary service or labor, as it now exists ;" not as they now exist ; not in respect to those that are there now ; but part of the same sort of slavery which now exists, shall continue to exist unchanged until the Territory becomes a State ; and in the mean time persons shall be admitted to go into that Territory and carry their slaves with them. Now, I submit it to my honorable friend if it is not entirely improbable that any such construction as he suggests can prevail before any court that seeks to attain the real intention of the parties who made this proposition? It is such slavery as now exists. Persons held to that service—you may carry as many there as you please. Put them both together, and they would read so ; and they being in the same instrument, can there be a doubt that ought to alarm us here, that the construction will be given to it which I place upon it, that it was intended not to be confined merely to persons now there and held to servitude, but as well to those who might be carried there hereafter? This is all I will say in reference to that ; and I submit it to the candor and the judgment of my honorable friend from North Carolina, in which I have entire confidence, whatever result he may come to, that if we put the two propositions together, all doubt would seem to be removed.

Now, sir, my friend from Virginia will argue this question as if the question of slavery was to be decided according to the course of the common law, and then refers us to the express declarations and decisions as though the common law decided that slavery could not exist. What sort of construction would that make of this provision? Here they have provided that the law establishing slavery shall exist, that the property of the master in him shall be recognized as it is there established by law ; and then the gentleman supposes that to be exactly contradictory, to refer to the common law as furnishing the rule of decision, which common law says there can be no property, as he interprets it, in man, and that when trover was brought for a slave—

Mr. MASON :—Not as I interpret it, but as interpreted in England.

Mr. CRITTENDEN :—I know that. He says it may be so interpreted ; that when trover was brought for a slave in England, the judges decided there was no property in man. Could the same judges, sitting in a court in New Mexico, have given that decision when the law there established such property? In such a case, their decision must be different. They are referring, according to him, to two contradictory rules: one establishing slavery and acknowledging property in the master, and the other the common law denouncing and deciding against the right of property in man. This could not have been their intention, nor can this be the construction. We cannot consider these gentlemen to have changed their opinion from one sentence to another, to have left an incongruity and a contradiction expressed upon the face of the same section.

Nor, sir, do they refer—and that is my answer to my friend from Virginia—to the common law as furnishing the rule of decision at all. The proceedings shall be according to the course of the common law; that is all. If any violation is done to the rights of the master, he may sue; and, for his greater security, he may sue in the Federal courts; and, for greater security still, the law shall be administered according to the course of the common law. The common law is referred to as determining the mode of trial. We say according to the course of the civil law, and we say according to the course of the common law. What do we mean? We mean this marked and characteristic and essential difference: the course of the civil law is for the judge, without the intervention of a jury, to decide facts as well as the law. The common law takes away from the judge the power of deciding the facts, and demands a trial by jury. What this convention mean, therefore, by this provision is, that trial shall be by jury, according to the course of the common law. That is the explanation of the difficulty, and thus all doubt is removed. By these plain provisions—plain in themselves, and made plainer still by being taken with the context—they say you shall have your rule of right, according to the law of the Territory, which is in your favor as to the right to hold persons as property; that law shall be your security; you shall have a remedy for any violation of that right in the Federal courts, and you shall have that remedy, not according to the course of the civil law, in which the judge is to decide, who might be against you, but in which a jury shall be called to decide the fact according to the course of the common law. That is the whole of it.

Mr. MASON:—Mr. President—

Mr. POLK:—If the Senator will allow me, before the Senator from Kentucky sits down, I will ask him if the Mexican law establishes slavery, or if it does any thing more than to protect the right of the master to his slave? If that is the only establishment of it, then it is established by implication merely.

Mr. CRITTENDEN:—I really do not know whether the gentleman would consider it as establishing or merely protecting. I do not know that there is a law in any State of the Union that *eo nomine* establishes slavery; I do not know.

Mr. POLK:—The object of the inquiry was this: it has been contended heretofore that, by the law of Mexico, there could be no slavery there; and then there is another law of New Mexico professing to protect the right of property. I have never seen that New Mexican law.

Mr. CRITTENDEN:—I believe I have answered the gentleman as far as my information extends. I have examined that law. It is as strong in favor of the master as the laws of Kentucky or Missouri. I believe it is the law of Mississippi transcribed literally, *verbatim*. That is my understanding. The law is as complete on the subject as the law of any State that I know of.

Mr. MASON:—Mr. President, if the Senator from Kentucky is right, and, in the interpretation of this section, the courts are necessarily to consider the expression, "according to the course of the common law," to which slaveholders are referred for the enforcing of the relation of master and slave, as referring only to common law remedies, then I am at no loss to conceive, after our experience of judicial interpretation against slavery, by what sort of artificial and sophistic reasoning those judges of the Federal courts may feel themselves bound to withhold the remedy. Why, sir, are we to shut our ears and our eyes against experience passing before us every day? What is the present Constitution? The second section of the fourth article is in these words:

> "A person charged in any State with treason, felony, or other crime, who shall flee from justice, and be found in another State, shall, on demand of the executive authority of the State from which he fled, be delivered up, to be removed to the State having jurisdiction of the crime."

That is the text of the Constitution. What is the interpretation in the free States? In the State of Kentucky an African is property, under their laws and usages, and has been so for two hundred years; for it was so when it was a part of Virginia; and did it ever enter into the mind of man to conceive that this plain text of the Constitution would be resisted, upon the ground that property in man was not acknowledged? And yet it is done. If I am not mistaken, the honorable Senator from New York [Mr. SEWARD], not now in his seat, when Governor of New York, made that very question with the Governor of

Virginia; and seeing this, are we to be willingly blind to this as the actual, judicial, and executive interpretation in every thing that affects the question of slavery as it stands in that section, and that, too, while we are seeking equality? Sir, it never entered into the mind of man, at the time this Constitution was formed, to credit that the time could ever come in the relations of these States when a man who fled from the State of Kentucky because he had stolen a negro into the State of Ohio, was screened from the operation of the Constitution, because in Ohio they do not deem a negro to be the subject of property; and yet that is the fact, the very issue now depending between those States; and we are asked to be blind, willingly blind, to all that experience at the very time we are attempting to secure a guarantee for violated rights!

Now, I said, Mr. President, that, if I were to tax my ingenuity, I might find a mode, even if the honorable Senator is right in ascribing to this clause of the section the necessary interpretation that it refers to remedies only. The Senator says the previous part of the section establishes the relation, as he construes it, not directly like the resolution of the honorable Senator which we offer here as an amendment, which establishes directly that there is property in slaves. This does not; but designedly avoids it; not from any improper motive—I do not ascribe that—but it is not only silent, but it avoids the very question. I suppose the honorable Senator is right in saying this language, judicial cognizance, according to the course of the common law, refers only to the remedy. Now, I tax my ingenuity to know how a court, in one of the free States, always leaning, of course, against slavery, would reason out that proposition, whether the remedy could be applied. Suppose an action of trover is brought. The inquiry would be, what is the remedy? We are told this is the remedy for which you are to apply to the law. A remedy is nothing in the world but a redress for wrong. Before you can apply the remedy, therefore, you must ascertain whether a wrong has been committed for which the remedy is adequate. Well, it comes from one side: the wrong was in taking the negro from the possession of the owner, against the local law of the Territory. The answer would be, "that may be true as far as the local law of the Territory is concerned; but here the Constitution adopts the common law as part of its text, and points the judges to the common law, and it applies the remedy." Now, the remedy is redress of the wrong, and we are bound to see that the wrong is one to which the remedy is applicable. The remedy is to recover property in the possession of one who is not entitled to it, and the common law, which applies that remedy to that wrong, says there is no wrong inflicted by taking the negro from the possession of his owner. It comes to that. It is suggested to me by the honorable Senator from Vermont [Mr. COLLAMER], that the common law, as a remedy, is one applicable to a common-law wrong. I do not say that the reasoning is just; I do not say that it is juridical; but I say, in our experience, we should be willingly blind if we take that for a security which will only be a snare.

Mr. PUGH:—Mr. President, it is very well known to the Senate that I prefer the proposition of the Senator from Kentucky, as a matter of individual choice, to the proposition which is proposed by the Peace Conference. Nevertheless, that Conference having been authorized, if not by Congress, at all events, so far as my State is concerned, by the act of her Legislature; and an overwhelming majority of the commissioners having agreed to this proposition as it stands, I shall hesitate very much in departing from it, whatever might be my individual opinion; but certainly if I thought the two Senators from Virginia had given it a correct interpretation, I should not agree to it. Now, as to this clause, it, in my judgment, had better have been omitted:

"The same shall be subject to judicial cognizance in the Federal courts, according to the course of the common law."

I suggest that the common law is referred to as fixing a right simply. The course of the common law is a phrase defined for more than two hundred years, in Latin, in English, and in Norman French. It means the formula of proceeding. I understood the Senator from Virginia [Mr. MASON] to say that it had been decided in several of the courts that an action of trover could not be brought for a negro slave in England. I think I am familiar with the case. It is reported in Salkeld's Reports, Lord Raymond's Reports, and in the Modern Reports—the same case reported three times; but the same court which decided that trover would not lie, because trover included the idea of property in the man himself, in the same opinion said that trespass on the case would lie for the loss of the service; so that it was all a question of pleading, and no question of right at all. It is within my recollection—and I believe the case was brought to the Supreme Court on a writ of error, and can be found in Howard's Reports—that a citizen of Kentucky declared in trespass on the case for taking away his slaves, and added two counts in trover. What is trover but an action of trespass on the case? Nothing more; and it never was any thing more. The measure of damages is the same in both actions—the value of the service of the servant; and yet that controversy on mere pleading—which, in nine-tenths of the States of this Union, has ceased to be of any value, because they have a code of procedure, is made a terrific objection here.

Now, sir, I have never read the code of New Mexico, and I do not propose to read it; but it is perfectly understood that that Territorial Legislature, pursuing the privilege, if you call it privilege, conferred by the compromise measures of 1850, has established the relation of master and slave, or master and servant, as perfectly as it is established in any of the fifteen so-called slaveholding States. I do not admire this word "*status*," which we find in the report of the Peace Conference; but as to the meaning of that word, I cannot be in any doubt. It does not refer to any persons in particular; it refers to a legal relation of servitude as between master and servant, and it provides that that relation, or condition, or *status*, shall not be changed; that for all wrongs or controversies arising out of that there shall be a remedy through the Federal judiciary.

I can see why the commission made this distinction. There have been many who have insisted that the Congress of the United States should pass laws for the protection of the right of the master to the services of his slave in a Territory; but it has always been my opinion, that the worst thing the slaveholding States ever could have would be to have that; for there would be a perpetual controversy here from session to session, and from day to day, whether the law went far enough in giving protection or went too far; and they would be remitting their right to the adjudication of the Senators and Representatives from the non-slaveholding States. Others have insisted, as the propositions of my honorable friend from Kentucky provided, that the relation should be protected by the legislation of the territorial authority. I would rather it were so, individually, if they chose to establish it. The peace commission do not want that. They evidently do not want to quarrel with the Territorial Legislatures about the measure of legislation; but they declare the right, and then say that this right shall be enforced in the Federal judiciary according to the course of remedies and forms of the common law. I do not see how there can be a doubt; and yet, as I have said, it seems to me that a great deal of it is unnecessary verbiage. I do not mean to debate that; I am not one of the peace commissioners; I am not to select my words to express the idea; but I am here; and my State with other States, having appointed commissioners in view of a crisis like this, as they esteem it, and as I esteem it, and they having agreed upon a great variety of propositions, some of which commend themselves to my judgment and some do not; but taking it altogether as one proposition, I am satisfied that I must either vote for all of it, or let all of it fall. I would rather vote for the proposition of my honorable friend from Kentucky. I said that sixty days ago; and I have said it in season and out of season. I have expressed my views frequently. I think the proposition of the commissioners would be better expressed, though it would come to the same thing, in these words: "in all the territory south of that line, it is hereby declared that no law or regulation shall ever be made or have any effect denying or impairing the right of the inhabitants to the service or labor of such persons as were held in that condition in any State of the Union; and thence taken into the said Territory." That would have expressed my idea more clearly, yet I am satisfied with this; it amounts to that. Whether the word "*status*" be good Latin or good English, the meaning is very clear.

I believe I admonished the Senate two hours ago that time was very precious; and I shall not detain them myself.

Mr. BAKER:—Mr. President, I mean to vote for the passage of these proposed amendments, just as they are, without any change; and I propose to give very briefly a few of the reasons which govern my judgment in that act. I will do it as pointedly as I can, and I will certainly do it very briefly.

In the first place, I feel that I am but submitting to the people of the whole country, amendments which they, and they only, can incorporate in the present Constitution; and I do not believe that, in any state of the case, I can do very wrong in doing that; but when I consider the immediate condition of the country, I feel that I am doing very right. Twenty States assemble in what is called the Peace Convention. They recommend to us, in times of great trial and difficulty, the passage of these resolutions. They are eminent men; they are able men; they are—very many of them, at least—great men; they have been selected by the States which they respectively represent, because of their purity of character and ability. The country is in great trouble. Six States have seceded; and I am told by very many men in whom I have great confidence, that their States are to-day trembling in the balance. I believe it. I am told—and upon that subject I have not yet made up my mind—that the adoption of these measures by the people will heal the differences with the Border States. I do not believe that I can do wrong, therefore, in giving the people of the whole Union a chance to determine these questions.

In the beginning, I voted against the propositions of the distinguished Senator from Kentucky. Even then I did not perceive any great harm in submitting any propositions to the people of the United

States which circumstances might appear to render necessary for any good purpose. I refused to vote for them, for two reasons: first, I believed something better might be attained; and second, I did not believe that the people of the States would agree to them. I do not believe that now, and for one simple reason: I think I may consider myself in some respect a representative of the opinion as well as the power of my own people. I am a Republican, a zealous and determined one. I have all my life been of the opinion that Congress ought not to protect slavery, and to extend the dominion of this Government for that purpose or with that possibility. A great many in the North, who are not Republicans, but are what we call DOUGLAS men, have shown, at the last election, under something of trial and sacrifice, that they too, do not believe that the Constitution does or ought to extend slavery. I am not disposed to give up that opinion; I do not believe they are. I was not disposed to give up when six States were in the Union who are now out, as they say; and I am not disposed to give it up yet. Independently of pride of opinion, I do not believe that kind of sacrifice would accomplish any good result.

These are the reasons in brief which induced me to vote with regret against the propositions of the distinguished Senator from Kentucky in the earlier portion of this session. But now, we are within two days of adjournment. Propositions essentially variant in their character to those are submitted here; and I am asked: "Will you, in your representative capacity, submit these to your people for their decision, either to accept or reject?" Now, why not? I need not dwell upon the fact that, while we are a representative, we are at the same time a democratic Government. I will not shut my eyes to the fact that twenty States appeal to us; I will not shut my eyes to the fact that there is imminent danger of permanent dissolution; I will not shut my eyes to the fact that, though the Republican party is in a constitutional majority, it is not yet, and it never has been, in an actual majority; and I do not believe that it is possible for one-third of the people to coerce the opinion of two-thirds.

Mr. WILKINSON:—I wish to ask the gentleman a question.

Mr. BAKER:—Do, sir.

Mr. WILKINSON:—I understand him as saying that the whole of the twenty States which were assembled in this Peace Convention agreed to this proposition.

Mr. BAKER:—My distinguished friend was writing, instead of listening, when he understood that. I did not mean to say that, and I did not.

Mr. WILKINSON :—I understood the Senator to say that twenty States appealed to us.

Mr. BAKER :—Yes, sir ; just as I say that the Government appeals to another Government, I do not say every individual in it ; just as I say that Congress appeals to another Government, not every individual member of Congress ; but I do say, in the words of the proposition before us, that "they," the Peace Convention, composed of the States recited, "have approved what is herewith submitted, and respectfully request that your honorable body will submit it to conventions in the States, as article thirteen of the amendments to the Constitution of the United States." That is all I said, or, at least, it is all I meant to say.

Now, sir, suppose every argument that the distinguished Senators from Virginia have brought to bear on this proposition was true : what then? Is that any reason why it should not be submitted to the people? Suppose they do not approve of it : what then? It is their business, not ours. Suppose they should : it is a measure of peace, of security, of union. Sir, I know, as you do, many of the members of that Convention. I have acted with them as Whigs in old times, and I wish they could come back. I know they have proved in old times, as they will prove again, that they love this Union to the very depth and core of their hearts. I do not propose to give them up ; I do not propose to weaken them ; I do admire, with my whole heart, the sacrifice of opinion which they make, and which is typified by the noble expression of the distinguished Senator from Kentucky to-day. Party or no party, North or no North, I, at least, will meet him half way. My State is very far distant. She had no members in that Convention. I do not know whether she will approve this measure ; but I know it will neither hurt that State nor me to give her a chance to determine. I know very well that the Senators from Virginia do not approve it. That is the very reason I do. [Laughter.] If I was sure they would not think me guilty of disrespect, I would remind them of what was said by a distinguished man in old times. Phocion, in the last days of his Republic—and I hope in that respect, at least, there will be no parallel—Phocion was once making a speech to the Athenian people, and something he said excited very great applause. He turned around to gentlemen, friends near him, and said : "What foolish thing have I been saying, that these people praise me?" Sir, if Virginia, represented as she is to-day—not as I believe she really is—but if Virginia, represented as she is here to-day, and as she has been during this session, were to approve these propositions, I should doubt them very much indeed.

I was surprised, however, to hear some things that the distinguished Senator from Virginia—I do not know whether to call him junior or senior—said. I do not mean the Senator who spoke last. He [Mr. Hunter] says that this proposition here is worse than the old Constitution. If that be really so, what in the world has he been complaining of so bitterly? He tells us, now, that under the old Constitution slavery was secure. Then, why do you grumble? He considers it as secure, not only wherever it is, but wherever it can go—nay, more than that; wherever the Stars and Stripes of the American Republic can float. I have been telling my people that, as a Republican, for a long while, and complaining of the Dred Scott decision; but he says slavery is secured. All the complaint that the other Senator from Virginia [Mr. Mason] makes, is against the decision of the courts in the free States we have been in the habit of making, which he insists are against the decision of the Supreme Court, constituted other than we wished it was. We have been in the habit of believing that one of the great evils we complained of was under the old Constitution, and that a new construction was given to it, alien to the intention, wish, construction, of our fathers; and we have complained that the Supreme Court was so constituted that it could not be reversed. We complained, as partisans, that now this Senate and the other House were so composed that we had no power in the Government, save through the President. Now, the Senator from Virginia indorses the whole of it, and says they were very well off, and did beautifully. Then why dissolve; why threaten; why make a Peace Conference necessary?

Mr. President, let us be just to these propositions. As a Republican, I give up something when I vote for them; but remember, sir, I am not voting for them now; I am only voting to submit them to my people; and I shall go before them, when the time comes, being governed in my opinion and advice as to whether they shall vote for them or not, as I see that Virginia, Tennessee, Kentucky, North Carolina, and Missouri, by their people, desire. To be frank, sir; if this proposition will suit the Border States, if there will be peace and union, and loyalty and brotherhood, with this, I will vote for it at the polls with all my heart and with all my soul; but if I see that the counsels of the Senators from Virginia shall prevail; if my noble friend from Tennessee [Mr. Johnson] shall be overwhelmed; if secession shall still grow in the public mind there; if they are determined, upon artificial causes of complaint, as I believe, still to unite their fate, their destiny, and their hope, with the extremest South, then, perceiving them to be of no avail, I shall refuse them. Therefore, at the polls at last, I shall be governed as an individual citizen by my conviction at the moment of what the ultimate result of these propositions will be; but I am not voting for that to-day. I am saying: "People of the United States, I submit it to you; twenty States demand it; the peace of the country requires it; there is dissolution in the very atmosphere; States have gone off; others threaten; the Queen of England upon her throne declares to the whole world her sympathy with our unfortunate condition; foreign Governments denote that there is danger to-day that the greatest Confederation the world has ever seen is to be parted in pieces, never to be reunited." Now, not what I wish, not what I want, not what I would have, but all that I can get, is before me. I know that I do no harm. If the people of Oregon do not like it, they can easily reject it. If the people of Pennsylvania will not have it, they can easily throw it aside. If they do not believe there is danger of dissolution, if they prefer dissolution, if they think they can compel fifteen States to remain in or come back, or if they believe they will not go out, let them reject it. I repeat again, it is their business, it is not mine.

But, sir, whether I vote for it at the polls or not, in voting for it here it may be said that I give up some of my principles. Mr. President, we sometimes mistake our opinions for our principles. I am appealed to often; it is said to me: "You believed in the Chicago platform." Suppose I did. "Well, this varies from the Chicago platform." Suppose it does. I stand to-day, as I believe, in the presence of greater events than those which attend the making of a President. I stand, as I believe, at least, in the presence of peace and war; and if it were true that I did violate the Chicago platform, the Chicago platform is not a Constitution of the United States to me. If events, if circumstances change, I will violate it, appealing to my conscience, to my country, and to my God, to justify me according to the motive. [Applause in the galleries.]

The PRESIDING OFFICER (Mr. FOSTER in the chair). Order will be preserved in the galleries, or they will be cleared.

Mr. BAKER:—Again, sir, let us see how, as a Republican, I give up any thing. First, suppose I did: I would give up a great deal to preserve a great Government; I would give up a great deal to be able to shake hands with Kentucky and Tennessee as friends for the rest of my life, as I have in all that has gone before. I would not be ashamed to give up. I would not at least be giving up to traitorous secession, such as Louisiana, Mississippi, and South Carolina are guilty of to-day; but I would be giving up to loyal and affectionate brethren, who implore me for the love of a common Union to do something to satisfy the doubts and fears of their people. I can stand that; I will do it.

Again, sir; how much do I give up? I have said, as a Republican, that Congress has the power to prohibit slavery in all the Territories of the United States. I believe it to-day. Talking about giving up, there are a good many other people that give up something here. Gentlemen on the other side, who have been contending that Congress had no power whatever to prohibit slavery, acknowledge that they were mistaken; at any rate they go for it; they do prohibit it by law, by the Constitution itself. Therefore I am not the only one that gives up.

Again: I believe it is wrong, politically wrong—I am not now discussing the social and moral question—but I believe it to be politically very wrong to establish slavery in the name of freedom. Sir, twelve years ago or more, it was my fortune, perhaps, to wander in a foreign land beneath the Stars and Stripes of my country. I went there, as I think, impelled by motives of patriotism, perhaps having mingled with them not a little desire of adventure, love of change, and that feverish excitement for which we people of this country are always and everywhere remarkable; but I believe, if I know myself, that I did suppose I was doing something to repay the country for much that she had done for me. Sir, often and again, wandering sometimes beneath

"Where Orizaba's purpled summit shone,"

sometimes by the dark pestilential river that marks the boundary between the two countries, often and often have I wondered to myself whether I was wandering and suffering there to spread slavery over an unwilling people. I am not sorry to see that now that is rendered impossible. I am not sorry to see that it is impossible, first, in the course of events; but if it were not so, I know, if these propositions shall pass, that the foul blot of slavery never will be extended over one foot of territory to be stolen or conquered by the people of the United States.

But I am asked, "What do you say about New Mexico?" I will tell you in twenty words. I am an older Republican than many of those I see around me, who vote to-day differently from me; not a better but an older. I voted in 1850, on the floor of the other House, against the compromise measures of that year. I did so, among other reasons, because I was not willing that Utah and New Mexico should become slave or free according to the wishes of their people, believing as I did then (I have changed my opinion in some respects since), that that was not best for the whole country. Contrary to my wishes, those compromise measures prevailed. New Mexico is nominally now, I believe, a slave Territory; that is, to use the words of the distinguished Senator from New York [Mr. SEWARD], there are some twenty slaves in the whole Territory. There they may, they probably will, remain. I submit to my people a proposition, that if they approve it as a compromise, as a concession, for peace for the Union, as it happens that that little Territory includes all that possibly can be slave territory, they will let it alone till the people are able and willing to make their own State constitution. That is all. Do I state it fairly? Does it go beyond that?

First, I contend that I give up but little. I give it up, as I understand, for purposes of freedom; and the distinguished Senators from Virginia agree with me. They say, in substance, that I am getting a great deal more than I give; and I confess, taking that view of the subject, at least in part, I wonder that a good many more of my Republican friends do not go with me.

Again: it is said on the Republican side that we protect slavery. In one sense we do, and in another sense we do not. In the offensive idea to me and to you of protecting slavery, I do no such thing, and I would die first. When the resolutions of the Senator from Kentucky were up the other day, I voted for the amendment of the other Senator from Kentucky [Mr. POWELL], in order to make them clear, to show what I was voting against. I was unwilling that territory hereafter to be acquired should be rendered slave territory; and I put that proposition distinctly in it, in order that when I voted against them, it might be seen why and how I did it. As I have said, this proposition renders that impossible. First, it refers only to the territory we now possess; that is, New Mexico alone. As to the territory north of 36° 30′, I need not speak. We know that God Almighty has registered a decree in Heaven that that shall never be slave. We, on our part, want no WILMOT proviso there; we all agree that we are willing to let it alone. South, there is but the barren Territory of New Mexico. Beyond that, who knows? If we are to acquire it, we are to acquire it by this proposition, by the assent of a majority of the States of both sections and two-thirds of the whole; and I do not know a man living who believes that with that proposition incorporated in the Constitution, slavery is probable, or even possible.

Therefore, Mr. President, I agree that in the compromise I, as a Republican, do give up to that extent, and no more, what I have said; but doing that, I believe that I consecrate all the territory between here and Cape Horn to freedom, with all its blessings, forever and forever.

So far, sir, as the discussion as to the meaning of this phrase about the common law is concerned, I do not care to indulge in it, and for this simple reason: first, according to the legal view of the Senator from Ohio, everybody knows that this expression, "the course of the common law," means the duly established forms of procedure known to the courts; that is all. In the next place, I am not afraid of the common law. I have been reared under it. With all its imperfections, and they are many, I love it. While it may be an objection to Virginia to quote it, to me it is full of guardianship and blessing. I do not stop to talk about the Somerset case, nor the decision in Salkeld, nor the Modern Reports. It is enough for me that I know, taking the whole proposition together, that slavery is impossible beyond where it now is, and, as a Republican, I can justify myself to my conscience in giving that vote.

Mr. President, I add very few more words. I should have been excessively pleased, as a partisan and a man, if the inauguration of Mr. LINCOLN could be one at which all the States would attend with the old good feeling, and with the old good humor. I have seen six States separate themselves, as they say, from us, and form a new confederacy, with great pain and greater surprise. I cannot shut my eyes, if I would, to the existing state of things. I listen to the warning of my friend from Kentucky. I listen to the warning of my friend from Tennessee. I have been in both States. I know something of their people. I believe that there, even there, the Union is in danger; and I believe if we break up here without some attempt to reconcile them to us, and us to them, many of the predictions of friends and foes as to the danger will be accomplished. I said, in the earlier part of the session—I repeat it—I would yield nothing to secession. When the Representatives from South Carolina and Mississippi and Alabama and Louisiana came here invoking war, telling us that if we did not yield to them they would secede, they would confederate with foreign Governments, they would break this Union, they would hold us as aliens and strangers and enemies, I believed then, as I believe now, that that was too dear a price to pay even for Union and peace; but to-day the case is altered. Virginia, Kentucky, Tennessee, reiterate their love for the Union. They tell us in unmistakable terms that they desire to remain; and in every county, nay, in every township of those States, we have staunch and true and ardent friends who would be willing to seal their devotion to this Union with their blood. It is they to whose appeal I would listen. It is from them that I would take counsel and advice; and when they tell me, "pass these resolutions; they are resolutions of peace; submit them to your people; listen to what ours say in reply; if it appears to you at the polls that these resolutions will produce peace, restore union, create or renew fraternal, kindly feeling, pass them; let us settle this question, and be one people," I agree; with all my heart, I will do it.

Now, as I close, let me ask what evil; who will be hurt? Suppose, when I get home, I find that the Senators from Virginia are on the stump and they are convincing their people that they are a great deal worse off; the more they convince Virginia that she is worse off, the more Pennsylvania and New York will be convinced that they are better off; and every argument they make against it in Virginia will have a twofold weight North and West. I could not make half as good a speech in favor of these propositions of Union, even in Oregon, or California, or Illinois—I speak of the States I know best—as I should make if I were to read their objections to these propositions.

But suppose—which I do not think possible—they could succeed, not only in Virginia (which I do not believe), but in Kentucky and Tennessee; suppose they were to swear, by the throne of God, they would not take them, but would dissolve and go off whether we passed them or not: we could very easily refuse to vote for them and be in as good a condition as we are to-day, and, in the mean time, next Monday, Mr. LINCOLN will be inaugurated. I desire to see around him thronging, nay forming the procession, every augury of hope and peace.

I expect to hear from his lips words of manly trust and confidence in the Union, and of concession, kindness to all its constituent parts. I have hoped that, in response to what he shall say, I shall hear from every part of what is now acknowledged everywhere yet as our Confederacy, a perpetual hymn of hope and praise rising from all parts of the Union; and, above all things else, I have hope and trust in time and patience. Therefore it is that I shall do no harm.

I know that there are very excited feelings upon this subject North and South. I understand that Massachusetts, an honored State—let me say, to qualify what I am going to say, first, that I believe that Massachusetts is the pattern of a community in the world; as well represented here as any State can be; representing herself better than anybody else can do it for her—I know that there are excited feelings in Massachusetts, and I think she has good cause. The act that more than any other else, perhaps, leads to this proposition of a Peace Convention—that "Congress shall provide by law for securing to the citizens of each State the privileges and immunities of citizens in the several States"—was an act which I abhorred and condemned from the beginning, and which I am not sorry to perceive that Massachusetts remembers now. Many gentlemen on the floor know to what I allude. On the other hand, South Carolina and Louisiana are ferocious for disunion; and I am afraid that their young men do want war. There is not excitement enough on the plantation and the farm, and in the streets of the towns; but they really want contest, excitement, and bloodshed. What they want I do not; I am trying to keep from it. I do not apprehend, therefore, that the sentiments which I have expressed here to-day will meet the approbation of the extreme men upon either side. I have no doubt my republicanism may be doubted. I think I can see in the look of my friend on my left now [Mr. King] that he has various convictions that I am very far from being sound in the faith. [Laughter.] Sir, it may be. I come from the midst of a people not directly concerned in this controversy; a population about half northern, half southern. We have intermarried together. Our interests, our fears, our hopes, our recollections, are mingled North and South; and I believe I am expressing their opinions—which perhaps form my own—when I say that I can see no possible harm to anybody anywhere in submitting these propositions to the people, who are, and ought to be, sovereign.

Besides, sir, what else can I do? As I sit down, let me ask Senators upon every side, what else can any of us do? Shall we sit here for three months, when petition, resolution, public meeting, speech, acclamation, tumult, is heard, seen, and felt on every side, and do nothing? Shall State after State go out, and not warn us of danger? Shall Senators and Representatives, patriotic, eloquent, venerable, tell us, again and again, of danger in their States, and we condescend to make no reply?

Sir, there is other business to be done here besides the mere ordinary business of the Government; besides the voting of supplies, and the raising of means by which to buy them. We have questions here to-day, as I believe, of peace and war, and I have waited long to see some mode of their solution. I repeat, I go for this proposition, and agree to submit it to the vote of the people, not because I believe it the best that can be done. I believe, however, that, to-day being two days from the close of this session, it is all I can do. When my people ask me, on my return, "Sir, have not States gone out?" I will say, "Yes." "Do not more threaten it?" if that is the word (I trust it is not the best one), I say, "Yes." They say, "Sir, do you believe they will do it?" "On my honor and on my conscience," I say, "if something is not done, yes." They then ask, "What have you done?" Mr. President, what have we done? I believe that is the question the country will ask of us; and I, for one, will vote for this proposition, that I may be able to respond.

Mr. GREEN:—Mr. President, I regard the consideration of this question as one of the most important which has ever been presented to the Senate since I have been a member of it. The Union is in danger; the fate of the country is at stake; and whatever the Senate or the House of Representatives or Congress combined can do, ought to be done to save the country. I have very little faith or hope, and I would express the reason why. But as little as there is, I will cling to the last remaining straw, and sink with it grasped fast in my hands, if I have no other resource. This country is of too much importance to me, to my family, to my friends, to my State, to my associates everywhere, to give up without a struggle. That struggle may prove to be fruitless; it may prove to be unavailing. The taunts and jeers thrown out are calculated to stir up ire and ill-feeling; I shall pass them by with disregard. I choose to sacrifice my feelings, and to make myself a burnt-offering on the altar, if I can do any thing to save the country.

What, then, shall we do? These propositions, presented by what is called the Peace Conference, are not to be compared to the propositions of the Senator from Kentucky; and I will not vote for a single one of them, while I will vote for his. They amount to a sacrifice of my honor, and a destruction of the rights of my State. I am permitted to say that the representatives from my State in the Peace Conference condemned them all, while they are willing to go for the proposition of the Senator from Kentucky. We cannot stand by this, and we will not.

Let us not deceive each other; let us not undertake to practice a system of deception which will sound pleasant to the ear, but will be bitter to the taste. I will not do it. Here is a positive prohibition of slavery north of 36° 30′, and then a doubtful question whether it is recognized south of 36° 30′. The Senator from Kentucky thinks it is; but I will not act upon a doubt. We have had too many doubts heretofore, and out of those doubts have grown many difficulties. I shall never permit, so far as my action is concerned, another question of doubt.

Mr. CRITTENDEN:—Will the gentleman allow me to interrupt him? Did he understand me as admitting that it was a doubtful recognition of slavery?

Mr. GREEN:—Not at all. I said expressly that the Senator from Kentucky contended that it did amount to a recognition, but others denied it, and that made it a question of doubt. I will not misrepresent anybody if I know it. Now, sir, I will not act upon a question which admits of doubt. We have passed along in our career for so many years that we have arrived at a point when we must understand each other distinctly and unequivocally, and I will not leave a single point open to equivocation. It must be expressly settled, and settled not only in express words, not only in unmistakable language; but I go further than that; it must emanate from the hearts of a people disposed to stand by it; and if they will not stand by it, I will not associate with them.

I want to preserve this Union; I want to maintain the constitutional rights of all classes, North and South; but to give me a mere written guarantee on parchment, and file it in the office of the Secretary of State, with a predetermination in the hearts and minds of the northern people inculcated and instructed to violate it, I cannot live with, and I will not. I would rather go where I naturally belong, with southern men; but if the true-hearted, the patriotic, and the honorable portion of the North will reverse this inculcated spirit of hostility to southern institutions, and bring them up to the mark where they will recognize constitutional guarantees, then I say, "Hail, thou my brother, we can go together;" but never till that comes to pass. We have approached that period in our country's history when there should be no cheating or attempt to cheat. We must understand each other, and make a permanent, lasting Union, or a permanent, lasting, peaceful separation.

This proposition presented by the Peace Conference, as it is called, I think the merest twaddle—and I use the term with entire respect to the members—the merest twaddle that ever was presented to a thinking people. The proposition of the Senator from Kentucky has some sense in it. If he chooses to desert his own, I shall not complain of him; for I know that warm, patriotic impulses move him in all his action; but I cannot accept the other, and I shall vote against every one of its provisions. When it is said to me that the territory south of 36° 30′ has adopted slavery—that New Mexico has—I must reply to Senators that they misunderstand the law. New Mexico has never adopted slavery. New Mexico has done this: she has provided remedies for redress of wrongs, including wrongs affecting slave property; but she has never established slavery; nor has Utah. Utah has never even recognized it by implication. Utah passed a law of this character: apprentices bound to service for a period of years may be held there; but when their servitude has expired, according to their articles of apprenticeship, they are free; so that the law of Utah absolutely, if it has any effect, prohibits slavery.

Senators overlook these facts. I take the broad and the bold and the unmistákable ground, not that the Constitution establishes slavery anywhere, but that the Constitution, extending over a Territory, will protect me in all my rights not prohibited by a local competent authority; that my rights are to take any property which I own in any part of the Union, Yankee clocks from the North, polar bears from the Rocky Mountains, mules from the Middle States, and slaves from the South; and that, unless there is a competent local authority to prohibit my rights in these respective classes of property, I am to be protected. The second step is that there can be no local authority as long as the territorial condition remains, competent to prohibit slavery in any Territory.

These are my positions; and hence, so far from this extraordinary position that slavery is local being true, the reverse is true. It may be local in the United States, but so far from its being local to the Territory in the United States, the reverse is true. Talk about freedom being national, and slavery local! I have a right to pass through Pennsylvania, and my right of transit is as perfect this day as it was when Pennsylvania was a slave State.

* * * * * * *

I have been anxious from the beginning of this session to stave off public action, to hold the public pulse still, and give an opportunity for reaction of northern sentiment. I want no reaction south. It has been my only hope, and my last hope, and that hope has failed.

* * * * * * *

These resolutions are intended to lull old Virginia, Maryland, Missouri, and Kentucky, until we are hand-cuffed and tied fast, and then action is to commence. They are all designed simply to lull us into a fancied security; but if we are wise betimes, and look forward to coming events, we will at once strike the blow, and separate from a Confederation which denies us peace, denies us protection, denies us our constitutional rights, and seek them in some other association of States.

* * * * * * *

Now, Mr. President, I want all these propositions voted down, and I hope my friend from Kentucky will revive his propositions and bring them up again. There is some vitality in them; there is some point in them; but as for these wishy-washy resolutions, that amount to nothing, it is impossible that any Senator here will, for a moment, entertain the idea of supporting them. The Peace Conference! And the smallest peace that ever I have heard of. Let the Senator adhere to his original propositions; let the Senator bring them up and press them upon the attention of the Senate. That is as far backing down as I will go. It is a little more than I want; but still, as a last effort to save the Union, I would go that far. Talk about these measures! These measures that have no vitality—these measures that amount to a total surrender of every principle—I never will vote for; and let the consequences of the future be what they may, I stake my faith and reputation upon the vote I intend to cast.

Mr. WADE:—I move that the Senate adjourn.

Mr. LANE:—I hope the Senator will give me the floor before he makes that motion.

Mr. TRUMBULL:—I ask the Senator from Oregon to yield to me a moment.

Mr. LANE:—For a motion to adjourn, I will.

Mr. TRUMBULL:—Yes, sir; I desire the floor with a view to make that motion. It is apparent that no good is to come out of the discussion of the proceedings of this Peace Conference. It is a proposition got up for the purpose of satisfying the Border States; and the Border States, Missouri and Virginia, say they will have none of it. The first section is a proposition establishing slavery—

Mr. MASON:—I rise to a question of order.

The PRESIDING OFFICER:—The Senator from Illinois will pause. The Senator from Virginia rises to a question of order, which he will state.

Mr. MASON:—I understand the motion to adjourn has been made.

Mr. TRUMBULL:—I have not made the motion yet. I stated that I would make that motion, and I was merely going to give the reason. The Senator from Oregon will have the floor to-morrow. I was stating the reason why I should make the motion to adjourn, which I intend to make in the course of a minute, and I merely made that statement to show that there was no object in sitting here and punishing ourselves in regard to resolutions which manifestly cannot command the assent of this body. I now move that the Senate adjourn.

Mr. DOUGLAS:—I call for the yeas and nays on that motion.

The yeas and nays were ordered.

And the Senate refused to adjourn, and, for special business, the peace propositions were set aside. The same day they were introduced, as follows:

Mr. LANE:—Mr. President, my object in getting the floor, was to give the reason why I cannot vote for the resolution now before the Senate. You are aware, sir, that I did vote for the propositions of the Senator from Kentucky to amend the Constitution, with the hope, if they could be adopted, that peace, perhaps, might be restored to the country; but those propositions have been superseded, and the Senator from Kentucky himself says that he is willing to sacrifice, on the altar of his country, as he terms it, his own propositions, and take the amendments which are proposed to the Constitution presented by the Peace Congress to the Senate. The resolutions proposed by the distinguished Senator from Kentucky were as low down as I could go. They did not secure to every State that right they have under the Constitution, as I understand it; but the resolution now before the Senate, to speak modestly, as I look at it, with all due respect to the great men who met here to consider this matter, who deliberated for many days, and presented this as the result of their deliberations, is a cheat, a deception, a humbug—nothing that any State can take as a final settlement of the questions that are now giving trouble to this country, nothing that can settle permanently those difficulties. We must have something more definite, something more certain, or there can be no Union even of the States that now remain in the Union, as I believe.

Mr. GREEN:—Mr. President—

The PRESIDING OFFICER:—Does the Senator from Oregon give way?

Mr. LANE:—Only for an adjournment.

Mr. GREEN:—I rise to make that motion, that the Senate do now adjourn.

So the motion was agreed to; and the Senate by a vote—23 to 22—adjourned.

March 2d.—Senator LANE having secured the floor, made the following speech on the report of the Peace Conference:

Mr. LANE:—Mr. President, I hope I shall be permitted to proceed without interruption, and I trust not to consume much time. While I had the floor yesterday, I stated some of my objections to the proposed amendments to the Constitution which are now before us. They are: that they do not do justice to the whole country—that they do not do justice to all the States. I have always held that the territory is common property; that it belongs to all the States; that every citizen of every State has an equal right to emigrate to, and settle in, the common Territories; and that any species of property, recognized as such in any State of the Confederacy, should have a like recognition in the Territories, and be guaranteed, protected, and secured in its full integrity, to the owner thereof. That this should be so, was the intent of the revolutionary fathers who shaped and framed the Constitution; and it was this principle, more, perhaps, than any other, which called into being that noble compact, which has so long been a bond of Union and goodness between all the States. It is the very life-blood and vitality of the Constitution. It is the ligament that has held us together heretofore, and which, if cut now, will result only in hopeless and immutable disruption. I have never deviated a single iota from this correct doctrine. Had we lived up to this equitable principle—the foundation upon which the Constitution rests, upon which only this Union can be maintained—we should have had no trouble in this country to-day. It is not my fault that trouble and dissatisfaction prevail; it is not my fault that secession has taken place, and that further secession will take place, unless Congress shall recognize this great principle of justice, of right, and of equality. That is the doctrine upon which this Union rests; and it must be maintained, or the connection will be severed.

While upon this question, Mr. President, I may be permitted to allude to my course in the Senate last session, and I shall do so very briefly, upon a series of resolutions introduced by the Senator from Mississippi [Mr. DAVIS]—a series of resolutions that were considered in this body, after having been previously maturely and deliberately adopted by a caucus composed of the Democratic Senators, and agreed upon by them, as setting forth the principles necessary to be maintained in order to secure the existence and perpetuity of this Confederacy. It has been charged upon this floor that, on the 25th day of May last, I voted against the right of protection to slave property in the Territories. In order that the Senate may know how I voted, and that I may show you and every other man that I stood then as I stand to-day, and as I have always stood upon this question, I will read some short extracts from the discussion upon this series of resolutions. The fourth resolution was in these words:

"*Resolved*, That neither Congress nor a Territorial Legislature, whether by direct legislation or legislation of an indirect and unfriendly nature, possesses the power to annul or impair the constitutional right of any citizen of the United States to take his slave property into the common Territories, but it is the duty of the Federal Government there to afford for that, as for other species of property, the needful protection; and if experience should at any time prove that the judiciary does not possess power to insure adequate protection, it will then become the duty of Congress to supply such deficiency."

Now mark! this resolution states that all the property of all the people of any State, whether slave or otherwise, has an equal right to protection; and if experience should at any time prove that the courts had not the power to afford that protection, then it was the duty of Congress to enact such laws as were necessary to protect every man in his legal and rightful property, no matter of what description or characteristic. Sir, not long since, upon this floor, a Senator was hardy enough to say that I voted against protecting property in Territories; and he desired to know what had happened that States should be concerned; what had occurred to alarm the States that were seceding from the Union? I will show you, sir, very briefly, what I said upon that question then; and I will repeat it now, for I have never changed my sentiments on this subject. No living man can assert, and in so doing tell the truth, that I ever uttered a word against the equality of the States, and their equal right in the common territory of our common country; and any charge that I voted then to refuse protection to property in the territory *is false.* I have always held that the territory belonged to all; that it was acquired, as I knew, at the expense of the Southern States as well as of the Northern; and upon the battle-fields where I had witnessed the good conduct of Northern and Southern troops, I found the soldier from the Southern States pouring out his blood as freely, and certainly in very much larger quantity—for there were very many more from the Southern States who participated in the battles of our country in the war which resulted in the acquisition of territory, than there were from the Northern States. Then, so far as the acquisition is concerned, it is joint, and it was for the joint benefit of all portions of the country. Consequently, I have held, and I hold now, that the Territories should be so appropriated. And when those resolutions were up last winter, I said what I will now read:

"I only desire to say, in relation to the series of resolutions, a portion of which I have already voted in favor of, that I shall vote in favor of the rest; for the whole of them together meet with my hearty approbation. They assert the truth; they assert the great principle that the constitutional rights of the States are equal; that the States have equal rights in this country under the Constitution; and, as I understand it, they must be maintained in that equality. These resolutions only assert that principle; and I say that it is a misfortune to the country, in my opinion, that the principles laid down in these resolutions had not been asserted sooner. They ought to have been asserted by the Democratic party in plain English ten years ago. If they had been, you would have had no trouble in this country to-day; the Democratic party would have been united and strong, and the equality and constitutional rights of the States would have been maintained in the territory, and in all other things; squatter-sovereignty would not have been heard of, and to-day we should be united. It is the fault of the Democratic party in dodging truth, in dodging principle, in dodging the Constitution itself, that has brought the trouble upon the country and the party that is experienced to-day."

I believe, if we had asserted and maintained these great truths ten years ago, and placed ourselves upon them boldly, as it was our duty to have done, we would have no trouble in this country to-day; but instead of declaring the great truths enunciated in these resolutions, we went off upon issues unbecoming the Democratic party. A portion of our leaders wandered and went astray, and asserted that the people of a Territory had the right to prohibit slavery whenever, in their judgment, it ought to be prohibited; a power which Congress even does not possess, and consequently cannot confer upon a Territorial Legislature, unless the creature becomes greater than the creator. It was this kind of trouble, and this sort of heresy introduced into the Democratic party, that has broken it up, and brought the disasters upon our country which we experience to-day. I say, then, let the blame fall upon the guilty; I am innocent of it; for I have held but one doctrine upon this question from the beginning to the present hour, and I shall hold that doctrine to the end. In the speech from which I have already read, I also used the following language:

"Sir, it appears to me to be very singular indeed, that any man can hold that the territory of this country belongs to a portion of the people, and that the people of one portion of the Union can go there and enjoy their property, when the people of another portion cannot enjoy the right of property in that territory—territory common to the whole country; territory that was earned or acquired by the common blood and common treasure of all; territory that is sustained by the common treasure of all; and to say that all shall not have an equal right there, is to deny a fact so plain, a principle so just, a right so manifest, that I can hardly see how any man who professes to be a Democrat can deny it, or how he can attempt to embarrass the adoption of the correct principles announced in these resolutions. I shall therefore vote against all the amendments, and every thing that is offered to obstruct their passage, upon the ground that they assert justice, that they assert truth, that they assert the equality and constitutional rights of all the States, which principle must be maintained, or this Union cannot be preserved."

That was my doctrine then, it is the doctrine which I have held and advocated for twenty years. It is the doctrine I hold now; and I so notified the Senator from Tennessee, who arraigned me here as voting against protecting property, and who did me willful and gross injustice in it—for I voted for it and he voted against it. That is to say, I voted against the resolution introduced by Mr. CLINGMAN, declaring "that slave property did not need protection in the Territories," while the

Senator from Tennessee voted for it; and when the motion was made to reconsider the vote adopting it in lieu of the fourth resolution of the DAVIS series, I voted to reconsider, and the Senator from Tennessee voted against it, showing clearly that he was against affording that protection to slave property which the fourth resolution provided for. Did I not maintain the truth? Was I not prophetic in the announcement that I made in this Senate Chamber then? I said, that unless this great principle of justice, of equality, of the right of every man to the common territory should be maintained, this Union would be broken up. This great principle has not been maintained, but the Union has been destroyed.

But, sir, to go to the votes. It will be borne in mind, and every Senator on this floor will bear me out in my statement, that while the DAVIS resolutions—the series of which I speak—were up, various propositions were made to amend them, and I voted against all amendments. There are Senators here at this moment who will sustain me when I say that, when in caucus and we had under consideration this series of resolutions, I said, and said it boldly and in plain terms, that if every man from every Southern State of this Union would come here and say, for the sake of peace, if you please, or any other reason, he was willing to abandon his equality, his right in the common territory, then, if alone, I would stand and protest against it; protest that he had no right to surrender a constitutional right; that none but a coward would do it; that every man had a right in the common territory; that it was his privilege, and he should never surrender it with my permission. On the other hand, I said that if every Northern man in the Senate Chamber—nay, but even every Northern citizen—expressed a desire to surrender his right, his equality, his privilege, to go to the common Territories with his property, I should enter my solemn protest against it, and insist that he had a constitutional right to go there, which he should never surrender with my consent, Then, how any man could assert that I ever entertained the opinion that slavery did not need protection from aggression, is to me the strangest, falsest thing in nature. I said, as I have shown you, that I had voted against all amendments, and would continue to vote against all amendments, or any attempt whatsoever calculated to obstruct the passage of the resolutions; for they asserted the right of the people to go to the Territories, asserted the power of the court to protect them in the possession of their property, and that if the court failed to protect them, Congress should afford the necessary authority to do so.

But, sir, allow me to observe, there was a resolution that I never voted for, and that no man can charge me with ever having voted for. Senators will recollect—and whoever has read the proceedings of the Senate will recollect—that an amendment was offered as a substitute to the fourth resolution, in these words:

"That the existing condition of the Territories does not require the intervention of Congress for the protection of property in slaves."

I did not vote for that resolution; but the Senator from Tennessee did. That amendment was adopted in lieu of the fourth resolution of the series that I have read, which insured protection to slave property in the Territories. It was adopted not entirely by Democratic votes; and that there may be no mistake, I will read what the Senator from Massachusetts said when he moved a reconsideration:

"I wish simply to say that I voted for that resolution because I believed the condition of the Territories requires no such law now or ever, and I do not believe in the enactment of any such law; but my friends on this side of the Chamber have put that resolution in the series; and for myself, I do not wish to be responsible for any portion of these resolutions, and I therefore wish the vote to be reconsidered."

This was the language of the Senator from Massachusetts, when he found that the Republicans, united with some Democrats, had stricken out the fourth resolution of the series, and inserted this as a substitute. I said to Mr. Wilson on that occasion:

"I desire merely to tender my thanks to the honorable Senator from Massachusetts. The series of resolutions, as introduced by the honorable Senator from Mississippi, are germane one to the other. They are a declaration of principles by the Democratic party. This amendment, as the Senator has said correctly, has been fastened on the Democratic resolutions by the votes of the Republican Senators. I feel grateful, indeed, to the Senator for making the motion to reconsider. I hope the vote will be reconsidered, and the resolution voted down."

The motion was put, and on the yeas and nays the vote was reconsidered. I voted for the reconsideration, and I voted against the amendment when it was adopted as a substitute for the fourth resolution. Among those who voted in the affirmative for reconsideration were Messrs. Benjamin, Brown, Chesnut, Clay, Davis, Fitzpatrick, Green, Gwin, Hammond, Harlan, Hunter, Iverson, Johnson of Arkansas, and Lane. Among those who voted against it, I find Johnson of Tennessee. I did not vote to continue in the series a resolution that refused protection to all the people in the common Territories. Portions of the Journal have been paraded to show the vote on Mr. Brown's amendment to Mr. Clingman's amendment. I said, in several speeches, that I should vote against all amendments, because the series had been considered not only here, but in a caucus composed of the Democratic Senators of this body, and we had agreed to take them as a whole, and to vote them through altogether if we had the strength to do so. I voted against every proposition to amend. I voted against Mr. BROWN'S, and I voted against Mr. CLINGMAN'S, and I voted against every other amendment that was calculated to weaken or embarrass the passage of the resolutions. Yet I am represented here as having voted against affording protection to slave property in the Territories! I ask again, if any Senator, if any man who can read, can say that the fourth resolution, for which I did vote and for which I struggled and contended, does not declare that slave property shall be protected in the common Territories of our country.

Could any thing be stronger than the fourth resolution? Could any man desire a more direct declaration of principles than that? Upon the yeas and nays I voted for it. I voted against the amendment that was adopted, and afterwards reconsidered. How, then, can a man arraign me before the country as having said upon oath, on the 25th of May last, that slave property should not be protected in the common Territories with other property? I have always held that all property should be protected, slave as well as other property; that it should have the same protection as, and no more protection than any other property. That they do not secure all this, is the objection I have to the amendments to the Constitution proposed by the Peace Conference. They are ambiguous, loose, and deceptive. I do not know that the people can comprehend them. There will be no certainty under them; and they would, if adopted, result in endless trouble and litigation. I trust no amendments will ever be made to the Constitution, unless they are made upon principles of right, justice, and equality, so that there can be no mistake in construing them hereafter. If we amend the Constitution, let us do it with a view to the peace of the country, with a view to the harmony of the country, with a view to the security of every interest, and of every State in the Union. If we could do that, and this day amend the Constitution so as to provide expressly that every State should have equal rights in the Territories and elsewhere within the Union, this Confederacy would last forever, the States that have left us would come back, and we should have then a great and a lasting Union indeed. Without it, we never can have a permanent Union. We must do something that is clearly right, or the States that have left us will never return. They never ought to return, unless they can have the right of equality secured to them by the Constitution. I claim for my State just that which she is entitled to, and not a particle more. I would concede to the Southern States, that to which they are entitled, and not a particle more. That, they must have, or there can be no peace, no union, no harmony, no security, and no perpetuity of this Confederacy. Such amendments to the Constitution, securing these objects and principles, are indispensable to the maintenance of the Government as it was formed.

Then why not do right? Why not every southern man ask just that which he is entitled to, and no more? He ought to be content with nothing short of what he is entitled to; and if he be, he is untrue to his section and his constituents; untrue to the people whose servant he is; and untrue to the institutions of the country; for the country can exist only upon the triumph of such principles. He who is unwilling to deal fairly by the North and the South, is a man who is guilty of shattering and ruining the Confederacy; destroying the peace and harmony and success of this great experiment of ours.

Mr. President, in the State of Connecticut the Democracy assert the correct principle, and they charge the trouble in the country to the right quarter. I stated, on a former occasion, that the Democracy of old Connecticut would never join the Republican party in any attempt to coerce the Southern States; and I am now authorized by their own declaration to say again, what I said before, that they, like the Democracy of Oregon and of every other Northern State, will never join a party that has refused justice; that has refused equality and right; that has refused to protect property in the Territories, or wherever the jurisdiction of the United States extends, in putting down those who contended for their rights and for the equality to which they were entitled. Sir, the loyal Democracy of this country fully understand the question, and they assert the right.

Now, sir, these great principles were not carried out. The platform on which the Democracy presented their candidates for President and Vice-President was not heeded, though based upon the Constitution. I will say to the Senator who has boasted of his efforts in Tennessee in behalf of the BRECKINRIDGE ticket, that I shall notice that hereafter; but I have only to say now, that, for the sake of the country, I would to God the ticket had succeeded. We should then have had those principles endorsed upon which the Government is established, and the country would have been at peace. For that alone I wished it to succeed.

I will say only a word, now, as to the amendments proposed to the Constitution. I had the pleasure of listening, yesterday, to the distinguished Senator from Kentucky. I know his patriotism and his devotion to the Union. I know his willingness to take any thing, however small, however trifling, however little it might be, that would, in his opinion, give peace to the country. Sir, I am actuated by no such feeling. We should never compromise principle nor sacrifice the eternal foundations of justice. Whenever the Democratic party compromised principle it laid the foundation of future troubles for itself and for the country. When we do, then, amend the Constitution, it ought to be in the spirit of right and justice to all men and to all sections. I voted for the Senator's propositions, and I will do so again, if we can get a vote, because there is something in them; something that I could stand by; but there is nothing in the amendments proposed by the Peace Conference. He proposed to establish the line of 36° 30′, and to prohibit slavery north of it and protect it south of it, in all the present territory, or of the territory to be hereafter acquired. In that proposition there was something like justice and right; but there is nothing in the amendments proposed by the Peace Conference that any man, North or South, ought to take. They are a cheat; they are a deception; they are a fraud; they hold out a false idea; and I think, with all due respect to the Senator—for I have the highest regard for him personally—that he is too anxious to heal the trouble that exists in the country. He had better place himself upon the right and stand by it. Let him contend, with me, for the inalienable and constitutional rights of every American citizen. Let him beware of "compromising" away the vital rights, privileges, and immunities of one portion of the country to appease the graceless, unrelenting, and hostile fanaticism of another portion. Let him labor with me, to influence every State to mind its own affairs, and to keep the Territories entirely *free* to the enterprise of all, with equal security and protection—without invidious distinctions—to the property of every citizen. Thus, and only thus, can we have peace, happiness, and eternal Union.

I could not avoid noticing the anxiety of the Senator from Kentucky to accept any thing, and the readiness of the Senator from Oregon to pledge his people—"my people"—to any thing that he chooses. Now, I know there are many free people in the State of Oregon. They generally do as they please. They have no master. No man owns them; and no man can claim to control them. But this I am warranted in asserting—for I know long, well, and intimately, the gallant men of Oregon—that they will not be found ready or inclined, at the Senator's and his master's beck, to imbrue their hands, in a godless cause, in fraternal gore.

Mr. President, the principles asserted in the resolutions adopted by the Senate, last winter, have not been carried out. We see the consequences. We see a dissevered country and a divided Union. A number of the States have gone off, have formed an independent Government; it is in existence, and the States composing it will never come back to you, unless you say in plain English, in your amendments to the Constitution, that every State in the future Union has an equal right to the Territories and all the protection and blessings of this Government—never! I tell you, sir, although some foolish men and some wicked ones may say I am a disunionist, I am for the Union upon the principles of the Constitution, and not a traitor. None but a coward will even think me a traitor; and if anybody thinks I am, let him test me. This Union could exist upon the principles that I have held and that are set forth in the DAVIS resolutions; but upon no other condition can it exist. Then, sir, disunion is inevitable. It is not going to stop with the seven States that are out. No, sir; my word for it, unless you do something more than is proposed in this proposition, old Virginia will go out too—slothful as she has been, and tardy as she seems in appreciating her own interests and her rights, and kind and generous as she has been in inviting a Peace Congress to agree upon measures of safety for the Union. The time will come, however, when old Virginia will stand trifling and chicanery no longer. Neither will North Carolina suffer it. None of the slave States will endure it; for they cannot separate one from the other, and they will not. They will go out of this Union and into one of their own; forming a great, homogeneous, and glorious Southern Confederacy. It is and it has been, Senators, in your power to prevent this; it is and it has been for you to say (you might to-day, as it is the last day, say so), whether the Union shall be saved or not. I know, that gallant Old Dominion will never put up with less than her rights; and if she would, I should entertain for her contempt. I should feel contempt for her if she were to ask for any thing more than her rights; and so I would if she were to put up with any thing less than her constitutional rights. Then, sir, secession has taken place, and it will go on unless we do right.

Mr. President, in the remarks which I made on the 19th of December last, in reply to the Senator from Tennessee, I took the ground that a State might rightfully secede from the Union when she could no longer remain in it on an equal footing with the other States; in other words, when her continuance as a member of the Confederacy involved the sacrifice of her constitutional rights, safety, and honor. This right I deduced from the theory of equality of the States, upon which rests the whole fabric of our unrivalled system of government—unrivalled, as it came from the hands of its illustrious framers—a model as perfect, perhaps, as human wisdom could devise, securing to all the blessings of civil and religious liberty, when rightly understood and properly administered; but like all other Governments, and even Christianity itself, a most dangerous engine of oppression when, having fallen into the hands of persons strangers to its spirit, and unmindful of the beneficent objects for which it was framed, it is perverted from its high and noble mission to the base uses of a selfish or sectional ambition, or a blind and bigoted fanaticism. I said, on that occasion—referring to this fundamental principle of our Government, the equality of the States—that "as long as this equality be maintained the Union will endure, and no longer." I might here undertake to enforce, by argument and the authority of writers on the nature and purposes of our Government, this, to me, self-evident proposition. But I deem it unnecessary to consume the time of the Senate in discussing that branch of the subject.

I propose, Mr. President, to confine what I have to say in regard to the right of secession to the question, Who must judge whether such right exists, and when it should be exercised? According to the theory of every despotic Government, of ancient or modern times, there is no such right. A province of an empire, how much soever oppressed, is held by the oppressor as an integral part of his dominions. The yoke, once fastened on the neck of the subject, is expected, however galling, to be worn with patience and entire submission to the tyrant's will. This is the theory of despotism. What are its fruits? We have seen, in modern times, some of the bloodiest struggles recorded in history growing out of the assertion by one party, and the denial by the other, of this very right. Hungary undertook to "secede" from the Austrian empire. Her right to do so was denied. She constituted an integral part of the empire—a great "consolidated" nation, as some consider the United States to be. Being an integral part of the empire, according to the theory of the Austrian Government, she must so remain forever. Austria not having the power to enforce an acquiescence in this doctrine, Russian legions were called to her aid; and Hungary, on whose gallant struggle for independence the liberty-loving people of this country looked with so much admiration and sympathy, soon lay prostrate and bleeding at the tyrant's feet. You may call this attempt of Hungary to regain her independence revolution. That is precisely what Austria called it. I call it an effort on her part to peaceably secede—to peaceably dissolve her connection with a Government which, in her judgment, had become intolerably unjust and oppressive. Her oppressors told her it was not her province but theirs, to judge of her alleged grievances; that to acknowledge the right of secession would strike a fatal blow at the integrity of the empire, which could be maintained only by enforcing the perfect obedience of each and every part.

We have, in the recent struggle of the Italian States, an instructive commentary on the now mooted questions of secession and coercion. Indeed, history, through all past ages, is but a record of the efforts of tyrants to prevent the recognition of the doctrine, that a people deeming themselves oppressed might peaceably absolve themselves from allegiance to their oppressors. When our Government was formed, our fathers fondly thought that they had made a great improvement on the despotic systems of modern Europe. They saw the infinite evil resulting from coercing the unwilling obedience of a subject to a Government which he abhorred and detested. They accordingly declared the great truth, never enunciated until then, that "Governments derive all their just power from the consent of the governed." A Government without such consent they held to be a tyranny.

Now, Mr. President, this brings us to the very point in issue. Who is to determine whether this consent is given or withheld? Must it be determined by the ruler? If so, the proposition just stated is an absurdity. Clearly it was the meaning of those who enunciated this great truth, that the subjects of a Government have the right to declare or withhold their consent; otherwise no such right exists. They, and they only, must judge whether their rights are protected or violated. If protected, every consideration of interest and safety impels them to consent to live under a Government which secures the blessings they desire. If, on the other hand, in their judgment, their most sacred rights are violated, interest and honor, and the instinct of self-preservation, all conspire to impel them to withhold their consent; which being withheld, the Government, as far as they are concerned, ceases.

Here I would call the attention of the Senate to the first of the Kentucky resolutions of 1798–'99, written by Mr. JEFFERSON, in which he says distinctly, that the parties to a political compact must judge for themselves of the mode and measure of redress, when they consider the compact violated and their rights invaded:

"*Resolved*, That the several States composing the United States of America, are not united on the principle of unlimited submission to their General Government; but that by compact, under the style and title of a Constitution for the United States, and of amendments thereto, they constituted a General Government for special purposes, delegated to that Government certain definite powers, reserving, each State to itself, the residuary mass of right to their own self-government; and that whensoever the General Government assumes undelegated powers, its acts are unauthoritative, void, and of no force; that to this compact each State acceded as a State, and is an integral party; that this Government, created by this compact, was not made the exclusive or final judge of the extent of the powers delegated to itself, since that would have made its discretion, and not the Constitution, the measure of its power; but that, as in all other cases of compact among parties having no common judge, each party has an equal right to judge for itself, as well of infractions as of the mode and measure of redress."

Here Mr. JEFFERSON asserts that a State aggrieved shall judge not only of the mode, but the measure of redress. Is this treason? If the measure of redress extends to secession, how can the Senator from Tennessee [Mr. JOHNSON] do less than denounce the great apostle of liberty—as Mr. JEFFERSON has been called—a traitor?

No less clear and explicit on this point, is the language of Mr. MADISON. Being chairman of a committee to whom the subject was referred—the resolutions having been returned by several of the States—he says in his report:

"It appears to your committee to be a plain principle, founded in common sense, illustrated by common practice, and essential to the nature of compacts, that where resort can be had to no tribunal superior to the authority of the parties, the parties themselves must be the rightful judges in the last resort, whether the bargain made has been pursued or violated. The Constitution of the United States was formed by the sanction of the States, given by each in its sovereign capacity. It adds to the stability and dignity, as well as to the authority of the Constitution, that it rests on this legitimate and solid foundation. The States, then, being the parties to the Constitutional compact, and in their sovereign capacity, it follows of necessity, that there can be no tribunal above their authority, to decide, in the last resort, whether the compact made by them be violated, and consequently that, as the parties to it, they must themselves decide, in the last resort, such questions as may be of sufficient magnitude to require their interposition."

In the remarks which I made on the 19th of December last, I referred to the fact that Virginia, in accepting the Constitution, declared that the powers granted under that instrument "being derived from the people of the United States, may be resumed by them whenever the same shall be perverted to their injury or oppression." I referred, also, to the fact that New York had adopted the Constitution upon the same condition and with the same reservation. I may here quote the language of Mr. WEBSTER, distinctly recognizing the right of the people to change their Government whenever their interest or safety require it. He says:

"We see, therefore, from the commencement of the Government under which we live, down to this late act of the State of New York"—

To which he had just referred—

"one uniform current of law, of precedent, and of practice, all going to establish the point that changes in Government are to be brought about by the will of the people, assembled under such legislative provisions as may be necessary to ascertain that will truly and authentically."

If the people of a State, believing themselves oppressed, undertake to establish a Government, independent of that to which they formerly owed allegiance, and the latter interferes with the movement, and employs force to prevent such a consummation, no one who acknowledges the great truth that the basis of all free government is the "consent of the governed," will deny that such interference is an act of usurpation and tyranny. Those only who borrow their ideas of political justice from the despotic codes of Europe, and are more imbued with the spirit of METTERNICH and BOMBA than of JEFFERSON and MADISON, will attempt to justify, palliate, or excuse such violation of the sacred rights of the people. I have observed that often the noisiest champions of popular rights are the first to trample those rights under foot. The word "freedom" is continually on the tongues of gentlemen on the other side of the Chamber; and I believe the Senator from Tennessee has been suspected of a decided leaning to agrarianism, so zealous has he been in advocating the rights, so entirely devoted is he to the interests of the "dear people." But now, when the *people* of the seceding States have pronounced, in tones of thunder, the fiat which absolves them from allegiance to a Government which they no longer respect or love, these same gentlemen all lift their hands in horror, roll up the whites of their eyes, as did old Lord NORTH many years ago, and exclaim "Treason!" "Treason!" Then, boiling with patriotic rage, they rise up and declare that "this treason must be punished; the laws must be enforced." History tells us that this was the language of King GEORGE and Lord NORTH when the colonies renounced their allegiance to the mother country. The former of these worthies, we are told, spent much of his life in a state of mental darkness—in other words, he was a lunatic. The other received from nature a narrow intellect, and inherited prejudices common to the aristocracy of that period and of all other periods of the world's history. Their errors were the natural offspring of incapacity and the false teaching received in their youth. While, therefore, we cannot admire or approve their conduct, these circumstances incline us more to sorrow than to anger, disarm our resentment, and dispose us to forgive what, under other circumstances, would deserve the severest censure.

But what excuse can we find for the peculiar champions of popular rights in this Chamber; these zealous servants of the people, forever ringing in our ears, "Let the voice of the people be heard; respect the will of the people; *vox populi vox Dei!*" Sir, I say too, let the voice of the people be heard and respected. And I think, for the sake of consistency with all my past professions as a Democrat, I am bound to respect the declared will of the sovereign States which, for reasons satisfactory to themselves, have seceded from the Union and established a separate and independent Government. Whatever the causes may have been which impelled them to a separation from the other States, I am bound to respect the expression of their sovereign will; and I heartily reprobate the policy of attempting to thwart that will under the pretence of "punishing treason" and "enforcing the laws." We are told that the design is to attempt nothing more than to collect the revenue in the ports of the seceded States. To say nothing of the justice or injustice of the attempt so to do, I ask Senators from the North, and the Senator from Tennessee, *will it pay?* Will it not be a declaration of war against the seceding States, involving the people of all the States in a long and bloody conflict, ruinous to both sections? Are their ethics not the ethics of the school-boy pugilist, "Knock the chip off my shoulder"?

One of the framers of the Constitution [Mr. MADISON], whose expositions of that instrument all classes, all parties, have heretofore received, and still receive, or pretend to receive, with profound deference and respect, has left on record his views of the injustice, impracticability, and inefficacy of force as a means of coercing States into obedience to Federal authority.

Among the statesmen of the Revolution—those who participated in the formation of our Government—there was no one who had such exalted notions of the power and dignity of the Federal Government, as the great HAMILTON. He was a consolidationist. The advocates of coercion might naturally expect to obtain "aid and comfort" from the recorded declarations of one of his peculiar political faith. But an examination of his writings will show, that instead of favoring coercion, instead of being the advocate of force, he was the advocate of leniency and conciliation towards refractory States, and deprecated a resort to force as madness and folly.

If the great names of MADISON and HAMILTON have not sufficient weight to restrain the madness of those who urge a coercive policy against the seceding States, then, indeed, I see no escape from that most dreadful of all calamities which can befall a nation—civil war. If those in this Chamber who talk so flippantly of war, had seen, as it has been my lot to see, some of its actual horrors, they might, perhaps, heed the warnings and respect the counsels of the sages and patriots whose language I have quoted. They would at least refrain from ungenerous insinuations against the patriotism of those northern Democrats, who, like myself, reprobate the policy of coercion as destructive of the peace, the prosperity, and happiness of every part of the country, north as well as south.

But to return to the remarks of the Senator from Tennessee. In the pamphlet report of his speech, page 7, JEFFERSON is quoted; but the concluding part of the quotation is repeated in the *Globe* report and not in that of the pamphlet. That part is:

"When two parties make a compact, there results to each a power of compelling the other to execute it."

JEFFERSON is here quoted to show that the Confederation has a power to enforce its articles on delinquent States. But the citation is unfortunate for the Senator from Tennessee, He had just previously asserted that Vermont and other States had, by personal liberty bills, violated the Constitution. Well; can he tell us how Virginia and South Carolina could enforce the Constitution on Vermont in that respect? It cannot be done. What follows? Why, as Mr. WEBSTER said at Capon Springs, "a compact broken by one party is broken as to all." Hence, according to the doctrines of JEFFERSON and WEBSTER as to the actual case which, according to the Senator, has occurred, the compact having been broken, the Southern States have a right to retire—are absolved from further obligations under the constitutional compact.

The Senator complains that I replied at all, as I was a northern Senator, and a Democrat whom he had supported at the last election for a high office. Now, I was, as I stated at the time, surprised at the Senator's speech—because I understood it to be for coercion, as I think it was by almost everybody else, except, as we are now told, by the Senator himself; and I still think it amounted to a coercion speech, notwithstanding the soft and plausible phrases by which he describes it—a speech for the execution of the laws and the protection of the Federal property. Sir, if there is, as I contend, the right of secession, then, whenever a State exercises that right, this Government has no laws in that State to execute, nor has it any property in any such State that can be protected by the power of this Government. In attempting, however, to substitute the smooth phrases of "executing the laws" and "protecting public property" for coercion, for civil war, we have an important concession, *i. e.*, that this Government dare not go before the people with a plain avowal of its real purposes, and of their consequences. No, sir; the policy is to inveigle the people of the North into civil war, by masking the design in smooth and ambiguous terms.

Now, sir, I want it distinctly understood, as I have already shown, that during the last session I stood firmly by the DAVIS resolutions. I voted against every amendment. I voted against an amendment that he voted for, because I believed it was partial, and did not do justice.

But the Senator from Tennessee proceeded with an air and tone of great triumph to bring forward my vote on the amendments proposed to the DAVIS resolutions. I think I have said all that it is necessary for me to say upon that subject. I have shown that I have voted for them under all circumstances, and against every amendment. Those resolutions assert the right of property in the Territories, and that when the courts fail to afford protection, then it is the duty of Congress to come forward and provide that protection. I wished to put slave property upon the same footing as other property. That is where I then stood, where I now stand, and where I intend to stand. The Senator asks, with a kind of triumphant air, what has happened since that day? Mr. President, I have said that I have done all in my power, by standing firm to the resolutions agreed to by the Democratic party, to afford protection. The Senator misrepresented my vote on those resolutions. I never voted against the DAVIS resolutions, nor did their substitute ever come up as a separate proposition. It was an amendment to one of that series of resolutions I voted against; and I would vote against any thing and every thing that would embarrass their passage, for they contained just what I thought was right.

What has happened since? Why, a thing has happened that never happened before. The denial of any and all protection to slave property in any and in all the territory; the denial of the right to take slave property to any of them has been proclaimed and affirmed at the ballot-box by a majority of the States, and a majority of the electoral votes of this Union. What has happened? Why, the thing has happened that has been three times before attempted, and three times before failed; the first attempt having endangered the formation of the Union, and the second and third its continuance. The first attempt was made in 1784, to exclude slavery from all the Territories. It was abandoned in 1787 by excluding it only from the territory northwest of the Ohio, leaving it to colonize that portion southwest of that river. The same thing was again attempted in 1820, as to the territory acquired from Louisiana; and after a terrible agitation, was abandoned by adopting the Missouri line. The third attempt was made in 1850, as to the territory acquired from Mexico; and then also the Union narrowly escaped destruction; but the compromise measures were adopted. And now it comes again, but in a more formidable way than ever. A President has been elected on that issue; for the first time the people of the North, after all previous compromises and warnings, have voted on the question, and every Northern State has pronounced for the spoliation.

Mr. President, perhaps the most signal instance of the evils of compulsory union between dissimilar people, is that of Ireland and England. The people of Ireland—the home and heritage of my ancestors—have, as the South has, a representation in the national Legislature; but being also, as the South is, in a minority in that body, have no power to protect themselves from the aggressions of England. The consequence is, that they have been excluded from the common benefits of British legislation, commercially, and even religiously, to say nothing of their exclusion from official station in the empire. And, accordingly, Ireland has been impoverished, degraded, and discontented. She has been trampled upon, outraged, insulted, treated like Cinderella. The people of this country have always sympathized with the wrongs of Ireland, and her struggles for independence. Yet there is now a greater difference between the people of the South and of the North than between those of England and Ireland, and greater antagonism of opinion and feeling. Nevertheless, it is proposed to hold the South in political subjection to the North, and for that purpose to employ naval and military force.

Sir, I might mention many other cases: the subjection of Greece to Turkey; of Poland to Russia; of the Netherlands to Spain; Italy to Austria. In all these cases we have sympathized with, and, in many of them aided, the secession from the common government, by contributions and individual service. Yet those Governments were not founded on consent, and there was no compact conceding the right of secession.

Sir, in conclusion, whether the course the seceding States have seen fit to take be right or not, is a question which we must leave to posterity, and the verdict of impartial history. Our time will probably be more profitably employed in considering how we shall deal with secession than in discussing the causes which have produced it. Secession, right or wrong, justifiable or unjustifiable, is an accomplished fact; and it presents to us no less an alternative than that of peace or war. Sir, I believe that, in the general ruin which would follow coercive measures against the seceding States, all sections, all classes, all the great interests of the country, without any exception, would be involved. How much better, Mr. President, that, in so fearful a crisis as the present, instead of passing "force bills," and preparing for war, instead of "breathing threatenings and slaughter," and preparing implements of destruction to be used against our brethren of the South, how much better, I say, for ourselves, for posterity, for the cause of civil liberty throughout the world, that our thoughts should be turned on peace? Peace, not war, has brought our country to the high degree of prosperity it now enjoys. The energies of the people up to this time have been directed to the development of our boundless resources, to the mechanic arts, to agriculture, mining, trade, and commerce with foreign nations. Banish peace, turn these mighty energies of the people to the prosecution of the dreadful work of mutual destruction, and soon cities in ruins, fields desolate, the deserted marts of trade, the silent workshops, gaunt famine stalking through the land, the earth cumbered with the bodies of the dying and the dead, will bear awful testimony to the madness and wickedness which, from the very summit of prosperity and happiness, are plunging us headlong into an abyss of woe.

Sir, in God's name, let us have peace! If we cannot have it in the Union, as it existed prior to November last, let us have it by cultivating friendly relations with those States which have dissolved their connection with that Union, and established a separate government. Though we and they may not, and, perhaps, in the nature of things, cannot live harmoniously under the same Government, it is our interest, no less than theirs, that we should at once endeavor to establish between our Government and theirs those amicable relations which should ever exist between two neighboring Republics. War, with its attendant horrors, being thus happily averted, the people of each Republic will be left at liberty to pursue, undisturbed, their several vocations. A mutually advantageous commerce will grow up between the two nations; treaties, such as regulate our intercourse with the Canadas, will be formed; confidence in all branches of business will be restored; a new impetus given to every variety of industry; the march of improvement accelerated, and the cause of humanity, of civilization, and of Christianity, advanced throughout the world. The people of Europe, accustomed to refer the settlement of their slightest differences to the bloody arbitrament of the sword, will behold with silent wonder and amazement the spectacle of a great people unable to agree in reference to one of their peculiar domestic institutions, peacefully separating, as did the patriarchs of old; resolving themselves into two distinct political communities, not hostile, discordant, belligerent; but each, animated with a spirit of generous rivalry toward the other, pursuing a more successful and prosperous career in its own chosen path, than when, united under the same Federal head, they painfully sought together the same common destiny.

Mr. President, we are living at a day and at a time when a Northern sectional party have obtained possession of the power of this great Government, who have declared in their platform, in their speeches everywhere, and in their press, that slavery shall never go into another foot of territory; that no other slave State shall ever be admitted into this Union; that slavery shall be put in the course of ultimate extinction. We have the announcement of the party that the foot of a slave shall never press the soil of one of the Territories; that no new slave State shall be admitted; and, in addition to that, that no slave State shall go out of the Union. Who ever saw such a party as that? Who ever knew any thing like it in the world before? They will not let slavery go into the Territories; they will not let a slave State come in; and they will not let one go out! They will not let them go out because they could not carry out their programme of placing slavery in the course of ultimate extinction. They want to keep the slave States in for their benefit—to foot the bills, to pay the taxes—that they may govern them as they see fit, and rule them against their will. Well, sir, I wish to say one word to that party, in all kindness; for I shall not trouble them again on this subject. I shall be a private, independent citizen before long. But I will say to that party, they had better change their tactics; they had better change front, and do it speedily. Let them place themselves upon the high ground of right and justice, and adopt such amendments to the Constitution as will not only hold old Kentucky, which has produced the greatest "compromiser" of us all—that good old State where I was raised, and that I am proud of—but the other Southern States also. I am afraid Republicanism will not do this. I know those old Kentucky people from terrace to foundation. They will endure much—very much—peaceably and quietly; but if they are goaded too far; if, by repeated wrongs, they are compelled to fight, then I would say to their enemy "beware!" There are chivalry and patriotism in Kentucky which is neither in the power of accident nor nature to subdue. You had better not press them too far. Do not drive them to the goal of last resort. Give them justice while you have it in your power to do so. Satisfy them that ultimately they shall have equality in this broken Government, or Union, if you will. But, sir, I leave the patching up of the Constitution to the distinguished Senator from Kentucky and other gentlemen, especially my friend from Pennsylvania [Mr. BIGLER], who has labored harder to patch up the

Constitution than any man I ever knew, except my friend from Kentucky, and I wish him God speed in the work. Let it be upon just principles; let it be right; let us have justice; and I shall be content.

Now, Mr. President, I have paid all the attention to the attempt that was made to place me in the wrong that I deem necessary. I can only now repeat, in the conclusion of my speech, that neither the Senator from Tennessee, nor any other Senator, nor can any man, tell the truth and say that I have, by any vote, word, or act of mine, at any time or on any occasion, refused protection to all property alike in the Territories. I have made it a point always. Indeed, the doctrine of the equal right of property, whether slave or any other, in the Territories, and its equal right to protection, is as strong in me as life itself. I have never uttered a word against that principle; but I have said, upon all occasions, that that doctrine must be maintained, or this Union could not stand. I have fought for it; but as I said in the outset, while I deeply deplore the condition of the country, it has been caused by no act of mine. And with this remark, I part with him, who, in imitation of Esau, seeks to sell his birthright. I would, if there was time, give a little advice to all sides, to every Senator on this floor. I would say: Senators come up to the great importance of this question; meet it; adopt, by a two-thirds vote—as we could do if Senators would deal rightly—amendments to the Constitution, placing all the States upon an equality in the Territories, and on every other question; submit them to the people; and by such amendments I believe we could prevent, or stop, a further rupture of this Union.

In a reply to the speech of Senator LANE of Oregon, the following remarks on secession, coercion, the Territorial question, and the Peace Conference propositions, are furnished by

Senator JOHNSON, of Tennessee:—Mr. President, it is painful for me to be compelled, at this late hour of the session, to occupy any of the time of the Senate upon the subject that has just been discussed by the Senator from *Oregon*. Had it not been for the extraordinary speech he has made, and the singular course he has taken, I should forbear from saying one word at this late hour of the day and of the session. But, sir, it must be apparent, not only to the Senate but to the whole country, that, either by accident or by design, there has been an arrangement that any one who appeared in this Senate to vindicate the Union of these States should be attacked. Why is it that no one, in the Senate or out of it, who is in favor of the Union of these States, has made an attack upon me? Why has it been left to those who have taken both open and secret ground in violation of the Constitution, for the disruption of the Government? Why has there been a concerted attack upon me from the beginning of this discussion to the present moment, not even confined to the ordinary courtesies of debate and of senatorial decorum? It is a question which lifts itself above personalities. I care not from what direction the Senator comes who indulges in personalities toward me; in that, I feel that I am above him, and that he is my inferior. [Applause in the galleries.] Mr. President, they are not arguments; they are the resort of men whose minds are low and coarse. Cowper has well said:

"A truly sensible, well-bred man
Will not insult me; no other can."

Sir, have we reached a point at which we cannot talk about treason? Our forefathers talked about it; they spoke of it in the Constitution of the country; they have defined what treason was; is it an offence, is it a crime, is it an insult to recite the Constitution that was made by WASHINGTON and his compatriots? What does the Constitution say:

"Treason against the United States shall consist only in levying war against them, or in adhering to their enemies, giving them aid and comfort."

There it is defined clearly that treason shall consist only in levying war against the United States, and adhering to and giving aid and comfort to their enemies. Who is it that has been engaged in conspiracies? Who is it that has been engaged in making war upon the United States? Who is it that has fired upon our flag? Who is it that has given instructions to take our arsenals, to take our forts, to take our dock-yards, to take the public property? In the language of the Constitution of the United States, have not those who have been engaged in it been guilty of treason? We make a fair issue. Show me who has been engaged in these conspiracies, who has fired upon our flag, has given instructions to take our forts and our custom-houses, our arsenals and our dock-yards, and I will show you a traitor. [Applause in the galleries.]

Mr. President, if individuals were pointed out to me who were engaged in nightly conspiracies, in secret conclaves, and issuing orders directing the capture of our forts and the taking of our custom-houses, I would show who were the traitors; and that being done, the persons pointed out coming within the purview and scope of the provision of the Constitution which I have read, were I the President of the United States, I would do as THOMAS JEFFERSON did, in 1806, with AARON BURR; I would have them arrested, and, if convicted, within the meaning and scope of the Constitution, by the Eternal GOD I would execute them. Sir, treason must be punished. Its enormity and the extent and depth of the offence must be made known. The time is not distant, if this Government is preserved, its Constitution obeyed, and its laws executed in every department, when something of this kind must be done.

The Senator from Oregon, in his remarks, said that a mind that it required six weeks to stuff could not know much of any thing. He intimated that I had been stuffed. I made my speech on the 19th of December. The gentleman replied. I made another speech, and now he has replied again; and how long has he been "stuffing"? How often has he been "stuffed"? [Laughter.] He has been stuffed twice; and if the stuffing operation was as severe and laborious as the delivery has been, he has had a troublesome time of it, for his travail has been great and the delivery remarkable. [Laughter.]

We know how the Senator stands upon popular or squatter sovereignty. On that subject he spoke at Concord, New Hampshire, where he maintained that the inhabitants of the Territories were the best judges; that they were the very people to settle all these questions; but when he came here, at the last Congress, he could make a speech in which he repeated, I cannot tell how many times, "the equality of the States, the rights of the States in the Union, and their rights out of the Union;" and he thus shifted his course. If the conflict between his speech made in Concord in 1856, and his speech made here on the 25th day of May last, can be reconciled, according to all rules of construction, it is fair to reconcile the conflict. If the discrepancy is so great between his speech made then and his speech on the 25th of May last, of course the discrepancy is against him; but I am willing to let one speech set off the other, and to make honors easy, so far as speech-making is concerned.

Then, how does the matter stand? There is one speech one way, and there is another speech the other way. Now, we will come to the sticking point. You have seen the equivocation to-day. You have seen the cuttle fish attempt to becloud the water and elude the grasp of his pursuer. I intend to stick to you here to-day, as close and as tight as what I think I have heard called somewhere "Jew David's Adhesive Plaster." How does your vote stand as compared with your speeches? Your speeches being easy, I shall throw in the scale against you the weight of what you swore. How does that matter stand? I intend to refer to the record. By referring to the record, it will be found that Mr. CLINGMAN offered the following as an amendment to the fourth resolution of the series introduced by Mr. DAVIS:

"*Resolved*, That the existing condition of the Territories of the United States does not require the intervention of Congress for the protection of property in slaves."

What was the vote on the amendment proposed to that resolution by Mr. BROWN, to strike out the word "not." I want the Senator's attention, for I am going to stick to him, and if he can get away from me he has got to obliterate the records of his country. How would it read, to strike out the word "not."

"That the existing condition of the Territories of the United States does require the intervention of Congress for the protection of property in slaves."

Among those who voted against striking out the word "not," who declared that protection of slavery in the Territories by legislation of Congress was unnecessary, was the Senator from Oregon. When was that? On the 25th day of May last. The Senator, under the oath of his office, declared that legislation was not necessary. Now where do we find him? Here is a proposition to amend the Constitution, to protect the institution of slavery in the States, and here is the proposition brought forward by the Peace Conference, and we find the Senator standing against the one, and I believe he recorded his vote against the other.

But, let us travel along. We have only applied one side of this plaster. The Senator voted that it was not necessary to legislate by Congress for the protection of slave property. Mr. BROWN then offered the amendment to the resolution submitted by Mr. DAVIS, to strike out all after the word "resolved," and to insert in lieu thereof:

"That experience having already shown that the Constitution and the common law, unaided by statutory enactment, do not afford adequate and sufficient protection to slave property—some of the Territories having failed, others having refused, to pass such enactments—it has become the duty of Congress to interpose, and pass such laws as will afford to slave property in the Territories that protection which is given to other kinds of property."

We have heard a great deal said here to-day of "other kinds," and every description of property. There is a naked, clear proposition. Mr. BROWN says it is needed; that the court and the common law do not give ample protection; and then the Senator from Oregon is called upon; but what is his vote? We find, in the vote upon this amendment, that but three Senators voted for it; and the Senator from Oregon records his vote, and says "no," it shall not be established; and every Southern man, save three, voted against it also. When was that? On the 25th day of May last. Here is an amendment, now, to protect and secure the States against any encroachment upon the institution within the States; and there the Senator from Oregon swore that no further legislation was necessary to protect it in the Territories. Well, his speeches in honors being easy, and he having sworn to it in the last Congress, I am inclined to take his oath in preference to his speeches, and one is a fair set-off against the other. Then, all the amendments being voted down, the Senate came to the vote upon this resolution:

"That if experience should at any time prove that the judicial and executive authority do not possess means to insure adequate protection to constitutional rights in a Territory, and if the territorial government should fail or refuse to provide the necessary remedies for that purpose, it will be the duty of Congress to supply such deficiency, within the limits of its constitutional powers."

Does not the resolution proceed upon the idea that it was not necessary then; but if, hereafter, the Territories should refuse, and the courts and the common law could not give ample protection, then it would be the duty of Congress to do this thing? What has transpired since the 25th day of May last? Is not the decision of the court with us? Is there not the Constitution carrying it there? Why was not this resolution, declaring protection necessary, passed during the last Congress? The Presidential election was on hand.

I have been held up and indirectly censured, because I have stood by the people; because I have advocated those measures that are sometimes called demagogical. I would to God that we had a few more men here who were for the people in fact, and who would legislate in conformity with their will and wishes. If we had, the difficulties and dangers that surround us now, would be postponed and set aside; they would not be upon us. But in May last, we could not vote that it was necessary to pass a slave code for the Territories. Oh, no; the Presidential election was on hand. We were very willing then to try to get northern votes; to secure their influence in the passage of resolutions; and to crowd some men down, and let others up. It was all very well then; but since the people have determined that somebody else should be President of the United States, all at once the grape has got to be very sour, and gentlemen do not have as good an opinion of the people as they had before; we have changed our views about it. They have not thought quite as well of us as we desired they should; and if I could not get to be President or Vice-President of all these United States, rather than miss it altogether, I would be perfectly willing to be President of a part; and therefore we will divide—yes, we will divide. I am in favor of secession; of breaking up the Union; of having the rights of the States out of the Union; and as I signally failed in being President of all, as the people have decided against me, we have reached that precise point of time at which the Government ought to be broken up. It looks a little that way.

I have no disposition now, in concluding what little I am going to say, to mutilate the dead, or add one single additional pang to the tortures of the already politically damned. I am a humane man; I will not add one pang to the intolerable sufferings of the distinguished Senator from Oregon. [Laughter.] I sought no controversy with him; I have made no issue with him; it has been forced upon me. How many have attacked me; and is there a single man, North or South, who is in favor of this glorious Union, who has dared to make an assault on me? Is there one? No; not one. But it is all from secession; it is all from that usurpation where a reign of terror has been going on.

I repeat, again, the Senator has made a set-to on me. I am satisfied if he is. I am willing that his speech and mine shall go to the country, and let an intelligent people read and understand, and see who is right and who is wrong on this great issue.

But, sir, I alluded to the fact that secession has been brought about by usurpation. During the last forty days, six States of this Confederacy have been taken out of the Union; how? By the voice of the people? No; it is demagogism to talk of the people. By the voice of the freemen of the country? No. By whom has it been done? Have the people of South Carolina passed upon the ordinance adopted by their Convention? No; but a system of usurpation was instituted, and a reign of terror inaugurated. How was it in Georgia? Have the people there passed upon the ordinance of secession? No. We know that there was a powerful party there, of passive, conservative men, who have been overslaughed, borne down; and tyranny and usurpation have triumphed. A convention passed an ordinance to take the State out of the Confederacy; and the very same convention appointed delegates to go to a congress to make a constitution, without consulting the people. So with Louisiana; so with Mississippi; so with all the six States which have undertaken to form a new Confederacy. Have the people been consulted? Not in a single instance. We are in the habit of saying that man is capable of self-government; that he has the right, the unquestioned right, to govern himself; but here, a government has been assumed over him; it has been taken out of his hands, and at Montgomery a set of usurpers are enthroned,

36

legislating, and making constitutions and adopting them, without consulting the freemen of the country. Do we not know it to be so? Have the people of Alabama, of Georgia, of any of those States, passed upon it? No; but a Constitution is adopted by those men, with a provision that it may be changed by a vote of two-thirds. Four votes in a convention of six, can change the whole organic law of a people constituting six States. Is not this a *coup d'état* equal to any of Napoleon? Is it not a usurpation of the people's rights? In some of those States, even our Stars and our Stripes have been changed. One State has a palmetto, another has a pelican, and the last that I can enumerate on this occasion, is one State that has the rattlesnake run up as an emblem. On a former occasion I spoke of the origin of secession; and I traced its early history to the garden of Eden, when the serpent's wile and the serpent's wickedness beguiled and betrayed our first mother. After that occurred, and they knew light and knowledge, when their Lord and Master turned to them, they seceded, and hid themselves from his presence. The serpent's wile, and the serpent's wickedness, first started secession; and now, secession brings about a return of the serpent. Yes, sir; the wily serpent, the rattlesnake, has been substituted as the emblem on the flag of one of the seceding States; and that old flag, the Stars and the Stripes, under which our fathers fought and bled and conquered, and achieved our rights and our liberties, is pulled down and trailed in the dust, and the rattlesnake substituted. Will the American people tolerate it? They will be indulgent; time, I think, is wanted, but they will not submit to it.

A word more in conclusion. Give the Border States that security which they desire, and the time will come when the other States will come back; when they will be brought back—how? Not by the coercion of the Border States, but by the coercion of the people; and those leaders who have taken them out will fall beneath the indignation and the accumulating force of that public opinion which will ultimately crush them. The gentlemen who have taken those States out are not the men to bring them back.

I have already suggested that the idea may have entered into some minds, "if we cannot get to be President and Vice-President of the whole United States, we may divide the Government, set up a new establishment, have new offices, and monopolize them ourselves when we take our States out." Here we see a President made, a Vice-President made, cabinet officers appointed, and yet the great mass of the people not consulted, nor their assent obtained in any manner whatever. The people of the country ought to be aroused to this condition of things;

they ought to buckle on their armor; and, as Tennessee has done (God bless her!), by the exercise of the elective franchise, by going to the ballot-box under a new set of leaders, they will repudiate and put down those men who have carried these States out and usurped a Government over their heads. I trust in God that the old flag of the Union will never be struck. I hope it may long wave, and that we may long hear the national air sung:

> "The star-spangled banner, long may it wave,
> O'er the land of the free and the home of the brave!"

Long may we hear old Hail Columbia, that good old national air, played on all our martial instruments! long may we hear, and never repudiate, the old tune of Yankee Doodle! Long may wave that gallant old flag which went through the Revolution, and which was borne by Tennessee and Kentucky at the battle of New Orleans, upon that soil the right to navigate the Mississippi near which they are now denied. Upon that bloody field the Stars and Stripes waved in triumph; and, in the language of another, the Goddess of Liberty hovered around when "the rocket's red glare" went forth, indicating that the battle was raging, and watched the issue; and the conflict grew fierce, and the issue was doubtful; but when, at length, victory perched upon your Stars and your Stripes, it was then, on the plains of New Orleans, that the Goddess of Liberty made her loftiest flight, and proclaimed victory in strains of exultation. Will Tennessee ever desert the grave of him who bore it in triumph, or desert the flag that he waved with success? No; we were in the Union before some of these States were spoken into existence; and we intend to remain in, and insist upon—as we have the confident belief we shall get—all our constitutional rights and protection in the Union, and under the Constitution of the country. [Applause in the galleries.]

The PRESIDING OFFICER (Mr. Fitch in the chair):—It will become the unpleasant but imperative duty of the Chair to clear the galleries.

Mr. JOHNSON, of Tennessee:—I have done.

[The applause was renewed, and was louder and more general than before. Hisses were succeeded by applause, and cheers were given and reiterated, with "three cheers more for Johnson."]

The PRESIDING OFFICER:—The Sergeant-at-Arms will immediately clear the galleries, and the order will not be rescinded.

The order having been executed by clearing the galleries and locking the doors leading to them, the Presiding Officer announced that the business of the Senate would be proceeded with.

The Senate, having disposed of several bills, was about to take action on a proposed amendment to the House resolutions, when the Peace Conference amendments were adverted to as follows:

Mr. MASON:—Now, I desire to say a word. There was a commission from twenty or twenty-one States summoned here by the State of Virginia to take into consideration the state of the country, and they have proposed an elaborate amendment to the Constitution, which they ask this body, in connection with the other House, to refer to the States. That has been under consideration for two days; no vote has been taken upon it; and the Senator from Illinois now proposes to postpone that in order to give precedence to a resolution from the House of Representatives proposing to amend the Constitution by prohibiting Congress from interfering with slavery in the States. His motion is, at this stage of the session, to put aside any further consideration of this amendment to the Constitution proposed by that Peace Conference, presented in the impressive manner in which it was done by the honorable Senator from Kentucky, in order to give precedence to this joint resolution of the House on this the last day of the session. Sir, I shall vote against giving it that precedence. I think it is due not only to those honorable gentlemen who came here and have submitted to us the result of their labors that we should give it that precedence, but I feel that it is due to the State of Virginia, who invited the Conference, that no precedence should be given over it. For that reason, I shall vote against it.

Mr. DOUGLAS:—I am glad to find that the Senator from Virginia has become such a warm advocate of the report of the Peace Conference. How many hours is it since we heard him denounce it as unworthy the consideration of Southern men or of this country? How long is it since these denunciations were ringing in our ears? We do not hear the praises of the Peace Conference sounded until we are about to get a vote on another proposition to pacify the country; and for fear we may have a vote that will quiet the apprehensions of the Southern States in respect to the designs of the North to change the Constitution, so as to interfere with slavery in the States, we find now that the Peace Conference is to be pushed forward to defeat this. Sir, if he is a friend of the proposition of the Peace Conference, let him act with me and sit as long as I will in urging it upon the Senate. I am for both; but this one is within our reach. We can close this much in five minutes. We should have had it passed before this time, if the Senator from Virginia had not interposed objections. If the amendment to the Constitution which furnishes guarantees to the border slave

States fail, it will be the result of the efforts of the Senator from Virginia. My object is to take that up; we can dispose of it in a very few minutes; and then, when we have secured thus much, we will proceed immediately to take up the report of the Peace Conference; and I tell the Senator from Virginia he will find me standing here adhering to it as long as he will; and when the vote comes, I think I shall show that I am as friendly to it as he; and that I have as much respect for and appreciation of the services of the great men who reported it.

Mr. MASON:—The Senator from Illinois and I construe our duties in a very different way. I have no parliamentary ends to obtain here by dexterous motions to give preference. The Senator has never heard me express the slightest approbation of these resolutions from the Peace Conference. On the contrary, he has heard me point out, with whatever ability I might, the objections that would compel me to vote against them. I intend to vote against them; but I deem it due to the character of these resolutions, and the way in which they were brought before the Senate, that their precedence should not be taken from them, and that we should have the first vote upon them. The Senator from Illinois will not find me taking back one word that I have said of objection to the resolutions that came from the Peace Conference; but I protest against their precedence being taken from them—a matter which has engaged the attention of the Senate for the last two hours to effect it. Now that it is done, I shall vote against the motion to give precedence. The resolutions of the Peace Conference should not be thrust aside by this resolution of the House; but that is the motion now before us, to thrust aside these resolutions in order to give place to the resolution of the House, and I shall vote against it.

Mr. CRITTENDEN:—I shall pursue, on this occasion, the course I have pursued throughout. My object is to attain a great end, and, if possible, to give entire satisfaction to the country, and restore it to peace and quiet, or to go as far in that direction as it is in my power to go. I shall vote to take up the resolution of the House, because we can act upon it immediately. I am an advocate of the resolutions from the Peace Conference. I have shown it; I have expressed it, and my determination to vote for them, and so I will; but I confess that I feel somewhat as the gentleman from Illinois does—surprised at the great zeal with which gentlemen want to keep up these propositions merely to strike a blow at others, claiming a precedence for a thing they mean to trample and spit upon.

Mr. MASON:—It has precedence, if the Senator will allow me, and he took it from it.

Mr. CRITTENDEN :—And he wants to continue that precedence. Sir, the way to manifest respect for their proposition is to vote for it. I do not understand this sort of proceeding on the part of gentlemen who desire to afford any means of pacification to the country. I am for this resolution of the House of Representatives; and I hope the Senate will vote to take it up. We can act upon it, and we can vote upon it, and we know well that we cannot pass these propositions of the Peace Conference. There are but two hours more of session in the other House—from ten to twelve o'clock on Monday morning. I cannot indulge in a hope, sanguine as I have been throughout, of the passage of those resolutions; and, indeed, the opposition here, and the opposition on this [the Democratic] side of the Chamber to those resolutions, are confirmation strong as Holy Writ that they cannot pass. Do gentlemen want to press them forward in order to prevent a vote on this resolution of the House? I hope not. I hope the motion of the gentleman from Illinois will prevail, and that we shall take up the House resolution.

Mr. BAYARD :—Mr. President, I have forborne to take any part in this discussion about the merits of any of these propositions before the Senate, nor do I intend to do so now. I shall reserve what I may have to say to another occasion. I shall not occupy the time of the Senate now. I shall vote against this motion, because, while I feel I do no injustice to others, I must necessarily exercise my own opinions. I consider the resolution passed by the House of Representatives as not worth the paper on which it is written, for the purpose of adjusting the difficulties in this country. I shall not detain the Senate by any attempt to give the reasons. Sufficient for me to state the ground of my objection, why I shall not vote to give preference to a resolution which, as it stands, I think will lead to no attainable result as regards peace or quiet in the country. As regards the other propositions, for which it is sought to be substituted, I express no opinion now, except to say, they are not exactly those that I should have preferred; but that I would gladly and willingly vote to adopt the distinct resolutions offered originally by the Senator from Kentucky. As to attaining a vote and disposing of this House resolution at once, of course, as I do not attach any importance to the measure, if passed, for the purpose for which it is to be passed, that would be a sufficient answer; but further, it will not stop debate, and it cannot prevent amendments. Amendments may be made; one substitute after another may be offered, and you can be led into debate quite as much as on the other. I would rather see the other proposition discussed; and on the whole, not thinking the particular resolution of the House entitled to preference as being of any great importance, I am not disposed to give it precedence.

Mr. SEBASTIAN, in speaking on the House resolutions, said: "It is now past four o'clock in the morning of the 4th of March, and it is evident, from obvious causes, that it is utterly impossible that any expression of preference for any other resolution than this can now have any effect, or receive even the notice of the House of Representatives."

At different stages of the proceedings of the Senate, in proposing and voting in relation to various amendments, the following among other things said and done, occurred with reference to the Report of the Peace Conference:

Mr. JOHNSON, of Arkansas:—I beg leave to offer as an amendment, and I presume it will be the last, the propositions submitted by the Peace Conference. I offer them not with a belief that they will be accepted or sustained at all. I should be glad to see even that step taken by the party who are to have, and who, in point of fact, do have possession of this Government. I offer them for the purpose of obtaining a vote upon them. I offer them, stating frankly that I shall not vote for them. I offer them with the conviction that there is between the Representatives on the other side of the Chamber, and those on the southern side, an irreconcilable difference; and it ought to be proclaimed, and it ought to be made frank and unmistakable. I offer it because it evolves truth. There is nothing left here to this Senate, on this the last night of the session, but this: to declare to the American people what is true, in order that they may know it, and may prepare themselves to meet it; that they may prepare, if they can, to reconcile it with peace, or to reconcile it to themselves; to stand by all the sorrowful consequences that shall otherwise come. This is the reason why I present this amendment. I believed when I voted for them that the propositions of the Senator from Kentucky were fair, were just to the people of the South, and to my own State among that number; and it is but honest that I should say now in presenting this amendment, that I consider these propositions a thousand fathoms beneath the propositions of the Senator from Kentucky.

It is in that condition that I offer this amendment. I hope Senators will have the courage and the nerve, if they have faith in and regard for their constituents, to whom they have taught their doctrines heretofore, to adhere to them and to stick to them now; and while they will vote against this amendment, I will stand by them also and vote against it, as one person who for fourteen years has represented his State in one or the other branch of this Congress. In saying this, I say it as the last act of my political life, and it is one upon which I put my faith, and on which I would put the last hope I have on earth. I know from the bottom of my soul that I am not averse to the continuation and the preservation of the present Union of States, which I have always considered sanctifies the continent of North America to peace and to prosperity forever. I feel from the bottom of my heart that whenever it shall be divided, it will be given up, from petty causes, and from petty irritations and misapprehensions, to the contingencies of war and the contingencies of blood and disaster, which have followed the divisions and separations of every other continent in the whole wide world.

Then, Mr. President, I offer this amendment from the conviction that common honesty of purpose, and the common frankness of men of nerve and of honor, will give us one vote to show that there is among us an irreconcilable difference, or that will give hope to those who, like the Senator from Kentucky, it seems to me, can hope against hope, that there is something to be done. I cannot believe that any thing is gained by this resolution. I cannot conceive that the proposition of the House gives security to my people. I will not stop to comment upon it, and to show why it is that I cannot vote for it. I sincerely hope that we may have a vote of the Senate upon the amendment I now offer; and I call for the yeas and nays upon it.

The yeas and nays were ordered.

Mr. JOHNSON, of Tennessee:—I wish merely to repeat again, before the yeas and nays are called on this amendment, that I shall vote against this, as I have voted against all preceding amendments, with the distinct understanding that I am not committed for or against any proposition contained in those amendments. I hope we shall vote them all down.

Mr. DOUGLAS:—I will merely state that when we have disposed of this resolution, I hope we shall take up the Peace Conference propositions immediately, and get through with them.

The Secretary proceeded to call the roll.

Mr. CRITTENDEN (when his name was called):—I desire to say that, although preferring this amendment, I shall vote against it, as I have against all others, in order to pass it as it came to us from the House.

Mr. JOHNSON, of Arkansas:—I should like to have made a further explanation; but I will not do it. I vote "nay."

The result was then announced—yeas 3, nays 34; as follows:

YEAS.—Messrs. Foot, Nicholson, and Pugh—3.

NAYS.—Messrs. Anthony, Baker, Bigler, Bingham, Bright, Chandler, Clark, Crittenden, Dixon, Doolittle, Douglas, Durkee, Fessenden, Foster, Grimes, Harlan, Hunter, Johnson of Arkansas, Johnson of Tennessee, Kennedy, King, Latham, Mason, Morrill, Polk, Rice, Sebastian, Sumner, Ten Eyck, Trumbull, Wade, Wigfall, Wilkinson, and Wilson—34.

So the amendment was rejected.

Other amendments—of which some were approved and some rejected—were offered to the joint resolutions, and, finally, the proposals of amendments to the Constitution from the Conference Convention were again brought forward in this manner:

Mr. CRITTENDEN:—I intend to be perfectly consistent in my course on this subject. I look upon the result of the deliberations of the Peace Congress, as they call it here, as affording the best opportunity for a general concurrence among the States and among the people. I determined to take it in preference to my own proposition, and so stated to many of the members of that Convention. I now propose the propositions agreed to by them as a substitute for my own.

I came here this morning, without the least expectation of any vote being taken on this proposition of mine. It has never been in a condition before where I was prepared to offer amendments to it. I had amendments which I intended to propose, not intending to make material changes, as I supposed, in substance and effect, but changing the phraseology, particularly of the first article, in which I propose to substitute an amendment, to declare merely that the *status* of persons held to servitude or labor under the laws of any State shall continue with the laws thus unchanged, as long as the Territory remains under a territorial government; and when it forms a constitution, to come into the Union as a State, to be received with or without slavery. All my papers and the amendments which I prepared are at my room, not here. That is the condition of the thing.

Mr. HUNTER:—The resolution stands now as several States have instructed for it, and I hope we shall have a vote on it.

Mr. CRITTENDEN:—I now move to substitute the resolutions of the Peace Convention. I have declared that I would do this; that I would abandon my own resolutions, and take that proposed by the Peace Conference.

Mr. HUNTER:—Then I call for the yeas and nays on the amendment of the Senator from Kentucky.

The PRESIDING OFFICER:—Does the Chair understand the

Senator from Kentucky to offer as an amendment to the resolution now before the Senate, the resolution of the Peace Conference?

Mr. CRITTENDEN :—Yes, sir.

Mr. HUNTER :—That is an amendment, and on that I ask for the yeas and nays.

The yeas and nays were ordered.

Mr. CRITTENDEN :—I wish to say a word in explanation; of course I shall make no speech at this hour. I have examined the propositions offered by that Convention; they contain, in my judgment, every material provision that is contained in the resolution called the CRITTENDEN resolution. The resolution that I offered contained nothing substantial that has not been adopted by the Convention, except in one particular, and that particular is this: they reject so much of the resolution offered by me as embraced future acquired territory. They said it was enough to settle in regard to the territory we now hold; and they have substituted a provision which, I think, ought to be perfectly satisfactory, as to acquisition of future territory. They say none shall be acquired, unless it be by a two-thirds vote of the Senate, which two-thirds vote shall include a majority of the Senators from the slaveholding States, as well as a majority of the Senators from the North. That gives ample security to the South; it gives ample security to the North. No territory can be acquired without the approbation of both sections of the Union, and having this in their power, they can then make any previous arrangement in regard to slavery that they please, before the acquisition of territory. That is the way they dispose of future acquisitions. I prefer it to the disposition made in the resolutions which I submitted to the Senate. I therefore offer them, and for other reasons: out of deference to that great body of men selected on the resolution of Virginia, and invited by Virginia herself. The body having met, and being composed of such men, and a majority of that Convention concurring in these resolutions, I think they come to us with a sanction entitling them to consideration; therefore I have moved them.

Mr. GWIN :—I hope the substitute will not be adopted. The very reason the Senator has given in favor of it, with reference to the acquisition of future territory, I think should be the cause of its being voted down. I am sure Senators from Northern States should not vote for such an amendment as this; because the first acquisition, if we get any at all, will be the very kind of acquisition that the Northern States want. It is well known that if we had had the same counsels in 1854 that we had in 1803, we should have acquired the whole Russian

Pacific territory to Behring Straits. If THOMAS JEFFERSON had been President, we should have got the whole of the Pacific possessions of Russia, as we got Louisiana from France, on the same principle; and I believe the first acquisition of territory we shall get will be the Russian possessions to Behring Straits. I hope this amendment of the Constitution will not be voted for by those who are in favor of acquiring territory, especially which will give us such important advantages on the Pacific Ocean. I am utterly opposed to restricting all acquisition hereafter; especially on the Pacific coast of the United States, both north and south. I hope this amendment will be voted down.

Mr. DOUGLAS:—I was exceedingly anxious to get a separate and distinct vote, first on the Peace Conference propositions, and then on the CRITTENDEN proposition, as perfected by the Senator from Kentucky. I have announced several times to-night, that that was my purpose; but after what the Senator from Kentucky has said about his obligations to the Peace Conference, to give priority to their proposition, I must follow him, although I should be delighted if we could make arrangements for separate votes. I prefer his perfected amendment to the Peace Conference proposition; but still, I cannot separate from him on this question, when he thinks he is bound to bring it forward.

The Secretary proceeded to call the roll on the amendment.

Mr. NICHOLSON (when his name was called):—I greatly prefer the resolution of the Senator from Kentucky, because it is unequivocal, unambiguous in its language, and embraces future as well as present territory; but I am willing, if that cannot be got, to vote for the other; and I do not concur in the criticisms that have been made on it to the full extent, though there are features in it to which I very much object. I shall, therefore, vote "nay" on this proposition.

Mr. POWELL:—As I have before announced, I have paired with the Senator from Pennsylvania [Mr. CAMERON]. If I were not paired, I should vote "nay."

Mr. GWIN:—He would vote with you, if he were here.

Mr. POWELL:—I cannot tell; he is not here.

The result was announced—yeas 7, nays 28, as follows:

YEAS.—Messrs. Crittenden, Douglas, Harlan, Johnson of Tennessee, Kennedy, Morrill, and Thomson—7.

NAYS.—Messrs. Bayard, Bigler, Bingham, Bright, Chandler, Clark, Dixon, Fessenden, Foot, Foster, Grimes, Gwin, Hunter, Lane, Latham, Mason, Nicholson, Polk, Pugh, Rice, Sebastian, Sumner, Ten Eyck, Trumbull, Wade, Wigfall, Wilkinson, and Wilson—28.

So the amendment was rejected.

No. IV.

[The action of both houses of Congress in relation to the Peace Conference, and the propositions of amendments therein adopted, would seem to form a portion of its history. I shall endeavor to furnish their action so far as it can be separated from other matters connected with the propositions presented. Immediately after the adoption of the resolutions of Virginia, under which the Conference was called, and on the 28th of January, 1861, the following proceedings took place in the House of Representatives of the United States.]

House of Representatives,
Washington, Monday, *January 28th*, 1861.

The Speaker, Hon. Wm. Pennington, laid before the House a message from the President of the United States, which was read by the Clerk, as follows:

To the Senate and House of Representatives of the United States:

I deem it my duty to submit to Congress a series of resolutions adopted by the Legislature of Virginia, on the 19th inst., having in view a peaceful settlement of the exciting questions which now threaten the Union. They were delivered to me on Thursday the 24th inst., by ex-President Tyler, who has left his dignified and honored retirement, in the hope that he may render service to his country in this its hour of peril. These resolutions, it will be perceived, extend an invitation "to all such States, whether slaveholding or non-slaveholding, as are willing to unite with Virginia in an earnest effort to adjust the present unhappy controversies in the spirit in which the Constitution was originally formed, and consistently with its principles, so as to afford to the people of the slaveholding States adequate guarantees for the security of their rights, to appoint Commissioners to meet, on the 4th day of February next, in the City of Washington, similar Commissioners appointed by Virginia, to consider, and, if practicable, agree upon some suitable adjustment."

I confess I hail this movement, on the part of Virginia, with great satisfaction. From the past history of this ancient and renowned Commonwealth, we have the fullest assurance that what she has undertaken she will accomplish, if it can be done by able, enlightened, and persevering efforts. It is highly gratifying to know that other patriotic

States have appointed, and are appointing Commissioners to meet those of Virginia in council. When assembled, they will constitute a body entitled, in an eminent degree, to the confidence of the country.

The General Assembly of Virginia have also resolved "that ex-President John Tyler is hereby appointed by the concurrent vote of each branch of the General Assembly, a Commissioner to the President of the United States; and Judge John Robertson is hereby appointed, by a like vote, a Commissioner to the State of South Carolina, and the other States that have seceded or shall secede, with instructions respectfully to request the President of the United States and the authorities of such States to agree to abstain, pending the proceedings contemplated by the action of this General Assembly, from any and all acts calculated to produce a collision of arms between the States and the Government of the United States."

However strong may be my desire to enter into such an agreement, I am convinced that I do not possess the power. Congress, and Congress alone, under the war-making power, can exercise the discretion of agreeing to abstain "from any and all acts calculated to produce a collision of arms" between this and any other Government. It would, therefore, be a usurpation for the Executive to attempt to restrain their hands by an agreement in regard to matters over which he has no constitutional control. If he were thus to act, they might pass laws which he should be bound to obey, though in conflict with his agreement.

Under existing circumstances, my present actual power is confined within narrow limits. It is my duty at all times to defend and protect the public property within the seceding States so far as this may be practicable, and especially to employ all constitutional means to protect the property of the United States, and to preserve the public peace at this the seat of the Federal Government. If the seceding States abstain "from any and all acts calculated to produce a collision of arms," then the danger so much to be deprecated will no longer exist. Defence, and not aggression, has been the policy of the administration from the beginning.

But while I can enter into no engagement such as that proposed, I cordially commend to Congress, with much confidence that it will meet their approbation, to abstain from passing any law calculated to produce a collision of arms pending the proceedings contemplated by the action of the General Assembly of Virginia. I am one of those who will never despair of the Republic. I yet cherish the belief that the American people will perpetuate the Union of the States on some terms just and honorable for all sections of the country. I trust that the mediation of Virginia may be the destined means, under Providence, of accomplishing this inestimable benefit. Glorious as are the memories of her past history, such an achievement, both in relation to her own fame and the welfare of the whole country, would surpass them all.

JAMES BUCHANAN.

The "series of resolutions" referred to, and transmitted in President BUCHANAN'S message to Congress, are in the body of this book on pages 9 and 10.

The following communication by the Governor of Virginia to the General Assembly thereof, was also submitted with the President's Message:

The Commonwealth of Virginia,
to all to whom these presents shall come, greeting:

Know you, that the General Assembly of the Commonwealth of Virginia, having, by joint resolution, adopted on the 19th instant, and hereto attached, appointed ex-President JOHN TYLER a Commissioner to the President of the United States to carry out the instructions conveyed in said resolution: therefore, I, JOHN LETCHER, Governor, do hereby announce the said appointment, and authenticate the same.

[L. S.] In testimony whereof, I have hereunto set my hand, and caused the great seal of the State to be affixed, in the City of Richmond, this 20th day of January, Anno Domini 1861.

JOHN LETCHER.

By the Governor:
GEORGE W. MUNFORD,
Secretary of the Commonwealth.

Mr. STANTON:—I move that that message be printed, and referred to the Standing Committee on Military Affairs.

Mr. JOHN COCHRANE:—I move as an amendment to that motion, that it be referred to the special committee of five.

Mr. HOWARD, of Michigan:—I would suggest that whatever committee the message is referred to, ought to have power to report it back at any time; otherwise it will be locked up where the House cannot control it.

Mr. BURCH:—The gentleman from Virginia only yielded the floor for the reading of the message, and is now entitled to the floor.

The SPEAKER:—It is proper that the message should be disposed of in some way.

Mr. STANTON:—If the House will allow me, I will move that

the message be referred to the Standing Committee on Military Affairs, with power to report on it at any time.

The SPEAKER:—That motion is not in order. A motion has been made to refer the message to the Committee on Military Affairs, and the gentleman from New York moves, as an amendment, that it be referred to the special committee of five.

Mr. BOCOCK:—If there is to be any debate on this motion, it should be allowed to go over until my colleage (Mr. PRYOR) makes his speech.

Mr. STANTON:—I move the previous question.

Mr. CURTIS:—The question should first be taken on the motion to refer to the Committee on Military Affairs.

The SPEAKER:—That statement is correct. The question is on referring the message to the Military Committee.

Mr. BOCOCK:—I am bound to interpose on behalf of my colleague, who says he only yielded to have the message read.

Mr. STANTON:—The previous question is demanded, and that will put an end to the matter at once.

Mr. MILLSON:—I think the question deserves some little consideration. I therefore move to postpone the further consideration of the President's message till to-morrow.

Mr. STANTON:—Very well; let that course be taken.

The motion was agreed to.

After the report of the Peace Conference had been transmitted to the House of Representatives, and while the joint resolutions were under consideration, several ineffectual attempts were made to get the labors of the Conference before the House. Here is one of the first:

Mr. MAYNARD:—It is known, I suppose, to most members of the House, informally and unofficially, that what is known as the Peace Conference, to which the country has been looking for several days, has concluded its labors and dissolved. [Cries of "Order!"] I desire to make a proposition.

Mr. BINGHAM, and others objected.

Mr. MAYNARD:—I have a right to make a proposition.

Mr. CRAIGE, of North Carolina:—I call the gentleman to order, and insist upon the enforcement of the rules.

Mr. MAYNARD [amid loud cries of "Order!"] moved to postpone the vote upon the pending propositions until to-morrow after the morning hour.

The motion was not agreed to.

And again, the same day, February 27th, the following effort was made:

Mr. McCLERNAND:—I wish to state that I understand there is on the Speaker's table a communication from the president of the Peace Conference. I ask the unanimous consent of the House that it be taken up and read.

Mr. LOVEJOY:—I object.

So action was further delayed.

March 1*st*, 1861.—When a communication from the Navy Department came up for consideration in the House, the motion to postpone the special order brought out the following action on the communication of the Peace Conference:

The SPEAKER:—There is a communication, which has been for some time lying upon the Speaker's table, from the president of the Peace Conference. The Chair thinks it is right that it should be taken up.

Mr. LOVEJOY:—I object.

Mr. GROW:—I call for the regular order of business.

The SPEAKER:—The Chair has not thought proper to present it until the propositions of the Committee of Thirty-three had been disposed of; but he thinks it right that they should now be presented.

Mr. STEVENS, of Pennsylvania:—I object, on behalf of John Tyler, who does not want them in. [Laughter.]

Mr. McCLERNAND:—I move to suspend the rules.

Mr. GROW:—I call for the regular order of business.

The SPEAKER:—The Chair thinks he ought to have the privilege of presenting these papers.

Mr. GROW:—I rise to a question of order. The territorial business is the special order. I am entitled to the floor; and I submit that it cannot be taken from me by any motion to suspend the rules.

The SPEAKER:—The Chair thinks the motion to suspend the rules is in order.

Mr. GROW:—The Chair can hardly understand my question of order. It is that the territorial business is the special order, made so by a suspension of the rules. While that is pending, therefore, by the uniform decision of the House, no motion can be entertained to suspend the rules.

The SPEAKER:—The territorial business was made the special order for the two succeeding days after the propositions reported by the Committee of Thirty-three had been disposed of.

Mr. BOTELER:—I want to know if there is any business, or can be any business, that should take precedence of these propositions of the Peace Conference?

Mr. LOVEJOY:—Yes, sir; there are ten thousand things that should take precedence.

The SPEAKER:—The Chair decides that the gentleman from Illinois [Mr. McClernand] has the floor, and is entitled to make the motion to suspend the rules.

Mr. GROW:—Do I understand the Chair to decide that the business of the Territories does not come up to-day?

The SPEAKER:—The Chair is of opinion that, under a strict construction of the rule, it would properly come up to-morrow.

Mr. GROW:—I appeal from the decision of the Chair.

Mr. HATTON: I move to lay that appeal on the table.

Mr. HICKMAN:—Upon that motion, I call for tellers.

Mr. WASHBURNE, of Illinois:—Before the House divides upon the appeal, I desire the Chair to state precisely what the point of order is that we are to vote upon.

The SPEAKER:—The Chair decided that the gentleman from Illinois [Mr. McClernand] had the floor, and was in order in moving to suspend the rules for the purpose of receiving the communication the Chair desired to lay before the House. From that decision an appeal was taken, and a motion made to lay the appeal on the table. The question is now upon the latter motion.

Mr. GROW:—I rise to a question of order again. The Chair has not stated my question of order correctly. My point of order was, that the business of the Territories was set down as a special order immediately after the disposal of the business of the Committee of Thirty-three.

Mr. HATTON:—I call the gentleman from Pennsylvania to order.

Mr. GROW:—I have the right to state my point of order.

The SPEAKER:—The gentleman from Pennsylvania will state his point of order.

Mr. GROW:—It is, that the Territorial business having been made the special order, comes up now as the regular order of business.

The SPEAKER:—The Chair decides that the gentleman from Illinois obtained the floor, and had the right to submit the motion to suspend the rules.

Mr. GROW:—He had no right to take the floor from me for any such purpose.

The SPEAKER:—The Chair overrules the question of order.

Mr. GROW:—And from that decision I take an appeal.

The SPEAKER:—The appeal is already pending; and a motion has been made to lay the appeal on the table.

Mr. GROW:—I call for tellers on the motion.

Tellers were ordered, and Messrs. ADRAIN and GROW were appointed.

The House divided; and the tellers reported—forty-seven in the affirmative.

Mr. HOWARD, of Michigan:—I move that the House adjourn.

Before the vote had been taken on the motion, the hour of five arrived; and

The SPEAKER declared the House had taken a recess until seven o'clock.

EVENING SESSION.

The House reassembled at seven o'clock P. M.

COMMUNICATION OF THE PEACE CONFERENCE.

Mr. GROW:—What is the regular order of business?

The SPEAKER:—The Chair had decided that the gentleman from Illinois [Mr. McCLERNAND] was entitled to the floor, to move that the rules be suspended to receive a communication from the Peace Conference. From that decision the gentleman from Pennsylvania [Mr. GROW] appealed; and a motion was made to lay the appeal on the table.

Mr. McCLERNAND:—I think we can perhaps agree to an arrangement that will be satisfactory to gentlemen upon both sides, by which any difficulty upon the question of order can be avoided. If gentlemen upon that side of the House will allow the propositions to be presented, we are willing that they shall be referred, and the House then proceed to the consideration of the territorial business.

Mr. KELLOGG, of Illinois:—I hope that will be done.

Mr. LOVEJOY:—I object to the reception of the proposition.

Mr. HICKMAN:—There are but few members present. I move that there be a call of the House.

The motion was disagreed to.

Mr. HICKMAN:—I ask the Chair for his judgment whether there is a quorum present or not.

The SPEAKER:—In the opinion of the Chair, a quorum is not present.

Mr. McCLERNAND:—I inquire whether there is any objection to the propositions of the Peace Conference being taken up and referred?

Mr. LOVEJOY:—I certainly object in *toto cœlo* to any such proposition.

Mr. BOTELER:—I desire to ask this question: can any member object to the reception of a communication from the Peace Congress?

Mr. LOVEJOY:—It is not a Peace Congress at all. There is no such body known to this House.

Mr. BOTELER:—I merely ask the question for information, for I do not profess to be familiar with the rules; I desire to know whether the objection of a single member can defeat the reception of such a proposition, especially when that single member is known not to be a conservative man, but a man opposed to all compromises?

The SPEAKER:—The Chair will suggest that a great deal of time will be saved by having a call of the House, as there is evidently no quorum present.

A call of the House was taken. A quorum having appeared, the House proceeded to dispose of several special orders, when, on a motion of postponement, it returned in this wise to the Peace Conference:

Mr. LOGAN:—I demand the yeas and nays on the motion to postpone.

The yeas and nays were not ordered.

The special order was then postponed.

Mr. McCLERNAND:—I now move to suspend the rules of the House, for the purpose of receiving the memorial of the Peace Congress, which assembled lately in this city.

Mr. GROW:—To be received? What for?

Mr. McCLERNAND:—For reference I suppose.

Mr. BURNETT:—No; but to get it in, and put it upon its passage.

The SPEAKER:—The Chair understood the proposition to be, that the rules should be suspended, in order that the paper should be received for reference.

Mr. McCLERNAND:—I withdraw that part of the proposition.

Mr. SICKLES:—If it be received, it is then in the power of the House to do with it what it pleases.

Mr. GROW:—The understanding was that the motion should be made for the suspension of the rules only to receive the proposition.

Mr. SICKLES:—That is all right. When the paper gets in, the House can do with it what it may deem fit.

Mr. LOVEJOY:—I demand the yeas and nays.

The yeas and nays were ordered.

Mr. SHERMAN:—Is it proposed to act on the memorial of the Peace Congress?

Mr. SICKLES:—If it comes before the House, it will be for us to say what disposition shall be made of it. [Cries of "Call the roll!"]

Mr. CRAIGE, of North Carolina:—This motion is merely for the suspension of the rules to receive the proposition, and this, therefore, may be considered a test vote. [Cries of "Call the roll!"]

The question was taken; and it was decided in the negative—yeas 93, nays 67; as follows:

YEAS.—Messrs. Charles F. Adams, Green Adams, Adrain, Aldrich, William C. Anderson, Avery, Barr, Barret, Bocock, Boteler, Brabson, Branch, Briggs, Bristow, Brown, Burch, Burnett, Campbell, Horace F. Clark, John B. Clark, John Cochrane, Corwin, James Craig, John G. Davis, De Jarnette, Dunn, Etheridge, Florence, Foster, Fouke, Garnett, Gilmer, Hale, Hall, Hamilton, J. Morrison Harris, John T. Harris, Haskin, Hatton, Hoard, Holman, William Howard, Hughes, Jenkins, Junkin, William Kellogg, Killinger, Kunkel, Larrabee, James M. Leach, Leake, Logan, Maclay, Mallory, Charles D. Martin, Maynard, McClernand, McKenty, McKnight, McPherson, Millson, Millward, Laban T. Moore, Moorehead, Edward Joy Morris, Nelson, Niblack, Nixon, Olin, Pendleton, Peyton, Phelps, Porter, Pryor, Quarles, John H. Reynolds, Rice, Riggs, James C. Robinson, Sickles, Simms, William N. H. Smith, Spaulding, Stevenson, William Stewart, Stokes, Thomas, Vance, Webster, Whiteley, Winslow, Woodson, and Wright—93.

NAYS.—Messrs. Alley, Ashley, Bingham, Blair, Brayton, Buffinton, Burlingame, Burnham, Carey, Case, Coburn, Colfax, Conway, Burton Craige, Dawes, Delano, Duell, Edgerton, Eliot, Ely, Fenton, Ferry, Frank, Gooch, Graham, Grow, Gurley, Helmick, Hickman, Hindman, William A. Howard, Hutchins, Irvine, Francis W. Kellogg, Kenyon, Loomis, Lovejoy, McKean, Morrill, Morse, Palmer, Perry, Potter, Pottle, Christopher Robinson, Royce, Ruffin, Sedgwick, Sherman, Somes, Spinner, Stanton, Stevens, Tappan, Tompkins, Train, Vandever, Van Wyck, Wade, Waldron, Walton, Cadwalader C. Washburn, Ellihu B. Washburne, Wells, Wilson, Windom, and Woodruff—67.

So (two thirds not voting in favor thereof) the rules were not suspended.

During the vote,

Mr. WOODSON said:—I rise for information. What are we voting on? [Cries of "Order!"] I cannot for my life imagine how this can be regarded as a test vote. I will vote to receive the proposition of the Peace Conference; but on its passage I will vote against it.

The SPEAKER:—The motion is, to suspend the rules for the reception of the memorial.

Mr. CRAIGE, of North Carolina:—I understood the gentleman from Illinois to state that this was a test vote.

The SPEAKER:—The Chair cannot undertake to decide whether it is a test vote or not.

Mr. JOHN COCHRANE stated that his colleagues, Mr. CLARK B. COCHRANE and Mr. LEE, were paired.

Mr. CRAIGE, of North Carolina:—I would have no objection, Mr. Speaker, to permit this resolution to come before the House, but I understood the gentleman from Illinois to proclaim that this was a test vote. Utterly opposed to any such wishy-washy settlement of our national difficulties, I vote "no."

Mr. CURTIS stated that he was paired with Mr. ANDERSON, of Missouri.

Mr. FOSTER:—While I am willing to vote for the reception of the memorial of the Peace Congress, of which I was a member, still I am unwilling to be considered as favoring their proposition. Is this vote a test vote on that proposition?

The SPEAKER:—The Chair does not think that it is; but each gentleman will decide for himself.

Mr. HALE:—I am willing to receive this memorial in courtesy to the Peace Conference; and not regarding this as a test vote, I vote "ay."

Mr. LEACH, of Michigan, stated that he had paired with Mr. ENGLISH, or he would have voted in the negative.

Mr. LEAKE (when his name was called) said that he regarded this *thing* as a miserable abortion, forcibly reminding one of the old fable of the mountain and the mouse; nevertheless, he was willing to let the mouse in, in order to have the pleasure of killing it.

Mr. RUFFIN:—As it is announced that this is a test vote, I am compelled to vote "no." Otherwise, I would have been willing to let the matter be brought before the House for its consideration.

Mr. JENKINS:—Who can make this a test vote? Certainly no man in this House. This is a vote to receive the memorial, and nothing more.

Mr. WILSON stated that Mr. VALLANDIGHAM was paired with Mr. BEALE.

Mr. JUNKIN stated that his colleague, Mr. MONTGOMERY, was detained at home by illness.

Mr. NIXON stated that his colleague, Mr. STRATTON, was detained at his room by illness, and that if he were present, he would vote to receive the memorial of the Peace Conference.

Mr. ELY stated that his colleague, Mr. LEE, was detained at his room by indisposition.

Mr. PENDLETON stated that his colleague was detained at his room by indisposition.

Mr. CAMPBELL stated that his colleague, Mr. SCRANTON, was absent from the Hall because of illness.

Mr. POTTER :—As this is a test vote, I vote "no."

Mr. BRAYTON :—I understand this to be a test vote, and therefore vote "no."

Mr. HOARD :—These papers are not before us. They are not printed, and we cannot be supposed to know any thing of them; and I would ask, therefore, how they can be regarded as a test vote? I vote "ay."

Mr. BOCOCK :—Mr. Speaker, out of deference to the Peace Conference, called as it was by my State, I vote to receive this report. But unless the report, as it appears in the papers, can be amended, it cannot receive my approval.

Mr. SHERMAN :—I vote against this, simply because we have no time to consider it.

Mr. HINDMAN :—I vote against suspending the rules, because I desire to defeat the proposition of the Peace Conference, believing it to be unworthy of the vote of any Southern man.

Mr. COX (not being within the bar when his name was called) asked leave to vote.

Mr. WASHBURNE, of Illinois, objected.

Mr. GARNETT :—Mr. Speaker, intending and desiring to express my abhorrence of these insidious propositions, conceived in fraud and born of cowardice, by giving a direct vote against them, yet from respect for the conference which reported them, I am willing to receive them, and therefore now vote "ay."

Mr. HARRIS, of Virginia :—I vote "ay," because I am in favor of the resolutions as a peace measure.

Mr. MAYNARD :—Believing these propositions eminently wise and just, I will let my vote stand in the affirmative.

Mr. BURNETT :—I hope the Chair will enforce the rules.

The SPEAKER :—I am trying to, all I can; and I hope gentlemen will keep their seats and preserve order.

Mr. DE JARNETTE :—I vote "ay," with the hope of having an opportunity to vote against the propositions of the Peace Conference.

Mr. BOTELER :—I vote "ay," to introduce these propositions,

because I believe it to be my duty to do every thing, consistent with honor, to preserve the peace and save the Union of my country.

Mr. COX:—I desire to ask a question of the Chair.

The SPEAKER:—The Chair will hear you.

Mr. COX:—I desire to know whether or not it will be in order to move to suspend the rules to enable me to have my vote recorded?

Mr. SPEAKER:—No, sir.

Mr. COX:—I would like very much to have it recorded in favor of these peace propositions. I vote "ay," if there is no objection.

Mr. HINDMAN:—Consent is not given to the gentleman from Ohio to have his vote recorded.

The SPEAKER:—It is not received.

Mr. ROBINSON, of Rhode Island:—Believing that this is a test vote, I change my vote, and vote "no."

Mr. JOHN COCHRANE:—I wish to know whether the vote of my colleague, CLARK B. COCHRANE, is recorded.

The SPEAKER:—It is not.

Mr. JOHN COCHRANE:—I think he has retired from the House on account of sickness in his family; and I believe he is laboring for the Union in other quarters.

Mr. MILLSON:—I desire to vote.

Objection was made.

Mr. MILLSON:—I am entitled to vote, having been absent upon a committee of conference. I vote "ay."

Mr. HINDMAN:—Is the gentleman entitled to vote under the rules of the House?

Mr. BARR:—Objection comes too late.

The SPEAKER:—It has been usual to allow gentlemen to vote under such circumstances.

Mr. HICKMAN:—Do the rules allow him to vote?

The SPEAKER:—The Chair supposes that is the rule of the House.

Mr. HINDMAN:—I ask to have the rule read.

Mr. MILLSON:—No rule of the House could take away the right of a member to vote when he is absent by order of the House. If the rules deprived a member of the right to vote under such circumstances, it would be void.

The result was announced as above recorded.

Mr. McCLERNAND:—This vote divides the Republican party, and sounds its death knell.

No. V.

REPORTS OF DELEGATES TO STATES.

Report of the Peace Commissioners to the Legislature of Virginia.

To His Excellency JOHN LETCHER, *Governor of Virginia:*

The undersigned Commissioners, in pursuance of the wishes of the General Assembly, expressed in the resolutions of the 19th day of January last, repaired in due season to the City of Washington. They there found, on the 4th day of February, the day suggested in the overture of Virginia for a Conference with the other States, Commissioners to meet them from the following States, viz.: Rhode Island, New Jersey, Delaware, Maryland, New Hampshire, Vermont, Connecticut, Pennsylvania, North Carolina, Ohio, Indiana, Illinois, and Kentucky. Subsequently, during the continuance of the Conference, at different periods, appeared likewise Commissioners from Tennessee, Massachusetts, Missouri, New York, Maine, Iowa, and Kansas. So that before the close twenty-one States were represented by Commissioners, appointed either by the Legislatures or Governors of the respective States.

The undersigned communicated the resolutions of the General Assembly to this Conference, and, both before its committee appointed to recommend a plan of adjustment, and the Conference itself, urged the propositions known as the CRITTENDEN resolutions, with the modification suggested by the General Assembly of Virginia, as the basis of an acceptable adjustment.

They were not adopted by the Conference, but in lieu thereof, after much discussion, and the consideration of many proposed amendments, the article with seven sections, intended as an amendment to the Constitution, was adopted by sections (not under the rules, being voted on as a whole), and by a vote of the Conference (not taken by States), was directed to be submitted to Congress, with the request that it should be recommended to the States for ratification, which was accordingly done by the President of the Conference.

The undersigned regret that the Journal showing the proceedings and votes in the Conference has not yet been published or furnished them, and that consequently they are not able to present it with this report. As soon as received it will be communicated to your Excellency.

In the absence of that record it is deemed appropriate to state that on the final adoption of the first section, two of the States, Indiana and Missouri, did not vote, and New York was divided, and that the votes by States was, ayes 9, nays 8—Virginia, by a majority of her Commissioners, voting in the negative.

The other sections were adopted by ranging majorities (not precisely recollected), and on the fifth and seventh sections the vote of Virginia was in the negative. The plan, when submitted to Congress, failed to receive its recommendation, and as that body, having adjourned, can take no further cognizance of it, the undersigned feel the contingency has arrived on which they are required to report, as they herein do, the result of their action.

Respectfully,

JOHN TYLER,
G. W. SUMMERS,
W. C. RIVES,
JAS. A. SEDDON.

The above report having been read and ordered to be printed, Mr. SUMMERS stated that the reason it was not signed by Judge BROCKENBROUGH, the other Virginia Commissioner, was because that gentleman was not in Richmond. Mr. SUMMERS presented a communication in which Judge BROCKENBROUGH stated his views at length on the propositions adopted by the Convention, and it was printed, by vote of the Legislature, in connection with the report.

After reviewing the different sections of the propositions adopted by the Peace Conference, Judge BROCKENBROUGH, in his letter, states that the said propositions, *as an entirety*, would have received his vote, and therefore the vote of Virginia, in the Peace Conference, if it had been submitted to a vote in that form.

Reports of the New York Commissioners to the Legislature of that State.

MAJORITY REPORT OF THE COMMISSIONERS TO THE PEACE CONVENTION.

March 23d, 1861.

To the Honorable the Legislature of the State of New York:

The Report of the Commissioners appointed by the Legislature of the State of New York to meet Commissioners from other States in the City of Washington on the fourth day of February, 1861, upon the call of the State of Virginia, by resolutions passed by the General Assembly of that State on the nineteenth day of January, 1861.

A copy of the Journal of the Convention is submitted herewith, from which it will be seen that prior to the presence of the Commissioners from New York, that body had been completely organized, rules of order adopted which excluded all persons other than members from witnessing its deliberations, forbidding any publication or other communication of its proceedings, and the taking of any entry from its Journal without leave; in short, requiring all its debates and acts to be kept secret. A committee had also been organized of one from each State to be appointed by the Commissioners from such State, to which the Virginia resolutions were referred, "with all other propositions for the adjustment of existing differences between the States, with authority to report what they might deem right, proper, and necessary to restore harmony and preserve the Union;" and this committee had been in session two days before your Commissioners were enabled to appoint any one of their number upon it. This was done on the eighth of February by the appointment of Mr. Field.

William E. Dodge, one of your Commissioners, took his seat in the Convention on the seventh day of February, 1861, and Messrs. Field, Noyes, Wadsworth, Corning, King, and Wool, on the eighth of February, Mr. Smith on the eleventh, and Judges James and Bronson on the twelfth day of February, and Mr. Granger, who was appointed in the place of Judge Gardiner, who declined, on the eighteenth day of February, 1861.

It was deemed advisable by your Commissioners that the proceedings of the Convention should be open to the public and the press, and hence they advised and concurred in resolutions introduced for that purpose, which were laid on the table on the motion of a Commissioner from the State of New Jersey. On a subsequent day they also concurred in a resolution authorizing the employment of a stenographer, to "preserve accurate notes of the debates and other proceedings of 'the Convention,' which notes should not be communicated to any person, nor shall copies thereof be taken, nor shall the same be made public until after the final adjournment of this Convention, except in pursuance of a vote authorizing their publication;" but this was refused, and the resolution laid on the table on motion of a Commissioner from the State of Pennsylvania, by a vote of eleven to eight, all the Slave States represented voting against it, with the addition of the States of Connecticut, Rhode Island, New Jersey, and Pennsylvania. Before the Convention closed its session, the following states, twenty-one in all, were represented in the Convention: Delaware, Maryland, Virginia, Kentucky, Tennessee, North Carolina, Missouri, Connecticut, Rhode Island, New Hampshire, Maine, Massachusetts, New York, Vermont, Illinois, Ohio, Indiana, Iowa, Pennsylvania, and Kansas. With the concurrence of a majority of your Commissioners, Mr. Field offered in the committee of one from each State, on the fourteenth of February, the following proposition:

> "Each State has the sole and exclusive right, according to its own judgment, to order and direct its domestic institutions, and to determine for itself what shall be the relation to each other of all persons residing or being within its limits;"

but it was rejected by a majority of the committee, and formed no part of its report.

That committee made its report on the fourteenth of February, unaccompanied by any written observations, in the shape of an amendment to the Constitution of the United States, in the following words:

ARTICLE 1. In all the territory of the United States not embraced within the limits of the Cherokee Treaty Grant, north of a line from east to west on the parallel of 36° 30′ north latitude, involuntary servitude, except in punishment of crime, is prohibited whilst it shall be under a Territorial Government; and in all the territory south of said line, the status of persons owing service or labor, as it now exists, shall not be changed by law while such territory shall be under a Territorial Government; and neither Congress nor the Territorial Government shall have power to hinder or prevent the taking to said territory of persons held to labor or involuntary service, within the United States, according to the laws or usages of the State from which such persons may be taken, nor to impair the rights arising out of said relations, which shall be subject to judicial cognizance in the Federal Courts according to the common law; and when any Territory north or south of said line, within such boundary as Congress may prescribe, shall contain a population required for a member of Congress, according to the then Federal ratio of representation, it shall, if its form of government be republican, be admitted into the Union on an equal footing with the original States, with or without involuntary service or labor, as the constitution of such new State may provide.

ART. 2. Territory shall not be acquired by the United States, unless by treaty, nor except for naval and commercial stations and depots, unless such treaty shall be ratified by four-fifths of all the members of the Senate.

ART. 3. Neither the Constitution nor any amendment thereof shall be construed to give Congress power to regulate, abolish, or control, within any State or Territory of the United States, the relation established or recognized by the laws thereof touching persons bound to labor or involuntary service therein, nor to interfere with or abolish involuntary service in the District of Columbia without the consent of Maryland, and without the consent of the owners, or making the owners who do not consent just compensation; nor the power to interfere with or prohibit representatives and others from bringing with them to the City of Washington, retaining, and taking away persons so bound to labor; nor the power to interfere with, or abolish involuntary service in places under the exclusive jurisdiction of the United States, within those States and Territories where the same is established or recognized; nor the power to prohibit the removal or transportation by land, sea, or river, of persons held to labor or involuntary service in any State or Territory of the United States to any other State or Territory thereof where it is established or recognized by law or usage; and the right during transportation of touching at ports, shores, and landings, and of landing in case of distress, shall exist; nor shall Congress have power to authorize any higher rate of taxation on persons bound to labor than on land.

ART. 4. The third paragraph of the second section of the fourth article of the Constitution, shall not be construed to prevent any of the States, by appropriate legislation, and through the action of their judicial and ministerial officers, from enforcing the delivery of fugitives from labor to the person to whom such service or labor is due.

ART. 5. The foreign slave-trade and the importation of slaves into the United States and their Territories from places beyond the present limits thereof, are forever prohibited.

ART. 6. The first, third, and fifth articles, together with this article of these amendments, and the third paragraph of the second section of the first article of the Constitution, and the third paragraph of the second section of the fourth article thereof, shall not be amended or abolished without the consent of all the States.

ART. 7. Congress shall provide by law that the United States shall pay to the owner the full value of his fugitive from labor, in all cases where the marshal or other officers, whose duty it was to arrest such fugitive, was prevented from so doing by violence or intimidation from mobs and riotous assemblies, or when after such arrest such fugitive was rescued by force, and the owner thereby prevented and obstructed in the pursuit of his remedy for the recovery of such fugitive.

Mr. Field, the member of the committee from New York, dissented from this report, as also did Mr. Baldwin, of Connecticut, and Mr. Crowninshield, of Massachusetts, and Mr. Seddon, of Virginia.

This report was under discussion, and various amendments were proposed to it until the twenty-seventh day of February, a majority of your Commissioners steadily opposing all its provisions except that prohibiting the foreign slave-trade, and most of such majority being opposed to the submission, by the Convention, of any amendment of the Constitution of the United States at the present time, and in the present excited state of the public mind. During the consideration of the report various independent propositions were made by the consent, and with the concurrence of your Commissioners; among which was one by Mr. Baldwin, of Connecticut, presented on the fifteenth of February, in the form of a minority report from the committee upon the plan of adjustment, which concluded with a resolution, "That the Convention recommend to the several States to unite with Kentucky in her application to Congress to call a Convention for proposing amendments to the Constitution of the United States, to be submitted to the Legislatures of the several States or to Conventions therein, for ratification, as the one or other mode of ratification may be proposed by Congress;" and this proposition, after being discussed at length, was lost on the twenty-sixth of February, by a vote of thirteen States against to nine in its favor, a majority of your Commissioners casting the vote of New York in favor of it.

A proposition somewhat similar, embracing an address to the people of the United States, and containing a resolution for calling the Convention, was also submitted to the Convention, with the like concurrence of a majority of your Commissioners, by Mr. Tuck of New Hampshire, on the eighteenth of February, and on the twenty-sixth was also defeated by a vote of eleven States against nine.

It will be seen, therefore, that your Commissioners, with those from several other States, offered to unite in a call for a Convention, to be convened in pursuance of the Constitution of the United States; and that the slave States uniting with several of the free States, uniformly opposed, and at last defeated it.

On the twenty-third of February Mr. Vandever, of Iowa, offered the following resolution:

"*Resolved*, That whatever may be the ultimate determination upon the amendment to the Federal Constitution, or other propositions for the adjustment approved by this Convention, we, the members, recommend our respective States and constituencies to faithfully abide in the Union."

A motion to lay it upon the table prevailed by a vote of eleven to nine, a majority of your Commissioners voting in the negative.

On the twentieth of February, Mr. Field, one of your Commissioners, at the instance of a majority of them, offered, as an amendment to the Constitution to be adopted by the Convention, and proposed with any other amendments, that it should recommend the following:

"The Union of the States, under this Constitution, is indissoluble; and no State can secede from the Union, or nullify an act of Congress, or absolve its citizens from their paramount obligation of obedience to the Constitution and laws of the United States."

On the twenty-sixth of February, after several ineffectual attempts to get rid of the proposition, on points of order, it was negatived by a vote of eleven States against ten, a majority of your Commissioners casting the vote of New York in its favor.

Mr. Wilmot, of Pennsylvania, moved the following as an amendment to the seventh article, on the twenty-first of February.

"And Congress shall further provide by law, that the United States shall make full compensation to a citizen of any State, who, in any other State, shall suffer by reason of violence or intimidation from mobs or riotous assemblies in his person or property, or in the deprivation by violence of his rights secured by this Constitution."

A motion was made to insert the word "white" before "citizen," but it failed by a vote of eleven to ten; and on the twenty-fifth of February the entire amendment was defeated by a vote of eleven to eight; your Commissioners, by a majority, casting the vote of New York in its favor.

Several other propositions upon other subjects were also submitted to the Convention, as will appear by the Journal; but it is not deemed necessary to refer to them more particularly, except, that on the eighteenth of February, Mr. Reid, of North Carolina, proposed to amend the first section of the committee's report by inserting after the word "line" in the seventh line thereof, the words "involuntary servitude is recognized; and property in those of the African race held to service or labor, in any of the States of the Union, when removed to such territory, shall be protected," and which was lost by a vote of seventeen States against to three for it. On the twenty-sixth of February, he also moved to insert in the same section, after the words "common law," the words, "and such rights shall be protected by all departments of the Territorial Government during its continuance," which the President ruled out of order, as the section had been previously gone through in detail, and was only before the Convention on its final passage.

The Report of the Committee on a plan of adjustment, already mentioned, came up for consideration on its final passage, after many amendments had been made to it, as will appear by the Journal, on the twenty-sixth of February, in the following form, and was ultimately thus adopted, by the votes stated at the end of each section:

Article XIII.

Section I. In all the present territory of the United States north of the parallel of 36° 30′ of north latitude, involuntary servitude, except in punishment of crime, is prohibited. In all the present territory south of that line, the *status* of persons held to involuntary service or labor, as it now exists, shall not be changed; nor shall any law be passed by Congress or the Territorial Legislature to hinder or prevent the taking of such persons from any of the States of this Union to said Territory, nor to impair the rights arising from said relation; but the same shall be subject to judicial cognizance in the Federal Courts according to the course of the common law.

When any Territory north or south of said line, within such boundary as Congress may prescribe, shall contain a population equal to that required for a member of Congress, it shall, if its form of government be republican, be admitted into the Union on an equal footing with the original States, with or without involuntary servitude, as the constitution of such State may provide.

YEAS.—Delaware, Illinois, Kentucky, Maryland, New Jersey, Ohio, Pennsylvania, Rhode Island, and Tennessee—9.

NAYS.—Connecticut, Iowa, Maine, Massachusetts, North Carolina, New Hampshire, Vermont, and Virginia—8.

DIVIDED.—New York and Kansas—2.

NOT VOTING.—Indiana.

SEC. II. No territory shall be acquired by the United States except by discovery, and for naval and commercial stations, depots, and transit routes, without the concurrence of a majority of all the Senators from States which allow involuntary servitude, and a majority of all the Senators from States which prohibit that relation; nor shall territory be acquired by treaty, unless the votes of a majority of the Senators from each class of States hereinbefore mentioned be cast as a part of the two-thirds majority necessary for the ratification of such treaty.

YEAS.—Delaware, Indiana, Kentucky, Maryland, Missouri, New Jersey, Ohio, Pennsylvania, Rhode Island, Tennessee, and Virginia—11.

NAYS.—Connecticut, Illinois, Iowa, Maine, Massachusetts, North Carolina, New Hampshire, and Vermont—8.

DIVIDED.—New York and Kansas—2.

SEC. III. Neither the Constitution nor any amendment thereof shall be construed to give Congress power to regulate, abolish, or control, within any State, the relation established or recognized by the laws thereof touching persons held to labor or involuntary service therein, nor to interfere with or abolish involuntary service in the District of Columbia without the consent of Maryland, nor without the consent of the owners, or making the owners who do not consent just compensation; nor the power to interfere with or prohibit representatives and others from bringing with them to the District of Columbia, retaining, and taking away, persons so held to labor or service; nor the power to interfere with, or abolish involuntary service in places under the exclusive jurisdiction of the United States, within those States and Territories where the same is established or recognized; nor the power to prohibit the removal or transportation of persons held to labor or involuntary service in any State or Territory of the United States to any other State or Territory thereof where it is established or recognized by law or usage, and the right during transportation, by sea or river, of touching at ports, shores, and landings, and of landing in case of distress, shall exist; but not the right of transit in, or through any State or Territory, or of sale or traffic against the laws thereof; nor shall Congress have power to authorize any higher rate of taxation on persons held to labor or service than on land. The bringing into the District of Columbia of persons held to labor or service for sale, or placing them in depots to be afterwards transferred to other places as merchandise, is prohibited.

YEAS.—Delaware, Illinois, Kentucky, Maryland, Missouri, New Jersey, North Caroline, Ohio, Pennsylvania, Rhode Island, Tennessee, and Virginia—12.

NAYS.—Connecticut, Indiana, Iowa, Maine, Massachusetts, New Hampshire, and Vermont—7.

DIVIDED.—New York and Kansas—2.

SEC. IV. The third paragraph of the second section of the fourth article of the Constitution shall not be construed to prevent any of the States, by appropriate legislation, and through the action of their judicial and ministerial officers, from enforcing the delivery of fugitives from labor to the person to whom such labor or service is due.

YEAS.—Connecticut, Delaware, Illinois, Indiana, Kentucky, Maryland, Missouri, New Jersey, North Carolina, Ohio, Pennsylvania, Rhode Island, Tennessee, Vermont, and Virginia—15.

NAYS.—Iowa, Maine, Massachusetts, and New Hampshire—4.

DIVIDED.—New York and Kansas—2.

SEC. V. The foreign slave-trade is hereby forever prohibited; and it shall be the duty of Congress to pass laws to prevent the importation of slaves, coolies, or persons held to service or labor, into the United States and the Territories, from places beyond the limits thereof.

YEAS.—Connecticut, Delaware, Illinois, Indiana, Kentucky, Maryland, Missouri, New Jersey, New York, New Hampshire, Ohio, Pennsylvania, Rhode Island, Tennessee, Vermont, and Kansas—16.

NAYS.—Iowa, Maine, Massachusetts, North Carolina, and Virginia—5.

SEC. VI. The first, third, and fifth sections, together with this section of these amendments, and the third paragraph of the second section of the first article of the Constitution, and the third paragraph of the second section of the fourth article thereof, shall not be amended or abolished without the consent of all the States.

YEAS.—Delaware, Illinois, Kentucky, Maryland, Missouri, New Jersey, Ohio, Pennsylvania, Rhode Island, and Tennessee—11.

NAYS.—Connecticut, Indiana, Iowa, Maine, Massachusetts, North Carolina, New Hampshire, Vermont, and Virginia—9.

DIVIDED.—New York.

SEC. VII. Congress shall provide by law, that the United States shall pay to the owner the full value of his fugitive from labor in all cases where the marshal, or other officer, whose duty it was to arrest such fugitive, was prevented from so doing by violence or intimidation from mobs or riotous assemblies, or when after arrest such fugitive was rescued by like violence or intimidation, and the owner thereby deprived of the same; and the acceptance of such payment shall preclude the owner from further claim to such fugitive. Congress shall provide by law for securing to citizens of each State the privileges and immunities of citizens in the several States.

YEAS.—Delaware, Illinois, Indiana, Kentucky, Maryland, New Jersey, New Hampshire, Ohio, Pennsylvania, Rhode Island, Tennessee, and Virginia—12.

NAYS.—Connecticut, Iowa, Maine, North Carolina, Missouri, and Vermont—7.

DIVIDED.—New York.

NOT VOTING.—Massachusetts.

When the question was first taken on the first section, it was lost by a vote of eleven States against it to eight in its favor, a majority of your Commissioners casting the vote of New York against it. A motion was immediately made to reconsider, which was advocated by Mr. Granger, one of the Commissioners from New York, and was carried by a vote of fourteen States for, to five against it—a majority of the Commissioners from New York again casting its vote in the negative, and the Convention adjourned. On the next day it again came up on its final passage, and was then carried by a vote of nine States for, to eight against it—the vote of New York not being given. Why it was not given is left by the Commissioners to be stated by Mr. Field, on his own responsibility. (*See note*, p. 596.)

The vote of New York was not given upon any of the sections except the fifth, for the reason already stated; but upon that section we all voted Aye, as all her Commissioners then present were in its favor.

After the several votes had been taken, it was objected that the whole article should be put to a vote upon the question of its final adoption before it could be regarded as properly passed, but the President of the Convention decided that this was not necessary, and no such vote was taken. At the close of the discussion on this subject your Commissioners were prepared to cast the vote against the entire article, if any question had been taken upon it as a whole, as a majority of your Commissioners think it should have been.

Soon after the adoption of these proposed amendments to the Constitution, and after voting down and laying on the table various propositions made by a minority in the interest of freedom and the free States, the Convention adjourned—having adopted an address to Congress requesting that body to submit the amendment, to Conventions of the several States, for ratification, according to the Constitution of the United States; and they were accordingly communicated to Congress on the same day. In the Senate, they were referred to a committee, and were recommended for adoption by a majority of that committee; but Messrs. Seward and Trumbull, a minority of the committee, reported against the amendments, and in favor of a National Convention; thus following out and approving the proposition which had been made in the Convention by your Commissioners, and the entire minority of that party, nearly three weeks before, and for which the majority which controlled it, if it had chosen to do so, could at any time have obtained an unanimous vote. The amendment of the Convention, however, failed to secure the approval of either branch of Congress.

The labors of your Commissioners having thus terminated, it is due to those whom they represented, and to themselves, that the majority should state briefly the reasons why the proposed amendments to the Constitution did not meet their approbation.

First.—In their judgment, no amendment of that sacred instrument in the interest, and for the purpose of the extension and perpetuation of the slave power—an interest which has wielded the whole political power of the United States during almost the entire existence of the Government—was either expedient or necessary. They preferred it should remain and continue just as it came from the hands of our revolutionary fathers; a Constitution establishing freedom and not slavery.

Second.—The Convention would scarcely listen to, much less adopt, any amendment in the interest of freedom or of free labor, or of the rights of citizens of the free States; the only one of that character—that in relation to securing to the citizens of each State the privileges and immunities of citizens of the several States—having been voted down as a direct proposition when offered by Mr. Wilmot, and only adopted in an indirect way at the end of the section requiring payment to be made by Congress for rescued slaves. In like manner the absolute right of secession in every State as inherent under the Constitution of the United States was claimed to exist by members of the Convention from the slave States, accompanied by a denial of any right in the General Government to coerce obedience to it, or to enforce the laws for the collection of revenue. And although all the delegates from the slave States did not take this ground, yet in several instances a majority of the delegates from several of them did so, and the States themselves generally voted against all propositions to the contrary. The article proposed by your Commissioners denying the right of nullification and secession was defeated in accordance with these views; so that in effect slave States, and such of the free States as voted with them, would not consent so to amend the Constitution as to deny the right of nullification and secession, even if all the guarantees demanded by the slave interest were accorded to it. In addition, many of the delegates from the slave States declared that it was the fixed determination of those States to stand by the States that had seceded from the Union, and to aid them in resisting it, even if such guarantees were given; and that they would resist any attempts to coerce them, or to enforce the revenue, or any other laws within their limits, without their consent. In other words, they claimed a right to remain in the Union under the Constitution, with its new guarantees of slavery, and yet to obstruct the operations of the Government, to prevent the execution of the laws, and to aid those who were in open rebellion against, and had made war upon it. Under these circumstances your Commissioners did not deem it consistent with justice, or the respect due to their own State, to give their assent to any of the proposed amendments, except that prohibiting the slave-trade—and even that, in their opinion, was unnecessary, as no enlightened legislative body would dare to propose to reëstablish that infamous traffic.

Third.—By the first section of the proposed amendments, slavery is *constitutionally* established in all of the territory south of the line of 36° 30′, and all control over it by Congress or the territorial legislatures is absolutely taken away during its territorial condition. In effect, there is to be no law for slavery, its permanency and existence being provided for, except the will of the master and the present odious slave code of New Mexico. These are fastened upon every inch of the soil of that immense region, beyond even the power of the people to remove them, however much they may desire to do so, prior to the formation of a State government. Slavery must therefore be the normal condition of the territory, while the State is in the process of formation and organization; and the inevitable result must be, that free labor and free institutions will be excluded, and no free State formed within its limits. As the territory was free from the blight of slavery when acquired, your Commissioners could not assent to its being changed into slave soil by an amendment to the Constitution of the United States.

Fourth.—The second section of the proposed amendments gives to the slave States an absolute negative upon the acquisition of free territory in every possible mode by which it can be acquired; and in giving reciprocally the same right to free States as to acquiring slave territory, also fetters the operations of the General Government both in peace and war, depriving it to some extent of the exercise of perfect sovereignty, and at the same time sanctioning, and perpetuating in the organic law, an odious discrimination in favor of an institution peculiar to the slave States, and at variance with the humane principles of the age. The free States do not need any such veto power in their favor, and the slave States would not demand it except to maintain and preserve for slavery a balance of power hitherto claimed, and to some extent exercised by them, for which they secure by this amendment a constitutional perpetuation. No well-founded objection seems to exist in regard to the acquisition of free territory, unless it be that it is obtained in order to convert it into slave soil; and your Commissioners could not consent to give to a single interest, that of slavery, a negative upon such acquisitions. They have always regarded slavery as a local institution, depending solely upon the laws of the States in which it was permitted for its existence; and they did not deem it expedient or just to recognize it as, or elevate it to, the rank of a positive governmental power, by clothing it with the right to interrupt one of the ordinary and most essential functions of the Government. Slavery, except as a limited basis of representation, has now no political power or authority under the Constitution; the wise and good men who framed that instrument cautiously withheld it in all other respects; and your Commissioners find in the history of the aggressions of the slave interest, only additional reasons for confining it within its original limits.

Fifth.—To so much of the third article as declares that the Constitution nor any amendment of it, shall be so construed as to give Congress the power to regulate, abolish, or control slavery within any State, there was no objection, as it has never been seriously claimed that any such power was given; but this provision is connected with so many objectionable, not to say odious ones, that your Commissioners felt themselves bound to vote against it. These surrender all the power of Congress over the District of Columbia, and over other places within its exclusive jurisdiction, in respect of slavery and its ultimate extinction, however much the people of the United States in the progress of civilization and humanity may desire it; and by the sixth section this provision is made unalterable without the consent of all the States. The influences produced by the existence of slavery at the National Capital, upon public men and public measures, are well known; and while they may be tolerated, as they have been, without any desire to exercise the power of eradicating the cause of the evil, still a sound policy requires that the power should not be abandoned. Connected with this surrender of a well-defined and necessary power, are other provisions in regard to the transit of slaves through the free States; in effect, permitting the carrying on of the internal slave-trade through these States, unless they pass laws forbidding it. This trade through the free States is not made dependent upon the consent of the States, but is made lawful without dissent; and the result is, that if this amendment shall be adopted, every free State will find it necessary to legislate for its exclusion, or to permit and regulate the transit by its own laws. These laws would be deemed odious by the slave States, and would produce dissatisfaction and irritation. Besides, in most of the free States, the normal legal condition of every person is that of freedom; this constitutional provision would at once change the local law of the State, and operate as a positive recognition of slavery in the absence of any new enactment. Thus, every free State would find itself compelled to adopt a slave code, more or less extensive in its character, regulating or excluding the inter-state slave-trade. Taking this in connection with the fourth section, authorizing the States to legislate upon the subject of fugitive slaves, and by their judicial and ministerial officers to enforce their delivery, contrary to the decision of the Supreme Court of the United States, which declares all such interference on the part of the States unconstitutional, it is apparent that the legislatures of all the free States would be beset by hordes of persons in the interest of the slave power for the passage of laws protecting slavery within their limits. No means, however impure, would be omitted to obtain them; and it is easy to see that a slave code upon the subject of transit of fugitives, more or less stringent in its character, would soon find its way into every statute book. When the States now free abolished slavery within their own limits, they intended to get rid of the evil entirely, not only in practice but as a necessity of legislation; these provisions compel a return to it, and involve the adoption of new laws for its regulation or exclusion.

Seventh.—The sixth section makes most of the amendments which give a constitutional protection to slavery, unalterable without the consent of all the States. It also includes the second section of the fourth article, which provides that "representatives and direct taxes shall be apportioned among the several States according to their respective members," including three-fifths of all slaves, &c.; and that portion of the fourth article which requires the delivering up of fugitive slaves. Thus, a preference is given to the slave interest over every other; these may all be affected by a constitutional amendment, ratified or adopted by three-fourths of the States; but the slave clauses are to remain, except by universal consent, fixed and immovable. No such protection is given to freedom; none to the property of free men, unless it be what is called property in slaves; none to the freedom of the press; none to the religion of the citizen, or to the rights of conscience. These rights, more sacred than any other, are deemed of less importance, and are secured by less guarantees than the right to hold a fellow man in bondage and to traffic in his flesh. Moreover, the three-fifth representation of slaves, and only the same rate of direct taxation, are perpetual by the same rigid provision. This not only gives to the slave States a representation of three-fifths of their slave property, but it secures to them an exemption from taxation on the same property to the extent of two-fifths. But no property whatever, in the free States constitutes a basis of representation, and all of it is liable to, and may be taxed. Unequal and unjust as was this discrimination in favor of the slave States, still as it formed a part of the original Constitution, it should be maintained; but when it is sought to extend it to new States, and to make it unchangeable without the consent of all the States, the attempt should be resisted by every freeman. There are other property interests more important than that of slavery, but none of them have been so arrogant as to claim such exclusive privileges and perpetuation.

Finally.—Other objections of a grave character might be stated, but it is not deemed necessary. The great purpose of the Convention was to amend the Constitution of the United States, so as to recognize and protect slaves as property. As a direct proposition this was negatived, but the same end was sought to be attained by indirect means, and its friends exulted in having accomplished it. Such is the obvious effect of these amendments. If adopted, slaves must everywhere in the Union be regarded as property, and entitled to the same legal protection as other property. The necessary result will be, that all State laws forbidding the bringing of slaves within their limits, will be void, the sovereignty of the States in that respect will be destroyed, and the National Constitution will recognize and protect property in man.

We do not believe that the people of the State of New York will, under any pressure of circumstances, however grave, recognize a claim so repugnant to humanity, so hostile to freedom.

We commend to your honorable body the careful consideration of these proposed constitutional amendments. We believe that they will, if adopted, engraft upon our Constitution the odious doctrine of property in man; that they will extend slavery over a vast domain once free; that they will change the whole spirit and character of our organic law, making that to protect and foster slavery which was intended to establish freedom; making that irrevocable and perpetual which the framers of the instrument intended should be temporary.

DAVID DUDLEY FIELD,
WM. CURTIS NOYES,
JOHN A. KING,
JAMES S. WADSWORTH,
A. B. JAMES,
JAMES C. SMITH.

NOTE OF MR. FIELD.

The following statement shows why the vote of New York was not given upon the first question taken in the Peace Convention, on the twenty-seventh of February. The Journal represents the vote as divided. *It was not divided.* The vote was ordered to be cast, *and should have been cast* in the negative.

On Tuesday, the day preceding, a message came to me from the clerk of the Supreme Court of the United States, that the Court was waiting for me in a case which had stood upon the docket since December, 1859, and was now for the first time reached in its order. The case was of great importance, for upon its result depended the closing or reopening of a litigation which I had conducted for nineteen years, which had embraced in its different forms more than eighty suits, and in the course of which the Courts of the State and of the United States had come into direct conflict. All the tribunals of the State of New York, where the question had been raised, had decided against my clients. The Supreme Court of the United States, by a majority of two, had once decided in their favor.

The present case was to determine whether the Court would adhere to its former decision. The stake of my clients was therefore immense, and I was their only counsel.

The case being called after my arrival in Court, the Chief Justice observed that, as it was too late to begin that day, the argument would proceed first the next morning, at eleven o'clock, unless the Attorney-General should claim precedence in another case. Then, thinking that the Convention would close its business during the day, I hastened back, and the question being soon taken, I cast the vote of the State against the proposition before the Convention, and it was rejected by 11 to 8.

A reconsideration was moved and carried, and an adjournment taken to half-past seven in the evening. At that hour I returned to the Convention, but to my disappointment, and in spite of my efforts, it adjourned to the next morning at ten o'clock, a majority of my associates voting for the adjournment.

The next morning I endeavored to procure a meeting of the delegation before ten o'clock, that I might obtain a formal instruction to the Chairman in my absence to cast a vote of the State against the proposed amendments. Not being able, however, to obtain the earlier attendance of all the members, I waited till they appeared in the hall of the Convention, and there, shortly before eleven o'clock, I called them together, and, all being present, a resolution, in contemplation of my absence, was moved and carried, that "the Chairman declare that New York voted No on each section." Thereupon requesting Mr. King to act as temporary Chairman in my absence, and when New York was called to cast the vote in the negative, pursuant to the resolution, I left the hall and drove to the Capitol as rapidly as possible, that I might be present at the opening of the Court.

Was it reasonable, nay, was it possible, that I should do otherwise? It is known to be a rule of the Supreme Court not to postpone an argument for other engagements of counsel. If neither counsel is present, the case goes to the foot of the docket, to be reached again only after two or three years; if one of the counsel only appears, he makes an oral argument, and a printed brief is submitted on the other side. In my view, it would have been trifling with the rights of my clients either to submit their case on a printed brief or to postpone it for two years. I had no one to send to the Court in my place. To despatch a letter with an excuse was a liberty I did not feel justified in taking, and if taken, it might fail of its object, as the Court, when informed of the circumstances, must have believed that no member of the delegation would take advantage of my absence if he could, and that he could not if he would, since the vote had been already determined in a meeting of the delegation, and that determination could not be reconsidered or changed without the desertion to the minority of one of the majority.

But whatever might be the opinion of others, my duty appeared to myself extremely plain. There was nothing to be done in the Convention but the merely ministerial duty of declaring what had already been determined, which duty could certainly be performed by another as well as myself, while, on the other hand, no one but myself could act in Court for my clients. It is true that some of my associates expressed to me their apprehension that the minority might appeal to the Convention, and that the Convention might arbitrarily overrule the delegation; but I answered them as I repeat now, that neither the minority of the delegation nor the Convention itself had any right to interpose. We were not asking a favor, but exercising a right. Whether a person not present could vote was not the question. Persons did not vote except on unimportant questions and by general consent. States voted; the vote of each State was delivered by its Chairman, who collected the voices of his delegation and announced the result. There was nothing in the reason of the thing, nothing in any rule or usage of the Convention, which required the voices of the delegation to be collected at the instant of announcing the result. They might be collected one minute beforehand, or, as in the present instance, ten minutes, or twice ten minutes. All that could be required was, that each member should give his own judgment upon the particular proposition, and the sum of these judgments it was the sole province of the Chairman to make known. There could be no occasion for their standing by his side while he performed this duty unless he needed their support or they feared his weakness.

I have said that there was no rule of the Convention which ordered the matter otherwise; on the contrary, the rule as to the mode of voting—the 18th—was as follows:

"18. MODE OF VOTING: All votes shall be taken by States, and each State to give one vote. The yeas and nays of the members shall not be taken, or published—only the decision by States."

On the twenty-first of February, Mr. Dent, of Maryland, moved the adoption of the following rule:

"When the vote on any question is taken by States, any Commissioner dissenting from the vote of his State may have his dissent entered on the journal."

Mr. Chase, of Ohio, offered the following as a substitute for Mr. Dent's rule.

"The yeas and nays of the Commissioners of each State, upon any question, shall be entered upon the Journal, when it is desired by any Commissioner; and the vote of each State shall be determined by the majority of Commissioners present from each State."

Mr. Chase's substitute was rejected, and Mr. Dent's rule adopted,

The usage of the Convention may be understood by a single example. The Maine delegation consisted of her two Senators and six members of the House of Representatives. One member only attended for the greater part of the Convention, and cast the vote of the State. Indeed it was a frequent practice for members to absent themselves and leave their associates to act for them.

The State of New York had, moreover, decided for herself in what manner her Commissioners should speak for her, by declaring in the joint resolution of the Senate and Assembly that they should cast their "votes to be determined by a majority of their number," not the majority of those who should happen to be present at a particular instant on the floor of the Convention, but a majority of the whole number. Suppose, upon a question being put, the delegation had met for consultation, and by a formal resolution determined that the vote of the State be No; then, instructing their Chairman to cast the vote accordingly, had separated, and all but the Chairman retired from the hall, could he thereupon have changed the vote to Aye, because he disagreed with the majority and alone remained on the floor? Or could the

Convention have refused this vote of the State? And if not, how is that question different from the one here?

It was, therefore, I must think with good reason, assumed by me when I left the hall, that if the question should be put in my absence, which by the way I considered uncertain, as the debate then going on might last for hours, and I hoped still to find some means of deferring my argument to the next day, I might certainly depend on the vote of New York being declared again as it had been declared before, never doubting for a moment the ability and the will of my associates to defend against all opposition the rights of the State, their own rights, and mine.

On my arrival at the Court I did not succeed in my desire to defer my argument to the next day; but had I done so, it would have made no difference, as the vote in the Convention must have been called before I reached the Capitol.

What occurred in my absence I can only know from report. Five different statements are given: one by Mr. King in a published letter, another by the secretary of the delegation in the minutes kept by him, the third by the chairman of the Massachusetts delegation, who had the best opportunity to observe what was passing, the fourth by the secretary in a correspondence with me, and the fifth in the published Journal of the Convention.

Mr. King's statement of what occurred in my absence is as follows:

> "The vote on the amendment soon followed, and before New York was called I asked my colleagues what vote should be given, and the reply was that in the absence of Mr. Field the vote was divided. Nevertheless, I stated the case to the Convention, and asked permission to cast the vote as before. This was objected to by one of the Commissioners of the minority, and permission having been refused by the Convention, by direction of my colleagues when the State was called I answered that the vote was divided."

The other statements are subjoined, and numbered, 1, 2, 3, 4, and 5.

From a comparison of these statements it appears.

First: That the direction given to Mr. King, when the whole delegation were together, regularly convened, in contemplation of my absence, was to "declare that New York voted No."

Second: That instead of confining himself to that duty, he began immedietely upon my departure, and before the vote was demanded, to ask anew, "what vote should be given?" and when the vote was demanded, instead of voting No, "stated the case to the Convention, and asked permission to cast the vote as before."

Third: That Mr. King's colleagues, though they had just resolved, in expectation of my absence, that he should "declare that New York voted No," yet "before New York was called," and of course before any intimation from the Convention or its President, in answer to his question, "What vote shall be given?" replied, "that in Mr. Field's absence, the vote was divided," and directed him so to declare.

Fourth: That the Convention never "decided that no person could vote who was not present." Whatever was done, was done between the delegation and Mr. Tyler. No order was taken by the Convention, but, on the contrary, the objection on the part of the minority of the delegation was that "the Convention had no control or authority in the matter."

What caused this departure from the course of proceedings prescribed by the resolution does not clearly appear. The delegation did not rescind the resolution; the Convention did not reverse it. I do not understand that my associates consider it a nullity—certainly they could not have so considered it when it was passed. I have not sufficient evidence that they changed their minds within ten minutes, or that they have changed them yet. That the resolution was not a nullity, but an authoritative act, binding upon every member of the delegation, until duly reconsidered, I believed then, and believe still.

I submit, therefore, that my reason for attending court, at its opening, was not only sufficient but imperative; and if I had not yielded to it, I should have incurred the reproach of my clients, and the censure of all right-thinking men; that before I left the Convention, I did not only all that could have been done, but all that was necessary, to make the vote of New York certain against the proposed amendments of the Constitution; and that the omission to record the vote of New York as it was ordered, was owing not to any act or omission of mine, but to the efforts of the minority of the delegation, or some of them, to prevent an expression of the opinion of the majority, and to the failure of my associates of the majority to execute in my absence what had been resolved when I was present.

It is certainly with regret that I write this note. My preference was for a statement in which we all could join, but my associates refused to enter into any joint relation of the facts.

I hope, also, it will not be inferred from any thing I have written, that I do not regret the omission to record New York as voting against what appeared to me an unwise and pernicious proposition. Though the importance of the vote has been greatly magnified, and the result in my opinion would not have been different if the vote of New York had been counted, as I believe some of the States not voting would, if necessary, have voted in the affirmative; and even if it had been otherwise, I think the action of the Convention was of no importance whatever; yet, I should wish this State, of which we are so proud, to appear always, even in a matter of ceremony, on the side of Freedom; ever loyal to the Constitution as it is, but against placing there a guaranty to slavery beyond the guarantees of our fathers.

DAVID DUDLEY FIELD.

NEW YORK, *March 20th*, 1861.

I.—*Extract from the Minutes of the New York Delegation, kept by their Secretary.*

"WEDNESDAY, *February 27th*, 1861.

"New York delegation met in the room, and Mr. Wadsworth moved that the New York delegation vote No on each of the sections of the committee's report. Messrs. Corning, Bronson, Granger, Wool, and Dodge opposed, urging that the vote of New York be given on each section as it was called. The majority overruled, and decided to have the Chairman declare that New York voted No on each section.

"The question on the first section being called, Mr. King stated that one of the members of the delegation being called away to the United States Court, the delegation had taken a vote before he left, and he appealed to the justice of the Convention to have it so cast, stating that the vote of the delegation had been so cast on the previous day.

"The Convention decided that no person could vote who was not present.

"The delegation was divided."

II.—*Letter from the Chairman of the Massachusetts Delegation.*

"WASHINGTON, *March 8th*, 1861.

"MY DEAR SIR:—Your favor of the 6th instant is before me. After alluding to the fact that 'my seat in the Peace Convention was at the table directly under the President's chair, between him and the New York delegation,' you desire me to inform you what took place on the occasion of the vote of New York being called on the morning of the 27th February. What I observed was this:

"When the vote of New York was called for, Governor King rose and stated in substance that you had a short time before left the Convention to argue a case in the Supreme Court, which had been assigned for that morning, and asked the permission of the Convention to give the vote of the State in your absence, the same as though you were present. To this one of the Commissioners, Mr. Corning I think it was, objected, saying that the vote of New York was to be given as her Commissioners who were present should decide, and that the Convention had no control or authority in the matter. Some conversation was then had between the Commissioners who favored and those who opposed the pending proposition, which I did not hear with sufficient distinctness to understand, and in a minute or two Governor King announced that the vote of New York was divided.

"This is the substance of what occurred, so far as I observed it.

"With great respect, your friend,

"J. Z. GOODRICH.

"To David Dudley Field, Esq., New York."

III.—*Letter to the Secretary of the Convention.*

"New York, *March 4th*, 1861.

"Dear Sir:—Was any resolution passed by the Convention on Wednesday, the 27th of February, respecting the right of New York to vote, or affecting the vote of that State in the absence of any of her Commissioners? On one side I am told that there was such a resolution passed, or vote taken, in my absence; on the other side, I am told that there was not. If one was passed, will you do me the favor to give me a copy of it, and oblige

"Yours truly,

"DAVID DUDLEY FIELD.

"Crafts J. Wright, Esq., &c., &c."

IV.—*The Secretary's Answer.*

No 135, Willard's, Washington, *March 5th*, 1861.

"Dear Sir:—I have your letter. When New York was called, the inquiry was made whether an absent member could vote, stating that one member of that delegation was absent. The President stated that an absent member could not vote. New York was stated divided, and did not vote.

"Respectfully, &c.,

"CRAFTS J. WRIGHT."

V.—*Extract from the Journal of the Convention.*

"*February 27th*, 1861.

"The question on the adoption of said section resulted in the following vote:

"Yeas.—Delaware, Illinois, Kentucky, Maryland, New Jersey, Ohio, Pennsylvania, Rhode Island, and Tennessee—9.

"Nays.—Connecticut, Iowa, Maine, Massachusetts, North Carolina, New Hampshire, Vermont, and Virginia—8.

"So the section was adopted.

"On calling New York, the members stated that one of their number was absent, and the delegation were divided. Inquiry was made of the President whether an absent member could vote. The President decided he could not, without general leave.

"New York, Indiana, and Kansas were divided."

To the Legislature of the State of New York:

The undersigned beg leave to submit a reply to the statement of Mr. D. D. Field, to the report of the majority of the Commissioners to the Conference Convention at Washington, respecting his absence on the final vote in that body, on the proposed amendments to the Constitution of the United States.

The fact of his absence is admitted by Mr. Field, and attempted to be defended at great length, but Mr. Field has omitted to state that, by the 14th Rule of the Convention, "no member should be absent from the Convention, so as to interrupt the representation of the State, without leave." Mr. Field neither asked nor obtained leave of absence, and hence, under the rule, he failed to discharge his duty, both to the Convention and his colleagues. Mr. Field does not state that he made any application to the court for a temporary postponement of his case, in view of the important vote then about to be taken in Convention. But, on the contrary, argues to show that his duty to his client was paramount to his duty as Commissioner of the State of New York, in a question involving constitutional principles. After Mr. Field had stated, in the presence of his colleagues in the Convention, that he was obliged to go immediately to the Supreme Court of the United States, he was urged by those who agreed with him in opinion, to remain, and give the vote of the State against the proposed amendments, and was repeatedly told that his absence would divide the vote; this was so stated to him, by the minority of the Commissioners, and that it would be so claimed by them before the Convention. He refused to remain, and with the full knowledge of the effect of his absence on the question about to be taken, he left the Convention, and thus defeated the vote of his State. We who remained in our places, felt deeply the embarrassment, and the remarks which were made in consequence of Mr. Field's withdrawal. We had steadily, up to that time, sustained with him, our own, and what we believed to be the sentiment of the State, in favor of freedom, and were, therefore, entirely unprepared for such a determination on his part. Nor is our surprise lessened by the manner and the certificates by which he has at great length attempted to defend his course on this occasion. The vote of New York was not declared until after the vote which had been previously taken in its delegation had been stated, nor until an appeal had been made to the Convention, and refused by its President, to enable his colleagues to protect its vote in the absence of the Chairman of the delegation. By his absence the vote of New York stood 5 to 5, and it was under the decision of the Convention alone, that the vote was declared to be divided. Mr. Field has stated that the omission to record the vote of New York against the amendments was not owing to any act or omission of his, but to the efforts of the minority of the delegation, or some of them, to prevent the expression of the opinion of the majority. The objection was made after notice to him that it would be made, and the Convention sustained it, hence the vote was lost by his absence. Nor is the opinion of Mr. Field entitled to consideration when he imputes to the majority a want of fidelity to him, in not claiming and adhering to the vote which had been taken when all were present, and which was afterwards rendered null, by his absence. They did adhere to it, and endeavored to cast the vote accordingly. It was his duty to have been present, and to have thus given effect to that which had been previously agreed to. Mr. Field states, and truly, that his colleagues refused to unite in a joint relation of the facts of the case. They refused, because they were not satisfied with his course, and would not be responsible for it in any way. Up to the moment of his leaving the Convention, Mr. Field had manifested great zeal and ability in sustaining and defending the principles which a majority of the delegation desired to advocate, and his failure at the last, and decisive vote, was as unexpected as it was indefensible.

JOHN A. KING,
WM. CURTIS NOYES,
A. B. JAMES,
JAS. S. WADSWORTH,
JAS. C. SMITH.

NEW YORK, *March* 28*th*, 1861.

To the Legislature of the State of New York:

Informed by the newspapers of this morning that five of my associates in the Peace Convention, after waiting nearly three weeks, made yesterday to the Legislature a communication purporting to be an answer to the note which I thought it my duty to append to the report, explaining why the vote of New York was not given at a particular time, I beg leave to submit the following in reply:

I do not perceive that my associates impugn a single statement of fact contained in my note. My engagement in Court, the importance of the engagement, the necessity for my keeping it, the meeting of the delegation in contemplation of it, their resolution directing how the vote should be cast in my absence, the neglect so to cast it, are all, by silence, admitted. Nor do I perceive any denial of the proposition that the delegation had a right to pass the resolution, which thus became binding on all its members until reconsidered and reversed.

Perhaps I ought to make one exception to this use of admissions. My associates apparently wish to have it believed, yet hesitate to assert, that the Convention made a decision respecting the right to vote. In one place they say, "that an appeal had been made to the Convention, and refused by its President;" in another, that "it was under the decision of the Convention alone that the vote was declared to be divided;" and in a third, that the objection of the minority was made after notice to me that it would be made, and the "Convention sustained it, hence the vote was lost," by my absence. They should have reflected that there could have been no "decision of the Convention" if the appeal to it was "refused by its President." The truth beyond question is, that although my associates imagined that the Convention decided something, it did in fact decide nothing.

My associates say further, that I argue to show that my duty to my client was paramount to my "duty as Commissioner of the State of New York, in a question involving constitutional principles." This is an idle calumny. My note can be read as well as theirs; and in general will be read by the same persons, and there is not a word in it to justify or excuse their assertion. I never thus argued. I claimed that I had two duties to perform, and that I performed both. I did not claim that my duty to my State was subordinate to any other duty whatever.

When my associates assert that their Chairman left the Convention "with full knowledge of the effect of his absence on the vote about to be taken," if they mean that I knew or supposed that they intended to reverse their own action, or that Mr. King would not announce the vote as it had been resolved, or would declare the vote divided, or that they would support him in it, or that the Convention would overrule the delegation, then they assert what they could not know to be true, and what is not true in fact. My note sets forth what I was told, and what I replied.

My associates argue that I failed to discharge my duty, because I did not obtain leave of the Convention before going into the Supreme Court. Though I do not remember to have heard before of leave granted by a deliberative body to a member to go out for half an hour, or for one or two hours, I will observe, by this Convention absence was expressly allowed, if it did not "interrupt the representation of the State." My associates do indeed claim that, when I left the hall, the State ceased to be represented, ten Commissioners only remaining behind. The argument of this strange position appears to be, that a State is not represented when its vote can be divided, and that the vote of New York was divided. Here is a double fallacy. To say that the vote was divided, begs the question. It was not divided so long as the resolution passed by the delegation remained valid, and its validity is not denied. The other part of the proposition is equally fallacious. A State is represented when there are in the body delegates authorized to represent it, whatever be their number. The arguments of my associates seem to be, that a State could only be represented in the Peace Convention by odd numbers, and that if it sent eight or ten representatives, it would have no representatives at all.

But what shall I say to the following sentences:—"Nor is the opinion of Mr. Field entitled to consideration, when he imputes to the majority a want of fidelity to him, in not claiming and adhering to the vote which had been taken when all were present, and which was afterwards rendered null by his absence. They did adhere to it, and endeavored to cast the vote accordingly. It was his duty to have been present, and to have thus given effect to that which had been previously agreed to." Would any one imagine that the authors were speaking of a vote, given in expectation of my absence, and to determine what should be done when I was away? The vote was taken because I was to be absent, and directed the Chairman how to act in that event, but it is nevertheless pretended that the moment I became absent, the vote became null. They might better have said that the vote would have become null, or rather that there would have been no occasion for it in case of my continued presence. Then they say that they adhered to it. How did they adhere? The resolution directed the Chairman to cast the vote in the negative. He did not obey the resolution. His associates and mine did not insist that he should. Nobody prevented his answering "no," when the vote was called. No reason has ever been given for his not so answering. That he should instead have entered voluntarily into a discussion with Mr. Tyler on the subject, and that his associates should have looked quietly on, can only be accounted for by supposing them indifferent or bewildered.

It is not an agreeable task to write thus of old friends; but I must defend myself when attacked, and defence cannot always be made pleasant to an assailant.

My late friends profess to think me responsible for the loss of the vote of New York on a certain occasion. I think them responsible for it. Which side is right the Legislature and the people of the State will judge.

DAVID DUDLEY FIELD.

NEW YORK, *April 11th*, 1861.

Report of a Minority of the Commissioners of New York.

IN SENATE, *March 25th*, 1861.

THE undersigned, constituting a minority of the Commissioners, appointed by the Legislature of the State of New York, under resolutions responsive to those of the State of Virginia, referred to in the report of the majority of the Commissioners of said State of New York, admitting the correctness of the record of the proceedings presented by said majority, but differing from them in much of the reasoning which they present, respectfully report:

That they entered upon the duties assigned to them, earnestly desiring to carry out the patriotic spirit of said resolutions as therein expressed, which said original resolutions are herein embodied as a part of this report:

NEW YORK.

CONCURRENT RESOLUTIONS *appointing Commissioners from this State to meet Commissioners from other States at Washington, on invitation of Virginia.*

WHEREAS, the State of Virginia, by resolutions of her General Assembly, passed the nineteenth instant, has invited such of the slaveholding and non-slaveholding States as are willing to unite with her, to meet at Washington, on the fourth of February next, to consider, and if practicable, agree on some suitable adjustment of our national difficulties; and whereas, the people of New York, while they hold the opinion that the Constitution of the United States, as it is, contains all needful guarantees for the rights of the States, are nevertheless ready, at all times, to confer with their brethren upon all alleged grievances; and to do all that can justly be required of them to allay discontent; therefore,

Resolved, That David Dudley Field, William Curtis Noyes, James S. Wadsworth, James C. Smith, Amaziah B. James, Erastus Corning, Addison Gardner, Greene C. Bronson, Wm. E. Dodge, Ex-Governor John A. King, and Major-General John E. Wool, be and are hereby appointed Commissioners on the part of this State, to meet Commissioners from other States, in the City of Washington, on the fourth day of February next, or so soon thereafter as Commissioners shall be appointed by a majority of the States of the Union, to confer with them upon the complaints of any part of the country, and to suggest such remedies therefor as to them shall seem fit and proper; but the said Commissioners shall at all times be subject to the control of this Legislature, and shall cast five votes to be determined by a majority of their number.

Resolved, That in thus acceding to the request of Virginia, it is not to be understood that this Legislature approve of the propositions submitted by the General Assembly of that State, or concede the propriety of their adoption by the proposed Convention. But while adhering to the position she has heretofore occupied, New York will not reject an invitation to a conference, which, by bringing together the men of both sections, holds out the possibility of an honorable settlement of our national difficulties, and the restoration of peace and harmony to the country.

Resolved, That the Governor be requested to transmit a copy of the foregoing resolutions to the Executives of the several States, and also to the President of the United States, and to inform the Commissioners without delay of their appointment.

Resolved, That the foregoing resolutions be transmitted to the honorable the Senate, with a request that they concur therein.

The foregoing resolutions were passed in the House of Assembly by a vote of seventy-three ayes to thirty-nine noes, and in the Senate by a vote of nineteen to twelve, those in the negative, in both Houses, being all members of the dominant party, and those in the affirmative composed of the members of the opposition, and of those Republicans who were supposed to be prepared to meet the State of Virginia and other sister States, in the spirit of the resolutions adopted by the States of Virginia and New York.

A single point in the record, to which reference has been made, requires some consideration before proceeding to the reasoning of a majority of the Commissioners upon the propositions finally adopted by the Convention. The majority of the Commissioners state that most of said majority were opposed to the submission by the Convention of any amendments of the

Constitution of the United States at the present time, and in the present excited state of the public mind.

Not only was that ground assumed by a majority of the New York Commissioners, but some of their number argued with great ability against the danger of touching that sacred instrument, consecrated by memories so dear to every patriot heart.

The propositions, presented as amendments, were clear and distinct—their adoption would in no manner disturb the general harmony of the Constitution; yet, strangely enough, to an ordinary mind, the majority of the Commissioners who found such danger in adopting the specific amendments proposed, voted with a united action for a General Convention to remodel the entire Constitution—exposed to all the hazards that must attend such a Convention—by whose action a form of government might be presented, in which could not be found a single trace of that Constitution for which they professed such high veneration.

The undersigned will now consider the reasons presented by a majority of the Commissioners against the proposition: The majority declare that the Convention would not listen to, much less adopt any amendments in the interests of freedom, or of free labor, or of the rights of citizens of the free States, the only one of that character, that in relation to the securing to the citizens of each State the privileges and immunities of the citizens of the several States, &c., &c. As the undersigned have no recollection of the propositions to which reference would seem to be made, other than that embraced in the last clause, which they have quoted, they would call the attention of the people of the State of New York to this subject, as one deeply interesting in its character, and upon which it is supposed that there is very little difference of opinion. As this statement is thrown out by a majority of the Commissioners, in a manner to carry a belief that the harsh and cruel enactments which deprive colored citizens of the North of the privileges they claim in Southern States under the Constitution, it may be well for our people to consider that such enactments are not confined to the States fostering the institution of slavery, but exist and are enforced in some States making peculiar claim to love for freedom and the rights of man. The State of Illinois has a code of laws against free colored persons, citizens of other States, as severe as those of South Carolina or Louisiana. These laws have been recently enforced, and yet the North does not hear one word of the wrongs inflicted upon colored citizens of other States found within the borders of Illinois.

It will be recollected that the Constitution first presented by the State of Oregon, contained a clause prohibiting free colored persons from residing within that State. That Constitution received the votes of both the Senators from New York—each expressing his views of that instrument, yet the public censure has not fallen upon either of those gentlemen, by reason of such action. Nor is it necessary to go beyond the election polls of this State, claiming its fifty thousand majority for the cause of freedom and of equal rights—and yet counting from the ballot box an hundred thousand majority against securing the privilege of suffrage to colored persons, upon the same conditions that it is secured to whites. These facts are presented with the hope that they may create a spirit of charity in the public mind toward those States whose peculiar position renders such harsh legislation certainly not more censurable than it is in free States.

The undersigned differ entirely from the majority of the Commissioners, as to the action of the Convention upon subjects interesting to the North. It is known to all that Virginia, Kentucky, and it is believed all the Southern Border States instructed their delegates to insist on the Crittenden propositions, a material feature of which was, that in all future acquired territory, south of 36° 30′, slavery should be permitted; and yet when this material clause was found repugnant to the Northern sentiment, a distinguished Commissioner from Maryland moved to limit it to *present* territory, which proposition was adopted. Surely this was an important surrender to Northern sentiment that should not have been forgotten.

The majority say, that by the first of the proposed amendments, slavery is constitutionally established in all the territory south of the line of 36° 30′, as if such recognition of slavery there was now for the first time to be established by the proposed amendment. The majority of these Commissioners are counsellors of eminent ability, and yet, for some reason not easily comprehended, they have seen fit to ignore a decision of the Supreme Court of the United States, which declares that slavery can be carried into all the Territories of the United States, whether south or north of the line of 36° 30′. The famous Dred Scott decision, to which reference is here made, was often referred to in the debates of the Convention, and was insisted upon by many gentlemen, holding views and opinions similar to those of a majority of the New York Commissioners, as affording all the protection that the South could require, and claiming that the proposed amendment was unnecessary, by reason of such protection.

The Territory of New Mexico was declared open to slavery by the compromise act of 1850. The public mind of the North was deeply agitated upon that subject. A distinguished statesman, who was removed from earth before his eyes were forced "to rest upon a dismembered Confederacy," was violently assailed for declaring that slavery could work no practical evil in New Mexico; and yet the recent census has vindicated that assertion, showing that in the ten years that have passed since that compromise, only twenty-four slaves were to be found in what the majority of the committee are pleased to call the "immense region" of New Mexico; more than half of whom were servants of army officers, to be removed when they should be ordered to other stations.

The Territorial Legislature of New Mexico has declared the existence and passed laws for the protection of slavery throughout that entire Territory, while the proposed amendment of the Constitution would exclude it from all that portion of said Territory north of 36° 30′.

The undersigned are not only ready to vindicate their votes for that proposed amendment, but claim that such an amendment to the Constitution would be a great gain to the cause of freedom; taking from the action of the Dred Scott decision, and of the Territorial Legislation, all territory north of 36° 30′; and they challenge a comparison of their votes, with the course of those who preferred to leave this question subject to the action of that decision, and to the legislation to which reference is made.

The *second* section of the proposed amendments, touching the future acquisition of territory, met the approval of the undersigned, as certainly not less important to the North than to the South. The history of our country shows how hastily the assumed powers of Congress have been exercised upon this question, and at this moment presents a startling example, of a State of vast territory, acquired by a joint resolution of Congress, sustained at an enormous expense, and now withdrawing from the Confederacy, seizing upon and applying to its own use all the Government property found within its borders. Every reflecting citizen can determine for himself where there is the most danger to the cause of humanity, and whether territory is more probably to be acquired from the North, and consecrated to freedom, or from the Southwest, upon which these exciting contests might be revived.

This proposed amendment is presented with entire confidence for the decision of our people.

As the majority of the Commissioners do not dissent from the general principles of the *third* article, but object to some of its provisions, the undersigned would remark that the principal difference between them and the majority would seem to be whether Congress shall be denied the power of abolishing Slavery in the District of Columbia, without the consent of Maryland and without the consent of the owners, or making the owners who do not consent just compensation. Ever since the formation of the Government, this has been a subject upon which the friends of freedom have been divided. In the opinion of the undersigned, this question should be permanently settled.

The power of removing slaves from one section of the country to another, is secured by this section, but cannot be exercised against the wishes of the State through which slaves would otherwise be taken. The power to touch at ports, shores, and landings, with vessels having on board persons held in bondage, and of landing, in case of distress, is embraced in this proposed amendment, the latter clause of which will, certainly, receive the approval of every friend of humanity. The undersigned do not join in the fears expressed by the majority, that a resort to "impure means" could ever secure from the Legislature of New York any laws upon these subjects, not entirely consistent with the honor and dignity of the State.

The *Fourth* proposition was adopted by a vote so large as to make comment here unnecessary.

As the *Fifth* proposition received the unanimous vote of your Commissioners, it requires no comment.

The *Sixth* proposition is upon a subject that has been discussed ever since the formation of the Government, and need not be dwelt upon.

The *Seventh* proposition presented itself with such force to the Convention as to receive a strong vote, but seven States declaring against it. It will be seen that this section requires Congress to provide by law for securing to citizens of each State the privileges and immunities of citizens in the several States.

Many other propositions were presented to the Convention, some of which received the full concurrence of the undersigned; to others they were opposed, and those who shared in the deliberations of the Convention do not doubt, and will not deny, that propositions were presented whose only object and effect could be to embarrass its proceedings.

The action of the Convention failed to secure at the hands of Congress the legislation necessary to present it to the people of the different States, in the manner prescribed by the Constitution. Still it is in the power, and the undersigned trust will be in the disposition of the representatives of the people of New York, in both Halls of its Legislation, to present them for the acceptance or rejection of her people.

Whatever differences of political opinion may exist, there can be but one mind as to the present critical condition of our country, or that it is the duty of every citizen to give all the aid in his power, to sustain an administration that has entered upon its complicated duties under circumstances of more embarrassment than have ever before existed in our country's history.

The undersigned not only as deeply regret, but as severely condemn, the action of those States who have attempted to withdraw from the Union, as do the majority of the Commissioners who opposed the adoption of the measures of conciliation presented by the Peace Convention.

Those who are conversant with the political action of the seceding States, will have observed how strong is their desire to draw the Southern Border States into this new Confederacy. With each of those Border States are large bodies of active politicians, constantly influencing the public mind, and misrepresenting, to a great extent, the opinions and designs of those who have wrought out this revolution in the national administration. The public mind is fearfully agitated upon these issues, and the refusal of the Legislature of New York to present the propositions of the Peace Convention, for the suffrages of her people, will greatly diminish the power of the Union men of the Border States to sustain themselves in their present trying position.

It is believed that Virginia is about to submit these propositions to her people; let New York, who so nobly responded to the call of Virginia, show that she, too, will be governed by the wishes of *her* people, and that if those ties which have so long held these powerful States in the bonds of brotherhood, must be severed, it shall be done only by the verdict of their people as recorded in the ballot box.

FRANCIS GRANGER,
ERASTUS CORNING,
GREENE C. BRONSON,
WM. E. DODGE.

Report of the Rhode Island Peace Commissioners.

To the Honorable General Assembly of the State of Rhode Island:

The undersigned Commissioners on the part of this State, appointed upon the request of the State of Virginia, to meet Commissioners from the other States to confer upon the best mode of adjusting the unhappy differences which now disturb the peace of the country, respectfully beg leave to report:

That on the 4th day of February last, at Washington, the day and place named for the opening of the Conference, they met Commissioners from other States, and remained with them in conference until the 27th day of February, at which time twenty-one States were represented, when having agreed by a majority of States to submit to Congress, to be by Congress submitted to conventions in the several States, the annexed article in amendment to the Constitution of the United States, the Convention finally adjourned.

This article, it will be seen, applies the old line of 36° 30′ of North latitude to all the present Territory of the United States, prohibiting slavery north of that line, whilst it recognizes and secures its existence south of that line during the territorial government, and provides for the formation of new States out of such territory with or without slavery as their constitutions may direct.

As this partition of territory was not disadvantageous, at least to the free States, as it disposed of the agitation consequent upon a recent decision of the Supreme Court of the United States upon a celebrated case, and followed a precedent which had given peace to the country upon this most dangerous subject of controversy for upwards of thirty years, your Commissioners gave their assent to it as the best practical solution of all difficulties growing out of the territorial question.

New territory is no further dealt with by this article than to require, except in certain specified cases, a majority of all the Senators from each side of said line, to concur in its acquisition, whether made by act of Congress or by treaty, thus giving to each class of States a check upon the cupidity of the others.

The other sections of the article were designed in general so to define and limit the rights, powers, and duties of both Congress and the States, with regard to the subject of slavery, as to prevent further controversy, and to enable and induce those most opposed in opinion and interest, by the practice of mutual forbearance, to live in peace and amity under the same Federal Government. It is believed that in no essential particular will this article change the present actual state of things; its value consisting in the security therein which it gives to all, and in the settlement made by it of present and probable subjects of controversy.

In a great practical matter of this sort, your Commissioners deem these results of far more importance than strict adhesion to any theory, however plausible in the abstract, and especially than to any party declaration of principles of a sectional cast, however vehemently argued, or numerously adopted on either side. To deal well and wisely with the actual and real, and whilst consulting the past and looking to the probable future for guidance, to base his action on what *is*, comprises the whole duty of a statesman; leaving to political philosophers to dream of what might have been, or in the abstract of what ought to be. Reform, it is true, in this way comes slowly, but it comes without the disturbance of material interests, without agitation of human passions, and without the violent outbreaks which these occasion—hindering and obstructing its progress in that grand and orderly procession of moral causes and effects which expresses and marks the providence and government of God.

It was apparent to all that, whatever may have been the motive and origin of the present alarming movement in the extreme Southern States, the instrument successfully used to promote it was the agitation of their people upon the safety of the institution of negro slavery in the States and Territories; and various conflicting opinions with regard to the best course to be pursued to allay this agitation were elicited in the course of this long conference. Extremists were not wanting on the one hand, who seemed inclined to construe the anomaly of slavery of the negro race, found in the Constitution of a free people, into a general rule; and who proposed or voted for propositions which they knew could not be accepted, that their assertion might aid in the remaining States the cause of secession. Extremists were not wanting, on the other hand, who were opposed to doing any thing upon the subject of slavery, especially at present, lest such action should compromise the incoming administration, and the Republican party, and even the character of the Government itself. Without suspecting the purity of the motives of either of these extremists, who beyond doubt represented the views of large and respectable bodies of men in their different sections, your Commissioners found themselves equally unable to agree with either.

They could not ignore the fact that seven States had separated themselves from the others and set up a federal government of their own; and that these were ceaselessly agitating the people of the remaining Southern States by inflammatory speeches, and writings skilfully addressed to their interests and sympathies, to induce them to join in this new movement. They could not doubt the assurances given to them by able and patriotic men from the States of Maryland, Virginia, North Carolina, Kentucky, Tennessee, and Missouri, that these attempts upon the loyalty of the people of their States had met at least with partial success; nor, indeed, blind themselves to the evidences of this found in the speeches and votes of individual Commissioners from these very States. Above all, they could not be insensible to the touching appeals of men, venerable in years, distinguished in public service, and whose reputation for ability and patriotism was national, to give them something in the shape of a constitutional security with which to allay the startled fears of their constituents, beat back the attacks of *their* enemies and *ours*, and even bring again to their duty thousands of men in the States of the extreme South, who had been led astray by the popular fears and impulses of the hour, and who, with the loyal but overborne, might well look to them for support, since no other had been afforded them in the reign of terror under which they were suffering. In the circumstances in which the country was placed, it seemed to your Commissioners that true policy ran in the course of generous impulse; that in this matter we were dealing not with treason, but with the most devoted loyalty which invoked our aid against it; that the concessions we made, if concessions indeed they were, were made to our friends that they might be strong enough to triumph over *their* enemies and *ours*, because the enemies of the country.

If, as is true, in this view of their duty your Commissioners stood in the main alone amongst the Commissioners from the Northern States, and ranged themselves by the side of the Central States of the Union, upon whom the weight of the civil strife must come if come it must, they need not assure you that no dastardly fears, no feelings of base compliance, dictated the position thus taken by them. Such motives to action neither became them nor those whom they represented. It was because of generous faith and earnest sympathy, of ties which no distance of time or space, and no difference of institutions can weaken; which in our fathers' days and our own led our heroes to *hazard all for all*, and at Guilford Court House, and Eutaw, and at Erie, with desperate valor to snatch victory for our common country out of the very lap of defeat; it was because our little State, with a warm heart and a ready hand, has never failed in counsel or deed to stand with the whole country in all dangers and in extremest disasters, that your Commissioners conceived that they best represented her by averting danger from those with whom they knew she would hasten to share it. If it be true that the time has arrived when our sympathy for an alien and a subject race has extinguished all sympathy for our own, and has hidden from us the ties of a common origin, common interests, and of a common glory, then, indeed, are we separated from our brethren, and the curse of slavery has fallen upon us as well as upon them. Your Commissioners found nothing in themselves to justify them in attributing such sentiments to the people of the State; and unitedly recommend the adoption by you of the amendment to the Constitution proposed by the Conference of Commissioners, as best fitted to give security and ensure peace to the country.

Among the measures strenuously enforced by some of the Commissioners, in lieu of that adopted by a majority, was the calling of a General Convention. To this measure your Commissioners opposed their most earnest and determined resistance. As a measure of peace, if for no other reason, because of the long delay which it implied, it would be utterly fruitless. But the possible danger of exposing a Constitution, framed and adopted in the earlier and more conservative days of the Republic, to be torn in pieces in these times of lawless irreverence and change, is too great for any wise man willingly to encounter. The very equality of the States in the Senate, which was won by the revolutionary sacrifices and valor of the smaller States, now almost forgotten, would, in the judgment of your Commissioners, be thereby greatly endangered; and your Commissioners earnestly represent to your Honorable body that under no circumstances should this State consent to a measure which might lead to her own extinction. The Constitution of a great country, adopted, as this was, on account of diversity of interests and views, with great difficulty, should be sacred. It may and should from time to time be amended to suit a change of circumstances, but never exposed to the danger of being uptorn. It is the symbol of our strength, because the ligament of our Union. It has collected about it the reverence of three generations of our people. It is the only rallying point now for the loyalty of the remaining States; the only hope of the restoration of the States which have left us; and, in its main features, it should be, as it was designed to be, perpetual. At no time should a General Convention be invited to invade it; and, of all times, this, in the judgment of your Commissioners, would be the most dangerous.

Finally, it will be found upon an inspection of the Journal of the late Conference of Commissioners, that the undersigned voted against many propositions in themselves just and expressive of *their* sentiments and *yours*, because inopportune and useless; and against others, because introduced for the very purpose of sowing dissension among the Commissioners and to prevent an agreement by majority upon any thing. In this they must ask your candid construction of their conduct, looking to the crisis, the occasion, the purpose and effect of the matter upon which they were called to act; and their unwillingness to hazard an agreement upon that deemed by them necessary, by tacking to it that which, however true, was at least useless, and might in the result be dangerous.

All which is respectfully submitted by

SAMUEL AMES, for self, and
ALEXANDER DUNCAN,
G. H. BROWNE,
WILLIAM W. HOPPIN,
SAMUEL G. ARNOLD,
Commissioners.

PROVIDENCE, *March 4th*, 1861.

COMMONWEALTH OF MASSACHUSETTS.

EXECUTIVE DEPARTMENT, COUNCIL CHAMBER,
BOSTON, March 25, 1861.

To the Honorable the Senate:

I have the honor to transmit to the General Court, for its use and information, a Report just received by me from John Z. Goodrich, Charles Allen, George S. Boutwell, Theophilus P. Chandler, Francis B. Crowninshield, John M. Forbes, and Richard P. Waters, Esquires, who were appointed Commissioners on the part of Massachusetts, under a Resolve passed the fifth day of February last, to attend a Convention of delegates from the several States of the Union, recently held at Washington.

And I embrace this opportunity to congratulate the people of the Commonwealth upon the fidelity, judgment, and ability with which the Commissioners, by whom they were represented, conducted their share of the duties of that deliberation.

And I trust that a similar intelligent, manful, and, at the same time, charitable and patriotic adherence to principles, fundamental both in morals and politics, will characterize the people of Massachusetts, and all their representatives, by whatever experiences of danger or difficulty their devotion to truth and duty may hereafter be tried.

I ask leave to call the attention of the General Court, also, to the fact that, as yet, no provision has been adopted for the payment of the expenses incident to the service with which the Commissioners were charged, and to recommend that a suitable appropriation for that purpose be made at the present session of the Legislature.

JOHN A. ANDREW.

To His Excellency JOHN A. ANDREW, *Governor, &c., &c.:*

The undersigned, Commissioners appointed by your excellency, in pursuance of certain resolutions passed by the Legislature at its present session, to attend a Convention to be held in the City of Washington, with authority to confer with the General Government, or with the separate States, or with any associations of delegates from such States, having, agreeably to your excellency's instructions, repaired to Washington and conferred with the delegates of twenty other States of the American Union, now respectfully submit the following report of the proceedings of the said Convention, and of the action of the Commissioners from Massachusetts.

The Convention commenced its sessions on the 4th of February, and closed its deliberations on the 27th of the same month. The Massachusetts Commissioners repaired to Washington as early as practicable after their appointment, and presented their credentials on the 8th of February.

The sessions of the Convention were secret; although repeated efforts were made, with the concurrence of the undersigned, first, to remove the injunction of secrecy, then to admit the public to witness the deliberations, and then to procure a complete and accurate report of the debates and doings. These efforts failed, and the undersigned are therefore able only to transmit a copy of the Journal of the Convention.*

On the 6th of February a resolution was adopted, upon the motion of Mr. Guthrie, of Kentucky, that a "committee of one from each State be appointed by the Commissioners thereof, to whom should be referred the resolutions of the State of Virginia, and the other States represented, and all propositions for the adjustment of existing difficulties between the States." Mr. Crowninshield represented Massachusetts upon this committee. At the earliest practicable moment he called for a specific statement of the grievances complained of by the discontented States of the Union. This call elicited much dis-

*** An authentic copy of the Journal was not received until the 21st instant and the Commissioners did not feel prepared to make a report without an opportunity for consulting it.**

cussion, but no definite response to the demand was ever made either in the committee or in Convention.

On the 15th of February, Mr. Guthrie, from the committee of one from each State, made a report recommending certain amendments to the Constitution of the United States. This report was adopted in committee by a majority of five States, the delegates from Kansas not having then taken their seats in the Convention.

A copy of this report may be found upon the twenty-second and twenty-third pages of the Journal. After much discussion and many amendments, the several sections of the proposed article of amendment to the Constitution were finally adopted on the last day of the session. It is to be observed, however, that the report as a whole never received the sanction of the Convention, although the several sections of the article of amendment were separately approved by a majority of the States voting; and it may well be doubted whether the entire article would have been adopted by the Convention.

The first section was adopted by a vote of nine States to eight; four States—New York, Indiana, Missouri, and Kansas—not voting.

The other sections were approved by larger majorities.

The undersigned declined to vote upon the last section, but the vote of Massachusetts, with the unanimous consent of its Commissioners, was given in the negative upon all the others. This course seemed to be demanded, whether regard was had to the constitution of the Convention, the circumstances under which it assembled, the nature of the propositions submitted, the solution of the difficulties in which the Government and people are involved, or to the character and peace of the country in the future. The two Pacific States, whose loyalty to the Constitution and the Union is unquestioned, could not have been represented in the Convention. Other States failed to appoint Commissioners. The resolutions of the State of Virginia were passed on the 19th of January; and it was expected that within sixteen days thereafter the representatives of this vast country would assemble for the purpose of devising, maturing, and recommending alterations in the Constitution of the republic. As a necessary consequence, the people were not consulted in any of the States. In several, the Commissioners were appointed by the executive of each without even an opportunity to confer with the Legislature; in others, the consent of the representative body was secured, but in no instance were the people themselves consulted. The measures proposed were comparatively new; the important ones were innovations upon the established principles of the Government, and none of them had ever been submitted to public scrutiny. They related to the institution of slavery; and the experience of the country justifies the assertion that any proposition for additional securities to slavery under the flag of the nation, must be fully discussed and well understood before its adoption, or it will yield a fearful harvest of woe in dissensions and controversies among the people. Nor could the undersigned have justified the act to themselves, if they had concurred in asking Congress to propose amendments to the Constitution unless they were prepared also to advocate the adoption of the amendments by the people.

It is due to truth to say that the Convention did not possess all the desirable characteristics of a deliberative assembly. It was in some degree disqualified for the performance of the important task assigned to it, by the circumstances of its constitution, to which reference has already been made. Moreover, there were members who claimed that certain concessions must be granted that the progress of the secession movement might be arrested; and on the other hand there were men who either doubted or denied the wisdom of such concessions.

The circumstances were extraordinary. Within the preceding ninety days the integrity of the Union had been assailed by the attempt of six States to overthrow its authority; seven other States were disaffected, and some of them had assumed a menacing and even hostile attitude. The political disturbances had been associated with or followed by financial distress.

The Convention was then a body of men without a recognized and ascertained constituency, called together in an exigency and without preparation, and invited to initiate measures for the amendment of the Constitution in most important particulars, and all at a moment when the public mind was swayed by fears and alarms such as have never before been experienced by the American people.

In these circumstances the undersigned thought it inexpedient to propose amendments to the Constitution, believing that so important an act should not be initiated and accomplished without the greatest deliberation and care. Nor could the undersigned satisfy themselves that any or all of the proposed amendments would even tend, in any considerable degree, to the preservation of the Union. Although inquiries were repeatedly made, no assurance was given that any propositions of amendment would secure the return of the seceded States; and it was admitted that several of the Border States would ultimately unite with the Gulf States, either within or without the limits of the Union, as might be dictated by events yet in the future. Indeed, no proposition was in any degree acceptable to the majority of delegates from the border slave States that did not provide for the extension of slavery to the Territories, and its protection and security therein.

And further, as appears from the Journal, the Convention was not prepared to deny the right of a State to secede from the Union. Mr. Field, of New York, introduced the following proposition, which, on motion of Mr. Ewing, of Ohio, was laid upon the table:

"The Union of the States under the Constitution is indissoluble; and no State can secede from the Union, or nullify an act of Congress, or absolve its citizens from their paramount obligation of obedience to the Constitution and laws of the United States."

After much debate and repeated attempts to avoid a direct vote, the following proposition was rejected:

"It is declared to be the true intent and meaning of the present Constitution that the union of the States under it is indissoluble."

AYES.—Connecticut, Illinois, Indiana, Iowa, Maine, Massachusetts, New York, New Hampshire, Vermont, and Kansas—10.

NOES.—Delaware, Kentucky, Maryland, Missouri, New Jersey, North Carolina, Ohio, Pennsylvania, Rhode Island, Tennessee, and Virginia—11.

On the last day of the session, Mr. Franklin, of Pennsylvania, moved the adoption of the following resolution:

"*Resolved*, as the sense of this Convention, that the highest political duty of every citizen of the United States is his allegiance to the Federal Government, created by the Constitution of the United States, and that no State of this Union has any constitutional right to secede therefrom, or to absolve the citizens of such State from their allegiance to the Government of the United States."

Mr. Ruffin, of North Carolina, moved to postpone the consideration of the same indefinitely, and the resolution was thereupon postponed by the following vote:

AYES.—Delaware, Kentucky, Maryland, Missouri, New Jersey, North Carolina, Ohio, Rhode Island, Tennessee, and Virginia—10.

NOES.—Connecticut, Illinois, Indiana, Iowa, Maine, Massachusetts, and Pennsylvania—7.

For these reasons and others the Commissioners from Massachusetts supported the proposition originally made by Kentucky, and introduced by Mr. Baldwin, of Connecticut, recommending a national convention for the purpose of revising the Constitution, and of providing for the exigencies likely to arise from the changed and perilous condition of the country. This measure offered an opportunity for consideration by the people, and for careful deliberation by the convention that might be constituted for the purpose. It is highly probable that, after the lapse of three-fourths of a century, a convention of delegates from all the States would by general consent propose amendments to the Constitution; and it is also probable that such a convention would at once tend to strengthen the feeling of brotherhood among the people of various sections, while the discussion of the principles of the Government would render its preservation of paramount concern to all. This measure of peace and union was rejected.

The undersigned are constrained by the force of many facts and circumstances to believe that an exciting cause of the present difficulties, and a serious obstacle to their removal, is the possible acquisition of Mexico and Central America.

The proceedings of the Convention furnish evidence upon this point.

The proposition to restore the Missouri Compromise, which guaranteed freedom north of the parallel 36° 30′ north latitude, but furnished no protection to slavery south of that line, was rejected by the aid of the unanimous support of the slaveholding States.

The proposition to settle the territorial question by the admission of New Mexico as a State, was summarily discouraged by the South in the committee.

The suggestion of one of the Commissioners from Massachusetts, that if the Convention would leave the territorial question out of view, the difficulties concerning the rights and relations of the existing States might be adjusted, did not meet with a favorable response from the slaveholding section of the country.

It is to be observed further, that the various propositions and amendments which were in any degree acceptable to the slave States guaranteed slavery south of said line.

It did not seem to the undersigned of signal importance, whether this guarantee was limited to our present territories, or made in words to apply to all future acquisitions. Whenever the line of slave States from the Gulf of Mexico to the Pacific Ocean shall be formed, an effectual barrier will have been raised against the migration of freemen southward. Nor can it be assumed, that either with or without constitutional prohibition, the limits of the republic are not to be further extended; and if the proposed line be established by the Constitution, the fairest portions of North America will be given up irrevocably to African slavery. Nor is the limitation of the right of a sovereign State to fix its own boundaries, which involves the right to acquire territory, consistent with its honor in peace, or compatible with its dignity and necessities in time of war. The American people are fully forewarned that it is unwise to rely upon constitutional prohibitions against the acquisition of territory; nor can such prohibitions always withstand the assaults of a determined and desperate majority when acting in harmony with the tendencies of public opinion, and the real or supposed necessities of the country.

With these views, and with this experience in mind, the undersigned did not regard with favor the provisions contained in the second section of the proposed article of amendment. It is also to be observed that by this section territory may be acquired for *naval and commercial stations, depots, and transit routes*, without a resort to the treaty-making power. These provisions seem to be broad enough to permit the summary annexation of Cuba, and portions of Central America and Mexico, by a simple law or joint resolution of Congress.

Thus, these two sections considered together, furnished no additional securities against territorial acquisitions, while they effectually established and protected slavery in all territory, present and future, south of the parallel 36° 30′ north latitude. By the first section, the common law was to be so changed, that a condition of slavery would be assumed in regard to all the African race within the Territories, and the laws of the several slave States would be enforced against all persons of that race who might be carried from the existing slave States into the Territories. The language is ambiguous, but this interpretation seems to be warranted; and, in the opinion of the undersigned, the courts would render an interpretation adequate to the result just indicated. It is thus seen that the only method of establishing and protecting slavery in the Territories, is to provide for the execution, within their limits, of the laws of the several slave States.

This section also incorporates into the Constitution of the United States the existing laws and usages of New Mexico relating to slavery, and renders them irrepealable during the territorial condition.

By the second section, the Senators are divided into two classes, those who represent the slaveholding, and those who represent the non-slaveholding States of the Union, and a majority of each class is required as a part of the two-thirds majority necessary for the acquisition of territory by treaty. A full exposition of this proposition would show that it is a complete and dangerous departure from the principles of the Government, and sure to effect its complete dissolution. When the Senate becomes two separate and distinct bodies, and when the existence of the institution of slavery determines where the line of division shall be, then the Government, for all practical purposes, is at an end. This proposition was introduced by Mr. Summers, of Virginia; and Virginia, by its delegates, also introduced and supported a kindred proposition, by which "all appointments to office in the Territories lying north of the line 36° 30′, as well before as after the establishment of Territorial Governments in and over the same, or any part thereof, shall be made upon the recommendation of a majority of the Senators representing at the time the non-slaveholding States; and in like manner, all appointments to office in the Territories which may lie south of said line of 36° 30′, shall be made upon the recommendation of a majority of the Senators representing at the time the slaveholding States."

We cannot hesitate to declare the opinion, carefully formed, that this policy of dividing the Senate into two classes, is fraught with dangers to the country more to be dreaded than the bold and defiant measures of those men and States that are arrayed in open hostility to the Union. This measure is a part of the policy of Mr. Calhoun, by which the Government was to be changed, and the executive department so divided that nothing could be done without the concurrence of two Presidents, one representing the slaveholding and one representing the non-slaveholding States.

The third section contains several provisions for strengthening and securing slavery in the District of Columbia and in the several States and Territories. It gives to representatives and others the right to bring their slaves into the District of Columbia, retain, and take them away, even after slavery may have ceased to exist in that District by the constitutional action of Congress. It secures the slave-trade between States and Territories in which slavery is established or recognized by law or usage, with the right of transit through free States, by sea or river, and of touching at ports, shores, and landings, and of landing in case of distress; reserving, however, to the States and Territories the power to prohibit the transit of slaves and the sale or traffic therein. Thus the transportation of slaves would be a right as broad as the limits of the republic, unless it should be restrained by the laws of individual States, which acts might readily be regarded as a breach of comity.

The fourth section of the article gives to the States the power of concurrent legislation with the United States for the rendition of fugitive slaves, thus introducing a new topic of agitation into every State, without in any degree relieving Congress of its duty in this particular.

The fifth section prohibits the foreign slave-trade, and makes it the duty of Congress to pass laws to prevent the importation of slaves, coolies, or persons held to service or labor. As Congress has already, by the Constitution, full power to regulate the migration or importation of persons from other countries, there is no reason for such constitutional provisions upon the subject. It alone remains to enact proper laws and secure their faithful and prompt execution.

The sixth section declares that certain sections of the proposed article of amendment, and certain provisions of the Constitution relating to slavery, shall not be amended or abolished without the consent of all the States.

The undersigned, being of opinion that no such stipulation ought to be made, and that if made, it would not be binding upon the country, did not hesitate to give the vote of the State against the proposition.

The seventh and last section of the proposed article of amendment is in the following words:

"Congress shall provide by law that the United States shall pay to the owner the full value of his fugitive from labor, in all cases where the marshal, or other officer, whose duty it was to arrest such fugitive, was prevented from so doing by violence or intimidation from mobs or riotous assemblies, or when, after arrest, such fugitive was rescued by like violence or intimidation, and the owner thereby deprived of the same; and the acceptance of such payment shall preclude the owner from further claim of such fugitive. Congress shall provide by law for securing to the citizens of each State the privileges and immunities of citizens of the several States."

In a Convention duly called and assembled for the revision of the Constitution, the undersigned would have assented to this section; and in declining to vote thereon they intended to so declare to their associates from the slaveholding States.

The undersigned thus set forth the doings of the Convention, and some of the reasons by which their conduct was controlled. It was not their fortune to concur with the action of the Convention. The concessions demanded by the discontented States, seemed to be inconsistent with honor, justice, and freedom, and calculated to render permanent the existing causes of disturbance. A Union restored by unmanly concessions, would be productive of bitter criminations and lasting hostilities, and would contain within itself the seeds of a violent death.

But the undersigned are bound to say that the differences in the Convention were, in the main, differences of opinion, and not of purpose. Loyalty to the Constitution and the Union was general; and the undersigned do not doubt that the act of Virginia, in inviting a conference with her sister States, will be productive of beneficial results to the country.

The Commissioners from Massachusetts were much impressed by the fact, which their personal intercourse with gentlemen from all the slaveholding States brought to their knowledge, that the present difficulties of the country were not caused by the pressure of grievances supposed to be actually existing; but rather by the fear of future interference with Southern rights, caused by entire misapprehension of the purposes of the people of the free States. Misrepresentation of those purposes, proceeding from among our-elves, whether prompted by ignorance of Northern sentiment, or by sinister otives, are greatly to be deprecated.

The undersigned entertain no doubt that the intercourse between the ifferent sections of the country, through their representatives in Convention, ad a most salutary influence in correcting false views of Northern sentiment, nd in assuring our brethren of the South that there is no purpose among he people of those States, who, upon principle, oppose the extension of lavery, to disturb or touch with an unfriendly hand the domestic relations f any other States of the Union.

In the present exigency of public affairs, each State should be careful to erform its whole duty freely and faithfully to its sister States and to the ountry; and then may it well and fearlessly demand, whether the Union ontain many States or few, that the Government shall be administered ccording to the principles of equality and justice which characterize the onstitution formed by our fathers, and which will prove a sufficient security n all the trials and perils of our national existence.

JOHN Z. GOODRICH,
CHARLES ALLEN,
GEO. S. BOUTWELL,
T. P. CHANDLER,
F. B. CROWNINSHIELD,
J. M. FORBES,
RICHARD P. WATERS.

BOSTON, *March* 22*d*, 1861.

INDEX.

INDEX TO THE APPENDIX.